Founding
God's Nation

Founding God's Nation

Reading Exodus

LEON R. KASS

Yale UNIVERSITY PRESS/NEW HAVEN & LONDON

Published with assistance from the foundation established in
memory of Calvin Chapin of the Class of 1788, Yale College.

Yale University Press books may be purchased in quantity for
educational, business, or promotional use. For information,
please e-mail sales.press@yale.edu (U.S. office) or
sales@yaleup.co.uk (U.K. office).

Set in Minion type by Westchester Publishing Services.
Printed in the United States of America.

Library of Congress Control Number: 2020937463
ISBN 978-0-300-25303-0 (hardcover: alk. paper)

A catalogue record for this book is available from the
British Library.

This paper meets the requirements of ANSI/NISO Z39.48-1992
(Permanence of Paper).

10 9 8 7 6 5 4 3 2

To My Study Partners

Nathan Laufer
Richie Lewis
Daniel Polisar
and
Hannah Mandelbaum

with Deep Gratitude

An astonishing and truly unique spectacle is to see an expatriated people, who have had neither place nor land for nearly two thousand years . . . a scattered people, dispersed over the world, enslaved, persecuted, scorned by all nations, nonetheless preserving its characteristics, its laws, its customs, its patriotic love of the early social union, when all ties with it seem broken. The Jews provide us with an astonishing spectacle: the laws of Numa, Lycurgus, Solon are dead; the very much older laws of Moses are still alive. Athens, Sparta, Rome have perished and no longer have children left on earth; Zion, destroyed, has not lost its children. . . . What must be the strength of legislation capable of working such wonders, capable of braving conquests, dispersions, revolutions, exiles, capable of surviving the customs, laws, empire of all the nations, and which finally promises them, by these trials, that it is going to continue to sustain them all, to conquer the vicissitudes of things human, and to last as long as the world? . . . Any man, whosoever he is, must acknowledge this as a unique marvel, the causes of which, divine or human, certainly deserve the study and admiration of the sages, in preference to all that Greece and Rome offer of what is admirable in the way of political institutions and human settlements.

—*Jean-Jacques Rousseau*

Contents

Preface

This commentary on Exodus, a work of my old age, is the fruit of twenty years of studying the book with students, friends, and colleagues in Chicago, Washington, DC, and Jerusalem. It is intended as a sequel of sorts to my commentary on Genesis, *The Beginning of Wisdom,* which likewise grew out of twenty years of studying and teaching that text with students at the University of Chicago. Given where I started out in life, I am amazed to be finishing it so deeply engaged with the Hebrew Bible. A first-generation American, I was raised in a secular—though Yiddish-speaking and proudly Jewish—home. For many years I studied Yiddish language and culture after school three days a week. But I had no bar mitzvah, followed the path of science and medicine, and never read, much less pondered, any part of anyone's Bible. Though I was taught at home to respect believers, by the time I was in college I regarded all religion as superstition, someday to be replaced by the fruits of Enlightenment reason and a vaguely Kantian universal morality of peace and justice. So what happened?

I have no single epiphany to report. Many events and experiences have moved me, too numerous to recount here. Intellectually, the most significant were the opportunities to teach Genesis and Exodus as "great books," in the spirit of liberal education, at the University of Chicago over a period of thirty-four years. But this book is more than a merely intellectual commentary on Exodus. Looking back, I now see that a different seed was inconspicuously planted in Cambridge, Massachusetts, on a Saturday morning in February 1967.

Our first child had just been born, on Christmas Day 1966. I was engaged in writing up my doctoral research in biochemistry, but brooding also on how my wife and I should raise this child. The Yiddishist education I had enjoyed with other first-generation Americans in the '40s and '50s was, I could see, no longer viable in the United States. My closest friend, Harvey Flaumenhaft, had insisted for years that the strong moral teachings of my home—righteousness, self-restraint, duty, and *menschlichkeit*—were in fact parasitic on traditional Judaism: the prophets, so to speak, without the law. Taking advantage of my condition as a new father, Harvey invited me to join him at Harvard Hillel for a regular Shabbat service. "What do you have to lose? They will read the weekly portion from the Torah, and someone will then say something interesting about it. You love discussions of books. Come. You might even learn something." So I went. I had been to a synagogue perhaps three times in my life—a cousin's wedding, another cousin's bar mitzvah, and my own wedding (held there to please my mother-in-law). Knowing nothing about the Sabbath service, I sat patiently awaiting the Torah reading.

As luck would have it, the weekly portion was Terumah (Exodus 25–27), devoted entirely to the detailed and boring instructions for building the Tabernacle. I remember thinking, let's see anyone make something interesting out of *this*. To my astonishment, Rabbi Ben-Zion Gold more than delivered. The instructions for the sanctuary, he pointed out, and the later account of its construction according to these instructions, sandwich the story of the golden calf, an eruption of wild and dangerous passions that the sanctuary is built to contain, regulate, and control—precisely through the measure, order, and rule prescribed by the detailed and necessarily boring instructions. Not bad, thought I. If a text this unexciting harbors such ideas, what might not the rest contain? (Some thirty years later, when we met at the bat mitzvah of a daughter of mutual friends, I was able to thank Rabbi Gold for his great gift to me.) Six months later, after a move to Maryland, we joined a Conservative synagogue and began to light Sabbath candles, preparing ourselves to offer our children an experience of Jewish tradition that they could later embrace or reject as they wished. Better, we thought, to be something rather than nothing, and *our* something was nothing to be ashamed of.

It would take another decade before I began seriously to engage the Bible in an intellectual way, first as a result of having to teach Genesis and Exodus (among other great texts) to first-year undergraduates in a year-long common core course at Chicago. The biblical stories took hold of me and became regular topics at the family dinner table. I eventually got up enough nerve to offer a full course just on Genesis, and fifteen years later, another on Exodus, both read in search of wisdom regarding human nature and human good. Suspending disbelief, approaching the Bible with an open mind, I was astonished to discover an account of human life that can more than hold its own with the anthropological and ethical teachings offered by the great poets and philosophers.

I discovered in the Hebrew Bible teachings of righteousness, humaneness, and human dignity—the source of my parents' teaching of *menschlichkeit*—that had been missing from my philosophizing. In the idea that human beings are equally Godlike, equally created in the image of the divine, I saw the core principle of a humanistic and democratic politics, respectful of every human being. In the Sabbath injunction to desist regularly from the flux of getting and spending, I discovered an invitation to each human being, no matter how lowly, to step outside of time, in *imitatio dei,* to contemplate the beauty of the world and to feel gratitude for its—and our—existence. In the injunction to honor your father and your mother, I recognized the foundation of a dignified family life, for each of us the nursery of our humanity and the first vehicle of cultural transmission. I satisfied myself that there is no conflict between the Bible, rightly read, and modern science. And I was moved to new postures of gratitude, awe, and moral attention.

According to the biblical account, just as the world is summoned into existence under intelligent and order-creating command, so to be a human being in that world—to be a *mensch*—is to live in search of an intelligible and order-creating summons. It is to recognize that we are here not by choice or merit but as an undeserved gift from powers not at our disposal. It is to feel the need to justify that gift, to make something out of our indebtedness for the opportunity of existence. And it is to stand not only in awe of the world's and our existence but also under an obligation to answer a call to a worthy life, a life that does honor to the special powers and possibilities—the divine likeness—with which our otherwise animal existence has been, no thanks to us, endowed.

In studying Exodus in this spirit, seeking its teachings regarding a worthy life for an individual and a community, I have had wonderful companions. I learned a great deal from outstanding undergraduate and graduate students in five classes at University of Chicago, among them Robert Abbott, Kristen Balisi, Jonathan Baskin, Jeremy Bell, Anastasia Berg, Lauren Bergier, John Ellison, Harriet Fertik, Rita Koganzon, Ruth Martin (Curry), Alex Orwin, Daniel Owings, Jeremy Rozansky, Aaron Tugendhaft, Margarita Zaydman, and Etay Zwick. In 2007 and 2008 I benefited immensely from a yearlong weekly study group with family members and close friends in Washington, DC: its members were Eric Cohen, Harvey Flaumenhaft, Amy Kass, Sarah Kass, Adam Keiper, Yael Levin (Hungerford), Yuval Levin, and Judah Mandelbaum. A seminar I gave in 2016 as visiting scholar at Shalem College, Jerusalem, brought new insights, especially from Amir Blumenkrantze, J. J. Kimche, Niv Liel, and Avia Sandak. Line-by-line explorations the following year (over FaceTime) with my Israeli granddaughter Hannah Mandelbaum were regularly illuminating. Finally, in 2017–2018, I benefited enormously from a group of Jerusalem friends who gathered weekly at Shalem College to read and comment on early drafts of each chapter in this book: Sagi Barmak, Amiad Cohen, Nathan Laufer, Richie Lewis, Jerome Marcus, and Dan Polisar (whose idea this was). Invariably, I would show up with a draft that I thought was sound enough, only to learn (especially from Nathan, Richie, and Dan) that three or four major revisions were in order; working with this group proved to be the most fruitful and satisfying intellectual experience of my life. When I returned to the United States, Nathan, Richie, and Dan continued to meet with me weekly on Skype to get me across the finish line. They gave me the benefit of their enormous biblical learning while entering sympathetically into my most untraditional way of reading the text. I remain in awe of their generosity and filled with gratitude for their friendship.

Thanks largely to these more recent experiences, the book I have written is not exactly the book I set out to write. When I began my study of Exodus twenty years ago, I came armed with questions that grew out of nearly twenty prior years of studying Genesis. I was eager to follow the story of how God's Way for humankind—begun with Abraham and transmitted to the households of Isaac and Jacob—would be instituted on a national scale. I wanted to see how the new national arrangement would address the troubling human tendencies—psychic, familial, social—that had come to light in the tales of Genesis. My primary questions came from political philosophy. I looked for insights into political founding and people formation, freedom and order, law and morality, the leader and the led. This book in part conveys what I have discovered about these matters.

But having dwelt at length with Exodus, through many readings with diverse companions and under different life circumstances, I finish in a different place from where I began. As a result of reading after the fashion I always recommend to my students, I have lived *with* the book and allowed it to work on me. My experience of Exodus, especially in the last few years, has revised my sense of what it is about. And it has changed me. I still see great merit in the philosophical questions I have raised, but I now appreciate the book's more-than-philosophical answers. Exodus surely illuminates the process of people formation. Its laws surely address the evils that lurk in the hearts of men. It surely offers wise guidance for communal life, against the technocratic and hedonistic temptations—once associated, respectively, with Egypt and Canaan—that still sing their seductive songs. But it also examines and nourishes deep longings of the soul for which law and politics are insufficient, longings that I was not fully aware I harbored when I first began this study. Two things especially have altered my outlook.

In Autumn 2016, as mentioned, I taught a discussion-seminar on Exodus at Shalem College. The students were second-year undergraduates, men and women in their early to late twenties, all of whom had completed their required national service. They were a mixed group, some religiously observant, most not. I taught in English from Robert Alter's translation; nearly all of them read the text in the original Hebrew. Everyone could understand what I said, but only a few could express any complicated thoughts in English. So I allowed them to speak in Hebrew, and others translated for me. Although the students did their best to accommodate me, none had prior encounters with a philosophical approach to the Bible. The experience was often frustrating for all of us. Yet for the entire time, I lived with one overwhelming feeling: I was enjoying the unbelievable privilege of reading with noble Israeli youth, and in Jerusalem, the founding text of the Jewish people—a text whose teachings had preserved the national identity of their devoted ancestors for two thousand years of exile, during which those ancestors not only studied the text but also lived by it. Moreover, the students were reading and discussing the text in the Holy Tongue (*lashon haqqodesh*), a language that had not been spoken on the street anywhere in the world for hundreds of years before the twentieth century. These facts not only defied political philosophy; they defied all reasonable expectations of how the world works. Even a devout atheist might suspect this was a miracle.

The second thing happened more recently, as a result of my work with Nathan, Richie, and Dan. I have lately found in the text itself true things undreamt of in my—or any—philosophy. Ironically, it was mainly studying about the Tabernacle that brought about this change. Until last year, I had never paid the Tabernacle much attention, even though thirteen of Exodus's forty chapters are devoted to it. The long account of its construction is at first glance—and at second and third glances—repetitious and boring. Since my eye-opening visit to Harvard Hillel in 1967, I had assumed that the Tabernacle was a concession to human weakness, serving mainly to cabin the ineradicable Dionysian impulses that erupted at the golden calf and that ordinary law can do little to satisfy—impulses whose significance I had undervalued. But to complete this commentary, and believing the text to be an integral whole, I forced myself to do due diligence on the Tabernacle. Over several months, I went line by line in the company of my three friends, trying to live with the text narratively and from the inside. By the end, I was astonished to discover that I had formed a more capacious and elevated idea of the Tabernacle and its purposes. I came to see that the founding of the Israelite nation—and of the Jewish People—rests on not two but three pillars. There is the story of slavery in and exodus from Egypt, providing the national narrative and memory of common history, suffering, and deliverance. There is the covenant and the giving of the Law, the moral-legal foundation of everyday conduct within the political community. But there are also the ritual enactments in the Tent of Meeting that speak to the human soul's deep longings for transcendence and that—quite mysteriously—can bring a numinous Presence into the daily lives of ordinary human beings. Only in this way, suggests the text, can the Creation be completed. Only in this way can human life in the world be made whole.

To help you with your own due diligence, I offer this book in the hope that your experience might be the same as mine.

—Jerusalem, February 2020

About the Text

Translation and Transliteration

In studying Exodus and in preparing this book, I have consulted many translations of the Hebrew text. I have most frequently used those provided by Robert Alter, Umberto Cassuto, Dr. J. H. Hertz, Joseph Magil, and Nahum M. Sarna. Occasionally I have looked also at the King James Version and the Revised Standard Version. The translated excerpts of Exodus that appear throughout this book are often composites of versions found in different sources, selected and modified according to my own sense of what seems most fitting. As far as possible, I have sought the most literal translation compatible with readable English.

Transliterations of Hebrew words largely follow the rules of *Encyclopedia Judaica*, 2nd edition. Therefore, aspirated ב and פ are rendered *v* and *f*, respectively; aspirated כ is indicated by *kh*, and aspirated ג and ד forms are rendered as *g* and *d*, respectively. However, aspirated ת is indicated as *th*. I deviate from the *Encyclopedia Judaica* rules in avoiding diacritic markings: therefore ח is rendered *ch*, and צ is rendered *ts*. Furthermore, א and ע are both indicated with an apostrophe (' and ', respectively) when they appear in the first position in a syllable. Final unvoiced ה is indicated by *h* at the end of the word. Furthermore, ק is rendered *q*, not *k*. As in the *Encyclopedia Judaica* system, the dagesh forte is indicated by a doubled consonant, except when it appears on the letters *shin* or *tsade,* in which cases it is not indicated. Silent *yod* (as in צאינה) is not indicated. Where this book refers to a Hebrew verb, the form given is usually the third-person masculine perfect (past tense) form, which is the form usually used in dictionaries. Where I refer to a Hebrew root, I indicate the three root letters in sequence (where necessary, separated by hyphens).

Citations from Exodus will be given numerically, chapter and verse. Citations from other biblical sources will first identify the book.

The Notes

To improve the reader's experience of the printed page, nearly all notes—including many (often lengthy) comments that extend or qualify what is in the text—have been placed in the Notes section at the back of the book, listed chapter by chapter. All citations and attributions appear there as well. A few substantive comments that demand more proximate placement appear as asterisked footnotes on the same page as the relevant text.

Pronouns

Throughout this book, I consistently use the male third-person singular pronoun to denote an unspecified human individual. I am keenly aware that this practice will raise eyebrows and not a few hackles. Some readers may be offended; others may conclude (I think mistakenly) that they are being excluded from my book or from the teachings of the book of Exodus. Acknowledging the difficulty, I offer my readers this explanation.

First, some forty years after this usage became politically fraught, we still do not have a gender-neutral third-person personal pronoun. "It" denotes something soulless (or nonhuman). The plural "they" is grammatically incorrect. The frequent use of "he or she" (or similar formulations) is cumbersome and would not only disturb the book's readability but also obtrude gender as an issue where it is irrelevant. Moreover, with today's consciousness of nonbinary gender identities, "he or she" is neither neutral nor inclusive enough. Unhappy with these alternatives, I reverted to the simplest and oldest usage, fully aware that it is not completely satisfactory but convinced that all the available alternatives are even less so.

In the same spirit, I also use the word "man" as an exact synonym for the less elegant "humanity"—again, to mean all of us collectively, without regard to gender.

Second, Biblical Hebrew is an inflected language. All nouns have gender, and verbs denoting their actions have matching gendered endings, yet their denotation is generally comprehensive. Sometimes when the Bible says "he," it quite literally means a male and not a female or both; in most places, "he" (or the grammatically masculine 'adam, "man") clearly means "any human being, regardless of gender": "And God created 'adam in His image; in the image of God created He him; male and female created He them." Readers today may disapprove of the Bible's gendered language and thought, but it is a matter of historical fact that I feel obliged not to alter.

I therefore ask for the reader's forbearance and good will in exchange for my assurance that I mean for this book to speak equally to every reader. Where I use "he" generically, the reader should understand that I mean the universal human being, regardless of sex or gender.

Founding
God's Nation

Introduction

This book offers a commentary on the book of Exodus, approached in a philosophical spirit. It aims to be useful to any thoughtful person—believers and unbelievers, seekers and citizens, Jews, Christians, and others—interested in questions about the good life and the just society and, regarding Exodus in particular, about the foundation, character, and purposes of political communities. Exodus not only recounts the founding of the Israelite nation, one of the world's oldest and most consequential peoples. It also sheds light on enduring questions about nation-building and peoplehood. It invites us to think about the moral meaning of communal life, the nature of political leadership, and the standards for judging a social order as better or worse.

Why Read Exodus?

Exodus, the second of the Five Books of Moses (The Torah), contains some of the most famous stories in Western literature: the enslavement of the Children of Israel by Pharaoh in Egypt, the rescue of baby Moses from the Nile by Pharaoh's daughter, God's call to Moses out of the burning bush, the ten plagues that God sends against the Egyptians, the midnight exodus of the Israelite slaves from Egypt as God passes over their houses while slaying every Egyptian firstborn, the splitting of the Sea of Reeds and the drowning of Pharaoh's army, manna from heaven in the wilderness, God's pronouncement of the Ten Commandments at Sinai, Israel's worship of the golden calf, and the building of the Tabernacle, a sanctuary for the Lord. Yet the power of these stories lies not only in their drama. They are here because each plays an indispensable part in the book's overarching purpose: to narrate the birth of the Israelite nation and to present the moral-political founding of a people called to carry God's Way for humankind. Exodus is therefore a work of enormous importance, both for the Bible as a book and for the world that bears its influence.

Within the Hebrew Bible, Exodus is *the* foundational political text. It moves us from the anarchic familial world of the patriarchs in Genesis to a new order of law and peoplehood. The rest of the Bible explores the trials and tribulations of the Israelite nation in the world that Exodus brings into being. Those books recount their turbulent wanderings in the wilderness, their entrance into the Promised Land, their battles with their enemies, their internal struggles and divisions, and their efforts—mainly failures—to follow the Law they received in Exodus. Yet even in times of decay and decline, the Founding Law given in Exodus remains a benchmark. When, centuries later, the prophets chastise the people for their moral failings, they do so in the name of the Torah, summoning them to return to God's Way.

Exodus has played an enormous part in the history of the world, well beyond its role in forming the people of Israel. Its stories and teachings have attracted followers and served as models for other "Israels," beginning with Christianity, which regarded itself as the "New Israel" and which eventually brought the Ten Commandments to much of the world. Ideas first put forth in Exodus—the principles of human dignity and human equality; the demand for justice, tempered by mercy; the injunctions to honor one's father and mother, to care for the vulnerable, and to respect the stranger; the summons to righteousness and holiness—became the moral, political, and spiritual wellsprings of Western civilization. For more than two millennia, the teachings of Exodus have guided millions of human beings, and its moral and political influence on the peoples of the West is unsurpassed. For it is the story of a particular nation with universal—and permanent—significance. And if read philosophically, Exodus still offers thoughtful readers rich material for thinking about nation-building and people formation, slavery and freedom, morality and law, man and God.

In Quest of Wisdom

I should explain what I mean by "philosophical" and by reading "philosophically." I mean, quite simply, "wisdom seeking" and "wisdom loving," after the literal meaning of the ancient Greek term *philosophia*, "the love and pursuit of wisdom." In this sense, philosophy refers not to some specialized academic subject matter ("the field of philosophy"), to some finished doctrine ("my philosophy of life"), or to some method of reasoning practiced by card-carrying professional philosophers ("the discipline of philosophy"). Rather it denotes the activity—epitomized by Socrates, Plato, Aristotle, and their descendants—of whole-hearted pursuit of the truth about the world and our place within it, in search of guidance for how we are to live. This book results from my efforts to read the Hebrew Bible in this spirit, the same spirit in which I read Plato's *Republic* or Aristotle's *Nicomachean Ethics*—indeed, any great book—seeking wisdom regarding human life lived well in relation to the whole.

It is, I know, highly unusual today to read the Bible in this spirit and with these aspirations. Neither academic scholars nor devoted readers of Scripture incline toward a philosophical approach. But both have much to gain from it.

Current academic prejudices reject the belief that the Bible—or any old book—can still serve as a vital source of human understanding and moral-political instruction. Since the nineteenth century, most biblical scholars have seen the Hebrew Bible not as a unified literary whole but as an aggregate of documents derived from diverse sources. They read it not as a possible source of wisdom regarding enduring human questions but as documentary evidence of the sensibilities and beliefs of an ancient people. More recently, politicized scholars, inclined to blame the Bible for Western ideas and practices they oppose, have attacked its teachings as racist, sexist, or anthropocentric. For them, the Bible is a source not of wisdom but of dangerous error.

Devoted readers of Scripture continue to take guidance from it. But because they regard the Good Book as the revealed word of God, they are disinclined to interrogate it like any merely great book. There is evidence to support their view.

The Bible is not a work of philosophy, ordinarily understood—though it is hard to say exactly what kind of work it is. Neither its manner nor its manifest purpose is philosophical. Its entire approach appears to be *anti*-philosophical. Philosophical inquiry seeks wisdom by looking to nature and relying on unaided human reason; biblical religion offers wisdom based on divine revelation and relying on prophecy. Philosophy begins in wonder and seeks understanding for its own sake; biblical wisdom begins in the fear of the Lord and seeks righteous and holy conduct. Over centuries, the great sages of the Jewish Tradition, deeply steeped in the Bible, read the text—especially the book of Exodus—not as a platform for universal speculation but as a source of law and morals for the Children of Israel. Jerusalem is not Athens.

Objections to reading the Bible philosophically—seeking universal wisdom—have force and merit but are not, in my view, decisive. For one thing, the book of Exodus does not say that it can be understood only from within the Tradition. For another, the giving of the Law to Israel is embedded in a much larger narrative of the human story, part of whose function is to make the *necessity* of the Law intelligible and its content acceptable to the reader. Besides, even a parochial text can be profitably read for its universal insight. The *Iliad,* written by a Greek for Greeks, remains for readers everywhere the deepest story of the relationship between man's awareness of mortality and his heroic quest for glory. If there is wisdom in the Hebrew Bible, it should be available not only to Jews and Christians but to all.

The Bible agrees. The text provides strong indications that the Lord's intention for His political founding is not merely parochial. Although He is directly concerned with the Children of Israel, He appears also to have the whole human race in mind. It is as an alternative to the failures of human beings uninstructed that He summons Abraham to initiate His Way for humankind, promising him that "*all the families of the earth* shall be blessed in you" (Gen. 12:3; emphasis added). He enters into a contest with Pharaoh (the plagues) in order that "the *Egyptians* shall know that I am the Lord" (7:5). He establishes His covenant with Israel, that it might become a "kingdom of priests and a holy nation" (19:6), with a people that His prophets will later call "a light unto the nations" (Isa. 49:6). And when Moses at the end of his life repeats the Law to the Children of Israel as they prepare to enter the Promised Land, he tells them that their statutes and ordinances are "your wisdom and your understanding in the eyes of the peoples: when they hear of these statutes they will say, 'Surely this great nation is a wise and understanding nation'" (Deut. 4:6). The wisdom of the Torah is said *by* the Torah to be accessible to everyone, even to those on whom it is not binding.

Many great thinkers, religious and not, have looked at Exodus in this spirit, seeking its wisdom about political founding, leadership and law, justice and morality. Figures as diverse as Machiavelli and Rousseau used the example of Moses in discussing national founding and legislating. In the seventeenth century, political thinkers like Peter Cunaeus found in the ancient "Hebrew Republic" guidance for modern political reform, and jurists like John Selden found in the Hebrew Bible the foundations for universal natural right and natural law. The biblical idea that the best body politic rests on covenant entered the American colonies with the Mayflower Compact, and the tradition of civic republicanism in America owes much to the Puritan devotion to the Hebrew Bible. In all sorts of formal and informal ways, the teachings of Exodus have written themselves into the moral and political life of the West, from the principles of the Decalogue to the condemnation of slavery, from wars of national liberation to the humane treatment of strangers. Anyone interested in human affairs stands to learn much from a serious engagement with Exodus by approaching the book open-mindedly and thoughtfully.

On no subject is Exodus more useful than the questions of nation-building and peoplehood.

What Makes a People a People?

What makes a people a people? What forms their communal identity, holds them together, guides their lives? To what do they look up? For what should they strive? Can there be an enduring and thriving people without a communal story, shared moral norms, or common national aspirations?[1]

Exodus is a wonderful text for thinking about these questions. It is at once a narrative account of and the normative text for the birth of the Jewish people—a parochial people that bears a universal teaching. Exodus tells the story, begun in Genesis on the plane of families, of how God (working through Moses) tries to address the evils and miseries of uninstructed human existence by instituting His Way for humankind: an alternative to the ways of the Mesopotamians, the Egyptians, and the Canaanites, it is a Way devoted to decency and dignity, righteousness and holiness. Beginning with the Children of Israel enslaved in Egypt, Exodus is mainly about the founding of the Israelite nation through three decisive events: their deliverance from bondage, their receipt of the Law at Sinai, and their building of the Tabernacle as a Tent of Meeting with their God.

The narrative account offers abundant material for reflection on subjects of universal interest: the best beginnings for founding a people (why start them in abject slavery, in a strange land?), the qualifications for leadership (why Moses and why Aaron?), the virtues of civic life (how do slavish people acquire moderation, courage, and fidelity?), the bond of civil society (what is the meaning of covenant and the nature of consent?), the source of law (reason or will, human or divine?), the forms of law (parsing cases or absolute commandments?), the reach of law (limited or totalitarian?), the purposes of law (securing rights or teaching duties, limiting wrongdoing or promoting excellence, justice or holiness?), the forms of governance (hierarchic or democratic, charismatic or bureaucratic?), the sources of trouble and the causes of rebellion (foreign influence or domestic schism, fear or envy, distrust or faithlessness, weak leaders or stiff-necked people?), and the relation to the divine (immanent or transcendent, what need for ritual and sacrifice?).

In a word, Exodus, like the rest of the Torah, speaks to the same vital questions that occupy the great works of Western philosophy and literature: Why are we here? How should we live? What can we know? What is a good human community? How can it be formed and sustained? How does it stand, generally, between human beings and the cosmos, between human beings and the divine?

Exodus explores none of these subjects thematically, as a treatise on political founding or law might do. Straightforward answers appear nowhere in our text, nor do the questions themselves. But insight is often more accessible through stories than through argument. Precisely because our questions arise out of a concrete narrative, we get to think about the universal through the particular, without losing the lived reality of the subjects of our reflection. Exodus supplies lively and vivid material for thinking about all these matters—provided we pay close attention and read in quest of wisdom.

This is also why we need (more than) a few words about attending and reading—especially because I read the Bible not in the usual ways.

How I Read

The Hebrew Bible, no matter who reads it, is not self-interpreting. To get at its meaning requires the hard work of exegesis and interpretation. The task of interpretation is complicated by the fact that the Bible, like most great books, does not provide rules for how to read it. As with the content, so with the approach: the thoughtful reader must find his own way. The path he takes will reflect his assumptions and intuitions about the nature of the book, as well as his own predispositions and purposes as a reader—all of them alterable over many readings and re-readings, not to speak of other changes in his experience. I owe my own readers an account of my accumulated assumptions and intuitions about Exodus and of my predispositions and purposes in reading and writing about it.

To begin with, I assume that Exodus is a *book,* an integrated whole, with a coherent order and plan; it is not just a collection of stitched-together fragments from different sources. While its story depends in part on what came before, as reported in Genesis, and while it continues meaningfully (and seamlessly) into Leviticus and the rest of the Torah, it is also a discrete unit with a beginning, middle, and end. It begins with the descent of the Children of Israel into—and, later, their deliverance from—involuntary servitude to Pharaoh in mighty Egypt; it peaks with the Lord's revelation and giving of the Law in the wilderness at Sinai; and it concludes with the raising of a Tabernacle that the

Children of Israel have erected in service to the Lord. As I will try to show, everything proceeds according to logical, not merely chronological, necessity. If this is true, it follows that the meaning of each part must be considered in relation to the whole; episodes taken out of context and sentences cherry-picked for special purposes may be misunderstood.

Next, I have come to see that every word matters. So do word order, first or unique uses, nearby repetition of words or phrases, puns and echoes of previous uses of the same term, and shifts from prose into poetry and back again. Juxtapositions are especially important. What precedes or follows a given sentence or story may be crucial for discovering its meaning. It matters, for example, that the commandment to commemorate Passover night from generation to generation is given to the people *before* the event actually happens. It matters that the visit to the Israelites by Moses's father-in-law Jethro occurs in the text right after their battle with the attacking Amalekites and immediately precedes the giving of the Law at Sinai. It matters that God's orders to build the Tabernacle come on the heels of an ambiguous sacrifice offered by Moses and that the story of worshipping the golden calf is sandwiched between those instructions and the reported construction of the Tabernacle that follows His prescribed orders precisely. Some biblical scholars find many of these juxtapositions incoherent and attribute them to different original sources; I find the text coherent and encourage the reader to join me in explaining the perplexing appositions.

Lacunae, absences, and silences also count. Why does the text say nothing about Moses's life growing up in Pharaoh's house during the decade and more between his adoption by Pharaoh's daughter and his manly appearance on the world stage, or about his decades living with Jethro in Midian before God calls him at the burning bush? Why is God not mentioned during the battle with the Amalekites? Does He play no part in the Israelite victory? Why does Moses say not a word during God's seven-chapter monologue about building the Tabernacle, and why is Aaron but lightly reprimanded for his egregious role in the people's idolatry with the golden calf? It is precisely the text's sparseness, lacunae, ambiguity, and reticence that invite and require the reader's engagement—about which, more soon.

A controversial assumption: I believe that, like any great book, Exodus carries its persuasive power in itself. Access to the truths it might contain does not require prior faith, prior traditional or religious commitments, or reliance on outside authorities. As already noted, nontheistic thinkers have learned much from studying the text on their own. And although much can be learned from the many wonderful commentaries that have been written about the book (I will make liberal use of them, here and there), the meaning and teachings of the book—a book that someone must have read before there were any commentaries—should be approachable without intermediaries.

To do so most profitably, I try to approach the text as naively as possible. I force myself to read it as if for the first time, ignorant of what happens later in the story, so as not to distort what is taking place before my eyes. In reading about any episode or interpreting any passage, I try to admit into evidence only what I have read before in Genesis or in the preceding parts of Exodus. I do not assume that the story's characters have read the Bible or know anything at all other than what the text has told us they have seen or heard or done.

Thus, for example, although the reader knows from the beginning of Genesis about the Creation of the world in six days, no one in the story learns about it until God pronounces the Ten Commandments to the Israelite people at Sinai. Unlike readers within the Tradition, who know where the book is going and who use materials from everywhere in the text to illuminate any given passage, I almost never use later passages to explicate earlier ones—although I may point out how a present episode or a novel expression, intelligible on its own, is *also* pregnant with future possibilities. I try to exclude concepts, even worthy ones, that are foreign to the text—which is hardest to do when they are part of the way I normally see the world. If I am to learn *from* the text, however, I cannot find only what I have unthinkingly inserted by way of question or answer. (I will, however, occasionally step back from the text to illuminate what I have found there by comparing it with teachings from other books and traditions.)

I am acutely aware of the great danger that hangs over all efforts at interpretation: that one will find in the text not what the author intended

but only what one has put there oneself. For these reasons, a philosophical reading of Exodus must proceed with great modesty and caution,
not to say fear and trembling. If I sometimes forget myself and seem
too bold, it is out of zeal for understanding. Moreover, I make no claim
to a final or definitive reading. The stories are too rich, too complex,
and too deep to be captured fully, once and for all. One can therefore,
as I hope to demonstrate, approach the book in a spirit that is simultaneously naïve, philosophical, modest, and reverent. As the example
of Socrates reminds us, humility before mystery and knowledge of
one's own ignorance are hardly at odds with a philosophical spirit.

I assume that the teachings of the text—including the divine
commandments—are not utterly opaque to human reason, even if God
and other matters remain veiled in mystery. Even though, as we shall
see, the text takes a dim view of the sufficiency of unaided human speech
and reason, it presents that case to our minds through intelligible speech
and in a most powerful way. And while obedience to the laws seems to
be required only because God commanded them, and reasons for them
are rarely provided, I assume that the commandments had to make
enough sense to the Israelites in the story that they were willing to consider giving their consent to obey. As centuries of rabbinic interpretation of biblical law demonstrate, finding reason and purpose in the law
surely does not undermine its claim on conduct. Moreover, contrary to
those who think that only the obedient and the faithful can understand
the text, anyone can fruitfully approach it in search of wisdom, even if
by so doing one comes to learn the limitations of such philosophical activity or even of thinking altogether.

I assume further that, like any great book read often and openly,
Exodus will eventually show us how it wants to be read. After long experience with the book, I now believe that the text has been written not
merely to inform the reader *about* the narrated events. It has been written mainly to form him—to educate him—not only by means of its explicit content and dramatic enactments but also and especially by the
ways in which it manages to draw him into its orbit. The book aims not
just to teach *about*, but to be lived *with*. Precisely through its manner of
writing and its need for interpretation and reinterpretation, it causes the
reader to enter into its content and make the book his own.

To be sure, the events described in the story happened millennia ago to a strange people living under very different circumstances from our own. But the story itself is addressed to unspecified and nameless readers whom it invites into its midst, century after century. We can—we should—enter sympathetically into it and inhabit the hearts and minds of all of its characters, including those who initially repel us. With some effort of imagination and sympathy, we can live with Moses at the burning bush, with Pharaoh during the plagues, with the people backed against the Sea of Reeds or hearing the Decalogue at Mount Sinai, with Moses on the mountain, with Aaron at the golden calf, with the people bringing gifts for the Tabernacle. We can try to understand them as they understand themselves.

Yet the text also gives us the distance the characters lack for assessing the story in its entirety. It rarely pronounces judgments but works to develop our sympathies and sensibilities as well as our understanding—if we let it.

In short, I have come to regard myself as an integral participant of the book. I am not a character in the story, but my vicarious participation is required for the text to come fully to life. This is, of course, true of other books. It is notoriously true of a Platonic dialogue, which *truly* exists only when the reader vivifies the conversation he is auditing by entering sympathetically into every person's speech—considering carefully for himself what it means, why the person said it, and the degree to which he speaks truly.

This is admittedly easier to do with a Socratic conversation than with the variegated text of Exodus. But having now for years entered sympathetically into the story, inhabited the characters, discussed their experiences with diverse colleagues and generations of students, pondered the law, and thought *with* the text and not just about it, I have felt it change my feelings and thoughts about important matters. Precisely because the world of the text is so different from my own—so spare, so unsophisticated, so awe inspiring—it has proved to be a powerful mirror in which to look at my own complacent understandings of significant subjects. By giving me a world that is not graspable by my familiar concepts, it has forced me to reconsider many previously unexamined notions and prejudices—for example, about the putatively clear distinction between ethics and ritual or between "secular" and "sacred"; about the primacy of such philosophical categories as "being and essence," "soul and body," "freedom and necessity," "cause and effect"; and, of course, the biggest mystery of all, about God, in the text and out.

Setting the Stage

Unlike Genesis, which begins at the very beginning, when the whole earth "was without form and void, and darkness was upon the face of the deep," Exodus begins *in medias res*. Even for readers familiar with Genesis, a brief review of what came before may help set the stage for what is to come in our reading of Exodus.

Genesis begins with Creation, offering an account of the createdness of our intelligibly ordered world. One of the main purposes of this account is the demotion of the earth, heaven, and the heavenly bodies—worshipped everywhere as gods by people who have not heard the account given in Genesis—from divinities themselves to mere creations of a divine higher power. Genesis ends with the incipient nation of Israel, bearing the seeds of God's Way and settled in Egypt—the peak of civilization and the highest human possibility that knows not the God of the Bible; a civilization boasting agriculture, architecture, art, science, technology, bureaucracy, wealth, and prosperity; and oriented precisely toward the worship of nature, especially the sun and the Nile.

The mythic stories of the first eleven chapters of Genesis—Adam and Eve, Cain and Abel, Noah and the Flood, Noah and his sons, the city and tower of Babel—quietly convey an anthropology, an account of the psychic and social elements of human life in all their moral ambiguity, that shows us why human life, if left to its own devices, leads to disaster. Simple innocence, anarchy, primitive law under paternal authority, and the universal rational city all fail. We are afforded insights into the problematic character of freedom and reason, cleverness and craft, pride and envy, *eros* and ecstasy. We learn of troubles within families, between strangers, and between men and God. We are therefore eager, when God calls Abraham in Genesis 12, to see if there can be found an alternative to the dismal prospects of untutored human life.

Beginning with Abraham (whom we vicariously join on his journey), God embarks on such an alternative, in which one nation is to be
instructed in His Way and then to bear this Way to all the nations of
the earth. The bulk of Genesis describes the beginnings of God's Way
through the three patriarchal generations. The trials of Abraham, Isaac,
and Jacob—and of the matriarchs Sarah, Rebekah, Leah, and Rachel—
begin to educate them, as well as the reader, regarding Who this God is
and what He might want of them. Each generation must face anew the
dangers of fratricide and patricide, and the temptations of hubris, assimilation, and God-forgetting.

It is tough work: the women are barren, there is famine in the land,
there is sibling rivalry and domestic strife, there are foreign dangers. In
the third generation, Jacob—renamed Israel for struggling with God and
man, and prevailing—manages to sire a clan whose members are variously unified, for better and for worse, in avenging the rape of their sister
Dinah, in hating (and then reconciling with) their brother Joseph, and
in burying their father Jacob in the ancestral cave in Canaan. At the end
of Genesis, they are an incipient nation, living comfortably not in the
Promised Land but in Egypt.

As an incipient nation called to carry God's Way, they have little
to go on. They may have memories of divine encounters with their ancestors and of God's promises of great fertility and the Promised Land.
They may have heard tales of the deeds of the previous generations of
Abraham, Isaac, and Jacob; they may have a vague awareness of God's
presence. But they have received to this point only one commandment:
the duty to circumcise newborn sons, in commemoration and reenact-
ment of the covenant that God made with Father Abraham. Culturally
speaking, it is not a lot: other than circumcision, there are no given laws
and no prescribed rituals to shape their lives in this foreign land of good
and plenty. They are alive and thriving in Egypt, and for now that
suffices.

The architect of their descent into Egypt—and, it turns out, the foil
for Moses who will bring them out—was their brilliant brother Joseph,
at first singled out for rule in Israel by their father Jacob but then rising
to become prime minister to Pharaoh in Egypt. Although already largely

lost to his people, he settles them in a favored location in Goshen under his protection. At the same time, he consolidates Pharaoh's power, centralizes all land ownership, and purchases the servitude of the Egyptian masses as the price for seed grain. In his own eyes a divine instrument and savior—as well he may be—he is also the architect of the eventual enslavement of his people.

This is not quite fair to Joseph. Early in His relationship with Abraham, God had foretold to him a period of 400 years of his descendants' servitude in a strange land, as the precondition of inheriting the Promised Land (Gen. 15:13–14). In His last speech in Genesis—and presumably His last speech to anyone for several centuries, until He speaks to Moses at the burning bush—God tells old Jacob, "Fear not to go down into Egypt, for I will *there* make of you *a great nation.* I will go down with you into Egypt, and I will surely bring you up again" (Gen. 46:3–4; emphasis added). Israel will become a great nation *only* in Egypt.

What was begun or founded in the households of Abraham, Isaac, and Jacob, in the Promised Land, must be re-founded on a national level, re-founded in exile, re-founded specifically in, against, and out of Egypt. The questions we therefore bring to the book of Exodus are these: How does this come about? What does it take to create this nation and form this people? What is required to enable Israel to embody and show to the world God's Way for humankind? And what has all this to do with Egypt? With this background and these questions in mind, we are (almost) ready to start reading, awaiting only a brief preview of what lies ahead—and a few words about God.

Preview

What you are about to read is a commentary, tied to the text and going nearly line by line, that proceeds from the first verse of Exodus 1 to the last verse of Exodus 40, with intermittent risings from the text to take stock of where we are and to explore larger themes. We will be guided throughout by the overall narrative, considering even the legal and architectural sections in the context of the unfolding human and national story. We will not only look in from the outside—from our safe distance in the twenty-first century—but will also, where possible, read sympathetically and personally as participant observers.

In that capacity, we will suffer with the Israelites under Pharaoh and travel with Moses from his birth until he takes up God's mission (in this book, Chapters One to Five), marvel at the plagues (Chapter Six), rejoice at Israel's deliverance from bondage and rescue at the Sea of Reeds (Chapters Seven and Eight), struggle on the journey through the wilderness to Sinai (Chapters Nine to Eleven), stand in awe while receiving the Law (Chapters Twelve to Fifteen), cautiously celebrate the ratification of the covenant (Chapter Sixteen), dutifully get instructions for the Tabernacle (Chapters Seventeen to Nineteen), rebel in Moses's absence and feel remorse after breaking the Law in worshipping the golden calf (Chapters Twenty and Twenty-One), and experience exhilaration at building the Tabernacle (Chapter Twenty-Two).

Along the way, we will explore central aspects of nation-building: the value of starting out in abject servitude, devoid of memory of the past and hope for the future; the character and education of Moses, the "outsider" liberator; the difficulties in mobilizing the slaves and in moving their master Pharaoh to release them; the rhetoric of signs, wonders, and chastisements, superior to speech; the vote for deliverance on Passover eve; the educative clash of civilizations, Pharaoh's against God's; the importance of song, dance, and story for national identity; the basic requirements for community survival—food, water, and self-defense; getting Egypt out of the slaves and the need for moderation, courage, and justice; a divinely ordained law; the deeper longings of the national soul and the impulse to sacrifice; inevitable rebellion and idolatry, followed by revelation, restoration, remorse, and return; a place in which to worship and experience the Divine Presence.

We will also have opportunities to study the emergence and improvement of the people, the education of Moses to the task of leadership, the importance of Aaron and Joshua and of Bezalel and Oholiab, and the emerging relationships between God and Moses, Moses and the people, and the people and God.

Finally, we will discover the three pillars on which the nation of Israel is founded. First, a shared historical narrative of slavery and deliverance, commemorated in story and in the annual festival of Passover, each element identifying the people with their difficult past and reminding them of their personal and enduring debt to their divine deliverer. Second, a comprehensive law, covering not only crimes and torts but also moral and spiritual matters, intended to guide everyday life and to shape national character and sentiment in the direction of holiness. Third, the creation of a Tent of Meeting, addressing the human soul's deep yet undisciplined longings for connection with the divine, providing an opportunity for God to dwell among human beings, and for human beings, through ritual practice, to experience God's Presence in their everyday lives.

A Few Words About God

Although I profess that the Bible may profitably be read as a great book, I must (finally) acknowledge that it is also unique among the great books because of its chief protagonist. God is different from any other character in any work of Western literature, mythic or realistic: different in power and authority, complexity and solicitude, and in the demands that He makes on His followers. To paraphrase the text, there is none like Him, anywhere. Also, because the teachings attributed to God in the Bible have reached the lives of millions of human beings, it is difficult to treat Him as we might treat Zeus in the *Iliad* or Marduk in *Enuma Elish,* the Babylonian creation myth. The very presence of such a figure in the story makes many atheists and others unable to read the Bible at all. Similarly, preconceptions about Him among more pious readers make it difficult for them to learn about God by reading in the wisdom-seeking spirit I advocate here. Having had neither of those difficulties, but beginning with my own skepticisms, I have found my own way of addressing this matter.

Almost anyone who comes to the Bible comes with some notion, however inchoate, about God—Who or What He Is or isn't and whether He "exists" or not. Whether we "believe in Him" or not, we think that the "entity" called God is almost by definition eternal, unchanging, omniscient, omnipotent, incorporeal, ineffable, infinite—crudely caricatured as an invisible but truly super Superman. To my great surprise, I discovered that *none* of these attributes—which were "given" to God by medieval theologians—are predicated of Him in the biblical text. In the places where He gives Moses a glimpse of "Himself," these are not at all the attributes that are mentioned. Finding my own preconceptions unsupported, I thus had to come to terms with the character called God or Y-H-V-H without the benefit of accurate prior knowledge or experience.

So how to proceed?

My modest suggestion, born not of philosophy or theology, comes from reading the text. No question, God is *the* prominent character in the story. He plays decisive roles in delivering His people, feeding them in the desert, forming a covenant with them, and giving them their laws. He develops a special relationship with Moses, who serves as His champion against Pharaoh and His agent with the people. These things I learn from the text's surface. But my modern mind wants to know more about *Him*. The text is aware of that desire and speaks indirectly to address it.

When Exodus begins, God is absent from the story—for almost all of the first two chapters. He makes His first real appearance in Chapter 3, as a voice speaking to Moses out of the burning bush. Although awestruck—and who wouldn't be?—Moses wants to know who or what is speaking to him and why.

I am more than a little sympathetic to Moses. As a reader of the Bible, invited from the start to hear the words and to watch the doings of this special character called God, I find myself always in Moses's position. Who is the mysterious voice speaking to me out of the text? What is His purpose? I also want to know just who or what *is* this character "God," who or what *is* this character "Y-H-V-H"? Not having had the Bible to read, Moses wants to know God's name; we readers have His "name," at least as a verbal placeholder in the text. But we want to know Who or What this Name signifies.

The answer Moses gets is the one we should take to heart: "I Will Be What I Will Be." Do not ask for My being or essence, or even about My existence or My person. Pay attention to what I say and do. That, according to the text, is the way of coming to know the character who is variously called God (*'elohim*) or the Lord (*Y-H-V-H*).*

---

*We need straightaway to acknowledge the difficulty in translating the Tetragrammaton, the so-called four-lettered Hebrew name of the God of Israel. Most

What is required for a wisdom-seeking reading of God's doings, and of the text itself, is not dogmatic belief but openness, a willingness to see "What He Will Be." We should adopt the skeptical posture of "Let's wait and see," instead of the cynical or suspicious posture of "What's the catch?" And as with the character of God, so with the text that teaches us about His doings on behalf of His people and the human race: we should suspend disbelief; we should pay close and careful attention; we should open ourselves to seeing and hearing what it has to show and tell us.

These last reflections should explain why I am not much bothered by the question of who wrote Exodus. The Bible has no title page, and it lists no author. The beginning of Genesis speaks confidently about the Creation, describing God's doings in the third person, yet speaking about an event to which there could not have been any human witnesses. Exodus likewise speaks confidently of things for which there can be no independent corroboration—for example, the conversations between God and Moses. Tradition ascribes authorship of the Torah to Moses, who must have learned it all from God. Perhaps that is true, but the text never says so. Still, why does it matter for the account's veracity? The truths of the *Iliad* are available to us without our knowing anything about its author or anything about the ancient Mediterranean world outside the text itself. Homer—about whom we know nothing—tells the truth when he attributes his poem to the muse: "Wrath, goddess, sing, of Peleus's son, Achilles . . ." Who can say where inspired words of genius come from? Sufficient unto the day is our ability to recognize their presence and to respond.

English translations will use "the Lord," and I will mostly (but not always) follow that less than satisfactory usage, despite the fact that doing so removes the sense in which the Tetragrammaton *may* function as a "personal name," and hence also the implication of singular and personal intimacy between the God of Israel and His people. I do so because, as I will suggest in Chapter Thirteen in the discussion of the injunction against taking the Lord's name in vain, we should have scruples against trafficking in the so-called divine name, not least because, in the biblical account, the divine appears to be indefinable and, hence, beyond *ordinary* naming.

Part One
Out of Egypt:
Slavery and Deliverance

Exodus 1–15

Into the House of Bondage

The book we know as Exodus is known in the Jewish tradition as *Shemoth,* "Names," following the custom of naming the books of the Torah after the first important word to appear in the text. Unlike, say, Plato's *Republic,* Shakespeare's *King Lear,* or, for that matter, the biblical books of Judges and Kings, *Shemoth* does not appear to be a title in the sense of specifying a theme or subject or main character. It may therefore be risky to make too much of it. Yet when we recall that the Hebrew names of at least three of the four other books of the Pentateuch are thematically predictive of our experience of the whole book,[1] we should reconsider. So let us pause briefly on the threshold of our reading to consider the importance of names and naming and to anticipate some of the names that receive explicit consideration.

Names in the Bible are more than convenient handles. In the beginning, God created the world and its creatures by calling them forth through acts of speech. Naming the animals is the first human act, and the first quoted human sentence is an act of gendered self-naming: man and woman (*'ish* and *'ishah;* Gen. 2:23). Names carry meanings both for those who bestow them and for those who carry them. Not only can names given at birth be prophetic, as people "magically" grow into their names. More generally, names are often seen as expressing the true character or essence of a being—for example, 'adam meaning "earth-ling" or *Chava* (Eve) meaning "life giver." Knowing and calling the name are avenues to that essence, and perhaps thereby entrées to its powers. Names can also be gained or won, in the form of fame or glory for earned success (think of Jacob's earning the name of Israel in his famous wres-tling match with an angel) or in the form of infamy or disrepute for earned failure and worse (think of the builders of Babel, who explicitly sought to make a name for themselves). Although all such memorable people, like the prototype "earthling," must sooner or later disappear from the scene, their deeds and names live on in memory—as in this book.

We should therefore pay attention to the uses of names in the book called "Names," and especially to the tacit exploitations and explicit dis-cussions of their meanings, including the Children of Israel, Egypt, Moses, his sons, the Tabernacle, and, last but really first, the Lord God—about Whose name Moses explicitly inquires (and later sings), and which the Children of Israel are later told they must not take in vain. I therefore venture this speculative suggestion: the deepest purpose of *Shemoth* may be for its characters and its readers to learn, through ex-periencing His words and deeds, something of the meaning of the Di-vine Name, of the One Who says mysteriously of Himself (in answer to Moses's question about His Name), "I-Will-Be-What-I-Will-Be"; of the One Who does what He does so that "the Egyptians [and, let me add, everyone else] shall know that I am *Y-H-V-H*"; of the One Who orders the Israelites to build Him a sanctuary so that He may dwell intimately in their midst.

Fruitful in Egypt

The book of Exodus opens straightaway with Israel in Egypt.[2] More pre-cisely, the opening chapter gives a synoptic account of Israel's descent, first into Egypt and later into bondage to Pharaoh. The beginning seems innocent enough:

> Now these are the names (*shemoth*) of the sons of Israel (*be-nei yisrael*) who came into Egypt with Jacob, each man came with his household: Reuben, Simeon, Levi, and Judah; Issa-

char, Zebulun, and Benjamin; Dan and Naphtali, Gad and Asher. And all the souls that came out of the loins of Jacob were seventy souls; but Joseph was in Egypt [already]. And Joseph died, and all his brethren, and all that generation. And the Children of Israel (*benei yisrael*) were fruitful (*paru*), and teemed (*vayyishretsu*) and multiplied (*vayyirbu*), and waxed mighty (*vayya'atsmu*), with strength (*bime'od*), strongly (*me'od*), and the land was filled with them (*vatimmale' ha'arets 'otham*). (1:1–7)*

When the Children of Israel (*benei yisrael*) come down into Egypt, they come literally as the sons of one man, their father Jacob (renamed Israel), whom they accompany on his journey. They come not alone, but each man with his household. The immigration happens as a collection of *families*. Lest there be confusion as to the new arrivals, we are given the names of eleven of Jacob's sons, grouped according to their (only hinted-at) maternity: first, Leah's first four sons; then Leah's last two sons and the youngest son (Benjamin) of Leah's sister Rachel; and then the two sons born to each of the handmaids, first to Rachel's, then to Leah's.[3] Joseph, Jacob's beloved son, we are reminded—in a great understatement—"was in Egypt [already]." As prime minister to Pharaoh, he remains separate; although he had secured, from his high position of state, a protected habitat for his family in Goshen, he plays no future part in their story, and his benefactions do not endure.

No sooner are we told that "Joseph was in Egypt" than we learn—with telescoped passage of time—that "Joseph died," and so too "all his brethren, and all that generation." This elite generation—the first generation of Israel to become a multitude, the last to know any of the patriarchs, and the last whose names are all known to us and will be memorialized in the nation's eponymous tribes—disappears from the scene.

What they leave behind is again called, but in a new and different sense, "the Children of Israel" (*benei yisrael*); still the descendants but

---

*Citations from Exodus will be given numerically, chapter and verse. Citations from other biblical sources will first identify the book.

no longer literally the sons of Jacob, they are now instead the incipient (but-not-yet) *nation* of Israel: Israelites. Because they are now a mass, we do not know any of their proper names; their identity is given in terms of their singular common ancestor. Other than their common descent, all we know about the Children of Israel pertains to their remarkable fruitfulness, emphasized by the sevenfold description of their growth: fruitful, teemed, multiplied, grew mighty, strongly, with strength, and the land was filled with them.

Three aspects of this description deserve comment. First is the intimation of animal-like activity and profusion. The word translated as "teemed"—*sh-r-ts*, "swarming"—is often used to describe the teeming of fish and insects; it appears first in Genesis 1 to describe the swarms of the sea ("Let the waters swarm swarms of living creatures"; 1:20).[4] Second is the impression of might and strength—the central term, underscored by the next word, is *vayya'atsmu*, "waxed mighty"—yet this impression is somewhat misleading. While there is surely strength in numbers, the "mightiness" of their numbers is not sufficient to resist the troubles that their proliferation will bring them. Finally, there is a certain (I suspect deliberate) ambiguity regarding *which* land was "filled with them": only the land of Goshen (the eastern delta of the Nile), where they had settled, or the entire land of Egypt? Were they still living, albeit crowded, in their original "ghettoized" separation? Or had they burst out to live interspersed among the Egyptians? How in fact did they live in Egypt, and in what ways were they distinguishable from others?[5]

These descriptions of the multiplication of the Children of Israel underscore the crucial question: Are the Israelites at this stage already a people? The answer seems to be no. They are not called a people (*am*) or a nation (*goi*). Nor is there any mention of God or their attachment to Him; unlike the barren matriarchs in Genesis (Sarah, Rebekah, and Rachel), the new fruitful generations of Israel apparently did not need or seek divine assistance in order to multiply. To the contrary, Israelite fecundity seems to partake of the natural and hyper-abundant fertility that is characteristically Egyptian—a gift of the land where the overflowing river guarantees plentiful crops, where the land teems with life, and where even excrement appears to give birth: the scarab (or dung beetle) is sacred to the Egyptians, an emblem of immortality, because it seemingly springs from the deadest detritus. And while Israelite fertility takes center stage, the practice of circumcision, the sole covenantal obligation on the Children of Israel, is not mentioned. As far as we know, the descendants of Jacob are now a multitude sharing little beyond their common ancestor and their extraordinary fertility.

To be sure, their fecundity might be regarded as a divine gift and a realization of God's promise: we readers of Genesis remember that God told Jacob that He would make of him a great nation (*goy gadol*) in Egypt, and we suspect that we are seeing the first delivery on that promise. But there is no evidence that the Israelites themselves see anything remarkable or providential in their flourishing. Instead their swarming like locusts in a land teeming with life may appear to them as the work of bountiful nature. Indeed, the text, by its silence on their view of the matter, may be said to point to their failure to see God's providence in their success.[6] Their fruitfulness must appear to them as a kind of strength, but it need not be experienced as a God-send. Indeed, prosperity has a way of leading to God-forgetting. When, at the end of the next chapter, God at last enters their story, He does so in response to their misery and their crying out. Unlike the patriarchal generations, it is not childlessness and infertility, which are personal woes, but the communal misery of slavery that eventually turns their attention toward God. But before things go bad, the Israelites swarm happily on their own, flourishing like the Egyptian land that is now their home.

Pharaoh Calls Out the Children of Israel

It is in fact a new Egyptian Pharaoh who first regards Israel as a people. This will not be the only time in human history that a people is first defined by those who see them as alien and threatening:

> Now there *rose up* (*vayyaqam*) a new king *over* Egypt ('*al-mitsrayim*) who knew not Joseph (*lo'-yada' 'eth-Yosef*). And he said unto *his people* ('*ammo*), "Behold the *people* ('*am*) of the Children of Israel are too many (*rav*) and too mighty

(*ve'atsum*) for us. Come, let us deal wisely [that is, "craftily"]
with them, lest they multiply, and when it comes to pass that
any war befalls us, they also join themselves unto our enemies, and fight against us, and *go up out of the land.*" (1:8–10;
emphasis added)

In this book called "Names," in a chapter replete with proper
names, the Pharaoh responsible for deeming Israel a nation is himself
strangely innominate. He is defined only by his newness and by a special kind of ignorance: "a new king who . . . *knew* not Joseph."* What is
the meaning of his not knowing? Is it merely historical ignorance of the
former prime minister, an ungrateful forgetfulness of what Egypt owes
to Joseph's clairvoyance and administrative genius? Is it also (or instead)
a rejection of the tolerant and economically prudent policy toward the
Israelite minority that Joseph instituted—a policy that might eventually
yield their full assimilation to Egypt, which Joseph exemplified? Whatever else it means, it betokens ignorance: ignorance of Joseph and of the
God of Joseph's ancestors, Creator of heaven and earth—knowledge of
Whom is a major theme of the rest of the book.

However this may be, the new Pharaoh is most likely not a legitimate heir of the previous Pharaoh but an upstart ruler, a monarch of a
new dynasty. Not only is he called a "*new* king," but the expression
qum . . . 'al—here translated "rose up over"—is often used elsewhere in
the Bible to indicate the violent overthrow of one ruler by another.[7] Very
likely insecure, and unrestrained by any gratitude that an earlier Pharaoh might have felt toward his loyal minister Joseph,[8] the new king's
first reported act is to divide Egypt into an "us" and a "them." Speaking
to *his* people, he singles out the Children of Israel as a dangerous alien
people, hoping thereby to rally the Egyptians to his side and to consoli-

---

*This first use of the verb "to know" (*yada'*), at the dramatic opening of the
story, highlights one of the central themes of the book: knowing and not knowing.
Here the subject is "knowing Joseph"; on later occasions, it will be "knowing the
Lord," a central issue not only within the people of Israel but also in the contest between Israel and Egypt and between Moses and Pharaoh. The verb "to know" will occur more than twenty times in the opening fourteen chapters. It will figure
prominently also in the story of the Tabernacle. We will watch it closely.

date his rule by inventing an enemy for them to fear and hate. It is not difficult to use envy to arouse their enmity, for the Children of Israel are flourishing and privileged, living in the lush land of Goshen and (unlike the Egyptian masses) enjoying their freedom and the fruits of Joseph's former favoritism.

Summoning his own people (*'am*) to defend themselves against the threat, Pharaoh defines the Israelites not in cultural but in bodily terms. Because of their large numbers—a sign of their superior health and fertility in this land noted for fertility and devoted to health and longevity—the Israelites are to be feared. A people, in the new Pharaoh's view, are a group of numerous "others" who are a threat in case of war, capable of tipping the balance in favor of one's enemies. Or they may "rise up from the land," whether by leaving and hence depopulating it or by bursting out from the country in which they had been confined and ultimately ascending to political power. Bodily speaking, the Children of Israel are a people to worry about.[9]

Quite apart from any need to consolidate his power, the new Pharaoh faces a genuine dilemma. Egypt has a recurring political problem, in which an underclass of vigorous people threatens to become more numerous than a ruling elite that (characteristically) does not reproduce in large numbers. The teeming Israelite population really might have been on the way to outnumbering the native Egyptians. Moreover, unlike the Egyptian masses, who were already indentured servants to Pharaoh, the Children of Israel were still free, able to go their own way. Finally, although we know very little about their way of life, the Israelites could no doubt be clearly recognized as a foreign element, with foreign ways and practices.[10] They thus posed both a cultural-ideological and a demographic threat to the regime, which a prudent leader of Egypt would not be wrong to address.

At the same time, the Children of Israel were almost certainly useful to the regime; the previous Pharaoh had ordered Joseph to put his brothers in charge of Pharaoh's own herds of cattle (Gen. 47:6), and it is likely that they were still valuable contributors to the national economy. As long as the Israelites were few in number, living apart, minding their own business yet contributing to Egyptian prosperity, they could be tolerated without worry—even in the absence of any gratitude that was owed to Joseph and his kin. But now that they are becoming numerous, Pharaoh faces a familiar problem regarding growing minority populations: *he both needs and fears them.* Because they are alien, he is afraid that they will revolt or join the enemy; because they are useful, he is afraid that they will leave. This dilemma is reflected in the otherwise perplexing statement of Pharaoh's concerns: in a war, they might join the enemy or "rise up from the land" and leave. Seeing how the demographic winds were blowing, Pharaoh was not wrong to worry about Israelite proliferation and to see them (before they saw themselves) *as a people.*

It is hardly obvious what a wise ruler, confronted by such a problem, should have done. As we will see, the course that Pharaoh chose turned out to be a disaster. It was only his efforts to limit the Israelites' fertility that put them on the path to becoming a people in a more than biological sense. Increased numbers produced increased Egyptian enmity, which gave rise to dehumanizing servitude and efforts at genocide, eliciting from the Israelites cries of grief and pleas for assistance that eventually opened the people to God, leading ultimately to their departure from Egypt and their becoming a people wedded to God's chosen Way.

It is easy to say with hindsight that separation of Israel and Egypt would have been a more prudent course for Pharaoh to follow. Separation is, in fact, the solution God Himself will provide. People with opposing ways of life cannot easily be accommodated in one land, and close association always promises trouble, especially when one group is more fertile. But Pharaoh, not having read the book of Exodus, may be excused for not discovering this expedient (as his successor may be excused for resisting it when Moses asks him to let the Israelites go). Not having the benefit of Genesis or recorded lore in the palace, he may be excused also for "not knowing Joseph" or for his way of handling a comparable political difficulty by making use of population transfer and the nonviolent purchase of loyal servitude. Like many a proud ruler, Pharaoh wants to have his cake and eat it too. He wants to eliminate the threat posed by Israelite growth while keeping and even expanding the benefits of their presence and labor. He decides to "deal craftily with them."

Against Israelite Fertility

The assault on Israelite fertility comes in three progressive stages, none of them successful. Pharaoh's first approach is indirect:

> Therefore they set over them taskmasters in order to afflict [or "abase" or "humble"; 'inna] them with their burdens, and they built cities of storage for Pharaoh, Pithom and Raamses. But the more they afflicted them, the more they multiplied and the more they broke forth (yifrots), and they [the Egyptians] dreaded the presence of the Children of Israel. (1:11–12)

Responding to Pharaoh's exhortation to deal craftily with the Israelites, the Egyptians set over them captains of work gangs to compel them into forced labor and wear them down with burdens. Their forced labor was used to build storage cities for Pharaoh, devoted exclusively to hoarding surpluses of grain, wine, and oil. In this little vignette, we see a deep truth about Egypt: in a land of excessive fertility and growth, many people spend their lives increasing the ruler's wealth and power, measured in his control over the necessities of life.

Although this arrangement is economically useful to Pharaoh, the bondage's true purpose is to crush the Israelites' spirit and keep them from procreating. Theirs was not the ordinary bonded labor under which the Egyptian masses had been living. This servitude is intended to humiliate, debase, and degrade: the verb 'inna, here translated "to afflict," has a root sense of "to depress" or "to put down," and in this context, it means "to abase, to lower, to humble."[11] Not content merely to exploit the Children of Israel, Pharaoh seeks also to degrade them. By compelling them to build for him the cities of storage, Pithom and Raamses, Pharaoh forces the Children of Israel—in an act that we readers may see as poetic justice—to repeat the labors Joseph (acting on behalf of a previous Pharaoh) imposed on the Egyptian masses to protect against a prophesied famine: take that, tit-for-tat, you lazy Hebrews.

But the plan backfires. The Israelites do not take their humiliation lying down: "the more they afflicted them, the more they multiplied and the more they broke forth" (1:12). How the Israelites manage to resist this plot against their fertility one can only guess, but resist it they did.[12] Far from allowing their misery to lead them into despair, they embrace the goodness of life and tacitly express hope for their own future. Their reproductive success is no longer described in the animalistic language of "swarming" or "teeming." And the language of "breaking forth" or "spreading out" treats their proliferation as if it were deliberate defiance, with the added suggestion that, "breaking forth," the Israelites now are surely spreading beyond Goshen into all of Egypt. The imagery even suggests something beyond natural procreation, perhaps divine solicitude and assistance. No wonder the Egyptians "were [now] in dread of the Children of Israel" (1:12).

In response, the Egyptians turn the screws, initiating the second phase of bondage. They "made the Children of Israel work (or 'serve'; 'eved) with crushing toil (befarekh; from a stem p-r-k, which means 'to crush small' in post-Biblical Hebrew), embittering their lives with hard servitude ('avodah) in mortar, brick, and all manner of work in the fields, in addition to all their other work wherein they made them work with crushing toil (befarekh)" (1:13–14). But when this increased oppression again fails to break the spirit or stem the growth in the number of Israelite slaves, Pharaoh adopts a still secret but more direct attack on their birthrate: infanticide. The text reports, in direct folk-tale-like speech, a remarkable conversation in which the godlike ruler of Egypt orders a pair of Hebrew midwives to arrange covertly for the death of all male infants born to Israelite women:

> And the king of Egypt spoke to the Hebrew midwives (la-meyalledoth ha'ivriyyoth), of whom the name of one was Shifrah and the name of the other Puah; and he said: "When you deliver the Hebrew [women], you shall look upon the birthstool; if it be a son, then you shall kill him; but if it be a daughter, then she shall live." (1:15–16)

There is, one must admit, some method in Pharaoh's madness. Although the most direct strategy for curbing fertility would be to attack *female* children, Pharaoh's assault on the males makes even more sense.

Male infanticide eliminates all potential future soldiers while leaving hordes of women who must marry out and who will then bear many more Egyptian children. Also, in Egypt and much of the ancient world, only males carry the familial and cultural identity; women do not count. Yet no doubt mindful of the enormity and riskiness of his plan, Pharaoh wants the killing done secretly, at birth, so that the Israelite parents will think the infant was stillborn and no one else will know the difference.

But whom could Pharaoh get to carry out such a dastardly strategy? Israelite women would have access, but they would surely not be willing; some Egyptians might be willing, but they would not have easy access. Pharaoh hits on an expedient: a (representative) pair of "Hebrew midwives" whose deliberately ambiguous identity symbolizes the king's difficulty. Are they "midwives who *are* Hebrews" or "(non-Hebrew) midwives *to* the Hebrews?"[13]

Regardless of the midwives' ethnicity, Pharaoh's plan is once again frustrated. As if anticipating and celebrating this surprising result, the text identifies the heroic Hebrew midwives by name (Shifrah and Puah), while continuing to leave the despotic Pharaoh nameless. We immediately discover why the midwives deserve to be remembered and honored and how they won their deathless names.

The Midwives Fear God

But the midwives feared God [literally, "the god" or "the divine"; *vatire'na hameyalledoth 'eth-ha'elohim*] and they did not do as the king of Egypt commanded them, but they saved the boys alive. And the king of Egypt called both the midwives, and he said to them, "Why (*maddu'a*) have you done this thing, and have saved the boys alive?"[14] And the midwives said unto Pharaoh, "Because the Hebrew women are not as the Egyptian women; for they are lively (*ki-chayoth;* "animals"), and are delivered before the midwife comes unto them." And God dealt well with the midwives; and the people (*ha'am*) multiplied and waxed very mighty. And it came to pass, because the midwives feared God, that He made them houses. (1:17–21)

Mighty Pharaoh, for the first but not the last time, has one of his direct orders defied, and by a pair of humble women.

The defiance of the midwives is all the more noteworthy if we take them to be Egyptians, as many commentators do. Israelite midwives could be expected to refuse to kill their own people's children. The reason the text gives for Shifrah and Puah's refusal supports the claim that they were Egyptian women: "fear of [the] God" (or "fear of the gods" or "fear of Heaven") is often invoked as the reason people refrain from mistreating strangers.[15] Moreover, if we assume the midwives were Egyptians, we can see this passage both as a singular example of the relation between Pharaoh and his own people and an indication of the limits of his power. Try as he might, the king cannot turn a midwife true to her calling into a murderer of children. More generally, the one problem that defies masculine despotism is birth or procreation. This episode thus also affirms the importance of women—and what women stand for—even in this time, place, and culture where women are neither prominent nor highly regarded.

This first defiance of Pharaoh's order, based on "fear of God," is emblematic of the subsequent contest between Pharaoh and the Lord; it anticipates the Bible's answer to the questions about who or what is cosmically highest, what is morally right and good, and which passions and attitudes should govern the human soul. Whether Egyptian or Israelite, these remarkable women are restrained by reverence and awe for an authority higher than Pharaoh's, higher even than all man-made law. Like decent people everywhere, they intuitively recognize that the usually important distinction between kin and stranger, defined by *nomos* (convention), is not absolute: there is a power beyond man-made law and custom—and a notion of natural right—that sets limits on what law and custom can sanction or justify. More precisely, these midwives—patronesses of birth—will not turn themselves into child killers just because a king commands them to practice infanticide. The godlike Pharaoh, despite his aspiration to complete mastery, is not the master of birth and death.

If the Egyptian midwives are moved by fear of "god," it is surely not the God of Israel: they would not have known Him. The text's precise formulation, "fear of *the* god [or gods; *ha'elohim* is grammatically plural]," suggests that it was a generic fear or reverence for the divine in general—a natural piety—that restrained them.[16] Yet it is these decent, life-affirming, and naturally pious women—not the Children of Israel, never mind the Pharaoh—who first show awareness of a higher-than-political power that cares about justice and injustice. All honor to them.[17]

The decency and courage of Shifrah and Puah are matched by their quick-wittedness and cunning. When rebuked by the king for failing to carry out his orders, they do not speak of their "fear of the god," for they know that such an appeal would carry no weight with Pharaoh. Instead, they invoke the liveliness of the Hebrew women: "these Hebrew women deliver like animals, fast, before we can arrive." Pharaoh is not amused. Already angry and fearful of superior Israelite fecundity, he is now told that Israelite women are a mighty force of generative nature, beyond any human—or at least beyond his Egyptian—control.

Pharaoh's Madness Exposed

Outraged by this news, Pharaoh now commands his entire people to drown all the newborn sons of Israel, sparing only the daughters. The suppression of natural birth, sought unsuccessfully by guile, is now to be accomplished by overt brutality committed by the whole Egyptian people. Thanks to the midwives' heroism, the secret plot had been thwarted. The whole evil plan is now brought into the open, where it will again fail:

> And Pharaoh *commanded* his *whole* people (*lekhol-'ammo*), saying, "Every son that is born you shall cast into the river, and every daughter you shall save alive." (1:22; emphasis added)

At first glance, and thinking again only about his demographic predicament, Pharaoh's policy may seem to make some sense: if successful, it would eliminate the threat of a future Israelite uprising while capturing the Israelite women as future mothers of Egyptian children. The problem of the despised alien people is to be solved partly by elimination, partly by assimilation. The result will be *ein Volk, ein Reich, ein Führer.*

But on more careful inspection, Pharaoh's decree strikes us not only as heinous but also as insane, a desperate measure of a desperate king. A strong king would not foment a polarizing conflict within his regime based solely on an unfounded fear that a subgroup would someday rise up against him. And a sane king would never tell his entire people to turn on one segment of the population and kill their children. Ironically, Pharaoh produces the problem he was trying to forestall. He creates in the Children of Israel an enemy where none had existed, unifying them as a people. He thus converts his fearful imagination of their future enmity into a present reality. He also brutalizes his entire population by forcing them to practice infanticide on their neighbors.[18]

The half-crazed, half-idiotic character of his megalomaniacal plan to control birth is reflected in the curious wording of his decree: as quoted in the text, Pharaoh does not specify *whose* infant sons are to be killed at birth. Although the addressee of the decree and its context in the narrative make it clear that Israelite sons were the intended target, the nonspecificity of his blustering order ("Every son that is born") is a sign of Pharaoh's wild unpredictability: this is the sort of fellow who may one day demand similar infanticide of or child sacrifice from the Egyptian people. Another king just like him will, through his despotic intransigence, indeed bring about the slaying of all firstborn sons and the destruction of his entire people[19] when God exacts justice for, among other things, this very edict.

Yet despite these obvious difficulties, we must consider whether this policy could have worked. Absent a saving God, could the Israelites have survived? As we will see, the Israelites do not fight back against the decree, at least not directly or in any number—any more than they resisted their own enslavement and affliction. Yet even before God enters the picture to redeem and deliver the Children of Israel, we do encounter some signs of resistance—largely (but not quite exclusively) on the part of women. As it turns out, Pharaoh's decree of infanticide creates its own antithesis in the form of womanly compassion. Thanks to Moses's mother and sister, and especially Pharaoh's own daughter, the decree to kill all the male infants brings the redeemer of the Israelites into Pharaoh's own house, where, unbeknownst to everyone, he is being prepared to lead his people out of Egypt. How this happens is the theme of the second chapter.

Israel Versus Egypt

The opening chapter of Exodus begins with the names of the sons of Jacob but ends with the names and deeds of a pair of Egyptian women, midwives to the Hebrews. An unnamed king of Egypt attempts to crush and destroy Israelite manhood, and he succeeds in imposing a severe bondage and crushing toil on the entire people. Yet the one problem Pharaoh cannot solve is the problem of procreation. He will be undone by the fruit of his own decree against childbirth.

This is not an accidental error. On the contrary, the mistake is characteristic of Egypt altogether, and it clearly reveals the difference between that dominant civilization and the nascent people of Israel. The last chapter of Genesis contrasted the funeral of Jacob, buried in the ancestral cave at Machpelah in the Promised Land, with the embalming of Joseph, a mummy in Egypt awaiting reanimation. The well-known Egyptian effort to master death is matched in the first chapter of Exodus by a new Egyptian effort to master birth. Taken together, they represent the core of the human effort to resist change and decay through technology and magic, as well as the tyrant's wish both to be his own source and to live forever.[20] This widespread disposition to mastery of nature, typically masculine, is not to be the way of Israel. Its rejection is first demonstrated by the compassion and generosity of women.

Before leaving the first chapter of Exodus, let us note two of its important contributions to the project of people formation. First, the story of how the Israelites become a people begins with their enslavement in Egypt, and we may wonder why such a first step was thought necessary or desirable. The Lord could have chosen other ways to forge Israel's national identity and character. How might reduction to bondage contribute—positively and negatively—to people formation in general and to this people in particular? Several possibilities suggest themselves.

On the positive side, the people acquire a common enemy against which to define themselves and unite. They are largely emptied of their existing customs and ways and are a blank slate on which something completely new can be written.[21] A very important element in our text is their firsthand experience of the evils of oppression and the mistreatment of strangers; as a result, they may be less likely to repeat these actions when they obtain power or, if not less likely, are at least capable of being appealed to on this matter. (God and Moses will later frequently remind them, "Remember that you were slaves in Egypt.") Finally, they are in an ideal position to discover to Whom they owe their deliverance and to develop gratitude and lasting allegiance to their divine deliverer.

On the negative side, however, the condition of slavery generally produces "slavish people" who, having no taste for freedom and no experience of self-rule, will not know how to defend themselves and will run from difficulty and uncertainty, preferring the security of food and drink to the risks of freedom. Moreover, the mere liberation of slaves often produces anarchy, at least until order can be introduced by appropriate law and leadership. There is thus a danger that the people, terrified of chaos and lawlessness, may either long to return to the security of slavery or look for a charismatic strong man to lead them, exchanging one tyrant for another. As we will later see, the formation of the people of Israel will both exploit the benefits and suffer the harms of beginning its national story in bondage.

Second, we learn something about Egypt and why it provides a foil for the emerging people of Israel. The Egypt we meet in the first chapter of Exodus displays xenophobia, ceaseless enforced labor, massive construction projects for Pharaoh's profit, the hoarding of agricultural excess, various attempts to control and restrict fertility (including infanticide), and despotic rule. The Way of the Lord, which He later prescribes for Israel, will pointedly reject these attitudes and practices. It will teach the humane treatment of strangers, weekly Sabbath rest and seven-yearly sabbaticals for the land, a community-built sanctuary for worshipping the Lord who delivered the people from bondage, teachings against hoarding and excess, celebration of procreation in the service of the covenant, and the rule of law in the service of each and all.

But we are getting ahead of ourselves. For now, we have the Israelites immersed in their miseries and Pharaoh at war with procreation. We turn immediately to the defiance of his edict and the birth of Israel's redeemer.

The Birth and Youth of the Liberator

The opening chapter of Exodus concludes with the Children of Israel bound in slavery in Egypt, leaving readers to wonder how, if at all, they will be able to liberate themselves. Will a Spartacus arise from their midst to lead a slave revolt against Pharaoh? If not, from where and through whom will their deliverance come? What sort of person will their leader be? The second chapter begins to answer these questions, as the book shifts focus to describe the birth and early life of Moses, Israel's future liberator, leader, and lawgiver.[1]

The story is neatly symmetrical. It opens with an account of Moses's birth and his given family of origin; it concludes with a report of his marriage and the birth of his first son—his chosen family of perpetuation. In between we learn how Moses first entered into Pharaoh's house and what happened when he emerged from Pharaoh's house. Unlike Father Abraham, who was childless at age seventy-five when God first called him with a promise of becoming a great nation, and for whom the birth of a son (by his barren wife Sarah) served as the goal for his adventures, Founder Moses will have already established his family before he receives (in the next chapter) his God-given mission. This marked difference signals that we are no longer in the family-preserving phase of God's Way, but are in the more complicated nation-building phase.

With Moses, as with the Israelite people, fertility has been achieved. A populous Israelite nation is enslaved in Egypt; the man who will lead them out is from the start moved by something more than a desire for progeny.

The beginning of Exodus 2 has a more immediate connection with the opening chapter, which ended with Pharaoh's edict commanding his entire people to drown all newborn sons (of the Israelites). At chapter's end, we were left to wonder whether this heinous policy would succeed. Would the Israelites continue to procreate despite the decree? Would the Egyptians carry out Pharaoh's deadly order? The beginning of the second chapter provides immediate—if merely tacit—answers to these questions: "yes" and "no." We are first given an Israelite response. We wonder whether it was typical or whether this act of procreation and preservation, singled out for mention, was unique.

Baby Boy

The story, told with understatement, begins innocently enough:

> And there went a man from the house of Levi and he took [to wife] a daughter of Levi. And the woman conceived, and bore a son; and when she saw him that he was good, she hid him three months. (2:1–2)

In the face of Pharaoh's decree, there is at least some Israelite resistance.[2] A nameless, which is to say ordinary, Levite man takes a woman; a nameless, again ordinary, Levite woman conceives and bears a child (who is, for now, also nameless), sees that he is good, and hides him against Pharaoh's call for male infanticide.

We might think this event was mere happenstance, reflecting only the natural way of a man with a woman or of a woman with her child. But the identification of both man and woman as members of the house of Levi invites us to think again. Levi (along with his brother Simeon) was one of the two ringleaders of the attack on the Shechemites, waged to gain revenge for the rape—the abasing and humiliating—of their sister Dinah[3] (Gen. 34). Baby Moses, who will later impose God's chastisements upon the Egyptians for their oppression and humiliation of the Children of Israel and who will lead them out of Egypt, is descended on both sides from a spirited son of Israel who would kill to avenge injury and outrage to his own and who, with his brother, liberated their sister from captivity in a foreign place. Is it possible that his Levite parents, in bringing him to birth and hiding him, were themselves resisting Pharaoh's injurious and insulting decree: the man in taking the woman, the woman in bearing and protecting the child? (As we learn later, they were not childless.[4]) Yet even if their motive was not defiance, that was surely the meaning of their acts. Even if their "rebellion" owed more to erotic desire than to political will, it provides concrete evidence that Pharaoh's plan has not gained universal compliance. We even wonder whether this unnamed Levite couple was in fact a prototypical pair of "rebels" joined in their defiance by countless others. Although the text's interest (and ours) is necessarily the emergence of Moses, we can hardly believe that Moses was the only boy born and preserved after the Pharaoh's edict, and therefore the youngest Israelite to later leave Egypt.[5] Be this as it may, we will keep in mind that Moses is doubly descended from one who would kill to avenge injustice to his own.

Mother Love, Maternal Cunning

The Levite man takes the woman, but it is his Levite wife who occupies center stage:

> And the woman conceived, and bore a son; and when she saw that he was good (*vattere' 'otho ki-tov hu'*), she hid him three months. But when she could no longer hide him, she took for him (*vattiqqach-lo*) an ark (*tevah*) of bulrushes and daubed it with slime and with pitch; and she placed the child therein and placed it in the reeds (*suf*) by the river's edge. And his sister took her stand afar off, to know (*lede'ah*) what would be done to him. (2:2–4)

The baby's mother was as shrewd and resourceful as she was brave. First, instead of naming (that is, individuating) her newborn son,[6] she

takes his measure: "she saw that he was good (*ki-tov*)." This is a judgment that readers of the Bible first heard at the beginning of Genesis, in
the story of Creation, when God saw the light, His first creature, and said
"that it was good (*ki-tov*)" (Gen. 1:4).[7] The parallel of his mother's judgment on Moses with God's on light hints at another auspicious beginning, perhaps the start of a new and distinctive human order that might
complete the natural order of Creation by becoming a light unto the nations.[8] But what exactly did Moses's mother notice in reaching this
judgment?

The conventional view holds that the baby was placid and didn't
fuss or cry—and hence could more easily be hidden without detection.
But as we later learn, the baby's mother had other children: Moses's older
brother Aaron and his sister Miriam, who was already old enough to play
a vital role in the present story. Could the mother have recognized in
this baby a spirit and vigor not seen in her older son? Far from being
placid and docile, was he from the start spirited and assertive, one who
made his presence felt—including by crying out at confinement or dis-
comfort?[9] Perhaps here was a child who, even in his swaddling, displayed
his Levite proclivities.

Moved by fierce mother love, the baby's mother takes prudent action. Just as God had ordered the building of an ark to save Noah and
companions from the Flood, so this Levite woman builds an ark to save
her son who will later, following God's instructions, save the chosen
people, including at the Sea of Reeds (*yam suf*). In both cases, the one
worthy to be saved and to save others is rescued from drowning by an
ark: the Hebrew word for ark, *tevah,* is used in the Bible in only these
two places.

There is more to her cunning. She places the child-carrying ark in
the reeds by the river's edge, no doubt in a carefully chosen place—a
place where certain people are likely to come by and discover it. The ark
and child are not simply abandoned to the mercy of the river. Because
she cannot bear to see what happens or, more likely, because her presence would undermine the desired impression of an abandoned child,
the mother leaves the scene. But the baby's older sister (also nameless),
entering the story just when she is needed but surely following her
mother's orders, bravely takes her stand and sets up watch "to know what

would be done to him" but also awaiting the arrival of an opportunity to rescue the child.[10] It seems that mother and sister knew what they were doing. Other women—Egyptian women—arrive (likely where they often arrived) to play their anticipated role in this budding triumph over Pharaoh's decree.

A Conspiracy of the Compassionate

> And the daughter of Pharaoh came down to bathe in the river, and her maidens walked along the river edge; and she saw the ark amid the reeds, and she sent her handmaid to take it. And she opened it, and she saw it, yes the child (*hayyeled*), and behold, a lad (*na'ar*) crying; and she had compassion (*vattach-mol*) upon him, and she said, "This is one of the children of the Hebrews." (2:5–6)

Arriving as a possible answer to the mother's prayers, Pharaoh's daughter (she too is nameless) is no less sharp-eyed than the child's mother. She spots the ark, she has it fetched, she sees the crying child. This is a singular moment: Moses is the only crying baby in the Bible. Pharaoh's daughter seems to intuit that something wondrous has presented itself: she unaccountably refers to the baby as a lad (*na'ar*), a term used only for a much older boy. Perhaps he cried not like a baby but like an older and more spirited youth.[11] Yet it is the sight of his tears—and the sound of his crying—that most moves her soul: in the face of suffering innocence, womanly compassion takes over. Only then does she infer that the child must be one of the condemned Hebrew children. Given the opportunity, she reveals herself to be first a compassionate woman and only secondarily an Egyptian princess—and even then, she does not harbor her father's xenophobia. Like the midwives' fear of God, his daughter's compassion for this foreign child upon the waters subverts Pharaoh's decree. Whether or not she had previously opposed it, on first encounter with a river-cast child she resists and reverses the edict.

As soon as she hears Pharaoh's daughter's compassionate declaration, the baby's sister, very likely carrying out her mother's plan, leaps into action:

Then said his sister to Pharaoh's daughter, "Shall I go and call you a woman nurse from among the Hebrew women, that she may nurse *for you* the child?" And Pharaoh's daughter said to her, "Go." And the maiden went and called the child's mother. And Pharaoh's daughter said unto her: "Take away this child and nurse it *for me* and I will give you your wages." And the woman took (*vattiqqach*) the child and nursed it. And the child grew, and she brought him to Pharaoh's daughter and he became her son; and she called him Moses (*Mosheh*), and she said, "because *from the water I drew him out*" (*mashah*, "to draw out"). (2:7–10; emphasis added)

The sister's only speech is strategically ingenious. She places the idea of adopting the baby before the princess—"that she may nurse *for you* the child"—and she quickly proposes a Hebrew wet nurse for the baby, a hint that she and the baby's mother are in cahoots in this plot. Thanks to his sister's interventions, the baby is returned to his mother for nursing, now on behalf of Pharaoh's daughter. He will be in an Israelite home, with his Levite parents, perhaps absorbing something of their spirit along with mother's milk.[12]

But the more remarkable deeds belong to Pharaoh's daughter, who appears determined to rescue and adopt this Hebrew child, her father's express edict notwithstanding. Decisively, she accepts the plan proposed by sister and mother; one even suspects that she guessed that the nurse whose wages she would pay was the baby's own mother. She enters into a conspiracy of the compassionate, transcending ethnic difference and defying her own father—surely in deed if not also by intention.

What's in a Name?

The name of the remarkably saved baby is given him not by his birth mother but by his adopting mother, the Egyptian princess. In her last deed and speech noted in the Bible, she names him *Mosheh*, an Egyptian word meaning "one who is born" or, therefore, "son." Yet in an astonishing gesture, which the text reports as if it were quite ordinary, Pharaoh's daughter explains the name using a Hebrew word, *mashah,* "to draw out."[13] In adopting her Hebrew-born son, the princess names him according to his bicultural identity: an Egyptian "son," who is "Hebraically" drawn out from the water by his adopting Egyptian mother.[14]

In this book of Names, we should go a little deeper into Moses's name, for his is the first name we get in Chapter 2 and the only personal name we learn while Moses is still in Egypt. Leaving aside the bicultural aspects of his naming, what does it mean that he bears the name "Moses" in the house of Pharaoh? As understood by his adoptive mother, the name is hardly individuating: the child called Moses stands to her simply as "Son." On this reading, far from conveying a strong bicultural identity, Moses's name expresses no personal identity at all. It serves as a placeholder awaiting later revelation, the meaning of which he—and we readers—will be able to fill in only through what "Sonny" does in the future. More than most people, Moses will have to earn the meaning of his name. He will have to *gain* his identity.[15]

We should consider the princess's action more carefully. What does she intend by his putatively multicultural naming? Why does she adopt him, and with what intention does she bring him into the palace? From one perspective, Moses could seem to her a consummate Egyptian, for he appears as a gift of the Nile. Moreover, to have escaped drowning in the river, he must be a blessed child, with special magical qualities or else divine protection.[16] Yet Moses owes his survival only to her intervention, to her compassion in drawing him out, in defiance of current Egyptian policy. Perhaps she is already opposed to her father's rule, and perhaps, as indicated by the name she gives him, she intends to raise him in a way that will keep him aware of his Hebrew origins.

Whatever her intentions, Moses for his entire life will carry a name embodying his adoptive mother's compassion. Drawn out of the water, he will draw his own people out of the sea of their despair and literally out of mortal danger at the Sea of Reeds. Though he will display spirit and practice violence, the compassion of the women in his life will remain with him—not just in name but in deed.[17] For this reason too, he is a fit candidate to carry out the work of a strong, awesomely powerful, yet loving and merciful God.

Mysterious Silence: Moses in Pharaoh's House

Saved from the Nile, Moses enters Pharaoh's house at the time he is weaned—likely no later than age three—as the adopted son of Pharaoh's daughter. In the immediate sequel, we are told of certain incidents that take place years later, when Moses, then a grown man, emerges from the palace, leaving the society of women and children to enter the world of men. From the point of view of the unfolding saga of how Moses the pitiable Hebrew child became Moses the redeemer, the text seems to imply that nothing more needs to be known. Yet the inquisitive reader surely wonders about Moses's boyhood as a prince (or at least a noble) in the palace and wonders too about the reason for the book's silence on this subject.

This is no idle curiosity. For we suspect that it is not merely poetic justice that has the liberator of the slaves come from Pharaoh's own palace, rescued from the water and from Pharaoh's decree by his own softhearted daughter. Rather, believing that these Israelite slaves cannot emancipate themselves, we sense that leadership must come from someone who has been raised to rule. Moreover, if he is to be a leader for God's Way, such a ruler would need to know not only how to be a leader of men (and not, like Joseph, largely an administrator of things). He would also need to be prepared *intellectually,* to learn about the world and the powers that rule it, especially should there be competing claims regarding knowledge of what is highest; that is, of the divine.

Quite apart from these considerations, we are moved to speculate on Moses's palace years and on his princely education in matters practical and philosophic. We imagine that Moses was taught to ride the horse and chariot and to shoot the bow. We imagine he was introduced to the doings of Pharaoh's magicians. But we suspect that, as a rising prince, he was also initiated into the arcane knowledge of the Egyptian priests and sages—teachings about the heavens and the earth, about the soul and its peregrinations, about Being itself and its highest sources. He likely studied mathematics, astronomy, cosmology, metaphysics, and theology. He likely learned the Secrets of the Great Pyramid[18] and imbibed an Egyptian outlook on how and why to gain knowledge of the natural world. Only against this background can we fully appreciate how

God will later catch Moses and enlist him as His servant and messenger. Just as the Children of Israel can become a people only through, out of, and against Egypt, so Moses can become their champion and God's only through, out of, and against his rearing as a prince of Egypt.[19]

Yet even if Moses received a princely education, we wonder whether he was fully an insider. His origins as a Hebrew child would likely have been known to Pharaoh and to everyone in the palace. Would he not have been regarded with suspicion or condescension? Might he have acquired a sense of his Israelite identity, not so much from remembering his natural home (which he left as a toddler) but from his treatment by people in the palace, especially by his adoptive mother, who had preserved in his name clues of his Hebrew origins? Was there something about his appearance or character that *resisted* his complete Egyptianization—in contrast to Joseph, who had fully Egyptianized despite living his first seventeen years among his own people? Had Moses been circumcised from birth (and we have no reason to believe either that he was *or* that he wasn't), that alone might have betokened a deeper difference,[20] whose meaning might have aroused anxious curiosity during puberty when his marked sexual difference might have affected his real or imagined erotic prospects. Or were his Hebrew origins gradually forgotten as he imbibed the culture and cultivated the ways of the palace? Might not his adoptive mother have tried to assimilate him as much as possible to the ways of Egypt? As the (adopted) grandson of Pharaoh, might he, over twenty years, have become as fully Egyptianized as Joseph? About all of this—important though it surely must have been—the text preserves complete silence. Moses is in Pharaoh's house, but we know nothing about *how* he lives there or *who* he thinks he is.

Questions about such matters are surely raised when we meet him for the first time as he emerges from his cocoon, in the stories that the text most emphatically wants us to know. These, the text seems to imply, are the *essential* things you need to know about what the young man Moses was like before God called him to his task. Even if his Egyptian education were necessary preparation, it is only God's instruction, power, and deeds that truly prepare Moses for his role as leader. At the same time, however, thoughts about Moses's education and his intellectual bent will again come to mind when we see how God captures him in the episode of the burning bush.[21]

Moses's life, even more than that of most children, began in the world of women: the domain of birth, nurture, and human renewal. According to our story, Moses owes his life not to merely one woman but to five, each of whom bravely resists Pharaoh's radical attempt to extend his rule over their domain. The two midwives, restrained by "the fear of heaven," refuse to perform male infanticide. Moses's mother and sister, moved by love of their own, hide and protect the infant boy and cunningly arrange his possible rescue. Pharaoh's daughter, moved by compassion, saves not her own but a despised Hebrew child, in defiance of Pharaoh's edict: she names him, brings him into the palace, adopts him, and presumably gives him an Egyptian and princely education.

The compassionate and deeply life-affirming qualities that these strong women display will later find an honored place in Israelite law and teaching, not least because, as we learn later, they are also attributes of God. But these virtues, admirable though they are, cannot alter the Israelites' political situation in Egypt. The women have presided over the birth, rescue, adoption, and palace rearing of Moses, the future redeemer of Israel; but their womanly virtues are hardly sufficient to liberate the Israelites from bondage or to turn them, once freed, into a self-governing people. If Moses is to become a political leader and liberator of the Israelites, he cannot learn what he needs to know while confined to the domain of women and children. He must step onto the worldly stage, to join a world then dominated by men.

Young Man Moses in the World of Men

Precisely to explore this possibility, the account abruptly turns from baby Moses's rescue to young man Moses's entrance into the world of men, skipping over all the years in between. But Moses enters this world unprepared for what he will find. In addition, he goes with an ambiguous identity: by birth, he is an Israelite slave (but a Levite), yet by upbringing he is an Egyptian noble. More than most adolescents, he ventures out entirely on his own and uncertain of who he is. He—and certainly we—should seek to discover under what identity and self-understanding he will act on the world stage.

What does he find when he goes out? Then as now, the world of men is full of strife and conflict: smiting, brawling, bullying. How well does Moses, left to his own devices, fare in this world? And what is he like, this young man Moses, as he makes his independent debut? The three episodes that follow reveal—and also shape—something of his character and identity, the two matters of greatest importance for his future.*

> And it came to pass in those days, when Moses was grown up, that he *went out* unto *his brethren* and he *saw* their burdens; and he *saw* an Egyptian *man* (*'ish Mitsri*) smiting (*makkeh*) a Hebrew *man* (*'ish 'Ivri*), one of *his brethren*. And he *looked* this way and that way, and when he *saw* that there was no *man* (*ki-'ein 'ish*), he smote the Egyptian and hid him in the sand. (2:11–12; emphasis added)

Moses, in his first grown-up deed, *went out*—out from his home, out to the world. But not just anywhere: he went to his brethren. The formulation hints at a confusion. Which is Moses's true home, the inside place where he grew up and from which he went out, or the outside place where his brothers could be found? And who, exactly, are Moses's "brethren": only his biological siblings and kin or (far more likely) all his fellow Israelites—and if the latter, how would Moses have come to regard them as his brethren? These ambiguities echo the blurred character of Moses's familial and ethnic identity—as well as the blurred family relations in the story as a whole, with mothers giving up children, daughters

---

*A couple of suggestions about how to read these stories. First, we should read them not merely as historical events but (also and mainly) as paradigmatic. Singled out among many events in the life of young man Moses, these stories are presented mostly for their revelatory insights into *who* Moses truly *is, at this stage of his life*. Second, in reading these episodes, we have to choose whether to regard them as three occasions that all reveal Moses's set character and experienced identity or as episodes that induce changes in Moses's character or self-understanding. This choice is especially important for thinking about Moses's sense of his ethnic identity.

defying fathers and rearing children not their own, all the result of Pharaoh's edict to thwart normal procreation and to maim family ties. Equally uncertain is Moses's intention: Did he go out for the express purpose of finding his brethren, or was that meeting an unintended result of his going out? We do not know. We also do not know whether it is only *we* who know that they were his brethren or whether he himself recognized them as such—and if so, how. But despite these double ambiguities—whether he meets them intentionally or not, knowingly or not—Moses immediately encounters them. Moreover, he is moved by what he sees—their burdens—and readily acts on their behalf.[22]

Moses sees an Egyptian man smiting a Hebrew man, described by the text as "one of his brethren."[23] Why the Egyptian was smiting the Hebrew we are not told, and Moses does not ask. Because slave masters may be expected to beat their slaves, we readers are not shocked to learn that an Egyptian was beating a Hebrew. But Moses, who is new to the world of men and who may not have known previously of the oppression of the Israelites—or if he knew, not cared about it (or them)[24]—sees before him not so much slave master smiting slave but (Egyptian) *man* smiting (Hebrew) *man;* the latter, *we* are told, is one of his brethren, a fellow Israelite (or is he, rather, one of his fellow men?).

Immediately and speechlessly, Moses moves to act. Yet he moves not impetuously but (literally) circumspectly, looking this way and that; doing so, he *sees* "no man," neither Egyptian nor Hebrew. Very likely, Moses wanted to make sure that there were no witnesses. Perhaps he also wanted to make sure he would not be stopped. But perhaps he looked to see whether there might not be somebody else willing to intervene and stop the smiting: Is there no man else who will do something? If not, I must step forward and be a man. Whatever motivated his circumspection, we note for later that Moses looks around only for other *human* viewers or agents. He does not look for divine assistance; he does not even imagine that God may be a witness.[25] Seeing that "there was no man," Moses takes matters into his own hands: he acts decisively. Just as he has looked, seen, and thought as a man, so he acts: not as an Egyptian or as a Hebrew, but *as a man.* In his first manly act, Moses smites the smiter and then prudently hides him in the sand.

It is of course possible that Moses, despite his Egyptian rearing, has acquired and retained some identification with and sympathy for "his own" Israelite people ("his brethren"). If this were so, we might think that Moses, when grown, went out specifically to find and to be with them. On this reading, Moses is outraged over the mistreatment of one of his own and leaps to his defense, killing the Egyptian oppressor. It seems hard to shake the sense that Moses must have had *some* sense of his confused identity and therefore that he might have harbored some secret (even if unconscious) bond of affection and sympathy for his fellow Hebrews, a bond that seeing their burdens may have awakened and strengthened in him. However he had thought of himself before, he now identifies as an Israelite.[26]

On balance, however, I favor a different reading. I see no textual evidence that Moses is moved primarily by the love of his own people or that he acts here *as an Israelite*.[27] As already noted, there is no clear textual evidence that Moses even knew that he was—or might be—a Hebrew. It seems to me, rather, that Moses intervenes not so much out of concern for or in defense of his own (Israelite) people or even out of an abstract hatred of injustice in defense of the innocent. He acts instead mainly out of outraged fellow feeling, which leads him to take the side of the underdog in opposition to brutality and lethal oppression wherever he actually and concretely encounters it.[28]

Compassion alone does not lead one to action. Righteous indignation at the sight of oppression is required, along with the desire and the will to put a stop to it. True, Moses does not act impulsively out of uncontrolled rage: he looks around before stepping in, and we are not told that he acted in anger. Nor do we know whether he intended to kill the Egyptian; perhaps he merely wanted to deter or disable him, but not knowing his own strength—this is presumably Moses's first fight—he killed him by accident and hastily hid the corpse not only to avoid detection but also (repelled by the sight of a dead body) to get his deed out of his own sight. But these uncertainties do not disturb the main point: Moses's advent into the world of men is humanly very impressive.

In his first appearance as a grown-up, Moses shows himself to be a man of action. He sees the way things really are, things that others would rather not see. He acts on his own, promptly and directly, his deeds following almost immediately upon what he sees with his own eyes. He does not avert his gaze; he does not say, as many men would, "It's not *my* concern!" Unwilling to ignore or accept brutality, he decisively takes matters into his own hands and offers spirited defense of a fellow human being (and one of his Israelite brethren) who is being violated and abused.[29] He also acts without self-regard or concern for his own interests; although he looks around before acting and buries the body afterward, the act itself evinces little concern for his own safety. Moses is courageous, manly, and tough; he sticks up for the underdog. In these respects, Moses shows that he has the right stuff for leadership, perhaps even for rule.[30]

But, we are forced to admit, Moses's smiting of the Egyptian, even as it displays manly traits from which leadership might develop, is not an act of leadership or even sensible heroism. Yes, one Hebrew is saved from one day's (possibly lethal) beating, and there is one fewer taskmaster to beat him and his fellows. But the Israelites' political situation remains unchanged. Indeed, it may even worsen, if and when Moses's deed is discovered. Pharaoh, to teach the Hebrews a lesson and to crush any hopes of rebellion they might entertain from the killing of the taskmaster, would very likely tighten the screws of their oppression. And Moses, if his act were detected, would be at best a pariah in Pharaoh's house, at worst a hunted criminal facing a death sentence.

Yet the very next day—whether undaunted by what had happened, or emboldened to look for more injustice to combat, or eager to be seen as if nothing had happened—Moses goes out again:

> And he went out the second day,[31] and, behold, two men of the Hebrews were striving together; and he said to the guilty one (*rasha‘*), "Why (*lammah*) do you smite (*thakkeh*) your neighbor (*re‘ekha*)?" And he said to him [Moses], "Who made you a man ruler and judge (*'ish sar veshofet*) over us? Do you mean to kill me, as you did kill the Egyptian?" And Moses feared, and he said [to himself], "Surely the thing is known." Now when Pharaoh heard this thing, he sought to kill Moses. But Moses fled from the face of Pharaoh and dwelt in the land of Midian. (2:13–15)

Once again, Moses comes upon men fighting—this appears to be the way of the manly world. But this time it is two Hebrews who are brawling with each other. Once again, Moses inserts himself into the action—we know not whether as a Hebrew, as an Egyptian, or as a man—apparently in the confident belief that *he* can do something about it. But whereas yesterday he relied on speechless deed, today he relies alone on speech.

Speaking only to the *rasha'* (the guilty or wrong one)—is he the one who started the fight or the one getting the upper hand, and how would Moses have known?—Moses tries to deflect his attention by arresting him with a question. The *first* word we readers ever hear Moses say is "why." It is unlikely that Moses is merely curious about the reason for the quarrel, though he may be interested in finding out who was in the right or, even more simply, as a British bobby used to say in such circumstances, "What's going on here?" More likely, moved by the sight of wrongdoing, he is using the question rhetorically, to rebuke the man and to induce him to halt, reflect, and change his behavior. The meaning of the question is not altogether clear: Why do you fight with (or wrong) one of your own (Hebrew) fellows, or why do you fight with (or wrong) your fellow human being?[32] Either way, Moses's question implies that neighbors (perhaps especially jointly suffering Israelite neighbors) have no reason to fight or to wrong one another or at least that they should not do so. It also implies that speech and questioning—especially *his* speech and questioning—can induce unruly men to change their hearts and amend their conduct. Moses brings the voice of reason and a concern for right and peace to the brawling world of (Israelite) men.

Moses's aspirations are honorable and reasonable. And his question expresses a good ruler's (or judge's) concern to prevent wrongdoing. But his intervention is, again not surprisingly, ineffective. It is in fact utterly naïve. He quickly discovers that speech (or at least *his* speech) carries no weight with the fighting Hebrews, who treat him with contempt. He lacks the authority to impose order, and the slaves lack the capacity to be ruled by reason and speech alone, or at least by Moses's words. Thus, the *rasha'*—recognizing the implicit meaning of Moses's intervention—bluntly turns Moses's questioning back on him: "*Who* made *you* a man ruler and judge *over us?*"

Yet this crude question, which tells Moses to mind his own business, conveys a doubly helpful message, because the man speaks better than he knows: the people in fact *need* someone to rule over and judge them, and someone besides Moses (perhaps God) needs to appoint such a human ruler-and-judge (*'ish sar veshofet*), with authority to keep the peace and adjudicate disputes. When the man adds, mockingly, "Do you mean to kill me, as you did kill the Egyptian?" he unintentionally does Moses a favor. By warning him that his deed is known, he enables Moses to flee before he is caught.

Although young man Moses's first two actions on the world stage are not successful, we notice many fine qualities on display. He is a man of forceful deed and reasonable speech. He cares for the underdog, he cares for justice, he cares for peace. The elements of successful manhood and leadership are here, but they are not yet properly woven together. To pursue peace and justice, Moses must find a way to combine reasonable speech with forceful deed. To anticipate: in a word, he needs law—*speech with teeth*—the voice of reason backed up by the threat of force. He also needs prudence or practical wisdom, the capacity to discern and choose the best means to accomplish the best *possible* goals—not necessarily the best *simply*—all seen in light of the circumstances. Finally, Moses must also acquire personal authority, a special kind of power or weight that human beings respect and accept, one based on the perceived presence of superior reason, superior might, and some mysterious charm or aura.

Before turning to the third episode in the life of young man Moses, we pause to observe something about his identity as it comes to light in the first two episodes. Although Moses enters the world of men from Pharaoh's palace, dressed no doubt as an Egyptian nobleman, in neither episode does he act as a prince of Egypt. He does not command the Egyptian taskmaster to stop; he bothers himself with brawling Hebrews; no one in either episode recognizes his authority. The Hebrew battlers, who appear to know who Moses is, clearly imply that he is not at all Egyptian ("as *you* did kill *the Egyptian*"), but they also reject him as one of their own. These episodes display Moses's in-between and uncertain identity. They may make him feel, more strongly than ever, like the outsider he is. They may stir up intimations that he belongs to the Israelite people, but not as a welcome member. Like many a youth who ventures into the inhospitable world, Moses is prompted to examine more carefully, "Who am I? What is my place in the world? What am I meant to do?"

If Moses is perplexed about these matters, the Israelites for their part are not exactly ready to be delivered from bondage. Not only do they strive with one another. Fearing that their lot will become worse because Moses smote the Egyptian, they may even side with their masters against him. Very likely, one of them even ratted him out for the murder. Either the Israelite who was spared by Moses's deed or another witness, unseen by Moses, told his "brethren" of this marvelous occurrence; word then spread through the community,[33] and "Pharaoh heard this thing" and "sought to kill Moses." The Israelites are a slavish lot, inside and out. It will take much doing to deliver them from both sorts of bondage.

Moses in Midian

Moses's confusion about his identity and place in the world, we imagine, only increases when he is forced to flee Egypt to save his life. He settles in Midian (why, we are not told), where he encounters yet another situation of conflict (this time between men and women) and yet another opportunity to show who he is and what he is made of:

> And [Moses] dwelt (*vayyeshev*) in the land of Midian, and he sat down (*vayyeshev*) by a well. Now the priest of Midian had seven daughters; and they came and drew water, and filled the troughs to water their father's flock. And the shepherds came and drove them away; but Moses stood up and helped them, and watered their flock. (2:15–17)

Moses, now living in exile in Midian,[34] sits down at a well, a place that sustains life and serves sociability. And because wells are places of meeting, they are also places, as we know from earlier stories, where love is born and marriages are arranged.[35]

We do not know why Moses is seated at the well. Is he there to draw water? An isolated man, could he be in search of a wife? Regardless, when the seven (unnamed) daughters of the (as yet unnamed) priest of Midian, arriving in harmony to water their flock, are harassed by the local shepherds, Moses once again springs into action on the side of the underdog, this time asserting himself on behalf of vulnerable women, even though they are to him total strangers. He not only bravely stands up to the bullies; he also kindly waters the women's sheep. Moses shows himself to be gallant and generous, in addition to being a brave man distressed by strife and injustice. If we had any doubts about the basis or extent of Moses's fellow feeling, this episode makes it clear that he cares for more than his own people. He acts here not as an Egyptian man or as an Israelite man but as a manly gentleman.[36]

Unlike the two episodes in Egypt, Moses's actions here are entirely successful—perhaps because he has learned a thing or two from his previous encounters. In addition, he is rewarded for his deeds by Reuel, the priest of Midian:

> And when they [the seven daughters] came to Reuel their father, he said: "How is it that you are come so soon today?" And they said, "An Egyptian man delivered us out of the hand of the shepherds, and he also drew water for us, and watered the flock." And he said unto his daughters: "And where is he? Why is it that you have left the man? Call him, that he may eat bread." And Moses was content to dwell with the man; and he gave Moses Zipporah his daughter. And she bore a son, and he called his name Gershom; for he said, "I have been a stranger (*ger*) in a strange land." (2:18–22)

The daughters, having avoided the usual bullying from the local shepherds, arrive home earlier than usual, prompting their father to ask why. Taking their cue from Moses's appearance or perhaps his speech, the women tell of "an *Egyptian* man" who "delivered us out of the hand of the shepherds." Prefiguring his later role as a deliverer of his people from the hand of the Egyptians, Moses, now appearing (to them) as an Egyptian man, delivers an underdog group of women from their tormentors.

Although not seeking a wife,[37] Moses acquires one and finds a new home under the roof of Reuel, the priest of Midian, with whom, we are told, he is content to dwell. (We will soon learn that he also acquires honorable work: he tends his father-in-law's flock.) In addition, Moses's wife Zipporah later bears him a son, establishing him as a father and fulfilling him as a man in this respect. No longer on the run from Pharaoh, Moses, now a family man, has finally found a solid and friendly place for himself in the large inhospitable world.

Yet we sense that all is not really well with him. Look at the name that he gives his firstborn—Gershom, from *ger*, "stranger" + *sham*, "there"—and especially at the explanation he offers: "I have been a stranger in a strange land." Most likely Moses is referring to his time in Egypt. His new home in Midian enables him for the first time to recognize and name his earlier alienation. Yet we suspect that Moses's estrangement is not solely located in the past or abroad: even as he settles in Midian, he makes his estrangement the name he will always have before him in the person of his son. Gershom inherits from his father only a heartsick remembrance of alienation. Although settled in Midian, Moses is not truly at home.

Why might Moses *still* feel like a stranger in a strange land? Why, having wife and child, job and home—all won through manly and noble actions—is he not yet fully settled? Are these usual achievements of manhood not sufficient? What does he lack? The answer lies just over the horizon.

First Stirrings in Egypt

Having given us the story of Moses's birth, his rescue and adoption, his manly emergence from the palace, his flight to Midian, his marriage, and the birth and naming of his firstborn, the chapter concludes by returning to the condition of the Israelite slaves in Egypt.[38] What we are told both completes the background for the story of their deliverance and describes the first stirrings of change:

> And it came to pass, in [the course of] those many days, that the king of Egypt died, and the Children of Israel sighed from their servitude (*'avodah*) and they cried out (*vayyiz'aqu*); and their cry went up to God from their servitude. And God *heard*

their groaning, and God *remembered* his covenant with
Abraham, Isaac, and Jacob. And God *saw* the Children of Israel, and God *knew*. (2:23–25; emphasis added).

Time has passed since we last looked in on the Israelite slaves. Their long
servitude persists. They may even be more miserable than before—
perhaps because of the arrival of yet another new Pharaoh (after the
death of the one who used the Israelites as scapegoats to consolidate his
power). When the coming of this new Pharaoh brings the slaves no relief, they descend into hopelessness. But, ironically for that very reason,
not all is dark. For the first time, the Children of Israel give voice to their
suffering: they break their long silence; they cry out their agony and their
anguish.[39] They do not explicitly cry out to God, nor do they ask for His
help; after several generations of servitude, preceded by several generations of prosperity, there is no reason to believe they had preserved any
knowledge of the God of their ancestors. Nevertheless, this voice of protest against their lot is a sign that they now refuse to accept their abasement and humiliation in silence and, by implication, that they aspire to
something better. Only the aspirationally free can complain against being enslaved.

Although the cry of the Children of Israel seems to have been addressed to no one in particular, this protest against their oppression nevertheless reaches God, Who bestirs Himself to begin the process of
their deliverance. He *heard* their groaning, which led Him to *remember*
His covenant with the patriarchs Abraham, Isaac, and Jacob. He *saw* the
Children of Israel. And He *knew*—although what He knew, we are not
told. Perhaps, as the next chapter will say, He "knew their pains" (3:7).
Perhaps He knew that it was time to fulfill the promise to Abraham. Perhaps He knew in addition what it would take to terminate the enslavement of the Israelites and initiate a new covenantal relationship between
Himself and the newly liberated slaves. With the slaves now voicing their
discontent, the time seems ripe to summon Moses and to start the process of redemption and people formation, the story of which occupies
much of the rest of the Torah.

Much of that story involves bold action under Moses's political
leadership. But it also involves new thinking and unfolding knowledge,

including knowledge of the Lord and what He wants of us. As if to un-derline the importance of such knowledge, we are invited to think about the relationship among the four mental activities here attributed to God: hearing, remembering, seeing, and knowing. How will the Children of Israel come to know God? How will they learn what He requires of them? Which is the more reliable path to such crucial knowledge: Seeing? Hear-ing? Remembering?

The story of Moses at the burning bush, in the immediate sequel, offers important help with these questions.

Moses Finds God and (Reluctantly)
Accepts His Mission

W hen we left Moses, a few verses back yet many years ago, he had settled in Midian, a refugee from Egypt. He was newly a family man: husband to Zipporah—a daughter of the priest of Midian (*Reuel*, "Friend of god [*El*]")— and father of at least one son, Gershom, named, Moses said, to remind him that he was once a stranger in a strange land. Now, with God poised to act on behalf of His people, Moses must be in a state of mind to receive God's call and commission. In subtle ways, as we shall see, the text hints at Moses's readiness, but it gives no clue about what might have made him ready. We are left to speculate—and about some new but most important matters.

The last chapter taught us some crucial things about Moses that may be relevant to his future mission. We learned about his character, his ambiguous (or perhaps transnational) ethnic identity, and his life experience, from birth and adoption to young manhood and exile. But we learned nothing about his intellect or his view of the divine. These deficiencies we hope this new chapter will rectify.

Moses, Ripe for Catching

Just as the text was surprisingly silent on what happened when Moses entered Pharaoh's house and on what he might have learned there, so it is astonishingly silent on what happened after Moses settled down in Midian, beyond the bare facts of his marriage and paternity. This silence covers some fifty to sixty years, between the time Moses arrived as a young man, probably in his early twenties, and the time God first calls him, when he is nearly eighty years old.[1] How has Moses changed over these decades? Is he still a spirited man of action, movable by fellow feeling and inserting himself into other people's business to rectify injustice? Or has he become more contemplative and spiritual under the influence of his priestly father-in-law? What now are Moses's thoughts about the divine?

From reading Genesis we have some sense of what is revered in Egypt: both nature "gods" (from the Nile to the sun) and human masters who seek to control nature (from Pharaoh to his magicians). But what is revered in Midian and specifically by the father-in-law with whom Moses has lived (presumably) much of this time? Has Reuel (Jethro)[2] opened Moses up to some form of monotheism and the possibility of a supernatural deity? Or has Midianite theology left Moses perplexed and searching? Has he adopted a Midianite identity and outlook, or is he still a stranger in a strange land—restless, searching, eager for some transformative experience that might yield true knowledge of the divine and lend purpose to his life? As with his time in Pharaoh's house, the text seems completely uninterested in Moses's life in Midian before God calls him; for the unfolding story, it matters only that God called Moses and Moses answered. But as wisdom-seeking readers we are interested also in how Moses became Moses, and especially in the ruling passions and aspirations of his soul. We therefore accept the text's silence as an invitation to thought that may help us better understand the whys and wherefores of what comes next:

> Now Moses was *keeping the flock* of Jethro, his *father-in-law*, the *priest of Midian;* and he *led the flock* beyond (or "behind") the wilderness (or perhaps "the pasture"; *'achar hammidbar*), and he came to the mountain of God (*har ha'elohim*), unto Horeb. (3:1; emphasis added)

This solitary sentence gives us a few clues to Moses's situation just before God calls him. Moses is not a farmer but a shepherd; his is an anti-Egyptian occupation. He does not work the soil or settle upon land appropriated as his own; instead, he wanders alone out in the pasture-land, with nothing between him and the heavens. He works for Jethro, identified doubly as his father-in-law (pointedly, not his *father*) and as the priest of Midian: unlike Jacob in Paddan-aram, who from the out-set had only trouble from his deceitful father-in-law Laban, Moses even after many decades still works for his father-in-law and appears to be on good terms with him. He has gone from living in the palace with the ruler of Egypt to living in the fields with the priest of Midian—an ar-rangement whose implications we would dearly wish to know.

The story begins, then, with Moses all alone in the open, an ex-posed shepherd, leading a flock not his own, serving his father-in-law-priest of the local religion and deities. But on this occasion, Moses wanders to the edge of the wilderness (or "pasture land," the more com-mon biblical meaning of *midbar*) near the high level of the desert (Horeb means "parched, desolate") and comes to a liminal place, out of the way.[3] The reader is told that Moses has come to "the mountain of God," but this fact was likely unknown to Moses. The meaning of the moun-tain's name is, for now, obscure: a towering presence in the desert, the mountain could have been a local cult place, filled with mystique and aura; alternatively, its name may be an anticipatory announcement of the later mountaintop theophany and the giving of God's Law to the Children of Israel. But wittingly or not, Moses has wandered off on a journey to a numinous experience. And in what state of mind? Very likely, he is es-tranged and restless, psychically and physically searching, and open to discovering something higher than what he knows, something that will speak to his longings—for father and fatherland, for vocation and pur-pose, for great distinction, for knowledge about the god most high, or for "he knows not what." Moses, the searcher, is ripe for the catching.[4]

God Catches Moses: From Wonder to Awe

God knows just how to catch him: by means of a wondrous spectacle:

> And an angel (or "messenger"; *mal'akh*) of the Lord *appeared*
> unto him in a *flame of fire* out of the midst of a thorn bush

(*sneh*); and he *looked,* and, behold, the thorn bush [was] burning with fire, but the thorn bush was not consumed. And
Moses said [to himself]: "I will turn aside now and I will *see*
this great *sight, why* (*maddu'a*) the bush is not burned?" And
[when] the Lord *saw* that he turned aside to *see,* then God
called unto him out of the midst of the bush, and He said:
"Moses, Moses"; and he said: "Here am I (*hinneni*)." And He
said: "Do not come closer: put off your shoes from off your
feet, for the place upon which you stand [is] holy ground
(*'admath-qodesh*)." And He said: "I [am] the God of your
father, the God of Abraham, the God of Isaac, and the God
of Jacob"; and Moses hid his face: for he feared to *look* upon
God.[5] (3:2–6; emphasis added)

The sight of a bush burning in the blazing heat of the desert would not
be worth much notice. But a bush not consumed by the fire it sustained
is something remarkable, provided this is discerned. The sharp-eyed
Moses catches it at once. One commentator observes that the miracle is
not that a burning bush was not consumed but that Moses turns to take
notice of it. But I am inclined to think that Moses's turn to gaze is right
in character. Recognizing that the sight defies both experiential and rational expectations, Moses is mentally disposed not only to pay attention but also *to seek an explanation:* moved by both wonder and
curiosity, he turns aside not only to see but also to seek the cause. Unlike Abraham, Isaac, and Jacob, Moses wants to know the *why* of
things.[6] He turns away from shepherding, a matter of leadership and
rule, toward questioning and understanding, a matter of truth, to be
sought for its own sake. We readers wonder whether this natural
philosophical—"wisdom-seeking"—inclination will be reinforced or un-
dercut. Is Moses's interest in the truth and cause of things a prerequisite
for his mission, one that will then be properly elevated and redirected?
Or does it reflect a character trait that must be corrected or even
squelched?[7]

The wondrous sight may be said to offer an especially Egyptian
attraction. Fire, both a principle of life (animal heat) and destroyer of
life, here burns steadily without causing destruction. Like the sun, the

highest god of the Egyptians, the unconsumable burning bush, with its unquenchable flames, is luminous and seemingly self-sustaining, permanently and fully "being itself at work." The fire is a manifestation of what Aristotle would later call *energeia*, "being-in-its-work," which, in its purest form, is the essence of the divine: complete, fully itself, fully active. Someone initiated into Egyptian wisdom would be especially attracted by the ever actively burning (not to say immortal) bush, which would appear to be at least an image, if not an actual terrestrial instance, of the eternal and the divine.

Moses's suspicion that he is in the presence of something supernatural (or something supremely and fully natural) is not ill-founded, but as it turns out, it is something undreamt of in his philosophy. The spectacle holds more than meets the eye; as the reader has been told, it is a message from the Lord. Most amazingly, as Moses approaches it, the wondrous "sight" *speaks,* addressing Moses not through his wondering eyes but through his hearkening ears.

For openers, the talking fire addresses Moses intimately by name, not once but twice, emphatically and with authority.[8] No doubt astonished to be summoned by name from out of the flames, Moses eagerly answers the call with complete attention: *hinneni,* I am fully present to you, whoever you are; please speak on, I am all ears.[9] The perplexing sight that invited approach has become an invisible and arresting mystery, before which one must hold one's place, gripped by awe—too frightened to go any closer, yet too attracted to run away. Fittingly, the divine voice tells Moses to approach no further and to show proper respect by removing his shoes, as he stands on holy ground.[10] Moses very likely having acquiesced, the voice then identifies Himself as the "God of *your* father, the God of Abraham, the God of Isaac, the God of Jacob"—an answer, please note, that speaks powerfully to any longing Moses may have to know his father, his identity, and his god. Moses, on his own and without needing to be told, now hides his face, unwilling to look on the divine speaker out of awe-fear-reverence. Moses approached wide-eyed to see a natural sight, in Egyptian wonder, but shrinks from seeing his father's God, in Hebraic awe.

We pause a moment over this experience. Awe-fear-reverence (the hard-to-translate Hebrew word is *yir'ah*) is *the* central religious passion, and no story I know better exemplifies the phenomenon of its sudden appearance. *Yir'ah* is called forth by an encounter with overwhelming power, with great authority, with deep mystery, with grandeur and sub-limity—in short, with the "awesome," in its original, nondebased mean-ing. Awe-fear-reverence is not a congenial passion: it implies, and insists on maintaining, clear distance from the object that elicits it. It acknowledges our weakness and inadequacy before something much greater than ourselves ("do not come closer"; "put off your shoes"). And yet it does not—like simple fear or terror—lead us to flee. On the con-trary, despite the evident inequality, the very fact of our recognizing the superiority of the object builds a connection between us. We are both attracted and repelled; we want both to approach and to stand back; we oscillate in place, bound in relation to the thing that defies our compre-hension and makes us feel small. We hide our face, but we hold our ground. Paradoxically, thanks to awe-fear-reverence and the bond it builds across the unbridgeable divide, we also feel less small. We are, in fact, lifted up, enlarged, magnified. This surely has happened here to Moses.

Moses also experiences a challenge to his way of approaching and knowing the world. His encounter at the burning bush calls into ques-tion not only the reliability of *this* mysterious sight. It challenges the natural human presumption that seeing is the most trustworthy way of apprehending the world. Moses, relying on sight, had approached the bush hoping to take its true measure. He trusted that his vision would give him full access to the being and meaning of what the world put be-fore him: what you see is what there is, and it beckons you to know it. Instead, he encounters a voice before which one can be confident only that one is in the presence of a being, but without any clue regarding its totality, never mind its identity and nature. Through speech and hear-ing we learn—at most—only as much as the speaker chooses to reveal to us. The mystery of what is hidden is enough to inspire caution and even awe.*

---

*Readers interested in a fuller discussion of the differences between seeing and hearing, and the significance of those differences for human life, may read the appen-dix at the end of this chapter, "Appendix: Seeing Versus Hearing."

But when, as in the present case, the voice that speaks appears to know us personally, addresses us with commanding authority, and last but far from least, identifies Himself as the divinity of *one's father and one's venerable ancestors*—names to conjure with—anyone would be struck dumb with awe and humility. Moses, a man torn from his Israelite past and having little if any knowledge of his father, is summoned to stand in his father's place and in the place of the Israelite patriarchs, addressed by the God they revered and Who cared for them. Moses, exiled Egyptian prince and son-in-law to a Midianite priest, rootless and restless seeker after truth, is invited to resume his true identity by a voice claiming to be the god of his ancestors. Paradoxically, the awe-struck Moses, stranger in a strange land, is now more at home with himself than he has ever been.[11]

Having been attracted by wonder, now replaced by awe, Moses has been perfectly caught. His Egyptian (indeed, human) orientation to and expectation of the world have been overturned. He is ready to be instructed and commanded regarding the divine mission to the Israelites. From God's point of view, Moses has passed the test with flying colors. He has shown himself to be a man who cares about more than politics and who is interested in the truth for its own sake, but who is also capable of awe, open to the mysterious divine, and moved by words about his father and ancestors and the God they worshipped. As He had with Abram, God has again found His man.

The Mission

Finding His man is one thing, getting him to accept his mission another thing entirely. Moses will prove a harder sell than Abram, who immediately responded to God's call without saying a word. Yet Moses is ready to hear more, and he and God will not in the end be disappointed. What follows is the longest conversation in the Torah. Here is how it begins:

> And the Lord said: "*I* have surely *seen* the affliction of *My* people who [are] in Egypt, and their cry *I* have *heard* by reason of their taskmasters, for *I know* their sorrows. And *I* have come *down* to deliver them out of the hand of Egypt, and to

bring them *up* out of that land unto a good and broad land, unto a land flowing with milk and honey, unto the place of the Canaanite, and the Hittite, and the Amorite, and the Perizzite, and the Hivite, and the Jebusite. And now, behold, the cry of the Children of Israel has come unto *Me*, and *I* have also seen the oppression [with] which the Egyptians oppress them. And now, go, and *I* will send you unto Pharaoh and *you* shall bring *My* people the Children of Israel out of Egypt." (3:7–10; emphasis added)

Having gained Moses's attention by revealing something (but only something) of His identity, God now reveals His state of mind and His intention, including the role He has chosen for Moses to play. He begins by telling Moses what He has seen and heard and what He knows—respectively, the affliction of "My people" that are in Egypt, their cry because of their taskmasters, and their pain. He then states His twofold purpose: first, to deliver His people from the hands of the Egyptians, and, second, to bring them up unto the Promised Land, a land that is both good ("flowing with milk and honey") and large (spacious enough to hold six flourishing Canaanite nations[12]). Concluding, God summarizes (again) what He has heard ("the cry of the Children of Israel") and what He has seen ("the oppression wherewith the Egyptians oppress them"), and then gives Moses his twofold charge: "I will send you unto Pharaoh" so that "*you* may bring *My* people the Children of Israel out of Egypt."

God's speech is emphatically about *His* purposes and plans: He uses the first person nine times, six times as a verb subject ("I"), twice as a possessive ("My people"), and once as an indirect object ("come unto Me"). Yet the speech is also subtly crafted to appeal to Moses's soul: having told Moses that He is the God of Moses's father, He invites him to identify with the present Israelite victims and future beneficiaries of God's plan. He tempts him with an overly attractive picture of the Promised Land. By speaking twice of oppression, He appeals to Moses's capacity for righteous indignation and fellow feeling and his love of justice. Speaking to Moses's ambition, God offers him the opportunity to be a liberator: "that *you* may bring My people out" from their oppression in Egypt.

Moses does not take the bait. On the contrary, he begins a conversation comprising a series of questions ("Who am I?" and "What is your name?") and doubts ("They will not believe my words"; "I am not a good speaker.") that show his reluctance to accept the assignment.[13] His questions admittedly make good sense on the surface and seem to fit his own circumstances in relation to the grand mission for which God is summoning him: What power do *I* have for this undertaking? What power do *you* have? The Israelite people, believe me, will need answers and assurances. But at the same time, his responses—especially his first two questions—give voice to deeper concerns and interests: Moses's uncertainty about his identity and his desire to know and, in some degree, control the divine.

Moses's Questions: Who Am I? Who Are You?

Moses's first response to God's long speech and call, while not exactly a refusal, pushes back against some of the explicit points God had stressed:

> And Moses said unto God: "Who [am] I (*mi 'anokhi*) that I should go unto Pharaoh, and that I should bring out the Children of Israel out of Egypt?" And He said: "But I will be with you (*ki-'ehyeh 'immakh*); and this [shall be] to you the token, that I have sent you; when you have brought out the people out of Egypt, you shall serve God upon this mountain." (3:11–12)

Moses's question, "Who [am] I," is multiply intelligible. Responding to God's heavy emphasis on "I," he has cause to wonder, 'If *you* are going to do all of that, what need have you for me?' This is not an impertinent question. An alert reader may be wondering the same thing: Why does God need Moses? If *God,* as He says, has come down to deliver *His* people out of Egypt, why does He need to send *Moses* ["*you*"] to Pharaoh "to bring *My* people the Children of Israel out of Egypt"?

Surely He could extract them all by Himself. Something other than divine power must be required; something else is desired beyond just getting the deed done. Speech and explanation, prophecy and persuasion, may be needed if all the participants are to know what is going on and why. God, we surmise, needs a human champion and messenger, prophet and educator, who will convey the meaning and purpose of His manifestations of power. Although nothing like this is explicitly said in the text or to Moses himself, God is looking for a leader and teacher of His people.

Moses's "Who [am] I?" could also mean 'Why me? What business is it of mine?' God had spoken of "My people," having made it clear to Moses that, as the God of Moses's father, He regarded Moses as one of them. But Moses, distancing himself both from the Israelites and from God, does not speak of "my people" or "our people" but only of "the Children of Israel." Implicitly, he is saying 'They are *your* people, not my people, so why is this my concern?'*

Moses's question is even more fitting on practical grounds. He is concerned, not unreasonably, about his capacity. No longer a youthful zealot, he does not regard himself as fit for such a heroic assignment: I am but a humble shepherd; I lack the capacity for such a momentous task. Besides, even in my youthful vigor, I had no success in dealing with this slavish people.

Finally, and deeper down, Moses's question, "Who [am] I?" may manifest his own confusion of personal identity: am I Midianite, Egyptian, or Israelite? He has good reason to wonder, on this ground alone, why *he,* hardly a qualified Israelite, should get involved in the voice's plan for the Israelites: Why should he leave Midian (where he has a stable life) to go to Pharaoh (whose predecessor he fled) on this mysterious *voice's* behalf to lead the *Children of Israel* (an unreasonable rabble) out of Egypt?

God's answer, "I will be with you," is reassuring on several counts, although its meaning is not altogether clear.[14] Interpreting Moses's ques-

---

*It will be a very long time before Moses speaks of the Children of Israel as "my people" or "our people" or includes himself as one among them. I invite the reader to discover the time and place he does so for the first time.

tion as showing a lack of confidence in his suitability or capacity for the mission, God tells Moses not to worry: I will also be present during the undertaking, working with you, Moses—or is it simply through you? *My power* will be with you. Empowered by God's presence, Moses should have no reason to doubt his own competence or capacity for the task.

God's reply also answers the deeper question of identity embedded in Moses's "Who [am] I?" You, Moses? You want to know *who* you are? Let me tell you: You are the one *with whom I will be. That,* from now on, is your identity.[15]

Recognizing that Moses may need more than verbal reassurance, God offers him a sign that will show that it is indeed God Who is sending him on his mission. Yet the nature of that sign is also far from clear. Is "the sign" the present theophanic revelation at the foot of the mountain—the burning bush that speaks personally to him? Is it the just-uttered promise, "I will be with you"? Or is it, by anticipation, the prophecy of a future return to this spot, following the Exodus from Egypt, where the people shall serve God upon this very mountain? Could it be all three: a sign here and now, visible, verbal, and personal, that stands also for a sign there and then, into the future: "I-will-be" with you—and them, at this very mountain—as "I am" am now with you?

God's enigmatic answer only increases Moses's perplexity. Understandably not placated, he has more questions:

> And Moses said unto God: "Behold, [when] I come unto the Children of Israel, and I shall say to them, 'The God of your fathers has sent me unto you'; and they shall say unto me, 'What [is] His name?' what shall I say unto them?" (3:13)

On its face, this question seems perfectly reasonable, seeing as its answer appears necessary for the success of Moses's mission. (Please note how readily the supposedly reluctant Moses imagines himself in the role of deliverer, standing before the Children of Israel.) The dispirited Israelite slaves, told that some ancestral "god of your fathers" has summoned them to Him, would surely want to know more about Him. Not only are they likely to have forgotten His name (if they ever knew it), but their long and bitter servitude in Egypt also would have given them reason to doubt His care for them, not to say His capacities or even His very existence. Under the circumstances imagined by Moses, by asking "What is His name?" the slaves would be asking especially about His power, 'This so-called god of our fathers, what is He able to do for us?'

Yet Moses, even more than the Israelites, has a vital interest in the same question: If, to my "Who am I?" you answer, "*I* will be with you (*'ehyeh 'immakh*)," then Who, pray tell, *are you?* It is not enough for me to know that you are the god who was worshipped by my ancestors. I must also know your power. By learning your name, I hope not only to know your power but also to gain access to it. Avoiding the impertinence of putting this crucial question in his own name, Moses tactfully and indirectly seeks the answer also and especially for himself.

Although the question seems reasonable, asking for God's name is overbold, impertinent, and even misguided. It presumes undue familiarity. It seeks to know by defining, delimiting, or grasping the "essence," in apparent unawareness that the infinite or unlimited simply cannot be named or grasped.[16] It may even aspire to some control over God, calling upon Him for our own purposes.

Nevertheless, we should not judge Moses too severely for his nerve in asking this question. Even God does not rebuke him for doing so. In fact, He may welcome Moses's desire to know Him so that He can properly redirect that desire into more appropriate channels. He may welcome Moses's desire to know Him also because He wants *to be known*—to be sure, in the right way.

The question "What's your name?" is the most human of questions. Through it, we give voice to recognizing another's unique and independent existence. Through it, we seek a handle whereby to reduce somewhat the opacity and mystery of the other and to place ourselves in relationship to it. "What's your name?" often bespeaks a desire for intimacy.

To seek the name of something is part of an effort to know not only its "who" but also its "what"—to grasp its being, to know its "essence"—both in itself and in its relationship to us.[17] To know its name is an avenue of access and thereby, perhaps, of a modicum of control.

The interest in divine names is an especially Egyptian proclivity, for biblical Egypt is the pinnacle of civilization and human ingenuity—

celebrating mathematics, astronomy, technology, bureaucratic administration, and a highly elaborate theology. In Egypt, the gods are all named, formed, defined. They are emblems of ideas and natural powers; for example, the scarab or dung beetle, which appears to arise out of excrement, is, as we saw, an emblem of immortality. They can therefore be grasped in speech and represented in images and likenesses (such as the ideograms of Egyptian writing). Moses, who turned toward the burning bush to seek the cause of its mysterious persistence, continues to evince a speculative interest in knowing—and grasping—the nature of the mysterious divine voice. This will not be the last time that Moses seeks direct knowledge of God, after the fashion of would-be philosophers or master manipulators.[18]

The question of the divine name is crucial also for the Israelites' deliverance. In the past, God was known only to and by singular individuals—Abraham, Sarah, Isaac, Rebekah, and Jacob—when the nation of Israel was but a seed, literally a mom-and-pop operation. For subsequent generations of Israelites, His existence and care for human beings could be attested only through receding memory, in stories of God's having once been the solicitous personal god of their fathers and connected largely with fertility and procreation. Now, with Israel on its way to becoming a people, God's relationship to his people will change dramatically. A new covenant will be established, greatly supplementing (though not replacing) the personal one made with Abraham, which promised great fertility and a land. The new covenant ties God to Israel's redemption from Egypt and will summon them to be to Him a holy people. For these new purposes and for this new relationship to God, a new aspect of God—manifested in a new name—must now become known, first to Moses and then to the Israelites.[19]

The Name(s) of God

Before Moses, only Jacob had had the nerve to seek any direct knowledge of God: in his famous wrestling match, he sought to know the name of his more-than-human counterpart. But when Jacob demands to know the name of his mysterious opponent, he is gently but firmly rebuked: "Why ask you my name?"[20] Jacob boasts of having "seen God face-to-face" and lived to tell the tale, but we who read the account are inclined to believe he saw no such thing. Now, several hundred years later, with the Israelites long abandoned under the thumb of Egyptian despots, it would be a rare Israelite who possessed even an inkling of his god's existence, never mind of His name—which is to say, His character and power. If the Israelites are to enter into a new relationship with Him, it will have to be on a new footing and foundation. To make this possible, a crucial aspect of God's "being" must become known to them.

(Permit me to observe again that we readers also have much to learn from Moses's question and its answer. We have been hearing about "God" (*'elohim*) and "the Lord" (*Y-H-V-H*) since the beginning of Genesis. But the *content* of those mysterious "words" or "names"—they are, to begin with, mere placeholders—gets filled in mainly through watching and listening to His deeds and speeches, as these are recounted in the unfolding text. Like Moses, we too are on the verge of discovering a new aspect of the divine and a new relation between God and human beings, beyond what it was with the patriarchs and matriarchs.)

God's reply to Moses's inquiry is perfect. Responding simultaneously to all aspects of Moses's question, He gives answer in three expressions:

> And God said unto Moses: "I Will Be What I Will Be (or "I Am What I Am"; *'ehyeh 'asher 'ehyeh*)"; and He said: "Thus shall you say to the Children of Israel: 'I Will Be (or "I Am"; *'ehyeh*) has sent me unto you.'" And God said moreover unto Moses: "Thus shall you say unto the Children of Israel: 'the Lord (*Y-H-V-H*), the God of your fathers, the God of Abraham, the God of Isaac, and the God of Jacob, has sent me unto you: this [is] My name for ever, and this [is] My memorial to all generations.'" (3:14–15)

Addressing only Moses himself and *his* desire for knowledge of the divine, God first gives the notoriously enigmatic answer, *'ehyeh 'asher 'ehyeh*. Then, in the face of Moses's puzzled silence—or perhaps before Moses can give voice to his perplexity—God responds directly to Moses's explicit question about what to say to the Children of Israel: Tell them that "I Will Be" has sent me to you. With Moses still mute and very likely perplexed, God adds, more expansively: "And God said moreover unto Moses: 'Thus shall you say unto the Children of Israel: "Y-H-V-H, the God of your fathers, the God of Abraham, the God of Isaac, and the God of Jacob, has sent me unto you: this [is] My name for ever, and this [is] My memorial to all generations."'"

The first expression, 'ehyeh 'asher 'ehyeh, occurs nowhere else in the Hebrew Bible, and it is heard therefore only by Moses—and by us. On its face, it appears to be a deliberate *non*-answer to the request for a name, a rejection of the question. Nothing like a definite name that reveals the essence or gives rest to thought, it is instead an enigma, true to the inexpressible character of an unbounded and ineffable divine. Yet Moses (and we) can perhaps learn something about God from these enigmatic words.

As already noted, 'ehyeh is the first-person singular of the verb "to be," *hayah,* in the imperfect (that is, ongoing and incomplete) aspect: in bad English, "I am being" or "I will be being." (Y-H-V-H, Yod-hey-vav-hey—generally translated as "The Lord" but not even pronounced by observant Jews who say, instead, 'Adonai, "Lord," or Hashem, "The Name"—is the correlative *third*-person singular, imperfect, of the same verb: "He-is-being," "He-will-be-being.") 'Ehyeh 'asher 'ehyeh therefore suggests something not only incomplete and unlimited but also ongoing, progressing, free, and unpredictable; not *static* but *acting in time;* and "knowable" therefore only through watching "its" deeds and words: Ask not my name, just see what I do. At the same time, and conversely, it might also be read as saying, "I am [always] what I am"—in other words, true to Myself and true to My word, and hence true also to My creatures and people.

If this (very limited[21]) analysis is correct, Moses and we acquire an immensely important and revolutionary insight about how human beings should approach the deity. "Knowledge of God," or a relationship to God, should be pursued not through inquisitive speech or philosophical speculation (fruitlessly seeking the essence), but through attending to God's commands and deeds, to what God *will be in time.* We should redirect our desire to "know God" away from philosophy and theology (speech about God) and attend instead to what He reveals of Himself in "history," to what *He says* to and *does* for human beings.

Moses, at least for now and on the surface, appears to be content with this answer, for he does not press for greater clarity. Yet his desire to know God more directly, more fully, and more intimately is not permanently suppressed. It will emerge again, and with a vengeance, after the episode with the golden calf.

Whatever Moses personally makes of *'ehyeh 'asher 'ehyeh,* God's third formulation gives him exactly what he asked for and what he needs in dealing with the Children of Israel: "*Y-H-V-H,* the God of your fathers, the God of Abraham, the God of Isaac, and the God of Jacob." Moses has what God calls His "name for ever and ever." And the people will get something that really does look more like a personal name. It links *Y-H-V-H*—"He Is/He Will Be," bespeaking God's indeterminate present but portentous future—to His past relation to the Israelites' ancestors and patriarchs. The new, future-oriented addition to the "name" heralds for the Children of Israel—and for us—a new aspect of God's relation to human beings: God will become the author of a full-fledged people, through deliverance, covenant, and law.

The Divine Charge

With Moses's apparent acquiescence to this multifaceted answer to his question about the divine name—implying perhaps that his question about God's power has also been sufficiently answered—God proceeds, without pause, to issue at length the divine charge to Moses, along with a synoptic view of how things will turn out. He tells Moses to gather the elders of Israel, and He tells him what he should say to them. He also predicts that Moses's speech will be successful:

> "Go and gather the elders of Israel together, and say unto them: 'The Lord, the God of your fathers, the God of Abraham, of Isaac, and of Jacob, has appeared unto me saying: "I have surely remembered you, and seen that which is done to you in Egypt. And I have said: 'I will bring you up out of the

affliction of Egypt into the land of the Canaanite, and the
Hittite, and the Amorite, and the Perizzite, and the Hivite,
and the Jebusite, unto a land flowing with milk and honey.'"'
And they shall hearken to your voice." (3:16-18)

Continuing without pause, God then moves to the next part of Moses's mission, an appeal to the king of Egypt, and a prediction of initial
failure but of eventual, divinely crafted success:

"And you shall come, you and the elders of Israel, unto the
king of Egypt, and you shall say unto him: 'The Lord, the God
of the Hebrews, has lighted upon us. And now let us go,
please, three days' journey into the wilderness, that we may
sacrifice to the Lord our God.' And I know that the king of
Egypt will not let you go, not even with a mighty hand [yours].
So I will put forth My hand and smite Egypt with all My wonders which I will do in the midst thereof. And after that he
will let you go." (3:18–20)

God concludes by telling Moses that the Children of Israel, when
they leave Egypt, will leave with great substance[22]:

"And I will give this people favor in the sight of the Egyptians.
And it shall come to pass, that, when you go, you shall not
go empty; but every woman shall ask of her neighbor, and of
her that sojourns in her house, jewels of silver, and jewels of
gold, and raiment; and you shall put them upon your sons
and upon your daughters; and you shall despoil the Egyptians." (3:21–22)

A few things deserve notice. God tells Moses how things will turn
out: his preliminary success with the Israelite elders, his failure with
Pharaoh, and finally God's ultimate victory over Pharaoh, using raw
power and wonders. Moses is given advance notice of the difficulty of
his mission, the limits of his powers of speech and persuasion, and the
need for divine intervention—an implicit exhortation to trust in

God's providence. We are left to wonder why, if God could directly get Israel out of Egypt, he adopts this complicated plan. Clearly, something more important than mere physical separation and deliverance from Egypt is at stake.

We notice too that Moses is given a prepared speech to make to Pharaoh; we will want to see how closely he adheres to it. And we notice that the Israelites will go out of Egypt with great wealth, in the form of gifts from the Egyptian people. Like the manumitted slaves who will later be discussed in Deuteronomy, the ex-slaves will receive (just?) compensation for their long service, and they will go out with the means to build a new life in freedom. At the same time, however, we note—well in advance—that they will now have the means to build not only a Tabernacle but also a golden calf. Freedom and wealth, although clearly preferable to slavery and poverty, have their own hazards.

Moses's Doubts: The Weakness of Speech

Despite God's expansive response to his question about His name, and despite His preview of coming attractions with its highly favorable outcome, Moses is not ready to accept the mission. Instead, imagining himself before the Israelites, he expresses the first of two doubts about the efficacy of his speech:

> And Moses answered and said: "But, behold, they will not believe me, nor hearken to my voice; for they will say, 'The Lord has not appeared unto you.'" (4:1)

Surprisingly, Moses seems unconcerned about his appearance before Pharaoh. Perhaps remembering his ineffective encounter with the brawling Hebrew slaves and their challenge to his authority, he seems worried only about persuading the Israelites: they will call him a liar. Moses does not say, but very likely supposes, that the Israelites will not believe him because they are a slavish rabble, incapable of being led to freedom and perhaps unworthy of it. He directly challenges the Lord's prediction that, once having heard the speech God told him to make, the Children of Israel "shall hearken to your voice."

The Lord concedes the point without argument: Moses's speech alone cannot overcome the slaves' lack of trust, either in Moses or in some long-missing deity in whose name he claims to be speaking. For them, wondrous deeds will speak louder than words:

> And the Lord said unto him: "What is that in your hand?" And he said, "A rod." And He said, "Cast it on the ground." And he cast it on the ground, and it became a serpent (*nachash*); and Moses fled from before it. And the Lord said unto Moses: "Put forth your hand, and take it by the tail"—and he put forth his hand, and laid hold of it, and it became a rod in his hand—"that they may believe that the Lord, the God of their fathers, the God of Abraham, the God of Isaac, and the God of Jacob, has appeared unto you." And the Lord said furthermore unto him: "Put now your hand into your bosom." And he put his hand into his bosom; and when he took it out, his hand was leprous, as white as snow. And He said: "Put your hand back into your bosom." And he put his hand back into his bosom; and when he took it out of his bosom, behold, it was like his [other] flesh. "And it shall come to pass, if they will not believe you, nor hearken to the voice of the first sign (*ha-'oth ha-ri'shon*), that they will trust the voice of the second sign. And it shall come to pass, if they will not believe even these two signs, neither hearken to your voice, then you shall take of the water of the river and pour it upon the dry land; and the water which you take out of the river shall become blood on the dry land." (4:2–9)

The Lord gives Moses a pointed personal lesson in the power of visible wonders. Intended to dispel Moses's fear that the Israelites will not believe him, they also dispel any doubts Moses himself may have had about his interlocutor's power.

We, as vicarious witnesses, pause a moment to consider just how this demonstration works. As the Lord says several times, the wonders, visible to the eye, are also *signs:* they point beyond themselves to an invisible meaning to which the signifying wonder, it is said, gives voice:

"they will trust the voice of the . . . sign." Before our eyes, we see an in-animate rod (a shepherd's staff) turned into a living snake, and we see the process reversed. We see the sudden arrival of dread disease (attacking the tool of human agency) and its equally sudden cure. If necessary, we are told, we could see life-giving water turned into dreadful blood, spilled upon and polluting the ground. These wondrous sights all point to—and announce in the language of visibility—the power of God over life and death and over health and illness. As executed by Moses, the wonders also bespeak—in "the *voice* of the signs"—the Lord's power over the work of human hands, directing them to His own purposes.[23] In being shown how to convince the people, Moses gets a preview of how God will empower his hand and the staff it holds to gain victory over Pharaoh.[24] But to experience the Lord's power, Moses himself needs—and demonstrates—trust and courage: he yields to God's orders, grasps the snake in the most dangerous place, and submits his hand to leprous transformation.

One might think that Moses would now be ready to confidently embrace the mission. But as if having understood nothing, Moses reverts to complaining about the inadequacy of his speech:

> And Moses said unto the Lord (*Y-H-V-H*): "Oh Lord (*'ado-nai*), not a man of words am I, neither heretofore nor since You have spoken unto Your servant; for heavy of mouth and heavy of tongue am I." (4:10)

The wonders and signs may be helpful. But, Moses seems to insist, he will still need persuasive—even inspiring—speech to accomplish the mission. And I am not up to that task: I am a man of action, not of words. I am not a teacher, I am not a lawyer, I am not a diplomat or an orator. We wonder whether he is still thinking about leading the resistant people or about confronting the recalcitrant Pharaoh, and we agree that Moses is not wrong about the need for rhetorical excellence—which he so far has not demonstrated. But we also begin to suspect that he is trying one excuse after another in the hope of getting out of his assignment.[25]

Still, the Lord takes Moses's concern at face value and addresses it fully:

And the Lord said unto him: "Who has made man's mouth? Or who makes a man dumb, or deaf, or seeing, or blind? Is it not I the Lord? So now go, and I, I will be with your mouth (*'ehyeh 'im-pikha*), and teach you what you shall speak." (4:11–12)

I told you before that I will be with you. I tell you now that I will be (also) with *your mouth*. Not to worry. Your speech will be more than just *your* speech. I have your mouth; I have your back. Now go!

Moses Balks, Aaron Talks: Brotherhood and Rule

Despite God's reassurances, Moses balks: "Oh Lord (*'adonai*), send, please, by the hand of him whom You will send" (4:13). In short, says Moses, 'Send someone else; anyone but me.' In his demurral, we detect a touch of mockery: 'You say, "I Will Be What I Will Be"? Okay, say I, "then send whomever you will send."' For the first time, Moses's remarks draw divine anger:

> And the anger of the Lord was kindled against Moses, and He said: "Is there not Aaron, your brother the Levite? I know that he can speak well. And also, behold, he comes forth to meet you; and when he sees you, he will be glad in his heart. And you shall speak unto him, and put the words into his mouth; and I will be with your mouth, and with his mouth, and will teach you what you shall do. And he shall be your spokesman unto the people; and it shall come to pass that he shall be to you a mouth, and you shall be to him in God's stead. And you shall take in your hand this rod, wherewith you shall do the signs." (4:14–17)

Although God gets angry with Moses—we will soon consider why—He does not even acknowledge that Moses might refuse his mission; He does not repeat the charge or try to persuade him to go. Instead, He alters the original plan by offering Moses a partner: his Levite brother Aaron, about whose existence we learn here for the first time. Aaron, says the Lord, will be very happy to see Moses and (He implies) to join the mission, gladly becoming Moses's first follower and his mouth-piece to the people. Aaron will play the prophet to Moses, as Moses does to God. Because Aaron, a man of the people who had never left them for Pharaoh's palace or far-away Midian, can "speak well"—that is, persuasively—he will be Moses's intermediary with the people. Closer to their felt needs than Moses, a man who is too remote from their lived experience and too far above them, Aaron will later become the High Priest and the head of the priestly line, mediating between the people and their God.

To our surprise, Moses now accepts God's plan without comment or resistance. He has run out of objections; he is pleased to have a part-ner for the mission. He is glad that his partner is his brother, a Levite, who will give him entry to the Israelite nation. But Moses does not yet appreciate that divided leadership risks conflict and chaos or that the relationship between brothers does not lend itself to rule and subordi-nation. Instead it always carries a risk of contention, to the point of frat-ricide. Famous founding stories often include fratricide; for example, Cain and Abel, also Romulus and Remus. Why? Because an aspiration to rule and the activity of ruling tacitly deny the radical human equal-ity epitomized in the relationship of brotherhood. Even in the absence of overt rivalry or jealousy, the relation of rule and subordination kills the brotherly relationship. The ruler, as ruler, has no brothers.

The ubiquitous problem of fratricide, implicit in political found-ing, was in fact writ large in the book of Genesis, heralded by the story of Cain, the first man born of woman. In Israel's early story, fratricide has thus far been avoided, though there were close calls in each patriar-chal generation—Ishmael and Isaac, Esau and Jacob, Joseph and his brothers—and much attention was paid to both the threat and its avoid-ance. But now, with Israel on the threshold of peoplehood, the issue of fratricide silently returns, though not in an obvious way.

Moses and Aaron actually get along well together, and their part-nership for the most part runs smoothly. It looks as if the problem of fratricide that had plagued the patriarchal generations has been over-come and that the relations among brothers in Israel may possibly be governed hereafter by an attitude of brotherhood. But despite this harmony and the absence of fratricidal enmity, the danger of a fratricidal *result* lurks below the surface. Not only will Aaron be involved in the sin of the golden calf (Ex. 32), which leads to the death of 3,000 men on orders from Moses to "slay every man his brother." Aaron and Miriam will also directly challenge Moses's authority (Num. 12:1–2), and Korah and his confederates will revolt against Moses, complaining not of his leadership but of nepotism, of the supremacy of the brotherly pair. Most significantly, Aaron will die before entering the Promised Land precisely because of Moses's failure as a speaker, the very reason Aaron was brought into the picture.

In sum, Aaron will die—as will his sons Nadab and Abihu—because Moses refused to take on the job alone and God was forced to insert Aaron into the leadership as Moses's mouth and instrument. Perhaps God was angry because He anticipated these troubles.[26]

Moses Prepares for the Mission

With God's introduction of Aaron and his role, the long conversation at the burning bush comes to an end. Moses promptly returns to Jethro, his father-in-law, and asks leave to return to Egypt to see his brethren "whether they yet be alive" (4:18).[27] He says nothing to Jethro about his encounter with the God of his ancestors or about the real reason he is going to Egypt, likely never to return. "Go in peace," Jethro responds.[28] But Moses does not leave at once. So the Lord addresses him again and again directs him to go; He also reassures Moses with news that the men who had sought his life are now dead. Heartened by this report, Moses "took his wife and his sons,[29] and placed them upon an ass, and he returned to the land of Egypt; and Moses took the rod of God in his hand" (4:20), the rod with which the wonders had been performed at the burning bush. Alluding to the rod, the Lord addresses Moses as he departs, offering final instructions and a stark synopsis of what he must do, say, and expect.

And the Lord said unto Moses: "When you go back into Egypt, see that you do before Pharaoh all the wonders (*mofethim*)[30] that I have put into your hand; but I will

strengthen (*'achazzeq*) his heart (*lev*), and he will not let the
people go. And you shall say unto Pharaoh: 'Thus says the
Lord: "Israel is My son, My firstborn. And I have said unto
you, 'Let My son go, that he may serve Me'; and you have refused to let him go. Behold, I will slay your son, your firstborn."'" (4:21–23)

Moses offers no reply. Yet he may be puzzled—as we readers surely
are—by what God has just told him. I must perform all the God-given
wonders, but they will not persuade Pharaoh to let the people go? Why?
Because God Himself will make them ineffective, by strengthening Pharaoh's heart. So why, if the goal is getting the Israelites out of Egypt,
would God wish to delay its attainment? And why, if He can do it on
His own, does He give me these futile tasks to perform? I am encouraged by God's promise of presence and assistance, but what kind of
leader am I supposed to be? Am I an active agent supported by divine
power, or am I just to be God's mouthpiece—and an ineffective one at
that? And what is this business about firstborn sons, Pharaoh's and the
Lord's? Most puzzling of all, why has the Lord chosen to tell me all this
in advance, even before I start out for Egypt?

These questions, if they occurred to him, do not detain Moses from
beginning his journey. But we will tarry over them a little, for they can
illuminate the meaning of subsequent events in Egypt. Our perplexity
diminishes once we recognize that getting the Israelites out of Egypt is
not the only goal or even the most important one. *How* they are delivered, and by whom, matters almost as much: If Pharaoh freely and easily let them go, would not he, rather than the Lord, be seen as their
deliverer? There are also considerations of justice: shouldn't the Israelites' deliverance from Egypt involve retribution for their lengthy oppression? Finally, there is a decisive issue of knowledge: shouldn't the
Israelites—and the Egyptians, and also we readers—learn from their deliverance about the powers that be? Shouldn't they (and we) learn who
or what is highest and mightiest, and who or what governs the world
and the people in it?

For hundreds of years, the Israelites have lived and suffered in a
society ruled by a single human master—an autocrat who is both feared

and revered and who thinks and acts as one of the gods—atop the world's most advanced civilization. To correct their way of thinking, they need to witness a protracted contest between the Lord and Pharaoh through which he and all of Egypt are compelled to acknowledge the superiority of the Lord. Only in this way can the enslaved Israelites learn that Y-H-V-H, their God, is indeed God Almighty.

But if the contest is to be conclusively revealing, there must be no easy victory over Pharaoh. He must be at the top of his game and must not fold his cards too early out of fear or weakness. Pharaoh must remain Pharaonic at the highest level, both to reveal the full meaning of Egypt and his despotic rule and to provide knowledge of the Lord needed for founding the nation of Israel. Thus, Pharaoh must not become dis-*heart*-ened. If he cannot strengthen or harden his heart by himself, the Lord must help him stay true to himself to the bitter end. Only in this way can the differences between Egypt and Israel, and between the rule of Pharaoh and the rule of the Lord, be brought clearly to light.

Hardening Pharaoh's Heart: Its Meaning and Purpose

To develop these thoughts more fully, we need to address a common misunderstanding about God's "hardening" of Pharaoh's heart.[31] Many readers rebel against the idea that God would deliberately harden Pharaoh's heart so that He might keep punishing him for his obstinacy. Who would follow such a cruel and capricious deity? To correct this erroneous impression, we need to look more carefully at the text and the meaning of terms. There are two separate verbs that will be most often used to describe what is done to Pharaoh's heart: *chazaq,* "to be strong," "to strengthen," "to encourage," used twelve times, including here; and *ka-ved,* "to be heavy," "to make weighty," used six times. On one occasion (see 7:3) a third verb is used: *qashah,* "to be dense," "to toughen," "to harden." In none of their primary meanings do these verbs mean "to make stubborn" or "to make obstinate"; even were we to translate them as "hardening" Pharaoh's heart, we should not understand his hardheartedness to mean "pitiless" or "callous" or "cruel." And when we recall that *lev,* which we translate as "heart," is understood in Hebrew to be the seat of mind, spirit, and will, we understand that "being strong of heart" means "not despairing"; means "remaining as strong as possible in mind, spirit, and will"; means "being bold and resolute." To strengthen someone's heart, in a word, is to en-*courage* him.

Here, in announcing what is to come, God says that *He* will strengthen Pharaoh's heart, a formulation that will be used nine more times in the story of the plagues. But as we shall see, Pharaoh will three times be said to strengthen his own heart, and in six other places, we will be told simply that "Pharaoh's heart remained strong," without learning who, if anyone, was responsible for making it so. Some scholars argue powerfully that these different formulations all mean the same thing.[32] But I believe that the different formulations are significant: sometimes Pharaoh will not be able to encourage himself; sometimes he will need divine assistance to remain strong when he would otherwise yield to despair.[33] But whatever or whoever is responsible for providing encouragement, the result is the same: Pharaoh is enabled to remain fully Pharaoh, resolutely himself to the very end. He is always strong enough to say and do what he, in his heart of hearts, is disposed to say and do.

A little reflection on our own experience can provide personal evidence about the mysterious phenomenon of "re-heartening." When we get discouraged, when we lose heart, we are sometimes able to rally ourselves. By means of personal pep talks and sheer force of will, we pick ourselves up off the floor, we resolve to face our defeats and disappointments, we knowingly get ourselves out of our despair. But sometimes we have sunk too deep to pull ourselves out, and our usual means of self-encouragement fail. And then, not by our own effort but as if by a miracle, encouragement "flies in" as if from some outside source, God only knows from where. With the aid of this mysterious "outside" help, we rise up from the psychic floor and acquire the needed strength or weight to overcome despair. We can then carry on as before, facing what must be faced with a firm heart, focused mind, and resolute will. If such re-heartening happens to us, why not to Pharaoh?

Pharaoh's ability to ride out the first nine plagues makes it possible for justice to be done. He had severely oppressed the Israelites; his predecessor had decreed that their infant sons be drowned; and between them, they had ordered their own people to carry out oppression and to practice infanticide—and many were no doubt willing. Only if Pharaoh stays in the game to the end will the full and deserved punishment be delivered for the enslavement of the Israelites and the killing of their babies (note, please, *not* for his obduracy). For these crimes, retribution was in order, partly to punish the guilty, partly to demonstrate that right can defeat might, partly to prove to the world that there is a moral law and a Judge who enforces it.

This last point leads us to the second, more important matter of knowledge. By pushing the contest with Pharaoh to the limit, the Lord makes clear to everyone in the story, and to every reader *of* the story, that He is supremely powerful, mightier than nature "gods," mightier than human masters and their magicians; that He can defeat the strongest opponent competing at his best; that He is true to His word and keeps His promises; that He can triumph over evil; that He is a moral judge Who dispenses justice according to desert and Whose idea of justice, happily, accords roughly with our own.

Beyond considerations of justice and knowledge, there is also the crucial lesson of God's beneficent care for His people and His aspiration for them. Only if Pharaoh resists to the end can it be shown that it is God and not Pharaoh who redeems the people. This beneficent deliverance will then become the basis of a new covenant (*brith*) between the Children of Israel and God, going beyond the covenant He made with Abraham, Isaac, and Jacob. In the people-forming event at Sinai, the Children of Israel will be addressed and defined as followers of "*Y-H-V-H* your God, who brought you out of the land of Egypt, out of the house of bondage" (20:2).

Firstborn Sons: Pharaoh's and God's

In concluding His speech to Moses, the Lord hints at the last plague that will finally bring about the deliverance of the Israelites: the slaying of Pharaoh's and all Egyptian firstborn sons. In doing so, the Lord speaks of Israel as "My son, My firstborn," which is the first time that the Torah uses the metaphor of God as father and His paternal relation to

Israel. Two different meanings of "firstborn" are at work: Pharaoh's (Egypt's) firstborn are the *first by nature,* the first to open the womb. God's firstborn, by contrast, is a people, not an individual, and this "son" is *first by choice* and *first by covenant.* He was "born" in a bond of agreement between the choosing "father" and the consenting "son" Abraham, a bond to which all the subsequent (natural) sons of the covenantal "son" are to be dedicated, generation after generation.

There is more to this contrast than metaphor: it heralds that nature is to be replaced by covenant and law as the supreme guide to human life. Except among God's chosen people, the natural firstborn is everywhere celebrated as the "womb opener": he is, quite naturally, the pride and salvation of both men and women. The father celebrates his potency and the continuity of his name and power; the mother celebrates her creative power that has, like God, brought forth new life.[34] For both parents, their heir is a new beginning and a future, a token despite mortality of preservation and rejuvenation, a guarantee of a cyclical "more of the same." By contrast, the covenantal "firstborn," the nation of Israel, is called to reject nature as a moral guide and the idea of human generation as "more of the same." Among the Children of Israel, the cycles of nature will be replaced by a forward-looking trajectory of history, lived under covenant and law, and aspiring not to natural potency but to national righteousness and holiness.[35]

We linger a moment longer to comment on the puzzlement about Moses's role. God has singled Moses out for a special mission, for which he must function both as God's messenger and mouthpiece and as leader of the incipient people of Israel. Are those two functions compatible? With God invisible and Moses and his rod performing wonders, is there not a risk that the people will confuse Moses with God? And on his side, might Moses forget that he is backed by divine power and is merely the Lord's agent? It is easy to state, a priori, what is required: Moses must acquire a standing high enough above the people to have authority with them, but not so high that either he or they will confuse him with God. But it is hard to get it right. Perhaps this is why God gives Moses this preview of what will happen with Pharaoh—the insufficiency of Moses's deeds and the necessity of divine action.[36] Pharaoh's strengthened heart will yield only to God's strong hand.

The "Bridegroom of Blood"

Just when we think Moses is really on his way to fulfill his mission in Egypt, he—and we—are arrested by a bizarre episode in which the Lord appears to threaten Moses's life:

> And it came to pass, on the way at the lodging place, that the Lord encountered him and sought to put him to death. Then Zipporah took a flint and cut off the foreskin of her son and touched it to his feet, and she said, "Surely a bridegroom of blood (*chathan damim*) you are to me." So He let him alone; then she said, "A bridegroom of blood, with regard to the circumcising." (4:24–26)

This exceedingly strange episode, presented in but three elliptical and confusing verses, has long challenged interpreters, even about the facts. Linguistically, there is pronominal ambiguity: Who is the referent for "met *him*," "sought to put *him* to death," "touched it to *his* feet," and "let *him* go"—Moses, his son, or, possibly even an angel of the Lord? The episode interrupts the narrative and seems to lack any logical connection to events before or after. Why would the Lord seek to kill Moses just after He sends him off on his mission? What is the meaning of Zipporah's deed and speech, and why does her action lead to Moses's rescue? Commentators over the years have suggested that these verses are fragments of a larger story, now lost, that would have been known to the earliest generations of readers. But even if this is true, what is this tale doing in the text and at precisely this point in the story?

An imaginative recent interpretation, by political scientist Jules Gleicher, focuses on the fact that Moses, sent on a political mission of the first order, chooses to take his family along, even though God had told him that Aaron would be his companion. God is angry, says Gleicher, because Moses is improvising, "turning a serious political mission into a family outing." Zipporah's act, which he interprets not as a *brith millah* (the circumcision marking God's covenant with Abraham) but as a Midianite healing ritual, keeps her son from further travel and forces Moses to continue alone. God relents because Zipporah's act "inadvertently promotes the divine intent. She and the boys return to Midian, whence Jethro brings them to Moses later, after the departure from Egypt."[37]

It is true that Moses's family does not accompany him to Egypt, and the episode at the lodging place is the likely cause of their turning back. By the time Moses meets up with brother Aaron, only a few verses later, he is alone; by contrast, in the comparable brotherly reunion in Genesis, Jacob—returning to Canaan and just renamed Israel—meets brother Esau accompanied by his large family. This difference fits with the momentous political goal of Moses's journey and with the replacement of the merely familial covenant made with the patriarchs (promising offspring, multiplicity, and land) by the people-forming covenant to be made at Sinai (comprising law, worship, and a national mission of righteousness and holiness). But Gleicher ignores the covenantal significance of the circumcision, which he treats only as an impediment to family travel. There are other, deeper matters at stake that his account omits. To discover them, we need a closer look at some linguistic features of the text, where links to antecedent and subsequent passages offer hints of thematic and substantive significance. In biblical narrative, the sequence is sometimes dictated not by chronology but, as here, by ideas suggested by the echoing of certain words and phrases.

We notice at least three linguistic connections, beginning with the verb *sought*. A few verses earlier, God had told Moses that "all the men who *sought* your life are dead" (4:19), reminding both him and the reader of Moses's as-yet-unpunished slaying of the Egyptian man who was beating the Hebrew man. Here, at the night camp, "the Lord encountered him and *sought* to put him to death" (4:25). Is this a reminder of Moses's previous willingness to shed blood? The theme of bloodshed—not only past but also future—is underscored by the repetition of the phrase "bridegroom of blood" and the use of the plural *damim* for blood.

The verb *encountered* provides a second linguistic connection, this time looking forward instead of backward. "The Lord *encountered* him" (4:24) will be echoed in the immediate sequel: "And he [Aaron] went and *encountered* him on the mountain of God and kissed him" (4:27). Could this threatening encounter with the Lord be in anticipation of the reunion of the brothers Moses and Aaron? We are reminded of the sus-penseful reunion of Jacob and Esau, preceded by the nocturnal encounter between Jacob and the attacking man-angel, which ends with Jacob limping away to an encounter in which fratricide is miraculously avoided. Just as the wrestling man-angel was perhaps a tutelary stand-in for Esau, could the Lord here be serving as a tutelary stand-in for Aaron?

Finally and perhaps most importantly, there is a linguistic connec-tion in the word *son* (4:25), which echoes the Lord's just-concluded in-struction about what Moses should say to Pharaoh (4:22–23): "My *son*, My firstborn, is Israel. . . . Send off My *son* that he may worship Me, and you refused. . . . I am about to kill your *son*, your firstborn." As already noted, this was the first biblical use of the paternal image for God's re-lation to Israel.

We cannot be certain that these three linguistic connections were intentional and, if so, whether they explain what this story is doing here. Nevertheless, they point to three corresponding issues, all pertinent to the situation in which Moses now finds himself and all worthy of our attention: bloodshed and its requital, brothers and fratricide, fathers and sons and the difference between a (merely) natural son and a son of the covenant. Using these clues, let us speculate as to why the Lord might here be threatening Moses. I proceed in reverse order.

Fathers, sons, and the covenant. Moses had previously failed to cir-cumcise his son: why, we have no idea. Some commentators blame his Midianite wife, given to him by her father, a Midianite priest who, they speculate, resisted Moses's wish to have it done; as evidence they point to the fact that it is she who finally yields under pressure and does the deed. But I am inclined to place responsibility on Moses. He named his son for his estrangement; before being called at the burning bush, he showed little evidence that he was connected with his people; and even after he is called by the God of his fathers, he does not really identify with them as "my people" or "our people." (We do not even know whether Moses was circumcised and, if so, whether it was done by his parents soon after his birth as a sign of the Abrahamic covenant or later in the palace as an Egyptian rite of passage.) But regardless of who was respon-sible, the failure to circumcise Moses's son meant that his son is dead to the covenant, and therefore that Moses is dead as a father within the covenantal bond to the Children of Israel whom he is supposed to lead out of bondage.

The speech God had just given Moses to make to Pharaoh distinguished between God's *covenantal* "firstborn" son, Israel, and Pharaoh's *natural* firstborn son, literally his eldest male offspring. Against that background, the questions this episode now pointedly puts to Moses are these: Your firstborn son, Moses, is he naturally yours (like Pharaoh's) or covenantally Mine (the Lord's)—and, by the way, whose son are *you?* In what sense are you—and yours—within the covenant? Are you willing to dedicate your son to Me and live within My covenant, identifying with your people? (The conflation of the questions about the identity of both Moses and his son may explain the ambiguity of the pronoun referent—although I am reading the story as if all the "hims" refer to Moses.) Before he heads to Egypt to bring forth God's covenantal firstborn, Moses must enroll his own son in the covenantal community; otherwise he is dead to the nation he is going to deliver ("the Lord sought to put him to death").

Brothers and fratricide. As I have noted, there is a tension between being a founder (or leader or ruler) and being a brother: the first is a position of superiority, the second a relation of equality. To rule over your brother is to "kill him" as your brotherly equal: that is the deeper meaning of the stories of Cain and Abel and of Romulus and Remus, in which the brotherly number "two" is shown to mean rivalry to the point of murder, and in which the founder of the city (Cain, Romulus) is shown to be a fratricide. Absent a teaching of brotherhood, all brothers are naturally rivals. Unlike the dyad of man and woman, whose complementary difference drives toward union, two brothers, lacking a forward-looking natural affinity, become heads of diverging lines that "meet" only in the past, in their common origin ("brother," in Greek, is *autodelphos,* "out of the same womb"). When a married man goes to defend the cause of his family or tribe of origin—as did Agamemnon, who took up the cause of his brother Menelaus, but to do so had to sacrifice his own daughter Iphigenia—he is ipso facto rejecting his wife, who thought she was getting a man who would start a line that began with them and who would defend *her* children, not his brother's or father's. Thus, part of the intrinsic meaning of coming to the aid of your brother is the willingness to sacrifice your own child: you either look forward (to your own line) or back (to your father's line). To reunite with your brother on nonrivalrous terms requires that you see your own son not as the pride-filled carrier of your name but as dedicated to something to which your pride has been submitted—and, in the best case, to the same something to which your brother and his sons are also dedicated.

In the present circumstance, Moses's pride must be humbled if he is to enter into a nonrivalrous relationship with Aaron—indeed, with *all* his "brethren" to whom he has told Jethro he is returning. Although born of the same father and mother, Moses by upbringing is not yet Aaron's covenantal brother: absent this kind of dedication of his son, their relationship remains on the natural plane of rivalry. Only after his son is circumcised can Moses be an *Israelite* brother to Aaron. Only then will their reunion not be fraught with danger, like the reunion of Jacob and Esau (where, after Jacob underwent a similar nocturnal ordeal, fratricide was narrowly avoided).[38]

Bloodshed and its requital. The repetition of the verb *sought* and the juxtaposed mention of two agents who sought Moses's death (first the Egyptian Pharaoh, here the Lord) invite the thought that Moses needs to atone for his earlier murder. There is blood guilt on him that needs to be expiated. But other bloody possibilities may be even more salient. First, the blood of the firstborn of the Egyptians, prophetically announced as a threat, may need to be expiated or at least acknowledged; Moses is going into a campaign in which innocent Egyptian babies are going to die. In consequence, the Israelites, as one of their first obligations, will have to redeem their firstborn sons, in part to acknowledge that their children, like their deliverance, are not their achievement or their property but are a gift from the Lord who passed over their houses on the deadly night of the exodus. The circumcision of Moses's son is a symbolic shedding of the blood of one's own, perhaps as anticipatory expiation and dedicatory expression of gratitude to the Lord. Second, and conversely, this may be less an expiation of guilt, propitiating an angry and dangerous God, than an acknowledgment and acceptance of the bloodshed to come. Moses is going into a campaign in which, thanks partly to his brother Aaron, more than three thousand of his Israelite "brethren" will be slaughtered by the Levites after the episode with the golden calf, *at Moses's own behest* (including the instruction "and each man kill his *brother* . . . his fellow . . . his kin"). The question for an incipient political leader is his willingness to kill and to be killed, and especially to have his own sons die for the sake of the covenant.

After Isaac was spared following Abraham's binding him as a sacrifice on Mount Moriah—showing that fear-awe-reverence for the Lord was higher in Abraham's soul than love of his beloved son—Abraham was told that "your seed shall possess the gates of your enemies," an indication that wholeheartedly embracing the covenant and serving the Lord mean dedicating and placing at risk the lives of your sons, who will forever have to defend the covenantal way of life. The question for Moses is this: Are you also prepared to place your son's life on the line for the Lord and His Way?

How, then, does Zipporah's deed address these concerns? Why she does what she does is a mystery, and we have no idea whether she regards the circumcising act as an Israelite covenantal sign—I suspect she does not. The mere fact that it is *she* who does it leads some interpreters to see the circumcision as a pre-covenantal, not especially Israelite deed, by which Zipporah hopes to propitiate an angry god who is threatening her husband. Others see it as a belated concession, after earlier resistance, to Moses's wish to circumcise his son—now that she sees Moses's life is in danger. Still others suggest that Zipporah, leaving her Midianite home for the first time, must embrace the covenant. Dedicating her son to the God of Moses, she "remarries" him by touching her son's foreskin to Moses's feet, making him a "rededicated" bridegroom through the blood of their shared child: to emphasize the point, she repeats the phrase, "a bridegroom of blood because of the circumcising."

But it may not matter why she does what she does or what she understands herself to be doing: the act has an independent meaning. Symbolically, Zipporah here dedicates the life of *her* son to the life and purpose of her husband; she has, wittingly or not, corrected his omission of the covenantal obligation; she has, again wittingly or not, placed their marriage on a different foundation. It is no longer the gift of the Midianite priest but a child-dedicating act of the mother. As a result of her action—deemed "good enough"—the Lord "let him go."

At the end of his night of danger, a revived Moses is more prepared, on all three fronts, for what comes next: he is ready for a peaceful reunion with Aaron (Aaron "kissed him"; compare the reunion of Esau with Jacob); he is ready (with the support of his foreign wife) to undertake his mission to his "brethren" the Israelites; and he is symbolically ready to shed blood—although he does not fully know it yet—and to place his son at risk in the service of the Lord. Following Gleicher, we must add that Moses will now head off on his political mission unencumbered by his wife and children, who (unreported by the text) return to Jethro in Midian.[39]

Enter Aaron

The reunion of Moses and Aaron follows immediately after the episode at the lodging place:

> And the Lord said to Aaron: "Go into the wilderness to meet Moses." And he went, and encountered him in the mountain of God, and kissed him. And Moses told Aaron all the words of the Lord wherewith He had sent him, and all the signs wherewith He had charged him. (4:27–28)

In response to the Lord's charge, a mere four words in Hebrew,[40] Aaron goes silently and without hesitation to meet Moses. After decades of separation, the brothers are reunited at God's mountain, presumably the site of the burning bush and, later, the giving of the Torah. The reunion is peaceful and smooth: Aaron kisses his long-lost brother. Moses, apparently not a kisser, is all business. He tells Aaron all that the Lord had charged him with and shows (or merely tells?) him all the signs that God had taught him. If Aaron had a response, it was out of our hearing. Without further ado, armed with these signs for persuading the people, Moses and Aaron head for Egypt.

Appendix: Seeing Versus Hearing

One cannot exaggerate the importance of the reordered priority of the senses, from seeing to hearing, for it makes all the difference in the world whether we approach life primarily through our eyes or through our ears.[41] Sight is the sense that preeminently inspires *trust* in the appearances. It is also the most philosophical of the senses, inviting and promising knowledge of the world: it conveys the impression of an enduring present comprising visible and self-evident wholes, all there all at once, that retain their identity through time and appear against a horizon of other visible beings. This horizon ultimately extends to the visible whole, overarched by the lustrous vault of heaven, populated by the beautiful luminaries that rise and fall, day and night, and move in perfect patterns, seemingly forever.

Not only in its content but also in its manner does sight invite a theoretical or contemplative orientation. Sight requires little effort on our part. We open our eyes and the world pours in on us, yet without (as with, say, touch) our feeling its force: wondrously, in sight we experience objects without feeling the cause or the mechanics of our seeing them. Moreover, we experience objects at a distance; we receive the "look" of the lion—its visible form, in Latin, its *species;* in Greek, its *eidos* or *idea*— even while the lion himself remains (mercifully) over there. This detachability of form or looks from its object, essential to the activity of seeing, becomes the basis of the *image-function* of sight: we can retain in memory mental pictures of objects or persons no longer present, and because images are always representations or likenesses, we can represent absent objects by making images or likenesses of them through drawing or carving, painting or sculpting. Following this capacity of our imagination—a faculty that works most gloriously when it deals with pictures—the mind grasps the distinction between image and original, and hence of the difference between the apparent and the true; as a result, it also can come to distinguish essence from existence. Together, recognition of these distinctions provides the foundation of philosophy, the search for the true being of things. Further, because the visible world impinges on us at a distance, and because in seeing the world we do not thereby alter it, sight makes possible an attitude of detachment and invites a relationship of restful contemplation—an activity said by the Greek philosophers to be the highest and most divine activity open to human beings, one in which the mind may be, in principle, filled with insight into the eternal whole.

At the same time, sight offers us an enormous field for exercising our freedom: in surveying the scene around us, we can turn our gaze to whatever we wish to bring into focus, whether as an object of beholding or as an object to pursue (or flee). If we do not like what we see, we can avert our gaze or, in the extreme case, close our eyes and make the noxious sights "disappear." More than any other sense, sight encourages us to feel that we are masters of all we survey. Regarding action as well as thought, sight flatters us into thinking that we can be as gods.[42]

Hearing is a different story. Sound assaults us even with our eyes closed. A hearing being is at the mercy of sound or voice, which intrudes upon him without his asking, even against his will: there are no "earlids" to protect us from unwelcome sounds or speeches. Where sight opens up options for attention, sound *compels* us to attend: we have no choice but to hear (even if we then choose not to listen). Yet what we hear never seems as complete as what we can see: sounds, unlike sights, are not images or likenesses of any originals. They do not give us beings or essences; they merely announce presences. Because the significance of sound—and especially of speech or music—is disclosed only through and over time, never all at once, the hearer must be brought to continuing attention to receive the sequence of sounds necessary for whatever intelligibility can be conveyed: the contingency of sound and speech—not under our command—makes us "all ears." We must strain to get what might come next. We are thus bound, through attention, not in a contemplative relation of static beholding but in a dynamic relation of hearkening; this relationship—if we are listening to speech—is based on intellectual content, not (as in touch) on bodily contact or (as in sight) on surface looks. Moreover, if vision invites the ideas of the enduring present, of being and essence, and of the cosmic whole before which we stand in wondering admiration, hearing invites the ideas of temporality, becoming, and historical directionality and also of the mysterious source whose existence sounds forth to us but to whose essence we have no direct access. The cause of the sound is beyond the sound, which represents only itself; the words that reach us convey no likeness of their author, whose nature remains obscure and whose reason for addressing us we can only guess. Where sights breed familiarity and invite reification and namings that "capture" the special being (that is, the species or look) of the seen, hearing breeds strained attention, perplexity, and bated breath. Fearful or reverent awe, rather than child-like wonder, is our proper response to the voice that calls—especially a voice that calls us by name and speaks with authority. Man's most natural disposition may be toward independence and beholding, but he may be better off if he can learn to hearken and heed.

F • O • U • R

Egyptian Overtures

Hitting Bottom

A ll of a sudden, without a word of transition, the text places us back in Egypt to witness the return of Moses and Aaron. We were last in Egypt decades ago, in the reign of an earlier Pharaoh (Moses's adoptive "grandfather"), when we witnessed revealing back-to-back episodes of young man Moses, newly emerged from the palace: Day One, his smiting of the Egyptian taskmaster; Day Two, his failure with the brawling Israelites. Upon learning from the latter that his deadly deed was known, Moses fled for his life. But as he left, he remembered—and surely still remembers—the stinging rebuke of the Israelite *rasha*: "Who made *you* a man ruler and judge over us?" Now, returning to Egypt, Moses comes with a possible answer to this question.

Moses returns no longer acting on his own. He comes as God's agent and prophet to mediate between God and Israel and between God and Egypt. He arrives with a memory of the theophany at the burning bush and with "I Will Be with You" still echoing in his ears. We immediately get to see how these experiences affect his conduct with Israel and with Egypt. In watching these interactions, however, we should remember that, except for Moses (and to some extent Aaron), none of the characters in the story knows what we know: neither Pharaoh nor the Israelites have read the text or directly heard the voice of God. Moses may be traveling with the Voice nearby, but we have no reason to expect that anyone else should believe or obey him. We are therefore interested to see how a man of God, with a specific mission and a national message, functions in a world that has no knowledge of the Lord.

The events in this chapter turn out to be crucial moments in Moses's education as leader. We will see him dealing with the Israelite elders and ordinary Israelites; we will see him before Pharaoh; we will see him confronted by the Israelite officers; and we will see him complaining to God. By the end, we should be able to say something about what he may have learned from these initial encounters during his first days on the job. And we readers may also be able to say what *we* have learned about leadership and its tribulations and discontents.

The last time Moses acted in Egypt, he dealt on a personal and moral level with two pairs of smiting men. This time he will deal on a national and political level with all of the Israelites but only with the one emblematic Egyptian, the (new) Pharaoh, Egypt's ostensibly divine "Smiter-in-Chief." We again get back-to-back episodes, but this time Day One begins among the Israelites. Both Moses and we are anxious to see whether he fares better this time.

Moses and Aaron Meet the Children of Israel

> And Moses and Aaron went and gathered together *all* the elders of the Children of Israel. And *Aaron* spoke *all* the words that the Lord had spoken unto Moses, and he did the signs in the sight of the *people*. And the *people* believed (*vayya'amen*); and when they *heard* that the Lord had remembered the Children of Israel, and that He had *seen* their affliction, then they bowed down and prostrated themselves. (4:29–31; emphasis added)

What an auspicious beginning! Moses and Aaron follow God's instructions to the letter (see 3:16, 4:15–16), and they convey accurately what God said or implied (see 2:25, 3:7–9, 3:16–17). Aaron is Moses's mouthpiece, as Moses is God's. After speaking with the elders, Moses (or was it Aaron?) did the signs—the rod/snake, the diseased hand, and perhaps also the water/blood—in the sight of the (entire) Israelite people. Just as the Lord had predicted, after seeing the signs "the people believed"— for the first time. Believed what? That the Lord had indeed appeared to Moses and that he and Aaron were indeed agents of God, channeling supernatural powers that would help deliver them from bondage. The scene ends spectacularly, with all the people prostrating themselves in gratitude to the Lord, grateful for His taking an interest in them and for the encouraging news that His agents Moses and Aaron had brought in His name. At long last, they are willing to believe, the Lord was going to do something about their affliction and abasement.

A skeptical reader, knowing how desperate people eagerly grasp at any promise of rescue and how weak people readily embrace assurances of help that require nothing from them, will be suitably suspicious of the depth and durability of the people's newfound faith. Their submission seems too quick, too impulsive, even too slavish. So too their being swayed by the signs and wonders. But reading sympathetically, we can also share their hope—always a virtue against the sin of despair—and their newfound willingness to listen to Moses and turn to the Lord. Any reader who has shared Moses's worries about gaining the trust of dispirited Israelite slaves might be forgiven, at this astonishing moment, for thinking that this project was going to be much easier than expected— at least with the Israelites.

That appears also to be Moses's view. At the burning bush, Moses had worried mainly about persuading the enslaved Children of Israel: "They will not believe me"; "I am not a good speaker." Yet with the help of brother Aaron and the wondrous signs, inspiring their trust has turned out to be remarkably easy, at least for the time being. Emboldened by— not to say drunk on—their success with the Israelites and without waiting for God's explicit instructions, Moses and Aaron confidently head straight for Pharaoh's palace, where a rude shock awaits them.

Before Pharaoh: Failed Diplomacy

Moses has been in the palace before, though many years ago. He probably knows the current Pharaoh, who very likely is his uncle, his Egyptian mother's brother (or half-brother). Moreover, he trusts that "I Will

Be" is backing him to the hilt. Moses believes, quite reasonably, that he therefore holds a very strong hand. But there is something wrong in the way he and Aaron play it:

> And afterward Moses and Aaron came, and they said unto Pharaoh: "Thus says Y-H-V-H the God of Israel: 'Let My people go, that they may hold a feast unto Me in the wilderness.'" (5:1)

Moses and Aaron begin abruptly—indeed, rudely—with none of the niceties or words of deference due his majesty. They address Pharaoh in a commanding tone. Freelancing, they speak in the name of the Lord, but they quote Him incorrectly and depart considerably from His previous instructions to Moses.* They apparently have neglected God's instruction to bring the Israelite elders; they appear alone before Pharaoh, lacking followers or any show of strength.[1] They speak of Y-H-V-H, a deity no Egyptian has heard of, and they call Him "the God of *Israel*," rather than "the God of *the Hebrews*"—the term by which the Israelites are known in Egypt. Instead of *requesting* in their own name ("please") a three-day leave, they demand (misquoting the Lord, and in the imperative mode) the release of the people for an undefined period. To put it mildly, Moses and Aaron have little appreciation of the delicacy of the situation and much to learn about how to work as ambassadors of God.[2]

They get the answer that such nervy speech would receive from any autocratic ruler:

> And Pharaoh said: "Who is Y-H-V-H, that I should hearken unto His voice to let Israel go? I *know not Y-H-V-H*, and moreover I will not let Israel go." (5:2; emphasis added)

---

*For ease of comparison, here is what God had told Moses about this encounter, when He first announced his mission: "And you shall come, you *and the elders* of Israel, unto the king of Egypt, and you shall say unto him: "The Lord, *the God of the Hebrews*, has *alighted upon us*. And now let us go, *we pray thee, three days' journey* into the wilderness, that *we* may sacrifice to the Lord our God" (3:18; emphasis added).

Pharaoh, believing in his own godlike status, is naturally skeptical about this so-called deity, whom he has never heard of and whose alleged speech he therefore need not heed. In two sharp utterances, one about knowledge, one about freedom, the Egyptian demigod—in the first words we hear him speak—emphatically rejects the demand made by Moses and Aaron: 'I do not know' and 'I will not release.' This simple declaration speaks volumes.

First, Pharaoh's statement beautifully articulates his starting positions—"No and No"—and vividly exposes the huge challenge for Moses and God: how to turn them into "Yes and Yes"—"Yes, I know Y-H-V-H," and "Yes, I will let them go." Second, without intending it, Pharaoh has enunciated in negative form a central teaching of the entire Torah: human freedom ultimately depends on knowledge of the Lord. Where human rulers do not know the Lord (and, therefore, each human being's equal and grateful relationship to Him), their subjects will not be free. Despotism is a child of ignorance of God.[3] And third, although presented as independent negations ("I do not know"; "I will not release"), the second one rests on the more important first one. Pharaoh's lack of knowledge of the Lord thus becomes the central focus of all subsequent events. Only if Pharaoh and Egypt come to know and acknowledge the Lord will the deliverance of the Israelites be rightly understood and compelling for everyone, readers included.

Suitably rebuffed, Moses and Aaron try again, this time speaking more modestly and following more closely God's earlier instruction. At the same time, we notice that they make no attempt to answer Pharaoh's question, "Who is Y-H-V-H?"

> And they said: "The God of the Hebrews has lighted upon us.
> Let us go, please, three days' journey into the wilderness, and
> sacrifice unto the Lord (Y-H-V-H) our God; lest He fall upon
> us with pestilence or with the sword." (5:3)

Moses and Aaron no longer speak as the Lord's messengers but as spokesmen for the people ("us"). They do not speak of Israel; they do not demand but plead ("please"); they ask for only three days away[4]— in all these ways, they are now following God's suggested words. But they conclude with their own invented reason why they must perform the sacrifices: if not appeased, their God will destroy them with plague and sword. Moses and Aaron appeal less to Pharaoh's possible mercy than to his self-interest: What use will the Hebrews be to him should their God decide to destroy them for lack of proper obeisance?

Pharaoh, no surprise, is not the least bit moved. He notices that Moses and Aaron have (he thinks, cravenly) moderated their tone and retreated in their demands. Taking this as proof of weakness, he goes on the offensive:

> And the king of Egypt said unto them: "Why (*lammah*) do you, Moses and Aaron, cause the people to break loose from their work? Get you unto your burdens." And Pharaoh said: "Behold, the people of the land are now many, and will you make them rest from their burdens?" (5:4–5)

Far from acceding to their request, Pharaoh ignores it completely. Instead, he rebukes Moses and Aaron for causing the people to shirk their labor. He adds insult to intransigence by insisting that Moses and Aaron are themselves shirking the duties of their Hebrew brethren: "Get *you* unto *your* burdens." And far from accepting the implied threat that God might destroy his slaves, Pharaoh subtly reminds Moses and Aaron that he has many slave laborers who are valuable to him, and he does not take kindly to releasing them from their tasks. The conversation is over; the first attempt at persuasive speech has failed. Moses and Aaron, speaking on their own, are impotent in dealing with Pharaoh and Egypt.

From Bad to Worse: Division and Despair

Pharaoh is not content with his verbal victory. Leaving nothing to chance, he immediately ("the same day") takes measures to prevent the people from ever heeding Moses and Aaron:

> And the same day Pharaoh commanded the taskmasters of the people, and their officers,[5] saying: "You shall no more give the people straw to make brick, as heretofore. Let them go and

gather straw for themselves. And the number of the bricks, which they did make heretofore, you shall lay upon them; you shall not diminish aught thereof; for they are idle; therefore they cry, saying: 'Let us go and sacrifice to our God.' Let heavier work be laid upon the men, that they may labor therein; and let them not regard lying words." (5:6–9)

Using a favorite tactic of despots, Pharaoh orders a heavier workload to forestall further restlessness. He acts ostensibly to cure the people's alleged laziness, but he actually seeks to show them who is boss and most of all to crush their spirit. Workers who, despite their servitude, might have felt a sense of accomplishment in making bricks for construction will now be reduced to scrambling hither and yon to fill their hands with straw. Once scavenging for straw breaks the people's will, they will be immune to the promptings of Moses and Aaron. Worse, they will blame Moses and Aaron for their new burdens, and like Pharaoh, they will regard the teachings about Y-H-V-H as false.

The plan works to perfection. The orders are delivered to the Israelite people, who then "were scattered abroad throughout all the land of Egypt to gather stubble for straw" (5:12). Yet the taskmasters insist that they fulfill their daily quotas "as when there was straw." When, to no one's surprise, they fail, the taskmasters punish their Hebrew overseers:

And the officers of the Children of Israel, whom Pharaoh's taskmasters had set over them, were beaten, saying: "Why (*maddu'a*) have you not fulfilled your appointed task in making brick both yesterday and today as heretofore?" (5:14)

What will the dispirited Israelite officers do now? Who will strengthen their hearts? To whom will they turn? Despite having expressed trust in the Lord in the first meeting with Moses and Aaron, the fickle Israelites cry out not to Him but to Pharaoh:

Then the officers of the Children of Israel came and *cried* (*yits'aqu*) *unto Pharaoh*, saying: "Why (*lammah*) deal you thus with your servants? There is no straw given unto your

servants, and they [the taskmasters] say to us: 'Make brick';
and, behold, your servants are beaten, but *the fault is in your
own people.*" But he [Pharaoh] said: "*You* are idle, *you* are idle;
therefore you say: 'Let us go and sacrifice to the Lord.' Go
therefore now, and work; for no straw shall be given you, yet
you shall deliver the [same] number of bricks." (5:15–18; emphasis added)

Hoping that Pharaoh would take their part against the unreasonable
taskmasters, the Israelite officers learn that the slave drivers were in fact
obeying his orders: "And the officers of the Children of Israel did see that
they were set on mischief, when they said: 'You shall not diminish aught
from your bricks, your daily task'" (5:19). So much for looking to Pharaoh.
Whom can we turn to now? Where, pray tell, is this *Y-H-V-H* about whom
Moses and Aaron spoke so hopefully? They must have been lying to us.

Straightaway, the officers have a chance to tell them off:

And they [the Israelite officers] met Moses and Aaron, who
stood in the way, as they came forth from Pharaoh; and they
said unto them: "The Lord (*Y-H-V-H*) look upon you, and
judge; because *you* have caused our odor to be odious in the
eyes of Pharaoh, and in the eyes of his servants, to put a sword
in their hand to slay us." (5:20–21; emphasis added)

Pharaoh's strategy is working. The desperate people turn on their would-
be leaders. They blame Moses and Aaron, rather than Pharaoh, for their
new troubles. They call upon the Lord not for His assistance but to pronounce judgment on Moses and Aaron. The bond between the leaders
and the led has been broken. The trust in the Lord, and in His champions, is gone.

Moses Hits Bottom

The people are not alone in their despair. It afflicts Moses even more
strongly. He makes no answer to the Israelite officers, but turns his
dispirited soul toward the Lord:

And Moses returned unto the Lord, and said: "Lord, why (*lammah*) have *You* dealt ill with *this* people? Why (*lammah*) is it that *You* have sent *me*? For since I came to Pharaoh to speak in *Your* name, he has dealt ill with this people; neither have *You* delivered *Your* people at all." (5:22–23; emphasis added)

Sharing as we probably do Moses's despair, we are likely not to notice what a radical speech he made. The Israelite officers blamed Moses (and Aaron), not Pharaoh, for their new troubles; Moses, for his part, shifts the blame to the Lord: Why have *You* dealt ill with *this* people (note, not "my people" or "our people")? Forgetting God's earlier warnings about Pharaoh's intransigence, Moses challenges the Lord to explain his own participation in the story: ever since I came to Pharaoh, speaking in Your name, he has abused them worse than ever.[6] This descriptive sentence contains a hidden accusation: it was what *You* said, through me, that caused all the trouble. So, not to mince words, comes the chief complaint: *You*, what have you *done* for *Your people* (again, not "my people" or "our people")? Implied is something even worse: You, Lord, have failed to keep Your word!

In but a few verses, comprising one short chapter of Exodus, the people's mood has gone from buoyant hope and worshipful gratitude to dejection and simmering anger. Moses, too, has gone from brisk confidence to sorrowful despair. How has this come about? More importantly, *why*? And what part might this descent into desolation play in the unfolding story?

A few matters deserve notice. First, the exchanges that Moses and Aaron had with the Children of Israel and later with Pharaoh took place on an entirely human plane. Although Moses and Aaron spoke *about* the Lord, He was completely silent throughout. We wonder why. Second, in dealing with the Children of Israel, Moses and Aaron carefully followed the Lord's instructions; they not only spoke but also performed the trust-inducing wondrous signs. But in dealing with Pharaoh, Moses and Aaron acted almost entirely on their own. They relied only on their own speech; they took liberties in what they said in the Lord's name; they were overconfident; they did not perform any signs or wonders.

Third, they did not remember that the Lord had foretold that it would take a very long contest, filled with many failures, before He would Himself deliver the Israelites from bondage. Fourth, they forgot that this very long contest required that Pharaoh remain unbowed and unbroken until the very last. It would help matters, therefore, if Pharaoh were at his maximum strength and confidence, feeling and exercising his supreme power and authority without fear or doubt. Finally, they did not reckon on perhaps the most important point: that trust in the Lord and hope for the future are most transformative when people are at rock bottom. Only once we recognize *completely* that our own powers do not suffice for our redemption—worse, that they have directly contributed to our misery—are we open to the possibility of having our hearts strengthened and our souls elevated by gifts divine.

Although we are not wrong to draw attention to Moses's shortcomings in this episode, we should not overlook a few crucial things in his favor. After his youthful failures in Egypt, he had fled for his life, but now Moses has no thought of fleeing, even though he has stepped into the lion's den armed only with invisible powers. He does not quit; he does not ask to be excused. Far from being a whiner and complainer, Moses asks God, his new partner, a perfectly reasonable question: Why have you allowed things to get so much worse for the people, and on my account?

For this last reason especially, we should not be surprised to discover that the Lord apparently was not disappointed by the sad turn of events. On the contrary, He was, metaphorically speaking, rubbing His hands with glee. He is pleased to see everyone at rock bottom; He is pleased that Moses expresses concern for the people's welfare; he is pleased that Moses does not even hint at wanting to leave. This teaching moment is precisely what He has been waiting for.

A New Revelation

And the Lord said unto Moses: "*Now* shall you see what I will do to Pharaoh; for by a strong hand shall he let them go, and by a strong hand shall he drive them out of his land." (6:1; emphasis added)

Now. Now that Pharaoh is feeling his oats and congratulating himself on his successful maneuverings. Now that the Israelites have hit bottom. Now that even you, Moses, are despairing of the mission. *Now* you will see what *I* will do. My strong hand—not your diplomatic speech—will compel Pharaoh to let the people go, to drive them altogether and forever out of his land.

To this promise, a stunned Moses has nothing to say. And we readers, who have shared his despair, are likewise now "all ears." What he and we hear next does not disappoint. Offering a new and more complete theophany, God addresses Moses in an unbroken two-part speech: the first part, with the Lord speaking about Himself, is for Moses's benefit; the second part tells Moses what, in the light of the first revelation, he is to say to the Children of Israel. Both parts deserve our most careful attention.[7]

And God spoke unto Moses (*vayedabber 'elohim*)[8], and said (*vayyomer*) unto him: "I am *Y-H-V-H.*

"And I appeared unto Abraham, unto Isaac, and unto Jacob, as God Almighty (*'El Shaddai*), but by My name *Y-H-V-H* I was not known to them.

"And also I have established My covenant with them, to give them the land of Canaan, the land of their sojournings, wherein they sojourned.

"And also I have heard the groaning of the Children of Israel, whom the Egyptians keep in bondage; and I have remembered My covenant.

"Therefore say unto the Children of Israel:
'I am *Y-H-V-H.*

'And I will bring you out (*vehotse'thi*) from under the burdens of the Egyptians, and I will deliver you (*vehitsalti*) from their servitude, and I will redeem you (*vega'alti*) with an outstretched arm, and with great judgments;

'and I will take you (*velaqachti*) to Me for a people (*'am*), and I will be (*vehayiythi*) to you a God; and you shall know that I am the Lord your God, who brought you out from under the burdens of the Egyptians.

'And I will bring you (*veheve'thi*) in unto the land, concerning which I lifted up My hand to give it to Abraham, to Isaac, and to Jacob; and I will give it (*venathatti*) you for a heritage.

'I am *Y-H-V-H*.'" (6:2–8)

The speech to Moses (and the speech within the speech that Moses is to make to the Israelites) begins with a formulaic announcement of God's identity: "I am *Y-H-V-H*." This is not, as Cassuto convincingly argues against the views of many scholars, the introduction of the Tetragrammaton as a new Name for the divine; that Name was already revealed to Moses at the burning bush. Rather, Cassuto suggests, this declaration of sovereign authority imitates the typical way in which rulers in the Ancient Near East introduced major proclamations to their people.[9] He continues,

> The opening formula *I am YHVH* serves also . . . to draw attention to the connotation of the Tetragrammaton, which is explained in the Torah . . . to mean: He who is with His creatures, and He who is constantly the same, that is, He is true to His word and fulfills His promises. I am *YHVH*, and My action shall be in keeping with My name.[10]

Upon hearing this declaration, Moses, we imagine, snaps to attention—as do we. Like him, we hearken not because we have learned a new Name for God but because we expect to have revealed to us something more about the meaning of the mysterious Name we already know. What it is that we—and Moses—now may learn?

We learn first that the patriarchs knew God only in His aspect of *'El Shaddai*, "Almighty God," but not in the aspect now coming to light, as conveyed in the Name *Y-H-V-H*. What might that mean? We can review all the passages in Genesis where "*'El Shaddai*" appears: the two places where God speaks of Himself as *'El Shaddai*[11] and the three (or four) places where one of the patriarchs uses this Name.[12] In all these cases, 'El Shaddai is invoked in connection with a blessing of fruitful-ness and fertility. The first (and paradigmatic) instance occurs in God's covenant-offering speech to Abraham, which begins, "I am 'El Shaddai; walk before Me and be wholehearted," and continues with His promise to "multiply you exceedingly." There follows quickly a promise that "you shall be the father of a multitude of nations," glossed further with "and I will make you exceedingly fruitful, and I will make nations come out of you, and kings shall come out of you" (Gen. 17:1–6).[13]

But that is not all. To the promise of great fruitfulness, God, still speaking as 'El Shaddai, adds a promise of land:

> And I will give unto you and to your seed after you the land of your sojournings, all the land of Canaan, for an everlast-ing possession; and I will be their God (vehayiythi lahem le'lohim). (Gen. 17:8)

The same linked promise of land and fertility is offered at the other time when God speaks explicitly as 'El Shaddai (to Jacob), as well as in two of the places where the patriarchs invoke that Name (Isaac blessing Jacob, Jacob telling Joseph of God's revelation at Luz). All the evidence points to the conclusion that the patriarchs knew God mainly—not to say only—for His promises of numerical greatness and the gift of land—what we might call *natural* goods, even if supernaturally guaranteed. The patriarchs did not know God as a lawgiver or a teacher of a way of life, and they were not in service to Him. Their sole covenantal obliga-tion was to honor His strong demand (though not called a command-ment) that they mark the sign of the covenant He made with Abraham in the flesh of their newborn sons—an early hint that the way of nature was in need of instructional correction or improvement through the giv-ing and acceptance of Law. But about law beyond the duty of circumci-sion, the patriarchs knew nothing or, more precisely, were told nothing in the reader's hearing. Nor did they know, beyond the promises of mul-tiplicity and land, what being the Children of Israel might mean, na-tionally speaking. As we shall see, it is these teachings, unknown to the patriarchs, that God in His aspect of Y-H-V-H is now going to provide, here and throughout the rest of the Torah. Finally, the patriarchs had received God's promise of their own land and of their return to that land, but neither they nor any of their descendants had seen that promise fulfilled.

(I hasten to forestall a possible misinterpretation. The Tetragrammaton [*Y-H-V-H*, usually translated as "The Lord"] in fact appears fairly often in Genesis, even on the lips of the patriarchs, even though before Moses, God had revealed it only once to anyone who was wide awake—in a statement about the land made to Abram just before the covenant between the sacrificial pieces: "I am *Y-H-V-H* that brought you out of Ur of the Chaldees, *to give you this land to inherit it*" (Gen. 15:7; emphasis added). Thus the point God is making here is not that the patriarchs never used the Tetragrammaton, but that they did not properly understand its meaning. The issue is not familiarity with the Name but knowledge of that aspect of the divine that the Name conveys. Note well: this knowledge now becomes available also to the reader.)

The Lord continues his prefatory remarks to Moses, adding to what He has just said about how He was known to the patriarchs:

> And also (*vegam*) I have also established My covenant with them, to give them the land of Canaan, the land of their sojournings, wherein they sojourned. And also (*vegam*) I have heard the groaning of the Children of Israel, whom the Egyptians keep in bondage (*ma'avidim 'otham*); and I have remembered My covenant. (6:4–5)

He informs Moses, for the first time, of His personal covenant with each of the patriarchs—Abraham, Isaac, and Jacob—an enduring bond in which (as an addition to, "*vegam*" or as an implication of whatever is involved in being known as *'El Shaddai*) He promised to give them the land of Canaan, the land of their sojournings. And He tells Moses what the reader has already been told, that He has also heard the groaning of the Children of Israel and has remembered His earlier covenant with the patriarchs. What is the point of these connected revelations? How do they address the dispirited condition of Moses and the people?

The point seems to be something like this, and it begins with strengthening Moses's heart: Do not despair, Moses. I, *Y-H-V-H*, have been waiting for just this moment to make Myself known more fully and to begin to deliver on My old promise to the patriarchs. I have been waiting for you to recognize fully your need of My help. And I have been waiting for the Children of Israel to cry out from despair at their bondage in Egypt. *Because* they are an oppressed multitude, they will be open to Me in My new self-revelation as their redeemer, protector, and guide— as someone Who keeps His promises to His people. I need you now to convey these tidings to them. But first, *you* must believe what I now tell you. You wanted to know my Name? You couldn't answer Pharaoh's question, "Who is *Y-H-V-H*"? You complained that I had not delivered My people? All right. I reveal to you here an added glimpse into Who I Am, which is to say, also, Who I Will Be and What I Will Do. Listen up.

A New Promise: Deliverance, Relationship, and Land

What follows, without interruption, is a speech God tells Moses to give to the Children of Israel on His behalf, a speech that begins and ends with His self-identification, "I am *Y-H-V-H*." The rest of the speech comprises a sevenfold, hope-filled promise to the Children of Israel, a promise that also reveals more of the character of the divine, as understood under the aspect of *Y-H-V-H*. The seven promises are each made with a distinct verb, always in the first-person singular, always linked to the next by "and": "And I will bring out . . . and I will deliver . . . and I will redeem . . . and I will take . . . and I will be . . . and I will bring . . . and I will give." The promises come in three groups: the first three deal with liberation from Egypt, the next two deal with a new and special national relationship between Israel and God, and the last two deal with the Promised Land. Let us look more closely at each of these groups:

> And I will bring you out (*vehotse'thi*) from under the burdens
> of the Egyptians, and I will deliver (*vehitsalti*) you from their
> servitude (or "bondage"; *'avodah*), and I will redeem (*vega'alti*)
> you with an outstretched arm and with great judgments. (6:6)

These three promises offer relief from three aspects of the miseries in Egypt: the elimination of burdens, the release from servitude or service, and the complete liberation of the people, redeemed by mighty deeds that also exact retribution for injustices suffered. The first two promises echo notions that we readers have heard before, but that the people have not.[14] The last promise—full liberation and redemption, accompanied by retribution, the "great judgments"—is altogether new.[15] God, speaking as *Y-H-V-H*, reveals that He is an emancipator, a deliverer, and a judge Who will redeem His people from burdensome servitude and punish their oppressors.

God's liberation of His people becomes the basis of the central set of promises, conveying a radically new teaching: the Children of Israel are to become a people, a special people bonded to the Lord:

> And I will take you (*velaqachti*) to Me *for a people* (*'am*), and *I will be* (*vehayiythi*) to you a God; and *you shall know* (*viyda'tem*) that I *Y-H-V-H* am your God, who brought you out from under the burdens of the Egyptians. (6:7; emphasis added)

Although the entire speech is addressed to all of the people collectively, it is only here that their future as a single and singular people is made known to them, in a promise that anticipates the covenant into which they will enter at Sinai. Speaking as *'El Shaddai*, God had entered into a *personal* covenant with Abraham to supply what he was missing: the ability to have children. That covenantal promise has now been largely fulfilled: the Children of Israel have become a swelling multitude, a great nation—but only in numbers and common descent. The promise that God, speaking as *Y-H-V-H*, offers here is made *with* and *to* that Abrahamic multitude, and it will supply what *they* are missing, what is keeping them from becoming a great nation in a deeper sense: deliverance from bondage.

Yet liberation from Egypt, they are now to be told, is just the beginning of their national future. *Y-H-V-H* promises that He will take them to Him as a special people. And He adds—using a phrase that both echoes and explicates the Divine Name—that "*I will be*" to you a God: *I will be* the One that you revere and worship. "You will be to Me a people; I will be to you a God": the "relational" aspect of *Y-H-V-H* is for the first time proclaimed loud and clear, in language that suggests nothing less than a marriage.

In this central pair of pledges, the Children of Israel are promised a national future—not just a personal or procreational future but also a political future that is a gift from *Y-H-V-H*—the gift that makes Him their God, the One they revere and worship. But their entire relationship with God and their future as a people will rest on their gaining knowledge of *Y-H-V-H* as their liberator from Egypt: "And you shall *know* that I *Y-H-V-H* am your God, who brought you out from under the burdens of the Egyptians" (6:7). The knowledge of that deed, and of the Lord's keeping of His promises, will be the foundation of the Israelite people.

This may be a good place to take up several conceptual complications raised, on the one hand, by the terms *bondage, servitude, service,* and *work*—all translating the Hebrew word *'avodah*—and, on the other hand, by the (properly translated) terms *deliverance* and *redemption,* as distinguished from *liberation* and *freedom,* terms that we regard as meaning the opposite of *servitude* and *bondage.* It may come as a shock to traditional readers who (with the assistance of the Passover *Haggadah*) have long read the story of the Exodus from Egypt as the triumph of freedom over slavery—never mind to our freedom-loving contemporaries for whom this is the paradigmatic story of national liberation—that the term Hebrew terms for *freedom* or *liberty* do not occur in the text, neither here nor anywhere else that the Exodus is discussed.[16] In light of this fact, some interpreters suggest that what is at issue in the Exodus is entirely a matter of *whom* to serve: the Children of Israel are to serve God, not Pharaoh. They support this suggestion by pointing to God's earlier comment to Moses at the burning bush: "when you have brought forth the people out of Egypt, you [plural] shall serve (*ta'avedun*) God upon this mountain" (3:12). In the passage we are now discussing, God is clearly proposing that the Israelites, once removed from service to Pharaoh, will be bound to Him ("I will take you to Me as a people"); even if this is but a marital image, it is not quite identical to autonomy or independence. For this reason, several of my zealously independent students argue that the Israelites, far from being liberated, are merely forced to exchange one form of service (not to say servitude) for another.

This question we shall carry forward and revisit later, when we are in a better position to see just what the Lord will require of His newly delivered people.

Yet there is one way in which the language of "liberation" is appropriate to understanding God's promises to Israel and the exodus from Egypt. Thinking about freedom not in personal terms—doing what you will, being autonomous—but in political terms, we gladly acknowledge that a nation cannot be free if it lives under the despotic rule of a human master. For this nation—or any nation—to find its own destiny, even if that turns out to be living under God's law, it must first be emancipated—liberated, freed—from tyranny, from service to a human ruler. This form of negative freedom is the condition of any national purpose. In the case of the people of Israel, that purpose will be defined not (as it is for Americans) in terms of enjoying rights to life, liberty, and the private pursuit of happiness, but in terms of seeking righteousness and holiness. Moreover, whatever its national purpose, a society under the rule of law is not in thrall to a human master. Liberation from a human overlord is the first requirement of peoplehood, just as it is in the promises *Y-H-V-H* makes here to the Children of Israel.

The unprecedented divine promise of peoplehood, defined through a special relationship with the Lord, is, however, not the end of the matter. The Israelites are meant to live as *Y-H-V-H's* people *in their own land*—a land that He promised to their ancestors and that has been waiting for their proper return. The final promises concern the land:

> And I will bring you (*veheve'thi*) in unto the land, concerning which I lifted up My hand to give it to Abraham, to Isaac, and to Jacob; and I will give it (*venathatti*) you for a heritage. (6:8)

God promises to deliver, at last, on His sworn pledge ("lifted up My hand") to the patriarchs. He will not only bring the Israelites to the land. He promises, for the first time in human hearing, that the land will be the people's national heritage indefinitely. The sevenfold promise completed, God signs off with His authoritative announcement of His identity, "I am *Y-H-V-H.*"

Moses, no doubt listening attentively, has learned several new things from God's revelatory speech, not only about His plans but also about Himself—What He Will Be. Most of these I have already pointed out, but one large item should not be missed. The order of presentation of God's sevenfold promise suggests that the goal of the entire enterprise is to fulfill the promise to the patriarchs by bringing their descendants to the Promised Land. While that may be the ultimate goal, it is not the defining one. According to this prophetic account, Israel must become a people *before* they arrive in the land: Y-H-V-H will first take Israel to Him as a people, and they will define themselves by revering Him as God. Unlike all the other peoples the world has known, Israel at Sinai will acquire its peoplehood before it has a land and before it has an economy. It will become a people with a special mission among the nations, owing to its special relationship with the Lord.

This is not to say that the land is unimportant.[17] On the contrary, the purposes and obligations that Israel will acquire through the covenant enacted at Sinai are meant to guide their lives as they govern themselves in their own land. It will be the acceptance of that covenant—those purposes and those obligations—that entitles the Israelites to live in the land that the Lord promised their ancestors. But even more than the people cannot fully be themselves apart from the land, the Promised Land cannot fulfill its promise until it is inhabited by people married to the Lord.

On Deaf Ears

His heart strengthened, and suitably encouraged, Moses goes off to deliver God's promises to the Children of Israel. Alas, they are not able to listen:

> And Moses spoke so unto the Children of Israel; but they hearkened not unto Moses for impatience of spirit, and for cruel bondage (*'avodah*). (6:9)

Broken in spirit, crushed by the increased Egyptian oppression, the Israelites turn a deaf ear to the good news that Moses brought. A radically new strategy will be required before they can be brought to believe.

From this point until the night of the Exodus, we will not again look in on the Children of Israel. We will not hear a peep from them until the Sea of Reeds. But as we read ahead, we must strive to remember their profound despair as we follow God and Moses into the contest with Pharaoh, a contest that will occupy the principals—and us—for a long time.

To Go Against Pharaoh

Ordering the Team

Moses failed in his attempts to rally the Children of Israel. His speech, in the name of the Lord, did not move their dispirited souls, and for good reason: they remembered what happened to them after his previous announcement of divine interest in their plight. Speech can no longer move them; deeds are required, and no ordinary deeds will suffice. The first venue for such wondrous deeds will be Pharaoh's palace. Moses must take the Lord's campaign into the home of the adversary.

The Problem of Uncircumcised Lips

And the Lord *spoke unto Moses,* saying: "*Come, speak* unto *Pharaoh king of Egypt,* that he send forth the Children of Israel out of his land." And Moses *spoke* before the Lord, saying: "Look, the Children of Israel have not hearkened unto me; how then shall Pharaoh heed me—and [besides] I am of *uncircumcised lips* ('*aral sefathayim*)?" And the Lord *spoke* unto Moses *and unto Aaron,* and gave *them* a *charge* (*tsivvah*) [not only] unto the Children of Israel, and [also] unto Pharaoh King of Egypt, to bring the Children of Israel out of the land of Egypt. (6:10–13; emphasis and square brackets added)

Responding immediately[1] to Moses's failure to persuade the Israelites, the Lord speaks to him (only), opening what will become another conversation about "speech" and "speaking." He orders Moses to "come"[2] and speak to "Pharaoh King of Egypt"—we notice this new formulation—that he should send the Israelites from his land. Moses, speaking back, understandably resists the suggestion. He remembers his first disastrous encounter with Pharaoh, and his most recent failure with the Israelites has left him in despair about his ability to persuade people who will not listen: My speech was ineffective with the Children of Israel, so how could it possibly move mighty Pharaoh, King of Egypt? Moses registers his reticence in a most peculiar way: "How then shall Pharaoh heed me—and I *am of uncircumcised lips* ('aral sefathayim)?"

What is Moses talking about? What is the impediment of "uncircumcised lips"? Is Moses just repeating, in different words, his earlier claim (in Exodus 4) that he is not a good speaker, that he is *heavy* of tongue and *heavy* of mouth? Or is he suggesting a different impairment? What is the meaning of "uncircumcised" as applied, metaphorically, to the lips?

God's response may provide a clue to the nature of the problem. As we shall soon see more clearly but as already hinted here (God spoke next to both Moses and Aaron, giving *them* a charge), the remedy—which accepts Moses's reluctance to speak—is the substitution of Aaron as speaker, just as it had been the remedy for Moses's earlier doubts about his ability to speak before the Israelites (4:14–17).

But we are reluctant to ignore the covenantal association of the reference to circumcision: Moses could be expressing doubts about his relation to the covenant and its people. Robert Alter writes that "the metaphor of lack of circumcision suggests not merely incapacity of speech but a kind of ritual lack of fitness for the sacred task (like Isaiah's 'impure of lips' in his dedication scene, Isaiah 6)," and he adds that the idiom is clearly meant to echo the Bridegroom of Blood story, in which Moses was not permitted to start on the mission until his son was circumcised.[3] On this reading, Moses could well be asking, "What sort of Israelite am I, lax about circumcision, that makes me eligible to undertake this difficult appeal to Pharaoh in the name of Israel and their God?" He returns not to his doubt about his speaking ability but to the doubt about his identity implied in his prior question: "*Who am I*, that *I* should go to Pharaoh and that *I* should bring out the Israelites from Egypt?" (3:11; emphasis added).

A second possibility worth considering builds on Robert Sacks's suggestion that Moses's claim not to be a man of speech "meant that in moments of righteous anger he (like Billy Budd) lost the power of speech." Sacks collects three compelling examples: Moses's speechless killing of the Egyptian taskmaster, his (later) speechless breaking of the tables of the law, and his (much later) speechless striking of the rock when told to speak to it—all three done in anger.[4] To be of uncircumcised lips may therefore mean "to be of untamed spiritedness or unrestrained manliness," hardly someone to send before Pharaoh on a diplomatic mission.

But there may be a simpler explanation, not directly tied to the circumcision of the Abrahamic covenant or to Moses's penchant for anger but related to the meaning of the word *'aral,* translated "uncircumcised," whose primary meaning is "to strip" or "to expose" and is connected with covering up and uncovering. Moses may be claiming that he has a congenital impediment (psychic as well as physical)—namely, "covered-up lips" and hence impaired speech—that cannot be corrected, "uncovered," "circumcised." But God had already addressed this concern, the last time Moses claimed to be a poor speaker: "Who has made man's mouth? . . . Is it not I the Lord? . . . I will be with your mouth" (4:11–12). Natural limitations, says the Lord, are irrelevant; the true power of speech is uncovered only when one aligns oneself, and thus also one's mouth, with the divine purpose.[5]

Perhaps for this reason, the Lord does not respond directly to Moses's comment about "uncircumcised lips" or to its implicit questions, whatever they are. Indeed, He does not answer Moses at all. We have passed the stage where God will try to persuade Moses by direct counterargument. Rather, for the very first time, He gives orders and not only to Moses. He speaks "unto Moses and unto Aaron" and charges them not only "unto the Children of Israel" but also unto "Pharaoh King of Egypt, to bring the Children of Israel out of the land of Egypt." In short, He deals with Moses's demurral by turning the proposal into a charge or command and by giving it to *both* Moses and Aaron.[6] A charge is not to be reasoned with: it can only be obeyed or refused. We are eager to hear how Moses and Aaron will respond.

Genealogical Interlude

The answer is postponed for many verses. Instead, for no apparent reason, the narrative is interrupted by a genealogical interlude. After a prolonged period of anonymity in this book called "Names," we are suddenly flooded with proper names and family trees. We are given a partial genealogy of the sons of Jacob, and especially of the line of Levi, which functions also as a genealogy of Moses and Aaron—the real point of the digression. The genealogy opens with two verses that give us the descendants of Reuben and Simeon, Jacob's eldest sons, after which we are given "the names of the sons of Levi according to their generations: Gershon and Kohath, and Merari" (6:16). Soon we are given the sons of Kohath: Amram, and Izhar, and Hebron, and Uzziel (6:18). Amram is of special interest:

> And Amram took him Jochebed his father's sister to wife; and she bore him Aaron and Moses. And the years of the life of Amram were a hundred and thirty and seven years.[7] (6:20)

Readers learn for the first time the names of Moses's (and Aaron's) parents, previously known to us only as "a man of the house of Levi" and "a daughter of Levi" (2:1): Amram and Jochebed. (Jochebed, Amram's wife, was also his aunt—such a union will later be forbidden under Israelite laws of sexual purity [Lev. 18:12].) Moses and Aaron are truly highborn: on their mother's side, they are grandsons of Levi and great-grandsons of Jacob (Israel); on their father's side, they are Jacob's great-great-grandsons. Understandably ignored in this genealogy is the fact of Moses's adoption by the daughter of Pharaoh or of his Egyptian rearing. We are supposed to be interested here only in the lineage of blood or, perhaps, lineage within the covenant.

But the real surprise of the genealogy comes next, in the account of the generations of Amram's and Jochebed's sons:

> And Aaron took him Elisheva, the daughter of Amminadab,
> the sister of Nachshon, to wife; and she bore him Nadab and
> Abihu, Eleazar and Ithamar. . . . And Eleazar Aaron's son
> took him one of the daughters of Putiel to wife; and she bore
> him Phinehas. These are the heads of the fathers' houses of
> the Levites according to their families. (6:23, 25)

We are told the name and partial genealogy of Aaron's wife and the names of their four sons.[8] We are told of the marriage of their son, Eleazar, and also of the birth of *his* son, Phinehas. We have the line leading down from Aaron to his grandson, Phinehas, and we have the origin of this line leading back to Levi (and Jacob, and by implication, through Isaac to Abraham). But about Moses's marriage (to Zipporah, daughter of Jethro) and about Moses's sons Gershom and Eliezer, both of whom we already know, we are given not a word. In this genealogy, Aaron is a father as well as a son; Moses is only a son. The tacit lesson is clear: Moses, and what he stands for, is genealogically a dead end. Aaron and what he stands for survive through the generations.

Why does this genealogy appear precisely here in the narration—so close to the revelation of God's name, so close to the enlarged importance of Aaron, so close to the soon-to-be announced division of labor between Moses and Aaron? How does this information about Moses's and Aaron's family tree help us understand their mission to Pharaoh and the problem of Moses's uncircumcised lips? Several things suggest themselves.

Most simply, we have arrived at a crucial point in a heroic story. Moses and Aaron have just been given their first charge and their heroic mission: they are now clearly defined as the leaders of the Lord's party. Moses has also just received a new revelation concerning the Lord's name. Moses and Aaron have arrived at their destiny, for the sake of which they are alive (more on this later). We readers are therefore eager and entitled to know their ancestry, with its names of memorable forbears (and pointing out in advance important descendants), as we prepare to see them take their starring roles in their people's heroic story. On this interpretation, what we have here is a Homeric genealogy of heroes on the threshold of their glorious exploits.

But given Moses's self-doubts and some details of the genealogy, there is more to say about its significance at precisely this point in the narrative. First, from this genealogy, we—but only we, not also Moses—learn that Moses's doubts about his Israelite identity have no foundation in fact: despite his having been reared Egyptian and having lived most of his life in Midian with a Midianite wife and father-in-law, despite questions about his circumcision and ritual fitness, the genealogy firmly establishes his lofty Israelite origins. Regardless of circumcision, he is very much a child of the covenant made with Abraham and the patriarchs, as much a son of Israel as his older brother Aaron. Moses and Aaron, both being sent to deliver the Children of Israel, are equally descendants of Jacob, the original "Israel."

But second, Moses's own line—and therefore his special contribution to the Israelite future—dies with him; what he brings either was not successfully transmitted or will no longer be needed. In contrast, the line of Aaron—and therefore his special contribution to the Israelite future—continues through the generations; what he brings will always be needed. Looking far ahead, we see the contrast between the unique lawgiver and the renewable priests, between a man who lives in one glorious deed as founder and men who live by renewing themselves in their progeny and by perpetuating also the rituals of the community. Moses, as Israel's founding father, sires politically rather than bodily, and his biological sons play no known role in perpetuating the covenant.[9] Aaron, later to be Israel's first High Priest, sires both in body and in spirit, and his biological descendants will follow him into the priesthood.[10] And looking right before us, we have the contrast between Moses, who cannot persuade others by speech and is ritually handicapped, and Aaron, who knows how to speak persuasively and is ritually comfortable. Given Aaron's new and crucial role, the genealogy exists to teach us who he is and to elevate his status.

This leads to a third, and perhaps most important, reason for this genealogical interlude. The emphasis given to Aaron and to his son and grandson—all later High Priests—suggests that he (and they) are in fact the answer to Moses's question about his lack of persuasive speech. Moses's kind of speech will never suffice to move either the people or Pharaoh. What will finally move them is not superior speech or better argument but meaningful deeds—including signs, wonders, rituals, gestures, and sacrifices—all of which are the domain of priests rather than philosophers (or prophets). The genealogical emphasis on Aaron, a man closer to the people, alerts us to the political limitations of rational (or prophetic) speech.[11] In the person and work of Aaron (and his like), we are invited to seek the needed instruments of effective rule.

Having located Aaron and Moses genealogically in relation to their forebears and descendants, the text concludes most matter-of-factly but insistently: these two are the very men we have been talking about.

> *These are that Aaron and Moses,* to whom the Lord said: "Bring out the Children of Israel from the land of Egypt according to their hosts." These are *they* that spoke to Pharaoh King of Egypt, to bring out the Children of Israel from Egypt. *These are that Moses and Aaron.* (6:26–27; emphasis added)

Aaron (mentioned first at first) and Moses; Moses (mentioned first at last) and Aaron. Both Levites. Both Amramites. Brothers. Seemingly interchangeable, but beneath the surface, poles apart. Yet also complementary and, for now, both necessary.

Solving Moses's Difficulties: Wonders, Signs, Judgments

The genealogy concluded, the text returns readers to where it had left us, eager for the next steps in the story and perhaps better prepared to see how the Lord will address Moses's worry about speaking to Pharaoh. The scene is re-created through repetition:

> And it came to pass on the day when the Lord spoke unto Moses in the land of Egypt, that the Lord spoke unto Moses, saying: "I am *Y-H-V-H;* speak you unto Pharaoh King of Egypt all that I speak unto you." And Moses said before *Y-H-V-H:* "Look, I am of uncircumcised lips, and how shall Pharaoh hearken unto me?" (6:28–30)

What follows is God's solution to Moses's difficulty. Not only does it address Moses's doubts and questions, but by giving detailed instructions for dealing with Pharaoh, it also clarifies the responsibility of each actor—Moses, Aaron, and God—and reveals more clearly the shape and outcome of the contest to come and why it matters:

> And the Lord said unto Moses: "See, I have set you in God's stead to Pharaoh; and Aaron your brother shall be your prophet. You shall speak all that I command you; and Aaron your brother shall speak unto Pharaoh, that he let the Children of Israel go out of his land. And I will harden Pharaoh's heart, and multiply My *signs* (*'othothay*) and My *wonders* (*mofethay*) in the land of Egypt. But Pharaoh will not *hearken* unto you, and [so] I will lay *My hand* upon Egypt, and bring forth My hosts [or "battalions"], My people the Children of Israel, out of the land of Egypt, by great *judgments* [or "retributions"; *shefatim*]. And the *Egyptians shall know that I am the Lord* [Y-H-V-H], when I stretch forth *My hand* upon Egypt, and bring out the Children of Israel from their midst." (7:1–5; emphasis added)

Moses, to repeat, had a two-part complaint: I can't speak, and Pharaoh won't listen. God's addresses both points directly. To the first problem, God tells Moses that he will not have to speak to Pharaoh. Instead, God will make Moses a (silent) god to Pharaoh, to whom Aaron will speak as his prophet. Previously, Moses had been told to function as a god in relation to brother Aaron (4:16), instructing him what to say to the Israelites. Now Moses is to appear as a god also to Pharaoh. Cassuto comments,

> Although Pharaoh is himself considered a deity, he is nevertheless accustomed to hear the prophets of Egypt address him in the name of their gods; now you [Moses] will appear before him as one of the divinities, who do not speak directly but through their prophets, *and Aaron your brother*

shall be your prophet, and he will speak in your name to Pharaoh. These words possibly contain a bitter ironic reflection on the Egyptian deities who "have a mouth yet do not speak."[12]

But Moses will not be wholly silent. He will speak (only) the words that the Lord commands, and Aaron will speak them to Pharaoh, telling him to release the Israelites from Egypt.

Having been straightened out on the question of his speech, Moses and we are surprised by the Lord's answer to Moses's second problem. God basically says, 'You're absolutely right, Moses: Pharaoh won't listen to you and he won't listen to Aaron.' Instead, He promises to multiply His *wonders* (portents) and *signs*—but, again, to no effect: Pharaoh still will not listen. So it will require that "*I will lay My hand* upon Egypt, and bring forth My hosts, My people, the Children of Israel, out of the land of Egypt, by great *judgments (shefatim)*."[13] In short, words will not be enough: an assemblage of wonders, signs, and (especially) judgments—the punishing force of the Divine Hand—will be needed to deliver the Israelites out of their bondage.

Let us consider more carefully the notions of wonder, sign, and judgment. A wonder or marvel is a remarkable spectacle ("Wow!"), so unusual that we would refuse to believe it had we not seen it for ourselves. Although a wondrous sight appears to speak for itself—some wonders may be *merely* wonderful—most of us, most of the time, will be curious about what is responsible for this implausible appearance and for its appearance to us right here and now. We wonder, that is, about the wonder's significance: Of what is it a sign? Does it point to its origin or source and, if so, to natural necessity or chance or to someone's deliberate intention, either human art and magic or divine intervention? Does it point (also or instead) to its meaning or purpose—for example, to warn, to threaten, to teach, to persuade, to punish? If to teach, what lesson is it meant to convey? If to punish, what has earned the chastisement? Different viewers may answer these questions differently; not everyone will rightly interpret the wonder's significance. Seeing might be believing, but it can lead us into error.

Knowledge Matters Most

The question of truth and error is in fact central to the contest that God, through Moses, will wage against Egypt by means of wonders, signs, and judgments. In concluding His response, the Lord reveals an additional—and most important—purpose, beyond getting the people out of Egypt: as a result of this deliverance, "the Egyptians shall *know* that *I am Y-H-V-H*." The practical act of deliverance—like the antecedent wonders, signs, and judgments—is at least partly for the sake of *knowledge*. Why is this so important?

Pharaoh had said to Moses: "I know not *Y-H-V-H*" (5:2). The Israelites too had turned a deaf ear when Moses told them of God's intent to make Himself known to them as the Tetragrammaton, with the promise that they would come to know Him. In this state of ignorance, no real improvement is possible, especially for the Children of Israel. If the Israelites are to come to know the Lord (6:7) and thus be willing to enter into a lasting relationship with Him, the prior testimony of the world's mightiest civilization will be indispensable.[14]

There is more. Egypt's coming to know the Lord will give the deliverance of the Israelites a universal significance, not only for Israel and Egypt but also for the entire world, then and now. The world needs to know that there exists a higher and mightier power than the mightiest human civilization and its so-called gods and that this power (unlike the nature gods of the Egyptians and other peoples) actually cares for and fights for human beings and keeps His promises to a hitherto downtrodden, oppressed, and despised people. The world needs to learn that ignorance of the Lord is the deepest cause of despotism, oppression, and despair. These theological, moral, and political teachings are perhaps the ultimate purpose of the contest of the plagues.

These reflections also provide the core of an answer to a question that bothers some readers: Why doesn't the Lord simply extract the Israelites from Egypt? Why the protracted and ineffective campaign of the first nine plagues? The whole array of plagues appears to be necessary for pedagogical purposes—for teaching the Egyptians, the Israelites, and the world the difference of *Y-H-V-H* and the difference it makes.[15]

There is, I hasten to add, yet one more audience for God's contest with Pharaoh, someone who has the greatest reason to know that "I am Y-H-V-H": Moses himself. Moses may have a head start on such knowledge compared with the slavish Israelites and the despotic Pharaoh. But if he is to play the role God has in store for him, he too must come to know more fully the One Who said, "I Will Be What I Will Be." He above all must learn to trust God's speech, learn His ways, and see how He works in the affairs of men. He must come to see His care and His justice and know His truthfulness and dependability. The "Egyptian" most in need of coming to "know that I am Y-H-V-H" is Moses himself.

To see how such knowledge is possible, we must take a more nuanced view of the insufficiency of speech. It is true that the speech of Moses and Aaron, as we are told in advance, will not produce the deliverance of the Children of Israel. But without the prophetic warnings given by Aaron and Moses, the signs and wonders and punitive hits might not be understood as the doings of an intelligent God Who is true to His word, Who cares for His people, and Who cares about justice. They could be explained away as manifestations of brute and arbitrary force. Pharaoh and Israel—and the world and Moses—need to learn that the word of the Lord is trustworthy and that His power bespeaks His promised care. For this lesson, speech is indispensable—the speeches of Moses and Aaron, and the speech of the text. We readers are given advance notice of the formula for success in Egypt: prophetic speech backed by divine force. Might this not be the formula also for the Law that Israel will receive at Sinai?

Moses raises no new objections or doubts following the Lord's response. We suspect that he now understands why he must go through the arduous process of unsuccessful speech and deed. It will pay off in the end, in the coin of knowledge of the Lord. Content at least for now, the brothers go off to Pharaoh, happily following God's instructions exactly:

And Moses and Aaron did so; as the Lord commanded them, so did they. And Moses was fourscore years old, and Aaron fourscore and three years old, when they spoke unto Pharaoh. (7:6–7)

With this final formulaic intimation of a momentous event, we are poised for God's contest with Pharaoh, with both redemption and knowledge hanging in the balance.

Time to Deliver: Moses and the Mission

Before going off to witness that contest, we pause to pull together what we have learned, first about Moses and then about the mission. To this point, we have never heard a word about Moses's age: we had wanted to know how old he was when he was weaned and entered the house of Pharaoh; how many years elapsed before he emerged from Pharaoh's house and came upon his brethren; how old he was when he got married and became a father; and how old he was when God called him at the burning bush. But in all cases, the text was silent. Why? Because none of those events was of decisive importance for understanding Moses's life. Often in biblical narrative, we are given the ages of heroes at the start of some crucial event or change in their lives, when they arrive at the destiny for which their entire life has been but preparation. For example, "And Abraham was ninety-nine years old when he was circumcised in the flesh of his foreskin" (Gen. 17:25), entering into the covenant with the Lord. Or, "And Joseph was thirty years old when he stood before Pharaoh king of Egypt" (Gen. 41:46), en route to becoming not a son of Israel but prime minister of Egypt. In the same way, we learn here that Moses has arrived at his heroic moment. Not only that. Moses arrives there at the age of twice forty, a number whose meaning derives from the weeks of gestation and is thus associated with a period in which silently, beneath the surface, a pregnant and world-altering event has been incubating. Moses, twice born (to a Levite mother and an Egyptian princess) and twice incubated (in the social wombs of Egypt and Midian), is at last revealed as the herald of the world's most momentous transformation since the forty-day Flood and the subsequent Noahide code and covenant. Everything in Moses's life before now must be understood in light of this heroic moment. His pregnancy over, Moses is now going to deliver. The world will never be the same.

The mission enters a new phase. Moses and Aaron are sent off officially, and everything feels promising. Unlike their first visit to Pharaoh, the new one will occur with the entire "team"—Moses, Aaron, and God—firmly in place and pulling in the same direction, each with his (His) distinct and carefully defined role, bent on the same purpose and sharing the same ideals: redemption (from bondage for the Israelites) and knowledge (of the Lord for all). Equally important, unlike the last time, Moses and Aaron are now prepared to try and fail and try again without complaint or discouragement, because they believe they will ultimately succeed, quite literally with God's help. The people lack faith in God's promises, but Moses and Aaron fully trust in Him. It is this trust that enables them to accept God's charge; it is this trust that makes them worthy of it. It is this trust that they will want to transfer to the people that it might become the motto and banner of Israel.

The Contest with Egypt

Before following Moses and Aaron into their extended confrontation with Pharaoh, let us remind ourselves of what we are doing and why. We are tracking two major questions of political founding: How do the Children of Israel, for now an oppressed multitude of slaves, become a free, self-governing people? And how does Moses, for now a stranger in a strange land, come to be their leader and founder? Both transformations require contact with and separation from Egypt, the world's premier civilization. More precisely, they require a contest with Egypt or, better, a contest between Moses and Pharaoh—Egypt's monarchic ruler, a god in his own eyes and to his people, the one who embodies fully what it means to be Egyptian. Only through a successful contest with Pharaoh can the Children of Israel become the people they are meant to be. Only through a successful contest with Pharaoh can Moses become Moses, leader and legislator of the Israelite people. And—we hasten to add—only through witnessing a successful contest with Pharaoh will we readers of the text come to know the Lord, and therewith also His plans for the people of Israel and for all humankind.

The confrontation with Egypt is, of course, more than political, and it is not mainly between Moses and Pharaoh, two human giants. It is fundamentally between *Y-H-V-H* and Pharaoh, two competing "gods," as it were, and the sources of competing views of the world and of human life.[1] In all its complicated aspects, the competition we shall witness is from start to finish in service to God's own purposes. One purpose, clearly, is to get the Israelites out of Egypt, but that goal alone, as we have noted, would not require the protracted and escalating infliction of the plagues. These plagues serve a second goal, explicitly stated: to enable people (first, the Egyptians, later everyone) to know the Lord. This educational goal is crucial for all parties in the story: to correct the theological pretensions of Pharaoh and the theological ignorance of Egypt (and the world); to enhance Moses's knowledge of God, Who He Will Be, so that he can help liberate the slavish souls of the Children of Israel; and to instruct and to inspire the readers of the story regarding their own views and sentiments about human freedom and the divine.

The contest with Pharaoh will be conducted by means of a series of wonders, signs, and judgments: marvelous appearances, pointing to significant meanings and effecting retribution upon Egyptian society. They also constitute the curriculum for the Lord's educational purposes. The contest will take place on several planes at once: power and might, justice and retribution, and knowledge of nature and the Lord. For the contest to be unambiguously conclusive, Pharaoh must compete until the very end, in full possession of his powers and wholly devoted to victory. His heart (read, also, his mind and will) must remain strong, weighty, and firm—with help if necessary—so that he can remain maximally himself, steadfastly and confidently devoted to thinking, being, and doing what he always wants to think, be, and do. When he finally yields, Pharaoh—exposed as *merely* King of Egypt—will become the most distinguished witness to the existence and superiority of *Y-H-V-H* God of Israel. When Pharaoh finally knows the Lord, so too will the Children of Israel. So will Moses and Aaron, all of Egypt, and—through word of mouth—all the other nations of the world.[2] So too will we, the readers.

A word of caution. Most readers of the story of Israel in Egypt are inclined to regard Pharaoh simply as a cruel and wicked despot, and not without cause. He enslaves and oppresses the Children of Israel; he crushes their spirit through added cruelties; he drowns their babies; he prevents them from worshipping their God; he eventually brings his entire nation to ruin. All this is true, and the plagues constitute retribution for these misdeeds. But it would be a mistake to regard the contest of the plagues as primarily moral, a battle of good versus evil. It is also and especially an intellectual contest, a contest about knowledge and truth.

For such a contest to carry weight, both interlocutors must be of superior intelligence, operating at the top of their game. Pharaoh may be an oppressor, but he is not therefore also stupid. On the contrary, we should regard him as very smart and confident in his knowledge of nature and human affairs. He is right to be skeptical of revolutionary assertions about how the world works or of radical claims about new gods and human communion with powers invisible. And he knows enough mass psychology to create a gulf between the "outside agitators," Moses and Aaron, and the people they claim to represent, burdening the people to weaken popular support for these would-be leaders. To make sure we do not underestimate Pharaoh, we will regard the contest we are about to witness as a battle between two intellectual heavyweights, both possessing knowledge of nature and craft. But it is a battle in which one of the contestants—Moses—will have, in addition, an inkling of and a devotion to a more-than-natural and more-than-human source of truth and goodness.

Let me add a related caution or, rather, a suggestion for the reader. In the story we are about to read, even more than elsewhere, we should try to imagine ourselves in the shoes of both Moses and Pharaoh, try to forget everything we know that they do not, and try to see the world through their eyes and with their knowledge. Moses and, of course, Pharaoh will not have read the Bible up to this point. Among other things, they do not know that the Lord God who figures prominently in this drama is also the Creator of Heaven and Earth. They surely lack our more developed notions of the Lord, formed from having read ahead in the Bible or from other teachings. And they do not know how the contest will end; even Moses, who has heard the plan from God, can at best only have faith in its fulfillment.

Prologue: Presenting of Credentials

As Moses and Aaron prepare to appear again before Pharaoh, this time heeding divine direction, God gives them a parting instruction:

> And the Lord spoke unto Moses and unto Aaron, saying: "When Pharaoh shall speak unto you, saying: 'Show for your-selves a wonder' (*tenu lakhem mofeth*); then you [Moses] shall say unto Aaron: 'Take your rod, and cast it down be-fore Pharaoh, that it may become a crocodile (or "sea dragon"; *tannin*).'" (7:8–9)

The Lord anticipates that in their first encounter with Pharaoh, he will demand that Moses and Aaron produce credentials in support of their claim to be agents or possessors of supernatural power. Pharaoh will not accept declarative speech; he will demand a spectacular deed: "Show for yourselves a wonder." He will insist on seeing a conspicuous spectacle that, on its own, will bespeak a more-than-natural power. In demand-ing that they show this wonder "*for yourselves,*" Pharaoh is perhaps implying—wittingly or not—that it must have a purely human source: the visible wonder proclaims the supernatural power of those (merely) human beings who created it.

Knowing that Pharaoh—even more than most people—will be im-pressed by a spectacular transformation of the lifeless into the living, the Lord gives Moses and Aaron instructions for setting such a trans-formation in motion. On Moses's command, Aaron is to cast down his rod—not Moses's rod, which had previously been turned into a serpent (*nachash*)—in front of Pharaoh, "that it may become a crocodile"—note, not by Aaron's doing. The Lord does not say, "and *you* shall turn it into a crocodile." Aaron—executing a gesture but not practicing magic—is merely to cast down the rod.

The choice of the *tannin* deserves comment. The term, read as "sea dragon" or "sea monster," has occurred once before in the text, in the first creation story of Genesis: "And God created the great sea monsters (*tanninim*)" (Gen. 1:21). These creatures embody the chaos of the sea; they are at home in the formless world before creation and are devourers of life and order. But here in Egypt, it is probably preferable to read *tannin* as "crocodile," famously a denizen of the Nile. The crocodile is a perfect symbol for dumb nature, even an emblem of natural divinity: it is a silent (tongue-less), impervious, but powerful creature; hidden in the reeds and master of his place; almost invisible to ordinary mortals but discernible by the sharp observer. But in Egypt, the crocodile has additional significance.

From ancient times through to the Roman period, the Egyptian pantheon included Sobek, the god of crocodiles, who to his worshippers was the god who created the Nile. He was a source of power and fertility and a symbol of Pharaonic strength and military power. Represented either as a crocodile-headed man or as a full crocodile, Sobek was both revered as protector against the dangers of the Nile and for his ability to ward off evil, and feared for his animalistic and violent nature—as were his patron animal and Pharaoh. The link between the Pharaohs and the crocodile was explicit in Egyptian writing: the ancient hieroglyph for "sovereign" includes two crocodiles.[3] Turning a staff of authority into a crocodile is thus a most fitting wonder to create in front of Pharaoh:

> And Moses and Aaron went in unto Pharaoh, and they did so, as the Lord had commanded; and Aaron cast down his rod before Pharaoh and before his servants, and it became a *tannin*. Then Pharaoh also called for the *wise men* (*chakhamim*) and the *sorcerers* (*mekhashefim*); and they also, [that is,] the *magicians* (*chartummim*) of Egypt, did in like manner *with their secret arts*. For they cast down every man his rod, and they became *tanninim*; but Aaron's rod swallowed up their rods. But Pharaoh's heart was strengthened (*chazaq*), and he hearkened not unto them; as the Lord had spoken. (7:10–13; emphasis added)

The scene before Pharaoh is presented to us without speech: only deeds are reported. Moses and Aaron do as they were told, presumably in response to Pharaoh's command, "Show for yourselves a wonder." Aaron's rod, cast down before Pharaoh and his courtiers, indeed becomes a *tannin*. Pharaoh calls on his wise men and sorcerers, his magicians who also perform wonders, to do the same. By means of "their secret arts," they succeed in turning their rods into *tanninim.* Pharaoh remains unmoved, as the Lord had predicted.

What has happened here? From Pharaoh's point of view, he sees that Moses and Aaron have some ability to alter nature and turn the lifeless into the living, an ability he mistakenly attributes to their secret arts. But their powers of animation are in no way superior to the secret arts and powers of his magicians. Trusting in appearances ("seeing is believing") and content with his knowledge and the powers under his command, Pharaoh confidently turns a blind eye to the meaning of Moses's and Aaron's wonder: insofar as it also a sign, he misreads it. He is (inexplicably) undaunted by the devouring of the Egyptian *tanninim* by Aaron's *tannin,* a possible omen of God's future victory over Egypt at the Sea of Reeds.[4] He ignores the possibility that something greater than human cunning is working through Moses and Aaron. He has no idea that he is up against a power that is the author of nature, Who brought order out of the watery chaos and Who is master of the monsters of the deep.

We readers should have a different understanding of what we just witnessed. We know that Moses and Aaron practiced no secret arts but were simply obeying God's instructions and awaiting His intervention. Along with them, we saw that God's power, channeled through human hearkening and faithful obedience, is compelling and effective. Human magic, spellbinding, and sorcery are unlikely to prevail against the order of the world and its Creator. If Pharaoh is unimpressed, Moses and Aaron must be awestruck. Having had no foreknowledge that Egyptian magicians could match the Lord's creation of the *tannin* or that the Lord would respond by causing Aaron's *tannin* to consume all the others, they are encouraged to proceed as they await further divine instruction.

This little episode, the presentation of credentials, serves as a prologue to the contest proper, with the sequential imposition of the famous ten plagues that the Lord sends against Egypt. As we have noted, these plagues will serve multiple purposes, including retribution and chastisement, and they will have an internal order that increasingly convinces all involved, readers included, of the relative merits and strengths of Pharaoh King of Egypt and the Lord God of Israel, and of the ways and

beliefs of Egypt and the ways and beliefs of nascent Israel. But once we
have gone through all the plagues and interpreted their significance, we
will discover that the episode we have just considered tells the entire
story in miniature. To appreciate that story, we need a thematic look at
the ways of Egypt.

What Is Egypt?

Egypt is not only the matrix out of which Israel emerges. It is also *the*
human alternative against which Israel will be defined. Because Israel
is to be the anti-Egypt, it is important to discover what Egypt is: its
worldview, its politics, its way of knowing, its gods. The narrative of the
plagues offers us wonderful material for considering these questions,
though their secrets are difficult to extract. In a few cases, we are not
sure what the plague really is; in each case, if we knew more about its
explicit target, we could learn a lot more. To better prepare ourselves for
learning about Egypt from the plagues, we should first collect things
readers already know about biblical Egypt from Genesis and the first
half-dozen chapters of Exodus, supplemented by a few additions from
outside sources.

First, Egypt is the fertile land, the place of agricultural plenty, the
place to which everyone turns when there is a famine. Its fertility is the
gift not of heaven-sent rain[5] but of the Nile, which seasonally floods the
land, nourishing each year's crop. Second, partly but not only for agricultural reasons, Egypt reveres the sun, which it treats as a god, *Ra,* the
immortal and glorious source of light, warmth, and growth, indispensable to Egypt's prosperity. Whereas the Nile is a parochial "deity," all
Egypt's own, worship of the sun expresses Egypt's opening to the universal. The mind of Egypt is hardly insular. Third, along with the regular movements of the Nile, the seasonal revolutions of the sun, absolutely
reliable, create the impression that the powers of nature are, at least in
part, friendly to human life. Nature is cyclical, dependable, eternal—and
to that extent worthy of reverence. Fourth, and on the other hand, Egypt
is obsessed with decay and death—two massive and most unwelcome
natural facts. It is culturally preoccupied not with morality but mortality: with the natural goods of life, health, fertility, ageless bodily beauty,

and, especially, longevity. We recall, from Genesis, Pharaoh's impertinent question to Jacob on their first meeting, "How *old* are you?" meaning perhaps, "Are you older than me?" (Gen. 47:8–10). We recall also the Pyramids, tombs of the Pharaohs awaiting reanimation, and the Egyptian customs of embalming and mummification, practiced also on Jacob's beloved son Joseph, as reported in the very last words of Genesis.[6]

Fifth, we learn from extra-biblical sources that many natural beings are regarded in Egypt as emblems of natural powers or ideas and are revered as deities for their "support" of the blessings of life, fertility, and longevity. The frog, for example, is an emblem of fertility, and the frog-headed goddess Heket is revered for her influence on childbearing; the bull (Apis) is an emblem of masculine strength and potency; the cow is an emblem of birth and maternal nurture, and the cow-headed goddess Hathor is revered as the source of rebirth and rejuvenation; the scarab or dung beetle, thought to emerge spontaneously out of excrement, is an emblem of immortality. The number of such emblematic creatures is very large. They should not be confused with the anthropomorphic gods that Homer and Hesiod introduced into ancient Greece, gods that made the indifferent cosmos appear less alien to human life, interacted directly with particular human beings, and could be appealed to for personal assistance. The gods of Egypt are best seen as signs of natural powers crucial to human life and therefore worthy of awe and reverence.

Sixth, an important corollary of this Egyptian polytheism[7] is the low cosmic standing of humankind and human affairs. Human beings have no special or exalted status in the cosmic whole. Egypt does not look beyond nature to any transcendent source, one that would be the intelligent cause and author of nature, one in relation to whom human beings would have special standing. Their cosmology includes nothing able to correct the silence of nature and nature gods about justice and other ethical goods important to human beings. Egypt is poles apart from the biblical teaching that the human being is the most godlike (*tselem 'elohim*) of the creatures, higher than all the others both on earth and in the heavens.

Seventh, partly but not only because of the problems of decay and death, *change is altogether unwelcome* to the Egyptian mentality. The men shave their bodies and heads to remove evidence of aging (as did

Joseph when, summoned from prison, he first came to Pharaoh). Egyptian hieroglyphs or ideograms are static representations of changing things. Stasis or recurrent cyclical movement (changeless change), not progress in time, is the preferred idea in Egypt.[8]

Eighth, and very important, the emphasis on picture writing and visible forms is connected with the epistemic preeminence of the sense of sight: seeing, for the Egyptians, is the royal road to knowledge, and seeing is believing.[9] Pharaoh sees wonders but does not listen to their voice (or to the speech of Moses), and he forgets them when they disappear. In contrast, the Israelites will get their truths largely through hearing, through memory, and through stories.

Ninth is the preeminence of technology, which goes beyond the very visible pyramids and storage cities. Although the public religion in Egypt officially worships nature and natural beings, the "wise men" of Egypt—working secretly in Pharaoh's palace—use their knowledge of nature to alter it. To make nature friendlier to human life, they develop "secret arts" (magic, sorcery) for controlling nature. As we will see from the deeds of the magicians we soon meet, they are especially interested in finding ways to convert the lifeless into the living and to reanimate the royal dead whom the palace physicians can only preserve from decay by embalming.

Finally, Egypt is politically an autocracy, presided over by one man who is regarded as a god and who rules according to his will and without external restraint.[10] Egypt also boasts an elaborate and centralized administration (first introduced by Joseph, "father to Pharaoh"), which is itself another form of rational mastery over things. But Egypt lacks any real politics (rule addressed to the souls of men). Administration and technology, not law and governance, are supreme.[11] Not incidentally, most native Egyptians are also indentured servants of Pharaoh—another of Joseph's gifts to a previous Pharaoh. Given the absence of a worldview in which human beings have a special relation to the divine, it is not surprising that Egypt practices a politics in which one man can lord it over everyone else and other human beings count for little or nothing at all.[12] As the contest with Pharaoh will make plain, his willful rule finally means accepting the destruction of the very people whose safety and well-being he presumably serves.

So what, then, is Egypt? We strongly suspect that the ten features we have just listed are not unconnected qualities. Rather, they appear to be interrelated aspects of a way of life that rests on a coherent worldview in which the cosmic powers appear to be hospitable but are finally indifferent to human life; in which human beings are orphans lacking special standing or purpose; and in which, finally, only man—only the *strongest* man—can be a god (that is, an awesome benefactor) to men. In subsequent passages, the Torah will sum up the meaning of Egypt in a single recurring epithet: the house of bondage (or "slavery"; *beth 'avadim*)—a house that is not a home; a bondage that enslaves not only the body but also the mind, the heart, and the soul. Where people think that human life is unendowed and only a powerful man can be a god to men, slavery—the absence of freedom in *all* its forms—is the only logical outcome.[13]

Against this background, we can see more clearly why the contest of the plagues is at once political, epistemological, psychological, and metaphysical-theological. It is not merely a strategic device for weakening Egypt and enhancing Moses's standing so that he may better defeat Pharaoh and deliver the Children of Israel from bondage. It is not merely a punitive system meant to dispense justice for Egyptian wrongdoing. And it is not merely a power struggle between Pharaoh King of Egypt and the Lord God of Israel. It is also and especially a program of education. It is a contest of ideas and worldviews—about god, man, and nature; about rulers and ruled; and about knowing itself—that will reveal the truth of these matters to Moses and the Children of Israel, to the surrounding world, and perhaps most especially to readers of the text.

The Nine Plagues (and One)

After Moses and Aaron successfully show their credentials to an obdurate Pharaoh, they are immediately enlisted by the Lord to initiate the series of wonders, signs, and judgments—the so-called plagues[14]—that will bring retribution on Pharaoh and his people and that will ultimately compel him to allow the Israelites to go free. The story of the first nine plagues is told in considerable detail over four chapters of Exodus (from 7:14–11:10), giving the reader a ringside seat from which to see the damage done by the sequence of hits and the effects they have on Pharaoh, on the Egyptians, and on Moses.[15] Then, after an interlude in which the text shifts back to the Children of Israel as Moses readies them for departure, we get in a very few verses the story of the decisive tenth plague and the physical exodus from Egypt (12:29–36).*

Despite their separation in the account, the tradition speaks of the ten plagues as a unity, and I will also occasionally do so. But there is a substantive reason for looking at them as nine plagues and one: the nine (three triads) all involve Moses and Aaron, do not produce the desired result, attack and defeat all but one of the major gods of Egypt, and conclude with Pharaoh isolated, defiant, and more godlike than ever. The tenth, administered by the Lord acting alone, produces the desired exodus and explodes Pharaoh's pretension to divinity, revealing him as the mere King of Egypt and a mere mortal.

Although there are many wonderful things to be discovered by mining the details of the account, I will depart from my usual practice and take a more synoptic view, only dropping down from time to time to consider some revealing particulars.[16]

The ten plagues, in order, are

1. *Blood (dam)*: the turning of the Nile and its tributaries into blood
2. *Frogs (tsefardea')*: an inundation of frogs throughout the land and into houses
3. *Gnats (kinnim)*: the dust of the earth that is turned into flying insects, all over Egypt
4. *Flies (ha-'arov)*: a swarming pestilence entering Egyptian houses and destroying the land[17]
5. *Cattle plague (dever)*: a lethal pestilence killing all domesticated animals
6. *Boils (shechin)*: ashes from furnaces, tossed upward, that become fine dust that descends to cause festering sores on the bodies of animals and human beings

---

*We will treat the tenth plague in the next chapter in the context of the Exodus.

7. *Hail* (*barad*): a destructive storm of hail and lightning, killing plants and all exposed animals and human beings

8. *Locusts* ('*arbeh*): an invasion that destroys all remaining plants and trees and overruns households

9. *Darkness* (*choshekh*): three days of complete darkness in which no one can see anything

10. *Slaying of the first-born* (*meth kol-bechor*): death of all firstborn sons and firstborn animals in every Egyptian household

Each plague affects the entire land of Egypt, save for this partial exception: beginning with the fourth plague, the land of Goshen, where the Israelites dwell, is pointedly exempt from the affliction and destruction.[18] As noted, none of the first nine plagues will yield the deliverance of the Israelites. Only after the tenth plague—different in kind—will Pharaoh let the people go.

The administration of the plagues follows a basic pattern: Pharaoh refuses to let the Israelites go; God tells Moses and Aaron to deliver a warning about an impending hit should he continue to refuse, which warning Pharaoh does not heed; the plague arrives as predicted; Pharaoh, at first obdurate but then moved to relent while the plague is upon him, promises to let the people depart if the plague is removed; the plague is reversed, but Pharaoh, his strength restored, reneges on his promise.

Let us examine the sequence and grouping of the plagues to try to discern their internal logic. The first nine can be divided into three cycles of three plagues each, based upon a tripartite literary form used in the preliminaries. For the first plague in each cycle (numbers 1, 4, and 7: blood, flies, and hail), Moses is told to deliver a warning to Pharaoh the next morning, when he comes down to the Nile River to bathe.[19] For the second plague in each cycle (numbers 2, 5, and 8: frogs, cattle plague, and locusts), he is told to warn Pharaoh in his palace. For the third plague in each cycle (3, 6, and 9: gnats, boils, and darkness), the blow comes with no prior warning. As Nahum Sarna suggests, "the controlling purpose behind this literary architecture is to emphasize the idea that the nine plagues are not natural vicissitudes of nature; although they are natural disasters, they are the deliberate and purposeful acts of divine will—their intent being retributive, coercive, and educative."[20]

But there is more to the order than such formal regularities. Considering the (ten) plagues according to their specific content, we see that they fall into five clear pairs of growing disorder and increasing misery. The first two—the waters turning to blood and the frogs emerging from the river—both have to do with the Nile, destroying or parodying its life-giving power. The second pair—gnats and swarms of flies—are irritating pests, thought to come from the ground, whose profusion makes terrestrial existence miserable. Continuing with a more direct assault on the central goods of life and health, the third (and central) pair—cattle plague and boils—are widespread diseases afflicting first domesticated animals and then also human beings. The fourth pair—hail and locusts—come from the sky to wreak havoc on Egypt's crops, her glory among the nations. And the final pair—three days of total darkness and death of the firstborn—betoken the end of the regime, if not also the end of the world: no sun, no son.

More important still, the plagues have cosmic—metaphysical and theological—significance. The chronological sequence across the first nine plagues moves cosmically upward from the waters, to the earth, to living things, to the heavens, to the sun itself. All domains of the world and all the powers they contain are subject to the Lord's power and influence. Looking at the plagues concentrically, we see an outer frame that attacks the revered Nile below and the revered sun above, moving inward in steps to an assault on the venerated cows and bulls in the center. The invasion of the insect pests, including the gnats "born" of the dust of the earth (*'afar ha'arets*),[21] mocks the Egyptian beliefs in spontaneous generation and reanimation. The attack from the sky on the land's vegetation shows the vulnerability of gods and goddesses of the earth and fertility. In a word, none of the so-called gods of the Egyptians—indeed, nothing in the cosmos—is immune from the Lord's power and control: everything in nature can become—or can be made—hostile to life.[22]

Scholars disagree as to whether the plagues should be seen as supernatural violations of the natural order of things—as "miracles"—or as extraordinary but still natural events that (although summoned by the

Lord) might rarely occur on their own: nature on steroids. Advocates of the latter, eager to square the biblical account with historical or scientific facts, suggest, for example, that the turning of the Nile into (what looks like) "blood" is not a miracle but rather a severe instance of the annual reddening of the river, caused by the deposit of red sediment flowing down with the spring-melted snow from the mountains of Ethiopia, augmented by a bloom of red and purple algae during the early autumn, befouling the water and killing aquatic life. Continuing in this spirit to "explain" the second plague, some suggest that the polluted river then causes the massive amphibious assault of the frogs, which invade the land to escape the toxic waters, while others suggest instead that there occurred an unusually large crop of frogs that are every year left behind on land when the waters recede after the inundation of the Nile. Even the darkness of the ninth plague has been attributed to the scorching sirocco winds that occasionally blow up from the Sahara or from Arabia, bringing thick sands and dust that can blacken the skies for days— although summoned in this instance, of course, by the Lord. From such interpretations we might argue that the plagues in their entirety constitute an attack on the worship of nature: they are intended to teach the nature-reverencing Egyptians—and, of course, us readers—that "big nature,"[23] far from being hospitable and friendly to human life, is deeply at odds with it.

A different interpretation, which sees the plagues as divinely caused distortions or violations of nature, holds that the Lord is not mocking, challenging, and correcting the Egyptians' reverence for nature but rather their effort to alter and control it so as to preserve and prolong human life. At the start of the contest, Pharaoh's magicians and sorcerers try to match the Lord's transformations, and for the first two plagues they succeed. They too can turn the water into blood; they too can produce an inundation of frogs. (Crucially, they cannot reverse these disasters: only the Lord can reverse the chaos He has created.) But beginning with the third plague (gnats), Pharaoh's magicians can no longer match the chaos-inducing transformations:

And the magicians did so with their secret arts to bring forth gnats, but they could not; and there were gnats upon man, and upon beasts. Then the magicians said unto Pharaoh, "This is the finger of God (*'elohim*)!" But Pharaoh's heart was strengthened, and he hearkened not unto them, as the Lord had spoken. (8:14–15)

The magicians recognize early in the contest that they are up against superhuman power (though they say "finger of *'elohim*," not "finger of *Y-H-V-H*"). But Pharaoh acts as if Moses and Aaron merely have superior technical skills, potentially available to his magicians if only they would study harder.

Thereafter, Pharaoh's magicians are out of the contest. Each succeeding plague brings increased natural disorder and greater miseries to man and beast—including the sixth plague, boils, which the magician themselves suffer (9:11). After each of the first nine plagues, the chaos caused by the Lord He also soon removes: just as each plague is a reversal or undoing of creation, so its removal is a re-creation of the world order. The plagues offer a panorama of "anti-creation," mocking the attempts of Egypt's secret arts to alter nature's workings and revealing both their limited capacities and their evil consequences: the sequence of hits reveals the tragic inner meaning of human attempts to control nature through technology. Such hubristic efforts are ultimately counterproductive: they destroy order, produce chaos, and lead in the end to a world inhospitable to earthly life (think especially of the cattle disease, boils, hail, locusts, and darkness). Clever men can destroy life-sustaining order; only God can create and preserve it.

Regardless of which interpretation one favors, the contest of the plagues shows from multiple angles the weakness of Egypt's nature "gods" and of the Egyptian view of divinity, as well as of Egyptian attempts to improve upon nature through craft. From one angle, we see that God is just more powerful than nature and the Egyptian magicians. From another angle, we see the dangers of trusting nature and human cunning: by magnifying some of the supposedly benevolent natural forces (fertility, for example, in the swarming of frogs) or some of the scientists' tricks (such as the creation of life out of dust or soot), the plagues show the destructive potential of both nature and human craft.

The fact that the Egyptian magicians can only duplicate the bloodying of the waters and the over-swarming of the frogs—and cannot reverse these evils—only proves the ethical weakness and physical frailty of their powers.

From yet a third angle, the Egyptians are shown in fact to be creators of chaos, not order. Several of the plagues signify an undoing of the Creation of Genesis 1, most especially the hail (which mixes fire and ice and threatens the earth's separation from the chaos-restraining vault of the heavens), the locusts (life that destroys the life-sustaining vegetation of the earth), and the darkness (which obliterates God's first creature, light). Only God is capable of restoring order out of chaos, as He did in the beginning—employing the principle of separation and distinction, which is connected directly with creating through speech. God's rational powers show themselves also in human affairs, where He detects differences among groups and individuals. He spares the territory of the Children of Israel during the later plagues. But as we will soon see, it is the tenth plague that spectacularly shows His intelligent uniqueness: What natural power can distinguish not only Israelite from Egyptian households but also a firstborn son from all other members of a household?

In addition to these cosmic and theological implications, the contest of the plagues carries a crucial moral and political teaching: it exposes the true meaning of Pharaonic rule. As already noted, Egypt is characterized not only by public worship of nature "gods" or by secret "magical" arts to alter nature. In the Ancient Near East, it is also politically distinctive in being ruled by one man who is regarded as a god. The plagues progressively reveal the inner meaning of this theologico-political arrangement. As they increase in severity and the land and people suffer more, some Egyptian functionaries either seek protection for themselves or urge Pharaoh to relent. After the plague of gnats, as we noted, the magicians declare that they are up against divine power. After the warning of the seventh plague (hail), some Egyptian courtiers "who feared the word of the Lord" sheltered their servants and cattle from the impending hailstorm, whereas the rest, "who did not regard the word of the Lord," left them out in the fields where they were destroyed. After Moses warns Pharaoh of the eighth plague (locusts), Pharaoh's remaining servants plead with him to let the Israelites go:

> "How long shall this man be a snare to us? Let the men go, that they may serve the Lord their God! Do you not yet know that Egypt is ruined?" (10:7)

At first, Pharaoh temporarily yields: he summons back Moses and Aaron and seems to offer them the chance to leave, but the offer is soon exposed as hollow when he declares that only the Israelite men may go. By the last plague, Pharaoh is isolated in his supremacy, playing his godlike part to the bitter end as his land and its people are ruined.

From Pharaoh's Point of View

Although things turn out badly for him, we should not casually allow hindsight to indict Pharaoh for his repeated refusals to yield. One might even wish to defend his actions as justified precisely by the national emergency caused by the arrival of a potent and crafty Israelite challenger: in the face of danger, when lesser people run for cover and cowardly souls counsel surrender, it falls to the powerful and august man-god to do all he can to save his country from ruin. So let us consider the matter more closely from his own point of view.

The demands Moses makes genuinely threaten the regime: not only is Pharaoh at economic risk of losing an enormous number of his slaves; his authority and divine status are at even greater risk should he be seen yielding to demands brought in the name of an unknown and alien deity. As the plagues proceed, Pharaoh loses, one by one, nearly all the sources of command and control. Outside forces are pushing him to surrender; his own supporters lose heart and counsel submission. But he rallies himself and doubles down on defending what is his. He relies increasingly on exerting his will, since his political authority over Egypt is all he has left; the last thing a ruler can prudently or decently do is to appear weak and helpless before his suffering people—especially if they believe he is a god. Pharaoh sometimes thinks of yielding, precisely when the plague is upon the land, and he briefly contemplates letting the people go in order to preserve Egypt. A couple of times he even admits that he has sinned, both against the Lord and against Moses and Aaron.[24] But when each plague again disappears, seemingly as a result of his disingenuous promises, and Egypt once again survives despite—or is it because of?—his stubbornness, Pharaoh is encouraged by this "success" to believe in his own wisdom. After all, we should remind ourselves, even the best king must sometimes resist his courtiers' fears and their calls for surrender. (Think of Lincoln's resisting his supporters' growing calls, after each new bloody battle, to stop the Civil War and to negotiate peace with the Confederacy—a peace that would have legitimated the rebellion and preserved slavery.)

In the end, however, the case for Pharaoh cannot stand. The refutation of his way—and of his divinity—is a major purpose of the protracted contest. Pharaoh's willfulness is finally not animated by a public-spirited concern for his nation and its people. Indeed, he willingly abandons his country to ruin precisely in order to show his own godly supremacy; in defending this ruling principle of the Egyptian regime, Pharaoh unintentionally reveals its catastrophic meaning. As each plague passes, so does his concern for the damage it has left behind. At no point does he attempt to heal the wounded or succor his people. At no point does he pray to any Egyptian deity; at every point he acts as if self-sufficient and all-important. After the ninth plague has left his country in frightful darkness for three days, Pharaoh is at his most defiantly godlike: he says to Moses, "Get away from me; take heed to yourself: never see my face again; for in the day you see my face you will die" (11:28). Nothing that affects the land or its people moves him; only with the tenth plague, which attacks the royal family itself, will he personally feel threatened and impulsively surrender.[25] In sum, the contest of the plagues demonstrates the deep truth of Pharaonic politics: to be Pharaoh means being certain of your own wisdom,[26] means being indifferent to your own people's dignity and well-being, and ultimately to their very existence. Adhering to his own wisdom and seeking ultimate control—and immortality—for himself, the resolute and self-sufficing Pharaoh is in fact an angel of death, unleashed finally against himself and his own.

The Rise of Moses

Until now we have considered the meaning of the plagues for the light they shed on the differences between mighty Egypt and nascent Israel—especially regarding worldview, gods, and political rule—and also on the ways of Y-H-V-H. But the contest of the plagues also educates Moses in the ways of the Lord and gives him on-the-job training for leadership in Israel. Moses's performance during the plagues, especially in his multiple negotiations with Pharaoh, shows his transformation from dispirited self-doubt to confident self-assertion. By the end, he is more than a match for Pharaoh King of Egypt and acts with almost godlike majesty. Although Moses's political standing derives largely from his growing understanding of the Lord's superior power and reliable support, we will be especially interested in how he takes the initiative as God's champion. In considering some of the moments of his transformation through the first nine plagues, we shall pay special attention to those words and deeds of Moses that were *not* specifically prescribed for him by the Lord.

In the case of the first plague—the turning of the Nile into blood—the text reports in great detail the Lord's instructions to Moses and the long speech of warning he is to make to Pharaoh. We learn of his strict adherence to these instructions—"And Moses and Aaron did so as the Lord commanded" (7:20)—and are told in detail what they actually did. But we do not get to hear Moses's speech to Pharaoh or any answers that Pharaoh might have given. When Pharaoh's magicians match the deed, Pharaoh, thinking he sees nothing more than matching secret arts, returns to the palace unmoved. But Moses, who knew better, could not help but be impressed, not only by the total pollution of Egypt's life-giving waters but even more by their rapid return to normal. Most mighty and truthful, Moses tells himself, is the Power that is with me.

We hear from Moses for the first time only after the second plague. Pharaoh, this time unimpressed because his magicians can also bring forth frogs yet annoyed that they cannot get rid of them, forcing him to ask mere mortals for help, summons Moses and Aaron. In a temporary show of humility, he tells them, "Entreat Y-H-V-H that He take away the frogs from me and from my people, and I will let the people go that they may sacrifice to *Y-H-V-H*" (8:4). To this, Pharaoh's first acknowledgment of the Lord,[27] Moses gives a spontaneous, uninstructed reply:

> Moses said to Pharaoh: "Have this triumph over me: for what time shall I entreat for you, and for your servants, and for your people, that the frogs be destroyed from you and your houses, [until] they remain only in the Nile?"
> And Pharaoh [instantly] said, "For tomorrow."
> And he [Moses] said, "According to your word, that you may know that there is none like *Y-H-V-H* our God. And the frogs shall depart from you, and from your houses, and from your servants, and from your people; they shall remain in the Nile only." (8:5–7)

Moses promises, on his own, to pray for deliverance at the time Pharaoh has specified, and he promises a successful outcome. Why? Says Moses, to prove to Pharaoh that "there is none like *Y-H-V-H* our God." It would also prove to Pharaoh, as Moses surely knows, that Moses is a man to be reckoned with: he can summon *Y-H-V-H*'s power at will.

A casual reader may not notice that Moses is taking a huge risk. What if his prayers are not answered? What if the Lord has other plans for the timing of frog removal? Not only Pharaoh but also Moses stands to learn something about the Lord: Will He, can He, does He answer my prayers? Never having prayed before, an anxious Moses "*cried out to the Lord*"—an expression, Cassuto points out, that is used in prayers for deliverance from danger[28]—"concerning the frogs that he had appointed [the time] for Pharaoh" (8:8). To what we imagine is Moses's great relief, his prayer is answered: "And the *Lord* did according to the *word of Moses*" (8:9; emphasis added). We note the pointed reversal of the usual formula: generally it is Moses who does according to the word of the Lord.

Moses's gambit, his first risky foray into independent speech, has succeeded. He has gained some credibility with Pharaoh. More importantly, his trust in the Lord has been vindicated. Moses learns that the Lord hears his prayers and has his back. True, once the frogs are gone,

Pharaoh reneges on his promise and refuses to let the people go. But Moses has gained in stature and confidence.

His confidence rises even more after the fourth plague of flies. Having learned after the third plague that his own magicians were incapable of ending the plagues, Pharaoh calls Moses and Aaron to gain relief, instructing them, "Go, sacrifice to your God *within the land*" (8:21; emphasis added). In response, Moses stands up to Pharaoh, pointing out that they cannot offer their sacrifices within Egypt, for the Egyptians would abominate the sacrifice of animals they hold sacred:

> "We shall sacrifice the abomination of the Egyptians before their eyes; will they not stone us? We must go three days' journey into the wilderness and sacrifice there unto the Lord our God as He will command us [that is, not as *you* command us]." (8:22–23)

Pharaoh is forced to accede to the request but adds a face-saving condition—"only you shall not go far away"—and then asks Moses once again to plead his cause to the Lord. Moses offers a dignified reply, adding a condition of his own and rebuking Pharaoh in the same breath:

> "Behold, I am going out from you and I will pray to the Lord that the swarms of flies may depart from Pharaoh, from his servants, and from his people tomorrow.
>
> *Only let not Pharaoh play false again* by not letting the people go to sacrifice unto the Lord." (8:25; emphasis added)

Once again, the Lord grants Moses's prayer—"And the Lord did according to the word of Moses" (8:27)—and the swarms of flies are removed. But Pharaoh, no surprise, does not keep his word. Moses is getting the picture, both about the reliability of the Lord's word and the unreliability of Pharaoh's. We expect his future conduct to reflect his growing knowledge and the confidence it inspires.

With the coming of the more frightening and devastating final three plagues—hail, locusts, darkness—there is much more conversation between Pharaoh and Moses, as they negotiate conditions for the Israelites' possible departure. Pharaoh, though chastened and increasingly isolated, tries to save face and maintain control; Moses, increasingly confident, proves to be at least Pharaoh's equal in bargaining and his superior in moral wisdom. When the hail is upon Egypt, a stunned Pharaoh confesses to Moses and Aaron, "I have sinned [only] *this time.* The Lord is in the [legal] right, and I and my people are in the wrong" (9:27; emphasis added); and he tells Moses, "Entreat the Lord: for there has been enough of this thunder and hail. I will let you go and you shall stay no longer" (9:28). Moses nobly responds, using his leverage also to give moral instruction:

> "As soon as I have gone out of the city, I will stretch out my hands [that is, I will pray] to the Lord, and then the thunder will cease and there will be no more hail, *so that you may know that the earth is the Lord's.* But as for you and your servants, I *know* that you do not yet fear/revere the Lord God." (9:29–30; emphasis added)

Moses is not taken in by Pharaoh's confession of mere legal wrongdoing in denying the Israelites permission to depart for worship. He will accede to Pharaoh's request to entreat the Lord not out of compassion for Egypt but to teach Pharaoh the supremacy of *Y-H-V-H.* Moses is becoming Pharaoh's teacher—and ours.

In the account of the eighth plague, we do not hear God telling Moses and Aaron what to say. Instead, we hear Moses, in a preface to his dire warning to Pharaoh about an infestation of locusts, improvise a speech for God: "Thus says the Lord, the God of the Hebrews, 'How long will you refuse to humble yourself before Me?'" (10:3). After giving the warning and without waiting for a reply, an emboldened Moses "turned and went out from Pharaoh" (10:6). Terrified, Pharaoh's servants remonstrate with him to let the Israelites go to worship the Lord their God: "Do you not yet know that Egypt is ruined?" (10:7). So Pharaoh recalls Moses and Aaron and seems to acquiesce: "Go, serve the Lord your God." But he adds a question, indicating that his permission is not unconditional: "But who are they who shall go?" (10:8). Moses answers with strength and dignity, brooking no compromise:

> "We will go with our young and our old; we will go with our sons and our daughters and with our flock and herds; for we must hold the Lord's feast." (10:9)

Pharaoh ridicules this answer, gives permission for only the men to go, and orders Moses and Aaron from his presence. Know that I alone may end a conversation, he is implying; I alone determine who may enter or leave my presence.

In consequence, the Lord sends an infestation of locusts, more severe than any before or since. The devastation is immense: "not a green thing remained" (10:15). A shaken Pharaoh summons Moses and Aaron in haste:

> And he said, "I have sinned against the Lord your God, and against you. And now forgive, please, my sin only this once, and entreat the Lord your God, only to remove this death upon me." (10:16–17)

Taking Pharaoh's confession as a possible turning point yet increasingly certain that he is not a man of his word, Moses, without replying, goes out and entreats the Lord for the cessation of the plague. The Lord grants his prayer. The locusts disappear. But once they are gone, Pharaoh, his heart again strengthened, still does not let the Israelites go. We come to the plague of darkness, in which the contest between Moses and Pharaoh reaches its peak. Pharaoh will not deceive Moses again.

After three days of thick darkness, which arrive without a warning and in which the Egyptians "did not see one another nor did any rise from his place" (10:23), Pharaoh summons Moses and gives him an enlarged permission to leave: "Go, serve the Lord; if only let your flocks and your herds stay behind, your little ones also may go with you" (10:24). Moses, in no mood to negotiate, makes clear that nothing less than a total exodus of man and beast will be acceptable:

"You must also let us have sacrifices and burnt offerings, that
we may make to the Lord our God; for thereof [of our cattle]
must we take to serve the Lord our God; we do not know [be-
forehand] with what we must serve the Lord until we arrive
there." (10:25–26)

Careful readers notice that Moses no longer speaks of a three-day journey. We wonder whether, once Israel can leave with its herds, he intends
to take the people out permanently. If so, we admire his cunning in inventing a (not very plausible) reason why all the cattle must leave with
the people.[29]

Pharaoh will have none of it. Seeing that Moses will not negotiate,
and perhaps also seeing through the ruse about the sacrifices, he explodes in anger at Moses, banishing him with a threat to his life: "Get
away from me. Take heed to yourself; never see my face again, for in the
day you see my face you will die" (10:28). Readers familiar with what
comes later will hear in Pharaoh's threat an anticipation of God's response to Moses's request to see His glory: "You cannot see My face, for
man shall not see Me and live" (33:20). But whereas God will be declaring metaphorically the impossibility of man's knowing God's glory or
essence, Pharaoh is literally threatening Moses with death.

Moses takes this sudden threat as a sign of Pharaoh's weakness,
and he answers fearlessly: "You have spoken well: I will not again see
your face" (10:29)—not because of your threat to me, but because of mine
to you. He then gives his warning of the tenth plague, the slaying of the
firstborn.

With Moses still standing his ground before Pharaoh, despite Pharaoh's threat still echoing in the air, the Lord—in a most unusual
address[30]—lets Moses know that the time has arrived for implementing
the tenth and decisive plague:

And the Lord said to Moses, "Yet one plague ("hit"; *nega'*)
more will I bring upon Pharaoh and upon Egypt; afterward
he will let you go hence; when he lets you go, he will drive
you away completely." (11:1)

And contemplating this departure ("drive you away completely"), the Lord repeats earlier instructions (given in 3:22) about how to prepare for it and predicts a favorable response from the Egyptian people:

> "Speak now in the hearing of the people, that they ask, every man of his neighbor and every woman of her neighbor, jewelry of silver and gold. And the Lord will grant the people favor in the eyes of the Egyptians." (11:2).

After this cheery thought about the way the Egyptians will regard the Israelites, there follows a striking comment on Moses's current standing:

> "The man Moses, too, is very great in the land of Egypt in the eyes of Pharaoh's servants and in the eyes of the people" (11:3).

Moses and we are told to bear in mind how his standing has risen with each plague and its removal, and how Pharaoh's counselors now recognize his superiority and even urge Pharaoh to yield to his requests. His heart "hardened," Moses must now feel his ascendancy, thanks to the Lord's help and support.

Emboldened by these reflections, Moses is now ready to announce the ultimate blow. What he now says, in the Lord's name, he says entirely on his own, without instruction. We listen in on the last words that Moses will ever say to Pharaoh:

> "Thus says the Lord: 'About midnight I will go out (*yotse'*) in the midst of Egypt, and all the firstborn in the land of Egypt shall die, from the firstborn of Pharaoh who sits upon his throne even to the firstborn of the maidservant who is behind the millstones, and every firstborn of the cattle. And there shall be a great cry through all the land of Egypt, such as there has never been, nor ever shall be again. But against any of the Children of Israel not a dog shall whet his tongue, neither against man nor beast, *that you may know what distinction the Lord makes between Egypt and Israel.* And all these ser-

vants of yours shall come down to *me* and bow to *me,* saying, "Go out, you and the people that are at your feet." And after that, *I* will go out (*'etse*).'" And he [Moses] went out from Pharaoh's presence in a flare of anger. (11:4–8; emphasis added)

Moses, who once complained of his heavy tongue and uncircumcised lips, speaks with force, majesty, and elegance. He paints vivid pictures, using touching images ("from . . . Pharaoh who sits upon the throne to . . . maidservant who is behind the millstones"; "great cry through all the land"; "not a dog shall whet his tongue"—all of these even more lovely in Hebrew). He prophesies the complete overthrow of Egypt's political and theological order, with its hierarchy leveled and Pharaoh suffering the same fate as a maidservant. He imagines the final scene, in which Pharaoh's servants bow down to *him* and urge his departure with all his people. And for the finale, Moses proclaims, "And I will go out"—using the same verb with which he began the speech, speaking for the Lord: "At midnight *I will go out.*" In this short speech, the first-person pronouns change their reference so that by the end, Moses and the Lord have almost become one. The man Moses is indeed very great in the land of Egypt.

Moses's business with Pharaoh is finished. He has acquitted himself with distinction. He has delivered the warning; it will be up to the Lord to make good on the threat.

Knowledge of the Divine

Before proceeding to the tenth plague and the exodus, we take stock of what we have learned so far (the story is not finished) about the theological question. As we have noted several times, the plagues, whatever else they are, constitute a political and theological argument, undertaken so "that the Egyptians may know that I am *Y-H-V-H.*" They are a direct attack on the Egyptian pantheon and the preeminent Egyptian "god," Pharaoh. They have shown the limits of his accumulated powers and reaffirmed the principles of order in the cosmos, an order that he did not create and cannot command. The plagues reveal not only the weakness but also the lack of goodness of Egypt's "gods" (including Pharaoh), and especially the maleficent character of Pharaonic rule. To revere only nature or the ruler, and to regard them as the source of right, is to recognize only morally neutral force and power. Denying the special dignity of human beings and knowing no authority higher than nature, Egypt's metaphysics and Egypt's politics both crumble.[31]

And what have we (and the "Egyptian Moses") learned so far about the Lord God of Israel? What "effective knowledge" have we obtained about "I-Will-Be-What-I-Will-Be" by watching what He has done in the world? First, the Lord is more powerful—over nature and over everything revered in Egypt, from the Nile to the sun—than Pharaoh and his magicians. Second, His power is guided by a discriminating intelligence and deliberate intention. His deeds are preceded by articulate speech; He can re-create order, by acts of separation, out of the chaos that He can produce; He distinguishes between Israel (protected from the plagues) and Egypt. (Later, we will see how He distinguishes, within each Egyptian household, between the firstborn and the others.) His power is totally unlike the naked power of the "nature gods," which neither speak nor make distinctions. Unlike the biggest natural powers—the causes of hurricanes, earthquakes, floods, and everything else that the Greeks called Poseidon—His power can selectively avoid harming His favorites. Third, He is truthful. He does what He says He will do, and unlike Pharaoh, He keeps His word. You can trust what He says—both when He promises good and when He promises bad. Fourth, He cares for His chosen "son," the Children of Israel, and He protects them from harm—all of them, not just the elite. (We wonder whether He cares for all human beings or only for the Israelites; can Moses yet tell that the Lord is more than just the God of the Hebrews?) Finally, He judges and punishes. He is a moral deity, a God of judgment Who dispenses justice.

The Lord's Justice

About this last claim, many readers disagree. Yes, He punishes the Egyptians for their mistreatment of the Israelites, but He does so severely, even cruelly, and seemingly without measure, striking the innocent as well as the guilty. The Egyptian masses, my students protest, do not all deserve the evils God brings down on them via the plagues. Although mindful of the easy answer that the Lord's justice is different from human justice, we feel obliged to consider whether His punishments are just, in human terms.

In looking at the plagues, including the tenth, as punishments or judgments (*shefatim*), we expect (or at least hope) that they are not just the expression of arbitrary or angry power but that they fit the "crimes" (abasing and brutal slavery, infanticide, and the like) and the "criminals" (Pharaoh, but who else?—all of Egypt?). About the fitness of punishment itself, we have Pharaoh's own testimony. In two places (after hail and after locusts), as we have noted, Pharaoh himself is moved to confess that he has sinned and (in one place) that the Lord (whom he recently said he did not know!) is in the right and that he *and his people* are in the wrong (9:27). The question is not whether they should be punished but how.

There are two ways of providing fitting punishment. The obvious one is measure for measure—*lex talionis,* "an eye for an eye," getting even—applied by an outside agent forcing the retributive measure. But there is another, subtler way: force someone to fully experience, as a result of his own deeds, the meaning of his own evil beliefs and actions. It is possible to read at least some of the plagues as forcing Pharaoh to bear witness against himself by making him responsible for the logical consequences of his opinions and actions. Like Midas and the golden touch, Pharaoh will get exactly what he wished for, only to discover that it was not what he wanted.

Both of these alternatives suggest ways to defend the justice of God's punishments. First, the suffering the Israelites experienced at the hand of Egypt was unspeakably harsh and long-lasting, and it could not have been carried out without the direct participation of many Egyptians (remember the taskmasters and the paradigmatic Egyptian smiting the Hebrew). Some of the plagues look like strict payback for those crimes: measure for measure, you drown my sons in the Nile, I bloody your Nile and kill your sons; you compel my people to slave away at brickmaking in furnaces, I turn the soot from the furnaces into boils that will punish your slave drivers.

Second, many more Egyptians were no doubt complicit in these crimes and thus indirectly guilty. They did not try to stop them, even though at one point they complained about the next evil they were about to suffer; they remained docile and complacent members of their society. They were in a sense guilty of what society did in their name. Like the non-slaveholding North before the American Civil War, all Egyptians, slave masters and others, enjoyed the economic benefits of slavery.[32]

Third, to generalize the point, communities prosper and suffer as one: that is what it means to belong to and to live in a community. Ascribing collective guilt for the deeds of political communities is not ipso facto unjust. In all matters of political justice—as God taught Abraham in the conversation about Sodom and Gomorrah—innocent individuals will invariably suffer unfairly because of the evils of the regime, just as they will benefit "unjustly" from any of its merits to which they have not contributed. The strict justice we expect as individuals, where each person gets *only* what he or she deserves (good and bad), is impossible in cities, nations, and empires. Political justice is rarely personally just.[33]

Fourth, this point is especially true when, as here, the whole nation is an extension of the will of one man, acting like a god (or tyrant). Thus—in the second way of punishment I mentioned earlier—*Pharaoh* is responsible for everything that happens to the Egyptians. Although the plagues are divinely sent, responsibility for their arrival rests mainly with Pharaoh. The Egyptian masses suffer more than they individually deserve only because Pharaoh refuses to bend to the Lord's demands. Because he remains stubbornly and fully Pharaoh, he exposes his people to the deep meaning of his tyranny: their suffering is both *his* doing and his punishment. Put another way, there is no justice under tyranny, only the rule of the strong; the people's suffering under Pharaoh supplies convincing evidence of this truth.

In this way, finally, the story demonstrates the injustice of Pharaoh's existence: his rule is in principle deadly to the very people for whose welfare he is responsible. To put it sharply, to rule like Pharaoh, without any "fear of God" or respect for human dignity, means that the people whom he rules count for nothing. A man who would kill newborn babies is himself a lethal plague upon the body politic. The panoply of plagues, including the death of the Egyptian firstborn, simply serves to make this plain, as Pharaoh is helped to bear witness against himself.

God intervenes in Egypt in part to show the Egyptians, the Israelites, and the world the deadly meaning of Pharaonic—despotic—rule.

Looking ahead to the tenth plague in light of these considerations, we can say that the death of the firstborns is finally on Pharaoh's head, not God's—and not only because he has refused to let the Israelites go when warned in advance. The principle at the heart of being a tyrant (a man who sees himself as self-sufficient and who seeks immortality for himself) is hostility to childbirth, to those who will take one's place. This anti-natal principle had in fact earlier escaped Pharaoh's lips: in the last verse of Exodus 1, Pharaoh, commanding all his people to drown their boys, forgot to specify "Hebrew." In the end, he was the cause of—he said yes to—destroying his nation's future, even in his own house. God's ultimate and fitting punishment of Egypt consists in exposing this deep truth about despotic rule: despotic rule means a blighted future and, ultimately, death to a civilization.[34]

There is yet one more—and deeper—way in which the plagues serve God's interest in establishing justice, beyond punishing the Egyptians for what they or Pharaoh have done. The plagues (and the ensuing encounter at the Sea of Reeds) teach the liberated slaves that they have the attention of an awesome cosmic power Who both cares and fights for them and opposes injustice and immorality. Knowing this, the Israelites will be much more likely, with appropriate fear and trembling, to accept God's offer of His covenant and His Torah—a giant step forward for the place of righteousness, decency, and holiness in human life. But to bring about this urgently needed moral and political change, God's approach required causing harm to some innocents among the guilty. For people who understand the evils of slavery and despotism and who would celebrate the advance of justice in the world, it seems to be a price worth paying—especially if the price is not overlooked.

Exodus

We come at last to the long-awaited deliverance of the Children of Israel from their centuries of bondage in Egypt. But for its own good reasons and not only to build suspense, the text does not go straight to the Exodus or the deed that produced it. Similarly, for our good reasons, neither will we. Before coming to the text itself, we offer a broad overview of what it is up to and why.

Liberation From and Liberation For

The departure from Egypt, soon to be accomplished in consequence of the tenth plague, is preceded among the Children of Israel (1) by the communal enactment of a ritual sacrifice and meal, here and now, following divinely given orders, and (2) by clear instructions regarding a commemorative practice that the Israelites must follow in the future, indeed forever: the annual seven-day festival of Passover. The departure is followed immediately by clear instructions regarding a second commemorative practice, also to be observed forever: the redemption of firstborn sons (and the sacrifice of firstborn animals). The one-time enactment is a modest (yet impressive) pre-deliverance people-forming event, as each family declares its willingness to be delivered by killing a lamb, marking the doorposts of their house with its blood, and eating the prescribed meal of fire-roasted lamb, flatbread, and bitter herbs. The annual commemorative practice is an elaborate people-renewing event, as each family relives the deliverance by telling its story and by re-creating its festive meal.

The commandments about annual celebrations of Passover and redeeming the firstborn are the first national Israelite laws (beyond the Abrahamic obligation of circumcision, which technically is the first [Israelite] paternal law, and beyond the Noahide rules about eating meat and retributing manslaughter, which, according to the Bible, are the first human laws).* The first national Israelite law commemorates the first step in the Children of Israel's becoming the *people* Israel: their deliverance by the Lord, as the Lord's people, from the land of Egypt and the house of bondage. On the eve of their redemption, and for seven days annually thereafter, the Israelites are to remember, reenact, and celebrate—family by family, yet all at the same time and in the same way—their emergence as a united community, independent and out of Egypt, and grateful to the Lord Who delivered them. This is the big picture of what the text is up to, and it is clear enough.

As to the *why* of this procedure, I have two suggestions. The contest with Pharaoh has been, to this point, inconclusive. We readers more than suspect, as Pharaoh does not, that the decisive conclusion will soon be upon him. But while we await the denouement, the text teaches us—as the Lord teaches the Children of Israel—that there is more at stake than getting the slaves out of Egypt. In framing the actual Exodus by the first pair of Israelite laws, the text clearly hints that the essence of

---

*Formulaically, we might say that the Noahide law (Gen. 9:1–7) established and instructed the true *human* difference (man, alone among the animals, is a creature that lives by law and not by might alone); that the law regarding circumcision (Gen. 17:9–14) established and instructed the true *paternal* difference (fathers are called to their work of perpetuation and transmission, away from that of gaining glory for manly prowess); and that the law regarding the Passover and the firstborn established and instructed the true *communal* (or *political*) difference (Israel is distinguished from other communities by its gratitude for worldly blessings and by its moderate mores and ways—against the opposed extremes of the rational mastering will and the chaos of Dionysian wildness).

the story lies not in mere (political) liberation from bondage but in liberation *for* a (more than political) way of life in relation to the Liberator. Even while still in Egypt, the people are being primed for Sinai and the giving of the Law. Why? Because getting Israel physically out of Egypt is the easy part; getting Egypt—both their slavish mentality and the allure of Egyptian luxury and mores—out of the Israelites' psyches will be much harder. The first national laws give them—and us—a foretaste of what should replace Egypt in their souls.

Second, until now the Israelite slaves have been almost entirely passive. They have cried out from their miseries. They have turned a deaf ear to Moses's promise of divine redemption. They have watched from a distance the destructive effects of the plagues on their Egyptian masters. But they have done nothing to show that they deserve emancipation or even that they want to be redeemed. If they are to make the transition from slavery toward the possibility of self-rule, the people themselves must do something to earn their redemption. The tasks they are given, both before and after their deliverance, are intended in part to make them worthy of being liberated: they are to act, and they are to act in obedience to God's instructions; they are to act trusting in God and in His servant Moses.

Obedience as the ticket to liberation seems paradoxical. But as we have already noted, the text never speaks of the deliverance of Israel from Egypt in terms of freedom. The biblical Hebrew words for liberty, *deror* and *chofesh,* do not even occur in the text. To be sure, the Israelites will be politically free from the house of bondage, in that they will not be slaves to Pharaoh in Egypt. And they will have the power and opportunity to exercise choice. But what they eventually will be invited to choose will not be "freedom" but something else: righteousness and holiness, gained through willing obedience. We will return to this matter at the end of this chapter.

Fundamental Regulations: Sacrificing, Eating, and Procreating

So much, then, for the goals of the prescribed rituals. But the details of each ritual reveal that there is much more going on, and we should not be surprised. We expect that the contents of the ritual enactments should be multiply meaningful. They should convey teachings and inspire attitudes that embody the way of life for the sake of which Israel is to be constituted as the Lord's people. They should simultaneously speak to the now-rejected alternative way of life that is Egypt. And they should address those permanently dangerous aspects of the human soul that, when unchecked, gain disastrous expression in Egypt and elsewhere but that, when regulated, carry the marks of God's Way for humankind.

This last suggestion requires some explanation. As I tried to show in my book on Genesis, the seemingly historical stories at the beginning of that book, before the call of Abraham, are also vehicles for conveying the timeless psychic and social roots of human life—of all human life, not just Jewish life—in all their moral ambiguity. The stories cast a powerful light, for example, on the problematic character of human reason, speech, freedom, sexual desire, the love of the beautiful, shame, guilt, anger, man's response to mortality, the morally dubious character of farming and the other arts, the impulse to sacrifice, and the human city. They cast an equally powerful light on the naturally vexed relations between man and woman, brother and brother, father and son, neighbor and neighbor, stranger and stranger, man and God. Adam and Eve are not just the first but also the paradigmatic man and woman. Cain and Abel are paradigmatic brothers. Babel is the quintessential city. By means of such stories, Genesis shows us not so much "what happened" as "what *always* happens" in the absence of moral and political instruction. Although God's Way, begun with Abraham, begins to address some of man's dangerous tendencies, several of them—such as sibling rivalry to the point of fratricide—plague each generation of the patriarchs. As a result, the wisdom-seeking reader coming upon Exodus hopes and expects that God's plan for humankind—a plan to be carried forward by His chosen people, Israel—will directly address the evils that naturally lurk in the hearts of men.

Not accidentally, therefore, the substance of the rituals and laws framing the Exodus from Egypt address the fundamental and highly problematic human matters of sacrificing, eating, and procreating: how we relate to the divine, how we relate to the rest of living nature, how we relate to our mortality and our future.[1] We first consider each of these matters as they appear in human life uninstructed, absent law and command.

The impulse to sacrifice has several conflicting roots in the human soul, deeper than some innocent desire to give thanks for bounties received: on the one hand, a Dionysian desire to unite with the primordial chaos, effacing all distinctions and order; on the other hand, an Apollonian desire to celebrate the source and principle of order by appealing to and acknowledging the rule and source of separation. And again, on the one hand, a wish to assert human power against and over the whole by trying to compel (through gifts or bribes) the highest power to do one's bidding; on the other hand, a wish to nullify one's own power before the whole by demonstrating our willingness to do the bidding of the highest power.

Many peoples in the ancient world practiced animal sacrifice, even child sacrifice; but the Torah is, at least to begin with, not at all keen on sacrificing, which it regards as a purely human invention. The voluntary offerings of Cain and Noah God neither requests nor even seems to want: He rejects the sacrifice of Cain, and He makes a most negative comment on the animal sacrifice of Noah.[2] Indeed, until this moment, God had asked only Abraham to bring a sacrifice. But from the experience Abraham learned that He does not really want child sacrifice, but only the father's dedicated awe and fear of God (*yere' 'elohim*).*

Eating, though necessary to all animal and human life, is also problematic: to sustain life and form, eating destroys the life and form of others, as voracity ultimately threatens the articulated world. The problem is especially severe in the omnivorous human animal. Man's un-delimited appetite—a manifestation of human freedom and reason— aspires in principle to do nothing less than devour the entire world and, through digestion, to transform it into himself.[3] Omnivorousness, an emblem of man's potentially tyrannical posture toward the world, extends also to cannibalism, just as the impulse to sacrifice extends also to human—and child—sacrifice.

---

*We shall have a fuller discussion of the subject of sacrifices in Chapter Eighteen, which treats of the sacrificial cult that is instituted in the Tabernacle.

Finally, regarding procreation, life's answer to mortality, the first-born son—as herald and emblem of the next generation—represents both the strength of the father, extending his potency beyond the grave, and a threat to the father's power, a living proof of his mortality and limited influence. Although fathers take pride in their paternity and in their sons, they and their sons often struggle for supremacy. We remember Ham's act of metaphorical patricide against the drunken Noah, and Noah's retaliatory curse of Ham's son Canaan. We remember Reuben's sleeping with his father Jacob's concubine. And we recall Pharaoh's ambivalent relation to and desire to control childbirth, and not only among the Israelites.[4]

In all these fundamental aspects of human life, absent the coming of moral instruction and law, there is the possibility—indeed the likelihood—of two extremely dangerous and wrong-headed tendencies. On the one hand, there is the danger of imposing human reason and will on the world through manipulating sacrifices to the gods, through omnivorous transformation of nature (as food), and through the denial of procreation. On the other hand, there is the danger of surrendering human reason and will to wildness and chaos, not only in the effacing of distinctions and the destroying of life that are involved in animal sacrifice but also in yielding to our souls' wildness and voracity in matters of eating, sex, and sacrifice—not excluding child sacrifice.

The way of life that the Lord has in store for humankind addresses both of these dangerous tendencies. Human life will be rationally ordered, but the order will not be man-made; it will not be willful, but reasonable. At the same time, the wilder and chaotic passions will be given room for expression, but within measure and under ritualized constraint. Our animals, the produce of the earth, and the fruit of the human womb will be recognized as ours, but ours no thanks to us. Rather, they embody and reflect an ordered world that we did not make and from which we profit largely as receivers of blessings. Our household "possessions"—our family members and servants, our livestock, and all of our "mere" things—we have as gifts; recognizing that fact enables us to treat them as sanctifiable aspects of a life devoted to a higher purpose, not merely as means of satisfying our infinitely expandable desires for pleasure and domination.

In Egypt, the supreme rule of one man imposing his will on the world wound up destroying the fertile land, its produce, and animal life. As we will soon see, it will destroy even the regime's own children, including the tyrant's own. Refusing to see the image of God in other human beings—which would mean recognizing their equal humanity—and refusing to acknowledge the more-than-human and more-than-natural source of all blessing, Pharaoh's actions, first against Israel and eventually against his own people, result finally in his saying yes to massive child sacrifice. This is arguably the true meaning of Egypt's denial of time and change and its pursuit of immortality.

Against the way of Egypt, the way of Israel begins with modest and restrained animal sacrifice[5]—animal, not human, and no more than can be eaten—with removal of the blood, the essence of life, which is used to consecrate the entire household in dedication to the Lord's command. The animal is roasted—simply, totally, without adornments, in purifying fire—and eaten in its entirety: its entrails are not offered in a shared meal to satisfy the appetites of a wild god believed to crave flesh and blood, but sacrificed as part of the whole animal, in response to and recognition of a benevolent God Who bespeaks order. The flatbread or *matsah*—modest, simple, uncorrupted human food, not proudly transformed by human artfulness, and made afresh each time as "mortal" bread—limits appetites, moderates our belief in our permanence and our conceit of self-sufficiency, and reminds us that the bread of the earth, no less than the deliverance soon to be procured, is a blessing, not a solely human achievement. It speaks of both the previous condition of enslavement and the gracious gift of liberation: the bread of affliction is also the bread of deliverance, because it is now commanded by, and will always be held as a remembrance of, the Deliverer.

Under the new way, the firstborn, including the human firstborn, will be seen as belonging to the Lord, not to nature or to our prideful selves—neither those who celebrate male potency nor those who celebrate maternal creativity in the opening of the womb. Yet the way of Israel eschews sacrificing the human firstborn, insisting squarely on reclaiming him from the Lord by an act of redemption. It is, for every household, a repetition of the teaching of the binding of Isaac: God does not want child sacrifice, nor does He want His people to wish to sacrifice their children. He wants them to be dedicated to rearing their children in His ways, beginning with the re-creation of the commemorative Exodus meal in every household at every Passover, reinforced by telling the children the story "because of what the Eternal did for *me* when He took *me* out of the land of Egypt" (13:8; emphasis added).

The practice of redeeming the firstborn commemorates not only the spared firstborns of Israel but (perhaps) also the common humanity of the lost sons of Egypt. Those Egyptian children may have been justly taken as punishment for Pharaoh's misdeeds and intransigence, and their deaths may have been necessary for Israel's deliverance and for Egypt's acknowledgment that "I am the Lord." But there is pathos, not to say iniquity, in this massive destruction of life, some of it surely guiltless: it is a fact that requires of Israel not so much atonement as acknowledgment. The Israelite lives that were saved and delivered, like the Egyptian lives that were destroyed, hang by a thread. Only by God's grace—and not solely for our own merit—do we ourselves still dangle.

Keeping this synoptic overview in mind, we now take up the text and examine some of its more revelatory details.

Preparing to Leave: Calendar, Passover Sacrifice, and Meal

Their work with Pharaoh completed, Moses and Aaron must now return to the Israelites to prepare them for deliverance. Their orders to do so come immediately. The Lord's detailed instructions, spanning twenty verses of uninterrupted speech, are sometimes surprising, especially at the beginning.

> And the Lord spoke unto Moses and Aaron in the land of Egypt, saying: "This month shall be *unto you* the beginning of months; it shall be the first month of the year *to you*." (12:1–2; emphasis added)

Before the Lord gives any orders about what the people must do, He declares in advance a change in the calendar: *for you*, this month (the spring month of *Aviv*) will be the first month of the year. This month launches your long-awaited destiny. A new age is dawning for you; therefore this month shall be forever reckoned as the beginning of your calendric year.

Time in Israel will have a new basis and a new meaning. With sun worship defeated and left behind in Egypt, Israel gets a calendar that will no longer be based on the sun's revolutions[6] in the heavens or the correlated seasons of the year and the earthly sproutings and harvests they provide. This seemingly unprecedented innovation completes the Bible's quiet but insistent polemic against living in thrall to the sun, the moon, and the stars—and the earth. The very beginning of Genesis had demoted the sun to a mere marker for the preexisting day and for seasons. It instituted instead a regular weekly seventh day, the Sabbath, independent of lunar change and commemorating instead the Creation and its Creator.[7] Similarly here, the annual calendar is redefined in commemoration of a historical rather than a natural event. The target is no longer Babylonian "moon time," but Egyptian "sun-and-earth" time.

At precisely the time of year when there is the greatest reason to celebrate nature, we get a celebration of God's beneficent action on behalf of His people. *Aviv* is made the first month, not because it is the time of renewed sprouting and growth but because it is the month of Israelite deliverance and the beginning of progressive history.[8] To put it another way, the month that is for everyone else the time of nature's springing forth will be for Israel the time of the people's "sprouting," a sprouting resulting not from natural necessity but from divine choice and deliberate intervention. This change in the calendar is not merely symbolic. The first step to freedom and dignity is to live not on nature's time but on your own.[9]

The Lord next gives Moses and Aaron orders to transmit to the people, beginning with instructions for a communal sacrifice:

"Speak you unto *all the congregation of Israel* (*kol-'adath yisra'el*), saying: In the tenth day of this month they shall take to them every man a lamb, according to their fathers' houses (*leveth-'avoth*), a lamb for a household (*bayith*); and if the household (*habbayith*) be too little for a lamb, then shall he and his neighbor next unto his house (*betho*) take one according to the number of the souls; according to every man's eating you shall make your count for the lamb. Your lamb shall

be without blemish, a male of the first year; you shall take it
from the sheep, or from the goats; and you shall keep it unto
the *fourteenth* day of the same month; and the *whole assembly of the congregation of Israel (kol qehal 'adath-yisra'el)* shall
kill it at dusk." (12:3–6; emphasis added)

In His striking beginning, the Lord refers to the Israelites for the very
first time as the *congregation* of Israel (not as the *Children* of Israel)—
using the term *'edah,* "a group fixed by appointment or agreement" (from
ya'ad, "to fix upon").[10] He continues by describing the common obligation that will earn them the new designation: by special appointment,
all the Israelites, albeit household by household, will at the same time
(the tenth day of the month and year just beginning) select an unblemished lamb (or kid) to sacrifice unto the Lord. And at dusk of the
fourteenth day the whole assembly (or convocation) of the congregation
of Israel shall kill the lambs together. Not since they first cried out in
complaint against their servitude (2:23) have the Israelites done anything
together. What they are asked to do here will be their first positive people-
forming event: an event comprising sacrifice, eating, and blood, each
element of which, as we noted, holds great significance. The planning
for this event itself builds a community of freedom, for only free people
are able to plan for themselves in advance.

The killing of the lamb is to take place on the night of the fourteenth
day of the new month: the night of the full moon.[11] The night of the full
moon, called *Shabbatu* by the Babylonians, was regarded by them and
other Ancient Near Eastern cultures as a night of dread, bad luck, and
evil. But in Israel, *this* night of *this* full moon will be the blessed night
on which the people will "vote with blood" for their deliverance. The
Lord, having given the instructions, will briefly "withdraw" from view
so that the congregation of Israel can assemble themselves as an identi-
fiable and united community, as the whole assembly of the congregation of Israel. What they have to do they will not do in secret; thanks to
the moonlight, the Egyptians may see them, even as they sacrifice animals that the Egyptians hold sacred.[12]

This is no small matter. During the New Kingdom (1550–1070 BCE),
the ram was the sacred animal of two Egyptian gods: Amun the king

of the gods, who was syncretized with the sun god as Amun-Ra, and Khnum, the god who made human beings on the potter's wheel. Sacrificing lambs would thus be offensive to the Egyptians and a danger to the Israelites.[13] But danger aside, as a symbolic gesture, the killing of the lamb represents the people's entrance into the battle against Egypt and its gods. Up until now, the Israelites have been passive and absent; the contest has been God against Pharaoh, acting through His agents Moses and Aaron. Now it is time for the people to join in, doing their (symbolic) part against all Egyptians. Their deed here foreshadows their willingness—which will not come easily to them—to take responsibility for themselves and not rely exclusively on Moses and God.

Although the sacrifice is to be performed by the whole congregation of Israel, assembled in its first collective act, we should not overlook its household-by-household character. The importance of this arrangement is highlighted by the recurrent mention of *bayith,* house or household, which occurs four times in these four verses and will occur eleven more times in this chapter (Ex. 12). There are several reasons for this emphasis, both positive and negative. In rejection of their situation in Egypt, where their families were threatened by crushing toil and the policy of infanticide, the Israelites, even before their liberation, will reaffirm the importance of family life. Israel will be a nation born of households (not, for example, of isolated individuals entering into a social contract). Although God is authoring a political revolution, unlike most revolutions this one will be family-affirming rather than family-denying: the attachment to the community and to the Lord will not require (as, for example, in Socrates's city-in-speech of Plato's *Republic*) renouncing the love of one's own flesh and blood. On the contrary, the family in Israel will remain the core of society and will have the educative function of transmitting the covenantal way of life. Far from aspiring only to feather their own nests, in Israel all families shall be devoted to something beyond family. Moreover, that higher devotion will enable families to be partners rather than rivals to each other: small households are told to reach out to one another, to make sure that everyone is able to eat, and to eat (only) to satiation, without excess, spoilage, or waste.

At the same time, the household principle is being subordinated to the communal principle and to divine service, in part to acknowledge and remedy the evils that (naturally) lurk in the uninstructed human family—the dangers of patricide, infanticide, and especially fratricide. Thus the familial offering tacitly acknowledges the impulse within families to bloody their own nest, an impulse that must and will be redirected and tamed (recall the Noahide permission to eat meat—but not the blood—in order to avoid homicide, or the substitution of the ram for Isaac in the story of his binding). It may also serve as belated, symbolic penance for the intended fratricide that brought Israel into Egypt in the first place: the story of Joseph and his murderous brothers, who brought his coat, stained with the blood of a goat, to their father Jacob as (phony) evidence that a wild beast must have devoured him.[14]

The Lord continues with instructions about what should be done with the killed lamb:

> "And they shall take of the blood, and put it on the two side posts and on the lintel, upon the houses wherein they shall eat it. And they shall eat the flesh in that night, roast with fire, and unleavened bread; with bitter herbs they shall eat it. Eat not of it raw, nor sodden at all with water, but roast with fire; its head with its legs and with the inwards thereof. And you shall let nothing of it remain until the morning; but that which remains of it until the morning you shall burn with fire. And thus shall you eat it: with your loins girded, your shoes on your feet, and your staff in your hand; and you shall eat it in haste—it is *the Lord's* passover (*pesach*). For I will go through the land of Egypt in that night, and will smite all the firstborn in the land of Egypt, both man and beast; and against all the gods of Egypt I will execute judgments: I am the Lord. And the blood shall be to you for a token upon the houses where you are; and when I see the blood, I will pass over (*ufasachti*) you, and there shall no plague be upon you to destroy you, when I smite the land of Egypt." (12:7–13; emphasis added)

The instructions begin with a directive about the blood and end with an account of its function: the houses whose doorposts are marked with blood will be spared the devastation of the Lord's final plague, the slaying of the firstborn. But the marking of the doors has additional significance, as does the use of blood for this purpose.

Did the Lord really need a marked door to tell an Israelite home from an Egyptian? Not likely. The exercise is for the Israelites, not for Him. Each Israelite household must earn its deliverance. Painting one's door was a freely chosen vote—in broad moonlight—for one's own redemption, an act at once obedient and faithful, as well as courageous and dignified. It was, to exaggerate but slightly, an act of liberation preceding actual deliverance. Every Israelite household had a free choice to make. Those who made it in accord with God's directive, trusting His promise of deliverance, were not only worthy of redemption but they were also already partly free of Egypt, where one's lot in the world was given, not chosen. Those who did not mark their doors, we never hear of. If there were any such, they presumably suffered the same fate as the Egyptians.

And why mark the doorposts with blood? Blood, which the ancient world widely regarded as "the life," was in some cultures eaten or drunk, often as part of wild cultic practices, as a way of augmenting one's own powers or communing with the gods. (It was perhaps in opposition to such practices that the Noahide code prohibited the eating of blood when it granted humankind permission to eat animal flesh.) In other cultures, precisely because blood is "the life," it was more than a physical liquid; it had metaphysical power and could redress the cosmic balance of such powers in mankind's favor. Putting blood on the door would, in those cultures, be a way of warding off evil forces—not by magic but by rebalancing or appeasing the powers-that-be. In stark contrast, this Israelite use of blood rejects—or, rather, transforms—those ideas and practices, even as it serves to protect the house. When used as God commands, it expresses a personal dedication to a known and benevolent deity and, especially, a trust in His promise of deliverance. "The life" is symbolically returned to its source or owner in a gesture of sacrifice that simultaneously consecrates the house. In addition, Israelite life is surrendered into God's care and protection through this symbolic substitute for firstborn sons who will not be taken by the Lord from their blood-marked houses. (The Paschal lamb may have a better claim to being such a symbolic substitute.) At the same time, like the "partial sacrifice" that is the mark of circumcision (see also the "Bridegroom of Blood" episode, Chapter Three) and that later becomes a prerequisite for participation in the Paschal sacrifice (12:43ff), the blood may betoken a willingness to dedicate the sons of the house to the Lord, and even to shed their blood—and the blood of others—in His defense. And unbeknownst to the Israelites who mark them, the bloodstained doors may even be a prior acknowledgment of the Egyptian lives that will soon be destroyed on Israel's behalf.

God's central instructions concern the Paschal meal,[15] whose main points have already been anticipated. The meal comprises (1) flesh, the food that (like blood) answers to the animal-like wildness and violence of the human soul, and (2) bread, the so-called human food, which bespeaks man's rational power to transform external nature for human use (by planting, harvesting, threshing, and grinding grain into flour and by baking moistened flour into bread) and to tame his own appetites through delayed gratification (toiling to sow today what he cannot enjoy for months). The meal also unites the produce of farmers and shepherds, rivals since Cain and Abel. In these instructions for the meal on the eve of the Exodus, the emphasis is on the meat (shepherds); in the forthcoming instructions for future celebrations of Passover, emphasis will be on the flatbread (farmers). This shift may be tied to the Israelites' anticipated move into their own land, which they will cultivate themselves, but, it is to be hoped, not in the exploitive fashion of Egypt.

The meal that the Lord enjoins is to be simple, only modestly embellished by culinary art. The meat is to be eaten not raw but fire-roasted—not boiled as a delicacy or eaten with sauces—and it is to be consumed that night in its entirety—not setting aside the entrails for the gods, not allowing for spoilage or waste. The modest bread is not to be leavened; the pure and plainest staff of life, it is nothing fermented or adulterated, puffed up or luxurious. Accompanying the meat and flatbread are bitter herbs (*merorim*), a reminder of the bitterness (*maror*) of the slaves' hard service in mortar and brick (1:14).[16] Taken all in all, it is a meal that meets necessity and rejects Egyptian delicacy and luxury.[17] The frugal meal before the Exodus is meant, among other things, to teach the Israelites to leave their Egyptian appetites behind.

The teaching of "leaving behind" is underlined by the manner in which the Paschal lamb is to be eaten: ready for departure, with loins

girded, shoes on feet, staff in hand, in haste. The anti-Egyptian meal is
to be eaten, so to speak, halfway out the door and not looking back. But
the point is not only to be anti-Egypt. Once again, God undertakes to
reconfigure the Israelites' experience of time. Please understand, He is
implicitly saying to them, this is not your ordinary meal, enjoyed in ordinary times. In fact, this is not *your* time at all: something much more
momentous is taking place, something that will change the time of your
lives and that of the entire world. Get ready. Get set. It is time to go into
a new, forward-looking age.[18]

The instructions conclude with a summary and explanation of
their significance: "It is the *Lord's* Passover" (*pesach*; 12:11; emphasis
added). The expression seems to imply familiarity with some preexisting (presumably Egyptian and naturalistic) festival of passover, which
is, like the sabbath and the calendar, here receiving a completely different meaning: it is the occasion of sparing—passing over—the houses of
the Israelites when the Lord crosses through the land of Egypt smiting
all the firstborn of man and beast and executing "judgment against all
the gods of Egypt; [for] I am the Lord" (12:12).

It is easy to see how the execution of this tenth plague will be a catastrophe for Egypt and, as God noted long ago, a fitting punishment
for Egypt's abuses of Israel, the Lord's "firstborn." But how, exactly, does
smiting the firstborn of man and beast constitute judgment against all
the gods of Egypt? To begin with, we note that the firstborn has a meaning beyond the birth order. The firstborn is the representative of the
whole class, a representative promoted by none other than nature herself. Second, all the so-called gods of the Egyptians had their sacred animal or animal emblem. To attack the firstborn of every animal is to hit
the representative emblem of the Egyptian pantheon. The Egyptian
"gods" are thus humiliated and exposed as powerless or indifferent, incapable of fulfilling their most essential duty: protecting the people who
worship them. In this sense too, the tenth plague constitutes judgment
against the gods of the Egyptians. But there is more.

To attack the firstborn is to attack taking direction from nature:
nature alone determines birth order. Bestowing social and political significance on birth order and the firstborn—for example, through primogeniture—is in effect living in deference to nature (not to say necessity

or chance). To kill the firstborn is a more than symbolic way of over-throwing the widespread human tendency to regard nature as primary and authoritative—which is to say, worthy of reverence or "divine."

With this reference to the gods of Egypt—the only one in the en-tire Egypt narrative—we have it confirmed from the Highest Authority that the contest with Egypt has ultimately been about the divine. When the Lord reveals His solicitude for His people, His keeping His word, and His utterly supernatural ability to distinguish not only Israel from Egypt but also, within each household, the firstborn from the rest, the so-called gods of Egypt—including Pharaoh himself—are exposed as nonentities. What "god" worshipped in Egypt can do all that?

Future Observance of Passover

In the remarkable next directive, issued without a pause or transition, the Lord moves from instructions for this one night to instructions for its annual commemoration.

> "And this day shall be unto you for a memorial (*zikkaron*), and you shall keep it a feast (*chag*) to the Lord; *throughout your generations* you shall keep it a feast by an ordinance (*chuqqath*) *forever*. Seven days shall you eat flatbread (*mat-soth*); surely, the first day you shall put away leaven out of your houses; for whosoever eats leavened bread from the first day until the seventh day, that soul shall be cut off from Is-rael. And in the first day there shall be to you a holy convo-cation, and in the seventh day a holy convocation; no manner of work shall be done in them, save that which every man must eat, that only may be done by you. And you shall observe the Feast of Flatbread; for in this selfsame day have I brought your hosts out of the land of Egypt; therefore shall you observe this day *throughout your generations* by an ordi-nance (*chuqqath*) *forever*. In the first month, on the fourteenth day of the month at evening, you shall eat flatbread, until the one and twentieth day of the month at evening. Seven days shall there be no leaven found in your houses; for whosoever

eats that which is leavened, that soul shall be cut off from the congregation of Israel, whether he be a sojourner, or one that is born in the land. You shall eat nothing leavened; in all your habitations shall you eat flatbread." (12:14–20; emphasis added)

In a directive probably unmatched in human affairs either before or since, a fledgling people—a mere mass of oppressed slaves—are told, *even before it happens,* how to celebrate *forever* the event of their (not-yet) deliverance. The reason is to educate the Israelites about how they are to regard time in the world and themselves in relation to it. The Children of Israel must leave Egypt already thinking about their children and their children's children, indeed, about their generations forever. Just as God is taking away Pharaoh's future, He teaches the Israelites how to think about theirs[19]: an unlimited future informed by memory of their God-delivered past.

The heart of the seven-day[20] memorial is a feast, *chag,* a word that comes to be synonymous with *festival.* Passover will be the only holiday in Israel's liturgical calendar for which a ritual meal is biblically prescribed and in which specific foods are designated as obligatory.[21] Unlike the meal on the original night of Passover, the annual Passover feast, as noted, emphasizes the obligation to eat flatbread. The bread of protracted affliction, turned by the Lord's hand into the bread of hasty exit and instant deliverance, embodies the essence of what needs to be remembered. Almost equal emphasis, however, is given to what is *not* to be eaten, indeed not even to be found in the house. In place of the blood-marked doors, there are to be leaven-free houses; twice we are told that anyone who eats leavened (read Egyptian) bread during the seven days of Passover will have his soul cut off from his people—a fate analogous to that suffered by those Israelites who failed, long ago, to mark their doors and consecrate their houses. All tokens of Egyptian indulgence, fermentation, and superfluity are to be banished. Those who refuse to banish them will themselves be banished, nay, will banish themselves. By clinging to the ways of Egypt, they effectively excommunicate themselves.

With these instructions about the future observance of Passover, the Children of Israel receive their deliverance on condition that it be understood as a forward-going enterprise in which their chief task is to be mediators. Gratitude and recompense for their deliverance must be expressed forward, by undertaking the tasks of instruction of and transmission to future generations. What they are to transmit is at this point almost completely unknown, but their orientation in the world has been established in advance. Their obligation to commemorate and reenact the people-forming act of their deliverance by the Lord stands as the keynote teaching. When Moses, after receiving these instructions, delivers them to the elders of the people, he makes the point explicit:

> "And you shall observe this thing for an ordinance to you and your sons forever. And it shall come to pass, when you come to the land that the Lord will give you, according as He has promised, that you shall keep this service. And it shall come to pass, when your children shall say unto you, 'What mean you by this service?' that you shall say: 'It is the service of the Lord's Passover, for that He passed over the houses of the Children of Israel in Egypt, when He smote the Egyptians and delivered our houses.'"[22] (12:24–27)

When the Lord finally completes his instructions to Moses and Aaron, Moses calls for the elders of Israel and gives them a condensed version of what the Lord told him to say. Given his equivocal experience with the elders,[23] Moses is eager to renew relationships, confident this time that he and the Lord will deliver on their promises and that the elders can help get the message across. In speaking with them, he adds specific instructions on how to get the blood on the doorposts and lintel (with a bunch of hyssop, dipped into the basin of blood), directs them not to leave their houses until morning, and tells them why: "For the Lord will cross through to smite the Egyptians; and when He sees the blood . . . the Lord will pass over the door, and will not suffer the destroyer to come into your houses to smite you" (12:23). Moses concludes by informing them of the ordinance about Passover to be observed by "you and your sons forever," finishing with lines just quoted: "for that He passed over the houses of the Children of Israel in Egypt, when he smote the Egyptians and delivered our houses" (12:27). In speaking to the people, Moses leaves himself and his deeds entirely out of the account (just as he is missing from the *Haggadah,* the text read at the Passover Seder). For the future people of Israel, the first nine plagues—performed through the agency of Moses and Aaron—do not count. All that matters is the Lord's mighty hand, taking them out Himself.

The Children of Israel

We hear again, at long last, from the Children of Israel. When Moses last came to them (weeks ago, before the contest with Pharaoh) bearing the Lord's new sevenfold promise, they had refused to hearken to his words, "for impatience of spirit and for cruel bondage" (6:9). This time it's a wholly different story. When Moses finishes, without saying a word,

> the people bowed their heads and prostrated themselves. Then the Children of Israel went and did as the Lord had commanded Moses and Aaron; thus they did. (12:27–28)

The nine plagues that wreaked havoc in Egypt have not moved Pharaoh, but it seems they have moved the Israelites. Having witnessed from afar the power commanded by Moses and Aaron, and having marveled at their own immunity from the devastation that power wrought, the Children of Israel have at last overcome their skepticism. They bow their heads in humble obeisance—we note, however, the text does not say to whom; could it have been to Moses?—and they then proceed to do as "the Lord had commanded Moses and Aaron." After expressing their homage, they obey. In doing so, they tacitly vote for and begin to earn their deliverance. They are ready to be redeemed.

Against this sanguine assessment of the Israelite masses, a skeptic will want to enter a word of caution. Once before, he would have us remember, the "people believed" Moses and Aaron when they promised the Lord's deliverance. Then too, "they bowed their heads and prostrated themselves" (4:31). But their faith was fickle, easily destroyed when Pharaoh increased their burdens: Might it be fickle again? In addition, one should probably not exaggerate the significance of their obedience or claim too much for their "freedom of choice." Their circumstances have long been desperate: What have they now to lose by hearkening? More relevant, they are threatened with destruction should they disobey and fail to mark their doors, and the evidence of the first nine plagues makes those threats quite credible. What looks to us like a free choice may have been experienced as compulsion.

Let us acknowledge these words of skeptical caution. But they do not finally persuade, provided that we try to imagine ourselves in the existential situation of the Children of Israel. Granted, they were between a rock and a hard place: marking their doors was risky, should the very visible Egyptians take notice; but so was leaving them unmarked, should the invisible Lord in fact pass through. Yet the Children of Israel did not waver. They unhesitatingly took the risk and placed their trust in the promise of the Lord, as communicated to them by Moses. It must have been a terribly anxious night, from dusk to deliverance; they could have had no certitude that the Lord would strike selectively as promised or that the Egyptians would not avenge their putting sheep's blood on their doorposts. But they were not paralyzed, they were not cowed, and they were not compelled: they chose, and chose freely.

The Plague of the Firstborn

Compulsion is precisely what the Lord has in store for Pharaoh. The day of reckoning has arrived:

> And it came to pass at midnight, that the Lord smote all the firstborn in the land of Egypt, from the firstborn of Pharaoh that sat on his throne unto the firstborn of the captive that was in the dungeon; and all the firstborn of cattle. And Pharaoh rose up (*qum*) in the night, he, and all his servants, and all the Egyptians; and there was a great cry in Egypt; for there was not a house where there was not one dead. And he called for Moses and Aaron by night and said: "Rise up (*qumu*), get you forth from among my people, both you and the Children of Israel; and go, serve the Lord, *as you have said*. Take both your flocks and your herds, *as you have said*, and be gone; and (or "but") *bless me also*." (12:29–32; emphasis added)

In elevated style, but with economy of expression, two verses suffice for the climactic tenth plague. Without warning, in the middle of the night, catastrophe strikes every Egyptian household, exactly as Moses has told Pharaoh. Also as predicted, there was "a great cry in Egypt" as the ubiquity of death and grief leveled all distinctions, from palace to pit. Overthrown symbolically are also the "gods" of the Egyptians, who—like the "divine" Pharaoh—are impotent to stave off the slaughter imposed upon Egypt by a more-than-natural power that can strike with discriminating accuracy. Pharaoh, whom we last heard banishing Moses with the threat "never see my face again; for in the day you see my face you shall die" (10:28), is compelled to summon Moses and Aaron in the middle of the night and, in abject capitulation, grant all their demands. He begins in the imperative mode: "Rise up, get you forth." But the content is entirely a humiliating concession to all of Moses's prior demands: separate yourselves from among my people; not only you but your children; go serve *Y–H–V–H* "as you have said"; not only your children but take also your flocks and herds "as you have said."[24] The end of Pharaoh's speech—his last ever to Moses and almost his last altogether—is full of pathos: it begins with a face-saving attempt to assert authority—"And be gone!"—but in a submissive about-face, recognizing that the Israelites have been blessed and that only the Lord of Israel can save him, Pharaoh pleads for a blessing also for himself.[25]

As did Pharaoh with Moses and Aaron, so do the terrified Egyptians with the Israelites: they press them hard to leave:

> And the Egyptians were strong (*chazaq*) upon the people, to send them out of the land in haste; for they said: "We are all dead men." And the people took their dough before it was leavened, their kneading troughs being bound up in their clothes upon their shoulders. And the Children of Israel did according to the word of Moses; and they asked of the Egyptians jewels of silver, and jewels of gold, and raiment. And the Lord gave the people favor in the sight of the Egyptians, so that they let them have what they asked. And they despoiled (*nitsel*) the Egyptians. (12:33–36)

Encouraged by their Egyptian neighbors, the Israelites do not need much convincing to leave. Hastily taking their unrisen dough, but keeping it under their clothes in the hope that their bodily warmth might cause it to rise, they make their exit from the land. But as they are leaving, they remember Moses's instructions—delivered long before, at his and Aaron's first meeting with them (4:29–30), when they repeated to the people the plan that God had presented to Moses (3:21–22)—to ask their neighbors for gifts of jewelry and clothing.* Exactly as the Lord had predicted, the Egyptians oblige, because "the Lord gave the people favor in the sight of the Egyptians."

What does this mean? Why, and in what spirit, do the Israelites ask for wealth? Why, and in what spirit, do the Egyptians oblige?

The alternative to asking is taking. The instruction to ask, whatever else it may be, is a means to prevent looting and pillage. Just because we are reading the Torah, with its high-minded teachings, we shouldn't imagine that this large mass of aroused, soon-to-be former slaves would, on their own, act differently from any other mob overthrowing their oppressors. They will want revenge and they will want payback for their labor and suffering, so they will take what they think is coming to them and more. Thanks to divine instruction, that does not happen here.

And what might they be asking for? Most likely, they are seeking compensation for their years of service. God had said, in his original prophecy and instruction, "When you go, *you shall not go empty*" (3:21; emphasis added), a phrase that will be repeated years later when Moses sets down the proper treatment in Israel of the manumitted Israelite slave:

> "And when you let him go free from you, *you shall not let him go empty*; you shall *furnish him liberally* out of your flock, and out of your threshing-floor, and out of your winepress; *of that*

*Here is that original formulation: "And I will give this people favor in the sight of the Egyptians. And it shall come to pass, that, when you go, you shall not go empty; but every woman shall ask of her neighbor and of her that sojourns in her house jewels of silver, and jewels of gold, and raiment; and you shall put them upon your sons and upon your daughters; and you shall despoil the Egyptians." (3:21–22)

> *wherewith the Lord your God has blessed you, you shall give*
> *unto him.* And you shall *remember* that *you* were *a bondman*
> *in the land of Egypt,* and the Lord your God redeemed *you;*
> *therefore* I command you this thing today. (Deut. 15:13–15; emphasis added)

Since the Israelite master has profited from the slave's service, the slave is entitled, when gaining his freedom, to some share of the accumulated profit. And the reason the master is given for his duty to be liberal is none other than "his own" bondage in Egypt, from which the Lord his God redeemed *him*—also not empty-handed.

The Egyptians comply with the request because, we are told, "the Lord gave the people favor in the eyes of the Egyptians." A rosy, not to say utopian, interpretation of this expression would suggest that comity, even brotherly feeling, had wondrously broken out between the Egyptians and their erstwhile enemies. Having themselves been terrorized and attacked, with slaughtered sons in every home, the Egyptians at last have fellow feeling for the brutalized and long-suffering Israelites. As if repudiating Pharaoh and his policies, they are eager to make amends for their complicity in the Israelites' oppression, and their gifts are intended as restitution and healing. On such a hopeful reading, however, we can only be terribly disappointed to learn at the end that the Israelites "despoiled the [neighborly] Egyptians."

I prefer a more hard-headed reading. The favor the Israelites win in the Egyptians' eyes comes from the fact that the Lord is clearly on their side. The disaster that has just struck every Egyptian household is all that is needed to show the Egyptians where power really lies. The multitudes always love a winner, especially when they have more to lose by clinging to the losing side. Thanks (only) to the Lord's display of matchless power, the Egyptians now look favorably upon His people. The gifts they give the Israelites are both tributes for victory and bribes to avoid further punishment. In the eyes of the Egyptians, the Israelites' request was an offer that they could not refuse. "And so they [the Israelites] despoiled the Egyptians," getting freely some portion of the recompense their former service deserved.[26]

There is a third, and perhaps better, interpretation of the Egyptians' behavior. At the penultimate stage in the contest of the plagues, just before Moses warned Pharaoh about the tenth plague, we readers were told that "the man Moses was very great in the land of Egypt, in the sight of Pharaoh's servants and in the sight of the people" (11:3). As Pharaoh's credibility and reputation sank with each mounting plague, the Egyptians—everyone other than Pharaoh—came to see that Moses was for real, and so, therefore, might be the people and the divinity he claimed to represent. Having previously thought of the Israelites as lowly and powerless, the Egyptians had not respected them, but their attitude was changing. Now, with the final attack on the firstborn, every Egyptian household can see that the Israelites are aligned with a powerful deity and therefore are worthy of respect. The Egyptian gifts, given on request, were not signs of affection but of grudging—and awe-ful—respect.[27]

The Departure

At long last, the Israelites leave Egypt. For such a momentous event, the text's description is almost anticlimactic:

> And the Children of Israel journeyed from Rameses to Succoth, about six hundred thousand men on foot, beside children. And a mixed multitude went up also with them; and flocks, and herds, even very much cattle. And they baked unleavened cakes of the dough which they brought forth out of Egypt, for it was not leavened; because they were thrust out of Egypt, and could not tarry, neither had they prepared for themselves any victual. (12:37–39)

The account is brief, spare, and straightforward. The numbers departing are staggering. Some non-Israelites—"a mixed multitude"[28]—joined the Exodus. From the start, they were undersupplied with food; what they had was but unleavened flatbread. They were free but hungry. Before long, they will regret their choice.

Israel is out of Egypt. The story of their servitude is over. In concluding this phase of Israel's experience, the text invites us to look back at the long history of exile:

> Now the time that the Children of Israel dwelt in Egypt was four hundred and thirty years. And it came to pass at the end of four hundred and thirty years, even the selfsame day it came to pass, that all the battalions of the Lord went out from the land of Egypt. It was a night of watching ["observance" or "vigilance"; *shimmurim*] unto the Lord for bringing them out from the land of Egypt; this same night is a night of watching ["observance"] unto the Lord for all the Children of Israel throughout their generations. (12:40–42)

The prophesied four hundred years of slavery (see Gen. 15:13) have ended.[29] The seventy Children of Israel who came into Egypt as the sons of one man leave as the battalions of the Lord. Their night of watching unto the Lord for His deliverance becomes, in the last sentence, the basis for observing a night unto the Lord "for all the Children of Israel throughout their generations," which is to say forever.

This last forward-looking remark is the link to the first of the text's two appendices to the Exodus, in which the Lord gives Moses and Aaron additional instructions about the ordinance of the Passover. Inspired perhaps by the presence of the "mixed multitude" among them, the seven succinct regulations are to make clear to the Israelites who is and is not eligible to participate in the Passover sacrifice. Participation in the sacrifice is to be restricted to Israelites, those within the Abrahamic covenant, including those who are willing to join the community (with their families) by being circumcised. Foreigners are not eligible to eat of the sacrifice; a manservant bought for money, when you have circumcised him, can participate, but settlers or hired hands who dwell among you but do not wish to join the community are to be excluded. The sacrifice is to be eaten in the house and not taken outside. The entire congregation of Israel—no exceptions—shall observe it. If a stranger sojourns with you and wants to keep the Passover, he may participate after all the males of his household are circumcised. After that, the sojourner shall be as a native of the land, but until then not: no uncircumcised person shall eat of it. The regulations conclude with a general rule regarding outsiders: "One law (*torah*) shall be to him who is native and to the stranger that sojourns among you" (12:49). There is to be no discrimination against strangers who are willing to join the community.

These regulations, easily overlooked because they seem anticlimactic, are in fact quite remarkable. As the Israelites set off on their journey to independent nationhood, it is not surprising that something should be said about how porous the boundaries of membership should be between them and their neighbors. What is striking is how open to accepting strangers the Children of Israel are encouraged to be and how generous are the criteria for allowing outsiders to join their ranks. The critical requirement for membership is not the blood tie of birth and ethnicity (or the ability to contribute to the gross national product) but commitment to the covenantal purposes to which the community is dedicated. One need not be a natural child of Israel to become a covenantal child in Israel. What is required is only circumcision, the voluntary acceptance of the (nature-altering) sign of God's covenant with Abraham and all his future descendants, a covenant intended from the start to establish, perpetuate, and transmit a way of life devoted, in the first instance, to righteousness and justice (Gen. 18:19)—and later also to holiness.

Israel's first national law, commanding the annual Passover festival to commemorate the deliverance from bondage, is here tied to Israel's very first commandment, as Abrahamic circumcision becomes the sine qua non for partaking of the Paschal sacrifice. Only people who willingly enter the covenant with God to do righteousness and justice can become full members of the nation that has been liberated from bondage in order to build a righteous and just political community—one where, among other things, strangers will be welcomed and justly treated.

These regulations having been communicated to the Israelites, the story of the deliverance comes to an end:

> Thus did all the Children of Israel; as the Lord commanded Moses and Aaron, so did they. And it came to pass the selfsame day that the Lord did bring the Children of Israel out the land of Egypt by their hosts. (12:50–51)

Consecration of the Firstborn

There is one more matter, pertinent to the deliverance from Egypt, still to be addressed: the status of the firstborn. The law prescribing future Passover observance immediately preceded the Exodus; the law prescribing redemption of the firstborn immediately follows it. It appears at the start of the second appendix to the story of the Exodus:

> And the Lord spoke unto Moses saying, "Consecrate [imperative, second-person singular] unto Me (*qadesh-li*) all the firstborn (*bekhor*), whatever is first to open the womb (*peter kol-rechem*) among the Children of Israel, both of men and of beast—it is Mine." (13:1–2)

The import of this requirement we discussed at the start of this chapter: to counter parental pride in producing and possessing offspring, as well as paternal (and cultural) impulses toward child sacrifice; to commemorate the sparing of the firstborn in Israel, purchased by the killing of the firstborn in Egypt; to overturn the widespread (including Egyptian) presumption that what is naturally first should be humanly first (primogeniture); to teach that children are a gift, not of nature but of the Lord.

The Lord's instruction, as far as we hear it, is contained in this single sentence. He asks that the firstborn (the *bekhor:* the one having priority according to birth or nature, the preferred one, and, again, whatever (naturally) opens the womb, both human and animal) be consecrated—be set aside, be dedicated, be made holy—unto Him. Why? Because they are all His! Looking ahead to the time of settlement in the Promised Land, the Lord demands that He be inserted into the relationship between a father and his son, and between a landowner and his animals, just at the proud moment when they will likely believe they are now on their own. Against the natural belief that my son and my calf and lamb are mine, the Lord insists that they are His. Moreover, He asks that they all be set aside or consecrated unto Him: if we read only this sentence, we would think that He is demanding that they be sacrificed to Him. What other form of consecration could embrace both humans and animals?

Only in the sequel, a fourteen-verse address by Moses, is this impression corrected. But the correction does not come right away. Before coming to the consecration of the firstborn, Moses sets forth the context in which this obligation is to be understood. That context, as we shall see in a moment, comprises memory and the education of children.

Before examining the content of Moses's speech, I must comment on the mere fact of it. Most interpreters assume that Moses is simply relating further instructions that the Lord gave him in private. I prefer to think that Moses is speaking on his own, perhaps intuiting what the Lord intends with his commandment about the firstborn, but mainly seizing the opportunity for basic cultural instruction. Here, and several times earlier, God has put into Moses's mind the need to think about the future, about the children, and about how the children should be related to God. Moses grabs the occasion to expand on the subject, whether from newfound confidence in the people or from fear of their waywardness. In the process, he creates the catechism for parents to use with their children. He turns their attention from liberation *from* to liberation *for*, to what they were liberated from Egypt to do: to their mission.

It is at this moment that Moses, the statesman, becomes Moses, the teacher, or, as he is known in the Tradition, *Moshe rabbeinu*: "Moses, our teacher." He uses his status as founding leader of the people to devolve some of the responsibility for national perpetuation onto the people themselves, family by family, fathers to sons. He teaches parents the central importance of teaching while also creating the national narrative that is to be taught.[30]

He begins with the obligation to remember the Exodus and to celebrate Passover:

> And Moses said unto the people: "*Remember* this day, in which you [plural] came out from Egypt, out of the house of bondage; for by strength of hand the Lord brought you out from this place; there shall no leavened bread be eaten. This day you go forth in the month Aviv [Alter translates, "the month of the New Grain"]. And it shall be when the Lord shall bring you [singular from here on] into the land of the Canaanite, and the Hittite, and the Amorite, and the Hivite,

and the Jebusite, which He swore unto your fathers to give you, *a land flowing with milk and honey,* that you shall keep this *service ('avodah)* in this month. Seven days you shall eat unleavened bread, and on the seventh day shall be a feast to the Lord. Unleavened bread shall be eaten throughout the seven days; and there shall no leavened bread be seen with you, neither shall there be leaven seen with you, in all your borders. And you shall *tell your son* on that day, saying: 'It is because of that which the Lord did for *me* when *I* came forth out of Egypt.'" (13:3–8; emphasis added)

The Children of Israel are told to remember this day, on which the Lord delivered them out of the house of bondage in Egypt, as a day for eating no leavened bread. Even (or, better, especially) when they come to the rich Promised Land, a land flowing with milk and honey—prosperous like Egypt (though the image is not agricultural)—they must keep this annual service ('*avodah*) to the Lord, a bulwark against any Egyptianizing temptation.* The essence of this service, repeated four times in two verses, is the eating of flatbread and the abstention from leaven. And what is the point? *To be able to tell your son* that you eat this flatbread and do this service because of your personal deliverance from slavery, a gift of the Lord. You are not only to remember but you are also to "remind" your children of your personal debt to the Lord.[31]

In reading this account, imagining ourselves among Moses's listeners, it occurs to us to ask: Are we eating flatbread and telling our children because God took us out of Egypt, or did God take us out of Egypt so that we could eat flatbread and tell our children—so that we could serve Him by keeping the memory of His beneficence alive from generation to generation? Have we been liberated not to be free but to have a story to tell—to ourselves, our children, and indirectly to the world? Have we been liberated so that everyone, forevermore, shall know and remember *Y-H-V-H*?

---

*We note that '*avodah* is the same word used for service and servitude to Pharaoh in Egypt: Have the Israelites simply exchanged one form of service for another? We will take up this question thematically in the last chapter.

The obligation of memory is the subject of Moses's next instruction:

"And it shall be for a sign (*'oth*) unto you upon your hand, and for a memorial between your eyes, *that the law (torah; teaching) of the Lord may be in your mouth;* for with a strong hand has the Lord brought you out of Egypt. You shall therefore keep this ordinance in its season from year to year." (13:9–10; emphasis added)

The concrete meaning of "sign upon your hand . . . memorial between your eyes" is unclear. We cannot be sure whether it is meant literally or metaphorically.[32] Either way, however, the sign upon the hand recalls the Lord's mighty hand; the memorial between the eyes recalls the deliverance from Egypt. But the main thing is the purpose of these reminders: that the (not-yet-given) law of the Lord may be in your mouth, to guide your life and teach your children, from year to year, indefinitely.

It is in the context of teaching the children the Lord's *torah* that Moses finally gets around to the consecration of the firstborn. He introduces a distinction, not present in God's original one-sentence directive, between what is to be done with the firstborn of beasts and with the firstborn of humans:

"And it shall be when the Lord shall bring you into the land of the Canaanite, as He swore unto you and to your fathers, and shall give it you, that you shall cause to pass over [that is, 'to be sacrificed'] unto the Lord all that first opens the womb; every firstling that is a male, which you have coming of a beast, shall be the Lord's . . . but all the firstborn of man (*'adam*) among your sons you shall redeem. And it shall be when your son asks you in time to come, saying, 'What is this (*mah-zo'th*)?' [that is, the meaning of these precepts about the firstborn] that you shall say unto him: 'By strength of hand the Lord brought us out from Egypt, from the house of bondage; and it came to pass, when Pharaoh was hard about sending us off that the Lord slew all the firstborn in the land of Egypt, both the firstborn of man, and the firstborn of beast;

therefore, I sacrifice to the Lord all that opens the womb, being males; but all the firstborn of my sons I redeem.' And it shall be for a sign upon your hand, and for frontlets between your eyes; for by strength of hand the Lord brought us forth out of Egypt." (13:11–16)

When the Israelites come to inhabit the Promised Land—lest they forget how they got it, what they owe, and to Whom—they will be obliged to sacrifice the firstlings of their flocks and herds, presumably as acts of thanksgiving, unto the Lord, to Whom all life belongs. But in repudiation of child sacrifice, including the sort that Pharaoh's recalcitrance yielded among the Egyptians, the Children of Israel will be obliged to redeem their firstborn sons, in memory of the Lord's redemption of His firstborn son, Israel, from the house of bondage. The human firstborn, no less than the animal firstborn, each a representative of its distinctive kind, is a creature of the Lord. But the human child may be redeemed—ransomed, bought back—because there are higher ways for him to be consecrated to the Lord.

The law regarding redemption of the firstborn in Israel has a distinctly political target: the practice, especially in settled agricultural societies like Egypt, of primogeniture, in which the naturally first is automatically the heir of his father's domain. The Bible has from the beginning silently inveighed against the father's prideful preference for his firstborn—favoring Abel over Cain, Isaac over Ishmael, Jacob over Esau, Ephraim over Manasseh—and making it clear that the naturally first is not the humanly best, especially if the standard is right, not might, especially if human affairs are not yet "set" according to God's plan. By claiming the firstborn for Himself and by insisting that consecration and redemption are the result of a human decision (imperative: "you consecrate unto Me," "you shall redeem"), God is warning Israel against the complacent view that things are permanently settled or that mindless nature will properly order human affairs, and against the prideful view that what we and nature produce suffices for human life.

But as the language of consecration implies, there is more here than politics or the teaching of moderation. The point is decidedly spiritual and God-centered. Human children can be consecrated unto the Lord in ways other than sacrifice. Moses connects this teaching—about the redemption of the firstborn in Israel—to the subject of teaching itself. Once again there is a child in need of instruction: he is puzzled by the laws of the firstborn and the different treatment of the animal and the human. The answer he gets explains the difference: we sacrifice the animal firstborn in gratitude for our deliverance from Egypt, and we redeem the human firstborn in memory of the price paid for our redemption. At the same time, we tacitly teach our children that, unlike other so-called gods, the Lord does not want child sacrifice. He wants only that our children be dedicated to His ways; He wants only that we remember gratefully His beneficence; He wants only that we continue to tell the story of how the world came to know Him. Consecrating our children to the Lord is not only compatible with their remaining alive: it will be the basic condition of their flourishing.

Coda

Israel is out of Egypt. Many of the Lord's additional purposes have been accomplished. The Children of Israel, formerly passive, have started to act, and to act communally. Pharaoh has been compelled to send the people away, and he seems (for now) to acknowledge the superior power of the Lord, even asking Moses for a blessing. The Egyptians have also come around, looking with favor on the Israelites, formerly the objects of their contempt. Moses's stature among both Israelites and Egyptians has risen; no longer worried about being a man with uncircumcised lips, he has gained confidence in his abilities to lead and to teach. We are tempted to conclude that the contest with Egypt is over, and we can move on to the next steps in nation-building. But there is unfinished business. One more act must follow. Still, we have seen enough to be able to add a few new thoughts on the subject of freedom—liberation *from* and liberation *for*.

As we noted at the start of this chapter, the actual departure from Egypt, described in very few verses, is surrounded by instructions regarding ritual enactments of sacrifice, eating, and procreation. Some acts (marking the doors, preparing and eating the Paschal meal) were prerequisites for being redeemed from Egypt, while others (the annual Passover holiday, the consecration of the firstborn, the teaching of the children) are perpetual obligations into the future, intended to memorialize God's deliverance of His people. Before they could be liberated, the people had to choose to mark their doors, to deny and defy the gods of the Egyptians, and to vote for their deliverance, manifesting in all these choices their obedience to the Lord and their trust in Him. After their liberation, the people were summoned to choose to keep the annual seven-day festival of eating flatbread (*matsah*) and to avoid leaven; they were called upon to choose to consecrate their firstborn sons and animals to the Lord; they were invited to remember the Lord's deliverance, to tell its story to their children, to educate their children in the meaning of the ritual observances by which Israel would forever define itself as a people—grateful to God for their existence as a people and devoted to keeping that relationship alive for themselves and future generations. In brief, they were to use their freedom from Egyptian despotism and their own free choices to relive their national beginnings—the Exodus always first among them—and thus reexperience God's presence in their lives.

Soon enough, the Israelites will be invited to enter into a covenant with the Lord in which they will be given many laws to guide their conduct toward each other and many additional rituals through which they are to relate to the Lord. The explicit goals of that covenant will be justice and holiness, the terms being defined by divine command, which terms they then freely choose to obey. They will be asked to choose to serve the Lord so that they may be lifted up to a higher plane of existence, making good on the promise inherent in their being made in the image of God. That is what liberation from Egypt is ultimately for.[33] The events and the teachings of the present chapter provide a beginning and put them on the upward path.

"Who Is Like You Among the Gods?"

The Lord, Egypt, and Israel at the Sea of Reeds

The deliverance of Israel from Egypt is not yet complete. Despite the devastating losses of all firstborn sons and the virtual surrender of the Egyptian multitudes, Pharaoh is not yet finished. The Israelites after their moonlit escape are still psychically in the dark, uncertain about who—Pharaoh? Moses and Aaron? The Lord?—was responsible for their hasty departure. Whether from fear, ignorance, or bewilderment, they also lack the proper disposition toward God and Moses, and toward their new independence.

All three difficulties are addressed in the immediate sequel, the famous story of the splitting of the Sea of Reeds, which settles the first two issues and begins to address the third. This episode drops the final curtain on Israel in Egypt—and on Egypt altogether as an actor in the Hebrew Bible. It makes perfectly clear to the Israelites that it was the Lord Who delivered them, and it begins to dispose them properly toward the Lord and Moses and toward their own national development.

The story is told in two parts: the contest and the aftermath. Together they constitute a crucial next stage in the formation of the Israelite people: the Children of Israel symbolically undergo a national rebirth by passing through the divided waters, and they celebrate and interpret this rebirth in the triumphant Song of the Sea. By the end of this epic experience, they are ready to start their journey to the Promised Land.

Starting Out—with Joseph's Bones

Once the ex-slaves are almost out of Egypt—at the border town of Succoth—the next question is which way they should go. The answer will be determined not by geographic convenience but by state of soul: cowardice or courage in the face of battle.

> And it came to pass, when Pharaoh had sent off (*beshallach*) the people, that God led them not by the way of the land of the Philistines, although that was near; for God said: "Lest peradventure the people repent when they see war, and they return to Egypt." But God led the people roundabout, by the way of the wilderness by the Sea of Reeds; and the Children of Israel went up armed [or, "in orderly array"; *chamushim*] out of the land of Egypt. And Moses took the bones of Joseph with him; for swearing he had sworn the Children of Israel, saying: "God will surely remember [literally, "remembering, He will remember"; *paqod yifkod*] you; and you shall carry up my bones away hence with you." (13:17–19)

The most direct route from Egypt to the Promised Land was the "way of the sea" to the northeast, the coastal route along the Mediterranean through present-day Gaza. But because this route was heavily fortified and inhabited by the Egyptians, God rejects this convenient alternative: should the people run into the need for battle, they would be unprepared and frightened and would seek a return to Egypt. Although the Israelites came out armed (*chamushim*)[1] and in battle array ("My battalions"; 12:41), they were psychically unprepared to face danger: their arms are useless without courage. God therefore leads them on a circuitous route, southeast into the Sinai Peninsula. When the Israelites enter the Promised Land forty years later, they will enter from the east, heading west—as it were, through the "back door."

The departing Israelites are not only armed with weapons. Moses, we are astonished to learn, is also carrying the bones of Joseph (!) in fulfillment of the deathbed promise Joseph had extracted from his brothers several hundred years earlier.[2] This little gesture, added almost as an afterthought, speaks volumes.

First, the bones of Joseph (who was previously embalmed) are the only available link the Children of Israel have to the patriarchs and the Promised Land; that is, to the original Children of Israel, the sons of Jacob. (Joseph's brothers are all buried—and lie rotting—in Egypt.) But Joseph's bones are more than a bodily link: their presence makes good on the sworn promise of Israel's sons, a promise about burial. A link to both flesh and spirit, bones and words, taking Joseph's remains is an affirmation of promise keeping and of living in time—both crucial to the Way of the Lord. Second, Moses's act honors the importance of memory in Israel. Joseph had prophesied that God would remember the Children of Israel, and he charged them to remember him. Moses remembers Joseph—how he learned of this obligation is a deep mystery[3]— and in doing so pays tribute also to God's remembering and keeping His promises. This is in sharp contrast to Pharaoh, whose words are written in water and who remembers nothing of what he has promised.[4] Third, the gesture is important to Moses's mission: it provides the ex-slaves with an edifying connection to their glorious past. Joseph was both a beloved son of Israel and a political power in Egypt. Taking Joseph's bones, in accord with his last request, shows the people Joseph's final preference: better to be buried in Israel than to be a mummy awaiting reanimation in Egypt. Joseph in the end chose Israel over Egypt, and Moses uses that fact to reinforce the same choice among the people.

The presence of Joseph's bones turns the Exodus into a funeral procession. It will recapitulate the journey that was followed by the burial procession for Jacob and was arranged by Joseph himself.[5] The Children of Israel are bringing Joseph home, redeemed from Egypt to which he was exiled by the (original) sons of Israel. At the same time, their deed represents the undoing of Joseph the Egyptian and all that he had wrought. By taking the bones for burial, the funeral procession is a repudiation of embalming and of Egypt altogether. It puts an end to the Egyptian diaspora, begun by Joseph, who was carried down to Egypt and sold into slavery owing to the (not undeserved) enmity of his brothers; who rose to become prime minister; who then introduced centralizing practices and indentured servitude into Egypt; which led to the enslavement of the Israelites; the end of which servitude is now marked when Moses and the Children of Israel redeem a promise made to Joseph, redeeming him for Israel and the Promised Land.

Considered in familial terms, Moses is doing a kindness to Joseph and fulfilling his brothers' promise to bury him in the Promised Land, just as Joseph did a kindness to his brothers by not avenging their mistreatment of him, and just as he fulfilled his own promise to bury his father in the cave at Machpelah. But looking at it in political terms, we see something deeper. Moses, the statesman and soon-to-be legislator, quasi-Egyptian-turned Israelite, prepares to bury the mortal remains of Joseph the administrator, Israelite-turned-Egyptian. In doing so, he symbolically rejects the Egyptian preoccupation with augmenting wealth and power. Instead, Moses will preoccupy himself with governing the souls of the Children of Israel, who, like the original sons of Israel, Joseph's brothers, are surely in need of such soulcraft.

The Children of Israel, their route selected, start their journey southeastward, moving from Succoth to camp at Etham, said to be on the edge of the wilderness. Traveling a path completely unknown to them and headed "for only God knows where," they are nevertheless not lost. They have direct divine guidance:

> And the Lord was going before them by day in a pillar of cloud, to lead them the way, and by night in a pillar of fire, to give them light; that they might go by day and by night. The pillar of cloud by day, and the pillar of fire by night, departed not from the people. (13:21–22)

Even for an impoverished imagination, the scene boggles the mind: six hundred thousand men, plus the women and children, plus the herds, traveling in formation led by the Lord in a cloud by day and a fire by night,* ceaselessly forging ahead: a most spectacular sight. Of the mood

---

*We should pay close attention to the company of the cloud and the fire, aspects of the Lord's Presence, which figures prominently in the rest of this story, in the rev-

and spirit of this human mass, we hear not a word and have no idea. Despite the presence of the cloud and the fire, our guess is that apprehension and anxiety were rampant, if not all the time, then surely in the sequel.

Entrapment

No sooner has the march begun than it is aborted. The Lord has other things in mind. He instructs Moses to tell the Israelites to "turn back"—presumably to the northwest—and to "encamp before Pi-Hahiroth between Migdol and the sea"; in fact, this site is "by the sea" opposite to Baal-Zephon, a pagan site of worship on its other (eastern) side.[6] Why this change of plans? The Lord has unfinished business with Pharaoh. As He tells Moses, when Pharaoh hears that the Israelites have started to return toward Egypt, he will say of them:

> "They are confused in the land,
> The wilderness has shut them in." (14:3)

Taking advantage of Pharaoh's interest in this news, the Lord reveals the purpose behind the change of route:

> "And I shall strengthen (*vechizzaqti*) Pharaoh's heart, and he will pursue them; and I will get *glory* (*ve'ikkavedah*; from *kaved*, "heavy," "weighty") over Pharaoh, and over all his host; and the *Egyptians shall know* that *I am the Lord*." (14:4; emphasis added)

By placing the Children of Israel in a place where they look lost, beleaguered, and easily attacked, the Lord is laying a trap for Pharaoh. Why? The case is overdetermined.

The stated purposes are two, one for Him and one for the Egyptians: the Lord will gain "glory" over Pharaoh and his host, and the Egyptians will come to know—to recognize, to acknowledge—the

------

elation at Mount Sinai, and in the account of the Tabernacle in our last chapter, where we will discuss them thematically.

(superiority of the) Lord. The former goal is new or at least newly stated, and at first glance it seems puzzling. Why would the Lord seek glory, and what does He need it for? Part of the difficulty is that there is no really good way to translate the Hebrew word *kaved,* which can mean "to be heavy," "to be weighty," "to be honored or glorified."[7] In the present context, we perhaps come close by suggesting that the Lord seeks to make His weight in the world manifest and known, seeks to be recognized for His gravity and significance in human affairs. It is not that He is insecure and craves recognition, but that being of the greatest weight, He wants that weight to be felt, known, and celebrated. How this goal is achieved, we will soon consider.

The second (and not unrelated) goal—that the Egyptians shall know the Lord—has always been the purpose of the contest with Egypt, from the plagues to the extraction of the Israelites (7:5). But this contest, with this purpose, was undertaken because the Children of Israel had refused to believe Moses's promise of deliverance (6:9). Thus, as we learn only at the end of the episode at the Sea of Reeds, its *ultimate* purpose has to do instead with the Children of Israel and their relation to God and Moses: "And Israel saw the great work which the Lord did upon the Egyptians, and *the people feared-revered* (yare') *the Lord;* and they *trusted* (vaya'aminu) *in the Lord and in His servant Moses*" (14:31; emphasis added). Immediately, Moses and the Children of Israel sing out the glory of the Lord. The true goal of the contest at the Sea of Reeds is the "conversion" of the Israelites.

To appreciate this conversion, we must remember the context. The Children of Israel, who rushed out of Egypt, lack a clear idea of who is responsible for their departure. The order was given by Pharaoh to Moses and Aaron in the middle of the night and then conveyed by Moses to the people. Even if they suspected that they had received more than human help, they—and we—have yet to witness an open, direct confrontation between the power of Pharaoh and the power of the Lord. The Lord's power had, of course, been evident in the plagues, but never before had Pharaoh mobilized—and personally led—all his forces to do battle against Israel and its god. The people had felt the lash of Pharaoh's taskmasters, but they had never had to fight for their lives against Pharaoh's armed forces directed fully against them. The entire context is military, and the newly released ex-slaves, not trusted to battle the Philistines, will soon have to confront the world's greatest military power—and with their backs to the sea. They are prepared to learn about courage and encouragement. They are prepared to learn that the Lord helps those who help Him help them.

Meanwhile back in Egypt, there is trouble brewing for Pharaoh:

> And it was told the King of Egypt that the people were fled; and the heart [or "mind"; *lev*] of Pharaoh and his servants was changed toward the people, and they said: "What is this we have done, that we have let Israel go from serving us?" (14:5)

By the light of day, very likely the morning after the Exodus (or, less likely, on the fourth day, since they originally sought to leave for only three days), the Egyptian people (presumably their officers or police) discover that the Israelites are gone. Believing that they have escaped from their masters, the Egyptians come running in dismay to tell Pharaoh the news (as if unaware that it was he who had sent them away). The people protest to Pharaoh, bemoaning the loss of their servants and complaining that nothing has been done to oppose their flight or to retrieve them.[8]

Pharaoh finds himself in a difficult spot. He not only faces an angry throng, demanding redress of grievances. He must also counter the implicit charge of weakness, not to say complicity, for failing to prevent the "flight" of the Israelites. Failure to act will be taken as proof of impotence; other groups might be inspired to revolt and leave. For all these reasons, Pharaoh must respond, promptly and vigorously. And so he does:

> And he made ready his chariots, and took his people with him. And he took six hundred picked chariots, and [with them] all the chariots of Egypt, and captains on all of them. And the Lord strengthened (*vayechazzeq*) the heart of Pharaoh King of Egypt, and he pursued after the Children of Israel; for the Children of Israel went out with a high hand [*yots'im beyad ramah*; "high-handedly," that is, with arrogant defiance]. (14:6–8)

For the first time since the contest of the plagues began, Pharaoh takes the offensive. Instead of passively suffering the slings and arrows of the Lord, Pharaoh will go to war in broad daylight against the Lord's people, personally leading the campaign. Egypt collectively asserts itself, pitting its all against the Lord. The day of final reckoning is imminent.

Before the Sea: Terror in Israel

The Egyptians, led by Pharaoh himself, are in hot pursuit. In a massive show of force—"all the horses and chariots of Pharaoh, and his horsemen, and his army"—they overtake the Israelites, finding them newly encamped before the Sea of Reeds. The beleaguered Israelites are terrified at the sight of the approaching host:

> And when Pharaoh drew nigh, the Children of Israel lifted up their eyes, and, behold, *Egypt* was marching after them; and they were sore afraid; and the Children of Israel cried out unto the Lord. And they said unto Moses: "Is it because there were no graves in Egypt, that *you* have taken us away to die in the wilderness? Why have *you* dealt thus with us, to bring us forth out of Egypt? Is not this the word that we spoke unto you in Egypt, saying: 'Let us alone, that we may serve Egypt?' For it were better for us to serve Egypt, than that we should die in the wilderness." (14:10–12; emphasis added)

We should not be too quick to condemn the Israelites. A ragtag multitude of newly released slaves—armed at best with lances and with no experience of battle, their backs to the sea—looks with horror on the approach of horsed chariots and the world's most powerful and sophisticated army: when they lifted up their eyes, behold, it looked as if all of Egypt ("Egypt," with singular verb) was coming after them. We too would have been terrified, and rightly so.

Once again, they begin by crying out, this time quite explicitly to the Lord, beseeching Him for help. But without waiting for an answer or receiving none, they turn against Moses, whom they hold responsible for taking them out of Egypt.[9] They accuse him of having deliberately brought them out to die in the wilderness. They claim, altogether falsely, that they had told him to leave them alone so that they might serve Egypt. In the crowning touch, they utter the credo of slavish souls: slavery before death.

Moses answers calmly, urging them to have faith in the Lord:

> And Moses said unto the people: "*Fear not ('al-tira'u), stand still (hithyatsevu),* and *see (ure'u)* the salvation of the Lord, which He will work for you today; for whereas you have *seen (re'ithem)* the Egyptians today, you shall *see (lir'otham)* them again no more forever. The *Lord* will fight for you, and you, you shall *keep still* (that is, "quiet"; *tacharishun*)." (14:13–14; emphasis added)

Moses's response reveals his growing stature and courage and his growing faith in the Lord, both the result of his experience of the Lord's doings (and his own) during the plagues and the night of Exodus. He shows no fear and tries to encourage the people with a faith-filled prophecy of what they are about to witness: you will *see* the Lord's salvation, thanks to which the Egyptians you *see* today you will never *see* again, forever.[10]

But looked at more closely, Moses's speech is problematic. In response to the credo of slavish cowardice, Moses utters the credo of passive piety: keep quiet, do nothing, and put your trust in God. To his surprise (but, I hope, not the reader's), the Lord takes issue with Moses's principle. Instead He proposes the principle of hopeful action:

> And the Lord said unto Moses: "Why do *you* cry out to Me? *Speak* unto the Children of Israel, that *they go forward.* And *you,* lift up your rod, and stretch out your hand over the sea, and divide it; and the Children of Israel shall go into the midst of the sea on dry ground. And I, behold, I will strengthen (*mechazzeq*) the hearts of the Egyptians, and they shall go in after them; and *I will gain glory* through Pharaoh, and through all his host, through his chariots, and through his horsemen. *And the Egyptians shall know that I am the Lord,* [only] *when*

I have gotten glory through Pharaoh, through his chariots, and through his horsemen." (14:15–18; emphasis added)

Objecting to the idea, "Let God take care of it," the Lord treats Moses as if he belonged to the mob crying out: he treats Moses's principle—"keep quiet, stay put, and place your trust in the Lord"—as, finally, indistinguishable from the slavish principle, "keep quiet, stay put, and place your trust in Pharaoh." Both principles ignore the possibility and necessity of human agency. The proper attitude is neither fear and despair nor hope for a miracle but, rather, *act in hope*.[11] The Lord will help (only) those who help themselves.

Let's look carefully at the positive parts of God's reply. You, Moses, must lead the people, and they must act. You must tell them, "Go forward. Advance. Walk—yes, exactly, into the water!"[12] There is more: you, Moses, must not only speak to them, but you yourself must act: you must lift up your rod (both the rallying insignia of leadership and a summons to divine assistance); you must stretch out your hand (the force of agency); you must divide the sea! Once you do that, the Children of Israel, who (bravely) have just entered the water, will go into the midst of the waters on dry land. That, Moses, is what you and the people must do. The rest will be up to Me: I will embolden the Egyptians, encouraging them to pursue the fleeing Israelites. But—not specified how—I will gain great glory by defeating Pharaoh and his Egyptian chariots, also thereby punishing them for mistreating my people. And when I have gotten glory by defeating Pharaoh, his chariots, and his horsemen, "the *Egyptians* shall *know* that *I am the Lord*" (14:18). And—we infer—once the Egyptians finally know it, so too will the Israelites.

Victory at Sea

Moses has received his instructions. The Lord arranges things so that he might carry them out. The pillar of cloud moves from a position in front of the Israelites to a position behind them, to shield them from the sight of their pursuers. As night descends, while still clouding the view of the Egyptians and preventing their approach, the pillar lights up the path of the Israelites going forward, as they get ready to enter the waters. It is time for Moses—and the Lord—to act:

> And Moses stretched out his hand over the sea; and the Lord led the sea with a strong east wind (*ruach*) all night, and He made the sea dry land, and the waters were split apart. And the Children of Israel went into the midst of the sea upon the dry ground; and the waters were a wall to them, on their right and on their left. And the Egyptians pursued and came after them, all Pharaoh's horses, his chariots, and his horsemen, into the midst of the sea. (14:21–23)

Familiarity with this famous scene should not make readers complacent about what we have just seen. Along with the Israelites beside the shore, and in the light cast by the pillar, we see Moses in action, stretching his hand and rod over the sea at nightfall. We then see—as what looks like the result of Moses's deed—a strong east wind that lasts all night, splitting the sea and opening a dry path between the built-up walls of water on either side. We see the Children of Israel courageously enter the sea on the dry land, no doubt relieved to have been given this route of possible escape; they brave the massive walls of water suspended on either side, which could come crashing down on them at any moment. Although the Lord does most of the heavy lifting, both Moses and the people do themselves credit. They embody the principle of dignified humanity: they act in hope.

The splitting of the Sea of Reeds is described in language and imagery that recall the creation story of Genesis 1. There, starting in darkness with a watery chaos (*tohu vavohu*), the *ruach* ("breath" or "spirit") of God hovered over the face of the waters; light was created and day was separated from night, and the waters were divided, above from below, to open a space for dry land to appear. The original coming-into-being of the world, through acts of separation, is re-evoked in this symbolic rebirth of the nation of Israel, passing through the waters from slavery under Pharaoh to freedom in relation to God.

Seeing their prey escaping on a path through the waters, the Egyptians come after them, once again intending to prevent "birth" in Israel. They fall eagerly into the Lord's trap:

> And it came to pass in the *morning* watch, that the Lord looked out over the host of the Egyptians through the pillar of fire and cloud, and He panicked the host of the Egyptians. And He took off the wheels of their chariots and drove them heavily; so that Egypt [singular] said: "Let us flee from the face of Israel; for *the Lord fights for them against Egypt*." (14:24–25; emphasis added)

As daylight returns, the Egyptians find themselves in the midst of the sea floor, metaphorically already in deep water. They start to panic, perhaps at the sight of the pillar of cloud and fire. Robert Alter explains what happened next: "As the water begins to seep back and before it becomes a flood that will engulf the Egyptians, it turns the dry ground into muck. The chariot wheels rapidly become stuck in the mud ("He . . . drove them heavily") and break off from the axles."[13] The Egyptians try to retreat, but it is of no use. In their one and only speech in the whole episode—and the last word we readers will ever hear from them—all the Egyptians, speaking as one ("Egypt"), at long last acknowledge the superiority of the Lord: "The Lord fights for them against Egypt."[14] God's oft-repeated purpose—that the Egyptians shall know *Y-H-V-H*—has finally been achieved. It is time for them to disappear:

> And the Lord said unto Moses: "Stretch out your hand over the sea, that the waters may come back over the Egyptians, over their chariots, and over their horsemen." And Moses stretched out his hand over the sea, and the sea returned to its strength when the morning appeared; and the Egyptians fled against it; and the Lord shook the Egyptians into the midst of the sea. And the waters returned, and covered the chariots, and the horsemen, even all the host of Pharaoh that went in after them into the sea; there remained not so much as one of them. But the Children of Israel walked upon dry

land in the midst of the sea; and the waters were a wall to
them on their right and on their left. (14:26–29)

"And there was evening and there was morning": a new day has dawned.
On command, with the people watching him, Moses again stretches out
his hand, this time to cause the waters to return. The flooding waters
cover the Egyptians. All are drowned; not one survives. Judgment is literally executed against all those who pursued the Lord's firstborn,
seeking to re-enslave them. And poetic justice is rendered against the
nation that sought to drown Israel's (literal) firstborn.

That Egypt comes to a chaotic and watery end is fitting in a still
deeper way. The Egyptians deserve to meet their end in the water not
only because they drowned the babies but also for their technocratic and
political practices. As we noted in the discussion of the plagues (Chapter Six), what looks in Egypt like technical mastery over nature turns
out to be a forerunner of chaos: here, the crocodile tries to conquer the sea
on wheels and gains his watery end. To rule by might and not by right is to
be the author of a mayhem that is finally self-engulfing. Egypt is finished
off in the formless chaos that is the true meaning of who she was.

The saga of Israel in Egypt is finally over. The Egyptians know the
Lord. The so-called gods of the Egyptians, including Pharaoh, are
smashed. The Egyptians are punished. The Egyptians are destroyed. In
the Torah, the Egyptians will never be heard from again.[15] But we have
yet to disclose the final purpose and meaning of the story: its effect on
the Children of Israel:

> Thus the Lord saved (*vayyosha'*) Israel that day out of the hand
> of Egypt; and Israel *saw* Egypt dead upon the seashore. And
> Israel *saw* the great work (literally, "the great *hand*") that the
> Lord did upon Egypt, and the people *feared-revered-felt awe*
> (*yare'*) [before] the Lord; and they *trusted* (*vayya'aminu*) in the
> Lord, and in Moses His servant. (14:30–31; emphasis added)

The story of the Sea of Reeds ends with this conclusion: "Thus the Lord
saved[16] Israel that day out of the hand of the Egyptians." Whereas the

entire story to this point had spoken of the *Children* of Israel, the conclusion speaks for the first time of *Israel*—a singularity, a collective, mature (not "children") and unified, a nation today and tomorrow—which exists as such only thanks to the Lord's salvation. Through this providential rebirthing process, the nation of Israel comes into being here.

But that is not what Israel sees or knows. What Israel sees, quite literally, are dead bodies, Egyptian corpses, washed up and littering the seashore. What Israel sees is how the Lord handled the Egyptians. As a result, it for the first time fears-reveres-feels awe before the Lord. The awe-fear-reverence that God's speech at the burning bush elicited from Moses, the sight of Egypt's dead by the water's edge elicits from Israel.[17]

The Israelites are not only awed by and frightened of the Lord. In addition, we are told, they trust in—have faith or belief in—the Lord and in His servant Moses. Why? Not only because of the Lord's demonstrated power but also because both He and Moses told them the truth, made good on their promises, and delivered them from their oppressors against all expectations. Moses spoke truly when he told them that God would save them and that the Egyptians they saw today they will never see again. Moses has acted fearlessly, never faltering, taking decisive and effective action with his outstretched arm and rod. For the first time ever (if only for the time being), the people are explicitly said to have placed their trust not only in the Lord but also in Moses, His servant: for the moment at least, they do not conflate Moses and God but see them in their proper relationship. For these reasons especially, the Lord's victory appears to be complete—again, for now.

We have yet to consider these events' effect on the people's courage, a major issue both in the lead-up to this episode and in the people's slavish response to their predicament. As the Israelites faced what they feared was their annihilation, the Lord fought for Israel in broad daylight and before their eyes, granting them a military victory that both was and was not theirs: they did their part, but victory belonged to the Lord, fighting for Israel. As a result, the Israelites may have learned several things relevant to all future battles: their need for courage, Moses's reliability, and the awesome superintending power and solicitude of the

Lord Who fights and cares for them. The crushing defeat and punishment of their former slave masters may have increased the conviction in Israel that a just God is on their side, Whom they should regard with awe and reverence and in Whom (and in Whose servant) they should trust, not just now but also in the future. But they are unlikely to reach these conclusions on their own, much less sustain them when evidence of the recent victory is no longer before their eyes. The sequel is intended to address this defect and to supply what is missing.

The Song of the Sea

The battle is over. Egypt is dead. The bodies of its champions litter the shore. Annihilation has been avoided. Victory is the Lord's—and ours. The time is ripe for celebration. But Moses makes sure that the celebration is turned to good purpose. He leads the Israelites in song:

> Then sang (*yashir;* [singular; imperfect]) Moses and the Children of Israel this song (*shira*) unto the Lord, and they said saying: "I will sing unto *Y-H-V-H*, for He triumphed, yes triumphed (*ga'oh ga'ah*)."[18] (15:1)

Why now a song? And why this one? What, after all, is song?

Song is humankind's venerable way of expressing—but also forming, directing, and educating—emotion. It bespeaks the heart; it lifts the soul; it shapes the sentiments. It provides a vehicle for lasting communal memory, especially of heroes and their deeds. "Sing, muse, the wrath of Peleus's son Achilles," begins the West's first and greatest epic, which celebrates and preserves forever the glory of the best of the Achaeans while also earning immortal fame for Homer himself. Song and heroism are twins—they are among the human race's "firstborn" offspring. In the Bible's first, and only previous, song, Cain's descendant Lamech, playing a poor-man's Homer to his own poor-man's Achilles, sang out his glory before his two wives, boasting of his own deeds, which he considered mightier than God's.[19] The deeds of man are as mortal as the doers; only in song have they any chance of living on. The world will little note nor long remember what they did here unless someone sings well about it.

But song not only preserves past deeds: it interprets them for us and teaches us what they mean. Such is the intention and genius of the Song at the Sea. Just now the people *saw* the Egyptian dead. They *saw* the work of the Lord's mighty hand. But what does it all mean, and what will it mean in the future when these sights are no longer available? Seizing the moment ("*Then*"), Moses takes advantage of the people's new trust in him, as the Lord's servant, to interpret what they have seen and put its lessons to future use. He provides memorable—and memorizable—words that will enable Israel to recall and share publicly the interpreted memory of this spectacular event long after the spectacle has vanished. The Song of the Sea is, like the Gettysburg Address (or perhaps better, "The Battle Hymn of the Republic"), Moses's attempt to teach the people the meaning of the war and inspire them for the great tasks remaining before them.

The text, it is true, does not say that Moses wrote the Song of the Sea. But I have never doubted his authorship. A multitude does not compose. And this multitude would have been incapable of anything as remarkable as this song. Only Moses knew the prophetic messages in the song, especially Israel's coming to the Lord's holy mountain. Only his great and prophetic soul could offer up—instantly and spontaneously—such astonishing poetry. Perhaps, as with Homer, the muse was singing through him, but if so she served Moses's rhetorical and pedagogical purposes perfectly. The text's disjunctive "sang Moses and the Children of Israel" suggests to me the distinction between author and chorus, even as it proclaims that they sang together—precisely what Moses would have wanted them to do. The verb "sang," *shir,* is in the singular.[20]

In pagan odes of triumph, Cassuto points out, "The glory of the victory is ascribed to the conquering king, but here there is not a single word of praise or glory given to Moses."[21] Astonishingly, Moses writes himself out of the song. It is from start to finish a song of praise to, an ode of triumph for, and a hymn of glory about the Lord. Through this song the Lord achieves one of His stated goals: His great glory. Lifted up in song, He gets it from Moses and His people.

The song is divided into three strophes (2–6, 7–11, 12–16),[22] preceded by a one-verse statement of purpose, looking backward, and followed by a two-verse epilogue, looking forward. We will consider only some of the highlights.

> I will sing unto *Y-H-V-H*, for He triumphed, yes, triumphed (*ga'oh ga'ah*); the horse and his rider He has hurled into the sea.
>
> My strength and my song [or "power"; *zimrah*] is *Yah*,[23] and He is become my salvation; this is my God (*'eli*), and I will glorify Him; my father's God (*'elohe 'avi*), and I will exalt Him.
> *Y-H-V-H* is a man of war (*'ish milchamah*; "warrior"), *Y-H-V-H* is His name.
> Pharaoh's chariots and his host He pitched into the sea, and his chosen captains are sunk in the Reed Sea.
> The deeps cover them—they went down into the depths like a stone.
> Your right hand, *Y-H-V-H*, glorious in power, Your right hand, *Y-H-V-H*, smashes the enemy. (15:1–6)

The song opens with its purpose—a song for *Y-H-V-H*—and its reason: because He has triumphed (surging up like the waters) and has pitched the Egyptian host into the sea. The battle is over; *Y-H-V-H* has won a decisive victory. Instead of singing about our relief, we will sing of His glory. In stating its overall thesis, the song exalts the Lord's name, while Pharaoh's is not mentioned. Moses's—or if you prefer, the poet's—first move is to hold up to view the invisible God, victor over the host now very visibly dead upon the shore.

The first strophe fills in this synoptic view, as the words both express and shape the Israelites' feelings. *Y-H-V-H* is our savior; he is clearly our God and the God of our fathers; we now know Him and therefore exalt Him as a "man of war," a "hero" who has earned in our eyes His glorious Name, *Y-H-V-H*. The terrified Israelites, only recently fearing annihilation, sing themselves into exhilaration by celebrating their champion in battle. They cast a vaunting look at the enemy: Pharaoh's chariots and his host are cast into the sea, the sea covers them over, they sink like a stone. The conclusion: *Y-H-V-H's* glorious power—"Your right hand"—smashes the enemy.

The second strophe reinforces the general conclusion of the first by reviewing some of the details of the completed contest:

> And in Your great mounting up, You throw down those rising up against You; You send forth Your wrath, it consumes them as stubble.
> And with the blast of Your nostrils the waters were piled up—the floods stood upright as a heap; the deeps were congealed in the heart of the sea.
> The enemy said: "I will pursue, I will overtake, I will divide the spoil; my lust shall be satisfied upon them; I will draw my sword, my hand shall destroy them."
> You did blow with Your wind, the sea covered them; they sank as lead in the mighty waters.
> Who is like unto You, *Y-H-V-H,* among the gods? Who is like unto You, glorious in holiness, awesome in praises, doing wonders? (15:7–11)

The strophe begins with *Y-H-V-H's* general ability to destroy His enemies, then moves to a poetic description of the splitting of the Reed Sea, in which the Lord's power ("the blast from His nostrils," or the east wind) brings the sea itself to heel.[24] The enemy is then concretely brought to life and given lines to express its malevolent intentions against Israel— invented lines the people never heard them say. (In the story of the encounter before the sea, the Egyptians never say anything at all.) But, again thanks to *Y-H-V-H's* wind and its mastery over the sea, the enemy sank as lead, never to be heard from again.

It is in its famous last verse that the people speak the monumental discovery, put first in the form of two rhetorical questions: "Who is like You among the gods, *Y-H-V-H*?" "Who is like You, glorious in holiness (*ne'dar baqqodesh*), awesome in praises, doing wonders?" Not only does *Y-H-V-H* have no peers among the gods that other people worship, but he also cannot even be counted in the same category: *Y-H-V-H* is altogether beyond "god-ness," beyond what the rest of the world understands as a "god." He is glorious precisely in His holiness; that is, in His separateness or apartness (*qodesh*, holiness: "set aside and apart").[25] *Y-H-V-H* is a singularity, doing awe-inspiring wonders that elicit our awe-filled praises.

The third strophe moves from the present to the future, and especially to the desirable effect the current victory over mighty Egypt will have on other nations, all of them potential enemies:

> You stretched out Your right hand—the earth swallowed them.
> You in Your love have led the people that You have redeemed;
>> You have guided them in Your strength to Your holy
>> habitation.
> The peoples have heard, they tremble; pangs have taken hold on
>> the inhabitants of Philistia.
> Then were the chiefs of Edom affrighted; the mighty men of
>> Moab, trembling takes hold upon them; all the inhabitants of
>> Canaan are melted away.
> Terror and dread falls upon them; by the greatness of Your arm
>> they are as still as a stone; till Your people pass over, *Y-H-V-H,*
>> till the people You made Yours pass over. (15:12–16)

After revisiting the effects of *Y-H-V-H's* mighty right hand, the strophe speaks of His love for His people and, in a single verse, leaps to the ultimate goal of the present deliverance: Israel shall dwell in the Promised Land and attend the Lord at His holy sanctuary—a goal to be attained through the Lord's guidance and strength.

To get there, however, other potential enemies must be defeated or neutralized. In its most triumphalist mood, the song imagines how the present victory strikes terror and dread in all the nations of the region: Philistia, Edom, Moab, Canaan. Conflating the present victory with imagined future ones, the song sees these possible future enemies made "still as a stone," while *Y-H-V-H's* adopted people again pass over safely, not through the Reed Sea but through hostile lands, to *Y-H-V-H's* holy habitation.

That distant goal is beautifully envisioned in the epilogue:

> You will bring them in, and plant them in the mountain of Your
> inheritance, the place, Y-H-V-H, which You have made for
> Your abode, the sanctuary (*miqqedash*), Y-H-V-H, that Your
> hands have firmly established.
> Y-H-V-H shall reign for ever and ever. (15:17–18)

At the end of this triumphal ode, celebrating Y-H-V-H as a man of war, the Israelites sing with hope of a future age of peace and tranquility in which they shall be securely planted on the Lord's holy mountain, the site of His sanctuary, and the kingdom of the Lord will be established on earth.

Though it expresses joy and exhilaration, the song is through and through an expression also of awe and gratitude—awe before, and gratitude for, the Lord's power, but also at and for His love and care for them, now and in the future. Absent awe and gratitude—and the encounter with truthful promises and beneficent care—the world would be only about force and power, winners and losers. The song is thus a hymn of triumph in more than a military sense. It teaches singers and hearers (us readers) alike that the defeat of Egypt is not only just punishment for "crimes" but also a triumph over a worldview that holds, in the end, that nothing matters but power.

The Accomplishments of the Song

What, then, has the song accomplished, beyond giving voice to the people's relief and exaltation? What purposes does it serve? First, as already noted, it provides verbal memory of an event whose traces will soon be invisible, and in danger therefore of being forgotten. Second, in commemorating the event, the song also teaches the people—and the reader—the event's meaning and future significance. Third, it unites the Israelites as a people: their first collective act is singing as one a song that, in both content and performance, shows that and why they are a people, all equally looking up to the Lord. Fourth, it inspirits these timorous souls for the next battle. The song inspires the people to believe that their future enemies are already afraid of them and their Lord. And it gives them an easily repeatable mantra—"Who is like you, *Y-H-V-H,* among the gods?"—with which to face them. The people sing themselves courageous, not just by rhythm and movement but also by inspiring words—words, I would say, expressly crafted for this purpose. True, their new confidence is based solely on the Lord's power, not on their own, but most people become more courageous in battle if they feel that God is on their side. Fifth, but in a way first, the song deliberately turns the people toward the Lord, to their future relationship to Him, and to His plans for them. They see that the Lord is not just another so-called god, and they see something of the meaning of His so-called name, "He Will Be." They mainly sing of Him as a "man of war" and return often to His powerful right hand, but they also speak of His love, His care, and His holiness. Even though it sings mainly of war, the song enables the people to envision a future of peace and tranquility unlike anything they have known. It quells their fears and feeds their hopes. It offers them a transcendent purpose, which becomes the object of their national aspiration: to serve the Lord on His holy mountain.

In singing of all these things, the people become (for now) better than they ordinarily are. They performatively manifest, here and now, the possibility of a communal order different from that of Egypt or any other place, an order made possible by looking up to and revering the Lord Who delivered them—an order reflected in their vision that they might come to serve Him and follow in His edifying ways, ultimately imitating His own holiness (*qedushah*).

But wait. I may have overdone it. I have let myself get carried away by the song, feeling its power, losing myself in its exuberance. Caught up in its triumphalist spirit, in sympathy with the need of ex-slaves to have Mighty Power on their (otherwise losing) side, and aware that only a military victory could make them fear-revere the Lord, I have ignored the human costs of any military victory, no matter how necessary or justified.

Coming down from that high, I must quickly acknowledge that there are dangers in this song, as in any song of triumph. There is the ugly spectacle of dancing on the graves of your enemies.[26] There is the dangerous unleashing of unruly passions and pride: despite humility before the awesome Lord, one can get drunk on the belief that He fights always on our side. There is danger even in thinking of the Lord only as a man-of-war—even if that view of Him is the one now most needed. And there is danger in singing itself: singing evokes the passions and often tries to direct them, but it may not be able to do so. Apollo brings measure and clarity, but Dionysus lurks with ecstasy and exuberance. The sequel shows that these are not idle concerns.

Miriam and the Dancing Women: Apollo or Dionysus?

The last words at the Sea of Reeds, themselves the last words on Israel in Egypt, give us a long-missing picture of the Israelite women, and of one woman in particular. Presented in only two verses, the picture is nonetheless pregnant with meaning:

> And Miriam the prophetess (*nevi'ah*), sister of Aaron, took the timbrel in her hand, and all the women went out after her with timbrels and with dances (*mecholoth*). And Miriam sang out unto them:
>
> > "Sing you to the Lord, for He has triumphed, yes triumphed (*ga'oh ga'ah*),
> > Horse and his rider He has hurled into the sea."
> > (15:20–21)

Out of nowhere, with no introduction, Miriam appears and for the first time by name. (The meaning of her name is ambiguous: either "bitter waters" [from *maror*, "bitter" and *yam*, "sea"] or "rebellion" [from "*marah*, "contentious" or "disobedient"].) We expect, therefore, to learn who she really is. She is introduced as a prophetess and as Aaron's sister, but we have met her before, at the start of Moses's Egyptian story. As Moses's unnamed sister, she had stationed herself by the Nile to see what would happen to him; she played a leading part in his rescue and his adoption by Pharaoh's daughter. Now, appearing at the end of Moses's Egyptian story, again by the waters, she is anything but stationary; she leads the women in celebrating the defeat of those who would have drowned (and later killed) him.

Miriam is called a prophetess—she is the Bible's first of three (followed by Deborah and Huldah)—because, as Alter surmises, "singing and dancing are an ecstatic activity, and one of the established meanings of the Hebrew term for 'prophet' is an ecstatic who typically employed dance and musical instruments to induce the prophetic frenzy."[27] Her designation as Aaron's, rather than as Moses's, sister has been explained by the ancient practice (called fratriarchy) in which a woman is identified in relation to her oldest brother. But in the present context, it may also mean that she is closer in spirit to Aaron than to Moses—and therefore also closer to the people, half of whom she leads in dance. Whereas Moses holds God's rod in his hand (a symbol of rule and authority), Miriam in her first named appearance—the one that reveals who she is—takes in her hand a timbrel or tambourine (symbol of release and abandon). With *all* the women following after her, she leads them in rhythm and dance (*mecholoth*). The women celebrate differently from the men. The question is their connection to the song of Moses.

In search of an answer, we start with some thoughts about dance,[28] which one might call voiceless singing with the whole body. In dance, the body is turned into a kinesthetic instrument of praise and joy, giving somatic expression to feelings beyond words. A manifestation of life and vitality, not just of mind, dancing expresses liberation and release from both ordered life and mental activity. With each dancing body moving synchronously with the beat, groups of dancers feel united, body and soul, all hearts beating—and not only figuratively—as one. Such a unified throng may, as here, celebrate a victory in battle; they can also seek ritually to merge with divine powers that they feel are already inspiring them.

If we imagine the scene by the sea, what sort of dancing do we see? Is it orderly, modest, and decorous; ecstatic, wild, and sexual; or something in between? We should resist the temptation of thinking that this throng of newly liberated Hebrew women will behave as if they were already living under the demanding teachings of the Torah or that they will practice the dances of Egyptian sophisticates. Rather, we should imagine that they dance as did (and do) peoples whose ways are less adulterated and constrained by the accretions of civilization.

The Hebrew word for dancing (*mecholoth*) comes from the word *chul*, a primitive root meaning, "to twist or swirl, circularly," and hence, derivatively, "to dance" (and also "to writhe in pain, especially from giving birth"). As I picture them, the women, wordlessly swirling, have cast self-restraint to the side; liberated from their recent terrors, they joyously give themselves over to the beat, body and soul, losing themselves in each other's motions. They are en route to a numinous experience, sensing and feeling and giving expression to the invisible divinity's great power, with which they are, as it were, seeking to unite. Should the spirit really move them, we might even see something like the frenzied and trancelike dances of the Maenads, the ecstatically whirling followers of Dionysus, with a strong sexual element, both expressing and provoking arousal.[29] An ecstatic activity seeking the holy is always at risk of becoming profane.[30]

Miriam, like prophets and priests, has stirred up the irrational and ecstatic passions, which she intends to give direction by turning them toward the Lord. Perhaps aware that things might be getting out of hand, in the midst of dancing she suddenly breaks out into song; she commands the women to praise the Lord in speech as she repeats verbatim the start of Moses's Song of the Sea.[31] She tries to redirect the ecstatic energy she has unleashed by reminding the dancers of the greatness of the Lord, by adding speech to their motion, and by getting them to sing parts of the Song of the Sea, perhaps as a chorus in counterpoint to the men.

What was the result? Did the women sing? The text lapses into silence. We are left in the dark. But a patient and careful reader may yet get an answer. The next time we hear of dancing—in its only other mention in the Torah—will be at the orgy around the golden calf (32:19), where Aaron, Miriam's brother, had "let the people loose." The dancing that Miriam led might represent the innocent version of which the orgiastic dancing around the golden calf may be the perversion. But the danger of the latter may be contained in the former. Dancing, as such, is pregnant with diverse offspring.[32]

Dancing, even more than singing, is an ambiguous exuberance of soul. Like joy, it is a great gift that elevates the spirit. But it is also dangerous to be released from one's right mind, to be outside of oneself, to merge with others in boundless energy. It may be that Miriam deliberately mobilized the wild spirit in order to give it direction (later, Aaron with the golden calf tries the same)—perhaps this was a cunning move of leadership or a risky gamble. Not being a philosophical treatise, the text does not discuss this subject directly. But by leaving the situation unclear and its conclusion unknown, it invites us to think about the wilder, Dionysiac passions in human life and the need both to give them expression and to hold them under rule—and the difficulty we all face in doing this successfully.[33]

However this may be, I do have a suggestion why this story is given the last word in the saga of Israel's Egyptian experience. Women get the last scene and the last words in the story of Israel in Egypt, just as women had the first scene and the first words, at the very beginning, where five of them defied Pharaoh's orders against life and birth. An astute student of mine has suggested that the dancing of the women is meant to reassert the supremacy of the principle of life against the largely masculine, battle-glorying singing of the men. The men, fixated on the dead Egyptian host, celebrate the Lord as a god of war and of battles; the women, she suggests, may be celebrating the rebirth, through the waters, of the Israelite nation. Even if they are not doing it self-consciously, they are emblematic of that vital regenerative element, lost from view in the male version of the event that both sexes have just witnessed.[34]

In the light of these insights, I should qualify my earlier suggestion that Moses's song interpreted fully the meaning of the event at the Reed Sea, providing a way for the people to remember what would soon fade from view. So caught up in its power and beauty, and so thrilled with the outcome of the battle, I did not pause to consider whether the Song of the Sea was entirely accurate in the meaning it chose to present. The distinctive activity of the women—who throughout the story of Egypt are the patrons and defenders of life—suggests that the Song of the Sea, glorious though it is, left out something vitally important. To the song of death-dealing victory in war must be added the dance of life and love in peace.

Looking Back, Looking Ahead

The story of Egypt is over. Looking back over the entire adventure, we may note considerable progress. Moses seems to have come into his own. He acts with less hesitancy, more confidence, unflinching courage, and greater trust in the Lord—yet also greater independence. No longer worried about his ability to speak, he composes exquisite poetry and gets the people to sing with him. He has earned their trust; he has put it to effective use, both in leaving Egypt and at the Sea of Reeds. When he first left the palace to look upon his brethren, he managed to kill one Egyptian oppressor and could not resolve a dispute between two fighting Hebrews. By the end—with massive assistance from above—he has killed off all of Egypt and united all the Israelites in song.

The people too have made progress. Having begun by crying out from their passivity to no one in particular, they conclude with growing agency and increased knowledge of and reverence for the Lord. On Exodus night, acting on their own behalf, they courageously marked their doors with the blood of an animal sacred to the Egyptians. At the Sea of Reeds, facing the full force of Egypt, they bravely entered the sea between two looming walls of water, trusting to Moses's promise of divine assistance. Having witnessed his courage and effective deeds, they have gone from blaming him for their increased burdens to trusting him in word and deed. The concluding episode with Miriam and the women completes the brother-brother-sister team of leaders and integrates the women into the emerging feeling of peoplehood.

Last but not least, Egypt, the oppressor nation and foil for Israel, is finished, acknowledging the Lord as it sinks into the sea.

Finally out of Egypt and with Egypt finally out of the picture, the Children of Israel must now head into the wilderness en route to the Promised Land. Given their nation-building accomplishments and given what the people have seen and sung at the Sea of Reeds, one might think that the worst was behind them and that the national way forward would be smooth. Alas, the people's courage, confidence, trust, and reverence are all short-lived. Necessity rears its head. The needs of life override pious remembrance and gratitude. Hymns of triumph cannot feed the hungry.

Part Two
From the Mountain:
Covenant and Law

Exodus 15–23

The Murmurings of Necessity

Having happily left wet and fertile Egypt and escaped through the waters of the Sea of Reeds, the Children of Israel now enter the dry and desolate wilderness (*midbar*). There they will remain for forty years, gestating a new way of life that will be delivered only when they enter the Promised Land.[1] The wilderness, an anti-Egyptian setting for acquiring an anti-Egyptian way of life, contains some land good for pasturage or driving cattle but is largely an arid and uninhabited no-man's land. In this barren place, the Israelites, wandering about, will be formed as a people before they enter the Promised Land, settle down for the first time, practice agriculture (the life of Cain, the life of Egypt), perfect tools, establish land ownership, and experience the inequalities that follow. Ancient Israel—alone among the earth's nations, then or since—becomes a people before they have a land and before they have an economy.

But people cannot live by God alone.[2] Survival requires attention to the necessities of life. Even though they are not yet in their own land, the Israelites must nevertheless address three basic needs of any people: (1) sustenance (food and water), (2) defense against external attack, and (3) provision of internal peace and order. Faced with these basic needs, they may begin to learn the correlative virtues of, respectively,

(1) moderation, (2) courage, and (3) justice. Fittingly, the first stories in the wilderness narrative—the murmurings about sustenance (15:22–17:7; treated in this chapter), the battle with Amalek (17:8–16; see Chapter Ten), and Jethro's visit (18:1–27; see Chapter Eleven)—address precisely these essential requirements of peoplehood. Putting sustenance first, the wilderness narrative begins with three episodes concerning basic necessities of life that loom especially large in the desert: first water, then food, then water again.

These episodes also shed light on several enduring questions of political founding and perpetuation, questions that appear here with special urgency because the polity is being formed from abased ex-slaves with no prior experience of decent political life.[3] First, the episodes are explicitly described as *tests* or *trials*: tests of trust and obedience (of the people, by the Lord) and tests of care and providence (of Moses/Aaron and the Lord, by the people). We meet for the first time some issues that face any new human community and will persistently confound God's attempt to embody His Way in His chosen people: the continuous testing of trustworthiness, the constant risks of ignoring the rules and doing your own thing, and the importance of moderation.

Second, these episodes provide a first opportunity to see how people and their leaders function on their own, in their newly independent state, under conditions of "anarchy"—that is, in the absence of any established social order or rules of conduct for everyday life. In Egypt, we saw strict despotism and slavery; we now get a look at lawlessness.[4]

Third, the Lord's responses to the people's complaints—especially His provision of manna—not only meet their needs and test their trust and obedience. As we will see, they also convey a fundamental—and anti-Egyptian—teaching about the relation between human need and the hospitality of the world: sufficiency, rather than scarcity or excess.

Finally, these episodes—again, especially the provision of manna—raise crucial questions about the relation between economics and politics and what it might mean for Israel that it begins its communal life without having to provide for itself.

With these matters in mind, we turn next to the three episodes. Afterward, we will revisit these themes and collect what we have learned about the people, Moses, and God.

Bitter Waters

From the Sea of Reeds, Moses led the people out[5] into the wilderness of Shur, on a route that he undertook apparently on his own. Newcomers to the desert, the Israelites are ill prepared for what they will find—and not find. For three days they encounter no water. They arrive thirsty at Marah (the name means "bitterness"; its location is today unknown). But they get restless when they discover that "they could not drink water from Marah, for it was bitter" (15:23).[6] For the first of many times, the people start to grumble:

> And the people murmured against Moses, saying, "What shall we drink?" And he cried (*vayyits'aq*) unto the Lord; and the Lord showed him a [particular] tree, and he [Moses] cast it into the waters, and the waters were made sweet. (15:24–25)

Who can blame the people, going three days without water, for murmuring? How should they know that the God of Battles, a good protector, is also a good provider, able to sustain them in the wilderness? Indeed, they murmur against *Moses* and express their complaint to him. We wonder: Was Moses, who will later go forty days on the mountaintop without eating or drinking, also thirsty? Does he understand the people's needs? No matter. He cries to the Lord on their behalf.

The Lord not only has a medicinal remedy for the bitterness.[7] By *showing* it to Moses, He illustrates the indispensability of divine instruction for meeting the needs of the liberated slaves. He is not just their Liberator and Champion; He is also going to be their Teacher and not only about food and drink. His first teaching follows immediately:

> There He made for them a statute (*choq*) and an ordinance (*mishpat*), and there did He test them; and He said: "If you [singular] will surely hearken (literally, "you will hearkening hearken"; *shamoa' tishma'*) to the voice of the Lord your God, and will do what is right in His eyes, and will give ear to His commandments (*mitsvoth*), and keep all His statutes (*chuqqim*), I will put none of the diseases upon you which

I have put upon the Egyptians; for I am the Lord that heals you." (15:25–26)

The lack of water, we now learn, was a test of their trust in the Lord, Who now instructs them that He can and will save them from threats to their health, just as He now cured the bitter water. But—in what anticipates the keynote of the later covenant at Sinai—He tells them that He will do so only on condition that they heed His commandments and keep His statutes and ordinances.[8]

The episode concludes with a seemingly unrelated fact, which may contain a subtle criticism of Moses's leadership: "And they came to Elim, where there were twelve springs of water and seventy palm trees" (15:27). This time, Moses is not said to have led them. The Israelites wind up not at bitter waters but at a bountiful oasis, and one that, as it were, had their name on it: one spring for each of the twelve tribes, one tree for each of the seventy Children of Israel who first came down to Egypt and from whom this huge multitude sprang.[9] Had Moses not yielded to the people's murmuring, had he not immediately cried out to the Lord, had he instead encouraged them to trust in the Lord and go a little farther, see, implies the text, how well the people's needs would have been met. Deliverance is often at hand if you do not despair and are willing to look for it.[10]

Give Us Meat and Bread

We next look in on the Israelites when they have arrived in the wilderness of Sin, between Elim and Sinai, one month after leaving Egypt. The issue this time is not thirst but hunger; the demand is not for water but for meat and bread, the food of Egypt:

> And the whole congregation of the Children of Israel murmured against Moses and against Aaron in the wilderness; and the Children of Israel said unto them: "Would that we had died by the hand of the Lord in the land of Egypt, when we sat by the flesh pots, when we did eat bread to the full; for you have brought us forth into this wilderness, to kill this whole assembly with hunger." (16:2–3)

Last time they just murmured; now we hear their spoken grievance. Last time their target was Moses; now it is Moses and Aaron. Most revealingly, this time they express longings for Egypt, their old home: they would rather be well-fed slaves than freemen starving to death.[11]

The text invites—almost demands—this question: Should we blame the people for this preference? They seem to convict themselves, out of their own mouths, of having slavish souls—no surprise to readers who remember how long they lived in bondage without even complaining, seemingly content just to have food to eat. Although physically liberated, they seem to still be psychically and morally in bondage. Yet no matter how much we may deplore their stated preference for Egypt, we must acknowledge the legitimacy of their needs. (As we shall see, God seems to agree.) Mind may dream of freedom, but stomach and blood insist on life. And when life is jeopardized by lack of food, all else is unimportant.

Against this view, one may argue that the people are too impatient; perhaps their trust in the Lord is not sufficient—although who could imagine anything edible appearing in the desert? But their behavior highlights a critical issue for any political order, even one founded by the Lord: the permanent restiveness in the human soul regarding the necessities of life, the fear of scarcity, and anxiety about getting enough. If not properly acknowledged and addressed, this anxiety can lead to grabbing all you can, hoarding what you have, and coveting what is your neighbor's. It can even lead to selling yourself into bondage for food— as the people here imagine doing and as the Egyptians did in Joseph's Egypt. It can also lead to rebellion, war, and plunder—ugly methods of gaining subsistence.

As if He had been waiting for such discontent, the Lord intervenes even without being asked, seizing the occasion for another teaching moment:

> Then said the Lord unto Moses: "Behold, I will cause to rain bread from heaven for you; and the people shall go out and gather a day's portion every day, that I may test them ('anassennu), whether they will walk in My Law (My Torah) or not. And it shall come to pass on the sixth day that they

shall prepare that which they bring in, and it shall be twice
as much as they gather daily." (16:4–5)

The Lord promises Moses that He will "rain bread from heaven" for the
people to gather, "a day's portion every day," to tame their hunger, but
He will do so in a manner "that I may test them, whether they will walk
in My law (*Torah*) or not." These remarks leave much to the imagination. For one thing, the nature of the test is not explicit. We suspect that
it will have something to do with the weekly calendar and with gathering and preparing food: on the sixth day (presumably counting from day
one of the manna), the food that they gather and prepare shall be twice
as much as they gather and prepare on the first five days. We will shortly
learn (six days later, and from Moses!) that this double portion is intended to provide for the seventh day, a day called *shabbat,* which is to
be free from gathering.[12] But remarkably, in speaking here to Moses, the
Lord does not mention *"shabbat"* or even "the seventh day." Neither is
there any hint that when this complicated story is complete, there will
be *three* restrictions placed on the gathering of manna: each should
gather only what he and his household need and can eat in a day; there
is to be no overnight storage or waste; and there is to be no gathering on
the seventh day. The point of all this—and the strange way it comes to
light—we will soon consider.

　　After hearing the Lord's promise to rain bread from the heavens,
Moses and Aaron address the people, redirecting their attention away
from themselves and toward God. They inform the people that Y-H-V-H
(not they) brought them out from Egypt; that He had heard their murmurings (which were, in truth, directed against Him, not them); and
that, in response, He means to give them flesh to eat in the evening and,
in the morning, "bread to the full" (16:8). They say nothing about any
limitations or about the double yield of "bread" on day six.

　　Completing their attempt to turn the people toward God, Aaron,
heeding Moses's directive, speaks to the "whole congregation (*'edah*) of
the Children of Israel" and tells them to come before the Lord.[13] In response, the people look out over the wilderness, "and, behold, the *glory
of the Lord (kevod Y-H-V-H)* appeared in the cloud" (16:10; emphasis
added)—perhaps a flash of fire or a "divine light"[14] is seen in the pillar

of cloud that was leading the people. Reassured that the Lord is still with them, the people are now prepared to heed His voice.

The Lord speaks to Moses, making it clear that He regards the people's murmurings as pleas for necessary help, rather than as signs of ungrateful rebellion:

> And the Lord spoke unto Moses, saying: "I have heard the murmurings of the Children of Israel. Speak unto them, saying: 'At dusk you shall eat flesh, and in the morning you shall be filled with bread; and you shall know that I am *Y-H-V-H* your God.'" (16:11–12)

Unlike Moses, the Lord hears the people's murmurings as prayers for His help. Gladly and graciously, He will feed their hunger. But not for nothing: as a result, if not also in exchange, Israel will come to know Him. The Egyptians came to know the Lord by experiencing His true and righteous power, exercised on behalf of Israel; the Israelites will come to know the Lord (also) for His caring and nurturing power, sustaining their lives by acts of grace.

Manna from Heaven

Sure enough, the Lord's word is His bond. His bounty rains from the skies:

> And it came to pass in the evening, that the quails came up and covered the camp; and in the morning there was a layer of dew round about the camp. And when the layer of dew lifted, and behold, upon the face of the wilderness was fine stuff, flaky, fine as the hoarfrost on the ground. And when the Children of Israel saw it, they said to each other, "*Man hu'*, What is it?"—for they knew not (*lo' yade'u*) what it was (*ma-hu'*). (16:13–15)

A massive flock of quail arrived in the evening, completely covering the camp and clearly fulfilling the promise of meat. But, *Man hu?*

What was this that appeared on the ground in the morning as the dew burned off?

Modern scholars, as puzzled as the Israelites but allergic to the idea of miracles, have tried to answer this question. A not implausible suggestion, formulated first by F. S. Bodenheimer, is that it was the sweet secretion of desert aphids that live on tamarisk trees in the region. The aphids exude the excess sugar they obtain from the trees in the form of droplets that, when dried by the desert air, become flaky sweet crystals. But in the present context, the daily appearance of such stuff in the huge quantities needed to feed more than a million people—like the nightly appearance of flocks of quail—is surely meant to be seen as miraculous.[15] On many levels, the people's unsophisticated expression of wonder is more apt—and more praiseworthy—than the scholars' search for scientific explanations. It is the people's first nonrhetorical question, their first utterance that is not a complaint, the first awareness of ignorance, the first sign of a nonslavish spark of curiosity in their souls—a small moment that may be compared to Moses's turning aside in wonder to see why the burning bush was not consumed. Their puzzlement is doubly rewarded: the substance will get its name, *manna,* from their question,[16] and their question, like Moses's, will get an answer that connects them to the divine:

> And Moses said unto them: "It is the bread which the Lord has given you to eat. This is the thing which the Lord has commanded (*tsivvah*): gather you of it every man according to his eating, an *'omer* a head; according to the number of your persons should you take it, every man for them that are in his tent." And the Children of Israel did so, and some gathered more, some less. And when they did measure it with an *'omer,* he that gathered much had no extra, and he that gathered little had no lack; and they took each man according to his eating. (16:15–18)

Moses's answer to the people's question both explains—the flaky stuff is bread, a gift of the Lord—and directs: take only what you need.

Although we readers did not hear it directly from the Lord, Moses here delivers His very first command to the newly freed slaves.[17] And it deals with how they go about satisfying their appetite: satisfy it, but limit yourself to that. Take what you need and what your household needs, but no more. The principle: to each (only) according to his needs. The implicit premise: there is enough for all.

This principle does more than satisfy hunger. It also teaches people to examine their desires. To follow it, you have to know what your needs are. In the absence of scarcity, we are thrown back on ourselves. We have an opportunity to curb our excess wants and to align our desires with our true needs, including those that might be peculiarly ours. We acquire moderation, that wisdom and measure embodied in our trained appetites.

The principle also has an economic and political point (which I will discuss more fully later). By preventing people from collecting more than they need, God precludes the emergence of markets through which some would gain wealth. He also prevents anyone from doing what Joseph and Pharaoh did: storing surplus food and using it to exploit the hungry, even to impose slavery. Having recently been slaves, some of the Israelites could easily have ended up imitating their former masters. Other Israelites would have succumbed to their slavish tendencies and given up freedoms for food security. At least for this "cooling-off" period, in which the people must unlearn their slavishness, God adopts the only workable arrangement to forestall these possibilities: unalterable equality.[18]

In a lovely ambiguity, it appears that the unit of measure recognizes the differences in people's hungers but only to equalize them. Everyone was to gather an ʿomer per person, yet some gathered more and some less—presumably because their actual sizes and needs were different. But since everyone took only what he or she could eat, none were left with excess or deficiency. Thus the size of an ʿomer seems to vary from person to person. For all other peoples, an ʿomer may simply be a mathematical unit of volume, but the biblical ʿomer becomes a unit of satisfaction—a measure of fitness between need and supply—and a unit of human equality.

Moses next adds a second obligation. Perhaps he is faithfully transmitting it on the Lord's behalf. Or perhaps, having grasped the principle, he has intuited the corollaries on his own:

> And Moses said unto them: "Let no man leave of it till the morning." But they hearkened not unto Moses, and some of them left over from it till morning, and it bred worms and rotted; and Moses was wroth with them. (16:19–20)

The target of the new directive seems to be both fear and waste. Some people, fearful that the Lord might not provide on the morrow, save some of their day's portion for the next day. In doing so, they unwittingly begin to embrace the Egyptian practice of storage and hoarding—a practice that Joseph introduced into Egypt and that this directive seeks to have the Israelites unlearn. But their lack of trust leads to waste. Both draw Moses's ire[19] because both show contempt for the Lord and His bounty.

A Day of Ceasing

The third obligation is the most important. On the sixth day there was much more stuff on the ground, and the people understandably took advantage, gathering twice as much manna, two 'omers per head. This behavior provoked the chiefs of the community, which is the first we hear of them: Who are they? The elders?—who come and report it to Moses, why, we do not know. Moses uses the occasion to introduce the idea of the Sabbath:[20]

> And he said unto them: "This is that which the Lord has spoken: Tomorrow is a day of ceasing, a holy sabbath (*shabbath-qodesh*) unto the Lord. What you will bake, bake [today], and what you will boil, boil [today], and whatever is left over leave for yourselves to be kept until morning." And they laid it up until morning, as Moses had charged, and it did not rot, nor were there any worms therein. And Moses [on the next day] said: "Eat that today; for today is a sabbath [*shabbath;* "a ces-

sation time"] unto the Lord; today you shall not find it in the field. Six days you shall gather it; but on the seventh day is the sabbath; in it there shall be none." (16:23–26)

This is the first time the Israelites hear about the sabbath—literally, a "cessation time"—a day of not doing, a holy (that is, a "separated" or "set-apart") day unto the Lord. It will be a prominent element of the Ten Commandments, and it becomes a central idea—perhaps *the* central idea—in the covenant that God and Israel will establish at Sinai, an idea that will be explicitly linked both to the Creation and (later, in Deuteronomy) to the deliverance from Egypt—to the Lord as Creator and to the Lord as Redeemer.* Here, in its original form, what becomes the exalted Holy Sabbath is introduced very modestly: a literal "separated day of cessation," it is but a guide for the people's gathering, preparing, and eating the extra manna that appears on the sixth day.

We should not, however, be taken in by the modesty of these instructions. A little reflection reveals the sabbath's deep implications. In Egypt, the slaves had toiled ceaselessly without respite. Each day would replicate the last and prefigure the next; monotony and inertia flattened the soul. The necessities of life, given the slaves by their masters, had been purchased with their freedom. All around them, Egyptians were engaged in acquiring, gathering, storing, hoarding—building storage cities for Pharaoh. Although "big nature" (the Nile, the sun) was revered, especially for its contribution to fertility and food, so too were the human additions to and technological improvements on what nature produced—beginning with yeast for the bread and boiled sauces for the meat.

Against this background, a regular day of cessation is a revolutionary innovation. It introduces the (anti-Egyptian) idea and practice of a caesura in time, a day of standing down; a day to desist from seeking, gathering, and preparing food; a day in which one may turn one's attention to other things. Against the monotonous regularity of the desert, the double portion of manna on the sixth day and the lack of overnight spoilage into the seventh reveal a philanthropically miraculous presence

*I postpone most of the discussion of the Sabbath until my treatment of the Ten Commandments in Chapter Thirteen.

in the realm of indifferent and mindless nature. The rhythm of human time is reckoned not on the basis of celestial events but on the Lord's rhythmic providence. Most impressively, the prohibition against gathering manna on the seventh day coheres with the fact that there will be none to gather: on the seventh day, the Lord ceases to produce it. Yet He has seen fit to provide in advance for that day. Taken all together, these aspects of the modest sabbath regulation invite people to turn with gratitude to the Lord, as the gracious source of bounty and provider of vital necessities.

Yet not everyone heeded the instruction about cessation:

> And it came to pass on the seventh day, that there went out some of the people to gather, and they found none. And the Lord said unto Moses: "How long refuse you [plural] to keep my commandments (*mitsvoth*) and my laws (*toroth*)? See that the Lord has given you the Sabbath (*hashabbath*); therefore He gives to you (*lakhem*) on the sixth day the bread (*lechem*) of two days. Sit (*shevu*) every man in his place; let no man go out of his place on the seventh day (*hashevi'i*)." So the people ceased (*vayyishbethu*) on the seventh day (*bayom hashevi'i*).[21] (16:27–30)

The habit of acquisition, of seeking and taking more and more, dies hard, and not only among ex-slaves who take nothing good for granted. Some of them went out on the seventh day but returned empty-handed, as there was nothing to gather. Moses had been angry when some untrusting people left manna over to the morning; here, the Lord is annoyed when some greedy people go gathering on the sabbath. Remonstrating with Moses, He speaks for the first time of His commandments and laws—even though none have been enunciated in our hearing—indicating the importance He attaches to the idea of a weekly day of cessation. Building a fence around the injunction against acquiring on the day of ceasing, He commands that everyone stay home in his place: no work, no commerce, a break in the workaday world.

The Lord's intervention is successful: the people cease—from gathering, from preparing, from going out—on the seventh day.

Remembering the Manna

The episode itself is over. There follow a series of notes to the story, most not needing comment: that the house of Israel called the stuff *manna*; that it was like coriander seed, white and sweet, like wafers made with honey; that the Children of Israel ate manna for forty years until they came through the wilderness and entered the land of Canaan; and that an 'omer is a tenth part of an 'efah. But in the midst of these notes, Moses introduces a significant community-forming directive.

Moses reports that the Lord has commanded the people to take an 'omer of manna to keep among them forever—"throughout your generations"—to allow all future Israelites "to see the bread wherewith I fed you in the wilderness, when I brought you out of the land of Egypt." Moses then commands Aaron to put an 'omer of manna into a jar and to place it before the Lord, to be kept throughout the generations. Aaron does as the Lord commanded Moses: "Aaron placed it before the Testimony, to be kept" (16:32–34).

We ignore the puzzling matters of where Aaron placed the jar and what can be meant by "before the Testimony" (or "Witness"; 'eduth) before the Tabernacle is built.[22] We focus only on the remarkable attention to commemoration, once again in the midst of the story. To the obligation to commemorate Passover night—the divine gift of liberation—is added here the obligation to commemorate the manna, the divine gift of sustenance. The Lord both frees and feeds His people, and one should never forget it.

The Torah of Manna

Encouraged by the charge to memorialize the manna, let us lift our heads out of the text to reflect on its meaning and its contributions to the founding of the Israelite nation. The provision of manna and the restrictions attached to its gathering and storage teach several important lessons. The condition of the world is not fundamentally one of scarcity but of plenty, sufficient to meet equally the (unequal) needs of every human being. There is thus no need to hoard against the morrow or toil endlessly, grabbing all you can; there is also no need to regard your neighbor as your rival who may keep you from your livelihood or whose need counts less than yours. Our condition in the world is one of "blessing": things are provided us not because we merit them but because we need them. Accordingly, one may—one should—regularly desist from acquiring and provisioning (*shabbat*) to express trust, appreciation, and especially gratitude for the world's bounty, which one must neither covet beyond need nor allow to spoil. In all these respects, the provision of manna in the wilderness stands as a correction of agricultural Egypt, where land ownership was centralized, inequalities were everywhere, acquisitiveness knew no respite, excesses were hoarded, the multitudes sold themselves into slavery to survive, neighbor fought with neighbor, and one man ruled over all as if he were god—eventually leading his entire people to destruction.

Against the former slaves' despairing belief that bondage is better than starvation and that serving Pharaoh offers the surest guarantee of life, but also against any simple pious reliance that God alone will provide, the Children of Israel are taught that they live in a world that can provide for their needs, but that the Lord helps those who help themselves—or help Him help them. They must work to gather,[23] but what they gather is a gift (later, when they labor, they should remember that what yields itself to their labor is not itself a product of that labor but also a gift). The world is marvelously hospitable to each person's needs, requiring only that this truth be acknowledged in a seventh day of desisting from work. In a world beyond scarcity and grasping, the choice is not freedom versus food and drink, but grateful trust versus foolish pride or ignorant despair.

Beyond these salutary teachings regarding the world's hospitality and proper attitudes toward freedom and necessity, the gift of manna also has political significance. It returns the Israelites to a gathering society, preagricultural and egalitarian, not unlike the bountiful Garden of Eden—before the division of labor, before property, and before the emergence of inequality. The community can thus be founded not out of organic economic growth, with households giving rise to villages and then cities, attaining economic self-sufficiency (Aristotle); not on conquest or plunder by the strong or an act of patricide or fratricide (Machiavelli, and the biblical example of Cain and the Roman example of Romulus); not on a social contract, entered into by fearful individuals who wish to escape from the war-of-all-against-all (Hobbes), who wish to protect private property (Locke) or who ratify a swindle pulled off by the weaker rich against the stronger poor (Rousseau)—but through a covenant based on human dignity, made with the Lord their God by free, equal, and well-provided-for human beings. The manna acknowledges the necessity of meeting necessity, but it does not give economics pride of place in thinking about how to make people orderly and good. Getting human beings out of slavery is easy; getting slavishness—and tyranny—out of human beings is hard. We also note in passing, given that the furnishing of the manna is followed by the war against Amalek, that the Israelites must become soldiers before they become farmers. When they must learn to fight, however, it is to defend something higher than property.

Manna, as the text notes here in advance, sustains the Children of Israel through their forty years of wilderness wandering until they enter the Promised Land—after which they will provide their own livelihood. For forty years, economic matters are set aside so that moral and spiritual ones may come to the fore. In keeping with its central mission (given later at Sinai) to become a kingdom of priests and a holy nation, Israel (to repeat) will be the only nation that becomes a people before inhabiting a land or having to provide for their common subsistence.

Peoplehood Before Economics: Is This Wise?

Is this uniqueness wholly good? Not everyone thinks so. Some argue that the subordination of landedness and political economy to morality and holiness is bad for the Israelites politically, once they have to live among the nations of the earth. Others claim that there are serious political costs of having God provide the people's sustenance. For one thing, they say, the Children of Israel are not being taught enterprise or self-reliance; instead they are learning to remain children. Unlike any genuine political community, this one starts out not having to provide for its basic needs. People do not take care of each other, nor do they really take care of themselves; and when they gather food, they gather only for their own households. A political community is more than the sum of its households, each with its own livelihood, each separately related to

God. And a political community cannot succeed if it cannot provide for its own people and if its people cannot provide for themselves. A relationship with God, wonderful though it be, is not enough to form a political community. It is true that self-support and independence will come later, after higher matters have been dealt with. When they enter the Promised Land, the Israelites will undertake to provide for themselves; the manna is but a temporary expedient, to feed the body in the desert so that the soul might learn moderation and be lifted up to higher purposes. Yet this beginning to their communal life has to affect the politics that ultimately emerges. Will the people be able to govern themselves? They will have a moralized politics that is God-fearing, but will their politics be successful?[24]

These points are well taken, but they may be answered. First, the manna was a temporary expedient, meant to correct for the desert's inhospitality during the year or so until Israel entered the Promised Land. Only later, after the incident with the spies, was the plan changed to forty years of wandering, so that the slavish generation might die out before their children entered the Land. Such temporary provisioning would be no more (but also no less) enfeebling or corrupting than the support parents give college-age children while they are in school.

Second, advocates of self-reliance who deplore the gift of manna must ask themselves what alternatives were available. Plunder of neighboring peoples is one option. Would this have had a better effect on the soul than God's providence?

Third, these practical rejoinders aside, this help comes very early in the process of people formation. At this stage, the most urgent task is to counteract the soul-crushing worldview that the ex-slaves imbibed in Egypt and replace it with the hope-filled worldview that can inform God's new nation. The manna addressed not just the people's hunger but also and especially their slavishness—their despairing urge to trade away their freedom for food, their lack of internal self-command. By contrast, a people that looks on the world with gratitude for plenty, rather than with fear of scarcity, will more readily embrace the higher purposes of freedom. That God should employ their belly's hunger to lift the people's gaze is ingenious and profound.

Fourth, economics is not the first business of politics. The first purposes of politics are to keep enemies at bay, to keep citizens at peace, and to attach people to the community; a people fitted for war and willing to fight to defend the whole community is a people capable of fending for itself. The higher purpose of politics is to safeguard and promote opportunities for a way of life that does justice to humankind's moral, intellectual, and spiritual possibilities. The problems that most need solving are not material but psychic. To put economics first in your soul is to be a slave.

Fifth, decent political life is, of course, imperiled by bad economics, especially, as we saw in Egypt, by massive inequality born partly of scarcity and partly of greed. To survive the lean years, the poor were forced to sell their cattle, their lands, and eventually their freedom. These economic manipulations—partly Joseph's handiwork—greatly increased Pharaoh's despotic power; the consequence was widespread degradation and dehumanization of the people. God's gift of manna prevents such inequality during the critical period of founding. By neutralizing opportunities for unequal acquisition and unequal allocation, He undermines possibilities for oligarchic and despotic rule. No one's need and no one's life are treated as more or less worthy than anyone else's. By feeding each person's needs equally, God's providence prefigures a politics that will respect our radical human equality: each of us a needy creature, each of us equally in the divine image.

Finally, contrary to appearances, the gift of the manna—though it revealed God's care for His people and encouraged their trust in Him—was not intended to teach the people to rely always on God's providence. Its purpose was to sustain them for a time so that they could be free to learn the more important lessons that the Lord wanted to teach them. Some of the people, as in today's welfare state, may have drawn the wrong conclusions from having their needs so effortlessly met; there is a risk that lazy people will learn to wait passively for God to take care of things. But it is a risk that must be taken. Only in this way will the people—equally—be able to survive in the desert while acquiring fundamental moral, political, and spiritual teachings, beginning soon at Sinai.

No Water

The final episode of the murmuring trilogy is again about water, this time not bitter water but none at all:

> And all the congregation of the Children of Israel journeyed from the wilderness of Sin, by their stages, according to the command of the Lord; and they encamped in Rephidim; and there was no water for the people to drink. And the people strove (*vayyarev*) with Moses and said: "Give us water that we may drink." And Moses said unto them:
> "Why do you strive (*riv*) with *me*?
> Why do you *test* (*nasah*) the Lord?" (17:1–2; emphasis added)

Directed now not by Moses but by God, the people arrive at Rephidim, which is, we surmise, an oasis in the desert. But finding the riverbed (wadi) dry, they face the dreaded disaster of all desert wanderers, worse than the lack of food. The situation is dire. No longer content just to murmur, the people rise up in quarrel against Moses as in a legal dispute, claiming their due: You brought us here; now give us the water we need!

Moses defends himself: Why are you disputing with *me*, when it was the Lord Who brought you out? Why have you so little trust in Him that you demand to test His care for you? As Alter observes, "the poetic parallelism [of Moses's reply] becomes a vehicle for expressing the inseparability of Moses's leadership from God's."[25]

Time passes. The people become desperate. Receiving no help from the invisible Lord, they murmur rebelliously against Moses, saying, "Why have you brought us up out of Egypt, to kill me and my children and my cattle with thirst?" (17:3). Moses, at a loss, instead turns to complaining about them to God:

> And Moses cried out (*vayyits'aq*) unto the Lord, saying:
> "What shall I do with this people?
> A little more and they will stone me." (17:4)

Moses is not only exasperated, he is also frightened. Remarkably, however, he shows not a grain of sympathy for the people's plight. To be waterless in the desert is for most people, if not for Moses, a life-and-death matter.[26] But in speaking with God, he does not mention the people's thirst or ask God to supply them water. The gap between leader and led is as wide as it has so far been.

Once again, the Lord responds in majestic and brilliant fashion. He does not enter into the dispute between the people and Moses; He does not address the charges or countercharges. Instead, with one shrewd order, He addresses both the water shortage and the leadership crisis:

> And the Lord said to Moses, "Pass on before the people and take with you some of the elders of Israel, and take in your hand the rod with which you struck the Nile, and go. Look, I will stand before you there on the rock at Horeb, and you shall strike the rock [with your rod], and water shall come out of it, that the people may drink. And thus did Moses do in the sight of the elders of Israel. (17:5–6)

God tells Moses to pass before the furious people, walking presumably in the dry riverbed. Frightened or not, he is to run the gauntlet between the ranks of the mob and brazen it out, with the potent rod in his hand and with the company of the elders as witnesses—perhaps also as buffers between himself and the people. As a sign, the Lord (pillar of cloud?) will hover over the rock at Horeb—the site of the first theophany at the burning bush. In the eyes of the elders, Moses's rod of destructive power turns beneficent: he strikes the rock and lifesaving water pours out of it, flowing into the wadi, which delivers it to the people.

The result is perfect. The crises have passed, the people have their water, and Moses has his authority restored—and his confidence. Everyone believes again, at least for the time being, that the Lord, Sustainer of His people, is (still) with Moses and Israel. We will soon have a chance to see whether this renewed confidence will last.

The story ends with another meaningful act of naming: "And he [who? Moses? God? someone else?] called the name of the place Massah and Meribah—Testing and Striving—because of the striving (*riv*) of the Children of Israel and because they tested (*nasah*) the Lord, saying, 'Is the Lord among us or not?'" (17:7). Unfortunately, the testing and striving will not be confined to these two places. They are perennial problems in any political order, especially under conditions of anarchy.

A Look at the Characters

Looking back over the three episodes, we attempt some generalizations about the participants. The people's restiveness and grumbling increased with each episode, from murmuring against Moses in the first, to murmuring against Moses and Aaron in the second, to disputing with Moses in the third, verging on rebellion—to the point that Moses fears, "Yet a little more and they will stone me." We gain here an important political lesson: the elite (as in Korah's later rebellion) may rebel against authority out of ambition or wounded pride, but the multitude will revolt over sustenance. Especially when hungry and thirsty and with their lives on the line, they will insist on knowing, "Is the Lord among us or not?"

Moses does not quite know what to do with the people's murmurings, in part, perhaps, because he had not expected to have to deal with their everyday needs. This task was not part of the job description when the Lord gave him his mission. In the first episode, about the bitter water at Marah, Moses cried out to the Lord—perhaps prematurely and with less than adequate faith, given that an oasis with twelve springs and seventy palm trees was but a short distance away. In the second episode, at the Wilderness of Sin, the Lord intervenes with the promise of meat and bread even before Moses can say anything, and Moses manages to remind the people that their quarrel is not really with him and Aaron, but with God. In the third episode, about the lack of water at Rephidim, Moses rebukes the people for disputing with him and for testing God but then, almost at his wit's end, complains about them to the Lord. Moses lacks sympathy with the masses' insistence on meeting their bodily needs. On each occasion, the Lord bails him out. But He does not endorse Moses's impatience with the people or with the need to care for daily necessities.

This is neither the first nor the last time that Moses, raised as an aristocrat, shows contempt for the mass of people. To become a worthy leader, he must learn to accept their limitations and their claim to equal humanity. (An earlier instance: recall how Moses at the Sea of Reeds, thinking the people incapable of doing anything, told them to stand still and wait for a miracle, whereas God rebukes him and tells him to lead and to have the people walk forward into the sea.) As he is learning here, being a leader is not just a matter of heroic deeds in times of crisis but also requires attention to the people's day-to-day welfare.

In one important respect, however, Moses shines in these episodes, especially if I am right in my reading of the way he teaches the people the rules regarding manna and the seventh day. From minimal explicit instruction—that God will provide each person "a day's portion every day" and a double portion on the sixth day—Moses catches on to the big picture. He intuits the implied rule against overnight storage; he sees that a seventh day of bounty is implied in the double-portioned sixth; he grasps the idea of a cessation of gathering, tied to the knowledge that the Lord Himself will cease raining manna on day seven. From all this, Moses intuits the importance of setting apart time out of time. He thus helps the Lord prepare the people for His singular teaching at Sinai: God's providence embraces not only His creative power but also His "standing down," His sanctified cessation, through which His creative work is brought to completion.

Unlike Moses, the Lord seems to be almost pleased with the people's murmurings, in that they provide an opportunity to teach them of His providence and care—and perhaps also to teach Moses to respect the people's (reasonable) demands. If the people are to trust in the Lord, He must be ready to answer their needs. This is most clearly seen in the middle episode about food—bread and meat. He does not even wait for Moses to transmit the people's complaint but acts at once to address it. He never remonstrates with the people for their murmurings, only for their failure to keep the rule against gathering on the Sabbath.

But God does not simply yield to the people's demands, nor does He overlook their slavish preference for the goods of the body. He takes advantage of their needs to elevate their gaze and, by means of obedience, to teach them important lessons: not only about His reliable providence and their need to trust in Him but also about the worldview they must come to adopt. This is the silent teaching conveyed in the rules governing collection of the manna.

Finally, we should consider the all-important matter of knowledge of the Lord. Can we say with any confidence that the people are permanently convinced about the Lord's existence? (That, after all, was supposed to be the ultimate goal of providing the quail and the manna.) This knowledge of the Lord is, unfortunately, hard to see. When times are tough, they seem not to know of Him and look only to Moses and Aaron as their leaders. Even though they have gained trust in the Lord and His servant Moses at the Sea of Reeds, that trust is fickle and frail. We know when the Egyptians finally came to know *Y-H-V-H*; we should be alert for the occasion when the Israelites do too.

Knowledge of the Lord is an important question not only for the people but also for us readers. If we are reading this book as an integrated whole, naively and as if for the first time, we are learning little by little Who and What He Is on the basis of what the character called "God" or "the Lord" says and does. We share, in other words, the position of Moses at the burning bush and also of the Lord-ignorant masses: we must watch and wait to see and know—slowly, slowly—that and What He Will Be. Speaking for myself, I am increasingly in awe of the Lord's sagacity, patience, power, grace, truthfulness, and—above all—His philanthropic beneficence.

"Is the Lord Among Us or Not?"

The Battle with Amalek

The murmuring episodes are behind us. In the midst of barren wilderness, water and food have been miraculously provided. Thanks to the Lord, the people of Israel are able to meet the first requirement of nationhood: obtaining the vital necessities of life. In the process, they received valuable instruction regarding the world's hospitality to human need, as well as some beginning guidelines to regulate their appetites and acquisitiveness in the direction of moderation. In addition—again, all thanks to the Lord—a rebellion against Moses's leadership has been avoided. His standing, we suspect, has actually improved. He not only stood up to the angry mob but, with the invisible help of the invisible God, also silently drew water for the people by smiting the rock with his rod.

But while the striving and testing are over, for now, we do not know what the people concluded from all this. Who did they think was responsible for their rescue at Rephidim—God or Moses? And could they distinguish the two in their minds? At the end of the murmuring tales, we were told that the people had been testing the Lord, saying, "Is the Lord among us or not?" But we were not told what they concluded. In the immediate sequel, beginning in the very next verse, the question recurs, this time not only among the people but also for the reader. The context is again a matter of survival. The issue now, however, is not food and drink but self-defense against an enemy bent on their destruction.

The encounter with Amalek is the first international test of the nascent community following their deliverance from Egypt. We expect that it will teach them—and us—something about what Israel may expect from other nations and what it must do to survive among them. Although extremely unwelcome to the Israelites, pedagogically speaking the test could not have come at a better time. So vital are those lessons, I suspect, that if Amalek had not attacked the Israelites, God might have arranged for someone else to do so.[1]

We turn, then, to the battle against Amalek, interested to see how this episode might contribute to forming the newly emerging people of Israel. Will the people have the courage to defend themselves in this first external attack, which threatens their very existence? What new qualities will appear in Moses's leadership and in his relationship with the people and with God? What lessons for the future might the Israelites—and we—draw from this story? Is the Lord among us or not, and if so, how?

Amalek

With the echo of the last verse—"Is the Lord among us or not?"—still hanging in the air, the story begins abruptly, with an attack out of the blue:

> Then came (*vayyavo'*) Amalek, and battled (*nilcham*) with Israel in Rephidim. (17:8)

Who is Amalek? And why did it attack? We are given no reason, so we must speculate.* The Amalekites were a nomadic Edomite tribe living

---

*Beginning with this minimalist statement, the entire account of this episode is highly (and I think deliberately) elliptical, with most important matters left to our imagination and for our speculation. In this respect, the account mirrors our lived experience: Who are these people? Why are they attacking us? What do they want? What shall we do? Is the Lord among us? We readers are given a ringside seat for a battle, but—like the participants—we receive no program notes disclosing the whys

in the desert in the south of Canaan. In that inhospitable place, they would have lived at least partly by plunder, making raids against their neighbors to capture animals for food, humans for slave labor or marriage, and assorted worldly treasure. The huge party of Israel, possessing all three, would be a perfect target.

For our purposes, however, more important than their way of life is their ancestry. Amalek was the grandson of Esau (Gen. 36:12, 16).[2] For more than twenty years, Esau nursed a murderous grudge—a perfectly reasonable one—against his twin brother Jacob, who had cheated him out of their father Isaac's blessing. Upon learning that Jacob was returning to Canaan from Paddan-aram, "Esau came ('*esav ba*')" to meet him with a war party of four hundred men, no doubt to finally exact revenge. When the brothers actually met (the morning after Jacob held his own in the nocturnal wrestling match against the man-angel, earning the name of Israel), Esau at the last minute underwent a miraculous change of heart. He fell on Jacob's neck and, instead of biting him, kissed him (Gen. 33:1–4). But for various reasons, we suspect that the reconciliation was incomplete and temporary. Esau never forgot or forgave, and his injury has not yet been avenged.[3]

Against this background, it seems possible that Amalek—not the long-dead eponymous founder but the people united in his spirit—has come to take revenge. Tribes carry smoldering grudges from generation to generation, waiting for an opportunity to get even. That opportunity comes when Amalek learns that the weakened ex-slaves, headed for Canaan, are in fact the descendants of Jacob/Israel. Like Esau with his returning brother Israel, the Amalekites do not wait for the Israelites to reach the Promised Land. "Amalek came ("*vayyavo' 'amaleq*")" from afar, from Canaan to Rephidim in the Sinai. Amalek came not to plunder, but to battle (the root meaning of the word for battle, *lacham*, means "to consume") "with Israel." This was, by Amalek's choice and action, a national battle: Amalek against Israel.

Cheating ever so slightly against our own rule not to import information that appears only later in the text, we might suggest that Amalek

---

and wherefores of what we are watching (or what they are doing). As in life, we must figure out for ourselves what is happening and why.

had heard—as Jethro in the next chapter will be said to have heard ("And Jethro heard . . . And came Jethro" [*vayyavo' yithro*; same verb]; 18:1 and 18:5)—of Israel's great victory over Egypt at the Sea of Reeds, with the Lord's help. The word is out: Israel has a mighty champion. As Ibn Ezra suggests, other kings heard what God had done and were sorely afraid. But not Amalek. Amalek heard but did not fear, either God or His people. Experienced in living by the sword, the Amalekites thought they could defeat them both. If one adds "no fear of heaven" to a smoldering grudge and an opportunity to satisfy it,[4] one has a perfect picture of what may have been responsible for Amalek's attack.[5]

We need not, of course, attribute any such conscious motive to the Amalekites for this attack to be read in the context of the Esau-Israel story. If the world is so arranged that the iniquities of the fathers are visited upon the children and the children's children—if the world hides old iniquities under rocks, letting them creep out when a time for payback is at hand—Amalek may be the avenging scourge of Esau completely without conscious intention. Such things really do happen: what goes around comes around, God knows how. But these thoughts, like the previous suggestions, are mere speculation.

Putting those speculations aside, what do we really know about Amalek and its motives? The text gives us very little. Amalek came. Amalek fought. Amalek fought with Israel at Rephidim (where it was quietly encamped). In sum, Amalek attacked Israel unprovoked. Perhaps this is enough to explain why the Lord will demand such harsh punishment of Amalek. Perhaps this is why, in the Jewish tradition, Amalek is regarded as the quintessential enemy of the Jewish people. Haman, the one man in the Bible (see the Book of Esther) who will explicitly seek to exterminate them completely, will be an Amalekite.

How will the Israelites respond to this attack? We have no reason to be sanguine. Just a little while ago, God had sent them on a long detour through the desert, fearing that, if faced with war, they would choose to return to Egypt. But since then, He has won a victory for them over Egypt at the Sea of Reeds, after which Moses sang them courageous. What will Moses and the people do now? Will Moses, as he did before the battle of the Reed Sea, tell the people to stand still and let the Lord deliver them? Or will he summon them to action?

Moses Takes Charge, Joshua Takes Command

This time, Moses does not dither or pray for a miracle. Without even seeking God's counsel, he springs immediately into action:

> And Moses said unto Joshua: "Choose for us men (*'anashim*), and go out, fight with Amalek; tomorrow I will stand on the top of the hill with the rod of God (*matteh ha'elohim*) in my hand."
>
> So Joshua did as Moses had said to him, and fought with Amalek; and Moses, Aaron, and Hur went up to the top of the hill. (17:9–10)

In a novel display of independent leadership without divine instruction, Moses for the first time takes the initiative. Although he has no military experience, he acts the part of a great wartime leader. He delegates authority and responsibility to Joshua (not to the elders), making him both military recruiter and general of the troops on the ground. And he assigns himself a presiding or conducting role, equipped with the rod of God, to be exercised on the remote heights well above the battle. Recognizing that he may need help, he does not go alone but designates others to accompany him. From the hilltop, with their help, he will show the people spirit and strength, encouraging them to believe that God is helping them.

So pleased are we to see Moses's executive energy that we do not pause to ask what made it possible. Only a few verses earlier, also at Rephidim, he was at a loss over the people's murmuring, crying out to God, frightened that his people would stone him. Now that he is facing a formidable army actually on the attack, what gives Moses the confidence to act on his own, setting things in motion even before the people had a chance to panic? What, from his point of view, were his options and prospects?

Escape was hardly an option, against a large (mounted?) army on the attack. Given the precedent at the Sea of Reeds, prayer was also contraindicated. Much better to stand and fight, trusting the Lord again for military assistance. Moses's confidence likely rests in the rod of God, which, he tells Joshua, he will take with him to the hill, the better to summon divine power. Previous results with the rod have been most encouraging. At the Sea of Reeds, with Israel's back to the water, God told him to "lift up your rod and stretch your hand over the sea and divide it" (14:16); when Moses stretched his hand over the sea, it was the Lord who—on Moses's cue—split the waters (14:21). More recently, Moses struck the rock in Horeb with the rod, and out came the water. The Lord was present but invisible, and He was not said to do anything. But Moses knows that it was not he but the Lord Who brought the water. After these successes, Moses must believe—or at least hope—that the rod of God can reliably summon God's needed power. Other than that, what hope could he have?

A careful reader will surely pause at the mention of Joshua, who has never before appeared in the text. Just when Moses and the people need a general, the fateful name of Joshua (*Yehoshua*; "God saves") appears out of nowhere, as does the man: Joshua is, quite literally, a godsend. We are not told his ancestry; indeed, Joshua may be said to earn his name by what he does here. At the end of the story, readers may well wonder: Who actually saved the Israelites—God or *Yehoshua*? More radically, as Joshua's name suggests, could these be two ways of saying the same thing? What is the relation between inspired human performance and divine assistance? (We will return to these questions later.)

Moses orders Joshua to choose men for battle, and somehow he does. Given what we had heard and seen of the ex-slaves, we marvel at his success at recruitment. The word here translated "men" is *'anashim*, males rather than human beings (*bene 'adam*), but a word whose root group, *'nsh*, suggests men in their frailty or mortality (*'enosh*, man, from *'anush*, "sick" or "feeble," as in Jer. 30:12)—not men of valor or warriors (*gibborim*) but "mortals." How Joshua could know which men might fight well (and which might not) we are not told, perhaps because such an ability is a great mystery, but more likely because Joshua was following instructions to choose ordinary men, "mortals." His recruits were unknown soldiers who rallied to the cause and acquitted themselves admirably, fighting better than they knew they could—though (to anticipate) the text at the end will tell us that it was *Yehoshua* and his sword (not the men nor Moses or the Lord) that won the day.

In Moses's Hands or God's?

When giving Joshua his orders, Moses, perhaps too old to lead men in battle and certainly having better options for his leadership,[6] says that he will ascend the hill overlooking the plain of battle with "the rod of God in my hand." The next day, when the battle starts, accompanied by Aaron and Hur (another previously unnamed character, whose name's meaning and his ancestry are uncertain[7]), Moses goes up the hill. We well imagine the imposing sight: Moses, standing on high with Aaron and Hur at either side, commands the scene, in full view of the myriad Israelites below. What Moses does up there is stunning:

> And it came to pass that whenever Moses held up his hand [arm; singular], Israel prevailed; and whenever he let down his hand, Amalek prevailed. But [or "And"] Moses's hands became [or "were"] heavy; and they took a stone, and put it under him, and he sat thereon; and Aaron and Hur held up his hands [plural], one on one side, and the other on the other side; so his hands were steady (*'emunah*; "faithful") until the going down of the sun. (17:11–12)

What is Moses actually doing in raising (and lowering) his hands? It is hard to say. But since this is a singular example of Moses's successful leadership, we should think about what made for his success. What do we readers think is going on?[8] One possibility is that Moses is summoning the Lord's direct intervention: by raising his hands, he brings God's power to bear on the battle. Or—a slight variation—Moses may himself be channeling divine power, and it is being passed through him to Joshua and the people. As the people perceive the difference between what happens when Moses's hands are up and when they are down, they will see (as will the reader) that "the Lord *is* among us" and that He is making the decisive difference, just as He did at the Sea of Reeds or with the manna.

Alternatively, Moses may be trying to inspire the people psychologically: when his hands are high, they function like a banner behind which soldiers rally. When the people see Moses's hands and his rod of power and authority raised (as it was at the Sea of Reeds), they *imagine* that he is either drawing down divine power in their direction or exercising some supernatural gift of his own, and they are inspired to fight harder.

There is also, I hasten to add, an attractive third possibility: maybe these are not really separate alternatives.

Consider: Moses plans from the start to go up above the battle, with the rod of God. Let us imagine that he hopes, but does not really know, that raising his hands with the rod will bring divine power to aid the fighters. Yet acting on that hope boosts his own morale when he sees the inspiring effect it has on the morale and fighting power of the people, who of course believe that God, thanks to Moses's rod, is now fighting for them. Question: Is God in this story or not? His name is not mentioned, but does that settle the matter?

How such extraordinary and mutually reinforcing effects happen is, in fact, a great mystery. But I dare to suggest that this is a perfect example of what someone may mean by "divine intervention" or "channeling divine power." Moses gestures with his rod in the direction of the Lord; the sight of his doing so inspires the people: hope and courage "fly" into them, as if from the outside, God knows how. The sight of the people's valor in turn inspires Moses: hope and confidence "fly" into him, also as if from the outside, again God knows how. Might this be an example of "God strengthening Moses's heart" and by that means strengthening also the heart of Joshua and the people? In the end, we may have no need to choose between saying that Moses himself was inspiring the people and saying that he was drawing down or channeling divine power.

Be this as it may, the fate of the battle seems to be quite literally in Moses's hands. Although still strong in spirit, Moses—no youngster— soon becomes tired; his hands become heavy from holding them up so long. The majestic Moses, God's own champion, is—like any mortal— not immune to human weakness. His compatriots, Aaron and Hur, find a large stone to sit him on, and for the rest of the day they prop up his arms, so that "his hands were steady"—literally, "steadiness," "faithfulness"; *'emunah*—until darkness put an end to the fighting.

Moses's fatigue and his need for assistance have suggested to some readers that this episode initiates the demystification of charisma and therefore constitutes a prelude to the coming of law and the embodiment of God's teachings in the *people* of Israel. Because the immanence of God's Way will finally depend on popular fulfillment of the law, not on the special deeds of a charismatic leader, it is important, say these interpreters, to prepare the people for the post-Mosaic era, for the rule of law (under God) in place of the rule of the glorious leader. After the Sea of Reeds and the smiting of the rock, the people may have been tempted to view Moses as himself divine. But they discover in this episode that he is just a human being: he gets tired, just like the rest of us; he needs the assistance of other people and cannot act all-powerfully on his own. Yes, we take some inspiration from him. But we are doing very well down here without him. We have agency; we have spirit; we are taking it to the enemy on our own.[9]

There may be something to this reading, at least for raising the issue of charismatic leadership's place in *this* national founding. But Moses is not yet on his way to the sidelines. He is now and will long remain indispensable to the birth of the nation. For their part, the people are far from feeling him dispensable or regarding him as a mere mortal. On the contrary, his role in this episode will have only increased their regard for him. As we shall see, they will soon come very close to deifying him.

Joshua and His Sword, Moses and His Hands

Despite his fatigue and need for help, the outcome of the battle relied decisively on Moses's leadership. As seen from our ringside seat, its success was, quite literally, in Moses's hands, faithful until the setting of the sun. Yet when the text describes the battle's conclusion, it singles out Joshua—and the sword in *his* hand, not the rod in Moses's—as the victor:

> And Joshua disabled (*vayyachalosh*) Amalek and his people [his army] with the edge of the sword. (17:13)

Joshua fights, not like Pharaoh's army with horse and chariot, but man to man, his sharp-edged sword[10] an extension of his mighty arm. The havoc he wreaks is considerable: Amalek is disabled.[11] Compared with

God's crusade against Egypt at the Sea of Reeds, the battle seems to have passed entirely into human hands.

But not so fast. Although we have treated the last two verses separately, the text has them side by side: "So his [Moses's] hands were steady until the going down of the sun" and "Joshua disabled Amalek . . . with his sword" (17:12–13). The sword was the sword of Joshua, but the hands were the hands of Moses. In Homer's *Iliad*, the heroes' greatest exploits on the battlefield occur only with the infusion of power and inspiration sent by gods. Might Moses's hands be mediating—in one of the ways already discussed—a divine power that enables Joshua to fight like Diomedes?[12]

Israel prevailed. Amalek's unprovoked attack was repelled and its army severely weakened—though not yet defeated. It was an extraordinary victory achieved by most ordinary men, but led by a gifted warrior, Joshua, who—as leader of the troops and master swordsman—is explicitly credited with the success.

How Did Israel Win?

How to understand what happened? How could this motley crew of untested and timorous ex-slaves have managed to hold their ground and repel their attackers? Who or what made the victory possible? The text offers few clues. Unlike in the battle at the Sea of Reeds, God appears to have played no direct role in this victory, and no Amalekite shouts in despair, "*Y-H-V-H* is fighting for them." The Lord's name is not even mentioned until after the battle, when, as we will see, He gives instructions on how it should be remembered.

Whether the Lord plays an *indirect* role in the victory is impossible to say—not least because we do not know what kinds of assistance may be attributable to Him. Who or what is responsible for strengthening the hearts of the disheartened? Who or what is responsible for their inspiration? (What, actually, *is* inspiration?) Who or what is responsible for the "faithfulness" of Moses's arm—or the "faithfulness" of his arm-propping comrades? Who or what is responsible for Joshua's appearance, just when he is needed, and his great success? Can we confidently answer the question, "Is the Lord in our midst or not?"

No, we cannot. The story does not provide an indubitable answer. But that may be its very point, both for the Israelites on the battlefield and for us looking on. In the absence of certainty about the Lord's presence, which way should we incline? Should we choose hope or despair? Do we act as if the Lord is with us, taking courage from this possibility even in the absence of certainty? Or do we act as if we are abandoned, quailing in fear because we lack proof of divine assistance? The story, it seems to me, invites this radical suggestion: one should trust in the Lord's presence, and the trust itself may produce it—nay, may constitute it.[13] In matters of the heart, the Lord is present whenever the heart trusts in Him. Could this be one meaning of the maxim, "The Lord helps those who help themselves"?

Consider, in this light, the conduct of the Israelites in the battle. The text says nothing about the people but focuses entirely on their leaders. Still, had the people lacked courage to accept battle and defend themselves, the story of Israel would have ended here. It seems that, if properly led, the people have hidden virtues that they do not know they have until they are called for. As was said of old, people acquire courage by acting courageously, by not giving in to their fears. To our delight, the Israelites have risen to the occasion. They agreed to fight, risking their lives; under duress they accepted the leadership of Moses and Joshua. What could have made that possible? How does it happen that people find their hidden virtues? What calls them forth?

At the Sea of Reeds, fearful and wishing they were back in Egypt, the Israelites experienced a victory that was none of their own doing (though they did bravely enter the sea between the looming walls of water, leading the Egyptians to their doom). Probably encouraged by that experience and especially by the stirring Song of the Sea, the people this time are less afraid. They do not cry out to God; they do not complain that they have been led here only to be slain by these invaders. The people show no fear; they do not hesitate—in part, perhaps, because Moses acted so quickly and decisively that they had no time to become faint of heart. The existential threat and the leadership of Joshua below and Moses above unify the people, and that unity further reduces their fear. Trusting that the Lord will fight *with* them—but not relying solely on Him—they rise to the challenge. They take courage from Moses's elevated arms and rod, likely thinking he is channeling divine power and assistance. Inspired by their own trust in the Lord's presence among them, they take the battle to the enemy, stay the course, and win. Even if He "did" nothing special to bring about the victory, was not the Lord among them?

The Arrival of the Lord

Only after the battle is over and the enemy is repulsed does the Lord explicitly enter the story. Appearing to endorse the enterprise, He (privately) offers Moses instructions about how it is to be regarded hereafter:

> And the Lord said unto Moses: "Write this for a memorial in the book (*bassefer*), and rehearse it in the ears of Joshua: for I will utterly blot out the remembrance (or "the name"; *zekher*) of Amalek from under heaven." (17:14)

These remarks are puzzling in several respects. What is to be memorialized: the story of the battle, the Lord's promise to blot out the memory of Amalek, or, as I suspect, both together? In what book is the writing to be done: a special book (or inscription) of remembrance written expressly for this purpose or the book we are now reading, the Torah or, perhaps, specifically Deuteronomy (in Hebrew, *Devarim*, "speeches")— the last book of the Torah comprising Moses's complete retelling of Israel's story, including the story of Amalek? If the story is to be written down, what is the need for rehearsing it orally, and specifically to Joshua? And most puzzling of all: How can one reconcile the injunction to remember Amalek with the divine purpose to obliterate the memory— the name—of Amalek from under heaven?[14] Before addressing these questions, we must note some unambiguous facts about God's speech.

The first thing to notice is the emphasis on memory. As with the Passover story, the Lord insists on the sacred obligation of remembering. But unlike the Song of the Sea, which poetically memorializes, interprets, and glorifies the Lord's victory at the Sea of Reeds, the Lord here calls only for an accurate recording of the event and of His plan for the Amalekites. Remarkably, the commemoration is to be made in writing: no one in the Bible has previously spoken of writing, and the verb "to write" (*kathav*) occurs here for the first time. Through the written word, memory can be safeguarded and transmitted limitlessly to future generations—exactly what God here intends. The written record, if it follows closely the account we have just read and analyzed, will pay tribute to the people and their human leaders; it will not be a song of glory for the Lord or, for that matter, anyone. But the important thing the Lord wants remembered is less the Israelite victory than the unprovoked and wicked attack of the Amalekites, the first nation to attack God's people and for no good reason ("Then came Amalek").

The written record of the attack and of God's plan to obliterate Amalek will preserve their memory for the people as a whole. But it will not suffice for their leaders, especially their generals, who need more than the dead letter of the written word. They need the living word, the spoken word, the animated word. It must be passed to them directly, and they must pass it on directly: God spoke it to Moses, Moses is to speak it to Joshua, and Joshua, we infer, will speak it to his successors.

God may be making an additional point by His special reference to Joshua. Joshua arrived on the scene—may we say providentially?—just when needed. Moses, singling him out, deputized Joshua to lead the battle. In summing up the battle, the text speaks only of Joshua's singular success with the sword. Now, as part of His post-battle comments, the Lord affirms Joshua's importance and makes sure Moses will pass the living word, for future reference, into only his ears. The Lord confirms, both for Moses and for us, Joshua's rising importance. The Lord, as it were, anoints Joshua as Moses's successor and seeks to ensure that Joshua believes He will be working with and through him against future enemies, the way He has worked with and through Moses.

Yet there remains a large and puzzling question: Why is the Lord so adamant about obliterating Amalek, and why does He make His intention known? Is Amalek to be obliterated for political and pedagogical reasons or for moral and theological ones? Is Amalek a uniquely guilty or incorrigible nation, punished for its own specific wrongdoing? If so, why does the Lord regard its evil as greater than that of Pharaoh's Egypt? Or is Amalek a paradigm or type, whose fate is a warning to other nations?

One plausible answer is pedagogical. Amalek was the first nation to make war on Israel, but alas, it will not be the last. A major reason for writing down this story and for rehearsing it in the general's ear is to teach young Israel that vigilant and courageous self-defense will be an eternal necessity. God knows that His people—and His Way in the world—will have inveterate enemies. "Giving" this enemy to the people through writing will enable them to remember, in good times and in bad, that they must always worry about their security. Taking encouragement from this surprising first success against Amalek, the Israelites must always be willing and able to resist their enemies, hopeful always of divine assistance and of an equally successful outcome.

A second possibility is political: the Lord intends to make an example of Amalek. The world needs to know what happens to those who threaten the Lord's people. Especially at the start of Israel's career as a nation, a strong message must be sent to all the nations of the world. It will be just as God promised Abraham: "I will bless them that bless you, and him that curses you I will curse" (Gen. 12:3). Hate the Lord and His people, and you will face utter destruction.[15]

But God is not just teaching lessons and giving warnings for the future. The extreme fate He promises Amalek calls for an explanation in terms of justice, a punishment that Amalek has earned not as a "type" but as itself, for an unspeakable "crime." What exactly did Amalek do that would warrant obliteration? Our earlier speculations on the meaning of Amalek's attack provide a plausible explanation.

Amalek comes without provocation to make war on nascent Israel, not to plunder but to destroy. Wittingly or not, it was in effect avenging its founding father Esau and carrying out his unfulfilled pledge to kill Jacob. Moreover, as we suggested, although Amalek had heard of the victory the Lord gave to Israel over Egypt, it showed no fear of God. On the contrary, Amalek attacked, among other reasons, precisely to demonstrate its fearlessness and win a victory also over the God of Israel. Pharaoh had waited to attack the Israelites at the Sea of Reeds until he saw them confused in the land, a sign, he thought, that the Lord was no longer with them. But Amalek, on hearing about the Lord's rescue at the sea, attacks directly.[16] Like Pharaoh before he was "enlightened," the Amalekites behave on the principle, "We know not the Lord—and even if we did, we would not fear-revere Him." Even if the Amalekites were not intentionally doing battle with God, their attack carries, implicitly, that very meaning. Those who intentionally attack the Lord's people are enemies of the Lord Himself; an attack on the people embodying the Lord's Way is ipso facto a direct attack also on Him. The Lord pledges to erase Amalek's name—its posterity—from the face of the earth, just as the Amalekites had hoped to do with His posterity and with Him.[17]

Moses Gets the Last Word

The episode concludes by reporting Moses's response to the Lord's instructions:

> And Moses built an altar, and called the name of it *Y-H-V-H-Nissi* ("The Lord is My Banner"). And he said: "The hand upon the throne of *Yah:* war for *Y-H-V-H* against Amalek from generation to generation." (17:15–16)

Moses hears from the Lord for the first time since the battle began. What he hears confirms his belief that the Lord was with him throughout the fighting. Having also learned of His intentions against Amalek, a grateful Moses—acting on his own—builds an altar, giving thanks for the victory. The altar is the first to be built among the Israelites; it will be not be the last that Moses builds spontaneously, without divine instruction. He names the altar "*Y-H-V-H* is my banner," acknowledging after the fact—and teaching the people—that the Lord was and is his inspiration, as well as the cause for which he was fighting and will continue to fight. Echoing the Lord's last words to him, Moses concludes—in a notoriously obscure passage—by celebrating the Lord's promise to wage war forever against those who hate Him and His people. Moses even imagines the Lord swearing an oath to do so—His "hand upon *Yah's* throne"—on His own seat of glory.[18] At the end of the story, Moses, who led the battle seemingly on his own, affirms for himself and teaches the people that the Lord was—and is—with him and among them. The Lord has once again helped those who, with trust in Him, have helped themselves. He will do so again and again and again.

Moses's last words in this story—"from generation to generation," which is to say, "forever"—invite a further reflection. Like the Israelite people, he has just had a brush with mortality. Death was all around, taking names. Too old to fight, Moses had to give command to a younger man, Joshua. Moses's own arms grew weary; he tired of standing; he needed assistance. The Lord's instruction to write down the story for posterity reminds Moses of his own finitude and the need to take steps for the people's welfare after he goes. To express the idea of "forever" in terms of "from generation to generation" is to bring Moses—and the reader—in mind of the need for transmission and perpetuation. It is perhaps no accident that the very next verses, which begin the new story of Jethro's visit, describe the arrival of Moses's father-in-law, along with Moses's wife and their two sons.[19]

The Leader and the Led

We learn, at the end of the story, what Moses, with God's help, makes of what has happened. He has gained additional insight into the Voice that called and now accompanies him everywhere. But what about the people? What have they learned, and how might this episode affect their relationship with Moses and his with them? The text, in its silence on this most important subject, once again invites our reflections.

From the point of view of the people, it might not have mattered what Moses was actually doing—or thought he was doing—during the battle. All they could see was the great figure of Moses high above them on the hill, his arms at first raised or not, as the battle ebbed and flowed, but then held aloft steadily and faithfully until victory. From the people's point of view, it looked as if he were responsible for their victory. If so, what should they think of him? Certainly, he seemed larger and more awesome than before. Might they be tempted to regard Moses as divine? Will his increased stature increase their regard for him and their willingness to follow? Do they now have an answer to the question asked long ago by the brawling Israelite: "Who made you a man ruler and judge over us?" (2:14).[20]

And what about Moses himself? Will he have a greater sense of his own power and standing? After such an event, most human leaders—

even great ones—would be sorely tempted to exult in their own personal triumph. But not Moses. The text gives us wonderful evidence to the contrary: his hands got tired (he may even have been discouraged), and he needed help from Aaron and Hur. Moses the great is also an ordinary human being, vulnerable in body, perhaps vulnerable also in spirit. He accepts help from his fellows, paradoxically, thereby increasing his own authority.[21] But lest there be any doubt, the Lord's speech to Moses after the battle settles the question, not only in readers' minds but also in Moses's. It is God's speech that leads him to the proper interpretation of what happened: that he has been fighting under the Lord's banner, and for the Lord. Moses, at least for now, is not confused about his relationship to either God or the people. By building the altar and by naming it as he does, he makes sure that the people know the difference between him and God.

The relation between the leader and the led is of vital importance in any political founding or regime. We should therefore (re-)articulate the problem, at least in outline. The leader must be high enough above the people that they will look up to and follow him, but not so far above them that they mistake him for a god (or that he so mistakes himself). He must not be so close to the people that he has to flatter and indulge them to maintain his position or that they feel that he is easily removable and replaceable by someone else no worse than he. For now, the relationship between Moses and the people seems to be in decent order: his standing in their eyes has risen, but not to the point that they regard him as God; he has growing authority but knows—and teaches the people—Whom he serves. But complications lie ahead, especially as the community is still anarchic—literally, lawless—and personal charisma may not be enough to maintain order. This is the question on the table when Jethro comes to visit, the subject of the next chapter.

Is The Lord Among Us? Inspiring the Leader and the Led

Throughout this chapter, we have frequently returned to the relationship between human agency and divine assistance, a subject at the heart of the story about Amalek. We have not only left behind stories celebrating the direct deeds of the Lord; we are left to wonder, for the first time in Exodus, whether the Lord is at work in human affairs—and, if so, how. As I have suggested, this is a recurring question, both in the text and in life. It strikes us most powerfully in times of great crisis, when human agency is pushed to its limits. To take but one notorious example: in the Book of Esther (the Bible's last story about Israel's confrontation with Amalek), Haman, an Amalekite, sought to destroy all the Jews. The people are saved through Mordechai's prudence and Esther's astonishing courage, and the name of God does not appear at all. Readers are left to wonder, there as in life, whether God was (is) present and active. To do so fruitfully, however, requires that we avoid having too narrow or too childish a view of the divine.

Though God is its leading character throughout, the Bible is not a work of theology: a *logos* about *theos*. As we saw with Moses's attempt to get theological knowledge, the Bible is not keen on speaking about Who or What God *is:* we come to know Him instead through His deeds and speeches. But having grown up in the wake of centuries of talk about God, we readers—believers and atheists alike—almost certainly come to the text with certain (largely unexamined) notions about who or what God is and how He works in the world—if He indeed exists and acts in our lives. (Even atheists must have an idea of the God in Whom they do not believe.) Most readers unavoidably first "conceive" God and His powers by extrapolating from human agency: we imagine Him as a very, very powerful agent—like Superman—Who can enter worldly affairs at will and move them as He wishes, by means that we can imagine only by augmenting our own human powers. We say, of course, that the Lord works in mysterious ways and that He is Himself beyond comprehension. But uninstructed, we tend to think of Him as possessing "superhuman human agency"—like ours, but vastly greater. How else could He act? There are, indeed, many places in the text where God and His doings are described in more or less these terms—in slaying the firstborn, in splitting the Sea of Reeds, in sending the quail and the manna—where we, as readers, should take the account at face value.

But the Bible speaks also of other ways in which God acts in the world. The Lord talks to various people and, here, especially to Moses; Moses has a Voice in his head, Who he knows is God. Later, God will speak to and through His prophets, making known His intentions, sometimes by direct speech and sometimes in a vision—and the prophets will all know Who is talking.[22] And very shortly, God will appear before all Israel (and all readers) as a lawgiver, pronouncing His commandments to His people and the world.

But most of the time, in the text as in life, God is silent. Yet even when He is silent, we are encouraged to think He is present, albeit in ways that differ from when He "plays Superman." People sense the presence of powers not of their making that touch them in unexpected ways. When they (we) need it, help comes from outside, God knows how. We feel the presence of mysterious forces in the world, forces that we engage and that "find us." We know "in-*spira*-tion," and we see its effects on others: we do not inspire ourselves.

If we readers are willing to part with our childish views of God as Superman, we might discover—in life, as in the story of the battle against Amalek—the other ways in which the divine is acting in our world. As I have suggested several times in this chapter, we may find God acting in the world even when He is not mentioned, when we see people acting as they do *because* they assume a relationship with God that will enable them to succeed.[23] God is present and active in human trust in Him. It is this—even more than learning to defend themselves against lethal enemies—that a free people needs to discover, and as soon as possible.

Jethro's Visit

Justice and the Need for Law

The battle with Amalek is over, on its way to becoming a national memory. The Israelites have shown their willingness and ability to defend themselves against outside enemies bent on their destruction, and they have been summoned to remember that they must be prepared to do so again and again. For the time being, the necessities of life are also taken care of, thanks to providential gifts of manna, quail, and water. What remains is the largest question confronting any stable human community: internal self-government. We readers are eager to learn whether and how these ex-slaves, formerly ruled by the despotic Pharaoh, will manage their own internal affairs, especially in the absence of law and established authority. Can these people be governed, and can they govern themselves? If not, what might enable them to do so? The saga's next episode, Jethro's visit, explicitly examines these issues.

Why Is This Story *Here?*

The story of Jethro's visit to Moses and the Israelites, the only subject of Exodus 18, covers several revealing incidents: Moses's reunion with his father-in-law and with his wife and children, the private conversation between Moses and Jethro about what occurred in Egypt and since, Jethro's initiation of sacrifices in the company of Aaron and the elders, and, on the second day, a review of Moses's judicial activities and practices, and Jethro's advice concerning them. We will examine each in turn, but we should first consider why this story occurs where it does in the narrative. Why does Jethro arrive just *now* and with Moses's family? How does this event relate to what comes before and after?

There is, in fact, much scholarly discussion about the timing and placement of the Jethro story, for it appears to be an anachronistic interpolation. The last chapter (Ex. 17) had the Israelites at Rephidim, and the next chapter has them arriving from Rephidim into the wilderness of Sinai and encamping before the mountain of God. But here, we are told, Jethro came with his entourage unto Moses "into the wilderness where he was [already] encamped, *at the mountain of God*" (18:5; emphasis added), a location that the people do not reach until the next chapter (19:2).[1]

This apparent anachronism should not bother us. Many times the biblical narrative departs from strict chronology to present matters in their logical or pedagogical order—following up suggestive verbal or thematic links, or introducing certain important questions that demand attention here and now, regardless of when the story actually took place.[2] A concern for effective truth, not literal chronology, governs the timing of storytelling.

There are many thematic and pedagogical reasons why the story of Jethro's visit occurs where it does. As noted in the last chapter, Moses has intimations of mortality, and his last words were "from generation to generation": it is fitting, therefore, for his own family's generations to arrive, as if summoned by his thoughts: "And came Jethro, Moses's father-in-law, with his sons and his wife unto Moses" (18:5). Also at the end of the last chapter, Moses, uninstructed, builds an altar: who should then show up but someone who knows what to do at altars: "Jethro, the priest of Midian" (18:1). It will be Jethro who initiates the sacrifices in the camp. His visit also continues the institution of delegated authority (from and by Moses) begun in the last episode: there, war was turned over to Joshua; here the sacrifices will be put in the hand of Aaron and the elders, and at Jethro's prompting, a cadre of judges will be appointed to handle less important judicial questions.

The story also carries implications for foreign and domestic politics. The Children of Israel should know that the rest of the world is not entirely against them; not all nations are like Amalek. Some will bless Israel as well as curse her. In the person of Jethro, the Israelites (and we) meet a nation that bears witness to the power of the God of Israel and is willing to be respectful and friendly. Just as the foreign priest Melchizedek arrives out of nowhere, right after the battle, to instruct Abraham about the theological meaning of his victory in the War of the Kings (Gen. 14:18–20), so Jethro arrives to instruct Moses and Israel about the theological meaning of the events they have just lived through. Here is a foreign priest, one who knows *'elohim* but not *Y-H-V-H*, coming to give his blessing to the interpretation that Moses has just given to these events ("*Y-H-V-H* is my banner") and who before all the Israelites attests to the truth of the story and the power of *Y-H-V-H*.[3]

But the chief function of Jethro's visit—for us readers no less than for Moses and the Israelites—is to shed light on questions of the internal ordering of communal life in peacetime. The necessities of everyday life having been provided for, and an external enemy having been vanquished, the arrival of a priest/ruler of Midian not only establishes a respectful and peaceful relation with a neighboring people. It also, and more importantly, bears witness to crucial internal matters regarding the arrangements of everyday life for this—or any other—nascent people: their relation to the divine, their conduct toward one another, the right way to govern, the need for law, the division of functions and the delegation of authority, and the relation between the leader and the led. Jethro's visit will touch on both sacrificing and judging—man's relation to God, and man's relation to man—as well as on Moses's relation to the people, all crucial matters for the overarching question of how to govern God's people.

Jethro's visit not only highlights these matters but also reveals—to Moses and especially to the reader—the inadequacies of the way they have been handled to this point. As we will see, Jethro proposes certain judicial reforms, which are largely administrative. But the limitations of Jethro's teachings show us that someone else must be Moses's teacher regarding the *content* of the law and its relation to the divine.[4] In a word, Jethro's visit shows us why what happens at Sinai is indispensable: we must move from anarchy and seat-of-the pants justice to given law, and from precarious charismatic leadership to authorized hierarchy. What's a small chronological discrepancy—if it really is a discrepancy[5]—compared with making clear to Moses and readers the need for the Law?

Family Matters—or Does It?

Jethro initiates the story:

> Now Jethro, the *priest* (*kohen*) of Midian, Moses's *father-in-law*, *heard* all that God (*'elohim*) had done for Moses, and for Israel His people, how *Y-H-V-H* had brought Israel out of Egypt. And Jethro, Moses's *father-in-law*, took Zipporah, Moses's *wife*, after he had sent her away (*shillucheyha*), and her two *sons*; of whom the name of the one was Gershom; for he said: "I have been a stranger in a strange land"; and the name of the other was Eliezer (*My-God-is-[my]-help*): "for the God of my father was my *help* (*'ezer*), and delivered *me* (*vayyatsi-leni*) from the sword of Pharaoh." And came Jethro, Moses's *father-in-law*, with his [Moses's] sons and his wife unto Moses into the wilderness where he was encamped, at the mountain of God. (18:1–5; emphasis added)

The story begins with rumor: Jethro heard something (the Hebrew text begins: "And he heard, Jethro . . ."; *vayyishma'*). He had in fact heard two things: what God (*'elohim*) had done for Moses and for His people and that *Y-H-V-H* had brought Israel out of Egypt. Just as *Y-H-V-H* had wished, word of His triumph over Egypt has spread beyond the immediate participants to the larger world.

We can imagine Jethro's surprise. He marries off his daughter to an "Egyptian" stranger; his son-in-law, going off after many years to see his "brethren" in Egypt, sends the woman and her children back to him and then disappears for a long time. But it turns out that this son-in-law of his has friends in very high places and is now back in the neighborhood. Suitably impressed but not content with hearsay, Jethro goes to see for himself.

Jethro is identified both as the priest[6] of Midian and as Moses's father-in-law, and he will function in this story in both capacities. But for now, and through much of the story, the familial function looms larger.[7] Very likely thinking that the danger of Egyptian retaliation has passed (or perhaps concerned about its effect on Moses), Jethro takes along Moses's wife—whom Moses had sent away, presumably after the "Bridegroom of Blood" episode at the inn (4:24–26)—and his two sons, to reunite them with Moses. The emphasis is on the sons. We hear again the origin of the name of Gershom, and we hear for the first (and only) time the name of Moses's second son Eliezer,[8] very likely the boy Zipporah circumcised at the inn. When the group comes to meet Moses in the Sinai wilderness, the order of mention is reversed: "And came Jethro[9] [first] with Moses's sons, and [then] with his wife, unto Moses in the wilderness" (18:5). Jethro may have been thinking "from generation to generation."

Upon arriving in the vicinity, Jethro sends Moses a message:

> "I your father-in-law Jethro am coming unto you, and your wife, and her two sons with her." And Moses went out to meet his father-in-law, and bowed down and kissed him; and they asked each other of their welfare (*shalom:* "peace" or "wholeness"); and they came into the tent. (18:6–7)

Jethro sends a message about the upcoming full family reunion. Moses, following well-established customs of respect and honor, goes out to the edge of the camp to meet his venerable father-in-law, bows down before him, and kisses him. Shockingly, the text is completely silent on Moses's greeting of his wife and children: no kisses, no words, nothing. As if to cover up this silence, some interpreters (including the careful Cassuto) suggest that Moses bowed to his father-in-law "as an expression of gratitude for his having brought him his wife and sons."[10] But there is no evidence in the text that Moses even acknowledges their presence. Indeed, we *never* hear Moses say anything to his wife or his sons, and we will never again hear of his sons.* For Moses, Jethro is the attraction.[11] The

---

*In a word, according to the plain sense of the text, Moses is not much of a family man. But this is not treated as a shortcoming. The point seems rather to be that

two men ceremonially exchange the socially obligatory inquiries about each other's welfare, then quickly retire into the tent where the important business can take place in private, one-on-one, leader to leader.

Moses and *Eros*

We pause to take note of the kiss that Moses gives to Jethro. Kissing is uncommon in the Bible, and this is the last kiss in the Torah. The most famous kisses in Genesis both involve Jacob/Israel: first, Jacob gives the beautiful Rachel a clearly erotic kiss at the well on their first meeting (Gen. 29:11; the only time in the Torah a man kisses a woman); second, Esau kisses his brother Jacob on their reunion (Gen. 33:4; a last-second, miraculous transformation of Esau's fratricidal hatred). The only two kisses in Exodus both involve Moses. The first was brotherly, when Aaron kisses him (4:27) on their reunion on the mountain of God, their first meeting since baby Moses was taken into Pharaoh's house. Here, with Jethro, Moses is not the kissed, but the—clearly non-erotic—kisser: the recipient is not his wife but her father. Reflection on these differences sheds light on Moses's soul.

Note the chiastic structure (in each half and overall): Jacob kisses Rachel; Esau kisses Jacob; Aaron kisses Moses; Moses kisses Jethro. Moses, a man of *thumos,* is not a man of *eros*—or, rather, his *eros* is not for woman. Jacob fell in love with Rachel at first sight at the well and then did a heroic deed to water her flock in defiance of the local shepherds. Moses rescued seven unmarried girls (Jethro's daughters) from bullying shepherds at the well, motivated only by righteous indignation and fellow feeling. From the women, he did not even get an invitation home.[12]

But it would be a mistake to say that Moses is without *eros.* Beginning with the name that Moses gives his younger son Eliezer, "My God is my help (*'ezer*)," the text hints in several places that Moses's *eros* is for God. The Bible's only previous use of the word *'ezer* refers to God's

---

the leader *as leader* has no family. The people *as a people* are his children; he is rather—like George Washington—the father of his *nation.* Yet, paradoxically, the absence of an ordinary family life may widen the gap between Moses and the ordinary people he is leading: he may seem to them almost self-sufficient and godlike; correlatively, they may be difficult for him to understand and empathize with.

creation of woman: "Not good (*lo' tov*) is it for the man to be alone: I will make him a help (*'ezer*) meet ("opposite"; *kenegdo*)" (Gen. 2:18).[13] God's help for man is woman; Moses's help for himself is God. Going forward, we will be watching for more overt signs of Moses's longings for God.

Beyond what they may reveal about his soul, Moses's two kisses have political implications. Both herald episodes in which Moses accepts partnerships and divides his authority, but the partnerships, though needed, are risky. Aaron was accepted only because Moses had rebelled against the mission. Jethro will urge Moses to depend on people who, like Aaron, are closer to the people than he is. In a crisis, these intermediates may come to do the people's bidding, in rebellion against Moses and the Lord. The kiss of closeness betokens the risks of closeness.

Jethro Testifies for the Lord

In the tent, Moses has much to tell, and he is especially eager to tell it to Jethro, in whose priestly company Moses first entertained religious thoughts and from whose house he went searching in the wilderness and came to this very mountain of God:

> And Moses told his father-in-law all that the Lord (*Y-H-V-H*) had done unto Pharaoh and to the Egyptians for *Israel's* sake,[14] all the travails that had come upon them by the way, and how the Lord *delivered* (*vayyatsilem*) them. And Jethro rejoiced for all the good that the Lord had done to Israel, in that He had *delivered* (*hitsil*) them out of the hand of the Egyptians. And Jethro said: "Blessed be the Lord (*barukh Y-H-V-H*), who has *delivered* (*hitsil*) you [plural] out of the hand of the Egyptians, and out of the hand of Pharaoh; who has *delivered* (*hitsil*) the people from under the hand of the Egyptians. *Now I know that the Lord is greater than all gods*; yea, for in this thing that they schemed [or "dealt proudly; *zadu*] against them."[15] (18:8–11; emphasis added)

Moses tells Jethro the whole story, in all its details. It is unclear whether the travails he reports are only those that Israel suffered in Egypt or (as

I think more likely) whether they include those suffered since (at the Sea of Reeds, in the wilderness, and with Amalek), and therefore whether the Lord's deliverance of which Moses speaks refers only to the extraction from Egypt or also to the divine assistance received in the other travails. For Jethro, it is the Lord's deliverance out of the hand of Egypt that twice draws singular attention: he rejoices at this news, and he blesses the Lord for this miraculous liberation (referring, there, twice to His "deliverance").

As we have said from the beginning of the Lord's contest with Egypt, victory over Egypt and the extraction of His people from Egypt's midst provide the best evidence for His existence and supremacy. We are therefore not surprised when Jethro concludes: "Now I *know* that the Lord is greater than *all gods*" (18:11; emphasis added). Jethro, the priest of Midian who introduced Moses to the divine, pronounces his alien blessing on the God of Israel. He completes his handoff of his daughter by returning her to a different god, the God of her husband, *Y-H-V-H*, the God of Israel.

One should not underestimate the importance of Jethro's testimony. Pharaoh and his drowning legions had good existential reasons for acknowledging the superior power of the Lord. But the testimony of an unaffected neutral party, and especially of a priest of the neighboring peoples, will carry much more weight—for Moses, for the Israelites, and for the wider world. Moreover, whereas Pharaoh and his men were impressed by the Lord's military might, Jethro emphasizes His care for His people: He rescued them from the world's greatest civilization, from the gods of Egypt, including Pharaoh. This unbiased patron of the divine attests to the superiority of the Lord.[16]

Jethro Feeds the Altar

What follows is the natural consequence of Jethro's conclusion—sacrifice:

> And Jethro, *Moses's father-in-law,* took a burnt-offering (*'olah*) and sacrifices (*zevachim*) for God (or "gods"; *'elohim*); and *Aaron came,* and all the *elders* of Israel, to eat bread *with*

> *Moses's father-in-law* before God (or "gods"; *'elohim*). (18:12;
> emphasis added)

Still identified as Moses's father-in-law and acting on his own initiative, Jethro brings a burnt offering and sacrifices to the divine. This is the first act of sacrifice in Israel since the liberation from Egypt, and it is begun by an outsider. Although Moses had sought permission for the Israelites to go out of Egypt so they could sacrifice to the Lord their God, there has been no word to suggest that they did so, even as part of the victory celebration at the Sea of Reeds. Moses built an altar (very likely with sacrifice in mind) after the battle with Amalek, but there is no report that he used it. Jethro, not Moses, brings sacrifice to Israel.

Yet there is something puzzling in the report of his sacrifices.[17] Jethro brings them not unto *Y-H-V-H* but unto *'elohim*. How should we understand this substitution? Perhaps Jethro respectfully refrains from invoking *Y-H-V-H* in public because he is not himself an Israelite. Perhaps, as some interpreters suggest, he is impressed with that aspect of God (denoted by "*'elohim*") that is associated with supreme natural power and that also punishes people who abuse strangers (people who have no "fear of heaven," *yere' 'elohim*). But I favor a third possibility, one that exploits the fact that *'elohim*, being grammatically plural, could be rendered as "gods," as well as God. Despite his stated recognition of the superiority of *Y-H-V-H*, Jethro seems to be offering a sacrifice to the divine more generally; that is, to his own god or gods, as well as to Israel's God.[18] His stunning testimony notwithstanding, he is not—or not yet—a convert; very likely, he regards the Lord as but one among the gods: a god of Israel, not the God of the whole. Could this be why, at the end of Jethro's visit, Moses will send him away?

There is another curious fact about the report of the sacrifice. In their only mention in this chapter, we are told that Aaron and all the elders of Israel come to join in the shared holy meal "with Moses's father-in-law" (not "with Jethro") before *'elohim*, before God or gods. A link is being established between Aaron and the elders and the practice of sacrifice. But where is Moses? Is he present? If so, he is present as an absence. His name is not mentioned, a fact underscored by the gratuitous repetition of "Moses's father-in-law" as a way of describing Jethro. Interpreters rush in to fill this silence: says the scrupulously careful Ibn Ezra, though Moses is not mentioned, he was naturally present, as the meeting took place in his tent. "With Moses's father-in-law before God," says Cassuto (treating the report of Jethro's visit as out of chronological order), means "at the entrance to the Tent of Meeting, which had already been erected before Jethro's visit."[19]

I not only find these explanations forced; I see no need even to look for them. Whether Moses is present at the sacrifices or not, the text has pointedly omitted him from the list of relevant attendees. It emphasizes its failure to say that Aaron and the elders came to eat bread with Jethro *and Moses* by telling us twice that they came to eat "with Moses's father-in-law" (instead of "with Jethro"). Why? To hint at the imminent division of function and of personal interest between Aaron and Moses. Aaron natively belongs to the sacerdotal realm of ritual observance; Moses natively belongs to the political realm of law and governance. Sacrifices and other "religious" functions that mediate between man and God—activities that express popular god-seeking aspirations and ecstatic passions—will later become the province of Aaron and his descendants, the *kohanim,* not of Moses.[20] By contrast, Moses, who has his own way of communicating with God, will bring and teach the law that will regulate and restrain human passions; he will govern the people.

So where is Moses? The next sentence tells us: he is serving as a judge and resolving peoples' disputes. Judging, not sacrificing, is Moses's métier.

Judge or Philosopher-King?

Jethro's visit, we are told, continues into the next day, which is a literary vehicle for signaling a change of subject. The focus shifts from the relations between man and God, in the ecstatic realm of worship and sacrifices, to the other dimension of community life, the sober realm of justice and judging—or, to use (somewhat inappropriately) our modern distinction, from matters of church to matters of state.[21] In a pivotal moment for the emerging nation, Jethro, dealing only with Moses, calls his attention to the need for a better system to administer justice and, more important, for explicit laws and teaching supported by divine approval, authority, and threat of punishment:

> And it came to pass on the morrow, that Moses sat to judge the people; and the people stood over (or "about"; 'al) Moses from the morning until the evening. And when Moses's father-in-law saw all that he was doing for the people, he said: "What is this thing (mah-hadavar hazzeh) that you are doing for the people? Why (maddua') are you sitting *alone*, while *all* the people *stand over you* from morning unto evening?" (18:13–14; emphasis added)

Let us try to picture the scene. Moses is enthroned on a seat of respect and authority as a horde of people wait all day long on his judgment. But the people hover near and over him, making him subject to their will. Moses delivers the word, but he is a prisoner of the people's needs and their unruliness. Worse, the situation is anarchic—literally "lawless" and "rule-less"—and precarious: Moses's ability to govern depends on people liking his judgments, on his not antagonizing them, on the sufficiency and durability of his charisma. For now, he has their trust and respect, based especially on his leadership at the Sea of Reeds and in the war against Amalek, and on their belief that he has divine connections or even godlike powers. The people seek him out for his judgments and instruction. But the people's trust is fickle. As he deals with disputatious people, some with angry grievances, many may lose their trust in him should his verdicts go against them. Although he appears to be in charge, Moses is in fact at their mercy. (Jethro, a tactful fellow, will soon delicately present this problem only in terms of Moses's becoming worn out, not of his being taken out.[22])

Moses, we recall, in his eagerness for peace and justice, early displayed a tendency to insert himself into other people's quarrels. He is now doing what he was inclined to do with the brawling Israelites: he is an 'ish sar veshofet, the one-man-ruler-and-judge (2:14)—though no one has yet *appointed* him to this role. Judging disputes was never part of the job description he received from the Lord. And the people, accustomed to being ruled by one man, relate to Moses (at least for now) as if he were a new and better Pharaoh. But Pharaoh-like or not, Moses embodies a permanent human possibility, celebrated in ancient myths of wise founding kings and embraced most famously by Socrates in Plato's *Republic* as the only just regime: the rule of one good and wise man—a "philosopher-king"—who has a god's-eye understanding of justice. Yet Moses sits not merely as a wise man but also as a divine-like lawgiver and judge, dispensing—is it intuiting, or is it channeling, or is it manufacturing?—divine teachings. That, we will soon see, is not the Torah's preferred political arrangement.

Jethro is astonished. Before commenting, he seeks explanations: What are you doing? Why are you sitting alone with the people over you? He is not mainly asking for information; he is challenging what Moses is doing.

God's Mouthpiece or Divining Judge?

Moses has a ready answer, which deserves most careful scrutiny:

> And Moses said to his father-in-law: "Because the people come to me to inquire of God (*lidrosh 'elohim*): when they have a matter (or "thing"; *davar*), it comes to me, and I judge between a man and his neighbor; and I make known the statutes of God (*chuqqe ha'elohim*), and His laws (or "His teachings, His Torah"; *torothav*)." (18:15–16)

When asked what he is doing, Moses gives an overview and then specifies its two parts. The people, he says, come to him for divine assistance in solving their difficulties.[23] Concretely, here is what happens: (1) When they have some matter, "it comes to *me*, and *I* judge between a man and his neighbor"; and (2) "*I* make known God's statutes and His teachings" (my emphasis). The people come to Moses as an oracle to get a ruling that will settle their disputes and answer their questions; they regard Moses as their only access to the divine, as someone who is at least plugged into some higher power. In rendering his judgments, however, Moses takes the occasion to teach the people God's statutes and laws (or "teachings").

The last clause is notoriously difficult to interpret. Has God already given Moses the Torah—either privately or, as we will soon learn, in public at Sinai—even though, in the text, we have not yet heard about it or seen it happen? Could Moses possibly be referring to a remark that God made to the people at Marah, about hearkening to His commandments (*mitsvoth*) and His statutes (*chuqqim*)?[24] Or did Moses intuit the spirit of God's justice by, for example, seeing how He punished the Egyptians and how He tended precisely to the people's needs? Or yet again—as I am inclined to believe—is Moses offering his own best judgments, intuiting or inducing—"divining"—from the cases before him the general legal and moral principles, which he then presents as God's statutes and teachings? It was evident from his first adult experiences that Moses has an innate sense of justice (or, better, of *in*justice) and is not shy about acting on it. By exercising that inborn gift to resolve the disputes before him, Moses finds—"divines"—the universal and eternal principles from within the particular cases.

True enough, God had told Moses that "I will be with you," and "I will be with your mouth"—though that was mainly in the context of dealing with Pharaoh—and Moses may in fact have believed himself to be a vessel for rendering divine judgment.[25] Nevertheless, we do not wish to attribute to Moses any additional knowledge—of God, of His laws, or of anything else—beyond what the text explicitly tells us he received (and that we have thereby also received). Why? Because when we actually get God's statutes and teachings, the case law or "bottom-up manner" of making law that Moses says he is following turns out to be upside down: God's way is to present the explicit statutes and teachings first, and only then their application to particular cases. Moses is surely doing the best he can in the absence of further instruction and in the absence of God's law, but at this point, *God's* law is not what Moses is teaching. He is dispensing his own intuitive wisdom about justice and treating it as sufficient.

If this is correct, the text also yields insights into the large question of how best to govern: it is not to get a better Pharaoh. The right way is not the rule of the best and wisest man, someone whom people will revere as a god. Whether he knows it or not, Moses is increasing the already dangerous gap between himself and the people, making it more likely that they will seek a replacement "god" when he is absent. The proper way is not rule of man but rule of law—not just any law, but divinely ordained law—equally applicable to the leaders and the led alike and administered by human beings for the benefit of all members of the community. Only this approach can hope to bring justice and civil peace.

The truth of these claims about the primacy of the rule of law gains definitive support much later in the text. When the Israelites are ready to enter the Promised Land to live under the Law, Moses the lawgiver must disappear from the scene. There must be no appeal from the law to the lawgiver.

Jethro's Advice

Having listened to Moses's explanation of his activities, Jethro immediately and thoroughly objects:

> And Moses's father-in-law said unto him: "*Not good (lo' tov)* is the thing that you are doing. You will surely wear away, both you, and this people that is with you; for the thing is too heavy (*kaved*) for you; you are not able to do it *alone*. Hearken now unto my voice, I will give you counsel, and may God (*'elohim*) be with you: (18:17–19; emphasis added)

Speaking as Moses's father-in-law (and perhaps concerned more for his welfare than for the people's), Jethro tells Moses that the job is too heavy for him and that he needs help.* In this indirect way, Jethro points up

---

*These remarks echo the situation on the hill at the battle with Amalek: Moses's hands grew *heavy*, and he needed help. There the issue was mainly bodily fatigue; here it seems to be what is called "burnout," a matter of the spirit. Also, as already noted, Jethro's first words—"*Not good* is the thing that you are doing"—have a more distant echo. God in the Garden of Eden had said, "*Not good (lo' tov)* is it for the man to be alone; I will make him a help (*'ezer*) opposite him" (Gen. 2:18). To correct Moses's aloneness, Jethro, like God, had already (twice) brought Moses his woman, both years ago and again on this visit; now, to correct a different aloneness, he will bring him lower-court judges.

the problem with letting one man be the sole ruler and judge: it is precarious for the leader and bad for the people. Jethro senses that Moses is at risk because he is alone and all the people are over against him; he needs to involve others in the process of judging so that they too will bear some of the responsibility. Jethro offers to give Moses specific advice but adds a codicil: "I shall give you counsel, and (or "but") *may 'elohim be with you*." In other words, may God approve my counsel and implement it. While giving his own political advice, Jethro keeps the divine in view; he reminds Moses of the need for divine approval.

As it happens, however, Jethro reminds not only Moses of the divine; he also puts God sharply in the reader's view, but with a twist. God, we notice, has not objected to what Moses is doing. We wonder: Does Jethro speak here for God? Is the advice he will give Moses sound—that is, sound from God's point of view? Could God perhaps be behind Jethro's visit? Even if He is not, could Jethro's arrival and his advice be a "godsend"? We read on, keeping these questions in mind.

Here is Jethro's advice:

> "Be you for the people before God, and you shall bring their matters (or "words"; *devarim*) before God. And you shall admonish them (or "warn them," "instruct them"; *vehizhartah*) about the statutes (*chuqqim*) and the laws (*toroth*), and shall make known to them the way wherein they must walk, and the deed that they must do. Moreover, you shall search out (or "prophesy" or "provide"; *chazah*[26]) from among all the people noble [or "valorous"] men (*'anshe chayil*), such as fear God (*yir'e 'elohim*), men of truth (*'anshe 'emeth*), hating unjust gain (*sone'e vatsa'*); and place such over them [the people], to be rulers of thousands, rulers of hundreds, rulers of fifties, and rulers of tens. And let them judge the people at all seasons; and it shall be, that every great matter they shall bring unto you, but every small matter they shall judge themselves; so shall they make it easier for you and bear the burden with you. If you shall do this thing, and *[if] God command you so*, then you shall be able to endure, and all this people also shall *go to their place in peace*." (18:19–23; emphasis added)

Having heard Moses's description of his work but perhaps interpreting it in a pagan way, Jethro gives him three suggestions, addressing the three formulations in Moses's account.[27] In response to Moses's (first) statement, that the people come to him (as to an oracle) to inquire of God, Jethro tells him to be the people's sole petitioner before God, the way that pagan priests bring petitions to the idols. In response to Moses's (last) statement that he teaches the people God's statues and His laws (Torah), Jethro advises him to admonish[28] the people about the statutes and teachings regarding how to live and act, but—note well—making no mention of any divine origin of these statutes and teachings. He is, as it were, separating the realm of justice from the realm of religion. But it is Moses's central statement about his judging that elicits Jethro's major advice: search out virtuous men ("men of valor"; *'anshe chayil*) and appoint them as judges over the people to handle all the lesser (graded) cases, leaving you, Moses, with only the great matters to decide on your own. Jethro concludes: "*If* you will do this thing, and [if] *God will charge you, then* you will be able to stand and also all this people will come to its place in peace"—which is to say, will be free of internal or domestic strife. In his final (and crucial) word, Jethro again puts the divine before Moses's mind: he needs at least to get divine approval of Jethro's plan ("may *'Elohim* be with you"), if not also divine authorization of it.

What should we think about Jethro's role here and about his advice? He appears to be the wise man of practical experience, bringing sound advice to correct Moses's errors born of inexperience. He sees, correctly, that the present arrangement is untenable. From past experience, Jethro knows Moses's penchant for independent self-reliance, especially regarding matters involving his strong sense of justice and injustice. He probably also knows that Moses's time in Egypt will have left him with only a monarchic model of rule and decision. He correctly discerns that Moses cannot manage the major affairs of the Israelite people—600,000 strong, counting just the men—if he is bogged down in resolving all their small disputes and judging each case, as it were, by the seat of his pants. Yes, he needs to admonish the people with statutes and laws that will teach them how to live and how to act. But mostly he needs help—massive help—in the administration of justice. From where we sit, heeding Jethro's advice looks like it would surely improve upon the present situation. His proposed decentralization of the judiciary seems wise. So too, at first glance, his criteria for selecting the judges: replace the traditional standard of age ("the elders," distinguished only by the accident of birth order) by the standard of character.

On reflection, however, we see difficulties. How can Moses—or anyone else—*know* the *'anshe chayil*, the men of valor or virtue? How can he know—especially by just gazing at them—who the really noble ones are, especially among this huge mass of former slaves? Individual Israelites may have stood out from the crowd in one of three ways: for their wealth coming out of Egypt (the size of their herds or the amount of their jewelry), for the vigor of their complaining, and for their prowess in the war against Amalek. Let us suppose that the *'anshe chayil* are the men of manly virtue who were visibly good in battle—or alternatively, as Rashi suggests, those of greater wealth. Does that mean they will be impartial and wise as judges? Can one see at a glance which of them fear God, love truth, and hate bribes? Yes, subordinate judges will relieve the burden on Moses, but will it be better for most people to have lesser men (whom they did not choose or approve) decide their cases?

We may also raise questions about the tiered bureaucratic structure that Jethro proposes, especially about the numbers. If one takes the numbers literally rather than symbolically, it turns out that roughly one out of eight men will be involved in judging: a population of 600,000 men will require 600 men to rule over the thousands, 6,000 men to rule over the hundreds, 12,000 men to rule over the fifties, and 60,000 men to rule over the tens—a total of 78,600 men handling judicial cases. (We note, in passing, the implication of Jethro's high numbers: the people are a mighty quarrelsome lot.) This elaborate bureaucratic structure seems ill-suited to a wandering desert existence.

There are still larger questions regarding Jethro's advice, apart from its feasibility and the difficulty of finding the right people to implement it. Is relying on the unaided wisdom or prudence of human beings—even an aristocracy of genuine natural virtue—the right way to govern this people, especially when they come under God's covenant made with *each and all* of the people equally? Is *character*—even if it could be properly recognized—*sufficient* as the principle of governing and judging for a people who will be called to aspire to something higher than avoiding reciprocal wrongdoing, to something beyond justice?[29] Jethro seems to be offering pagan ("Greek") advice for a people with a decidedly different mission.

The heart of Jethro's advice concerns the administration of justice. But the greater question concerns the *content* of justice and the instruction the people need to govern their lives. In Jethro's view, these vital tasks—too important to delegate to others—belong to Moses alone. It is Moses who should admonish the people, imparting to them the statutes and teachings that will guide how they are to live. Jethro clearly recognizes the need for law. But he speaks as if Moses himself can be the law's author and teacher: "And *you* shall admonish them . . . and [*you*] shall make known to them" (18:20).

But that is not the whole story. Twice in his remarks, as we have noted, Jethro puts Moses in mind of the divine. And he concludes by suggesting that his advice must first be ratified by God: "and *if God so commands* you (*vetsivekha*)" (18:23). He does not explicitly tell Moses to get God's approval of his plan, and he does not suggest straight out that Moses ask God to be the lawgiver. Yet in the end, he gently nudges Moses to seek divine guidance in matters of justice. This, more than his judicial reforms, may be his most important contribution. Jethro has emphasized administering justice, but God will emphasize being just.

Jethro puts Moses in mind of the need for divine approval (and even guidance) regarding the people's governance. And perhaps it is this thought that makes Moses susceptible to that guidance when it is offered. The law can only be given to the leader and legislator if and when he is ready to receive it. As we will see in the next chapter, when the people set up camp before the mountain, Moses (perhaps with Jethro's words still echoing in his ears) quite on his own immediately starts to ascend the mountain in search of God (*'elohim*). Only then does the Lord call out to him, to offer him and the people His law and teachings (19:2–3). Before He gives him guidance, God waits until Moses, on purely human grounds, realizes that he needs it.

Moses, it seems, thought well enough of Jethro's advice—better than we did—and moved promptly to implement the administrative suggestions:

> So Moses hearkened to the voice of his father-in-law, and did *all* that he had said. And Moses chose men of valor (*'anshe chayil*) out of all Israel, and made them heads over the people, rulers of thousands, rulers of hundreds, rulers of fifties, and rulers of tens. And they judged the people at all seasons: the hard matters they brought unto Moses, but every small matter they judged themselves. (18:24–26; emphasis added)

The text has Moses doing everything Jethro told him to do. But the description of Moses's action raises some doubt. Moses appointed men of valor, but nothing is said about whether he considered Jethro's other criteria: "fear of God (*yir'e 'elohim*), men of truth (*'anshe 'emeth*), hating unjust gain (*sone'e vatsa'*)." Should we understand that those traits were encompassed in the description, "men of valor"? Or was it not possible to identify—any, or many, or enough—people with those qualifications?

However this may be, the text tells us that the division of labor worked, and for a long time ("at all seasons"): the judges handled the small matters themselves while referring the big questions to Moses. About the promulgation of statutes and teachings, nothing is said.

At the end of Jethro's visit, several questions remain. Did Jethro's suggestions on their face—and Moses's following of his advice—solve the problems they were meant to solve? Does his plan moderate or aggravate the gap between Moses and the people? Does it trade the charismatic hierarchy of Moses's one-man rule for the more efficient but coarser hierarchy of the "aristocracy"? Do we not still lack the truly hierarchic element, without which the hierarchy Moses just instituted becomes highly problematic? Without the substance of the divine law—not yet given—might the new system be worse and less trustworthy than Moses judging alone? Might not creating a class that rules by whim, not by given law, be worse than what they had before?

Jethro, to repeat, gave Moses more than judicial advice. Regarding the big problem—rule by one man alone—he not only urged Moses to replace the rule of one by the rule of few but he also gently directed Moses from the rule by man to the rule by God. As if to anticipate difficulties of the sort we just listed, he explicitly pointed out the need for God's approval. What, the text cries out at us, will the Lord say?

The Lord has been completely silent during Jethro's visit, and Moses has yet to check with Him: that part of Jethro's advice Moses has yet to follow. Given our uncertainty, we readers are eager to find out, sooner rather than later, what He will make of all this. We rather suspect that Moses is even more eager than we.

Jethro's Departure

The story ends with Jethro's departure:

And Moses released (or "let depart"; *vayeshallach*) his father-in-law; and he went his way to his own land. (18:27)

The visit has been a success. Jethro has delivered Moses's wife and children (who presumably now stay with Moses—though the silence between Moses and his family roars at the reader). He has learned what he wanted to know about how Israel got out of Egypt. He has given testimony to the superiority of *Y-H-V-H,* God of Israel. He has initiated sacrifices and offered thanks to the divine for Israel's deliverance. He has given his son-in-law practical advice for dealing with the disputatious people. He has watched and perhaps supervised the selection and installation of the judges. It is time for him to leave.

"And Moses *let* his father-in-law *depart.*" Why might Moses have not wanted Jethro to stay? Was there a theological difference, perhaps revealed in the tent conversation or at the sacrifices? Why, once Jethro had pronounced the superiority of *Y-H-V-H,* did he offer sacrifices instead to the generic divine (*'elohim*)—and for that matter, why did he not "convert"? Was there a political difficulty, revealed in the advice he gave Moses (either about the judges or about his role as the people's petitioner before God)? Was Moses leery of having this venerable foreign priest in his midst, a possible threat to his authority or an obstacle to getting on with the mission to the mountain? Or was there in fact no difficulty at all? Do we have in Moses's behavior a perfect model for the relationship between two people with different ways and different gods, separate but equal and respecting one another? In sending Jethro away freely, was Moses modeling how Pharaoh should have treated Israel? As so often happens in the text, our inability to be sure about the correct alternative presents us with important matters to think about.[30]

Be all this as it may, the departure of Jethro closes the circle on the Midianite-Egyptian-Midianite, pre-revelation phase of Moses's life. That phase began with the burning bush episode at the mountain of God, after Moses wandered from Jethro's house; it finishes at the mountain of God with Jethro's departure from Moses's tent, shortly before the mountain is engulfed with another divine fire. Having at the start given his daughter to an Egyptian prince and perhaps having nudged him to start seeking the divine, Jethro at the end delivers her back to him, a champion now of *Y-H-V-H*. Jethro's work is done.

But his departure raises a profound question for the reader. We, like Jethro, have "heard" the entire story; about everything Moses told him, we too have "hearsay"—that is to say, reading—knowledge. Do *we* stay in the camp of Moses, or do we readers go back to our own "land"? When we come to the next chapter, will we place ourselves among the people at the foot of the mountain, ready to hear the covenantal offer? Jethro's embrace of Moses's account, coupled with his subsequent departure, suggests that merely hearing the story up to this point is not sufficient to attach someone to this nascent community. That a nation was rescued from some other nation would of course be important to its own members. But is there anything here of compelling and universal significance that could attract and attach outsiders such as our wisdom-seeking selves? Something else seems to be required.

Covenant from the Mountain

A Kingdom of Priests and a Holy Nation

W̲e have reached the threshold of the central event in the book of Exodus, indeed, the central event in the story of the people of Israel: the giving of the Law at Mount Sinai. Before proceeding to experience that event, we pause briefly to consider what it means, in relation both to what has come before and to what comes after.

What happens here will have the widest significance, not only for ancient Israel but also for the entire history of the West. Israel will acquire a comprehensive teaching regarding all aspects of human existence, a guide for its communal life in the Promised Land. Looking backward from centuries ahead, the peoples of the West (and thoughtful people everywhere) will have acquired a permanent source of guidance regarding how human beings are to live. The West became what it is through the creative tension between reason and revelation: on the one hand, a life lived according to human reason, exercised on the world around us, looking up to nature or to man's powers to alter it; on the other hand, a life lived in obedience to the revealed commandments that God has offered in part to correct for the limitations of the life lived according to reason. We need to remind ourselves why the second alternative was—and might still be—deemed necessary.

The Moral Weakness of Human Reason

From the start of the book of Genesis, wisdom-seeking readers will have noted the Bible's suspicion of the adequacy of human reason. The Garden of Eden story displays the text's doubts about unaided reason's ability to discover what is good and right; in subsequent stories, we have seen the text's doubts about unaided reason's ability to make right and good prevail against the restive waywardness of the human heart. Also from the start of Genesis, the Bible has denied the divinity and dignity of "nature," especially of the heavenly bodies, previously deemed everywhere to be divine. After the catastrophe of the Flood, we have witnessed at Babel the failed rationalist project of human self-re-creation. If not by reason or by looking up to or improving upon nature, how might human life be well guided?[1]

After showing us several disasters of the uninstructed life (Gen. 2–11), the Torah starts to give us an answer. It lets us watch as God embarks on a new approach with Abraham, from whom He promises to make a great nation and through whom *all* the families of the earth shall be blessed. Yet the content of that new way has remained sketchy. Apart from orienting their lives mindfully toward God (and apart from the recently acquired obligations to commemorate Passover, redeem the firstborn, and wear phylacteries), the only specific obligation on the descendants of Abraham is circumcision, an act dedicating newborn sons in fulfillment of their ancestor's covenant with God. Abraham, we learn, was summoned by God because He wanted him to teach his children to do righteousness and justice (Gen. 18:19). But the content of justice and righteousness has been entirely unspecified.

Yet although we have seen no specifics of God's Way, we readers of Genesis and Exodus have gotten many glimpses of the evils and iniquities that we hope this Way will correct: murder and fratricide (Cain and Abel, Jacob and Esau, Joseph and his brothers, Simeon and Levi and the men of Shechem); adultery (Abraham and Sarah with Pharaoh and Abimelech, Isaac and Rebekah with Abimelech); rape (Dinah); incest (Lot's daughters and their father, Reuben and his father's concubine, Judah and Tamar); rebellion against paternal authority and law (Ham); theft (Jacob and the blessing, Rachel and her father's idols); bearing false witness (Potiphar's wife against Joseph, Joseph and his brothers); mistreatment of strangers (the Sodomites and Lot, Egypt and the Hebrews); the temptation of apotheosis (Lamech, Babel, Pharaoh); worship of idols and false gods (Egypt); and despotism and slavery (Egypt). We will look carefully to see if and how the Law addresses these moral matters, for individuals and for the entire community.

Political Challenges for Leader and Led

Not only moral but also political issues are on the table as the Israelites approach Sinai. To embody His Way for human beings, God has chosen to create His new nation from a poorly formed and chaotic multitude of abased ex-slaves. The project faces several challenges. How to make out of the ex-slaves not only a people but a self-governing people: righteous, God-fearing, and—eventually—holy? How to do so while avoiding the injustices that usually afflict human communities, especially the mistreatment of strangers and iniquities toward family and neighbors, ranging from fratricide, adultery, and theft to slavery, exploitation, and despotism? How to prevent the lowering of communal aspirations and the deformation of desire, from excessive attachment to gain, comfort, and safety to the worship of idols and false gods? And how to bring order and measure to human life while leaving room for exuberance, ecstasy, and the nonrational energies of the soul?

There are also lingering issues regarding the leaders and the led. How to prevent too large a gap between the leader and his people, so as to avoid the twin dangers of contemptuous tyranny and servile idolatry? How to prevent too small a gap between the leader and his people, so as to avoid the twin dangers of appeasement and weakness, and rebellion and revolt? How to find a leader who, while knowing the highest, is able to attain and be satisfied with the highest possible? How to find a leader who can effectively mediate between God (or The Good) and the people's all too human needs and weaknesses?

Since the departure from Egypt, events have revealed several political difficulties bearing on God's project regarding both the people and their leader. The people's astonishing deliverance from Egypt, their rescue from the hands of the pursuing Egyptians, and the ensuing miracles in the desert have not prevented them from losing trust in Moses when their basic needs are unmet. They make trial not only of Moses but also of God, and they cannot be governed by persuasive speech alone. Like the Egyptians, they require signs and wonders, but all too easily forget them. They are unruly and quarrelsome; they need law, authority, and guidance to keep the peace. Yet even as they are ready to rebel against Moses, they are also at risk of confusing him with God.

A man of great self-command who esteems the power of speech and reason, Moses has shown himself impatient with the people's weaknesses and murmurings. He is slow to appreciate their needs; he disdains their lack of self-control yet is himself prone to anger; he looks down on their inability to be persuaded by reason alone. Until Jethro's visit, he was willing to sit, unappointed, as the sole judge and supreme ruler over the Israelites, embodying the rule of one man as wise—a philosopher-king, a better Pharaoh, an oracle channeling divine wisdom.

It was Jethro who questioned Moses's monarchic relationship with the people. He advised that judging be decentralized and authority delegated to men of virtue—an aristocratic expedient that Moses at least partly follows. But Jethro also encourages Moses to see the need for *codified law,* for *'elohim's* approval of the law, and for judicial delegation. When Jethro departs, Moses, with *'elohim* on his mind, is eager to remedy these deficiencies. He will discover that the Lord has bigger things in mind.

Moses to the Mountain

The story of Israel at Sinai begins by setting the stage:

> On the third new moon of the Children of Israel's going out from Egypt, on this day did they come (*ba'u* [perfect tense]) to the Wilderness of Sinai. And they journeyed from Rephidim and came to the Wilderness of Sinai, and they camped in the wilderness; and Israel camped there over against the mountain. But [or "And"] Moses had gone up unto God (*'elohim*). (19:1–3)

To indicate the unique and momentous character of the event to follow, the story begins abruptly, eschewing the narrative's usual connections with previous events. (The story does not start with "And" or with "And it happened" [*vayehi*].) On the day of the third new moon—three for completion, new moon for novel beginning—they arrive at the Wilderness of Sinai, opposite the mountain of God,[2] for what will be their transformative rendezvous with God. While the Israelites make camp below, Moses makes haste to go above. On his own initiative, he separates himself from the group and immediately starts up the mountain, seeking an encounter with *'elohim*.

We are not told what is on Moses's mind or what exactly he is looking for. But given that he is said to have gone up to *'elohim*, not to *Y-H-V-H*, we suspect that he is first of all seeking the divine as he was instructed to do by Jethro.[3] With Jethro's advice to get *'elohim's* support still fresh in his mind, Moses is almost certainly seeking divine counsel regarding law. Perhaps he also remembers God's remark at the burning bush: "When you bring the people out from Egypt, you [plural] shall serve *'elohim* on this mountain" (3:12). Finally, Moses may be personally eager to resume his association with the divine at *'elohim's* "holy mountain,"[4] an association that began so auspiciously at the burning bush. Perhaps for all these reasons—and now back at the mountain where it all began for him—Moses wastes no time in seeking to commune again with the divine.

As at the burning bush, Moses's eagerness to engage is fully requited, though not in the way he expected. It is not *'elohim* that responds, but (God in His aspect as) *Y-H-V-H*, with a new mission well beyond Moses's previous imaginings:

> And *Y-H-V-H* called unto him out of the mountain, saying: "Thus shall you *say* to the house of Jacob, and shall you *tell* the Children of Israel: 'You have *seen* what I did unto the Egyptians, and how I bore you on eagles' wings, and brought you to Me. Now therefore, if hearkening you will *hearken* (*'im shamoa' tishme'u*) unto My *Voice*, and keep My covenant (*brithi*), then you shall be Mine own *treasure* (*segullah*) from among all the peoples (*'ammim*); for all the earth is Mine; and

you shall be unto Me a *kingdom of priests* (*mamlekheth ko-hanim*), and a *holy nation* (*goy qadosh*).' These are the words which you shall *speak* unto the Children of Israel." (19:3–6; emphasis added)

Seeing Moses on his way toward Him, the Lord calls him from out of the mountain. Using high poetic speech and an unusual choice of words,[5] He immediately tells Moses what to say to the House of Jacob and what to tell the Children of Israel: Moses, speaking in His name, is to offer a new national covenant with Him.

The Shape of the Covenant

In the speech Moses is to make for Him, the Lord begins by reminding the people of what they have *seen:* they have witnessed with their own eyes the Lord's power over their enemies. Since then, they have witnessed His special care for them: using a beautiful image—how I carried you to Me on eagles' wings—the Lord offers the people a poetic interpretation (as did the Song of the Sea) of their rescue from Egypt and their recent wanderings in the wilderness. The image conveys perfectly the character and purpose of the Lord's providence. The Lord is like the high-soaring bird who lovingly carries its needy fledglings atop its wings, safe from predators and secure against failure, leading them upward to the loftiest heights, to its home in the mountaintop.

On the basis of this "witnessed" evidence, the Israelites should therefore know that the One speaking to them here, through Moses, is the same One Who delivered them from the Egyptians and has been nurturing them with manna. Because He is their protector and caretaker, they should now gladly entertain a proposal of a new relationship with Him—a relationship based not on seeing but on hearing and obeying. Wonders for the eyes lead to teachings for the ears.

The Lord offers the Israelites a covenant (*brith*), an agreement that binds together two parties that, absent such an agreement, would have no enduring relationship with each other.[6] As in all such agreements between a lord and his vassals, the Lord offers the Israelites protection and care in exchange for their allegiance, obedience, and tribute. The proposal is, also as usual, a take-it-or-leave it offer from the strong to the weak. But precisely because it is a covenant on offer, rather than an imposed decree, it is not being forced on the people. They must consent to the new relationship if it is to mean anything.

Before examining the specific content of the covenant, we must appreciate one crucial fact: the formal act of covenanting will itself be the decisive people-forming event. Made in public with all of the people united, the *brith* becomes a source of their identity: once they accept the offer, the Israelites will become God's "firstborn son," following in His ways. Unlike liberalism's "social contract," in which individuals give up certain liberties to safeguard the rest, the covenant will offer guidance for how everyone is supposed to act and live communally. Most important, it will give the people a purpose for their existence: they will gain an enduring national goal that will define and inspire them for generations to come—in principle, forever.[7]*

The agreement the Lord is proposing is conditional, presented in an if/then form: "If hearkening you will hearken to My Voice and keep my covenant" (if, in sum, you will obey My [not-yet-given] commandments), then several—in fact, three—things will follow: (1) *"you* will become *for Me* a treasure among all the peoples, for Mine is all the earth"; and *"you* will become *for Me* (2) a kingdom of priests and (3) a holy nation." What does all this mean: "The Lord's treasure among all the peoples"? "Kingdom of priests"? "Holy nation"? What would the Israelites have understood of these terms, and of the overall proposal?

*A community based on contract is in principle dissolved if the contract goes unfulfilled; if its basic terms are violated, the people have a right to revolt. But what about the binding promise of a covenant, especially one made with God? Individuals can leave the community, but can the community annul the agreement? Can God nullify His promise? We shall take up this question in connection with the story of the golden calf (see Chapters Twenty and Twenty-One). It will turn out that God's commitment is permanent, even though the people will have to pay and atone for falling short. Because the Lord will offer grace beyond merit and forgiveness beyond desert, the people can continue to aim high, even though they know that they will regularly fail.

We proceed slowly, working carefully with the text to consider each of the terms. Thereafter, we shall venture our own interpretive suggestion.

The Terms of the Covenant

The first thing to notice is something easily overlooked. Never mind all those ambiguous terms on offer, the Children of Israel learn here for the first time that they are a people, an *'am*. The Lord says to Moses, "Say to the *house of Jacob*" and "tell to the *Children of Israel*" that they are now (instead or also) a people: although Moses is told to address them in their pre-national (and pre-political) designations ("*house* of Jacob," "*Children* of Israel (Jacob)"), he must describe them to themselves as a people among the peoples, an *'am* among the *'ammim*. A previous Pharaoh—the one who knew not Joseph—had called the Israelites a people (to him, a dangerous "other"). But they had never spoken of themselves that way; nor had God or Moses ever referred to them as a people, a distinctive, self-governing group defined by a common culture, law, and way of life. According to the Torah, they have not previously been a people, and nothing they had done or experienced before this moment could make them one—not their extraction from Egypt or their deliverance at the Sea of Reeds, not their success against Amalek, not even their looking up to God and Moses. They become a people only here, as a consequence of the covenant with the Lord.

Despite the Israelites' late arrival on the scene (they are hardly the world's firstborn nation) they are poised to become *the treasured people*—the prized national possession[8]—of the Lord of all the earth. They are chosen not because they are worthy or deserving—even though they are the heirs to God's covenant with Abraham.[9] As the words of the offer make clear, Israel can become God's treasured people (only) through obedience. The sovereign of all the earth promises to select Israel as His special treasure, His favored people, but only if Israel hearkens to His Voice and keeps His covenant.

If, in relation to the Lord, Israel will become His treasured nation, in itself it will become a kingdom of priests and a holy nation. The meaning of these terms is, to say the least, puzzling—and, we suspect, also for the people who will shortly hear these words. How are they to be understood?

A Kingdom of Priests

To begin with, what is a priest (*kohen*), as the Israelites would have understood the term? Is he, as most modern readers will assume, a strictly religious figure who cares for (only) the "sacred things": who deals with the god-seeking passions of human beings, guards the sanctuary, and mediates between the people and their god(s) through, for instance, petitions, sacrifices, or other rituals? Or does a priest also have political functions, ruling over his people in their "secular" affairs (say, war or justice), in the name of the gods?[10] Clearly, whatever else they are, priests are persons of special standing in the community, enjoying special privileges and powers that are to be used only in service to the divine. By the same token, priests also incur special burdens and dangers as they stir up the people's passions, face the awesome powers aloft, and bear the iniquities of the community before the divine. They are custodians of purity and danger.

So what is on offer to Israel as a prospective "kingdom of priests"? We note first the unusual combination of "political" and "religious" terms—of the profane (kings) and the sacred (priests). The goal seems to be a union between the messy realm of human affairs, awash in imperfection, and the transcendent realm of God, beyond the foibles of humankind.[11] But whatever "kingdom of priests" turns out to mean, the phrase implies that Israel's way of life will be suffused with matters divine.

A first question about "kingdom of priests" (or about "holy nation") is whether the term is meant to distinguish the collectivity of Israel from other peoples ("the priestly people") or whether it is also meant to describe its individual members. In this latter sense, "kingdom of priests" would designate a special internal structure of the community—a kingdom *comprising* priests—in which everyone is a priest. Because the law and a relationship with God would belong equally to everyone, each person or household in the community would perform the priestly functions of sacrifice and ritual worship. (It is this interpretation of "kingdom of priests and a holy nation" that Korah and his followers will later exploit to justify their rebellion against Moses and Aaron.[12]) The text itself will soon present a difficulty with this interpretation: when instructing

Moses to keep everyone away from the mountain during the theophany, God Himself speaks separately about the priests and the people (even though a separate priesthood has yet to be appointed [19:24]). And later, only some Israelites (the hereditary line of Aaron and his descendants) will be given the special function of priests.[13] Nevertheless, according to an internal understanding of "kingdom of priests," everyone within the community would in some sense have the same status in relation to God and the holy things.

The idea of "kingdom of priests" could (perhaps additionally) have external reference. Israel, in its relations with other nations (the Lord's other "children"), would acquire the status and function that priests have within nations: it would mediate between God and the other nations of the world. Just how it might do so is completely unclear: would it, as the priestly kingdom, actively promote God's teachings to the other nations and seek to convert them by proselytizing? Or would it "minister" to the world by standing apart as a model or even just as a witness to a higher way of life? Should Israel, as a kingdom of priests, be actively involved with the other nations, or should it stay away, having a national life that is different from that of any other nation and even beyond politics altogether? If so, will it be able to defend itself in the nasty and dangerous domain of international affairs?

There is a third way to understand "kingdom of priests": a "kingdom" in which priests—not kings—rule or, better, in which God Himself is "king" and the priests rule as His ministers. A theocracy, in other words, not a monarchy. Such an understanding might be seen as providing a correction for Moses's "kingly" behavior. It would also suggest a nation in which the holy things are uppermost in the life of the community. With the building of the Tabernacle and the institution of the priesthood, both coming soon, a good case can be made for this theocratic rendering of "kingdom of priests."

A Holy Nation

Similar ambiguities attach to the phrase "holy nation." The Hebrew word for "holy," *qadosh*, has a root meaning of "to be set apart" or "separated."

It carries not only the negative sense of separated *from* but also the positive sense of separated *toward* and separated *for:* to be *qadosh* is to be distinctive because uniquely dedicated—in this case, "for Me, the Lord." From this understanding, *qadosh* readily comes to mean "sacred," "hallowed," "consecrated."[14] No doubt the former Egyptian slaves will have heard of sacred animals and hallowed places, but what could they possibly have made of the idea of their becoming a holy nation? Does it mean that Israel will become (externally considered) a nation set apart from the others, either in the way it lives or in relation to the divine? Or does this mean (also or instead) that Israel (internally considered) will have a "holy" character—either as a whole nation (*goy*) or each person individually, each person a *kohen*? If the latter, would this holy character be synonymous with obedience to God's commands? Or, in addition or instead, would there be some specific commandments whose observance could make the nation or the individual holy; for example, keeping the Sabbath and revering mother and father?[15] Does holiness mean something "spiritual," something higher than mere obedience to the laws, higher even than justice and righteousness? Did not the priestly Jethro's visit call attention to this distinction? Did he not, with his sacrifices, model the performance of special duties toward the divine and special activities to set apart place, time, and offerings?

Considering next the relation between the "if" and the "then" parts of the covenantal agreement, I suggest that the "then" parts are not to be understood as God's *rewards for,* but rather as the direct *results of,* obeying His commands. God does not say, "If you hearken, I will make you . . . ," but rather, "If you hearken, you will become. . . ." The logic of the presentation, with its three consequences of obedience, goes something like this. If you obey Me, I will treasure you most among the nations of the earth. Why? Because you will then have become to Me a priestly nation (*mamlekheth kohanim*). And what does it mean to be a priestly nation? It means that your people will be set apart as dedicated to Me (*goy qadosh*).[16] It means that they will embody holiness, or at least strive to embody holiness, by following especially those aspects of God's law that elevate human beings to a plane of existence higher than mere obedience.

An Interpretive Suggestion

Leaving all these linguistic perplexities to the side, it seems fair to say that the Lord is offering Israel something new under the sun. Given their experience, the people should recognize, in the very presentation of the offer, that it is a novel opportunity. And given all that we readers of the Torah have seen, so should we.

Hearing what the Lord, through Moses, tells them, the people should think as follows. We have seen the evidence. We know the truth of what the Lord has told us. We have arrived on the world stage thanks to His power against the Egyptians and His providence in bringing us ("on eagles' wings") to Himself, here at His "holy mountain." And now we know why He did it.[17] We are to occupy a special place among the nations of the world: to be a nation apart (holy), yet with a priestly relation to the others. In both aspects, we will bear ourselves in a special relationship to the Lord, a relationship that requires (only!) that we hearken to His Voice and keep His covenant.

We readers, having vicariously seen much more than the Israelites, should think as follows. One people will from now on be defined by their special relationship to the Lord, Who rules over all the earth. That special relationship will blur or at least reduce the distinction between the human and the divine, between the profane and the sacred. It will "mix" together the *holy* (*qedushah;* "separateness") with nationhood and with ordinary life (thus, paradoxically, making "the separate" no longer altogether separate): obedience to God's words sanctifies everyday life. The people will eventually be summoned to *be qadosh* as the Lord is *qadosh*. And through the devoted deeds of this people, He-Will-Be-What-He-Will-Be will acquire for the first time an established and acknowledged *national* place in the human world.

This covenantal arrangement is crucial for God's overall project for humankind and for addressing the obstacles that stand in its way. From the beginning of His relationship with Abraham and his immediate descendants, and more recently from the beginning of His relationship with the Children of Israel in Egypt, God has sought to form them into a people that will bear His preferred way for humankind, so that this people, living in accordance with this way, will be a blessing to all the peoples of the earth. Everything in the story so far has pointed to this purpose, which will now be made explicit in the people-constituting covenant to be enacted at Sinai.[18] The constitutive principle of the Israelite nation will be the people's covenantal relationship with the divine. Striving to fulfill its obligations under the covenant, Israel will then bear the truth and goodness of that relationship before the other nations of the earth.

The specifics of the covenant have yet to be revealed. But its overall form already lays down one crucial political principle: the covenant is to be made with the entire people—with each and every one[19]—not merely an elite. Jethro had suggested to Moses an aristocratic (or oligarchic) principle, at least as regards judges and judgment: the rule of the best human beings. Moses, although at first ruling monarchically, adopted Jethro's principle: he appointed 'anshe chayil, manly men or wealthy ones, to do the judging. But God's proposed covenant does not look to men of virtue or point to rule by philosophers or kings or prophets. It speaks rather of and to the entire body politic. In place of talk about personal virtue, it speaks of obedience and holiness, qedushah. Moses will remain God's agent and champion, but the founding event will constitute the people not around the manly virtues of the few but around the god-seeking aspirations of the many.

God has no illusions about the people. He knows their weaknesses and their propensity to stray. But He also knows that the excellence and self-command of a Moses are neither widely possible nor even sufficient to create a worthy human community. With the call to qedushah, to holiness, God is proposing a way of life that paradoxically embraces the limitations of all the people beneath the mountain. Though hardly heroic, and notwithstanding their periodic grumbling, each in his or her own (albeit limited) way has willingly embraced the project to this point. The call to holiness addresses directly the people's need to work through the human penchants for error and evil, so well exemplified in the stories of Genesis and Exodus. Later, specially appointed priests will mobilize and dramatize some of the passions that lead to chaos and will channel them into pathways that are at once cathartic, liberating, and elevating. Whatever it means, "a kingdom of priests and a holy nation" will be an entity in which ordinary human beings—not just the elite— can come as close to God as is humanly possible.[20]

God's project is not just to raise philosophers, aristocrats, or prophets to the heights of human possibility, but to enable all of us to live well despite our considerable limitations. Whatever holiness turns out to mean, God has in mind an elevated way of life in which not just a few but everyone can participate.

The success of His plan, however, first requires that the people accept the covenantal offer. We do not have long to wait for their answer.

The People's Response

And Moses came and called for the elders of the people, and set before them all these words that the Lord commanded him. And *all* the people answered *together* [literally, "as one"; *yachdav*], and said: "All that the Lord *has spoken* we will do." And Moses reported the words of the people unto the Lord. (19:7–8; emphasis added)

Moses descends the mountain, summons the elders of the people, and puts before them the Lord's entire proposal ("all these words"). The elders, we imagine, bring the divine offer to the various households under their authority. Perhaps exaggerating in the direction of the truth, the text tells us that *all* the people accepted the Lord's proposal in unison.

Why do they all say yes? Students of mass psychology will suggest that each one was influenced by his neighbor. Besides, what choice did they have? They are, at this point, utterly dependent on the manna God provides for them. Moreover, what kind of truly free consent can one expect or attribute to former slaves who are not yet free in soul? Reading the text in this spirit, a famous midrash imagines the Israelites giving their consent only because an entire mountain was held over their heads.

More hopeful readers will see the people's consent in a more favorable light. Precisely because of their prior condition of servitude, feeling lowly and empty, the people may have been genuinely attracted by the prospect of playing a part in a grand project, presented by the Power that delivered them from bondage. The offer awakens and appeals to their higher aspirations: a dream of greatness, a desire for holiness, a longing for the divine. Rising above their usual preoccupations with safety and comfort, they are stirred by the grandeur of their new and lofty national purpose: to bear always the Lord's great hope for humankind. Even if they have little idea what they are agreeing to and are prone to change their minds and neglect their promises, their consent still seems genuine and significant, and it does them credit. Once again, we may say, their agreement makes them worthy of the offer. Should they later fall short of their commitments, they will understand that they are violating not only God's commands but also their own covenantal agreement to obey them.

If the students of mass psychology read perhaps too cynically, the hopeful readers read too cheerfully. To their great credit, the people accept the covenant—unanimously, immediately, and without hesitation or conditions. But careful attention to their words calls their consent partially into question. They do not say what the covenant in fact calls for: "What the Lord *will say* we will do." They agree only to what He has *already said*. Their caution—or is it bewilderment?—reflects their ignorance of the precise terms of the agreement; they do not know what they are getting into or what will be expected of them.[21] Whether from desperate fear or enthusiastic hope, their consent is hardly informed. And their agreement, while admirable, is not sufficiently confident and forthcoming: they do not promise in advance to heed whatever the Lord *will* say.

These facts escape Moses, but not the Lord. Going again up the mountain, Moses simply reports the people's positive response and considers the deal done. But the Lord knows that the people's agreement was far too easy, their acceptance far from complete. Something more will be needed to bring them along: a new relation between them and Moses. What happens next is intended to get the people to accept Moses's authority as God's prophet for and teacher of His people. This will require spectacular pyrotechnics.

The Spectacle and Its Purpose(s)

The Lord begins to instruct Moses about His end and His means:

And the Lord said unto Moses: "Lo, I come unto you in a thick cloud, that the people may *hear* when I speak with *you,* and may have *trust (ya'aminu) also in you* forever." And Moses told the words of the people unto the Lord. (19:9; emphasis added)

The Lord will come to Moses in a thick cloud, so that the people may hear—but not see—when He speaks to Moses. Why? "So that the people may have trust *also in you* [Moses] *forever.*"

The scene on the mountain will be more than awe-inspiring. Seeing nothing clearly, the people will only hear voices, and they will not know whose voice they are hearing—especially when the ram's horn, God's Voice, and Moses's voice are all sounding at once. The whole scene is meant to flood the senses and overwhelm the ordinary ways through which people gain knowledge of the world. The people must know that Moses is invested with divine authority and actually speaks for God.[22]

Apparently perplexed by God's remark and thinking perhaps that He may not have understood him properly, Moses simply repeats what he said before: the people have agreed already. God is not moved. Moses does not yet appreciate what He is up to. God has in mind a permanent change in the relation between Moses and the people—and Himself. Yet on closer consideration, it is not obvious what God intends.

One possibility—in my view, the more likely one—is that God plans to use this experience to increase Moses's standing among the people, as part of a larger plan of passing agency more into human hands. At the end of the episode at the Sea of Reeds, the people were said to "trust *(vayya'aminu)* in the Lord and in *Moses His servant*" (14:31), but that trust became short-lived when water and food grew scarce. More recently, when Moses sat judging the people, they may have seen him as godlike, but they were at risk of turning against him, as they so often had. Jethro had told him: get codified law and get divine support. Here, in front of the people, Moses will soon get both. Being heard conversing with God atop the cloud-capped mountain, he will directly receive divine authority for all his future pronouncements. He will finally have answered the challenge of the Israelite *rasha'*: Who made you a man ruler and judge over us? He will receive, as it were, his divine commission in full hearing of the people: now they should trust *you*.

An opposite interpretation also makes sense. The people already regard whatever Moses does as coming from God, but he is in danger of being carried away with his own authority; for example, by presenting his intuitive judgments in the people's disputes as if they were God's teachings. Jethro had told him that he should tell the people God's words and laws, but Moses did not. What God has planned is a subtle criticism of Moses: the laws should not come from you but from Me. When the people hear us conversing atop the cloud-capped mountain, they will understand that you, Moses, are merely My messenger and prophet. They will trust in you *also,* but as My servant, and in Me first.[23]

Moses, seemingly dumbfounded, again simply repeats what he said before: "And Moses told the words of the people unto the Lord" (19:9).[24] The Lord ends the conversation by dispatching Moses with instructions to prepare the people for the big occasion.

Getting Ready for the Revelation

In many cultures and traditions, encounters between gods and men are regular occurrences. Where men worship nature gods, traffic between them is expected. Some traditional myths even speak about sexual relations between men and goddesses or between gods and women—even between gods and beasts. The boundaries between the human and the divine are as porous as those between man and nature. But as we have seen, the Bible from the beginning has set its face against such notions. Nature is not divine; the sun, the moon, and the earth are creatures, not gods. The world came into being through acts of speech and separation, from a single intelligent source, not through the sexual union of sky father and earth mother or any other divine duality.

Against such a background, a quasi-physical encounter between the Lord and human beings is a big deal, unprecedented in the Torah. The Lord has spoken to only a few characters: outside the otherworldly Eden, only Noah, Abraham, Sarah, Hagar, Rebekah, Isaac, Jacob/Israel, and Moses have heard from Him, sometimes in dreams. Abraham and Moses have conversed with Him; Moses lives with His Voice in his ear. In Egypt, at the Sea of Reeds and with the manna, the Lord effected "miracles" in full view of human beings. His messenger even manifested himself to Moses at the burning bush. But His direct "appearance" and "revelation" before human beings, never mind before an entire people, are simply unprecedented—and dangerous. Special preparations will be needed both to celebrate the unique character of this revelation and to guard against its dangers:

> And the Lord said unto Moses: "Go unto the people, and sanctify them (*veqiddashtam*) today and tomorrow, and let them wash their garments, and be ready against the third day; for the third day the Lord will come down in the sight of all the people upon Mount Sinai. And you shall set bounds unto the people round about, saying: 'Take heed to yourselves, that you go not up into the mountain or touch the border of it; whosoever touches the mountain shall be surely put to death; no hand shall touch him, but he shall surely be stoned or shot through; whether it be beast or man, it shall not live; when the ram's horn sounds long, they shall come up to the mountain.'" And Moses went down from the mountain unto the people and sanctified the people, and they washed their garments. And he said unto the people: "Be ready against the third day; come not near a woman." (19:10–15)

The two days of preparation required for the divine encounter serve two purposes: the people must show proper respect, and they must maintain proper distance. They are to sanctify or purify themselves "today and tomorrow" and wash their clothes, so that their outer appearance shall reflect the purity within. With the aid of these measures, they are to prepare themselves also psychically for the third day—the day of completion—when, in the sight of the people assembled, the Lord (in a thick cloud) will come down the mountain.

But against any impulse to rush the mountain and merge with the divine presence, the strictest boundary must be observed between the human and the divine, even as the divine appears in human company for this one and only time. Awe-filled keeping of distance, not ecstatic rushing to fuse, is the only appropriate human response to the presence of the Lord. In telling Moses what to say about this crucial matter, the

Lord does not mince words: an uninfringeable boundary between them and Me; death by stoning or arrow for any man or beast that violates it, even by the slightest touch. Only when the ram's horn sounds long, to indicate the end of the revelation, can the people again come up into the mountain, no longer sanctified by the divine presence.

Moses comes down the mountain and delivers the Lord's instructions. Following orders, Moses sanctifies the people, who, for the first time since they left Egypt, are asked to purify themselves. He tells them, we surmise, to put away all "strange gods" and idols, amulets, and fetishes that they may have brought with them from Egypt.[25] They are to avoid any activity that would detract from the purity of heart and mind that is appropriate for encountering Y-H-V-H. The people wash their garments as they would before any eagerly anticipated meeting. Making clear that this encounter will be noetic, not erotic—mental, not carnal—Moses adds in his own name the injunction to refrain from sex.[26]

Nature in Tumult

The third day arrives, not with a whimper but with a bang:

> And it came to pass on the third day, when it was morning, that there were thunders [literally, "voices"; qoloth] and lightnings and a dense cloud upon the mountain, and the sound ("voice"; qol) of a horn exceedingly loud; and all the people that were in the camp trembled (vayyecherad). And Moses brought forth the people out of the camp to meet God; and they stood at the bottom of the mountain. (19:16–17)

We should try to imagine ourselves in the crowd. The morning of the eagerly awaited day has arrived. But, My Lord, what a morning! A colossal storm erupts above and engulfs the mountain: there are flashes of lightning and peals of thunder; thick clouds cover the sky and the mountaintop. The exceedingly loud sound of a horn—or was it the fierce wind rushing around the mountain?—adds to the noise and commotion. The scene being far from what they had expected, all the people in the camp tremble at the turmoil. Who can blame them? We tremble with them.

But Moses is not afraid. He leads the people out of the camp. They station themselves at the base of the mountain, as close as they are allowed, awaiting the Lord's arrival:

> Now Mount Sinai was altogether in smoke, because the Lord descended upon it in fire; and the smoke thereof ascended as the smoke of a furnace, and the whole mountain quaked (*vayyecherad*) greatly. And when the voice (*qol*) of the horn waxed louder and louder, Moses spoke, and God answered him by a Voice (*beqol*). (19:18–19)

The people stand quietly, but the turmoil continues. The mountain smokes, it blazes, it trembles and rumbles and roars—like a volcano in the midst of a hurricane. At last, through the rising sound of the horn, verbal contact is finally made: Moses, standing with the people, speaks up to the fire, and God (*'elohim*) answers him, a Voice from on high.

But all is not yet ready for the revelation. The Lord has some final stage directions for Moses, primarily concerning who is to be where. As we shall see, the location of Moses himself will often be anything but clear:

> And the Lord came *down* upon Mount Sinai, to the *top* of the mountain; and the Lord called Moses to the *top* of the mountain; and Moses went *up*. And the Lord said unto Moses: "Go *down*, charge the people, lest they break through unto the Lord *to gaze*, and many of them perish. And let the priests also, that come near to the Lord, sanctify themselves, lest the Lord break forth upon them." (19:20–22; emphasis added)

The Lord finally "arrives," descending to the top of the mountain, to which He summons Moses up. Moses goes up, in the sight of the people, who look on in amazement, both at his courage and at his special access. But no sooner does he arrive, far above the trembling crowd, than he is told to go back down, again to warn the people against breaking through to the Lord. But there is a more explicit command: the people are not to gaze at ("to see"; *lir'oth*) the Lord, lest they perish.

Why the emphatic prohibition on seeing and gazing? Why is "seeing" forbidden? In part it is because the entire premise of the proposed covenant is "Hearken to My voice." In ordinary human affairs, as I have noted several times, seeing is believing. But in Israel, people are finally to trust their ears, not their eyes. They are to hear and heed the word of the Lord. The display of visual pyrotechnics is intended to overwhelm the sense of sight, so that the people will (only) listen.

There is a further problem—indeed, two problems—with "gazing," with "looking *at*": it can be a prelude to intimacy and merging, or it can be a form of disrespectful appropriation. One can gaze longingly, hoping to unite with the beloved. Or one can, like the voyeur (and viewer of pornography), capture the look for oneself with no respect or engagement of the heart. Both temptations of gazing are at odds with the relationship God wants Israel to establish with Him: not fusion, not appropriation, but reverent and joyous obedience in imitation of His holiness (apartness). As we shall soon see, being in relation to God will arise not through seeing or touching or merging—or making visible likenesses or using His Name—but through consecrating time, beginning with Sabbath observance.

The remark about "priests" is puzzling, since no priests have yet been appointed. Rashi and others suggest that the term refers to the firstborn. In traditional societies, the sacerdotal duties usually fell to the firstborn. But the passage, anticipating the appointment of priests, may also (or instead) be warning those who deal with sacred things, and who mediate between the people and God, to avoid the common and dangerous errors people make in trying to approach the divine.

Moses, either confused or annoyed at having to go back down so soon, tells the Lord that he finds the instruction redundant:

And Moses said unto the Lord: "The people *cannot* come *up* to Mount Sinai; for You did charge us, saying: 'Set bounds about the mount, and sanctify it.'" And the Lord said unto him: "Go, get you *down,* and *you* shall come *up,* you, and Aaron with you; but let not the priests and the people break through to come *up* unto the Lord, lest He break forth upon them." So Moses went *down* unto the people, and said to them . . . (19:23–25; emphasis added)

To Moses's demurral, the Lord replies, we imagine, with irritation. He wants the order repeated, so He says, to both the priests and the people. But we suspect that the Lord has an additional purpose for Moses's shuttling up and down: He wants the people to see that Moses has easy access to the Lord and that he can return from such encounters unscathed. The people have seen Moses go up the mountain; they have yet to see him return. God's order for Moses to descend allows them to do so. Such experiences feed God's larger purpose: He wants to establish Moses as His mediator, not only in battle but also at law.

Moses, obediently if perhaps reluctantly, goes down the mountain. "So Moses went down to the people, and he said to them (*vayyo'mer 'alehem*) . . ." What did he say to them? Did he tell them what came before or what comes next? Traditional Hebrew commentators assume that he delivered the warning that the Lord had just told him to give. But the verb "to say" (*'amar*), unlike the verb "to speak" (*dibber*), is almost always followed by the directly quoted speech. Here it is not. Alter suggests, "Perhaps 'to say' is used here for Moses in order to avoid any overlap with God's speech act in the very next verse: 'And God spoke (*vayedabber*) these words (*devarim*).'" But Alter adds, a little cryptically, "It should be kept in mind that the chapter breaks are medieval, so the original text moved directly from Moses's saying to God's speaking."[27] Or, to speak bluntly, what Moses may have said to the people was nothing other than God's "Ten Words," delivered by Moses speaking about God in the third person. Who can say what Moses said?

The chapter ends without clarity. It confuses and perplexes the reader, as does the entire account. Where is Moses, up or down, and why so much shuttling? How, among the multiple voices—the thunder, horn, Moses's, God's—can the people or the reader discern the Voice of the Lord? The reader's perplexing experience trying to make sense of these introductory moments mimics the awesome, bewildering experience of the people on the ground. They are surely disoriented, as are we. Where is Moses? Where is God? And most important, Who (who) is speaking, when, and for Whom (whom)?

Could such confusion—or, better, mingling—of Voices (voices) be precisely the purpose of the pyrotechnics? How does this serve God's goal regarding the people's attitude toward and trust in Moses? And, gentle readers, a pointed question arises also for us: How among the disorienting sounds and bewildering sights of our lives may any of us discern the authentic Voice of God?

We must wait a while to answer these questions. Keeping them in the back of our minds, we must first hear God's awesome pronouncement of the Ten Commandments.

Principles for God's New Nation

We come at last to the central event in Israel's national founding: the giving of the Law at Mount Sinai. The "Ten Commandments" (20:1–14), pronounced there by the Lord God to the assembled and recently liberated Children of Israel, constitute the most famous teaching of the book of Exodus, perhaps of the entire Hebrew Bible. Prescribing proper conduct toward God and man, the Decalogue embodies the core principles of the Israelite way of life and what would become known as the Judeo-Christian ethic. Even in our secular age, its influence on the morality of the West is enormous, if not always acknowledged or welcomed.

Yet despite its renown, the Decalogue is only superficially known, even by practicing Jews and Christians, partly because its very familiarity inhibits a deeper understanding of its teachings, but mainly because the teachings themselves are not easily understood. In aspiring to comprehend them, this chapter departs from our usual attention to the narrative to concentrate entirely on the content of the Decalogue—without regard to the speaker, the awesome presentation, or the way the words are received by the people on the ground. We will leave our place among the people and attend solely to the rational content of these famous words: we seek to know what they mean, what they intend, and why they matter.[1]

Before plunging into the text, I should emphasize in advance how unexpected and stunning will be the content of what is spoken. To this point, we have witnessed God's concern for His enslaved people, His recruitment of Moses, His successful contest with Pharaoh, His victory over Egypt at the Sea of Reeds, His attention to the people's needs, and His offer of a national covenant to the Israelite masses. Nothing has prepared us for an avalanche of intrusive and demanding principles, teachings, and obligations that will touch every aspect of human life. These principles, teachings, and obligations erupt into the world exactly as they now erupt into the reader's consciousness. Neither the world nor we will ever be the same.

Structure and Context

Let me begin by correcting some common misimpressions, starting with the name "Ten Commandments." Although most of the entries in the Decalogue appear in the imperative mode ("You shall" or "You shall not"), they are not called commandments (*mitsvot*) but rather statements or words: "And God spoke all these words (*devarim*)." Later in the Bible we hear about the ten words—in the Greek translation, *deka logoi* or Decalogue—but whether the reference is to these statements is far from obvious.

Counting is no help. Traditional exegetes (Jewish and Christian) have derived as many as thirteen injunctions from God's speech in Exodus 20, and because internal divisions within particular statements are unclear, even those who agree on the number disagree on how to reckon them. Furthermore, no mention is made in Exodus 20 of the famous stone tables on which, in traditional imagery, we see the Decalogue inscribed, five statements on each. When such tables are mentioned later in Exodus, we are not told what is written on them.[2]

What then do we know about the structure of these pronouncements? One group of them touches mainly on the relation between God and the individual Israelite: the first words spoken are "I *Y-H-V-H* (or, "I the Lord") [am] your God ('*anochi Y-H-V-H 'elohekha*)," and within this group we hear the phrase "*Y-H-V-H* your God" four more times. The second group (beginning with "You shall not murder") touches primarily on conduct between and among human beings; in this section neither God ('elohim) nor Y-H-V-H is mentioned, and the very last word of the Decalogue, "your neighbor," marks a far distance from the opening "I Y-H-V-H" (or "I the Lord").

Next, nearly all of the statements are formulated in the negative. The first few proscribe wrongful ways of relating to the divine—no other gods, no images, no vain use of the divine name—while the last six begin with lo, "not." Human beings, it seems, are more in need of restraint than encouragement.

In this sea of prohibition, two positive exhortations stand out: one about hallowing the Sabbath, one about honoring one's father and mother. Hallowing the Sabbath is also one of two injunctions that receive the longest exposition or explanation; the other long one concerns images and likenesses. Clearly, these three deserve special attention.

Far more important than structural features is the context into which the Decalogue fits. As we saw in the last chapter, this is the people-forming covenant proposed by God through His prophet Moses to the Children of Israel (19:5–6). It is only here, with the offer of a divine covenant, that this motley multitude of ex-slaves first learns that they can become a people among the other peoples of the earth and, further, that they can become a special people with a great purpose, a treasure unto the Lord. Moreover, this special place is defined in more than political terms: they are invited to become a kingdom of priests and a holy nation. This is a matter to which we will return, as we search for clues to what might render them holy.

Yet the Decalogue is hardly the bulk of the Torah's people-forming legislation. All of the laws specifying proper conduct and ritual observance come later: first in the ordinances immediately following the giving of the Decalogue, then in the laws regarding the building of the Tabernacle, and then, in Leviticus, in the law governing sacrifices and the so-called holiness code. So the Decalogue is a prologue or preamble to the constituting law. Like the preamble to the Constitution of the United States, it enunciates the general principles on which the new covenant will be founded, principles that touch upon—and connect—the relation between man and God and between man and man. Making clear in advance what it will mean to belong to this new people, the Decalogue is less a founding legal code and more an aspirational guide for every Israelite—and, perhaps, every human—heart and mind.

Y-H-V-H, Your God

The Decalogue is introduced[3] as follows: "And God spoke all these words, saying . . ." (20:1). Unlike most biblical statements reporting a divine act of speaking, this one does not identify the audience. The omission is fitting, for the speech is addressed simultaneously to all the assembled people and to each one individually: all of the injunctions are given in the second-person singular. Moreover, although pronounced at a particular time and place and uttered before a particular group, the content is not parochial. It is addressed to anyone and everyone who is open to hearing it—including, of course, to us, who read the text and ponder what it tells us.

If the audience's identity is unspecified, that of the speaker is plain: "I Y-H-V-H am your God, who brought you out of the land of Egypt, out of the house of bondage" (20:2). Later Jewish—but not Christian— tradition will treat this assertion as part of the first statement and the basis of a first positive precept: to believe in the existence of the one God, Y-H-V-H. But in context it functions more to announce the identity of the speaker—who, as would have been customary in any proposed covenant between a suzerain and his vassals, declares the ruler–subject relationship that governs everything that follows. On this understanding, "I Y-H-V-H am your God" emphasizes that the speaker is the individual hearer's personal deity: not just the god of this locale, capable of making the mountain tremble, rumble, and smoke, but the very One Who brought you personally out of your servitude in Egypt.

Unlike God's self-identification to Moses at the burning bush (3:6), there is no mention here of the patriarchs. The covenant offered to the Israelites is not with the God of their long-dead fathers but with the God of their own recent deliverance. The former covenant was for fertility, multiplicity, and a promised land; the new one concerns peoplehood, self-rule, and the goals of righteousness and holiness. It rests on a new foundation, and it is made not with a select few but with the comprehensive many.

Although the basis of the new relationship is historical, rooted in the Lord's deliverance of the Israelites from Egyptian bondage, His opening declaration also conveys a philosophical—that is, universal—message. He appears to suggest that for the Children of Israel—and perhaps for unnamed others—there are two great alternatives: either to live freely in relation to the Lord or to be a slave to Pharaoh, a human king who rules as if he were divine. Egypt, identified redundantly as "the house of bondage," is presented here not as one alternative among many but as the only alternative to living as men and women whose identity and freedom depend on embracing the covenant with the Lord.

How Not to Seek God

After the opening remark declaring God's relation to this people, the next statements concern how God wants them to conduct their side of the relationship. The instruction is entirely negative.

The first wrong way is this: "You shall not have other [or "strange"; 'aherim] gods before Me" (20:3). This is not (yet) a declaration of philosophical monotheism but of cultural monotheism.[4] God is claiming an exclusive, intimate I-thou relationship like that of a marriage, requiring unqualified fidelity and permitting no other to come between the partners. One might phrase it: "You shall look to no *stranger*-gods in My presence." This goes beyond turning an I-thou relation into a triangle. 'Aherim, the word translated "other" or "strange," suggests that all such putative deities would be alien not only to the relationship but also to its human partners. The only God fit for a relationship with beings made in God's image is the One Whose being they resemble and Whose likeness they embody. Only such a One would not be a "stranger."

It is true that powers regarded (not unreasonably) by other peoples as divine—such as the sun, the moon, the earth, the sea, the volcanic mountain, or the river—may play a decisive role in determining the character and events of human life. The powers that the Greek poets presented as anthropomorphic gods—Poseidon, earth-shaker; Aphrodite, source of erotic love; Demeter, source of crops; warlike Ares—must be acknowledged and respected for their place in human life. But one cannot truly have a relationship with them, for they are strangers to all those who look to them.[5] Only *Y-H-V-H* offers the possibility of genuine kinship.

Having established exclusivity, God then corrects a second error, the human inclination to represent the divine in artfully made visible images and to worship these likenesses:

> You shall not make unto you a graven [or "sculpted"] image, nor any likeness of any thing that is in the heavens above or that is in the earth below, or that is in the water under the earth; you shall not bow down unto them, nor serve them, for I *Y-H-V-H* your God am a jealous (or "zealous") god, remembering [or "visiting"] the iniquity (*'avon*) of the fathers upon the children unto the third or fourth generation of them that hate Me; and showing grace (*chesed*) unto the thousandth generation of them that love Me and keep My commandments. (20:4–6)

Intended to proscribe the worship of idols, this injunction builds a fence against such practices by forbidding even the making of sculpted images, especially of any natural being. It emphatically opposes the practice, known to the ex-slaves from Egypt, of worshipping natural beings—from dung beetles to the sun to the Pharaohs—and representing them in sculpted likenesses. But it also seems to preclude any attempt to represent, in image or likeness, God Himself. The overall message seems clear: any being that can be represented in visible images is not divine.[6]

What's wrong with worshipping visible images or the things they represent? Even if it rests on an error—mistaking a mere likeness for a divinity—it seems harmless enough, at worst a superstitious waste of time. But the practice and the disposition behind it are hardly innocuous. To worship things unworthy of worship is demeaning to the worshipper; it is to be oriented falsely in the world, taking one's bearings from merely natural phenomena that, although powerful, are not providential, intelligent, or beneficent. Moreover, such apparently humble submission masks a species of presumption. Human beings will have decided which heavenly bodies or animals are worthy of reverence and how these powers are to be appeased. The same human beings believe that they themselves, through artful representation, can fully capture these natural beings and powers and then, through obeisance, manipulate them. Worse, with increased artistic sophistication comes the danger that people will come to revere not the things idolized but the idols themselves, and even the sculptors and painters who, in making them, willy-nilly elevate themselves.[7]

Perhaps the most important objection is that neither the worship of dumb nature nor the celebration of human artfulness teaches anything about righteousness, holiness, or basic human decency. The worship of nature or of idols may even contribute to the problem. Making the connection explicit, the Lord vows to visit the "iniquities" of the fathers on the sons, unto the third or fourth generation.

An iniquity (*'avon*) in the Bible differs from a sin (*chet*). To sin is to miss the mark, as an arrow misses the target. To commit an iniquity is to do something twisted or crooked, to be perverse. Sin is not inherited, and only the sinner gets punished (see Deut. 24:16); iniquity, however, like "pollution," lasts and lasts, affecting those who come in its wake. It is not only that perverse fathers are likely to pervert their children; the children are inevitably stained by the father's iniquity.[8] How this comes about, the text leaves wonderfully ambiguous, thanks to the multiple meanings of the Hebrew verb *poqed,* which means both "visiting" and "remembering." Either the Lord promises to intervene directly, actively inflicting the father's twisted deeds on the sons, or He promises to let those deeds linger in the fabric of the world, contaminating the lives of the sons until there is some repentance or cleansing. Either way—and perhaps they amount to the same thing—the perversity of the father's deeds will reverberate through the generations.[9]

The Israelites are not yet told what behavior they are to regard as iniquitous. Is it idolatry itself, or does idolatry lead to such twisted practices as incest, fratricide, child sacrifice, bestiality, and cannibalism? One way or the other, the fathers (and mothers) are put on notice: how they stand with respect to divinity will affect their children and their children's children. God and the world care about and perpetuate our iniquities.

But not indefinitely—only to the third or fourth generation, the limits of any father's clearly imaginable future. Overshadowing all is the promise of God's bountiful grace "to the thousandth generation of those who love Me and keep My commandments." Just as the sons of iniquitous fathers suffer through no direct fault of their own, so a thousand generations of descendants of a single God-loving and righteous ancestor enjoy unmerited grace.[10] (It has been only 200 generations since the time of Father Abraham, for whose merit the children of Abraham are still being blessed.)

From this injunction against idol worship we learn that God and the world are not indifferent to the conduct of human beings; that our choice is between living in relation to the Lord and worshipping or serving strange gods, between keeping His commandments and living iniquitously; that the choices we make will have consequences for those who come later; but that the blessings that follow from worthy and God-loving conduct are more far-reaching than the miseries caused by iniquitous and God-spurning conduct. There will be perversity in every generation, but the world overflows with *chesed* or grace.

This surprising turn in the comment on idolatry and iniquity highlights the decisive (and perhaps most important) difference between idols or strange(r) gods and "the Lord your God." Under no other deity does the world embody the enduring grace and blessing foretold here. As humankind learned with the hope-filled rainbow sign after the Flood (Gen. 9:1–17), the token of God's first covenant with humankind, so here each Israelite learns that he will have reason to be grateful not only for his recent deliverance from Egypt but also for the enduringly gracious (and not merely powerful or dreadful) deity with whom he is covenanting.

The implications for how we are to live in the light of this teaching are clear. My children and my children's children are at risk from any iniquity I commit, but endless generations will benefit from the good I may do. An enormous responsibility, then, and yet we know also that we are not solely responsible for the world's fate and that redemption is always possible. Even if we fail, there will still be *chesed.* To walk with hope in the light of *chesed* offers the best chance for a worthy life.

The final error to be corrected concerns the use of the divine name. If visible beings are unworthy of worship and if, conversely, "*Y-H-V-H* your God" cannot be visibly depicted, all that remains to us of Him (when He is silent) is His name. Yet it is also not through His name that the Israelites are to enter into a proper relationship with the Lord:

> You shall not take up (*nasa'*) the name of the Lord your God in vain, for the Lord will not hold guiltless the one who takes up His name in vain. (20:7)

Without warning and for no apparent reason, the Lord now speaks of Himself in the distant third person. This distancing fits with the progressive distance from "your God," to "other/stranger gods before Me," to "images and idols" not to be made and worshipped, and now to "the name of the Lord your God" that is not to be taken in vain.

The prohibition, though seemingly straightforward, asks to be unpacked. What, exactly, is being proscribed? What uses of God's name are "in vain"? The concept embraces not only speaking falsely but also speaking emptily, frivolously, insincerely, contemptuously. The most likely occasion for such empty invocations would be in swearing an oath, calling on God to witness the truth of what one is about to say or the pledge one is promising to fulfill. A common instance of the contemptuous use of God's name, explicitly mentioned later in the Torah (Lev. 24:10–16), would be blaspheming or cursing: either reviling the Name itself or using it to curse another. But the injunction seems to have a larger intention.

The injunction's real target may be the attempt to live in the world assuming that "God is on our side." To speak the Lord's name, unless instructed to do so, is to wrap yourself in the divine mantle, to summon God in support of your own purposes. It is to treat God as if He were sitting by the phone waiting to do your bidding. In the guise of beseeching the Lord in His majesty and grace, one behaves as if one were *His* lord and master. One behaves, in other words, like Pharaoh.[11]

There is a deeper issue, having to do less with misconduct than with the hazards of speech itself. Treating a name as something one can "take up" or "lift" is also to take up the thing named, as if by its handle. Like making images of the divine, trafficking in the divine name evinces a presumption of familiarity and knowledge. To handle the name of the Lord risks treating Him as a finite thing known through and through.

Even if uttered in innocence, the use of the Lord's name invites the all-too-human error that attends all acts of naming: the belief that one thereby grasps the essence.

Called by God from out of the burning bush, we recall, Moses sought to know God's name. The profoundly mysterious non-answer he received—'ehyeh 'asher 'ehyeh, I Will We What I Will Be, or I Am That I Am—was a rebuke: the Lord is not to be known or captured in any simple act of naming. The right relation to Him is not through naming or knowing His nature but through hearkening to His words. To repeat: the right approach is not through philosophy or theology, not through speaking about God (*theo-logos*), but through heeding His speech.

Yet to this point, there has been no positive instruction regarding how one *should* relate to the divine. What does this God want of His people? The next utterance gives the answer.

The Sabbath Day

Of all the statements in the Decalogue, the one regarding the Sabbath is the most far-reaching and the most significant. It addresses the profound matters of time and its reckoning, work and rest, and man's relation to God, the world, and his fellow men. Most important, this is the only injunction that speaks explicitly of hallowing and holiness—the special goal for Israel in the covenant being proposed:

> Remember the Sabbath day, to keep it holy (*leqaddesho*). Six days shall you labor and do all your work (*melakhah*). But the seventh day [is a] Sabbath to the Lord your God.
>
> You shall do no manner of work (*melakhah*), you, your son and your daughter, your servant and your maidservant, your cattle and your stranger that is within your gates.
>
> For in six days made (*'asah*) the Lord the heavens and the earth and the sea and all that is in them; but He rested (*vayyanach*) on the seventh day; and therefore the Lord blessed (*berakh*) the seventh day and He hallowed it (*vayeqaddeshehu*). (20:8–11)

The passage opens with a general statement, specifying two obligations: to remember and to sanctify. Next comes an explication of the duty to make holy, comprising a teaching for the six days and a contrasting teaching for the seventh. At the end, we get the reason for the injunction, a reference to the Lord's six-day Creation of the world, His rest on the seventh day, and His consequent doings regarding that day.

Imagine ourselves hearing this simple injunction at Sinai. We might find every term puzzling: What is "the Sabbath day"? What does it mean to "remember" it? And what is entailed in the charge, "to keep it holy" or "to sanctify it"? And yet the statement seems to imply that "the Sabbath day" is already known to the Israelites. What might they have understood by it?

The word *sabbath* comes from a root meaning "to cease," "to desist from labor," and "to rest." Where have the ex-slaves encountered a day of desisting? Only in their recent experience with manna in Exodus 16 (discussed in Chapter Nine). In response to their murmuring against Moses born of their unmet need for food, the Lord caused manna to rain from heaven for the people to gather, "a day's portion every day." This He did not only to tame their hunger but also explicitly "that I may test them, whether they will walk in My law or not" (16:4). Of greatest significance was the Lord's injunction limiting work to six days: there was to be no gathering on the seventh day, for which a double portion was provided on the sixth.[12]

Aside from their experience of manna, the Israelites may have had another referent for a "Sabbath day." Before the coming of the Bible, many peoples in the Ancient Near East already reckoned time in seven-day cycles connected with the phases of the moon. Among the Babylonians, the seventh days were fast days, days of ill luck, on which one avoided pleasure and desisted from important projects for fear of inhospitable natural powers. This was especially the case with their once-a-month Sabbath, *shabattu* or *shapattu,* the day of the full moon.

Against these naturalistic views, the Sabbath teaching in Exodus institutes a reckoning of time independent of the motion of the heavenly bodies, in which the day for desisting comes always in regular and repeatable cycles and is to be celebrated as a day of joy and blessing. Readers of Genesis already know the basis of this way of reckoning time from the story of creation, whose target was precisely those Mesopotamian teachings. But the Children of Israel are only now learning that time in the world—and, hence, their life in the world—will be understood differently from the way nature-worshipping peoples understand it. The Sabbath day, blessed by the Lord, has existed from time immemorial, but the creation- and humanity-centered view of the world enters human existence only through the covenant being here enacted with the Children of Israel.

What, then, is the duty to remember the Sabbath? About some matters—such as their previous servitude—the Israelites will be exhorted to keep in mind what they have experienced. About the Sabbath day—whose original, of course, no human being since Adam and Eve could have experienced—the Israelites are told to keep present in their minds what the Lord is now telling them for the first time. Once they learn the reason behind the injunction, the duty to remember will link their future mindfulness with their recall of the remotest past: the creation of the world and the beginning, or pre-beginning, of time. Each week, going forward, the Children of Israel not only will be recalled to God's creation of the world but also will be invited symbolically to relive it.

Much later, when Moses repeats the Decalogue in Deuteronomy, he will enjoin the Israelites to "guard" (or "keep" or "observe"; *shamor*) the Sabbath day, to keep it holy, "as the Lord your God commanded you" (Deut. 5:12). Guarding and keeping are duties for the Sabbath day itself, but remembering it should take place all week long, reconfiguring our perception of time and its meaning. Under this radically new understanding, the six days of work and labor point toward and are completed by the seventh day and its hallowing. Mindfulness of sanctified time edifies the manner and spirit in which one lives *all* the time; this change in the meaning of time transforms and elevates all of human existence. Work is for the sake of a livelihood, but staying alive has a purpose beyond itself.

Again, the root meaning of *qaddesh*, to make holy, is to set apart, to make separate, to make separate toward some object of dedication. Other peoples have their own forms of separation or sanctity: sacred places, sacred rituals and practices, sacred persons or animals. But in

Israel, what is made holy is not a special object, place, or practice, but *the time of your life.*

How to make this time holy we learn in the sequel; here the Israelite idea of holiness is connected to the distinction between work and rest, as well as that between the things that are yours and the things that "belong" to God. The six days of work appear to be "for yourself and your own"; the seventh day is a Sabbath "to the Lord your God," on which "labor [*avodah*] for oneself" is replaced by "service [*avodah*] to the Lord."

Yet the form of devotion is odd. No rituals or sacrifices are specified; what is required is an absence, a cessation, a desisting, and this obligation falls on the entire household. From master to servant to beast and stranger, the worldly hierarchy is to be set aside; regardless of rank or station, all are equally invited to participate in the hallowing of the day. Nor do they need to travel or offer a sacrifice to encounter this sanctified time. Holiness has a central, ever-renewable place in their ordinary life at home, if they but keep it in mind.

And the key to the holiness that is the Sabbath's desisting from labor? It is nothing less than God's own doings in connection with Creation. Every week the Children of Israel are returned to the ultimate beginning and source of the world, summoned to commemorate its creation and Creator.

The Israelites are not only recalled to the Creation; their weekly cycle of work and desisting is also meant, symbolically, to reproduce it. Here is the most radical implication of the Sabbath teaching: the Israelites are, de facto, enjoined "*to be like God*"—both in their six days of work and especially on the day of desisting. Note well: their relationship to the Creator is no longer based solely on historical time and in their (parochial) deliverance from Egyptian bondage. It is ontologically rooted in cosmic time and in the universal human capacity to celebrate the created order and its Creator, and in our special place as that order's Godlike, God-imitating, and God-praising creatures.*

---

*It bears emphasis that God is here revealing Himself for the first time to the Israelites (or to anyone else *inside* the biblical narrative) as the Creator of heaven and earth. Before now, He has told Moses that He was the God of the patriarchs, and He has told the people that He delivered them from the Egyptian house of bondage—both aspects of His role in human history. Why, one wonders, is this the right time to

It is, of course, peculiar to command us to rest as God rested, because it is peculiar to speak of God "resting." Nevertheless, we can conjecture something of what it might mean.

In the original account of Creation, at the end of the sixth day, "God saw every thing that He had made and, behold, it was very good." But the true completion of Creation comes only after the creative work had ceased:

> And the heaven and the earth were finished and all their array. And God finished on the seventh day His work which He had made and He desisted (*vayyishboth*) on the seventh day from all His work which He had made. And God blessed (*vayevarekh*) the seventh day and He hallowed it (*vayeqaddesh 'otho*), because on it He desisted (*shavath*) from all His work which God created to make. (Gen. 2:1–3)

Here there is no talk of resting but only of desisting, blessing, and hallowing (setting apart) the seventh day. A complete world of created and contingent beings has been brought into being by a divinity Who then completes His creative efforts by standing down. In this mysterious blessing and hallowing of time beyond the world of making, God makes manifest in the rhythm of the world an acknowledgment of its mysterious and hidden source.[13]

Remarkably, this consecration of time—and this pointing to what is "out of time"—is something only we human beings can glimpse and participate in. It is open to us if and when we set aside our comings and goings, our getting and spending, and turn our aspirations toward the realm beyond our worldly being from which that being derives. It is open to us when we are moved by wonder and gratitude for the existence of

---

make known His authorship of the cosmic whole? Is it to teach the Israelites the more-than-parochial character of their god and to invite them therefore to see themselves in a more exalted and universal light? Or is this knowledge of God's awesome cosmic power deemed necessary to compel obedience to the teaching about the Sabbath and the following injunctions about conduct involving other human beings? What is the connection between the idea of God as Creator and the idea of God as giver of Law and teacher of morals?

something rather than nothing, for order rather than chaos, and for our unmerited presence in the story.

It may also seem odd to suggest that human beings would imitate God by feeling gratitude; why, and for what, would God be grateful? In seeing that His several creations were "good" and that "every thing that He had made" was "behold, *very* good" (Gen. 1:31), God appeared to be expressing His appreciation and gratitude for how well it all turned out.[14] Similarly, by being given Sabbath rest, we human beings can stand back from our everyday work to express wonder and gratitude at the miracle of our life and our creative powers. Any gratitude we feel is not itself part of the (six-day) created world; it is a manifestation of grace that stands us, however briefly, outside the flux of the world's ceaseless motions and changes. Although mobile beings ourselves, we alone—godlike among the creatures—are capable of contemplating the world and feeling gratitude for its goodness and for our place in it. In this respect too, Sabbath remembrance and sanctification permit us to be like God.

The existence of Sabbath rest offers a partial reprieve from the unremitting toil prophesied by the Lord at the end of the story of the Garden of Eden—a "punishment" of the human attempt to become like gods and know good and bad, undertaken in an act of disobedience. According to that account, our prideful human penchant for independence, self-sufficiency, and the rule of autonomous reason led us into a life that, ironically, turned out to be nasty, brutish, and short. This is still very much our lot. But here, with Sabbath desisting, we are not only permitted but also obliged to pause our life of toil, sorrow, and loss and accept instead the godlike possibility of quiet, rest, wholeness, and peace of mind.

This rise to godlike peace, unlike the self-directed "fall" into the knowledge of good and bad, depends on obedience, the only way a free and reckless creature like man can realize the more-than-creaturely potential given him at the Creation. It is in hearkening to a command to enter into sacred time that we may realize our human yet godlike potential. Doing as I say, teaches the Lord, is the route to "doing as I did" (or "being as I Am").

The Sabbath teaching has other profound implications for human life, especially for politics. Adherence to the Sabbath injunction turns out to be the foundation of human freedom, both political and moral.

By inviting and requiring all members of the community to imitate the divine, it teaches the radical equality of human beings, each of whom is understood to be equally God's creature and equally in His image.

Even if only in embryo, Sabbath observance thus embodies the principle and fosters the arrival of a truly humanistic politics. Although not incompatible with political hierarchy (including kingship), the idea behind the Sabbath renders illegitimate any regime that denies human dignity or enables one man or a few men to rule despotically as if divine.[15] And by reconfiguring time, elevating our gaze, and redirecting our aspirations, Sabbath remembrance promotes *internal* freedom as well, by moderating the passions that enslave us: fear and despair (owing to a belief in our lowliness), greed and niggardliness (owing to a belief in the world's inhospitality), and pride and hubris (owing to a belief in our superiority and self-sufficiency).

The deep connection between the Sabbath and political freedom is supported by the repetition of the Decalogue in Deuteronomy. There, the reason Moses will give for Sabbath observance is not God's creation of the world but the Exodus from Egypt:

> And you shall remember that you were a slave in the land of Egypt, and the Lord your God brought you out thence with a mighty hand and an outstretched arm; *therefore*, the Lord your God commanded you to keep the Sabbath day. (Deut. 5:15; emphasis added)

In place of the six days of God's creative work contrasted with the seventh day of divine rest and sanctification, Moses's Deuteronomic version contrasts the Israelites' enforced labor in Egypt with the Lord's mighty deliverance. This substitution invites us to see the second justification for Sabbath observance as the logical analogue of the first. Where men do not acknowledge the bountiful and blessed character of the world, as well as the special relationship of all human beings to the source of that world, they will lapse into worship either of powerful but indifferent natural forces or of clever but amoral human masters.

These seemingly opposite orientations—the worship of brute nature and the veneration of clever men—amount, finally, to the same thing: both deny the godlike standing and holy possibilities of every human being and of humanity as such. Called upon to remember what it was like to live where men knew not the Creator in whose image we are made and to remember the solicitude of the Creator for His suffering people, the Israelites will embrace Sabbath observance, and as a result their politics will be humanized and their lives elevated.

Honoring Father and Mother

The Decalogue moves next to its only other positive injunction, which is also the first to prescribe duties toward human beings and the last to mention "the Lord your God." Standing as a bridge between the two orders of duty—to God and to one's fellow men—it also invites us to consider what each has to do with the other:

> Honor your father and your mother,
>   so that your days may be long upon the land which the
>   Lord your God gives you. (20:12)

As children of the civilization informed by the Bible, we take for granted that the duty of honor is owed to both father and mother, and equally so. Yet this obligation is almost certainly an Israelite innovation. Against a cultural background giving pride of place to manly males and naming children only through their patronyms, the Decalogue proclaims a principle that regards father and mother equally. Well before there is any explicit Israelite law regarding marriage, this singling out of one father and one mother heralds the coming Israelite devotion to monogamous union,[16] with clear lines of ancestry and descent and an understanding of marriage as devoted to offspring and transmission. Moreover, the principle is stated unconditionally: God does not say, "Honor your father and mother if they are honorable." He tells us to honor them regardless. We will soon consider why.

As children of the civilization informed by the Bible, we probably also take for granted that our parents should be singled out for special recognition and respect. But this is hardly the natural way of the world. Not only is the natural family the nursery of rivalry and iniquity, even to the point of patricide and incest, but also honor in most societies is usually reserved not for mom and dad but for people out of the ordinary: heroes, rulers, and leaders who go, as it were, in the place of gods.

Calling for the honoring of father and mother is thus another radical innovation, a rebuke at once to the ways of other cultures, to the natural human (and especially male) tendency to elevate heroes and leaders, and to the correlative quest for honor and glory in defiance of human finitude. Instead of honoring the high and mighty, the way of the Lord calls for each child to honor his or her father and mother, elevating what they alone care for and do: the work of perpetuation. And by elevating both equally, each child also learns in advance to esteem his or her spouse, as well as their joint task as transmitters of life and of a way of living in which perpetuation is itself most highly honored.

The Israelites will shortly be told more about what it means *not* to honor father or mother and how seriously this failure is regarded. In the ordinances following the Decalogue, two of the four capital offenses (on a par with premeditated murder and kidnapping for the slave trade) are striking one's father or mother and cursing one's father or mother. But what it means to honor them is unspecified, perhaps for good reason. By not reducing that obligation to specific deeds or speeches, the injunction compels each son or daughter to be ever attentive to what honoring father and mother might require. What the Decalogue is teaching here is a settled attitude of mind and soul.

Consider two alternative terms that might have been used to describe what children owe their parents: *love* and *obedience*. One can love or admire without honoring, and conversely, one can honor without loving or admiring. Yet for the Israelite, the duty to honor parents remains even if love is absent. As for obedience, the duty to honor father and mother extends long past the time when we, their children, are under their authority. An adult child may disagree with his father and mother and choose to act in ways they would not approve; yet even when he does so, his unexceptional and enduring obligation to honor them is still intact and binding.[17]

Unlike the feeling of love and unlike the wonder of admiration, both of which go with the grain, the need to honor (to give weight to; *kabbed*) is not altogether congenial. Honor implies distance, inequality, looking up to another with deferential respect, reverence, and even some measure of fear. It is like what is owed to a god, for it is rooted in the feeling of awe—a link that will later be made explicit. When the Lord proclaims His central teaching about holiness, the injunction on the proper disposition toward father and mother will be renewed, revised, and placed in remarkable company:

> You shall be holy; for I the Lord your God am holy. You shall fear [revere] (*tira'u*) each man his mother and his father, and you shall keep My Sabbaths. I [am] the Lord your God. (Lev. 19:2–3)

Fear, reverence, and awe are, of course, the disposition that is appropriate toward the Lord Himself: it was "awe-fear-reverence of God" for which Abraham was tested and praised in the binding of Isaac on Mount Moriah (Gen. 22:12). Moreover, the command to fear/revere mother and father is now clearly coordinated with the command to observe God's Sabbath, making explicit the link between the two positive injunctions. What, then, links the honoring of father and mother to Sabbath keeping and to being holy?

The teaching about "father and mother" comes right on the heels of the reason offered for sanctifying the Sabbath day: God's creation of the world and His subsequent setting apart a time beyond work and motion. It thus extends our attention to origins and "creation," now in the form of human generating. God may have created the world and the human race, but you owe your own existence to your parents, who are, to say the least, co-partners—equally with each other, equally with God—in your coming to be. For this gift of life, you are beholden to honor them, in gratitude.

Gratitude toward parents is owed not only for birth and existence but also for nurture, for rearing, and especially for initiation into a way of life informed by the disposition to gratitude and reverence. The way of this "initiation" is itself a source of awe. Our parents not only teach us explicitly and directly regarding God, His covenant, and His commandments. In their devotion to our being and well-being—given to us not because we merit it—they are also the embodiment of, and our first encounter with, the gracious beneficence of the world and its bountiful Source.

Filial honor and respect are not only fitting and owed; they are also necessary to the parental work, whose success depends on authority and command. Exercising their benevolent power by invoking praise or blame, reward or punishment, in response to righteous or wayward conduct, yet forgiving error and fault and remaining faithful to their children, parents embody and model the awe-some, demanding, yet benevolent and gracious authority of the Lord God of Israel. In response, on the side of the child, filial piety expressed toward father and mother is the cradle of awe-fear-reverence (and eventually love) of the Lord.[18] Even when we no longer need their guidance, we owe them the honor due their office.

So the injunction to honor father and mother is fitting and useful. But why has it such prominence in the Decalogue, and why, paired with the Sabbath, is it at the heart of God's Way and the summons to holiness? On the assumption that God reserves His most important teachings to address those aspects of human life most in need of correction, we need to remind ourselves of the problems this injunction is meant to address: the dark and tragic troubles that lurk within the human household and that, absent biblical instruction, imperil all decent ways of life: the iniquities of incest and patricide.

The Bible's first (and almost only previous) mention of "father and mother" is found in a comment inserted into the story of the Garden of Eden—after the man, seeing and desiring the newly created woman, expostulates, "This one at last is bone of my bone and flesh of my flesh," and then names her as if she were but a missing portion of himself: "She shall be called Woman ('ishah) because from Man ('ish) she was taken." At this point, interrupting the narrative, the text interjects:

> Therefore a man *leaves* his father and his mother and cleaves unto *his woman,* that *they* may become as one flesh. (Gen. 2:24; emphasis added)

Many commentators have seen here the ground of a biblical teaching about monogamous marriage. I believe the context suggests something darker. The inserted exhortation comes right after a speech implying that love and desire—including especially (male) sexual desire—is primarily love and desire of one's own: "bone of *my* bone and flesh of *my* flesh." Leaving your father and mother to become "as one flesh" with an outside woman serves as a moral gloss not on monogamy but on the sexual love of your own flesh, which, strictly speaking, is the formula for incest.[19]

The danger of incest, destroyer of the distance between parent and child, is tied to a second threat: resentment of and rebellion against paternal authority, up to and including murder. The Bible's first story about the relation between father and sons, the story of Noah's drunkenness, is, in fact, a tale involving at least metaphorical patricide. Told as the immediate sequel to the establishment of the Lord's first covenant with all humanity, the story serves as a crucial foil for the teaching about family life that God now means to establish in the world.

Noah has just received the first new law, comprising the basis for civil society, away from the anarchic "state of nature" that was the antediluvian world. At its center is the permission to kill and eat animals but, in exchange, an obligation to avenge human bloodshed—an obligation said to turn on the fact that man alone among the animals is godlike:

> Whosoever sheds man's blood, by man shall his blood be
> shed; for in the image of God was man made. (Gen. 9:6)

It concludes with the command to procreate and perpetuate the new world order:

> As for you, be fruitful and multiply, swarm through the earth,
> and hold sway over it. (Gen. 9:7)

We look to the sequel to see how well this creature, made in the image of God, fares under the new covenant, and the result is not cheering. Noah plants a vineyard, gets blind drunk, and lies uncovered in his tent, stripped not only of his fatherly authority but even of his upright humanity. There he is seen in his shame by Ham, his hotheaded son, who goes outside and publicizes his discovery, celebrating his father's unfathering of himself. Without touching a hair on Noah's head, Ham kills his father *as a father*. Ham's brothers, Shem and Japheth, enter the tent backward and cover their father's nakedness without witnessing or participating in it. When Noah awakens, he curses Canaan, son of Ham, but calls forth a blessing on "the Lord, God of Shem," the son whose pious action restores his fatherly dignity and authority.

In explicating this story elsewhere,[20] I suggested that it is intended to show how rebellion, incest, and patricidal impulses lurk within the natural—that is, the uninstructed—human family. These dangers must be addressed if a way of life is to be successfully transmitted, especially a way of life founded on reverence for the Lord in whose image—as Noah and the human race have just discerned—we human beings are made.

The impulse to honor your father and mother does not come easily to every human heart.[21] Yet some appear to get it right even without instruction. Shem, who restores his father's paternal standing, seems to have divined the need for awe and reverence for his father as a pathway to and manifestation of the holy. And Shem's merit is visited upon his descendants: he becomes the ancestor of Abraham, founder of God's Way. Ham is the ancestor of the Canaanites and the Egyptians, whose abominable sexual practices will be the explicit target of the laws of sexual purity (in Lev. 18) that are central to Israel's mission to become a holy nation. It is at the end of this list of forbidden deeds, each proscribed as an iniquitous "uncovering of nakedness," that the Lord pronounces the connection among the call to holiness, awe and reverence for mother and father, and the observance of the Sabbath.

This analysis—that the order to honor father and mother targets the iniquitous sexual practices of the surrounding nations—also offers us the best interpretation of the enigmatic reason God gives for obeying this (and only this) injunction: "So that your days may be long *upon the land* which the Lord your God gives you" (emphasis added). What does this mean? And why does God tie long life on the land to honoring father and mother rather than, say, to not murdering? Surely this cannot mean that people who honor their fathers and mothers will personally live to an old age. It probably does not mean that people who honor their own fathers and mothers are more likely to have longer lines of descendants. Given our analysis and paying particular attention to "*upon the land,*" it most likely means that the land will not cast you out, as it will soon do to the Canaanites, precisely for these iniquitous practices. Honor your father and mother so that the land be not defiled and not vomit you out.[22]

Summing up: the injunction to honor father and mother constitutes a teaching not only about gratitude, creatureliness, and the importance of parental authority. It insists on sacred distance, respect, and reverence, precisely to produce holiness, *qedushah,* in that all too intimate nest of humanity that often becomes a den of iniquity and a seedbed of tragedy. Sabbath observance offers a correction against the (especially Egyptian) penchant for human mastery and pride that culminates in despotism and slavery. Honoring father and mother offers a correction against the (especially Canaanite) penchant for sexual unrestraint, including incest, that washes out all distinctions and lets loose a wildness incompatible with the created order and with living as a holy people. Adherence to these two teachings—each a summons to a life of moral gravity and reverent looking up—offers the best chance for vindicating the high hopes the world carries for the creature who is blessed to bear the likeness of divinity.

Parochially Universal

The connections between the Decalogue's two positive injunctions, and between both of them and the goal of holiness, shed light on two vexed questions: the universality versus the particularity of God's teaching to Israel and Israel's special standing among the nations. Our interpretation implies that the call to holiness, although made to the people of Israel, seeks to produce on earth a perfection not just of one people but also of human beings as such. This is perhaps already implicit in the Israelites' call to become a kingdom of priests, whether as example or as minister to the other peoples. The universality becomes explicit with the reason for Sabbath remembrance and sanctification, as the Israelites are summoned to adopt a Godlike perspective on the nature of time and the relation between motion and rest. All human beings can appreciate and imitate the divine activities of creating and hallowing, because we are all equally related to the Lord whose divine likeness each of us bears.

Yet paradoxically, we are immediately reminded that universality, like holiness, requires remaining true to the particularity of our embodied existence. What could be farther from universality than the utterly contingent and non-interchangeable relationship each person has to his singular father and mother? Granted, the parent–child relationship bears deep similarities to the relationship between the biblical God and any human being. But no one lives with the universal Father and Mother, only with his own very particular ones. A person can revere fatherhood and motherhood as such only by showing reverence for his own father and mother.

Beware the universalist who has contempt for the particulars; beware the lover of all humanity—or of holiness—who does not honor his own father and mother. For it turns out to be all but impossible to love your neighbors as yourself if you treat lightly your most immediate "neighbors," those who are most emphatically your own and also most able to guide you to your full humanity. The case for a parochial community that bears a universal way—hence the case for the distinctive nation of Israel—follows directly.

From the Lord's (or the Decalogue's) perspective, the contingent and parochial character of our existence is not a misfortune or a defect. In the Torah it is a blessing that we have bodies and live concrete and parochial lives, for it is only through our lived experiences, here and now, that we gain full access to what is universally true, good, and holy. Unlike a later scriptural teacher, the Lord of the Decalogue does not exhort you to leave your father and your mother and follow me (Matthew 10:34–38). Instead, He celebrates the fact that grace comes locally and parochially into the life each of us was given to live as well as we can, embedded in the covenantal community into which we are blessed to be born.

The "Second Table": Moral Principles for Neighbors

When we move to the statements of the so-called second table of the Decalogue, we find ourselves on more familiar legal and moral ground, which we can thus cover more briefly. But familiarity should not breed contempt. These principles, regarding the conduct of man with man, not only form the bedrock of biblical morality but also are arguably the indispensable foundations of any decent society.

Murder, adultery, and theft are outlawed by virtually all civilized peoples. These legal prohibitions not only form the necessary condition of civil peace; they also erect important boundaries between what is mine and what is thine: life, wife, property, and reputation. Because they stand to reason and because they were established already in the Ancient Near East, they need neither explanations nor promises of punishment for violation (or reward for compliance).

And yet the Decalogue is not a legal code, and it goes beyond existing Near Eastern law. Formulated in absolute terms, the lapidary two-word Hebrew style of these statements sets them forth as eternal and absolute moral principles, apodictic declarations that define what it means to belong to "us," and normative principles that everyone must accept as a member of Israel. In addition, packaged within God's preamble to the specific covenant with Israel, they acquire elevated standing as sacred teaching, ordained by a divine lawgiver and resting on ontological ground firmer than mere human agreement or utilitarian calculation:

> You shall not murder (*lo' thirtsach*).
> You shall not commit adultery (*lo' thin'af*).
> You shall not steal (*lo' thignov*).
> You shall not bear false witness against your neighbor (*lo' tha'aneh vere'akha 'ed shaqer*).
> You shall not covet (*lo' thachmod*) your neighbor's house;
> you shall not covet your neighbor's wife, nor his
> [man]servant nor his maidservant, nor his ox nor his ass,
> nor anything that is your neighbor's. (20:13–14)

The first three absolutes defend the foundational—rather than the highest—human goods: life, without which nothing else is possible; marital fidelity and clarity about paternity, without which family stability and responsible parenthood are very difficult; and property, without which one's chance of living well—or even making a living—is severely compromised.[23] These principles will receive further specification later in Exodus, when the ordinances of the covenant are pronounced.

Although stated in the negative and aimed at preventing interpersonal evils, these principles are not merely useful means to civil peace and order. They bespeak positive moral teachings that defend things good in themselves. Thus, the principle against murder implicitly teaches the preciousness of human life and the equal dignity of each person's share in it. It does not quite say that life itself is sacred or the ultimate or highest good: the Lord does not say, "You shall not *kill*," but "You shall not *murder*" (that is, kill wrongfully).[24] There will be circumstances where taking a human life is permitted, and others where it will even be commanded. But the ruling idea of all interpersonal relations is profound respect for the goodness of human life. The ground, not mentioned here but stated earlier, is that each human being bears the same God-like relation to the Lord.[25]

The proscription of adultery also has a meaning beyond its utility in promoting family stability. It implicitly teaches the ideal of faithful marriage in the community of Israel, as well as the need to respect the covenantal pledge on which all marriages rest, both one's own marriage and that of one's would-be adulterous partner. It celebrates human beings' ability to elevate their sexual natures by bringing them under vows of loyalty, exclusivity, and a commitment to raising together the fruits of sexual union. To steal a man's wife (or for a wife to commit adultery) is, in a way, a bigger blow than murder: by confounding paternity, it signifies the permanent removal of the man's descendants as his own.

Theft produces more than harm and loss, and it is more than a threat to peace and order. However small the loss, theft is also an injustice to the owner, an expression of contempt. Against such moral error, the statement proscribing theft implicitly teaches respect for other people's property. Property is, literally, what is proper or appropriate to a man (as is also his wife or, for a woman, also her husband). One's property is an extension of oneself, something one needs for life and something one has (likely) earned by one's own creative efforts ("Six days shall you labor"). Respecting another human being and the life he is able to lead includes respecting whatever is his own.

The proscription of bearing false witness carries a moral message that goes beyond its clear importance in judicial matters. At stake are not only your neighbor's freedom, property, and reputation but also the character of communal life and the proper use of the godlike powers of speech and reason. Echoing the earlier prohibition on taking the Lord's Name in vain, this injunction takes aim at wrongful speech—speech that is vain, light in weight, and empty of truth.[26] To speak falsely is to pervert the power of reasoned speech and to insult the divine original, whose reasoned speech is the source of the created order and the model of which we are the image.

If most of the prohibitions in the second table are familiar, the Decalogue concludes in a surprising turn by focusing not on overt action but on an internal condition of the heart or soul, a species of desire or yearning. The uniqueness of the proscription of coveting is suggested both by its greater length and by the spelling out of the seven things belonging to your neighbor that you not only must not steal but also must not even long for.

What is this proscription doing at the close of the Decalogue? As a practical matter, a prohibition against covetous thoughts and desires builds a fence against the other forbidden deeds. If you do not covet the things that are your neighbor's, you will be less likely to steal, commit adultery, or even murder; you will be less tempted to make your neighbor suffer harm or loss by bearing false witness against him. Implicit in the Hebrew verb we translate as "covet," *chamad*, is more than a mere delight in or desire for. The biblical psychology of coveting connotes also the (hard-to-resist) urge to *do*, spilling over into active planning to make the coveted object one's own.[27] Such was clearly the case in the first biblical use of this verb in the Garden of Eden story. After the serpent had undermined the Lord's command, the woman's imaginative soul soared quickly from seeing to coveting to disobedient action: "And the woman saw that the tree was good for food and a delight to the eyes, and that the tree was to be *desired* (*venechmad*) to make one wise, and she *took* of the [forbidden] fruit and did eat" (Gen. 3:6; emphasis added). Coveting is more than halfway to misconduct.

But beyond such practical considerations, the final injunction causes us to reflect about the meaning of possession and the nature of desire and neighborhood. A man who covets what is his neighbor's suffers, whether he knows it or not, from multiple deformations of his own desire. Not content with his own portion of good things, he cannot see them in their true light: as means to—and participants in—a higher way of life.

Moreover, some items appear both on the list of seven partakers in Sabbath rest and on the list of seven "covet-ables"—as if to indicate the mistaken direction of the coveter's desire. His heart is set on the possessions of another because he fails to realize that the things that matter most are not the unshareable things, but the things we and our neighbors have in common: knowledge of the Lord and what He requires of us, participation in His grace and the bounty of Creation, and the opportunity, despite our frailty and penchant for iniquity, to live a life of blessing and holiness.

Our neighbor's aspiration to or possession of these *higher* goods in no way diminishes our chances to attain them. On the contrary, to live among neighbors who yearn for the shareable goods is to live in a true community, in which all can be lifted up in the pursuit and practice of holiness. Such a polity, even if only an aspiration, is a light unto the nations.

It is therefore not an accident that the Decalogue, which began by highlighting the special and exclusive relationship Israel now has with the Lord, Who will tolerate no other "gods" before Him, should end with remarks about coveting and an implicit teaching about the true object of our desires. Coveting is ultimately a form of idolatry, an offense against both God and neighbor.[28]

What Has the Decalogue Accomplished?

At the start of the last chapter, we collected a laundry list of evils and iniquities, displayed in the stories of Genesis and Exodus, against which we readers hoped God's new covenant with Israel might take a stance. Listening now to God's words, we are not disappointed. Murder, adultery, theft, and false accusation have been specifically and directly prohibited, as have worship of false gods and rebellion against parental authority. Despotism, slavery, and mistreatment of strangers are indirect targets of the teaching of the Sabbath; avoiding incestuous relations is a crucial part of the purpose of the call to honor father and mother.

But beyond these obvious targets, the Decalogue's principles also address two of the biggest threats to peaceful and decent communal life, as they were revealed in the stories of Genesis: fratricide and coveting, and especially the kind of coveting that leads to fratricide. The dangerous sources in the human heart are pride and greed—the desire to be first and the desire for more—both of which lead to potentially lethal rivalry. Cain's (and Esau's) wounded pride pointed directly to fratricide. Sarah's envy of Hagar, and her rejection of Ishmael on her son Isaac's behalf, led to the painful banishment of Abraham's firstborn, a nonlethal form of fratricide. Jacob's acquisitiveness displaced his brother, duped his father, and destroyed his brotherly relationship with Esau. Rachel's envy of Leah, and Leah's of Rachel, gave birth to near-fratricidal enmity among their sons. Jacob's sons' envious hatred of Joseph and Joseph's trafficking in his fantasies of superiority were a recipe for disaster, averted only at the price of losing Joseph to Egypt. Joseph's acquisitiveness on Pharaoh's behalf led to indentured servitude that later ensnared the Children of Israel for four hundred years. In all these cases, people covetous of their neighbors' goods or places of honor bred anger and resentment in the place of brotherly (sisterly) love.

It is easy to see how the injunction against coveting speaks to these dangers. But they are also addressed, indirectly but profoundly, through the other foundational principle: honor your father and mother. Brothers as brothers may naturally be rivals, especially insofar as they embark on parallel lives and tend to forget their shared point of origin, their family of birth. But when summoned to honor common parents, a slumbering bond between them may soften their rivalry and prevent lethal hatred. Judah pledges his life for Benjamin's, not because he loves Benjamin but because he gives weight to his father's sorrow and anxiety. And thanks to Judah's eloquent speech to him, Joseph is finally moved by thoughts of his aged father to abandon his charade and reveal himself to his brothers, for whom he had harbored only a (well-deserved) enmity. Looking back to the common parental source—and then past father and mother to the ultimate Source, before Whom we can but stand humbly— lifts the gaze and tames the angry and iniquitous heart. Not for nothing is the teaching about father and mother the indispensable link between our relations to God and to our fellow human beings.

All to the good, these high-minded thoughts. Considering only ourselves, the readers of the Bible, we may attest to the enormous moral progress that the Decalogue represents. But returning to the biblical narrative from which we departed to examine the meaning of the Ten Words, we do not yet know what, if anything, the Decalogue will in fact accomplish for the people to whom it was directly addressed. It is time to give up our philosophical examination of the Decalogue as a stand-alone set of principles and return to the story in which they are embedded.

Reactions on the Ground and the Need for Sacrifice

When we left the people, just as the Lord began speaking, they were standing anxiously at the foot of the mountain. Above them was the awesome sensory extravaganza produced by God so that they might "trust also in Moses forever." Even as the Lord, in elevated language, is enunciating the august, monumental, and revolutionary guiding principles for Israel's national way of life, the thunder and lightning and calls of the horn continue full blast. As the Lord's final utterance dies away in the reader's hearing, the text returns us to the reaction of the assembled masses, among whom we again imagine ourselves:

> And all the people *saw* (*ro'im*) the thunderings, and the lightnings, and the voice of the horn, and the mountain smoking; and when the people *saw* it, they trembled, and stood afar off. And they said unto Moses: "Speak *you* with us, and we will hear; but let not God speak with us, lest we die." And Moses said unto the people: "Fear not; for God is come to test you, and that His fear may be before you, that you sin not." And the people stood afar off; but Moses drew near unto the thick darkness where God was. (20:15–18; emphasis added)

Instead of getting an account of the people's reaction to the words they just heard, we get an account of their sensory experience. Their senses were not only overwhelmed but also utterly confounded: they *saw* (!) the thunder and the voice and the smoke.[29] We strongly suspect that unlike us readers the people did not understand—or even hear—a word that was said.[30] They draw back from the mountain (perhaps as soon as God starts speaking), trembling in fear. Unlike Moses at the burning bush, they do not hold their ground in awe; they retreat, afraid for their lives. They turn instead to Moses—"Speak *you* to us and we will hear; but let God not speak to us, *lest we die*"—beseeching him to be their teacher and legislator.

In a remarkable response, Moses speaks directly to assuage their fear while endorsing its utility and redirecting its object: 'Do not fear that God will destroy you. On the contrary, know that He is giving you the "Fear of God" as a gift, to keep you from sin, the truly fearful thing.' The people do not respond. They remain terrified and stand away from the mountain, which is to say that they distance themselves from God. They look on in awed silence as Moses draws near to the thick darkness of the Lord's presence, perhaps to fulfill their request that *he* be the one to speak God's law to them.

We will never again have a clearer demonstration of the difference between Moses and the people, and it is precisely over the matter of how to relate to God. Moses seeks His presence and prefers His company; the people seek His absence and prefer Moses's authority. Moses is satisfied by a relationship with God carried on through intelligible speech; the people will require something else. By the people's choice, Moses is now going to speak for God. With their "consent" and with divine backing, he now has the authority for the divine law that "he" will give them.

Has God's sensory extravaganza achieved its purpose? Will the people now trust (also) Moses forever? "Forever," who knows. But certainly, they trust in Moses as never before. Indeed, God's experiment may have succeeded all too well. The people may trust Moses more than merely "also." In their terror, they seem close to regarding Moses himself as their god; that is, as the power most revered and most relied on for its potential benefits to human life. The gap between the leader and the led may have overshot its distance. We do not have long to wait before this question will be front and center.[31]

Yet for the time being, at least, we think that God's purpose for Moses and the people has been achieved. In the long run, God's goal for Israel may be a sociopolitical condition of "equity," with equal status for all, each equally under God's law. But to get there, the Israelites first must go through a stage of "hierarchy," with Moses in supreme command.[32] For this reason, the current elevation of Moses, however risky, might be an indispensable success for now, to be replaced much later, when Moses disappears from the community, by the unqualified rule of the law under the leadership of the priests.

Moses approaches the thick cloud. The Lord unclouds his understanding, responding precisely both to the danger that the people might divinize Moses and to their implicit desire for a different way to communicate with Him. Moses, who has no need for a mediated relationship with the divine, thinks that the "fear of God" will suffice for the people, but God knows better. He appreciates the people's need for other ways—non-intellectual and symbolically physical—to come closer to Him: He allows them to offer sacrifices. In the Decalogue, the preferred route to closeness to God is not by sacrifices or even specified worship but through imitation of Him, in the sanctification of time as prescribed in Sabbath rest. Sacrifices (at least here) are a concession; they serve man's needs, not God's:[33]

And the Lord said unto Moses: "Thus you shall say unto the Children of Israel: 'You yourselves have *seen* (*re'ithem*) [only] that *I* have *talked* with you from heaven. [Therefore] You shall not make with Me gods of silver, or gods of gold, you shall not make unto you. An altar of *earth* you shall make unto Me, and shall sacrifice thereon *your* burnt-offerings, and *your* peace-offerings, [of] *your* sheep, and *your* oxen; in *every* place [where you travel] where I cause My name to be mentioned I will come unto you and bless you. And if [when you come to the Land] you make Me an altar of stone, you shall not build it of *hewn* stones; for if you lift up your tool upon it, you have profaned it. Neither shall you go up by steps unto My altar, that your nakedness be not uncovered (*lo'-thiggaleh 'ervath-kha*) thereon.'" (20:19–23; emphasis added)

In giving Moses instructions regarding sacrifices, God also teaches him about the people's need for physical mediation. Moses is to remind the people that what they "saw" was nothing more—yet surely nothing less—than the Voice of the Lord Himself, addressing them from on high. Having seen no visible form and having no reason to make for themselves "gods" in place of or in addition to the Lord, they are not to make silver and golden idols to represent Him or to please Him. Instead, they are to connect with Him through sacrifices, offered on a primitive earthen altar.

"*Your* burnt offerings and *your* peace offerings, [of] *your* sheep and *your* oxen"—all *yours:* that is, for *you,* not for Me—shall go up. And in every place that you travel—not only here on this mountain, for I am not a god of place—where I cause you to invoke My Name with sacrifices (or, perhaps better, where I reveal Myself to you by Name), I will come *down* to you and bless you. Two-way traffic: sacrifices up, blessings down. Communication of the sort that is intelligible to and desired by the people.

But as with the Lord's gift of manna, the permission to offer sacrifices comes with instructions and limitations. The requirements address opposing deep-seated and dangerous tendencies in the human soul that were addressed already in the contest with Egypt and that are often expressed in places and practices of sacrificial worship: the rational penchant for mastery, for artful imposition of order and luxury through technology and aesthetic beautification; and the irrational passion for surrender, for ecstatic wildness, and orgiastic merging. There will be no artful chiseling of stones, no exposed nakedness during worship[34]—just a simple expression of your longing for Me, performed in unadorned and modest ways. The people get their closer connection to God; but no one yet knows that an opening has been created for their worship of the golden calf.

With these small adjustments to the relationships between Moses and the people, between the people and God, and between God and Moses, the people and we are ready to hear the full expression of God's law.

Ordinances for God's New Nation

Justice and the Civil Law

We are still at Mount Sinai. The Lord has pronounced majestic and revolutionary principles for His new nation. The people, overawed and frightened, stand far off. Moses, communing with the Lord in the thick darkness, is about to receive a profusion of specific laws or ordinances—in Hebrew, *mishpatim*—which he is to set before the people as terms of the proposed covenant. The rich and dramatic narrative of events turns abruptly into a legal rulebook occupying several biblical chapters (21–23), presented by the Lord without interruption, without comment, and without response from Moses. A few introductory remarks may ease the transition and show how this material fits into the story of Israel's national founding.

Introducing the Ordinances

It is not easy to know how to read these chapters and these ordinances. Coming right after the Decalogue, the Lord's general principles proclaimed in crisp second-person-singular imperatives, the ordinances seem at first glance like an expanded set of practical guidelines, conveyed in detailed laws (mostly in the third-person singular) for Moses to transmit to the people. And it is primarily as "law" that they have been studied and interpreted, both by Jewish codifiers of Rabbinic Law and by modern academic scholars of "biblical law," for whom the content of these chapters is known as the Book of the Covenant (*Sefer Habberith*).[1] But modern readers who encounter these ordinances without preconceptions or outside (scholarly or Traditional) assistance may well be perplexed. They—we—may find the text puzzling and troubling for several reasons.

For one thing, the ordinances are not a comprehensive civil code: many obvious topics (for example, marriage and divorce, and inheritance) are omitted. Nor do they read like any statutory legislation with which we may be familiar. Some of them prescribe proper conduct, as do our civil laws, and many specify fitting responses to wrongdoing or mishap. But they also contain ethical principles; they sometimes give reasons for the regulations; and in addition to covering topics that are everywhere part of civil law, they contain instructions for seasonal festivals and religious observances. What kind of "law" is this?

The format of the ordinances is also inconsistent. Like other ancient legal codes, many of the ordinances take a casuistic verbal form ("If someone does this, then . . ."), rather than (like the Decalogue) an apodictic form ("You shall not . . ."). Yet we do not get all the obvious cases touching a particular subject, and it is unclear what governs the selection of either the main case or the stated variations. Are these the most illuminating or the most common cases, or perhaps only (or also) are those the ones most needed by the people or most "acceptable" to them? Or are the cases chosen because they embody crucial principles that can later be extended to additional situations? There is a further formal difficulty: against the largely casuistic format, a few absolute prohibitions stand out. Why do *these* subjects admit of no exceptions? Why does the Lord present only these subjects in unconditional terms?

The overall organization and internal order of the *mishpatim* are sometimes difficult to discern, and parts of the sequence appear to be governed by word association and analogy rather than by logical structure. To many readers, large stretches of ordinances seem to be ordered at random. Yet if examined more closely, the early laws may be seen to move through a series of topics that are recognizably matters of civil law, both criminal and tort: masters and servants; interpersonal conflicts, from homicide and personal injury to theft and lesser disputes; damage to property, both livestock and other; testifying and judging. These "standard" subjects then merge with novel ones, including relations with outsiders, seasonal festivals and religious celebrations, and the practices and temptations of a soon-to-be agricultural people. I hope to show that careful attention to the order and content of these ordinances reveals a coherent structure and purpose. We will therefore read them—as we read the Decalogue—not as a disordered heap but as a unified whole, an integrated package informed by a singular intention.[2]

Another difficulty that modern readers may have with these ordinances is less easily dealt with: the alien and alienating character of some of the laws and many of the punishments. To our sensibilities, the subjects appear primitive and barbarous, the punishments harsh and cruel. The goring ox. Beating a slave. Knocking out his eye or tooth. Animal sacrifices. Death to sorceresses. Capital punishment for cursing father or mother. An eye for an eye, a tooth for a tooth. Even readers willing to embrace the demanding principles of the Decalogue will be repelled by some of the ordinances, especially by the retributions. Yet we must read these laws in their historical context and in relation to the prevailing customs at the time they were introduced. Considered against that background, God's ordinances for Israel represent a giant step toward a more humane jurisprudence and a more moral way of life.

Knowing some comparative law is helpful for appreciating the ordinances, even when considered on their own terms. The text is likely in silent conversation with contemporary Middle Eastern legal codes by (unspecified) ways of rejection, confirmation, or amendment. Given that the Torah elsewhere visits stories and practices known to the neighboring peoples (for example, cosmogony or the Flood), but only to transform them, we expect to find evidence here too for the distinctive moral and spiritual teachings of God's Way. And even if the Lord's ordinances do not explicitly target the laws of others, comparison with those laws may nonetheless reveal the Torah's revolutionary character.

Scholars of biblical law, comparing our text with ancient Mesopotamian and Hittite legal collections (unearthed in the Middle East during the nineteenth and twentieth centuries CE), have identified numerous points of contact but also significant differences, a few of which I will point out when we get down to cases. The largest, most comprehensive, and best known of the legal collections is the one composed by the Babylonian king Hammurabi (ca. eighteenth century BCE) some 250 years before the estimated date of the Exodus from Egypt.[3] Engraved in cuneiform on stone stelae, its intent was to glorify the king, but it was apparently little used as a basis for judicial rulings. It comprises 282 legal paragraphs sandwiched between a personal prologue and epilogue, is written in casuistic form, and touches on many recognizable matters of public and private law. Most of the former deal with preserving public order; most of the latter concern economic transactions, marriage and family matters, and inheritance of property. The stated purposes are conventionally political and utilitarian: "to establish justice," "to give good government," "to prosper the people," "to abolish enmity and rebellion."

Let me point out just one major difference between the two sets of laws. A characteristic feature of the Code of Hammurabi is its reference to three distinct, seemingly fixed social classes—roughly, "gentry," "commoners," and slaves—and there are laws that apply differently to members of different classes. The comparable ordinances of the Lord, by contrast, apply uniformly to all members of the community. As we will see, this difference reflects the more-than-political purpose of the laws: not only righteousness but also holiness, expressed in a special relationship between each Israelite and the Lord.

Comparison with neighboring legal codes takes us only so far in trying to understand the materials before us. Far more important for our purposes are the ordinances' biblical contexts. They appear not as a detached legal code but as part of the long, unfolding story of the human race and especially of the Children of Israel, through whom God is now attempting to address humankind's proclivities for folly and mischief. As we have seen, the fundamental weaknesses of human beings uninstructed have been brought to light through the stories of Genesis and Exodus, and it is precisely these unsavory tendencies and evil practices that the Lord's Way is meant to address: wounded pride leading to murder and mayhem; rebellion against paternal authority leading to patricide; unrestrained sexual desire leading to licentious behavior, rape, and incest; xenophobia leading to brutal oppression and chattel slavery; hubristic pride leading to self-worship; and despair leading to superstition and idol worship. In the same spirit, we must also relate the ordinances to the principles just enunciated in the Decalogue. Almost all its topics are elaborated in the ordinances, save only "coveting"—not a natural subject for legislation—and, surprisingly, adultery and the related issues of marriage and divorce.

But the most important biblical context to consider is the covenantal founding of the people Israel in relation to their God. The ordinances, all of which originate with God, are presented as specific responsibilities under the covenant the Lord has proposed to the Israelites, which will govern their lives when they reach the Promised Land.[4] If they hearken to His words, they will become for Him a "kingdom of priests and a holy nation." Unable or unwilling to hear the laws directly from the Lord Himself, they will now hear them indirectly from Moses, God's agent as lawgiver. Once Moses tells them what will be expected of them, they will be ready to give—or withhold—their consent to the covenant.

Yet precisely because accepting the covenant requires Israelite agreement to its terms, we expect that the God-given ordinances—and the mode of their presentation—are at least partly adapted to His primary audience: the people on the ground at Sinai. The ordinances must make sense in purely human terms: at the very least, they must not be utterly contrary to reason or unacceptable to the newly liberated masses, hardly paragons of virtue or moral self-command. We suspect that some of the rules and formulations have been chosen precisely to gain the acceptance of the ex-slaves, in part by making a vivid contrast with their experience under Egyptian despotism—which they know much better than they know the Code of Hammurabi.

The ordinances may also be addressed to future judges, offering guidance for adjudicating disputes and direction for sentencing wrongdoers. They will also advance the usual functions of legal courts: retribution for wrongdoing, compensation for victims, and deterrence of future offenders, all in the service of promoting civil peace and order. But the ordinances are surely addressed in the first instance to the people as a whole, for whom they serve as "teachers" of the Way of life to which the Lord is summoning them. Incomplete and primitive though they may be, they provide the people, at the beginning of their covenantal existence, foundational ideas and guidelines that they can later extend on their own, once the educative function of the founding law has done its work.

It is this pedagogical function that likely explains the choice of cases presented, especially, as we shall see, the Lord's emphasis on the proper treatment of slaves, pregnant women, widows and orphans, strangers, and the poor—the community's vulnerable members. It also helps explain the ordinances' spare formulation: enough is said to get across the principle but not enough to settle most cases that come to court. Adjudication will therefore require interpretation, which the terse ordinances, functioning as guidelines, both allow and direct. From the same compact formulation, the people get the desired moral-political-religious teaching and the judges get general directives.

Remembering the covenantal context into which the Lord's ordinances are introduced, we note another decisive way in which they differ from the typical legal code, ancient as well as modern. The laws governing relations between man and man, as we learned from the Decalogue, partly reflect the more primary relation between man and God. We therefore expect that this relationship will receive special attention and codified specification. It is not by accident that the ordinances are prefaced by instructions about building altars and offering sacrifices to God and that they conclude with discussions of the sacred festivals and pilgrimages to His sanctuary.

As it happens, the boundaries between the "religious" and the ("merely") civil or political ordinances are not sharply drawn. This suggests that the connection between the theological and the political may be stronger still. If it is through knowing and obeying *all* of His laws (and all the laws are His laws) that Israel will come closer to God, then the ordinances as such—and not only those dealing, say, with festivals and sacrifices—are a new avenue for knowing *Y-H-V-H*.[5] Proper treatment of indentured servants or strangers, no less than keeping the Sabbath or bringing first fruits to the sanctuary, is equally a mode of honoring the Lord and sanctifying one's life. As in the Decalogue, the "political" and "theological" ordinances are manifestations of the same thing: a teaching for living together as one people, self-consciously looking up to the Lord and His preferred ways.

This last point is not usually noticed by scholars of biblical law or by others who treat the ordinances as an isolated legal code.[6] But it is at the heart of the rabbinic tradition, for which the Torah is a seamless teaching about the relationships between man and God and between man and man. A word must therefore be said—yet again—about the relation between the interpretation I am attempting here and the centuries of rich treatment of these texts by Jewish law and commentary. The Talmud, the repository of rabbinic interpretation of the laws and still the basis of Jewish observance, elaborates at great length on the teachings of justice adumbrated in these beginning ordinances, among which are rooted 53 of the 613 biblically based commandments of the Tradition. A single, often cryptic verse from Exodus gets several talmudic chapters of elaboration, reflection, and refinement,[7] against which our naïve reading will unavoidably seem simplistic. Even my scant familiarity with these texts leaves me in awe of the wisdom and prudence of the rabbinic sages in their explication and extension of the law, filling in the lacunae and investigating every ambiguity and novel or related case. Here, more than in the narrative portions of Exodus, it is arguably impossible to understand the biblical text without extensive reference to the Oral Law, the traditional commentaries, and the legal *responsa*. Who better knows the meaning of the law than the Rabbis who kept it alive over centuries of Jewish diaspora?

Conceding this argument, and with apologies to readers learned in the Tradition, I will nonetheless try to explicate even this part of the text in its own terms, independent of later commentary.[8] The biblical ordinances are embedded in the narrative of Exodus, and they were written and read as part of this story before they entered rabbinic legal interpretation. Unlike the talmudic sages, who abstract the passages from the whole in order to grasp their *halakhic* import, the book we are reading presents everything in one seamless account. More important, Moses—and his audience on the ground—will hear no more than what we readers of the plain text see on the page. At some level, therefore, the ordinances must be intelligible to them without further commentary. Finally, since the ordinances are not a comprehensive legal code but are paradigmatic guidelines for living under conditions of sovereignty in the Promised Land, many of the subsequent accretions and interpretations, given under conditions of exile, are not necessarily relevant to the intent of the law as given here at Sinai. For all these reasons, I submit, we may approach the package of ordinances in its own context, expecting that we will be able to make sense of it. At the same time, however, I will occasionally note significant differences between my reading of the plain text and the rabbinic account and indicate where and why I think the rabbinic reading is better or deeper.

These preliminary considerations lead to important conclusions about what we are reading and how we will read. The ordinances of Exodus 21–23 supply constitutive teachings for national self-rule, looking up to the divine. They are addressed first of all to the Israelite people in the story, in anticipation of the time when Moses leaves the scene and the Law will take his place. The ordinances' purpose is not just legal but also cultural: to educate these former slaves in the conditions of human freedom and decency, to enjoin them to aspire to righteousness and holiness, and to prepare them to resist the evils that afflict human life in Egypt, Canaan, and everywhere else.

We readers of Exodus should hear the ordinances as guidelines for a New Way of life for humankind, crucial not only to the people in the story but also to ourselves. For we are vicariously taking a walk with the Israelites, eager to see whether and how God's Way for humankind finds a foothold in the human world. Accordingly, we will receive these teachings both with the ears of the Israelites and with our own ears, giving them as sympathetic a hearing as we can (despite our modern sensibilities) as we continue our search for wisdom about communal well-being and a life well lived.

The "Hebrew Slave"

The Lord begins[9] with a brief instruction to Moses: "These are the ordinances (*mishpatim*) which *you shall place before them* (*tasim lifenehem*)" (21:1; emphasis added). Where we might have expected "which you shall tell them" (or "teach them"), the usage "which you shall *place* before them" is noteworthy. Is this just a shorthand way of conveying God's desire that the people expressly agree to the laws, which He offers as a proposal for their consideration and approval? Or does this expression hint also at a tablet or book containing a permanent record of the ordinances, something that will become the Book of the Covenant (*Sefer Habberith*)? We must wait and see.[10]

The first ordinance that Moses must set before the recently liberated people concerns the matter of slavery:

> When [*ki*] you [second person singular] obtain [buy, possess; *qanah*] a Hebrew slave [indentured servant, bondman*; '*eved* '*ivri*], six years shall he serve (*ya'avod*), and in the seventh year he shall go out free for nothing (*chinnam*). (21:2)

Why do the ordinances begin this way? For a reason at once substantive and rhetorical: the subject of slavery (servitude) is the foundation of the relationship between the Lord and the Israelites; it is the great human evil from which He delivered them. The Decalogue begins with the Lord identifying Himself as the One who delivered the Israelites out of the land of Egypt, out of the house of bondage (*mibbeth 'avadim*)—an action that established the ground of their relationship and of the new covenant. Here, the first ordinance instructs the Israelites on the defining subject of servitude and deliverance. It will also be of immediate personal interest for every Israelite ex-slave—a rhetorical reason why it is addressed to every hearer in the second-person singular.[11]

---

*We must emphasize again the difficulty in translating the Hebrew word '*eved*, which we discussed earlier in the context of Egyptian slavery (see Chapter Four). Because it can mean everything from "chattel slave," to "bondman" and "indentured servant," to "hired worker," and (elsewhere) even to "servant of God," we must be careful not to allow the worst connotations of "slavery" to creep *automatically* into our reading. Were it not for this danger, I would consistently translate '*eved* as "slave." Instead, I will vary the translation depending on what I think the context requires, but always indicating the presence of the same Hebrew term. By "indentured servant," I will mean a person who has contracted (or been forced) to work for another for *a fixed period of time*, in exchange for food and other necessities. By "bondman," I mean any man *bound* to work for another without wages, but where the term of service is unspecified. When I use the word "slave" I will be emphasizing the relation to the master as "*owner*"; when I use the word "servant" I will be emphasizing the servant's "*work*" or "*service*."

The main teaching is radical and revolutionary: there is to be no permanent servitude, at least within the covenantal community.[12] All Hebrew "slaves" go free after a time. They are not chattel slaves but (temporary) indentured servants. Even though they may be "bought and sold" for service or work, the Hebrew servants do not constitute a permanent class of enslaved human beings. There are no "natural slaves," no category of inferior human beings who, with their descendants, "deserve" to remain in bondage and who are considered to be their master's property. The only thing the Hebrew slave shares with slaves elsewhere—and that differentiates him from non-indentured workers—is that he cannot decide to leave his service during the period of indenture. As we will see, subsequent additions to this ordinance convey other ways of recognizing the equal humanity of one's servant.

We pause to imagine how the Israelites at Sinai are likely to hear this radical opening statement and how it might color their hearing of the rest. In Egypt, the only other world they have known, society was divided impermeably into masters and slaves, many of them in permanent bondage to Pharaoh. Had the newly liberated Israelites thought to imagine their future, they might have looked forward to a society in which *they* could be masters—or, for the dreamers among them, from which slavery would be eliminated. In one sentence, both their old world and any imagined utopian new world are set aside. The Israelites are offered a new reality to which they can favorably relate: no permanent slaves, no permanent masters, and freedom on condition that one not live so irresponsibly that one must return to indentured service. From the opening sentence, all Israelites know that their way of life will be the antithesis of Egypt's.

To the dismay of many modern readers, the ordinance presupposes the continuation of servitude and does not call for its abolition. But we should remember that throughout the ancient world (and not only in Egypt) chattel slavery—where slaves were regarded simply as property—was a universal practice and almost always a cruel one.*

---

*Because slaves were regarded as the mere property of their owner, there were absolutely no restraints on what he might properly do to them. From a variety of classical sources, we get the horrible picture. Consider, for example, practices of corporal

Against that practice, the present teaching is a decidedly humane correction. And these ordinances about the Hebrew servant may gradually lead to a fuller realization of their humane intention and to the ultimate extinction of slavery.[13] Perhaps more to the present point, we are not told—though it bears heavily on how we should think about this form of "slavery"—how someone is bound into servitude in the first place.

There were several common routes, beginning with destitution: a person with no other prospects sells himself into (temporary) service, either to work off unpaid debts or simply to sustain himself (recall Joseph's acceptance of the destitute Egyptians into [permanent] bondage to Pharaoh in exchange for grain). Even though forced by economic necessity, such voluntary entrance into service appears more dignified than a life of begging or stealing, not to speak of the later institution of debtor's prison. A second scenario is explicitly mentioned in the sequel (22:2): a captured thief who cannot pay back what he stole must serve for a time to make restitution to the man he injured; this too, to my eyes, is arguably a more just arrangement than our practice of incarceration. Next, and more problematic, a poor man—again, to pay off his debts—may sell his son into service or a daughter into marriage or concubinage. If a man has many mouths to feed, a case can be made that it is better for him and for most of his family to remain free, even if it requires that one of his children must become for a time an indentured servant—although we now consider sexual slavery abhorrent and are extremely cautious about child labor. Finally, we imagine that a man might obtain

---

punishment and other abuses of the body. Fingers and thumbs were amputated for breaking pottery. Slaves who knew too much about their masters had their tongues cut out to keep them from talking. Prisoners captured in war were routinely blinded, so much so that blindness came to be a visible mark of slavery. Ears were removed for acts of disobedience, and in the Code of Hammurabi, ear removal was also prescribed as fit punishment for striking a free person on the cheek or for denying an order of one's master. Teeth were knocked out to curb appetite. Slaves who worked indoors were castrated. (Genesis speaks several times of Pharaoh's eunuchs, including Potiphar, Joseph's master.) So widespread were these practices that visible bodily mutilation was taken to be the mark of servitude, and the maiming was often done to mark one's own slaves. We shall keep these examples in mind when we come later in this chapter to the ordinances dealing with bodily harm done to slaves.

slaves from captives acquired in war or through kidnapping. The first of these alternatives is not explicitly mentioned, though it would be implicit in any reference, should there be one, to the *foreign 'eved*. The second option, as we shall see in a future ordinance, is strongly condemned: to kidnap for the sake of selling into slavery (the origins of the African slave trade) will be deemed a capital offense.

Although enunciated in the second-person singular, the point of this teaching about servitude is not merely individual and private but most emphatically social and political: Israel is not to be permanently divided into freemen and slaves. In the newly constituted community, all members will retain equal status as covenanters with the Lord, exactly as they are now in the wilderness. Even when they fall on hard times, they must be seen as retaining their dignity as free human beings, living under the God-given law to which their ancestors freely gave consent. As we recall from the Decalogue, slaves (both the man servant, *'eved*, and the maidservant, *'amah*) were included in the obligation and privilege of Sabbath rest. The requirement of six years of work and the seventh year of release from work echoes precisely the teaching about the Sabbath. And the verbs "he-shall-serve" and "he-shall-go-out" both bespeak the agency of the *servant*, not of his master. Despite being in service, he still partakes of the dignity (and eventual freedom) he possesses and deserves as a human being.

The keynote teaching, nullifying chattel slavery, refers to the "*Hebrew* (*'ivri*) servant," a phrase whose meaning is debated. Does it mean only Israelite servants, or does it include outsiders as well? Most traditional interpreters favor the first alternative, as if the text had read, "If you obtain a servant from among the Children of Israel"—although they do not try to explain why that unambiguous formulation was not used instead. In support, they cite later passages (not in this collection of *mishpatim*) that clearly distinguish between indentured servants from within the Israelite community and servants obtained from neighboring peoples. Only the latter may be treated as heritable property and made to serve forever (Lev. 25:39–46).

But we shall soon meet other ordinances about slaves in which the restrictive word "Hebrew" does not appear, which defend the equal humanity of every *'eved*, Israelite or not. And there are scholars who argue, regarding our present passage, that *'ivri*, Hebrew, should not be read as a synonym for "Israelite." Based on the uses of words akin to *'ivri* in Akkadian, Ugaritic, and Egyptian, as well as prior usages of the word "Hebrew" in Genesis and Exodus, Cassuto argues that it is not a racial or ethnic but a class category: a Hebrew is someone who is an *outsider*—someone from *'ever*, literally, "from across [the boundary]"—who is (therefore) fit to serve.[14] If this were correct—and I am unconvinced but glad for the question to be held open—we might have here a primary teaching about servants in general, to be heard in this way: "You were a Hebrew slave in Egypt; now, this is how you should think and act regarding your own Hebrew slaves." Or perhaps, "You should look upon any bondman of yours as if he were as you once were, a Hebrew slave in Egypt."

However this may be, this implicit reminder of their Egyptian servitude ends with the phrase, "go out *free for nothing*" (*yetse' lahafshi chinnam*)—"free for nothing" as opposed to "free by ransom." Never forget that you were once Hebrew slaves in Egypt. Should you have any of those in your house, they too—like you—will go out free for nothing, delivered without having to pay ransom. Unstated is the reason: you would still be there were it not for Me.

This tacit reminder of the Lord's deliverance closes the circle with a crucial implicit teaching at the root of Israel's unique attitude toward slavery: no human being can truly be another's master or another's servant. Why? Because the true Master—before whom all are equally called to service—is the Lord.[15] The converse is also true: because all human beings are equal in relation to the Lord, permanent human servitude—with its tendencies to arrogant oppression from above and slavish idolatry from below—is entirely illegitimate.

Slaves and Family Life

After presenting the basic ordinance and establishing the fundamental principle of no permanent servitude in Israel, the next four verses offer specifications and provisos—all introduced by the qualification "if," *'im,* not "when," *ki.* They generally address the indentured servant in relation to his family:

> *If* he comes in by himself, he shall go out by himself; *if* he be married, his wife shall go out with him. *If* his master gives him a wife [from among his other servants], and she bear him sons and daughters, the wife and her children shall be *her master's,* and he shall go out by himself. But *if* the servant shall plainly say (*'amor yo'mar;* literally, "saying he shall say"), "I love my master, my wife, and my children: I will not go out free"; then his master shall bring him unto God (*'el-ha'elohim*), and shall bring him to the door or the doorpost, and his master shall bore his ear through with an awl; and he shall serve him forever. (21:3–6; emphasis added)

Several things deserve comment. First, there is a presumption against breaking up marriages and families: if a married man must sell himself into service, his wife goes in with him and goes out with him. The second case, admittedly more complicated, continues a presumption in favor of marriages (and at least against fornication). Having acquired an unmarried manservant who may be with him for six years, the master may (prudently or generously) give his servant a wife from among his other servants.[16] Because he would hardly do so were the woman (and children born to her) to leave with the man when his six years are up, the wife and children remain with the master.[17] Unlike the first case, this rule seems cruelly indifferent to the breakup of families. But the text only says that [implied: when the time comes] the man shall go out by himself as he came in [implied: *free for nothing*]. The woman and her children do not automatically go *free for nothing,* but if they are to go out, they must be redeemed by payment. Nothing prevents the man from working thereafter to ransom the woman and the children.

As if reading the reader's mind, the last case addresses these very considerations: a man who, loving his master, his wife, and his children, chooses to remain in service forever. What to think about this case?

On the one hand, one could argue that the keynote principle of freedom ("no permanent servitude for anyone") admirably creates a humane exception for familial love—in the special case where the master is also lovable. Freedom is not an end in itself but the condition for higher devotions, including the familial love of one's own. (A cynical reader may suspect that the master—like Laban with Jacob—gave him the woman so that such familial affection might keep the man permanently in his service.) In addition, we may wonder whether a child could easily honor his father if his father choose his own freedom over paternal responsibility. On the other hand, one might find something disgraceful in choosing servitude over freedom—even with a noble master—especially if there exist other ways of redeeming one's family. Several things incline me to the latter view, prime among them being the ritual of drilling the ear at the doorpost.

The visible marking in the flesh, made in public, declares that this is a man who has chosen permanent servitude. One cannot tell from the mark itself why he has chosen to remain: Was it because he loves his family more than his freedom (a noble reason) or because he loves his security (a base reason, not unlike preferring a return to the flesh pots of Egypt)? It seems right to say that the choice of perpetual servitude need not be ignoble: it all depends on the circumstances and also on the goodness of the master, who might (in a rare case, like Sir Thomas More) be a God-fearing man who could lead his servant (perhaps, even, a former thief) to higher spiritual things. But to think this way is to forget who the real master is here. As I argued earlier, freedom from all human masters, in service to the Lord who delivered you from such servitude, is the foundation of the God's Way for Israel, and via Israel for humankind. The mark on the organ of hearing and obedience signifies an impaired orientation of the slave's soul.[18]

In any other context, we might argue that service can be ennobling, especially if the master is himself noble and worthy. Against the prejudices of modern times, we might seriously suggest that a servant (one who serves someone and something) may be altogether a higher human being than an employee (literally, a "tool"—something used—a mere "slave-for-wages"). Consider, for example, the case of Kent in *King Lear.* Kent, a most admirable nobleman and the best man in the play, degrades himself and enters in disguise into the service of the degraded Lear, because Lear was once a great king with regal and moral authority—and all readers admire Kent for doing so. But in the biblical context, only God has that kind of regal and moral authority; only God deserves lifelong devotion and service.

The case is settled by considering the place of ear piercing: the doorposts. Doorposts were marked on Exodus eve in blood (which is the life) as a vote for freedom. More precisely, they were marked in obedience to a command that was the necessary and sufficient condition for deliverance (of self and household), an election of liberation. Here, the man is marked at the doorpost—before God (or the court) as witness— as someone who prefers to remain in servitude to a *human* master. Even if his love of his family seems a noble reason for doing so, there is something shameful, even rebellious, in his choice. He voluntarily chooses to wear in disgrace his master's imprint on his ear.

Daughters Sold into Service

After the case of the male Hebrew servant, the next group of ordinances deals with daughters sold into service. Once again, there is a main case followed by qualifying circumstances:

> And when (*ki*) a man sells (*yimkor*) his daughter to be a maidservant (*'amah*), she shall not go out as the menservants do. (21:7)

Before trying to unpack this ordinance in search of its moral and political point, we must acknowledge our difficulty with the entire premise. As modern Western readers, we are offended by the practice of selling daughters or betrothing them without their consent. But we must remember that such customs were once the general norm,[19] and not only in the ancient world; they are still prevalent today in large parts of the Muslim world and in parts of Africa. For most of human history, alas, daughters have been under the thumb of their fathers, to be given or sold into marriage to whomever the fathers pleased. Against this background, the Israelite innovation may be seen as a giant step forward in defense of the woman's rights and dignity.

A daughter sold as a bondwoman goes not as a servant to labor but as a wife or concubine of her (Israelite) master.[20] The payment is, as it were, the equivalent of a bride-price, and by offering it to her father, the master espouses her to himself. For this reason, she does not leave as a manservant does. As the further stipulations make clear, the purpose of the rules is to protect the woman against deceit, dishonor, and abuse:

> If (*'im*) she pleases not her master, *who has designated her to himself,* then shall he let her be redeemed; to sell her unto a foreign people he shall have no power, *seeing he has dealt deceitfully with her.* And if (*'im*) he espouses her unto his son, he shall deal with her after the manner of daughters. If (*'im*) he takes him another wife, her food, her raiment, and her conjugal rights he shall not diminish. And if (*'im*) he does not do (*ya'aseh*) these three for her, then she shall go out for nothing, without money. (21:8–11; emphasis added)

If the young woman displeases her lord, whether as sexual partner or through some "fault" or act of indecency, he cannot sell her to an alien household; he must allow her to be redeemed,[21] because—note the reason given—he has dealt deceitfully with her. When he took her, he promised to keep her as his own, and now he has changed his mind. Should he instead designate her for his son, she shall be treated as a daughter, a full member of the family, notwithstanding her origins. If the master takes a second wife (for himself or for his son), her rights as a wife shall not be diminished. Should he fail to fulfill his three obligations to her,[22] she goes out free for nothing—and, in case you missed the point—she goes out without money (ransom). Whatever else one might say about this practice, the rules not only protect the unfortunate daughter of a poor man (or a thief) who gets sold into marriage or concubinage; the entire practice provides her an opportunity to marry and rise above her station. Against the background of the custom then prevailing, these are humane innovations.

Capital Offenses

After laying down the basic political law of slavery and freedom—greatly restricting indentured servitude and upholding the dignity of servants—God turns next to the all-important defense of human life and what He regards as equally capital matters.[23] These ordinances add specificity to the Decalogue's central principles regarding murder and honoring father and mother, and they put additional weight on the keynote teaching about freedom and slavery:

> Whoever strikes (*makkeh*) a man so that he dies, he shall surely be put to death. But if he lies not in wait, but God (*'elohim*) delivers him into his hand, then I will appoint you a place to which he may flee. But if [on the other hand] a man comes willfully upon his neighbor to slay him with guile, you [second-person singular] shall take him [even] from My altar that he may die. (21:12–14)

The main case baldly states the principle: a homicide pays with his own life. The ordinance echoes almost exactly the central teaching of the Noahide code: "Whosoever sheds man's blood, by man shall his blood be shed; for in the image of God was man made" (Gen. 9:6). But whereas the Noahide teaching was a strictly act-oriented principle—albeit a gigantic advance over the bloody-minded, vengeance-craving, antediluvian state of nature[24]—the new dispensation makes room for considering intent, not least because the life of the homicide also matters. If the killing was not planned or intended (like Moses's killing of the Egyptian overseer who was smiting the Hebrew slave; [2:12]), and if the blow was fatal only accidentally—a so-called act of God or chance—the killer may, indeed *must*, flee to a place or city of refuge. That he has shed human blood makes him a pollution upon the community, forcing him into exile; that he did not mean to do so allows him to find refuge, saving his life and protecting him from those who would seek revenge.[25]

But this immunity vanishes if the murderer acted deliberately and planned ahead (as did Cain with Abel). Not even God's holy altar provides refuge for one who would deliberately slay his neighbor or his brother. This again contrasts with neighboring ancient societies that gave absolute sanctuary to anyone who entered a sacred precinct, even had he willfully killed a man. In Israel, the holiness of God's Temple cannot outweigh the preciousness of human life. An assault on the creature made in God's image is an assault on God Himself.[26]

A similar kind of reasoning may be at work in the acts described in the next three ordinances, all of which, like premeditated homicide, are capital offenses:

> And he that strikes his father or his mother shall surely be put to death. And he that steals a man and sells him, or if he be found in his hand, he shall surely be put to death. And he that curses [or, perhaps, "contemns" or "dishonors"; *meqallel*, literally, "one that makes light of"[27]] his father or his mother shall surely be put to death. (21:15–17)

In keeping with the Decalogue's revolutionary statement of principle, two of these offenses, on a par with murder, concern one's father and mother. Much stricter regarding honoring (both) parents than the law of neighboring peoples,[28] God's Law for Israel prescribes an automatic death sentence for anyone who simply strikes either parent, seemingly regardless of whether the blow does any harm. If read legalistically, this seems unduly harsh: Is a slap in the heat of argument, perhaps in self-defense against an abusive father's blow or tirade, the capital equivalent of premeditated assault and battery committed against a decent father?[29] Clearly, there is much need for judicial discernment, and the rabbinic tradition supplied volumes on the subject. But the principle stands as a light in God's Way: to strike your father and mother is a crime equivalent to murder.

More remarkable still is the second deadly offense against parents: reviling or cursing one's father or mother, that is, uttering aloud a call for God or the cosmos to rain down evil upon their venerable heads. For people educated under such teachings, the reason seems almost obvious: to curse or even severely disdain your father and mother (as Ham disdained his drunken father Noah) is to kill them *as your parents*, people to whom you are indebted for your very existence. The denial of your "creators" is at once an attack on the Creator and a metaphorical self-annihilation. The punishment fits the crime.

Sandwiched between the two offenses against parents is the capital offense of kidnapping with the intent to keep as a slave ("found in his hand") or to sell into bondage—the crime of Joseph's brothers against him, which is not directly punished in the Genesis narrative. By a tortuous path, that crime led to Joseph's assimilation in Egypt and eventually to the 400-year enslavement of the Children of Israel, from which the Lord has only just redeemed them. To steal a fellow human being and sell him into bondage not only repeats that original offense and shows contempt for the Lord's deliverance. The offender embraces the despotism of Pharaoh, who profits from repudiating the dignity of his fellow man. The slave-trading (or slave-making) kidnapper gets what both he and Pharaoh deserve.

Bodily Injury

From crimes causing death or otherwise meriting the death penalty, the ordinances move to a series of nonfatal injuries brought about by fighting. These injunctions bespeak the Torah's regard for bodily wholeness as well as for civic peace:

> And when men quarrel, and [when] one strikes (*vehikkah*) the other with a stone, or [only] with his fist, and he dies not, but keeps his bed; if he rises again, and walks abroad upon his staff, then he that struck him shall be quit [of the capital punishment]; only he shall pay for the loss of his time, and shall cause him to be thoroughly healed. (21:18–19)

"When men quarrel, and [when] one strikes the other with a stone, or [only] with his fist." There is clearly no point telling these men[30] not to quarrel and fight; they must instead be told in advance that they will be held accountable for the consequences, should the fighting cause serious injury. If the injured party dies directly from the blow, the person responsible will be tried under the ordinances regarding homicide. But if the victim becomes bedridden only to rise again (even with the aid of his staff), his assailant must compensate him for his lost time at work and must pay for his care until he is completely healed.

It is easy to overlook the radical features of this seemingly banal teaching, all directed toward increasing the chances for civic peace by ignoring claims of offended honor and vengeful anger—both major causes of fighting. First, the ordinance shows no interest in who started the quarrel and why, or who was in the right. It does not care whether the blow was struck intentionally with malice aforethought or unintentionally in the heat of the moment. It treats fighting only insofar as it causes bodily damage, and it treats the damage (only) as personal harm rather than (also) as personal injury; that is, as a matter of *injustice* (Lat. *inuria*). Second, there is no compensation for insult or slight: don't show me your wounded pride, just your broken leg. In this way, conflicts among men that almost always begin with righteous anger over a perceived injustice are reduced to matters of economic loss and medical reparation. Everyone is put on notice: you will pay for harming your neighbor, whether you meant to or not and whether he deserved it or not. (Correlatively, if you are the wounded party, you will be compensated only for harm and lost time, not for the indignity of it all.) The goal is civic peace and physical safety, not upholding honor or *amour propre*.[31]

Given the Law's abundant concern for human dignity, its indifference to the indignity experienced by injured parties may at first seem strange. But there is no inconsistency. The high moral worth of every human being has nothing in common with the inflated social worth that prideful individuals claim for themselves and fight to uphold. The Torah's emphasis on the former may even be the reason it rejects the latter: because all human beings are equally in God's image, puffed-up personal pride and vanity are serious ontological errors. Pride is finally a species of idolatry.[32]

The remaining ordinances about bodily injuries address harms to persons who are socially more vulnerable than free men: one's servants and slaves, and pregnant women:

And if a man strikes (*yakkeh*) his bondman, or his bondwoman, *with a rod,* and he/she dies under his hand, *he/she shall surely be avenged (naqom yinnaqem)*. Notwithstanding, if he/she continues a day or two, he/she shall not be avenged *(yuqqam)*; for he/she is his money *(kesef)*. (21:20–21; emphasis added)

This ordinance is written entirely in the interest of the slave, not of the master. The bondman and the bondwoman—and not only the Hebrew ones—are not the master's property to be treated at will. At least with respect to their lives, they are independent persons before the law, with rights and interests the law seeks to defend.

A master, it is assumed, has permission to discipline his slaves. He might have occasion to strike his bondman or bondwoman with a rod (note: a rod, not a stone), the instrument of chastisement, perhaps with cause. But masters beware. Your slaves are human beings too, protected under our law, and should they die from your beating, you will answer with your life. You will be held guilty of willful murder, whether you intended to kill them or not. In this striking Israelite innovation, the ordinance that ordains capital punishment for killing one's fellow man (or woman) applies equally to anyone who kills his slave.[33]

The ordinance not only warns masters to respect their slaves' lives but also teaches the community a correlative duty. Unlike the previous statements on capital punishment, which spoke about the perpetrator— "he shall surely be put to death"—this ordinance speaks on behalf of the victim: "*he/she* shall surely *be avenged (naqom yinnaqem)*." Lest you think that a slave is merely property, you have an obligation to avenge his lost life. Never mind that he is a lowly foreign slave, far from home, with no one here who knows or cares about him: the whole community bears responsibility to retribute his murder.

But what happens if the slave's death does not occur during or immediately after the beating, but only after a few days? In this case, the death is not avenged, not because he is a slave but because there is reasonable doubt about cause and culpability: we cannot be sure this was intentional homicide. Since the master used the rod—not a lethal instrument like a stone—and since the slave did not die right away (as he would have done had the beating been excessively brutal), we cannot conclude that the master intended to kill him—not least because the slave's death would also be an economic loss for the master. (Consider the economics: one chastises only slaves one wants to keep.) Therefore, if the master cannot be shown to have either directly or intentionally caused the slave's death, justice does not require his death—since his life, too, is precious. Nor, having lost his slave, does he require any additional punishment. The loss of his bondman is sufficient material punishment: "for he/she is his money," now gone.[34]

Sometimes fighting men accidentally strike and harm innocent bystanders. Although we are not given such a (general) case, we imagine that should one occur the law of damages would apply: if you caused the harm, you pay for lost time and medical recovery. But in place of this general case, there is a special case that cries out for special treatment—and receives it:

> And if men strive together (*yinnatsu*), and strike (*venagefu*) a woman with child, so that her fruit departs, and yet no [additional] harm (or "damage"; *'ason*) follows, he shall be surely fined, according as the woman's husband shall lay upon him; and he shall pay as the judges (*bifelilim*) determine. But if any harm (*'ason*) follows, then you shall give life for life, eye for eye, tooth for tooth, hand for hand, foot for foot, burning for burning, wound for wound, stripe for stripe. (21:22–25)

The account raises many questions. Why the fuss over pregnant women but not other innocent bystanders harmed by brawling men? What do some of the difficult terms mean, beginning with *'ason*, "harm"?[35] Why, in this case, is a fine proposed by the husband yet also determined by the judge? Why haul out the frightful catalog of harsh punishments for what seems to be but an accidental injury? More simply, how should we—or the soon-to-be auditors at Sinai—think about the case itself?

Do the brawling men accidently knock into an unrelated woman who just happens to be passing by and just happens to be pregnant? Or might she be an interested party, related—as wife or lover—to one or both of the fighting men? Could they be fighting about (or over) her? Could they be fighting about her pregnancy—and, if so, about her possible infidelity? Or might she be trying to break up a fight, perhaps involving her husband, when one of the men (presumably unrelated to her) accidentally strikes her a blow intended for his opponent? We have no way to answer any of these questions. From the fighters' point of view they may matter a great deal, and a judge hearing such a case will likely want to get the whole factual story. But from the point of view of the ordinance and its implicit principle, these facts are irrelevant. The ordinance teaches us that the harm to the fetus and the woman is all that counts.

The exact nature of that harm is not altogether clear. We know that the woman miscarries—"her fruit departs." But what is meant by "and no harm (*'ason*) follows"? Does it mean only that the woman does not suffer any other damage? Or does it refer also to her prematurely delivered fetus, who might continue to live or not? Commentators differ on this question.[36] Yet there is no question that the law regards the mother–child dyad as an especially precious—and vulnerable—subject, regardless of social class.

Unlike the previous ordinances regarding homicide, which mitigated the severity of the punishment where the killing was unintentional, here the penalty for unintentional harm is *more* severe: if the woman dies, so does the man who brought it about, even if entirely accidentally.[37] Remarkably, in this patriarchal world in which a woman's social status is inferior to that of a man, her life is avenged more stringently. But nothing better conveys the importance the Torah attaches to protecting a pregnant woman and her nascent child than the stated punishment: the famous *lex talionis,* mentioned here in the Bible for the first time. What is this law, and why is this the crime for which it is initially introduced?

Modern readers are likely to be repelled by the law of the talion: an eye for an eye, a tooth for a tooth, strikes most of us as primitive, if not barbaric and cruel. Besides, what good can it do the victim if the perpetrator suffers an identical harm? In support of such negative judgments, there is little evidence that these punishments were ever meted out, as the Rabbis reinterpreted them as calling only for proportional monetary damages. But even if read literally, taken in context against the existing cultural and legal alternatives, the law of the talion is a giant step forward from the barbarism and mayhem of revenge cultures, even as it concedes something to popular demands for retributive justice.

First of all, the law of the talion establishes the principle of measure and fitness. It limits the impulse to take revenge by restricting the amount—no *more* than an eye for an eye—and the object of punishment: only the perpetrator shall be punished, not also (or instead) his wife or his children. (In the Code of Hammurabi, if an upper-class woman dies as a result of the blow, the daughter of the offender shall be put to death [209–210].) Second, the social class of the victim is irrelevant—another blow to the rule of honor and pride. (In the Code of Hammurabi, if the woman is lower class or is a bondwoman, the assailant pays only a fine, even if the woman dies from the injury [211–214].) Third, by announcing the punishment in advance, the ordinance removes it from the realm of discretion, limiting the ability of judges to favor members of their own class. The lives of all pregnant women (and their unborn babies) are of equal weight before the court. Finally, as in the previous ordinances, the law of the talion—though it might seem to be motivated by vengeful desires—in fact rejects the idea of revenge. It ignores the avenging motive of wounded pride and honor and addresses only the retribution of harm.

These considerations notwithstanding, the punishment for harming a pregnant woman and her child is severe, and deliberately so. We are meant to take notice that it is her safety (and perhaps also her child's) that is singled out for eye-for-eye retribution.[38] Men will fight, often about women, but they are put on notice that they will be culpable should their negligence and wildness harm the life-giving dyad. And since one can never be sure whether a nearby woman is pregnant, men are encouraged to be careful in the presence of all women. The general teaching about men in relation to women and children could not be clearer: when men fight, women and children are most at risk. The law seeks to build a wall of protection around them.

It is remarkable how far these ordinances on bodily injury go in acknowledging human hotheadedness while denying it any honored place in human life. In dispensing His divinely given law to these ex-slaves, summoning them to a righteous way of living, God seems to concede that He has limited power to shape the souls of men—at least at first. No matter how righteous the communal teaching and aspiration, nasty things will happen. Law or no law, God or no God, people are going to be bashing one another with stones (or their equivalent). Yet even while making this concession, the law has removed all recompense for insult or disdain, which is usually what makes people angry enough to fight. Loss and harm make people sad, but they become fighting mad because you treated them with contempt. (Like the other laws of personal injury, the law about harming the pregnant woman also treats such anger with its own silent contempt.) The law wants to know where you hurt, not what your rival said about you or why you are smiting your neighbor.[39]

Yet while wounded honor has no honored place in these teachings, it cannot be expunged from social relations. The law, to repeat, leaves room for men to fight. It does not teach, "You mustn't fight"; it says, "You shouldn't fight near a (pregnant) woman." It does not say, "Do not beat your neighbor"; it says, "Do not beat your father or your mother." God at Sinai does not create rules that are impossible for a human being to live up to, never mind ex-slaves reared in brutal bondage. A law that is too hard to obey puts everyone immediately outside itself. The ordinances about fighting are laws even hotheaded people can live with. Moreover, although limiting hotheaded demands for vengeance by the strict proportionality of the *lex talionis*, the ordinances also partly satisfy the all-too-human demand for retribution.[40]

The final case of personal injury reverts to masters beating their slaves, very likely prompted by talk of eyes and teeth. This time the bodily harm is not lethal, but as before the focus is on the victim:

> And if a man strikes the eye of his bondman (*'eved*), or the
> eye of his bondwoman (*'amah*), and destroys it, he shall let
> him (her) go free for his (her) eye's sake. And if he knocks
> out his bondman's tooth, or his bondwoman's tooth, he shall
> let him (her) go free for his (her) tooth's sake. (21:26–27)

What kind of a bondman (or bondwoman) is this? As before, the ordinance does not specify. Some commentators have argued that it must refer only to the non-Israelite slave (for example, nothing is said about the monetary compensation to which an Israelite injured in fight was earlier said to be entitled). Others maintain that the Hebrew servant is also included (for example, nothing in this ordinance prevents him from also seeking compensation from his master, after he goes free; in addition, even though he is under contract to work off his debt, he should not have to work for a master who has knocked out his eye or tooth). But I am inclined to think the lack of specificity is deliberate: whatever sort the servant or slave, the Lord has an important—and revolutionary—point to make. The Code of Hammurabi [199] and the Hittite Laws, regarding all slaves as property, both call for monetary compensation to the master should a man destroy the eye of *another* man's slave. But neither says anything about a master who harms *his own* slave. Perhaps more than any other, the present ordinance marks an important difference between the Lord's Way and the ways of the world.

The Israelite master who beats his own slave does not pay an eye for an eye. He pays instead with the slave's manumission, letting him go free for nothing. And lest the point be misunderstood, the slave goes free even for a knocked-out tooth (presumably even if it is knocked out inadvertently). Against the widespread abuse and deliberate mutilation of slaves in the Ancient Near East,[41] even the accidental loss of an eye or tooth puts an end to servitude in Israel. Israelite masters are put on notice: their slaves—*all* of them—must not be harshly beaten or maimed. You own their labor, but you do not own their bodies, still less their lives. They are not your property; they are, like you, human beings, whose embodied life deserves to be respected—and, we readers of Genesis can add, because we are all equally in God's image.

To this point the law has consisted almost exclusively of punishments for wrongdoing. But it has said nothing edifying about the goods these punishments defend: the worth of life and limb, the honor of parents, the preciousness of pregnant women and the innocent life they carry, the equal humanity of slaves. The ordinances take the occurrence of wrongdoing for granted and address its consequences in the fairest and least vengeful ways possible. Like most of the Decalogue, also stated in the negative, the ordinances continue to assume that human beings need to be restrained more than they need to be encouraged, and they seek to deter them by threat of clearly defined punishments. The ordinances simultaneously warn potential wrongdoers about the consequences of the most common kinds of wrongdoing and counsel those who must punish them. Like our own tort and criminal law, God's ordinances teach conduct not by modeling good behavior but by setting out what happens in cases of bad conduct—cases we can all recognize as coming with the territory of being human.

Implicit in all these laws, however, is a positive teaching of what Israel should look up to and esteem. Not only does the law punish, compensate, frighten, and deter. Tacitly and indirectly, it teaches us the community's idea of and ideals for leading a worthy life. And by the order in which the ordinances are presented, the law teaches us how to rank and prioritize the human goods it is striving to protect and promote: first, human freedom; then, human life and respect for parents; then, bodily wholeness—suffused throughout with a concern for everyone's human dignity, including respect for the life and limb of servant and slave and special care for pregnant women and their unborn children, and informed by a desire to promote civil peace. Yes, the law should be obeyed because it is the law. But well-made law reveals its reasons and purposes to the careful student, even if these are not explicitly stated.

Dangerous Animals

The ordinances conclude the subject of bodily harms with those caused by domestic animals. As in the Code of Hammurabi, the goring ox is chosen as the typical and exemplary culprit. We begin, once again, with the general case. The Israelite innovations will occur largely in the subsequent variations.

> And when (*ki*) an ox gores a man or a woman, that they die,
> the ox shall surely be stoned, and its flesh shall not be eaten;
> but the owner of the ox shall be clear [of further punishment].
> (21:28)

In keeping with the high value the Torah sets on all human life (woman's as well as man's), the man-slaughtering ox is put to death, even though it could have had no evil intention. To modern readers for whom "punishment" turns on culpable responsibility, and for whom responsibility, to be culpable, generally requires either intention or blameworthy neglect, this teaching will appear strange at best. But this biblical recompense was established already by the (innovative) Noahide code that provided the basic legal foundation of all civilized society, replacing the anarchic and bloody antediluvian state of nature:

> "And surely the blood of your lives will I require [a reckoning; that is, "I will require payment for it"]; *at the hand of every beast will I require it;* and at the hand of man, even at the hand of every man's brother, will I require the life of man. Whoso sheds man's blood, by man shall his blood be shed; for in the image of God was man made" (Gen. 9:5–6; emphasis added).

For homicide to be murder requires intent, but the foul deed of homicide is itself rank, without regard to its cause.

What is at issue in the case of the death-dealing ox is less what we call crime and more what we used to call defilement: the shedding of human blood and its boundary-defying "watering" of the earth.[42] Considered metaphysically, the spilling of human blood is arguably *worse* when spilled by an animal, who in doing so breaches a morally significant boundary by laying waste his cosmic superior. Here, as elsewhere, the pollution of human bloodshed must be cleansed and "undone" by removing the cause of the pollution. Moreover, in Israel the polluting animal must not be eaten, lest the eater be defiled by contact and incorporation (hence, death by stoning). In this standard case, the owner of the ox is not punished further, beyond the loss of his ox; in this last provision, the Code of Hammurabi agrees.

So much for an ox who gores for the first time. But if he lives and becomes a habitual gorer, his owner will be held responsible. Here the Israelite law is distinctive:

> But if (*'im*) the ox was wont to gore in time past, and warning has been given to its owner, and he has not kept it [in], but it has killed a man or a woman, then the ox shall be stoned, *and its owner also shall be put to death.* If (*'im*) there be laid on him a ransom (*kofer*), then he shall give for the redemption of

his life whatsoever is laid upon him [by order of the court]. Whether it have gored a son, or have gored a daughter, he [the master] shall be dealt with according to the same judgment. If the ox gores a bondman or a bondwoman, he shall give unto their master thirty shekels of silver, and the ox shall be stoned. (21:29–32; emphasis added)

The basis of the owner's responsibility is very carefully delineated. The ox has gored before; the owner knew about it and was warned to take precautions (say, by cutting off the ox's horns or by fencing him in); the owner failed to do so ("he has not kept it [in]"); and this time the ox not only harms but kills a man or a woman—then and only then will the owner be deemed responsible for manslaughter and punished accordingly. Where human life is lost, such blatant indifference is treated as tantamount to approval, and gross negligence as indistinguishable from intent: the owner, like a murderer, deserves to pay with his own life. In thus holding the owner capitally responsible for the death, the Torah goes beyond the neighboring laws, which merely fined the negligent owner of a death-dealing ox.[43]

But the Lord leaves open a less drastic outcome. Perhaps because the ox owner's life is also precious, perhaps because he did not *willfully* cause the death, or perhaps because the victim's family took pity on him, the law offers a possible way to avoid the death sentence. Although as a matter of strict justice he deserves to die, the court in its mercy may allow him to ransom his life back.[44]

The next variation of ox-caused homicide concerns the death not of an adult but of a child—a son or daughter. Lest you think that that the law holds only for adults, the ordinance prescribes the same judgment should the habitually goring ox kill a child (of either sex). Against the practice of neighboring peoples, which demanded the death of a man's son should the ox kill the son of another, the Torah will punish only the guilty owner. People are punished only for their own sins.

The final case of bodily injury deals with a slave (male or female) fatally gored by someone else's ox. Most interpreters regard this as continuing down a rank-ordered list of the ox's possible victims—from adults to children to slaves (almost certainly non-Israelite ones). On this reading, the negligent owner is not, for some reason, said to be capitally liable and merely pays the slave's master a fixed compensation—thirty shekels (= six-tenths of a mina)—for the loss of his slave, perhaps also as a set ransom. (The Code of Hammurabi [252], dealing with such a case, likewise prescribes a payment of one-third mina of silver to the slave's master.) But again uniquely in Israel, the ox is stoned as in all the other cases, because—as with all human beings—the shedding of a slave's blood must be requited. Even a foreign slave is never just property.

But this case of an ox killing a slave may not be part of the series, to be compared with the cases of killing man or woman, son or daughter. It may instead be a distinctly new case involving an ox not known to gore, to be read in relation to the original case of an ox who unexpectedly kills a man or a woman (21:28): case one, ox gores and kills man or woman; case two, ox gores and kills bondman or bondwoman.[45] On this reading, the ordinance teaches that even the lives of slaves killed unintentionally by a dangerous animal demand retribution from its owner: the slave's life is as precious as that of a free person. The offending ox is killed—just as it is when the victim is not a slave—and its owner pays substantial compensation to the slave's master for the loss of his service.

On either reading of the last case, however, the general teaching about dangerous animals stands. Their conduct, like ours, is scrutinized under a standard that esteems and protects all human life.

Harm to Animals

The foregoing ordinances demonstrate that God regards human life and limb—*every* human life and limb—as precious.* The rules He prescribes are clearly intended to make them more secure. But animal life, including the animal life of your neighbor, is also worthy of care and

---

*Precious, but not *sacred,* and therefore not always inviolable. The Hebrew Bible is notorious for the number of cases and instances that not only permit but even *mandate* the taking of human life, sometimes in large numbers. Human life can be forfeited by deeds that deny or contradict its own preciousness or the still higher things that human life is meant to serve. Life is the *fundamental*—foundational—human good, and certainly higher than property, for example, but it is not the highest of human goods.

protection. From dealing with oxen that injure humans, the ordinances move seamlessly to humans who injure oxen (and other domestic animals):

> And when (*ki*) a man shall open a pit, or when (*ki*) a man shall dig a pit and not cover it, and an ox or an ass fall therein, the owner of the pit shall make it good ("make it whole," that is, "make compensation"; *shallem*); he shall give money unto the owner of them, and the dead beast shall be his. And when (*ki*) one man's ox hurt another's, so that it dies, then they shall sell the live ox, and divide the price of it; and the dead ox also they shall divide. Or when (*ki*) it be known that the ox was wont to gore in time past, and its owner has not kept it [in], he shall surely pay ox for ox, and the dead beast shall be his own. (21:33–36)

A man is strictly liable for the harm he causes his neighbor's animals. Negligence in leaving open a pit is treated as if it were intentional or, more precisely, regardless of intent: the "care-less" man pays the owner for his dead ox or ass and reaps for himself the dead animal. If one's ox, not previously known to give trouble, fatally injures a neighbor's ox, it is regarded as an accident, but the owner, accepting responsibility, shares equally in his neighbor's loss. But if, as with a human victim, the ox was a habitual gorer and his master did nothing to keep him from other people's animals, the master must make full restitution, ox for ox. Once again, the dead animal comes to him. The Israelites are summoned not only to be their brothers' keepers but also to be keepers of their brothers' animals—or at least, not their destroyers. Life matters.

Against this reading, some will complain that I have sentimentalized what is purely an economic matter. Elsewhere in the ordinances, the Lord will explicitly promote kindness to animals.[46] But here, it will be said, the domestic animals are regarded as mere property—a special kind of property, to be sure, vulnerable (like the master) to injury and death. But in an agricultural society they are regarded mainly as tools—the ox for plowing, the ass for transporting—that are indispensable for their owners' survival and prosperity. Moreover, the deeds required in these ordinances are all economic: make compensation, give money, sell, divide the price, pay. In *this* case of a negligent owner with a goring ox, he pays no non-economic penalty, and his ox is not stoned.

All true, but not decisive. The fact that money changes hands by way of rectification does not mean that economic values are all that is at stake or that the animals are regarded solely as property. They are living beings that can be injured and killed, and not merely broken like pottery. Only a living thing is at risk from an open pit, into which it may wander and fall. Only a living thing can be killed by a dangerous animal. It is to the lives of living property that these ordinances are addressed.

Taken legalistically and in isolation, separate from their unfolding pattern, one might read these ordinances as merely economic. But looked at in context, they convey certain nonlegal values. They are organized mainly around the nature and severity of the harm to the victim—loss of freedom, loss of human life, loss of bodily integrity—and also according to the agent of the harm—human (deliberate or accidental) or animal (accidental or culpably predictable). When we descend to oxen and asses as victims, we again have the same array of agents—human; animal, accidental; and animal, culpably predictable. Harm to the animals is treated on the pattern of harm to humans. The value of their life is not equal to our own; their death on the horns of a goring ox does not call for retribution against the ox. But as we learned from the Sabbath teaching in the Decalogue, the cattle are entitled to Sabbath rest alongside the human household. The household pottery does not rest, but animals are never just property.

Protection of Property

The ordinances about harm to animals do, however, provide a smooth transition to ordinances about property as property—as goods considered solely under the aspect of ownership (proprietorship). Respect for persons includes respect for their possessions, for the things of their own: "You shall not steal" was also one of the Decalogue's cardinal principles. That principle is fleshed out in the following guidelines, beginning with simple theft. Once again, we suspect that the text is silently in conversation with the prevailing law of neighboring peoples.

Nothing better reveals the unique moral emphasis of God's Way than comparison with the Code of Hammurabi on the subject of property. Although the Code does not prescribe automatic capital punishment for homicide and allows for monetary compensation or pardon for the taking of a life, its protection of property is merciless. Hammurabi imposes death as the automatic penalty for breaking and entering, stealing, receiving stolen property, inability to repay stolen goods, aiding or harboring a fugitive slave, and looting at a fire. By contrast, theft is never a capital offense in Israel[47]:

> When (*ki*) a man steals an ox, or a sheep, and kills it, or sells it, he shall pay five oxen for an ox, and four sheep for a sheep. If (*'im*) a thief is found digging through, and is struck so that he dies, there shall be no blood-guiltiness for him. If (*'im*) [however] the sun is risen upon him, there shall be blood-guiltiness for him—he shall make restitution; if (*'im*) he has nothing, then he shall be sold for his theft. If (*'im*) the theft be found in his hand alive, whether it be an ox, or an ass, or a sheep, he shall pay double. (21:37–22:3)

The transition to the subject of theft involves stealing animals, indispensable to the livelihoods of both farmers and shepherds, and the objects of much care and attention.[48] In the model ordinance, the case involves the theft of animals—an ox or a sheep—that are either killed by the thief (presumably for food) or sold for profit. The substantial compensation—five oxen or four sheep for just one killed or sold—indicates that the law has more than restitution in mind. Given the ease with which untethered animals can be seized and the difficulty owners have in protecting them, the weighty penalty serves as a needed deterrent: a prospective animal thief will think four or five times before appropriating another man's sheep or ox. The stiff penalty compensates the owner for the insult of the theft, not only for the loss.

But the real meaning of this generous compensation becomes clear when we realize that the neighboring legal systems (including the Code of Hammurabi) sentenced thieves to death if they could not immediately pay back what they took (or if they stole by breaking in). The wish to correct this mindset about theft may explain the otherwise confusing order of the next three cases.

Following the model case of a thief caught after the fact, without the stolen goods, we expect to hear about compensation due when the thief is caught red-handed, still in possession of the goods. Instead, the next two ordinances consider the rights of the homeowner, should he catch the thief during the break-in. If the thief tries to enter at night, the homeowner may strike him dead without incurring the usual penalty for homicide. The presumption seems to be that a thief entering in darkness likely poses a threat also to life, and the homeowner may be excused for doing whatever is necessary to neutralize that threat.[49]

But if a man tries to steal in broad daylight, it is culpable homicide to kill him, for one must presume that he had no intention to attack the persons of the house and that the homeowner was not in danger for his life. To kill the daytime thief is murder. And here are the Israelite innovations, at once compassionate and morally challenging: rather than impose death on a thief who cannot make restitution for what he has stolen, he is allowed to sell himself—no, he *must* be sold—into indentured servitude to pay off over time what he owes. Mercifully, his life is spared. But as every ex-slave needs to learn, the path from slavery to freedom is not a one-way street, and freedom is contingent on good behavior. A thief is not only compelled to accept responsibility; through service, he also gets a chance to atone for his crime, to make restitution, and to rehabilitate himself. Human life and human character—even those of a thief—are both precious.

After these two cases, which teach the larger principles regarding the relative standing of human life and property and the importance of taking moral responsibility, the final ordinance returns to the matter of compensation for stolen animals. If the thief is caught red-handed, with the stolen animals alive and well in his possession, he gets off lightly: he pays back double. Why double? Because simple return of the stolen property would neither punish the misdeed nor deter anyone from attempting it. In addition, the penalty is exactly fitting: the thief suffers precisely the loss he would have inflicted on the owner. We have already been told what happens if the thief is not able to pay the price for the extra animal.

From damage to property—especially to one's domestic animals—resulting from theft, the ordinances proceed to deal briefly with damage done to a neighbor's cultivated land. In the ontological ordering of the "victims" of damage, agricultural crops stand lower than living things, human and animal. (Biblical Hebrew does not regard plants as living things [*chayoth*], but as the fruit of the earth—its "produce"—as hair may be considered the fruit of the head.) But thanks to the cooperative arts of agriculture, human effort enhances what the earth produces, thus making possible settled human habitation. Therefore, in the human ordering of damaged goods, the land and its produce rank very high indeed. They are at risk from beasts, from fire, and from human negligence and carelessness:

> When (*ki*) a man causes a field or vineyard to be eaten, and lets his beast loose, and it feeds in another man's field, of the *best* of his own field, and of the *best* of his own vineyard, he shall make restitution. When (*ki*) fire breaks out, and catches in thorns, so that the stacked grain or the standing grain or the field [itself] is consumed, he that kindled the fire shall surely make restitution. (22:4–5; emphasis added)

On close analogy with the cases of damage to human life and limb done by one's animals, the principle of strict liability applies also to damages to field and vineyard caused by the trampling or grazing of one's animals. The dumb animal feeds where it will. But as the language of the ordinance makes clear, its owner bears full responsibility: he "causes" the field or vineyard to be eaten; he "lets loose" his beast. His negligence is therefore treated as intent to harm his neighbor. For this reason, and because grain and grape are vitally important to his neighbor's livelihood and well-being, he must make restitution from the *best* of his own field and vineyard.[50]

Damage to a neighbor's crops caused by fire is treated somewhat differently. The fire "breaks out," it "catches in thorns," and the grain or field is (passively) consumed; no human agency seems to be involved. Nonetheless, the law places responsibility on the man who kindled the fire, almost as if he were guilty of arson; he must make restitution.[51] Playing with fire means paying for whatever it burns. It would be difficult to find a better expression of the importance the Torah places on personal responsibility for the well-being of your neighbor—and also for the bounty of the Promised Land toward which nascent Israel is headed and from which it will derive its livelihood.

Caring for Another's Property

From direct harm to personal property, both living and landed, caused willfully and accidentally, the ordinances move to the more complex and delicate matters of what the common law will later call "bailment": an arrangement in which the physical possession of some property passes temporarily into the hands of someone (the bailee) who is not the owner (the bailor). What kinds of protections are available to your property when it is not in your hands? And who is responsible should it be lost or damaged while in another's possession? The ordinances deal with several scenarios, hazards, and remedies. As with the previous ordinances, we do not get a comprehensive casebook, only enough to convey the principal legal guidelines and moral teachings.

> When a man delivers unto his neighbor money or goods for safekeeping (literally, "to keep" or "to guard"; *lishmor*), and it is stolen out of the man's house: if the thief is found, he [the thief] shall pay double. If the thief is not found, then the master of the house shall come near unto God (or "the gods"; *ha'elohim*), to see whether he has not put his hand unto his neighbor's goods. For every matter of trespass, whether it be for ox, for ass, for sheep, for raiment, or for any manner of lost thing, whereof someone says: "This is it," the cause of both parties shall come before God (or "the gods"; *ha'elohim*); he whom God (or "gods") shall condemn [plural verb] shall pay double unto his neighbor. (22:6–8)

The first case involves the theft of property (money or "stuff") left with the bailee for safekeeping, who presumably undertook to safeguard it as a favor. If the thief is found, the crime is handled like any other theft:

the thief pays double. But what to think if the thief is not found? Was it really stolen by a third party, or has the bailee lost it, destroyed it, or sold it to another for personal gain? In a word: Was the trusted bailee a thief? To allay suspicion, the bailee must approach the court—and swear before God as his witness—that he has not mishandled or misused the bailor's goods. Such an oath, either by itself or with a favorable judgment of the court, is apparently enough to relieve the bailee of the need to make restitution.

But the matter may surface again, should someone—the owner or another witness—claim that he has seen and identified the lost goods: "This is it!" If this happens, the original owner and the person in possession of the designated goods both approach the court, and each swears before God that he is the rightful owner of the property. The man who loses the case pays the other twice the cost of the item. As before, the double penalty serves as both punishment and deterrent—not only to theft of property but also to false accusation (attempted theft of another's reputation via bearing false witness).

The next scenario involves animals handed over into the care of a neighbor, who will tend them for the owner, presumably not as a personal favor but for compensation (as Jacob tended Laban's sheep and perhaps also as Moses tended Jethro's). Animals, being alive, are harder to tend than money and also more vulnerable. What to think and do if the animal dies, is hurt, or gets lost? And what if it is stolen or killed by a wild beast?

> When a man delivers unto his neighbor an ass, or an ox, or a sheep, or any beast, to keep, and it dies, or is hurt, or driven away, no man seeing it; the oath of the Lord shall be between them both, to see whether he have not put his hand unto his neighbor's goods; and the owner thereof shall accept it, and he [the neighbor] shall not make restitution. But if it is stolen from him, he shall make restitution unto the owner thereof. If it be torn in pieces, let him bring it for witness; he shall not make good that which was torn. (22:9–12)

If the bailed animal dies, suffers harm, or wanders off—as any living thing might do regardless of who was looking after it—resolution of the case requires the bailee to swear an oath (this time before *Y-H-V-H*, not *ha'elohim*), probably in court or before witnesses, that he did not directly cause the damage or loss. Absent such culpable responsibility, the owner must accept the loss as accidental, and the bailee is absolved of having to make restitution. But the bailee must compensate the owner for any loss via theft: he undertook to safeguard the animals for the owner, and he failed to do so. Should the bailed animal be killed and torn apart by a beast—an accident, with a wild and unpredictable cause—the bailee will be exempt from making restitution, provided that he produce the torn body of the animal in evidence.

The last cases involve property transferred not by bailment, which is initiated by the owner, but by borrowing, initiated by the neighbor:

> And when a man borrows anything of his neighbor, and it is hurt, or dies, the owner thereof not being with it, he [the borrower] shall surely make restitution. If the owner thereof is with it, he shall not make it good; if it be a hireling, it came for his hire. (22:13–14)

The borrower, unlike the bailee, is liable for loss from whatever cause, even accidental ones, but only if the owner is not also present (presumably joining his neighbor in the use of the borrowed animal).[52] Should the owner be present, working with his borrowing neighbor when the animal is hurt or dies, the borrower is exempt from making restitution. And if the animal was not borrowed but rented, the borrower is not liable for accidental damages, even if the owner is not present. The owner has benefited from the rental; the borrower has lost part of the animal's use. The strict liability of the borrower does not apply.

We are at the end of the ordinances regarding property and of the civil law more generally.[53] We have seen how these instructions address the basic conflicts that arise among human beings, adding their own humane glosses and innovations. But we are only halfway through the *mishpatim*. The ordinances of the second half, even more novel and far-reaching, reveal even more than the first half the revolutionary character of God's Way for Israel and humankind.

Beyond Civil Law, Beyond Justice

W e are in the middle of the long list of ordinances intended to govern the life of the people of Israel when
they arrive in the Promised Land. Until now, we have
mainly heard injunctions that come under our crimi-
nal law and torts—offenses and harms against persons and their property. Although the accents fall differently than in our own legal system,
we clearly recognize the attempt to establish justice, and we readily acknowledge that laws like these are necessary to address misdeeds committed by neighbor against neighbor, whether born of coveting and
greed or of wounded pride and anger, and whether committed against
free and equal men or against the weaker, more vulnerable members of
the community (women, children, servants, and slaves).

But according to the terms of the covenant God has proposed to
the Israelites, His Way for Israel aims to do more than rectify mutual
wrongdoing: it aspires toward holiness, *qedushah*. To feed this aspiration, the Decalogue addressed relations not only between neighbor and
neighbor but also between man and God. We therefore expect that the
ordinances too will at some point move beyond matters of legal justice
to address moral and spiritual matters. We expect to hear how the Israelites are to stand with respect to other cultures and to persons who do
not follow the God of Israel. We particularly expect to receive teachings

that contrast with the ways of the Egyptians behind and the Canaanites before. We expect a rejection of Egypt's hyper-rational aspiration to mastery of nature, seeking to efface the gap between man and God (and to conquer mortality), expressed in human self-worship (Pharaoh), hubris, and despotism. We expect opposition to Canaanite irrational surrender to mindless nature, seeking to efface the gap between man and animals, expressed in worship of earthy fertility gods, sexual licentiousness, and antinomian wildness. Following the Decalogue's strong condemnation of idol worship and its strong affirmation of Sabbath observance, we expect to encounter specific negative teachings about idolatry and positive teachings about ritual observance.

Rejection of idol worship was a major principle in the Ten Commandments, where it was connected with iniquitous behavior. It returns increasingly as the narrative moves toward Canaan, and it comes up prominently in the middle of the *mishpatim*, in the context of iniquitous—explicitly sexual—misconduct.

Seduction (and Marriage) of the Un-betrothed Virgin

The transition of subject matter is prepared by two verses dealing with the seduction of an un-betrothed virgin. Along with the ordinances protecting the rights of a daughter sold into bondage and the one about brawling men who harm a pregnant woman, this is the only ordinance that deals explicitly with sexual matters or the relations between men and women (and between fathers and daughters). No other ordinances in Exodus even come within hailing distance of the Decalogue's injunction against adultery, and there are no positive teachings about marriage.[1] We will therefore look carefully at what we are given here, hoping to extract a fuller teaching from this limited case of seduction:

And when (*ki*) a man seduces a virgin who is not betrothed, and lies (*shakhav*) with her, he shall surely pay a dowry (or "bride-money"; *mohar*) for her to be his wife. If (*'im*) her father utterly refuses to give her unto him, he shall weigh out money ("silver"; *kesef*) according to the dowry of virgins. (22:15–16)

This ordinance comes out of the blue, after a series of cases involving payment of monetary damages for harm done to property deposited by or on loan from its owner. Just possibly, payment of a fine for stolen or damaged goods provides the substantive link to the present example of seduction and deflowering of an un-betrothed virgin, who is therefore under the care of and taken from her father.[2] The case stands out for its special subject matter, yet it also lacks the expected context. This is about seduction—the man "persuades," the woman "consents"—but there is no law about rape. Likewise, there is no ordinance about the seduction of a betrothed woman, which, we imagine, would be handled as a case of adultery.[3] What might be conveyed, morally speaking, from this most incomplete treatment of the subject of men and women, sex and marriage?

Close examination reveals that we have here all the elements of marriage, but in a perverted order. In the proper case, a young woman, never having given herself to anyone, is betrothed to a man who has publicly declared his intention to make her his wife and has backed his offer with the promise of the bride-price, a fund reserved for the use of the woman on becoming a wife.[4] The marriage is then consummated through sexual union. In this case, in contrast, a man persuades a young woman—say, with gifts or the promise of marriage—to lie with him, skipping over the steps of betrothal and delivery of dowry; what is consummated is not marriage but its parody. There is no public statement of intent; there is no promise of commitment; there is no "earnest money" to protect the young woman's future. Given these violated conditions, the ordinance seeks to make things right for the young woman while also vindicating the (unstated, but tacitly present) right order for marriage.

The moral point seems to be this. A young woman (or girl[5]), seduced to give up her virginity, must not be condemned to abandonment by her seducer, not least because her eligibility to marry someone else is now greatly compromised. Since he has taken his pleasure with her or, rather, since he has lain with her as if she were already his wife, the seducer must marry her, paying also the proper dowry a bride normally receives at her betrothal. But even though he is obliged to marry her, she is not obliged to marry him. Her father may object to the marriage—a seducer begins under a cloud of ignominy and bears a large burden of proof as a prospective bridegroom—and the girl may be spared a bad match to which she might have felt drawn, whether out of infatuation or morning-after shame. And even if she does not marry him, he must pay the dowry price that she would have brought had he not seduced her.

Against this high-minded reading, some commentators see here only crass economic considerations. Indeed, the entire patriarchal picture, made worse by the emphasis on money, repels most modern readers. Daughters appear to be little more than their fathers' property, for sale into marriage; a deflowered daughter—under ancient custom, virtually unfit for marriage—is much less valuable. The present ordinance, on this reading, exists mainly to protect the father's economic interest: it gets him the bride-price for virgins even if he objects to the marriage, and the girl's wishes count for nothing.

There is something to this interpretation, but it is far from the whole story. Even the economic part of the tale needs to be properly understood. The ordinance exists to protect innocent girls from irresponsible men (and their own vulnerabilities), and it exists especially to protect the institution of marriage. There are good reasons to require men to pay a bride-price as proof of their seriousness and capacity to provide. The reasons are even greater in the present case, where the financial considerations do not so much enrich the father as they dower the otherwise unmarriageable daughter. They also serve to deter would-be seducers. The need to pay dearly for one night of pleasure will make men less careless, especially since there is no guarantee that the father will later consent to the marriage (and full dowry payment will still be required). True, fathers exercise authority over their daughters' sexuality and marriage prospects (and also profit economically), but not because the daughters are regarded as property. In a world in which unprotected girls and young women are easy targets of seducers and predators[6] (and subject to their own untutored appetites and poor judgments), paternal protection makes good cultural sense. It makes even more sense for a culture that is to be built upon the foundation of stable families, whose chief purpose is to perpetuate from generation to generation the way of life being introduced here at Sinai.

The Torah cares about sexuality not because it is prudish but because it cares about procreation and the rearing of children. It opposes sexual predation and sexual unrestraint—as it opposes incest—ultimately in the name of protecting the interests of women and children and the tradition into which children are to be initiated. For these purposes, it is crucial to know who belongs to whom and who is responsible for whom. Exogamous marriage, with daughters surrendered by fathers to outside suitors, puts an end to incest. The protection of virginity before marriage encourages men to take responsibility for the children born of their brides, confident that the children are their own. No worthy man will want to marry a woman who, even at the time of marriage, may be carrying someone else's child.

Such philosophical arguments, sound though they may be, are hard to make effectively and not only in modern times. Even those who are persuaded by them intellectually may find them weak bulwarks against sexual desire or seductive promises from handsome men. In place of argument, therefore, the culture provides economic incentives to get people to do what reasoning alone cannot. It gives fathers authority over, and financial stakes in, their daughters' sexuality not because daughters are their property but because they need paternal protection—and not least because fathers also need incentives to protect their daughters. The economic considerations are strategically linked to the larger cultural purposes.[7]

The case of the seduced un-betrothed virgin, fully unpacked, implicitly conveys the Torah's deep teaching about sex: sexuality is properly housed in marriage. A woman's virginity and her life-giving powers are not to be trifled with. Fathers must care for daughters as much as for sons.[8]

Abomination and Idolatry

This modest example of seduction and consensual sex, modestly discussed, brings us without warning to the more explosive aspect of the wild and ecstatic passions. The theme changes abruptly, as do the tone and form of presentation:

A sorceress (or "witch"; *mekhashefah*) you shall not let live.

Whoever (or "anyone who"; *kol*) lies with a beast shall surely be put to death (*moth yumath*).

He that sacrifices to gods (*la'elohim*) shall be utterly eliminated (or "banned" or "destroyed"; *yachoram*)—except to the Lord alone. (22:17–19)

These three strange passages—apodictic in form, absolutist in reach, uncompromising in tone, and each declaring death as punishment—burst onto the page without preparation.[9] They disrupt abruptly the casuistic style of the previous ordinances; they change the subject from interpersonal wrongdoing. Why are they here? What have they to do with each other? Properly understood, they provide a foundation for the wholly different set of ethical-political-religious teachings that immediately follow. These touch first on moral obligations to the stranger and the weak, then on religious obligations regarding the seasons and the land. We will proceed slowly, verse by verse, and then look at the whole.[10]

Why the condemnation of sorceresses? Who are they, and what do they do (or claim and attempt to do)? The word translated "sorceress," *mekhashefah*, comes from *kishef*, a verb meaning "to whisper a spell" and, derivatively, "to enchant" or "to practice magic." It implies secrecy, subtlety, and cunning, in the service of making some transformation in the ordinary course of things. The word and its cognates occur but three times in the Torah and nine more times in the prophets and writings.[11] The only previous use of the term occurred earlier in Egypt, at the beginning of the contest of the signs and wonders. Aaron, acting on the Lord's instruction, "flung down his staff before Pharaoh and before his servants, and it became a crocodile (*tannin*)" (7:10). Not to be outdone, Pharaoh summoned his own transformers, including his "sorcerers":

And Pharaoh, too, called for the wise men (*chakhamim*) and the *sorcerers* (*mekhashefim*), and they too, the magicians (*chartummim*) of Egypt, did in like manner *with their secret arts.* They flung down every man his staff, and they became crocodiles (*tanninim*); but Aaron's staff swallowed up their staff. (7:11–12; emphasis added)

In Egypt, the sorcerer is a person of high political position who uses "magical" techniques, based on hidden knowledge, to turn one thing into another. As we have seen, he does not accept but tries to alter the boundaries and distinctions of the given world, imposing instead an order of his own devising. Attempting to obliterate the difference between man and God (while serving a man who believes himself to be divine), the sorcerer promotes man to godlike power in an attempt to remake the world—ultimately, perhaps, to conquer death. Yet as the plague episodes showed, the sorcerers' secret arts were limited, and they could not reverse the changes they had made. Their practices led not to a superior order but to greater disorder, pathologically superabundant yet unsupportive of life.[12] Their attempt at re-creation proved to be *anti-*creation, restorative of the primordial chaos.

We should not ignore the fact that the sorcery under attack here belongs not to men but to women. Even if the condemnation applies also to male sorcerers (as Maimonides argued and as a passage in Deuteronomy 18 will later suggest), might female sorcery pose a distinctive danger that, in the present context, is being singled out for special emphasis? Might a female "wizard" work her magic by different means? Might she have different aspirations and purposes?

The text offers us little help, and we have had no prior example of feminine witchery. Nonetheless, in keeping with the direction of Israel's physical journey, our thoughts go forward from Egypt to Canaan, where we will encounter sorcery and witchcraft of a different kind.[13] There the dominant temptation will turn out to be not mastery of nature, but merging with it. And the resulting deformations will not be those of high civilization but of an earthier paganism, issuing in what the Bible regards as willing self-degradation and dehumanization. The bewitching powers will include various forms of sexual seduction and unregulated sexuality. The clear and present danger: wily women will use their sexual powers to seduce men toward forgetting their humanity, their responsibilities, and (especially) their god(s).[14] This is an old story, told in many traditions.

Homer's *Odyssey* is replete with beautiful and tempting women (and goddesses) who keep Odysseus and his men from returning to hearth and home. Odysseus dwelt for seven years with the beguiling nymph Kalypso. But it was the beautiful sorceress Circe who used her sexual allure and magical potions to turn Odysseus's men into swine, giving them the bodily form commensurate with their appetites. Odysseus was spared the transformation only because of his superior wit and knowledge, embodied in the "moly" root Hermes had given him, whose nature enabled him to resist.[15] Still, Odysseus stayed with Circe for a whole year and, according to non-Homeric versions of the myth, fathered several children with her.

In the Hebrew Bible, female sorcery is tied not only to swinishness and dehumanization but also to idolatry. Only one biblical woman is clearly charged with sorcery (and harlotry), and that is Jezebel, the Phoenician-born wife of Ahab, king of the ten tribes of Israel. She used her power over her weak husband to get him to abandon the Lord, to persecute His prophets, and to install the worship of Baal and Asherah.[16] Perhaps the present condemnation of female sorcerers also has this prospect in mind.[17]

Despite their differences, these forms of sorcery—the Egyptian and the Canaanite—have several errors in common. They both reject the articulated world as created, reject the Creator of that world, and reject the dignified place of human beings in that world: as neither beasts nor gods but god*like* creatures, yet not themselves divine.[18] Failure to respect the humanity of the human being is the problem explicitly addressed by the second injunction, the condemnation of bestiality: "Whoever lies with a beast shall surely be put to death."

Bestiality appears to have been practiced throughout the Ancient Near East—in Egypt, in Mesopotamia, and especially among the various Canaanite peoples.[19] In Egypt, scenes of sex with animals are found on sarcophagi of the elite, and sex with the bull "god" Apis was practiced during certain fertility festivals, presumably to imitate the cosmic watering of feminine earth by masculine sky. The Babylonians practiced bestiality widely until the Code of Hammurabi made all forms of sex with animals a capital crime. In Hittite law, it was a capital offense with some animals but permitted with others. Often connected with worship and sometimes with magic, as Cassuto observes, sex with animals crops up in many places in pagan mythology, even among the gods: "In Ugaritic poetry it is narrated that Baal had intercourse with a cow in order to be saved magically from death that awaited him as a result of the devices of Mot the king of the netherworld; and in the epic of Gilgamesh there are references to the relations of the goddess Ishtar with various animals."[20]

By contrast, the Torah, both here in Exodus and several times in Leviticus, condemns *all* such bestial relations in the strongest possible terms. The reason is hinted at in the Garden of Eden story. Setting out to make for man a "counterpart" ("help-opposite-him"; *'ezer kenegdo*) as a remedy for the problem of his "aloneness," God first makes the animals and brings them before him, but they are all found to be unsuitable. Only with the creation of woman, from his own flesh and bone, does the man find a suitable mate; he celebrates that fact in a lusty speech expressing his male desire.[21]

Bestiality, born of an earthy and licentious impulse toward merging, violates the sacrosanct boundary between humans and animals, and not only in sexual fusion. It also manifests a wild, unrestrained (beastlike) sexual appetite to which it gives unrestrained expression.[22] This twisted behavior is unworthy of any human being, and especially of a people aspiring to imitate the Lord in holiness.

The Lord's opposition to bestiality, along with His opposition to sorcery, will later be collected under the notion of "abomination (*to'evah*) unto the Lord," something the Lord regards as hateful and disgusting.[23] But His disgust is no mere matter of taste. It is elicited by transgressions of cosmic or anthropological principles, fundamental to the world He has created and the human world He seeks to perfect—for example, the distinctions between God and man, man and beast, male and female, the living and the dead. All traditional cultures make such distinctions and establish boundaries, both natural and human, that they regard as socially meaningful; the violation of these distinctions and the crossing of these boundaries they regard as abominations. For example, the Egyptians (as we were told in Genesis) abominate shepherds and find it abominable to eat with the Hebrews, presumably because the Hebrews eat lamb (Gen. 46:34 and 43:32). In Exodus, as we noted earlier, Moses insists that Israel must leave Egypt to make sacrifices unto the Lord, because the Egyptians will abominate the sacrifice of animals they hold sacred (8:26). Generally speaking, an abomination—even one involving only human beings—is not a violation of justice or an offense against another person or creature, but a defilement of oneself and a transgression against the order of being. It is, in other words, an iniquity or a perversity, and it offends against the Creator. There is therefore a close connection between all other abominations and idolatry, which one may call the ultimate abomination.[24]

Our interpretation of the first two condemnations—of sorcery and bestiality—in fact implies that the Torah opposes them not only as intrinsically problematic (which they are) but also because of their intimate connection with idolatry: not only the superstitious worship of statues but also revering other false "gods," from natural beings (such as the sun, the earth, and potent animals) to human masters, and even the "worship" of wealth, honor, and power. The third injunction attacks the problem of idolatry head-on: there are to be no sacrifices (no worship, no devotion) to any (so-called) gods—other than to the Lord. "Whoever sacrifices to gods shall be utterly eliminated—except to the Lord alone."

The uniqueness and importance of this injunction against sacrificing are suggested both by its odd structure (with the verb in the middle of the verse, rather than at the end, and the addition, almost as an afterthought, of the monotheistic exception made for the Lord) and especially by the unusual verb declaring what shall be done to transgressors. Instead of saying, as was said of the man committing bestiality, "he shall be put to death" (moth yumath), this ordinance speaks of "eliminating" (or "banning" or "destroying"; Hebrew root ch-r-m) the idol worshipper. This is the first use of this root in the Bible. Lexicographers tell us that it is related to the verb for "to catch" or "to seclude" in other Semitic languages; in the Hebrew Bible, it clearly means "to utterly destroy," leaving no trace or remains.[25] But however we translate it, the notion implies cleansing and purification rather than retribution, eliminating an abomination or pollution rather than punishing a criminal. We are now entering the realm of the sacred and the sacrilegious, beyond justice and injustice, where nothing less than complete eradication will do.

Yet the separation between the holy and the just must not be overdrawn, and idolatry has implications also for human relations. As we saw in the Decalogue's treatment of this practice, there is a connection between idolatry and iniquity. The rejection of both nature gods and human masters was shown to be crucial for teaching righteousness, holiness, and basic human decency toward your neighbor. To deny the Lord is to deny *each* man's special relation to the Creator and special standing in the world: human beings are—all of them—*betselem 'elohim*, in the image of God, the only beings that are "godlike." In contrast, to affirm the Lord is to affirm also this special relationship between man and God that, if properly respected and honored, becomes the basis of a humane and morally superior way of relating to all other human beings.

These three apodictic injunctions—all harsh and uncompromising, each important in its own right—serve also as a trumpet call for a new set of teachings, beyond those dealing with crimes and torts, which follow in the immediate sequel. These new teachings are embodied in novel ordinances regarding moral-political and spiritual matters—beginning with the proper stance toward three kinds of vulnerable human beings: strangers, widows and orphans, and the poor. Their treatment is informed by and dependent on the difference between the God of Israel and the gods and ways of neighboring peoples who use secret arts (mastery) or unrestrained sexuality (dissolution) as a means for negotiating the troubled place of human beings in the order of things. You are not a god, says the Torah, with magical transformative powers; neither are you a beast among the beasts. You are a creature capable of knowing and respecting the constitutive distinctions of the articulated world. And you are capable of having a relationship with the Lord God, Creator of heaven and earth and Deliverer of Israel. Knowing who you are requires seeing yourself as having been lifted up out of bondage in Egypt for the sake of such a special relationship and a call to holiness. As a consequence, you can now see the stranger as a fellow human being, and not merely in legalistic terms of the sort we left behind in the last chapter.

Duties Toward the Vulnerable: The Stranger

Immediately after the three apodictic ordinances, each seeking to eliminate a degrading and sacrilegious practice from the Israelite community, we get the first of the many famous biblical passages regarding the
proper treatment of strangers. Just as the "civil" laws began with solicitude for your fellow Israelites who might be compelled to enter indentured servitude (21:1–11), so these "ethical-spiritual" laws begin with
concern for the strangers among you, people who would everywhere else
be targets for enslavement:

> But (or "And") a stranger (*ger*) you [singular] shall not mal-
> treat, neither shall you oppress him; for you [plural] were
> strangers (*gerim*) in the land of Egypt. (22:20)

At first glance, the change of subject seems abrupt. Yet the presence of
the conjoining "*vav*"—"but" or "and"—at the start of the verse implies
a logical link to what came just before, the proscription of worshipping
any god but *Y-H-V-H*. How does a call for decent treatment of strangers
follow from the absolute rejection of their gods and, implicitly, their
whole way of life? And—a different sort of question—why does the Lord
suddenly address the Israelites in the second-person singular, a practice
that He will maintain through most of the remaining ordinances?

A little reflection shows that what at first looks like a contradiction is in fact a necessary entailment. Yes, in the name of the Lord, you
are to reject absolutely the gods and ways of foreign nations, both the
Egyptians behind and the Canaanites ahead. But precisely *as* followers
of the Lord, you are therefore able—nay, obliged—to see the humanity
of the stranger and to treat him decently. Let us see how this works.

The stranger (*ger*), we note to begin with, is not some abstract or
generalized "other," a favorite subject of much contemporary moral discourse. The *ger* is instead a concrete someone, a specific person who
dwells among you as an outsider. He is a foreign sojourner, a resident
alien, a person—and this is crucial—away from his own home and homeland. Because he is a stranger in a strange land, he is vulnerable personally and politically. In any ordinary host society, the attitude toward the

ger can range widely between tolerance and xenophobia, hospitality and exploitation. At the extremes, do you feed him or eat him? Do you let him be, or make him your slave?

The Bible's previous stories about how strangers are treated elsewhere suggest that, with few exceptions, mistreatment is the rule. In Genesis, we are shown the stark contrast between Abraham's eager and unstinting hospitality, offered through an open tent door, to the three visiting strangers (angels appearing as men) and Lot's more hesitant and guarded welcome of the same visitors when they come to his house in Sodom. In a frightening account, we see how all the men of that Canaanite city surround Lot's house and demand that he turn those visitors over for homosexual rape. When Lot pleads against such wickedness, offering them instead his own daughters, the Sodomites condemn Lot as a stranger to their community who now presumes to judge them; they threaten to treat him worse than the others. (He is saved only by the superhuman actions of the angels.)

There are many more examples. When sojourning in foreign places, Abraham (twice, in Egypt and in Philistia) and Isaac (in Philistia) feel constrained to pass their wives off as their sisters—each then taken by the ruling prince for his harem—for fear lest they themselves be killed for the sake of such appropriation. (Sarah and Rebekah are spared adulterous liaisons only by divine intervention.) We have already commented (see Note 4) on the fate of Jacob's daughter Dinah, a maiden who wanders alone into Shechem, another Canaanite city. (There is no divine intervention—God's name is not even mentioned in the story—and Dinah is not saved). Joseph, upon arriving in Egypt, is sold into Potiphar's service, and when he resists Mrs. Potiphar's repeated attempts at seduction, she condemns him as an impudent Hebrew outsider and has him cast into prison. Finally, in addition to these personal ordeals, we heard the Lord tell Abraham that his seed will be a stranger in a land not their own, whose people they will serve and who will afflict them for four hundred years (Gen. 15)—a prophecy that was, as we have learned in Exodus, precisely fulfilled. The picture is nearly universal: people who leave home and become strangers in someone else's land risk murder, sexual abuse, unjust accusation, imprisonment, and enslavement at the hands of the natives and their rulers.[26]

Those stories in Genesis and Exodus have impressed upon the reader the need for a different way. We are therefore delighted to encounter the present ordinance against the mistreatment of strangers, but we wonder how it may be connected to the just-announced summons to monotheistic worship of the Lord, a call that is explicitly and uncompromisingly hostile to worshipping other (so-called) gods. Unlike polytheism, which offers multiple objects for human reverence, monotheism does not tolerate such divided devotions ("You shall have no other gods before Me"; "I Y-H-V-H your God am a jealous god"). Those who follow the Lord are to have one God, one standard of conduct, and one way of life, rejecting all others. Yet unlike the stranger-abusing polytheistic societies, this singular God and way of life insist on hospitality and humanity toward the stranger. What is the basis of this rejection of xenophobia and abuse of the *ger*?

Earlier, in discussing the Ten Commandments, I suggested that the right relation to God as the Creator (say, in Sabbath remembrance) was the basis for defining the right relation to other human beings within the covenantal community, as these are articulated in the principles of the so-called second table. And we have just seen that protecting the metaphysical boundaries that make human beings human also depends on acknowledging no god but *Y-H-V-H*. By implication, we are now invited to see that the same (exclusive) relationship to the Lord—the Creator God of Whom all human beings are equally the image—is also the basis for humane treatment of the stranger and the vulnerable who dwell among us.

That metaphysical reasoning, however, remains merely implicit. It will impress intellectuals and readers who remember the teaching of Genesis 1 about humankind in the image of God. But the political instruction of this collection of ex-slaves requires something more personal and experiential. The explicit reason the Lord gives for treating strangers decently appeals not to theology and the Creation but to historical memory and sympathetic identification: you know what it was like to be a despised and oppressed stranger in a strange land; remember it, for God's sake, and do not impose such a fate on others. It is for this purpose that I have chosen you. And it is to serve this purpose that you will institute My Way in the Promised Land.

This is not an easy lesson for any nation to learn. The Torah must repeat multiple times its exhortation to the Israelites to remember their own experience in Egypt,[27] and there are also numerous additional injunctions to respect and care for the stranger. Why? Because ex-slaves might relish having a turn at taking out their past suffering on others. They might enjoy doing unto others as they had been done by, rather than as they wish they had been treated. Also, the Israelite ex-slaves, chosen by the Lord to be His people and taught to despise the gods of other peoples, might feel themselves called, or at least entitled, to treat strangers with contempt. But precisely because of the difference between Y-H-V-H and the strange "gods"—a difference at least as great as the distinction between man and beast—the Children of Israel must not maltreat or oppress strangers as other peoples have done and still do.

As we suspected from the start, this humanistic aspect of God's Way for Israel, and through Israel for humankind, is among the chief reasons why Egyptian servitude had to be the school for this political founding. Israel had to begin its national existence in bondage to learn firsthand the meaning of political suffering and oppression. Its path to a better way of life required that it encounter the Lord first as the Enemy of Slavery and Oppression. The fulfillment of the summons to be a holy nation—and the difference between holy and unholy politics—begins with the proper treatment of strangers and other vulnerable people. And it calls on each individual, one by one—"You, singular"—to answer the call to national holiness by striving for it personally.

The stranger who lives among you is welcomed not as "the other" or because he worships other gods or has a different culture. He is welcomed—or at least not abused and oppressed—not for reasons of theory but out of fellow feeling and empathy, extended to him because we recognize what it means to be vulnerable and exploitable away from one's own land. This empathic teaching of fellow feeling, though not based on universal maxims or abstract philosophy, can nonetheless be generalized to embrace all kinds of human beings, should they reside in your midst. As we shall see, it can even be extended to domestic animals.

One cannot exaggerate the importance of this novel—even revolutionary—teaching about the stranger. The love of your own is central to most human associations; it is the basis of our familial, civic, national, and patriotic attachments. But all political communities, from ancient times to today, are at risk of exaggerating the (merely conventional) distinction between who is in and who is out.[28] They are inclined to overstate—even absolutize—the difference between neighbor and stranger, born of an excessive love of one's own and an equally excessive fear and hatred of the other—a hatred that takes support from the belief that the ways of others are inferior, even immoral and indecent. Even today, xenophobia is the oldest politics there is. The Bible wades into this problem with a sophisticated and humane teaching: remember what it was like to be an oppressed stranger. Reject the stranger's ways, but honor his humanity. Be zealous in protecting the natural boundaries—between God and man, and between man and beast—that keep human life human. But be equally zealous in protecting the stranger from being treated as less human than yourself. The argument for doing so is written into your own people's flesh.

Duties Toward the Vulnerable: Widows, Orphans, and the Poor

From the stranger, God speaks next of the widow and the orphan, also without defenders in a man's world and for whom God also has special regard[29]:

> Any widow or orphan you [plural] shall not *afflict* (or "abase"; Hebrew verb *'innah*). If you [singular] afflict them in any way—when he *cries out* (*yitsa'aq*) at all unto Me, I *will surely hear* (*shamoa' 'eshma'*) his cry. And My wrath shall wax hot, and I will kill you [plural] with the sword; and your wives shall be widows, and your children fatherless. (22:21–23; emphasis added).

Although they are members within the covenantal community, the widow and the orphan are, like the *ger,* vulnerable to mistreatment. And although Israel's bondage in Egypt is not explicitly mentioned, the language used here recalls that experience. The verb "afflict" (*'innah*) is the same one that appears in the verse, "they [the Egyptians] set taskmasters over them to afflict them with their burdens" (1:11). The phrase, "he cries out (*yitsa'aq*) at all unto Me," uses a verb that is similar in both sound and meaning to that used in the verse, "the Children of Israel . . . cried out (*vayyiz'aqu*), and the cry came up unto God by reason of the bondage" (2:23). And "I will surely hear his cry" reminds us of God's words to Moses at the burning bush: "I have surely seen the *affliction* of My people (*'oni 'ami*) that are in Egypt and I have *heard their cry* (*tsa'aqatham shama'ti*) because of their taskmasters" (3:7; emphasis added). By these linguistic links, the new injunction assimilates the vulnerability of the defenseless widow and orphan to the vulnerability of the Hebrew slave in Egypt. As with the Israelite slaves in Egypt, God will not only hear the cry of the afflicted widow or orphan. Should the community allow the affliction to continue, the Lord will take matters into His own hands, with devastating consequences for all. In a lovely touch—pointed out by Ibn Ezra—even if only a single person afflicts a widow or orphan and the community does not rise up to defend her, the entire community ("you," *plural*) will share in and be punished for his guilt. Because the offense is held to be a matter of injustice rather than a lesser misconduct, retribution will be swift and fitting, measure for measure: you, the afflicters, will pay with your lives, so that your own wives and children shall become widows and orphans.

The final group in this triad of vulnerability are the needy members of the community, people who must borrow money from their better-off neighbors to get by. These unfortunates must also not be mistreated:

> If (*'im*) you lend money to any of My people (*'ammi*), even to the poor with you (*'immakh*), you shall not be to him as a creditor; neither shall you lay upon him interest. If (*'im*) you ever take your neighbor's mantle as a pledge [against the loan], you shall restore it unto him before the sun goes down; for that is his only mantle, it is his garment for his skin; in what shall he lie down (*yishkav*)? And it shall come to pass, when he cries unto Me (*ki-yits'aq 'elay*), that I will hear (*veshama'ti*); for I am gracious (*channun*). (22:24–26)

When your needy neighbor asks for your financial help, you lend it to him but not as a creditor, one who demands payment according to the law. Nor do you make money off his misfortune by collecting interest on the loan. The implicit reason is conveyed by the pun of 'ammi and 'immakh: the poor man *with you* is always one of *My people*. The distinction between debtor and creditor, like the distinction between the poor and the well-off, pales to insignificance because both are equally God's people. As God's people are His "children," all members of the Israelite community are like family, each a brother to all the others. Brothers who borrow from and lend to one another do not thereby regard themselves under the abstract legal categories of debtor and creditor, and the lender brother will not charge his borrower brother interest. Neither, according to this ordinance, will the Israelites.

A loan, of course, differs from a gift.[30] The receipt of a loan is generally accompanied by a deposit of collateral, to be held against payment. This is in itself a sensible and just practice: the lender is protected against total loss in the exchange, and the borrower has an incentive to redeem his pledged deposit. The entire practice of lending to those in need depends on these safeguards and incentives. Yet once again, in God's Way for Israel, the strict legal requirements of pledging collateral gives way to an empathic view of humane justice that takes into account the special circumstances, differential needs, and varying resources and capacities of one's fellows.

This teaching is conveyed in the exquisite final passage, which insists on just such sensitive consideration regarding pledges given by your poor neighbor: if he gives you the coat off his back as security for a loan, you must restore it to him daily before nightfall; that is, even before he has need of it. He will, of course, deposit it again in the morning, but you may not use your rights at law to cause your covenantal brother unnecessary suffering. Within the covenantal community, human relations call not for the exactitude of law but for decency and fellow feeling. How remarkable and wonderful it is to have a law that teaches that (mere) law itself must yield to human need!

What is the relation between this ordinance about lending to the poor and the two ordinances that preceded it? It does not speak of maltreatment or oppression, as did the ordinance about the stranger, nor does it speak about affliction, as did the ordinance about widows and orphans. Yet here too, the Israelites are meant to understand this teaching in light of their remembered bondage in Egypt. Like the mistreated widow or orphan, the poor man will cry out to the Lord, and the Lord will hear and respond on his behalf. Just as He would have Israel share His zeal against the boundary-denying abominations, so He would have Israel share His zeal against oppression, maltreatment, and inhumanity, first exercised on Israel's behalf against their Egyptian oppressors.

Although the three ordinances in defense of the vulnerable spring from a common source and reflect the Lord's concern for justice and humanity, careful readers will have noted one significant difference among them. The Israelites are summoned to treat the widow and orphan and the poor properly because they are God's people. But they are summoned not to oppress or mistreat the stranger for a different reason: because they themselves suffered such conduct as strangers in Egypt. At first glance, this difference makes perfect sense. The stranger—unlike the vulnerable Israelites—does not, and would not, call out *unto the Lord;* that is what, in the deepest sense, makes him a stranger. And only those who call out to the Lord are "My people." But does this mean that there are different notions of right for dealing with those who are not "My people"? For example, is an Israelite permitted to charge interest on a loan to a stranger? And must he return a stranger's mantle, deposited as a pledge, at nightfall? Is it okay to afflict widows and orphans who are not members of the covenantal community?

The text says nothing of the sort. And yet the question is pertinent: it lies behind complaints sometimes made against the Israelite way of life, which, despite its humane ordinances, still makes much of the difference between insider and outsider. Later ordinances will specify different obligations toward persons on different sides of this divide (including, for example, the permissibility of taking loan interest from a non-Israelite, and there will be different laws regarding manumission of an Israelite bondman and a foreign one).

The general question about whether ethical teachings must apply universally in order to be truly ethical is too large to take up here, although we touched on it briefly in our earlier discussion of the Decalogue. For now, we simply repeat that the Israelites, under the covenant with the Lord, become like a family. And family members have, in many matters, special moral obligations to each other. Family members have a stronger claim on us than do outsiders. The paradigmatic case: we have an inviolable duty of filial honor to our own father and mother, but not to everyone else's father and mother. To deny this is to make all moral obligations indifferent to the nearness or remoteness of human connection. And to act on such an idea may be immoral, at least in those matters where nearness morally counts.

Toward Holiness: Duties Toward Rulers, Human and Divine

From duties toward the foreigner, the unfortunate, and the poor—those who are socially "below us"—the ordinances move to duties toward those above us—our rulers and especially toward God. The first word forbids reviling or cursing them:

> God (*'elohim*) you shall not revile ("treat lightly" or "curse"; from the root *qll*), and a chief (*nasi'*) among your people you shall not curse ("execrate"; from the root *'rr*). (22:27)

Whatever else they mean, these injunctions may serve as a cautionary afterthought to the recent passages about people who cry out to the Lord in their distress. Some of them, out of misery and despair, will be complaining (only) against those who mistreat them and calling on the Lord for His assistance against them. But others, out of frustration and anger, will be tempted to curse God or their rulers for their troubles: the world (or society) is unjust, God (or the ruler) is to blame—damn them all.[31]

The oppressed and the poor are not the only ones who might be tempted to curse God. Lenders and creditors whose loans are not being repaid as promised might become annoyed with the Lord's rules about not charging interest and returning pledges. Damn it, God, why must it be at my expense that You have chosen to look after Your poor? In support of this interpretation, we note that the ordinances regarding the vulnerable are addressed to people having power, not to the vulnerable themselves; the present ordinances about cursing may still be speaking to them.

But whether we are rich or poor, creditors or debtors, all human beings, whenever the world is not going as we think we deserve, tend to find fault with—even to revile or curse—those in charge. Even if no words are uttered, our despair is ultimately a self-important complaint against God and His Creation. The present ordinance warns everyone against these disrespectful and despairing practices.

The negative injunction also carries an implicit positive teaching. We are tacitly admonished to show proper regard for—to honor and give weight to—those who rule and govern, human and especially divine. The remaining ordinances in this section deal more explicitly with what honoring God implies. The next one ascends from not cursing Him (for failing to arrange the world to our liking) to not delaying in bringing Him what He is owed (for His gracious providence):

> You [singular] shall not delay [to offer] of the produce-of-your-harvest (literally, "of your fullness"; *mele'athekha*), and of the outflow-of-your-presses (*vedim'akha*). The firstborn of your sons you shall give unto Me. Likewise shall you do with your oxen, and with your sheep; seven days it shall be with its dam; on the eighth day you shall give it to Me. (22:28–29)

In an expression of gratitude for the bounty of the field, the fruit of the vine, and the fecundity of the flocks, the first portions of each are to be offered to the Lord. Needless to say, these are not intended for His use or for the satisfaction of His "appetites." He desires instead that we acknowledge that the satisfaction of our needs and wants is a blessing owed to His providence. We live and flourish because of gifts we neither created nor merited. Before we satisfy our own appetites, we set aside first portions—whether from the earth or from the womb—as gifts of gratitude to God.[32]

The obligation to give to the Lord all firstborn sons will be heard by the assembled—and by the reader—in light of the earlier instruction, given at the Exodus from Egypt, that allows for the redemption of the human firstborn (13:13). (We discussed this matter at some length in

Chapter Seven, "Exodus.") Here the point seems to be this. Your first-born sons, like the first fruits of the earth, are properly Mine, to be sacrificed on My altar. But because of the preciousness of human life, you are allowed to redeem him from the priest. You not only may, you must: there is to be no child sacrifice in Israel. The firstborn of the flocks and herds, by contrast, cannot be redeemed; after a week's nurture by its mother—perhaps to assure viability and fitness—it is given up to the Lord.

Because the Israelites are being summoned to be a kingdom of priests and a holy nation, their everyday life—not only their special sacrifices—ought to reflect this special purpose. The final ordinance in this section makes the point precisely. This injunction is the first of many—most will be given in Leviticus—that define what holiness in Israel will consist of:

> And holy men (ve'anshe-qodesh) you [plural] shall be unto Me; [therefore] you shall not eat any flesh that is torn by beasts in the field; you shall cast it to the dogs. (22:30)

The general call is to be holy men—men set apart—unto the Lord. What better way to do so than in eating, the most everyday and vital of human activities? Though we are needy creatures like any other, we are not defined mainly by our needs but by our aspirations. Even the poor among us are summoned to realize our higher—holy—possibilities. We should therefore not live as scavengers of flesh torn from the kill of wild beasts, thus ratifying their deeds and participating in their violent and mindless ways.

This ordinance, like the later dietary laws of Leviticus that became the basis of the Jewish practice of *Kashrut,* builds on the original principle of the Noahide code, the humanizing law that took man out of the state of nature, replacing the rule of force with the rule of right. Homicide was outlawed, because human beings are created in the image of God; however, as a concession to—and restraint of—human bloody-mindedness, men were given permission to eat meat, but only on condition that we not eat the blood.[33] Now, in a further insistence that we do not belong to the dog-eat-dog world, the Israelites are not to eat any meat that comes to hand. Flesh torn by beasts is fit only for beasts.

This injunction aims not only to separate human beings from beast-like violence. It also teaches that we should not be slaves to our appetites. As we should not be ruled by our bellies (any more than we should be ruled by our groins), so we should not eat like ravenous beasts. Tell us what and how you eat, and we can tell you who and what you are.[34] If you would be holy, eat in ways that respect your special relation to the divine.

Sacred Obligations to the True, the Good, and the Right

The next ordinances deal with matters of judgment at law and with relations to enemies, to the poor (again), and to strangers (again). They continue to emphasize moral rather than strictly legal issues, summoning each Israelite (in second-person singular commands) to practice honest speech and just conduct. We therefore consider them as a continuation of the call to be "holy men." Holiness—standing apart from the modes and orders of human beings who know not *Y-H-V-H*—involves much more than eating (or not eating) the appropriate foods. What comes out of a man's mouth may also defile him.

God begins with three injunctions about speech. They spell out implications of two principles of the Decalogue, the one about bearing false witness and the one about taking the Lord's name in vain:

> You shall not bear ("take up," "utter"; *lo' thissa'*) a false ("vain"; *shav'*) report ("rumor"; *shema'*); put not your hand with the wicked (*rasha'*) to be an unrighteous witness (literally, "witness for violence"; *'ed chamas*). You shall not follow a multitude ("the many" or "the great"; *rabbim*) to do evil; neither shall you answer ("bear witness"; *velo'-tha'aneh*) in a dispute (*riv*) to turn after a multitude (*rabbim*) to pervert [justice]; nor shall you show deference (*tehdar*) to a poor man in his dispute (*riv*). (23:1–3)

These verses are hard to translate because of their odd syntax and usage. Nevertheless, most translators reach something like the following plausible teachings, applicable both to general speech or conduct and to disputes that may come before a court.

As a general matter, you should not spread falsehoods and rumors about your neighbors. All the more reason why, if summoned to be a witness in court, you should not join wrongdoers by giving false testimony on their behalf, thus doing violence to justice. You should not follow the herd (or the mighty) into evil deed or speech, no matter how numerous or prominent they are. All the more reason why you should not do so as a witness in court—again, perverting justice and denying the Lord (implicitly, by violating your sworn oath to be truthful). The true and the right, not the popular or the mighty, should be your guide. For the same reason, you are forbidden to give false testimony even on behalf of the poor. In speaking as a witness or when called upon to give judgment, you must no more abandon justice to show compassion for the lowly than to curry favor with the high and mighty. As Moses will later admonish the Israelites, "Justice, [only] justice shall you follow" (Deut. 16:20).[35]

Although there is nothing wrong with this interpretation of these ordinances, it may be slightly off the mark. And it may not go far enough. For one thing, it makes too little of the many linguistic clues that cry out for a broader and deeper teaching. I have already alluded to reverberations of the Decalogue: the verb *lo' thissa'*, "you shall not take up" and the word *shav'*, "vain" or "false" or "empty," both occurred in the injunction, "You shall not take up the name of the Lord your God in vain" (20:7); in addition, the verb *tha'aneh*, "answer" or "bear witness," occurred in the other injunction involving speech, "You shall not bear false witness against your neighbor" (20:13).[36] But the deeper echoes are prompted by the unusual use of the highly charged and heavily freighted words *chamas*, "violence," and *rasha'*, "wicked," both of which have previously been used in Genesis and Exodus only to describe the direst moral conditions. For example, *chamas* is used twice in Genesis to characterize the wholesale violence into which the world had descended before the Flood. And *rasha'* is used three times by Abraham in pleading with God not to slay the righteous with the wicked in Sodom, whose near-universal wickedness toward strangers is vividly shown when the angels come to Lot.[37]

What might we conclude from these linguistic reverberations? These allusions to lawlessness and violence suggest that the prime target of the present ordinances may not be disputes in the law courts but episodes of uncontrollable violence, vengeance, and vigilante "justice" that take place "on the street."[38] In this interpretation, we hear the ordinances differently. Do not spread rumors or speak falsely to stir up or support the wicked in their acts of violence. Do not join the many (or the high and mighty) in their evil machinations, and do not twist the truth to skew the outcome of a dispute toward the high and mighty (or toward the many). But for the same reason, do not twist the truth to show deference to the poor, whether singly or in the mass. Do not commit, aid, or abet violence and wickedness. In sum, remember what I just told you: Holy men you shall be unto Me; do not engage in beastly practices.

The next two injunctions teach proper attitudes and conduct toward your enemies and adversaries. Just as you are forbidden to make distinctions between rich and poor in questions of justice, so you are forbidden to make distinctions between friend and enemy in duties of humaneness:

> If you meet your enemy's (*'oyivekha*) ox or his ass going astray, you shall surely bring it back to him again. If you see the ass of him that hates you (*sona'akha*) lying under its burden, you shall forbear to pass him by; you shall surely release it with him. (23:4–5)

It is very common—perhaps endemic to uninstructed human nature—to make much of the distinction between friend and enemy, more even than the distinction between neighbor and stranger. Those we dislike, and those who hate and oppose us, we are not eager to see prosper, never mind to assist in their troubles. But those who intend to follow the way of the Lord must set aside these natural attitudes and practices; one's rivals and opponents are also members of the covenantal community, sharing a common fate. They, like you, are equally part of "My people."

This larger positive point is taught through simple but paradigmatic examples. Would you return a wayward animal belonging to a friend? It goes without saying that you would. But justice and respect for personal property and respect for the well-being of domestic animals require that you do the same for your enemy. Would you not pause to help a friend relieve his suffering donkey from an onerous or unbalanced burden? The same obligation in compassion and righteousness applies to a suffering animal belonging to someone who hates you. Who knows, you might even turn his enmity into affection.

This last possibility may in fact be the point of these ordinances, which otherwise seem a little out of context. If the three previous ordinances were intended to curb wicked speech and violent deeds, the present two seek to diminish the animosities that often spill over into misconduct and violence. In the service of civil peace and justice, the Lord seeks to root out baseless hatreds and eliminate vicious speech and savage deeds. While acknowledging the enduring fact of enmity between members of the community, He seeks to minimize its power by exploiting our compassion for dumb animals. Not only will your enemy be surprised and grateful for your good deed; as a consequence of your kindness, you too are likely to feel somewhat more warmly toward him. Generosity leads to affection, at least as much as does receiving it.[39] Although nothing is said explicitly about justice in the courtroom or injustice in the streets,[40] the context into which these ordinances fit may silently convey this added implication: impartiality and fairness are owed as much to your adversary as to your supporter, as much to your enemy as to your kin. In all cases, prefer what is right to what is congenial. Better, make most congenial (only) what is right.

These obligations to your adversaries do not, however, translate into a comprehensive teaching of "love your enemy," however much they tend in that direction. The ordinances seek to govern people's actions, not their feelings. The Lord says, "In these and these specific ways, act kindly to your enemy's animals." He does not say, "Love your enemy." Such a demand would likely be regarded as unreasonable, even if confined to your opponents within the covenantal community. Natural animosities and rivalries are bound to arise, often for good reason; it is sufficient unto the peace and justice of the community that they be held in check and that people not allow ill will toward their neighbors to pervert what justice and decency require of them.[41]

The final set of ordinances in this section (re)turns explicitly to matters of justice and judgment in cases at law, this time addressing the prospective judge more than a potential witness:

> You shall not pervert the judgment (*mishpat*) owed to your [singular] poor ('*evyonekha*) in his cause [at law]. From a false matter keep yourself far; and do not destroy (*harag*) the innocent and the righteous; for I will not acquit the wicked (*rasha*). And you shall take no bribe (*shochad*); for a bribe blinds them that have sight, and perverts the words of the righteous (*divre tsaddiqim*). And a stranger you [singular] shall not oppress (*lachats*); for you [plural] know (*yada*) the heart (or "soul" or "breath"; *nefesh*) of a stranger, seeing you were strangers in the land of Egypt. (23:6–9)

If you are a judge hearing a case, truth and justice shall be your only concerns. Do not fail to do right by your poor; they are, after all, *your* poor. Their poverty does not entitle them to special consideration, but neither does it diminish their claim to justice. Your failure to do right by them harms also yourself, for they are *your* people. Do not yield to false charges, and beware of convicting and destroying the lives of the innocent and the righteous; I, the Lord, will hold you accountable for such wickedness, and—lest you think your crooked result will stand—I Myself will punish the guilty whom you have corruptly acquitted.

The ubiquitous problem of bribery—rendering skewed or false judgments in exchange for gain received or favors promised—is addressed head-on. Most unusually, the Lord gives us the reasons why He is banning it, and they go beyond the harm done in any individual case: bribery corrupts the judge's soul. A judge who once saw clearly will have his vision clouded. His soul for sale and his mind on gain, he will be unable to see the undistorted truth. Although he was until now a righteous man, the bribe affects how he thinks and speaks. Instead of giving voice to what his righteous eye will have seen, he now finds sophistic ways to rationalize his corrupted vision with perverted speech. In every respect, he will have abandoned his rectitude. We sense, as before, an overarching concern with the goal toward which each Israelite (second-person singular) is being summoned: to be a holy human being to the Lord.

The unit concludes by returning to the matter of the stranger, the topic with which this entire section of ordinances began (22:20). This time, at least by implication, the beginning context appears to be judgments at law. In disputes before the court, the distinction between native and stranger, resident and sojourner, is irrelevant to the vocation of doing justice. Once again, you may rightly hate the strangers' ways and their beliefs and notions of divinity. But if one of them finds himself peacefully in your midst, he is accorded the equal protection of your law. In case you wonder why, once again a reason is given. This time it appeals not to your interest in avoiding self-corruption, but to your hard-won understanding and the empathy to which it should lead. You know from experience the soul of estrangement and the burdens of oppression. Do not repeat the errors and crimes of your former Egyptian oppressors.

Sabbatical Rest

The next set of injunctions serve as a transition between the ordinances intended explicitly to govern conduct among human beings, even if with concern for holiness in mind, and subsequent ordinances intended explicitly to delineate obligations to the Lord (even if with clear communal implications in mind). These transitional ordinances promote positive social goods by combining the ideas of sacred time with the nature of work—especially agricultural work. They apply the Decalogue's principle of Sabbath rest to the use of the Promised Land:

> And six years you [singular] shall sow your land and gather in its yield ("produce"; *tevu'ah*); but the seventh year you shall release it [the land] (*tishmetennah*) and you shall abandon it [the yield] ("let it lie still"; *unetashtah*); and the needy of your people may eat; and what they leave, the beast of the field [the wild animals] shall eat. In like manner you shall deal with your vineyard, and with your olive yard. (23:10–11)

The new ordinance begins with "And." We therefore expect it to continue the antecedent concern for the stranger and the need to remember Israel's own estrangement in Egypt. We are not disappointed: a humanitarian social good is immediately evident on the surface. But we should not miss the bigger picture, for the teachings here are simply revolutionary.

Just as this nation of ex-slaves, inured to ceaseless toil and the fear of scarcity, has been enjoined to desist from labor every seventh day, trusting instead to the world's bounty and God's providence, so this soon-to-be agricultural people is instructed to stand down periodically from wresting its livelihood from the earth and to release the land from exploitation.[42] Every seventh year, there is to be no planting or reaping, no harvesting of grape or olive. Every seventh year, land will be ownerless and unworked, and what the earth puts forth on its own will be available to all, including the poor. Even the wild beasts, creatures in their own right, are given a place at the land's table, should the poor leave anything behind.

Utilitarian arguments have since been adduced to justify the practice. Any plot of earth, given periodic rest, will remain more fertile. A full sabbatical for the entire land would save the soil from exhaustion. But sound land management would hardly call for resting the entire land at once. The injunction has prior, higher, and more far-reaching moral and spiritual purposes—among them, to elevate the people above their utilitarian and economic preoccupations.

One of those purposes might be called the sanctification of the land itself, which is "invited" to participate in sabbatical rest. The better-known Leviticus passage, where the Lord is reviewing His legislation previously given at Sinai, makes the point explicitly:

> "When you [plural] come into the land that I will give you, then shall *the land keep a Sabbath (veshavethah ha'arets shabbath)* unto the Lord. Six years you shall sow your field, and six years you shall prune your vineyard, and gather in the produce thereof. But in the seventh year there shall be a *Sabbath* of *solemn rest (shabbath shabbathon) for the land,* a Sabbath unto the Lord." (Lev. 25:2–4; emphasis added)[43]

In this later passage, the land is personified, called upon actively to "*keep a Sabbath*," and explicitly given "solemn rest." This beautiful teaching may be implicit in our present (Exodus) ordinance, but the explicit accents point to benefits not for the land but for those who work it. In the present passage, the land is not personified, the word "rest" (*shabbat*) is not mentioned, and the active verbs—the deeds that are commanded—belong not to the land but to the individual Israelite: *you* shall release the land; *you* shall abandon its yield. One explicit consequence is that the poor shall eat what the land spontaneously produces; unlike the previous injunctions about the poor, which proscribed their mistreatment, this one prescribes positive acts that redound to their benefit. But the benefits to the poor (and the wild animals) are a result, not necessarily the purpose, of releasing the land. The true target for this teaching is the land's "owner."

The first thing he needs to learn is that he is not in fact the owner of the land. As will be said later (see Note 45), the land belongs ultimately to God, and he must never forget it. But there are more existential lessons, which not surprisingly exploit contrasts with Israel's prior experience in Egypt.

First, there is a question of how he will live during the sabbatical year. The spontaneous crop will be meager because no work will have been done. What will he eat? (This obvious question is further encouraged by the fact that the text mentions only the poor and the beasts—not the owner—as eating the sabbatical produce.[44]) Barring a miracle—like the manna on which he now lives—he will have to anticipate necessity and make provision ahead of time. He must save for the future, so as not to find himself in danger of having to sell himself as an indentured servant.

We are reminded of the practice of Joseph and Pharaoh during the seven fat years. They bought and hoarded grain against the seven lean years to come. The people were not so prudent. When the famine came, they were at Joseph's mercy and eventually had to sell themselves (and their land) to survive. In Egypt, hoarding by those at the top of society was used to enslave those at the bottom. In the desert, hoarding of manna was forbidden, and people learned to trust in the Lord to provide. But in their homeland, things will be different: they will have to care for themselves. They will have to store food—not to enslave but to keep from falling into servitude.[45]

Mention of Egypt points to a second teaching that will distinguish the Israelites' life in their own land: all who work the land will get a sabbatical from toil, a release from enslavement to their work, an opportunity to renew themselves. The Sabbath day provides a weekly opportunity to turn one's body and soul away from getting and spending toward gratitude and communion with God; the sabbatical year provides a full year to turn one's body and soul away from producing and consuming, with an opening to something higher. It provides an extended occasion to experience gratitude for life in the land and to practice generosity and hospitality toward the poor; it provides an extended occasion to restrain acquisitiveness, exploitation, and indifference to the needy. Release of the land brings release for the landowner, a point made, as Cassuto observes, by the structural placement of this passage:

> This paragraph, the last of those dealing with ordinances and statutes, thus parallels the first, which speaks of the Hebrew slave (21:2–6); in both paragraphs reference is made to six years of labor and to release from work in the seventh year. Every Israelite resembles the Hebrew slave in this respect, that he, too, shall work for only six consecutive years, and after this period he also shall be freed, in the seventh year, from the yoke of hard toil.[46]

It is not a dog-eat-dog world. Rest, give, and be grateful to God—and care for those in need. As God much later will say, "Man does not live by bread alone."[47]

The sabbatical year conveys two more profound teachings, the first about the proper relationship between human beings and the earth. It does so by addressing the twin dangers of an agricultural people: for the ruling few, the belief that we are, through our ingenuity and efforts, masters of the earth; and for the toiling many, the belief that we are, because dependent on Goddess Earth, her servants and slaves. Those who work the land are at risk of submerging into it their entire identity.[48]

The sabbatical year corrects these dangerous tendencies. For one year of every seven, the Israelites will separate themselves from the land and put aside not only toil but also all ideas of mastery and bondage. They live on the land, they live off the land, but they are not the land, and they are destined for more than earthy things. They are like the prototypical human beings in the Garden of Eden: though formed of the dust of the ground, they live by the spirit of God.

The second profound teaching, admittedly only implicit, concerns human aspiration and the true objects of human desire. As I pointed out in discussing the Decalogue, there is a close connection between the teaching about the Sabbath and the injunction against coveting. Both seek to direct the soul away from its natural preoccupation with and desire for unshareable material things and to direct it toward the shareable goods of "knowledge of the Lord and what He requires of us, participation in His grace and the bounty of creation, and the opportunity to live a life of blessing and holiness, despite our frailty and penchant for error and iniquity." The sabbatical year is a recurring way to reorient the soul of the entire community to its highest yearnings.

With echoes of sixes and sevens, servants and strangers, and rest for the weary, an intertwined concern for the spiritual and the moral continues into the sequel, as God returns to the subject of weekly Sabbath rest.* The context this time is the sabbatical year under an agricultural way of life that easily distorts the relation between a man and his neigh-

---

*This is the first of several reiterations of the injunction to keep the Sabbath. One may wonder why it needs to be repeated so often. Two reasons suggest themselves. First, the idea and practice of Sabbath observance are, as noted in Chapter Thirteen, fundamental to Israel's way of life. Second, these practices are not easily embraced, for the demands of keeping a day without work go against the human grain. (In both these respects, Sabbath observance is similar to the teachings about the stranger and the teachings about idolatry, two other demanding injunctions that are repeated many times.) But the "repetitions" vary from one another, according to the context in which they occur. Attending to the context may shed light on the differences in formulation, even as the differences in formulation enrich the meaning and import of the teaching. The present case provides a particularly good example of what I mean.

bors and between man and God. As a result, the accents fall differently from how they did in the Decalogue:

> Six days you shall do your work, but on the seventh day you shall cease ("rest from labor": *tishboth*); *in order that* (*lema'an*) your ox and your ass may have rest (*yanuach*), and the *son of your bondwoman* and the *stranger* (*ger*) may be *refreshed* (or "may catch their breath"; *veyinnafesh*).[49] (23:12; emphasis added)

Unlike the Decalogue's principled introduction of weekly Sabbath cessation, there is no reference here to imitating God as Creator of heaven and earth. Nor is there (as we will see in Deuteronomy) explicit mention of the deliverance from Egypt as the reason for Sabbath observance. In keeping with the foregoing instruction, the emphasis—indeed, the explicit purpose—is entirely humanitarian and (regarding the animals) humane.

The teaching about the sabbatical year spoke of the poor and the (wild) beasts, who might live off the spontaneous produce of the unworked land (though those benefits were not stated as the purpose for releasing the land). Here, in contrast, the named beneficiaries are your own domestic animals, the lowliest of your servants ("the son of your bondwoman"), and the stranger. The gifts to them are the stated purpose of Sabbath cessation: "*in order that* (*lema'an*)" the lowly creatures in your power and under your control—not you—may have rest (animals) and refreshment (humans). If we add some verbal echoes, the teaching is even more stunning. In the original teaching about the Sabbath (20:10), the Israelites were ordered to imitate God's activities in creating the world, but the word "rest"—*nuach*—was ascribed to Him alone; here, the animals will be allowed to rest. In a later return to the teaching about the Sabbath, the reason will again be God's doings: "And on the seventh day He ceased from work and [He] was refreshed (*vayinnafash*)" (31:17). Your animals are to rest every seventh day, just as God did at the beginning; the lowly son of your bondwoman and the stranger are to refresh themselves every seventh day, just as God did at the beginning. You, landowner-to-be, I put on notice: those who work for you, those in your power, no matter how lowly, are not your tools but creatures of God, to be treated accordingly.

This is the only version of the Sabbath teaching that gives the animals such prominence; only here is "rest" attributed to them. Such emphasis is fitting for a people about to work the land, most of whom will not have servants but only animals to help with the work. They might well be tempted to exploit without limit the oxen that plow their fields and the asses that bear their burdens. Not so, says the Lord, Who with one motion serves the animals' well-being and teaches kindness to their human masters.

The emphasis on animals in this formulation also completes a reflection on the relation between man and the animals with which this entire section of *mishpatim* began, with the ordinance about bestiality. That ordinance placed the strongest possible emphasis on enforcing the boundary between man and the animals and insisting on the human's superior dignity. Here, the superior dignity of the human, in relation to the Lord, becomes the basis of humane and respectful treatment of the animals in our midst—just as the same relation to the Lord is the basis for humane and respectful treatment of the stranger living among us.

This transitional section concludes with an ordinance that speaks explicitly about the relationship between the foregoing civil and humanitarian legislation and attachment to the Lord. Like the previous ordinance, this injunction reprises one of the initial teachings: the proscription against acknowledging any gods but *Y-H-V-H*. The thought follows logically on what has come before and anticipates precisely what is coming next:

> And in all things that I have said unto you, you shall guard yourself; but the name of other gods you shall not even mention (or "invoke"; *thazkiru*); neither let it be heard out of your mouth. (23:13)

These are My laws; these therefore are the teachings you should follow: "guard yourself" to observe them—exclusively. I have repeatedly told you to be decent to the stranger who dwells among you. You shall not cheat or oppress him; you shall not deny him fair treatment in court; you shall see that he is refreshed on the seventh day. But do not, as a result of your contact with him, fall into acknowledging his "gods." Do not give them even the reality of verbal mention. Only the Lord is divine.

Once again, this more exacting repetition of the teaching about other gods—do not even mention their names—is both necessary and apt to the moment. The Israelites are a people set apart by a very demanding moral-spiritual teaching. They are about to enter a land inhabited by all kinds of people with less exacting "gods," who therefore fall more easily into sin and perversity. Yet the God of Israel demands that His people respect the humanity of the stranger while not falling into his ways. It is a very tricky business. No wonder the lesson bears repeating.[50] No wonder the people's attachment to the Lord needs to be magnified and strengthened.

Instructions for honoring the Lord, three times a year, follow immediately.

Sacred Times: The Seasonal Festivals

Although the Israelites must avoid all idolatrous worship, they are called upon to observe three seasonal holidays, analogous to the agricultural festivals celebrated by the neighboring peoples. This is, in one sense, hardly surprising: for the first time in their history, the Children of Israel will become an agricultural people. Their ancestors, the literal children of Israel, had lived in Canaan as wandering shepherds; upon returning to the Promised Land, they will live as settled farmers, and soon as city dwellers. Not only their means of livelihood but also their entire way of life will be transformed, and their relation to God must reflect that new civilizational reality. But whereas the pagan agricultural holidays pay homage to natural powers, especially the earth and the sun, the Israelite sacred festivals will be devoted to the Lord.

His preliminary instructions for marking Israel's calendar (details He will give them later) call for three seasonal pilgrimages:

> Three times (*shalosh regalim;* literally, "three feet") you shall-keep-a-feast (*tachog*) unto Me in the year. The Feast of Flat-bread (*chag hammatsoth*) you shall keep; seven days you shall

eat flatbread, as I commanded you [12:15], at the time appointed in the month of Aviv—for in it you came out from Egypt; and none shall appear before Me empty-handed. And the Feast of Harvest (*chag haqqatsir*), of the first fruits (*bikkure*) of your labors, which you sow in the field; and the Feast of Ingathering (*chag ha'asif*), at the end of the year, when you gather in your labors out of the field. Three times (*shelosh pe'amim*) in the year all your males shall appear before the lord (*'adon*) Y-H-V-H. (23:14–17)

As among the pagans, the cyclical fruitfulness of the land will provide occasions for Israelite celebration. As among the pagans, there will be a festival of planting, a festival of first fruits, and a festival of final harvest. But in Israel, each celebration will involve all adult males in a pilgrimage journey to an as-yet-unspecified sanctuary of the Lord, where their gratitude will be expressed in sacrifices offered not to "nature gods" but to Y-H-V-H. Moreover—and this is an equally important difference—the agricultural festivals will in time be connected to certain crucial events in Israel's early national history. Not the cyclical rhythms of bountiful Mother Earth but Israel's forward-looking covenantal mission becomes the cause of celebration and gratitude. We have already encountered this paradigm: the transformation of the spring festival of planting—here called the Festival of Flatbread—into a commemoration of the Exodus from Egypt, the first people-forming event.[51]

To this point, we know very little about the content or conduct of these festivals. The Hebrew word translated as "feast" or "festival," *chag*—"kept a feast" is *chagag*—comes from a Hebrew root meaning "to go around," "to dance in a circle." Perhaps because each of the designated *chaggim* requires that all males in the land journey to the Lord's designated sanctuary, the term also acquires the meaning of "pilgrimage." We imagine long processions of pilgrims, traveling with their prescribed offerings to greet the true "lord" (*'adon*), Y-H-V-H, not Baal ("master" or "lord"), the earthy god worshipped (at home) among the Canaanites. At the sanctuary, the pilgrimage culminates in sacrifice, feasting, and dancing, in grateful celebration of the Lord's bounty and beneficence. These pilgrimages, precisely because they take place at three set times, also serve a social purpose[52]: they help unify the dispersed people, who gather from all over the land and demonstrate by leaving their roots that it is not the earth they are celebrating. By bringing all the people to a common place in worshipful celebration, the seasonal pilgrimages will forge the nation's communal—spiritual—identity. Obeying in the sanctified place this divine injunction, given at Sinai, the Israelites will regularly renew and refresh themselves in the Lord's covenant as the covenantal community.

The section on sacred festivals concludes with three instructions about the sacrifices Israel is to offer to the Lord. In keeping with the different object of their devotions, the Israelites are to avoid certain practices that, one suspects, may have been common among their nature-worshipping neighbors:

> You shall not offer the blood of My sacrifice with leavened bread; neither shall the fat (*chelev*) of My feast remain all night until the morning. The choicest first fruits of your land you shall bring into the house of *Y-H-V-H* your God. You shall not seethe a kid in its mother's milk (*chalav*). (23:18–19)

The first and last of these ordinances, both dealing with animals, are not exactly clear. The first injunction recalls the specific requirements for the commemoration of Passover, although that holiday is not mentioned here.[53] Later, in Leviticus, the Lord will proscribe sacrificing on the altar any *meal* (grain) offerings that have been transformed with leaven.[54] But whether this is (as here) a specific requirement for the Paschal sacrifice or a general constraint on all altar sacrifices, the target is grain that has been deliberately fermented by human agents. Some interpreters see fermentation as an objectionable symbol of human corruption and a taste for luxury; what the Lord wants is a pure and unadulterated gift. Others suggest that leavening is objectionable because it implies that the sacrifices might literally be food for God—instead of evidence that His children will remember and acknowledge Him before enjoying any fruits of the earth. This interpretation is supported by the fact that (in the Leviticus passage just cited) an injunction against sacrificing honey—

thought by neighboring peoples to be a favorite food of the gods—will be added to the ban against sacrificing leaven.

The requirement to offer the best and choicest first fruits, as they come from the ground, seems unproblematic. It simply extends to the fruits of "mother earth," now in the context of the three sacred agricultural festivals, the principle that the "first-to-open-the-womb" belongs—as a gift given in gratitude—to the Lord (see 13:11ff). And it urges the farmers not to delay in offering thanks. Readers of Genesis may note that the injunction also tacitly corrects the sacrifice of Cain, the very first farmer, who was also the inventor of sacrifices. Suffering from the natural error of farmers, occupationally prone to attribute their produce to their own effort, Cain did not bring the *first* fruits of the ground, and what he brought he brought only in "the end of days"; Abel, by contrast, brought "the firstlings of the flock and of the fat (*chelev*) thereof" (Gen. 4:3–4).

The final injunction is puzzling, to say the least. This passage later became the basis of the extensive rabbinic injunctions against the mixing of meat and milk—a central part of *Kashrut*, the dietary laws still observed by traditional Jews today. But the point of the original injunction is obscure and contested, and carries no such explicit implications.

In context, this final instruction seems to be a tacit correction of some objectionable practice, either already known to the Israelites or to be found when they encounter the neighboring Canaanite peoples. Yes, the Lord seems to be saying, I have laid claim to the firstlings of the flock, but you are not to serve them up to me boiled as a delicacy in their mothers' milk.[55] But if there is a further explanation, it is hard to come by. Several suggestions have been offered over the centuries, none mutually exclusive.

Some interpreters (for example, Maimonides) see this rule as an attempt to keep the Israelites away from the idolatrous customs of the Canaanites, and there is some disputed evidence in the Ugaritic tablets to suggest that the Canaanites did indeed cook young animals in milk or butter. Other commentators (for example, Abravanel) see the rule as a humane measure designed to oppose hard-heartening cruelty, akin to other biblical injunctions against cruelty to animals. Still others (for example, Philo) see the injunction as preserving a strict boundary between life and death, one of the binary distinctions crucial to biblical ontology and ethics: there is something grossly improper in using the substance that feeds the living animal to season or flavor it after its death. Not everyone thinks a reason can be found or should be sought. Ibn Ezra held that the rationale for this prohibition is "concealed from the eyes of even the wise," while Moses Mendelssohn says that "the benefit arising from the many inexplicable laws of God is in their practice, and not in the understanding of their motives."

I confess to finding merit in all these suggestions (especially in Philo's), and I see no way—and also no reason—to choose among them. Given the disagreement among these weightiest of commentators, we should be content to acknowledge our ignorance and declare the matter a mystery. Perhaps it is fitting that the mysterious Author of these ordinances should conclude them with an injunction that leaves us would-be rationalizers in the dark.

Looking Ahead to the Land: Prospects, Risks, and Responsibilities

God's presentation of the ordinances appears complete. He has outlined the essential teachings that are to govern the lives of the Israelites within their distinctive and separate community, a community summoned to a holy life in the Promised Land. Their obligations to one another and to the Lord have been presented as complementary, intertwined, and mutually implicated aspects of a single way of life. But nothing has yet been said about how they are to acquire the land or how they are to relate to the alien peoples who now occupy it. The final section of God's speech—known to scholars as the "Epilogue"—addresses itself to these important matters. It offers hope, issues warnings, clarifies responsibilities, and envisions a favorable outcome regarding the encounter with the Canaanite peoples. In keeping with a basic yet paradoxical feature of God's relationship with Israel, it combines the Lord's unconditional promises with demands for Israelite obedience. Far from a mere "epilogue," it forms a crucial part of the covenant-forming message that Moses is to place before the people for their agreement and consent. We should listen to it through their ears as well as our own.

God begins by addressing the journey ahead and the roles He and the people will play in bringing it to a successful conclusion. Both He and they will have an "assistant":

> Behold, I send an angel (or "messenger"; *mal'akh*) *before you,* to *guard* you on the way, and to *bring* you into the place that I have prepared. Take heed of him, and hearken unto his *voice*; do not provoke (or "rebel against") him; for he will not pardon your transgressions (*pesha'*); for My Name is in him. But *if* you shall indeed hearken unto his voice, and do all that I speak; then *I* will be an enemy unto your enemies, and an adversary unto your adversaries. For My angel shall go before you, and *he* will *bring you in* unto the Amorite, and the Hittite, and the Perizzite, and the Canaanite, the Hivite, and the Jebusite; and (or "but") *I* will *destroy* ("efface" or "annihilate"; Hebrew root *k-ch-d*) them. (23:20–23; emphasis added)

To begin with, God announces that he will send an angel—His agent and messenger—to lead and protect the people on their way and to bring them safely to the Promised Land. For the first time since well before the Exodus from Egypt, God returns to the last part of His original sevenfold promise to the Israelite slaves: "And I will bring you in unto the land concerning which I lifted up My hand to give it to Abraham, to Isaac, and to Jacob; and I will give it to you for a heritage: I am *Y-H-V-H*" (6:8). There, God said that He would bring them personally; now He assigns that role to His messenger.

What does this mean? And what will Moses and the people make of this news? We must spend a little time on the vexed question of what is meant by "an angel," in general and in the present case. The term *mal'akh*, from a root meaning "to dispatch as a deputy," can mean anything from "messenger" to "angel" (God's messenger) to "prophet" to "the theophanic angel," a *direct* manifestation of God Himself (as with Moses at the burning bush, where the so-called angel speaks in the first person as the Lord [3:2ff]). Nothing obliges us to think of the otherworldly and winged creatures of medieval painting; an ordinary human being, if suitably empowered, may serve as God's messenger. When the term *mal'akh* is encountered in the Torah, interpretations vary. Some insist that it is a visible and fearsome (nonhuman) messenger of God; others treat it as a metaphor for providential guidance of a human agent; still others elide the distinction between God and His angel, calling the angel "in the final analysis . . . simply God's action."[56]

In a more radical interpretation, some suggest that the messenger who will go before the people, who will guard and bring them to the land, and whose voice must be heeded is none other than Moses himself—at least insofar as the people are concerned. Who has led them out of Egypt and through the Sea, has judged and admonished and taught them, and has been shuttling up and down Mount Sinai bringing messages from the Lord? The man Moses.[57] As the fearful people prepare to leave the mountain for the arduous journey to the Promised Land, they will need, this argument goes, to believe that the Lord will go with them, at the very least through his agent Moses. At the same time, as we have seen, Moses's authority with the people is precarious. Not that long ago, they were ready to stone him. God's remarks about the angel address these difficulties. By convincing the people that their leader is His messenger, God confers the needed authority on Moses, precisely when he is most in need of their trust. In addition, the message about the messenger will strengthen Moses's heart for the journey. Believing that God is with him, Moses will be inspired to ever greater heights of command and judgment, gaining the people's trust as never before. By saying to them, "I send a messenger before you . . . to guard you . . . to bring you to the place," the Lord gives the people language to think of Moses's conduct on a more-than-human plane. What emboldens the soul and elevates the voice of great men to heights beyond their known capacities, if not some "higher power"?

Attractive though this reading is, it is not finally persuasive. Several passages make it as difficult to collapse the difference between Moses and the angel as it is to collapse the difference between the angel and God. The angel will go before "you," second-person singular—at once before Moses and before the united people of Israel. The angel will carry God's Name and refuse pardon for the people's transgressions—neither tasks that are part of Moses's job description. The angel will lead them into the land of the Canaanite peoples—something Moses will not do.

I prefer to regard the angel as akin to the one we encountered in the one prior use of the term *mal'akh* in Exodus: God's personal agent, who guarded His people at the Sea of Reeds. As the Egyptians threatened to drive the Israelites into the sea, "the angel of God (*mal'akh ha'elohim*), who went [had gone] in front of the camp of Israel, removed and went behind them; and the pillar of the cloud went from in front of them, and stood behind them; and it came between the camp of Egypt and the camp of Israel" (14:19–20). Neither Moses nor God, but some mysterious third agent was present, keeping company with the traveling cloud and fire, leading from the front when possible, guarding from behind when necessary. Just such an agent, Moses here learns, will henceforth go with him and the people all the way to the Promised Land.

The announcement of a guardian angel will surely come as welcome news to the people. Even though they will depart from God's holy mountain, they will not be alone; a powerful agent of the Lord will lead and protect them on their journey. In addition, the Lord Himself will be near, ready to act once the people arrive in the land. The angel will lead, guard, and instruct, but the Lord Himself will take care of the fighting.

Yet the presence of God's messenger could turn out to be inconvenient for the people. They are exhorted to obey him and warned against rebelling or provoking him; bearing God's Name and presumably speaking for Him, the angel will not forgive their transgressions—which is to say, God will not forgive them. On the other hand there is a conditional promise that if the people do obey the angel and do all that the Lord demands of them, the Lord vows to take their side against their enemies and adversaries.

Readers may nod when hearing this, but for the Israelites, it is an arresting and bittersweet promise. Enemies? Adversaries? This is the first time they are told directly that they will have to face such difficulties when they get to the Promised Land. Moses, in the Song of the Sea, had sung of how "all the inhabitants of Canaan are melted away" once they heard of the Lord's triumph over mighty Egypt. But now the Israelites learn that several peoples are still in the land and will not take kindly to their arrival.[58] Okay, we remember the Amalekites. But who knew that we would face other enemy nations before we can come "home"?

The Lord gives them the good news before the bad. You will not face these enemies alone—provided you obey the angel and the Lord: should you do so, I will make your enemies My enemies and your adversaries My adversaries. My angel shall lead you into the midst of the six nations, but I, the Lord, will destroy them.

Moses and the people will no doubt be encouraged by this news. But readers with modern sensibilities will be distressed. What's this? The expulsion and annihilation of six resident Canaanite nations, simply to make room for the Children of Israel? The defeat of Egypt and the Amalekites we can defend, more or less, on grounds of justice. But how to justify the removal and destruction of indigenous peoples who, as far as we know, have done nothing to the Children of Israel—or anyone else— to merit their disappearance? We may not be able to justify it, but we can explain it.

Attempts at justification might take one of two forms: the Canaanites had it coming to them, or alternatively, the Israelites require it if they are to survive and flourish. The ground for the first justification was laid long ago. When Abram (during the covenant between the sacrificial pieces) asked God to tell him when he would inherit the Promised Land, God told him that not he but his seed would inherit it, after four hundred years of slavery in a strange land: "And in the fourth generation they shall come back *here; for the iniquity of the Amorite is not yet full*" (15:16; emphasis added). Now, after four hundred years of iniquitous living, the land of Canaan is ready to vomit out its inhabitants*— with help from the Lord.

---

*This language appears only later in Leviticus in the discussion of forbidden sexual unions, where the indictment and punishment of the Canaanites are presented in full: "Defile not you yourselves in any of these things; for in all these the nations are defiled, which I cast out from before you. And the land was defiled, therefore I did visit the iniquity thereof upon it, and the land vomited out her inhabitants. You therefore shall keep My statutes and Mine ordinances, and shall not do any of these abominations; neither the home-born, nor the stranger that sojourns among you—for all these abominations have the men of the land done, that were before you, and the land is defiled—that the land vomit not you out also, when you defile it, as it vomited out the nation that was before you" (Lev. 18:24–28).

In the present context, however, the other consideration seems more pertinent, as the sequel will make clear. The nascent people of Israel, newly chartered under a demanding set of laws, must learn to live apart, away from the temptations of the more easy-going (and iniquitous) Canaanite way of life. The removal of the Canaanites is the surest way to avoid the dangers of dilution and corruption.

Something close to this concern seems to be what God has in mind. To see it, we must stop thinking in terms of justice and consider instead God's long and arduous efforts to establish a beachhead in the world for His Way, a righteous and holy way for humankind. It was for this reason that he made a covenant with Abraham, renewed it with Isaac and Jacob, and saw to it that their descendants were delivered from Egyptian bondage after four hundred years. It is for this reason that He now proposes a covenant with Israel, to be filled out by giving her people an exacting Law under which they are to live. The history of the world, as God intends it, requires that the Children of Israel be established in a land where they can practice the Law and God's Way, and live as the covenantal community uncorrupted by other practices. Since there is no empty land in which to establish them—all land, including that of their ancestors, is occupied—a price of removal must be paid in order to establish Israel in its land. It is an unfortunate price, but if the Way is to take hold and survive, it cannot be avoided. God chooses to pay it by picking a particularly sinful people to cast out, thus justifying morally a matter of political and historical necessity.[59]

Modern sensibilities, informed, ironically, by biblical notions of justice and love of neighbor, will find this practice deeply flawed—condemnable as ethnic cleansing or, worse, genocide. Our recent history has seen horrendous examples of similar practices and worse, justified by murderous revolutionaries like Lenin and Mao as necessary to create "the new man" and the classless society. But we tend to forget that most nations are born in sin—in fratricide, conquest, displacement, forced removal, even genocide. It is to overcome these unjust ways of the world that the Lord is trying to establish a righteous alternative, a model and light unto all the others. Just as He needed to extract His people from despotic Egyptian rule, so He needs now to separate them from licentious Canaanite influence. Should we be dismayed by His practice here, it is only because, with His covenantal people, He managed to get His Way established.

We return to the text. The Lord's prophecy of success against the native peoples is followed immediately by yet another warning, this time about getting too cozy with the ways of the Canaanite peoples, among whom they must enter the land. The several general injunctions against idolatry are particularized in relation to the earthy gods of the Canaanites. This danger must be dealt with severely:

> You shall not bow down to their gods, nor serve them, nor do after their doings; but you shall utterly overthrow (*hares teharesem*) them, and utterly shatter (*veshabber teshabber*) their pillars ("their cultic monuments or steles"; *matsevothehem*). And you shall serve [only] the Lord your God, and He will bless your bread, and your water; and I will take sickness away from the midst of you. None shall miscarry, nor be barren, in your land; the number of your days I will fulfill. (23:24–26)

As I have noted several times, beginning in our discussion of the Decalogue, there appears to be a close connection between worshipping—bowing down to and serving—alien "gods" and committing iniquity (imitating "their doings"). This danger seems particularly great regarding the Canaanite gods and practices, because their earthy wildness and boundless, alluring sexuality are integral to their activities of worship. To avoid these temptations, a war must be waged against the shrines, images, altars, pillars, and monuments of the pagan "gods," leaving no stone erect.

In an echo of the verse about idolatry discussed near the beginning of this chapter (22:19), the Israelites are again admonished to serve only the Lord, their own God, Who promises them a different and bountiful future in the service of life and its perpetuation: blessings of food and water, removal of sickness (for the sake of the now living) and of miscarriage and barrenness (for the sake of the next generations), and a promise of long life in the land. The last of these promises echoes the

Decalogue's phrase, "that your days shall be long in the land that the Lord God has given you," appended to the injunction to honor father and mother—a phrase that we interpreted, exactly as here, to mean that the land will not vomit you out, as it will soon do to its current licentious and incestuous inhabitants. That cleansing of the land is the subject of the next promise:

> I will send My terror (or "dread"; *'emah*) before you, and will panic (or "vex" or "discomfit" or "destroy"; from the Hebrew verb *hamam*) all the people to whom you shall come, and I will make all your enemies turn their backs to you. And I will send the hornet before you, which shall drive out the Hivite, the Canaanite, and the Hittite, from before you. (23:27–28)

How to cleanse the land? Through fear of the Lord, seen fighting for Israel. The language recalls precisely the episode at the Sea of Reeds, the first great battle in which the Lord fought for His people.[60] His angel in the vanguard will cause the inhabitants of the Promised Land to turn and run in fear. To hasten the process, the Lord promises to send a plague of stinging insects to drive the inhabitants from their hiding places. In Egypt, plagues of insects helped Israel leave bondage. In Canaan, a scourge of insects will help drive out the detested natives.

The natives will leave, yes, but not quickly:

> I will not drive them out from before you in one year, lest the land become desolate, and the beasts of the field multiply against you. By little and little I will drive them out from before you, until you be increased, and inherit the land. And I will set your border from the Red Sea even unto the sea of the Philistines, and from the wilderness unto the River; for I will deliver the inhabitants of the land into your hand; and *you* shall drive them out before you. (23:29–31; emphasis added)

The turning over of the land must take some time.[61] The stated reason is the need to protect the land from desolation and returning to wilderness.

But there is also the suggestion that the people themselves must have a hand in conquering the land: Yes, "I will drive [the inhabitants] out before you," and, yes, "I will deliver the inhabitants of the land into your hand"; but finally, "*you* shall drive them out before you." The Lord will help the Israelites help themselves and prepare them to defend themselves against all adversaries. But they must from the start acquire the courage and skill to secure their land and protect themselves against all enemies.

This instruction tells the people, for the first time, the boundaries of the Promised Land. Although we cannot be certain of the exact geographic references, the commonwealth appears to extend from the Red Sea to the Mediterranean, and from the wilderness in the south to the Euphrates River in the north—a territory the size of ancient Egypt, which was attained only in the days of King David. It is not clear whether the boundaries should be taken literally or are only intended to feed nationalistic aspirations. But readers of Genesis will recall that when God made His first covenant with Abram between the sacrificial pieces, He told Abram that He had already given, to his seed, "the land from the river of Egypt to the great river, the river Euphrates"—an even greater domain, at that time home to nine nations rather than the current six (Gen. 15:18–21). Conquering this land and expelling its inhabitants cannot happen all at once.

The expulsion of the natives is not only a promise. It is an obligation, imposed on the Israelites to protect them against being corrupted by pagan ways. The Lord concludes by returning yet again, and most emphatically, to the tempting danger of foreign gods and practices. The final words of God's covenant with Israel proscribe making any other covenants:

> You shall make no covenant with them [literally, "to them"; *lahem*], or with their gods. They shall not dwell in your land—lest they make you sin against Me, for you will serve their gods—for they will be a snare unto you. (23:32–33)

In the present context—the anticipated conquest of the land—the Lord's warning about other covenants concerns the risk of population mixing, a consequence of an amnesty or of coexistence offered by the victorious Israelites to the peoples they conquer.[62] The defeated pagans must not be allowed to dwell in the land; they must be completely expelled. Why? Because otherwise the Israelites will be seduced into worshipping their gods and imitating their iniquitous practices. To avoid being ensnared and whoring after false gods, the only alternative is complete separation.

Yet we shall soon see that the Children of Israel are perfectly capable of ensnaring themselves, even before any contact with the Canaanites. The Lord has good cause for worry. Living up to His Way is demanding, and backsliding and falling away are ever-present possibilities. Warnings and exhortations will not be enough. The deep, problematic longings of the human soul must be addressed by additional measures.

Part Three
To the Tabernacle:
Worship and Presence

Exodus 24–40

Strange Goings-On

"Blood of the Covenant" and "Seeing God"

W
e have arrived at a pivotal point in our story. The momentous giving of the Law at Sinai appears to have ended. First, we heard the majestic Decalogue, pronounced by the Lord Himself before the assembled Israelites. Then we listened to the ordinances (*mishpatim*), spoken by Him to Moses, who must transmit them to the people. Finally we heard the Lord's instructions regarding travel to the Promised Land and how Israel is to behave toward the Canaanite natives upon arrival. But the event at Sinai is not finished. Although the Law has been given, the people have not yet heard most of it, nor have they given their assent to obey. In addition, the Lord has something more in mind, not for the people but for Moses himself and for others in the "leadership." As it happens, Moses also has a few extra things to attend to, quite on his own. But both Moses's and the Lord's "additional somethings" will expose important problems concerning the relationship between man and God that have yet to be addressed but will demand center stage for the rest of the book. The events described in this chapter—all reported in Exodus 24—bring closure to the previous rounds of lawgiving and precipitate a massive new addition to the Law: the construction of the Tabernacle and the institution of the sacrificial cult. How and why this comes about we must follow slowly and closely.

As I am offering a most unorthodox reading of the events reported in Exodus 24, readers may be helped by knowing in advance what led me to it—even though the explanation involves referring to, and reading backward from, matters that still lie ahead (a violation of my usual rule for reading). After Exodus 24, there are only sixteen chapters left in the book of Exodus, thirteen of which are devoted to the Tabernacle (*mishkan*). Chapters 25–31 contain the Lord's detailed instructions for constructing the Tabernacle and all its appurtenances; Chapters 35–40 report the actual construction, following the instructions exactly, much of the time repeating them letter for letter. Sandwiched between the instructions and their execution are three chapters (32–34) on the episode of the golden calf and its idolatrous worship. Just as the two accounts of the Tabernacle frame and contain the account of the golden calf, so, as we will see, the Tabernacle (a house of worship) addresses, cabins, and redirects—by bringing under elaborate and precise divine directions—the passions that erupt in that episode: a desire to close with the divine, the ecstatic passions of Dionysus, the aesthetic taste for visible beauty. Perhaps, as most interpreters believe, the Tabernacle was part of God's original plan for Israel; yet its elaborate structure is a far cry from the Lord's previous instruction—given after the Decalogue to address the people's stand-offishness—that He is to be worshipped on a *simple earthen altar,* something they will do for the first time, but without divine instruction, in Exodus 24, the subject of our present chapter.

The other crucial element in our interpretation is the Torah's deeply ambivalent attitude toward the human impulse to offer sacrifices, previously discussed in Chapter Seven and revisited at the end of Chapter Thirteen. In particular, we remember God's adverse judgment of Noah's uninstructed animal sacrifice upon leaving the ark ("The imagination of man's heart is evil from his youth"), a judgment that led immediately to the Lord's giving of the Noahide law (Gen. 8:20–9:17). By analogy, we notice that the law of the Tabernacle follows immediately upon the report of Moses's uninstructed animal sacrifice and the other events reported in Exodus 24. So we are led to ask what Exodus 24 is doing exactly where it is and how its events may connect to what God—perhaps in response—does in the immediate sequel. Might the episodes reported in this chapter reveal the problems that made the Tabernacle necessary?

Might it even contain the seeds of the golden calf? It was with these ideas in mind that I first noticed—and have here interpreted—several very disquieting elements in the events presented in Exodus 24, especially Moses's strewing of blood on the people, and the nobles "seeing God" and eating and drinking in His presence.[1]

Call for a Summit Meeting

The ordinances have laid down the law for all the Israelite people, each of whom was summoned (usually in second-person singular) to answer the call to be holy men unto the Lord. But there are no instructions regarding the administration of the law or how people are to be chosen for positions of leadership, either "political" or "religious." To be sure, Moses is the Lord's anointed, and several of the Lord's earlier efforts were intended to get the people to trust in Moses and "to believe [him] forever" (19:9). But now that the Law has been given, questions will likely emerge about how Moses will lead and who might help him do so, and especially in which activities. More important, although the Israelites have been repeatedly warned against worshipping—even mentioning—the gods of the Canaanites, little has been said about how they should channel toward the Lord their impulses to pay homage to the divine or who will mediate the "traffic." To address these matters, God appends to the ordinances (*"And* unto *Moses* . . .")[2] an additional order for Moses himself:

> And unto Moses He [had] said (*ve'el-Mosheh 'amar*): "Come up ("ascend"; *'aleh* [singular imperative]) unto the Lord, you, and Aaron, Nadab, and Abihu, and seventy of the elders of Israel; and worship you ("prostrate yourselves"; *vehishtachavithem* [plural]) from afar; and Moses alone shall come near unto the Lord; but they shall not come near; neither shall the people go up with him." (24:1–2)

The Lord orders a meeting on the mountain of what seems to be His designated leadership team: in addition to Moses, on one hand, Aaron and his eldest sons Nadab and Abihu[3]; on the other hand, a representative group of the elders, in the same "perfect" number as the seventy descendants of Jacob who first came down to Egypt (1:5). God's designated party does not include the judges whom Moses had appointed on Jethro's advice, nor does it include Joshua, who had distinguished himself in battle and who will later be Moses's replacement as the people's chief leader. We therefore suspect that God is interested in addressing "religious" matters, specifically the subject of worship.

This should not surprise us. The last time we heard about the group, all the elders and Aaron came together (uninstructed) to eat bread with Jethro, Moses's father-in-law, at the sacrifice that Jethro was offering to God (18:12). The Lord's summons to a reprise of that spontaneous occasion may be intended either as a continuation of that event or, more likely, its correction. This select group—likely including Moses—is to worship (literally, "prostrate themselves") "from afar," after which Moses is to complete his ascent into the divine Presence. The rest of the leadership party is not to go all the way up with Moses. And the people are not to go up at all.

Whatever the Lord has in mind for these encounters, the instructions clearly establish a tripartite division of the camp: first, Moses; second, Aaron, his sons, and the elders; last, the mass of the people. An intermediate and mediating group is being introduced between Moses and the people, an elevated group of nobles (led by Aaron) who can help out when needed, take charge should Moses be absent, and govern the formal practices of worshipping the Lord. In addition, this elite group may be able to bear witness, from its experience on the mountain, to Moses's special relationship to the Lord, thus supporting his credibility and authority with the people.[4] With this last command to Moses, the Lord finally finishes speaking. (He has been speaking without interruption or comment since Exodus 20:18.) He awaits Moses's compliance.

But Moses does not immediately do as he has been told. Pointedly, he does not ascend. Instead, probably remembering the previous charge to place the ordinances before the people (21:1), he descends (or returns) to the camp. The covenant, he thinks, needs to be ratified immediately.

Ratifying the Covenant

Arriving in camp, Moses wastes no time in seeking the people's consent to the covenant. He first makes sure that they know what it will oblige them to do:

> And Moses came and told the people all the *words* of the Lord, and [or, "that is"] all the *ordinances* (*kol-divre Y-H-V-H ve'eth kol-hammishpatim*); and *all* the people answered *with one voice,* and they said: "All the words (*kol-haddevarim*) that the Lord has spoken (*'asher-dibber Y-H-V-H*) will we do (*na'aseh*)." (24:3; emphasis added)

Commentators disagree about what exactly Moses told the people. Some say that the "words of the Lord" refer to the Decalogue (introduced by "And God spoke *all these words,* saying" [20:1]), as distinguished from the ordinances (*mishpatim*), clearly so named: thus, these interpreters argue, Moses told them everything. Others, noting that the people had already heard the Decalogue and that God had explicitly told Moses to set the ordinances before the people (21:1), suggest that "all the words" refers only to the ordinances (with the *vav,* usually translated "and," functioning here as "*vav* explicative," the equivalent of our "that is"). Either way, Moses presents all the words to the people, and all the people, in one voice and without hesitation, agree to do as they have been commanded. Their reply is similar—though not identical—to their response when Moses first brought them news of the proposed covenant.[5] But now, having heard in detail what the Lord requires of them, their acceptance of His offer seems more genuine.

But Moses is not yet satisfied. He wants to formalize the agreement and get their consent one more time. This is no ordinary covenant, to be sealed by a handshake between equal partners, or "cut" by having both parties walk ceremoniously between the cleaved parts of animals severed for that purpose. Moses wants a ceremony to ratify the agreement, a symbolic enactment of the covenant that will be commensurate with its incommensurable partners and its historic and fateful significance.

And he wants it done in a grand way that will engage the people where they live.

Moses wastes no time fulfilling his plans. Once again, he acts without instruction:

> And Moses wrote (*vayyikhtov*) all the words of the Lord, and rose up early in the morning, and built an altar (*mizbeach*) below the mountain, and twelve pillars (or "monuments"; *matsevah*), according to the twelve tribes (*shevatim*) of Israel. And he sent the young men of the Children of Israel (*na'are bene yisra'el*), who offered burnt-offerings (*'oloth*), and sacrificed peace offerings (*zevachim shelamim*) of oxen unto the Lord. (24:4–5)

Not trusting to memory, Moses puts into writing all the words of the Lord that the people had just agreed to obey, perhaps working well into the night and writing presumably on parchment. This is the first humanly initiated act of writing in the Bible,[6] and it should therefore arrest us. But we readers of this written account of "first writing," taking writing for granted, need prodding to pause and wonder at Moses's deed. We see that he is concerned about memory and forgetfulness. But whose? For whom is he writing? And in what language? Can the Israelite ex-slaves read? Could he be writing also and especially for himself, to preserve an accurate record of what the Lord has commanded and the people have agreed to? Is he writing also for future generations? If so, will a parchment record be sufficient? Is that what we have just been reading? And what, if anything, does the Lord think of this? We lack answers to all of these questions.

Traditional readers may be shocked by this line of questioning and by my calling attention to the ways in which Moses acts without—or even against—divine instruction. Since I will do so throughout this chapter, a word of explanation is in order. I try where possible to picture the events described as if I were a living witness, seeing them for the first time. I do not assume that everything done by the people, by the elders, or even by Moses himself is good and wise or in accord with God's will or plan. Any uninstructed deeds—against a background where almost everything else is explicitly commanded—are noteworthy and deserve serious examination. But neither do I assume that Moses's independent acts are necessarily improper or mistaken, against God's will, or blameworthy. When the Lord is silent, people must act as best they can; for the sake of at least the reader, it may be crucial to see how well—or badly—they manage. I have followed this intuition throughout, but it is especially important in this chapter, when so much of what happens is uninstructed—beginning with the sacrifice Moses now offers.

Eager to proceed, Moses rises early the next morning to prepare a sacrifice unto the Lord and to enact approval for the new covenant. On one side, he (by himself) builds an altar below the mountain, the channel to the divine; on the other side (or perhaps all around the altar), he erects the pillars* representing the Children of Israel according to their tribes (*shevatim*), named after the sons of Jacob.[7] In so doing, Moses establishes (or at least confirms) that the relevant subdivisions of the new people of Israel will be the genealogical tribes of the sons of Jacob. God neither supports nor opposes such a move—though He will later endorse the notion (Num. 1). Throughout this entire event, Moses acts wholly on his own; the Lord has not yet called for any animal sacrifice. Sacrifices initiated by human beings, we recall, have been problematic, both from God's point of view and eventually also from ours.[8]

The human and divine parties thus symbolically represented, Moses then arranges for the sacrifices—the first since leaving Egypt, save for the one offered by Jethro. To our surprise, Moses neither offers the sacrifices himself nor calls on Aaron or the elders to offer them, no priests having yet been officially appointed. Instead, the youth from each tribe—those who will inherit the land and will especially bear the responsibility of keeping the covenant—are given the honor and

---

*The word for Moses's pillars is *matsevoth,* the same word that named the erected monuments of the Canaanites, which the Lord had just commanded the Israelites to overthrow and shatter (23:24). What to make of Moses's improvisation in the light of that demand? What are pillars, and what do they represent? Do they have an independent meaning, or does their meaning derive solely from the intention of those who erect them and from the character of the deity they "serve"? (The Tabernacle will have no pillars.)

burden of offering sacrifices unto the Lord—sacrifices, we note again, that He has not called for.[9]

We can readily imagine what is on Moses's mind and why he proceeds as he does. God's Law, given through Moses to the people, must now pass into human hands. As leader of the people, he must figure out how to execute the transfer most effectively. He understands that he is ratifying with the Children of Israel a timeless covenant that will long survive him. Not he, therefore, but the people or their representatives must make the offerings to God. The people's heroic past must not be forgotten—hence the twelve eponymous tribes; yet the perpetuators are the men of the future—hence the youth bring the sacrifices, propitiating the Lord and invoking His assistance in all that is to come. But this is prologue to the ratification ceremony itself:

> And Moses took (*vayyiqqach*) half of the blood, and put it in basins; and half of the blood he threw (*zaraq*) against (or "upon"; *'al*) the altar. And he took (*vayyiqqach*) the book of the covenant (*sefer habberith*), and read it in the hearing of the people; and they said: "All that the Lord has spoken will we do and we will obey (or "hear"; *na'aseh venishma'*). And Moses took (*vayyiqqach*) the blood, and threw (*vayyizroq*) it on the people, and said: "Behold the blood of the covenant, which the Lord has made [literally, "cut"; *karath*] with you regarding all these words." (24:6–8)

We need several readings to understand what is going on, beginning with clarifying the facts. First, Moses does three things, each heralded by the verb "he took": he took (half of) the blood, he took the book, he took the blood. The acts of speaking—reading and answering—are sandwiched between two deeds of strewing blood. The Lord's speech and the people's answer are the heart of the matter; the throwing of blood is their frame and wrapping.[10]

The blood, obtained from an unknown number of slaughtered oxen, Moses collects and divides in two. He does not allow it to spill into puddles on the ground, as do those who thereby seek to feed the chthonic gods. Instead, he gathers it in basins, and saving one half for the people, he throws the other half upon the altar, symbolically "covering" or "immersing" the divine in sanctified lifeblood. Before doing the same with the people, however, he reads to them "the Book of the Covenant"—a new term, invented by Moses—and receives from them a ringing endorsement, fuller than the first: not only will we do; we will also hear (or "obey"). Their approval in hand, Moses now throws the rest of the ox blood on the people, declaring it—in another Mosaic invention—"the blood of the covenant," the covenant that the Lord has just made with the people.

We must ponder several ambiguities in the text, beginning with the "rational" or spoken elements.

First, what is "the Book of the Covenant"? We cannot be sure. From the context, it seems to be what Moses had written down the previous evening—whether it was just the ordinances, also the Decalogue, or, in addition, the Lord's original proposal for the covenant (19:3–8).[11] Whatever it is, it represents the content of the covenantal agreement here being ratified.

Second, what is meant by the people's two-part answer, "we will do" and "we will obey" (literally, "hear")? Traditional interpreters quite properly regard this as the perfect expression of submission to God's will and dedication to His ways: in deed and in word they unhesitatingly surrender themselves to the Lord. Yet we wonder why, if so, the order is not reversed: does not an obedient person first listen and hear (and heed) before he does? Are the people implicitly saying they will do as they have been told but are open to hearing more—even about the very things that they just agreed to do—or are open to *heeding* more, including any new commands that the Lord may issue later? Or are they tacitly affirming the view that, in moral matters, learning comes as a result of doing: first obedient performance, then understanding.

Third, what exactly did Moses do with the blood? Many translators, whether from squeamishness or to make the scene appear more decorous, say that Moses "sprinkled" the blood and only on the pillars—or at most, on the seventy elders—as representatives of the people: after all, they point out, it would have been impossible to sprinkle blood on all 600,000 Israelites. But the text clearly says that Moses *threw (zaraq)* the blood[12] and on the people, not merely their representatives. Each person was confirming and pledging his own agreement to abide by God's commands. If the "blood of the covenant" symbolically sealed the deal, each of the Israelites deserved to be so marked, bound each and all in a "blood oath." Moreover, the text does not say that Moses threw it on all the people: he threw it widely and broadly, even if not everyone was hit. We can imagine blood flying in all directions. The scene is anything but decorous.

Scholars are quick to see this enactment in the context of similar rituals practiced by other ancient, not to say "primitive," peoples. Robert Alter offers an anthropological reading of what he calls "the primal archaic power of the rite," and he adds literary evidence of its local significance:

> The idea of two parties to a solemn, binding agreement confirming the mutual obligation by dipping hands in the same blood, or exchanging blood smears, is attested in many cultures. In this covenant of ontologically disparate partners, the altar that is sprinkled with half the blood may serve as surrogate for the deity to whose service the altar has been erected. The covenantal rite of casting blood on the people is a climax of the sundry occurrences of blood in this narrative from the Bridegroom of Blood episode onward: the blood of circumcision (itself a covenantal act) that deflected the death to Moses or his child and the blood of the lamb that warded off the Destroyer in Egypt reappear here as the blood of the sacrifice that confirms Israel's everlasting bond with God.[13]

There is surely merit in these suggestions. Oaths and pledges were in many places sealed in blood—although usually in one's own blood—to symbolize the soul's earnestness and veracity. Moses, looking for ways to enlist the people's passions, may also be exploiting again the successful use of blood on the eve of their departure from Egypt, when each family gained protection and redemption by personally marking its own door in lamb's blood. Once again, Moses gets the people to participate in a physical act, this time to seal with blood the new agreement with the Lord, in the hope and expectation that the sworn covenant will again be redemptive.

But this account slides over relevant biblical facts about the previous use of blood—for example, that its use (on doorposts) in Egypt was commanded by the Lord, not improvised by Moses; or that a different word was used for "basins"; or that the people in preparing for the Exodus were active agents, not passive subjects, in the painting of blood, done carefully using branches of hyssop. It slides over that fact that, whatever the practices of neighboring peoples, none of the covenants previously recorded in the Torah involved the use of blood, not even the one God made with Abram between the sacrificial pieces (Gen. 15). More important, the account downplays several aspects of this episode that, when considered in light of Moses's character, his notion of leadership, and his view of the people, are disquieting and weird. Where might Moses have learned about such a ritual? Needless to say, he did not study cultural anthropology, and he was not, to our knowledge, a party to any previous blood-soaked covenantal confirmation—not as a prince in Egypt, not while living with Jethro in Midian. True, his father-in-law was a priest with experience in offering sacrifices (see 18:12); I have speculated that perhaps it was Moses's long association with Jethro that triggered his interest in the divine and opened him to God's call. But Jethro is a man of measure and peace, and there is no account of his engaging in blood-stained rituals or blood-sealed oaths. Moses was not involved in the one sacrifice—not bloody—that Jethro performed during his visit. More important, what moves Moses to this particular act? Measures are needed to ensure that the people will remember their free consent to the covenant, but why does Moses choose *this bloody* means of remembrance?

Moses, cut from cloth wholly different from the people, conducts his relation to God on the high plane of intellect. He himself has no need of physical signs and wonders[14]; he has no taste for sacrifices. For him, a verbal agreement would be sufficient. He has shown himself impatient with the people and their corporeal neediness and fickle ways. He remembers how they were overawed by the Lord's declaration of the Decalogue and stood far off, and how the Lord, in response, told Moses to give them altars as a means of approaching Him. Verbal consent will be insufficient, he seems to feel; they need some dramatic gesture that will forever impress upon their memories the agreement they have just made. Blood, not mere ideas—*that* will impress them, *that* will unite them, *that* will awe and inspire them.

Not a bad idea for a leader without prior experience in such things, but is it necessarily wise? What passions will be aroused, especially among these people, if they are bathed in blood with no prior warning or explanation? Can those passions, once aroused, be controlled? How can such a crude and bloody scene support a covenantal way of life that teaches order and measure, and that opposes exactly this human penchant for wildness and violence? In his effort to engage the people, Moses—forgive me for saying so—overdoes it.[15]

Perhaps I am misreading this. Perhaps, as Alter hints, this covering of blood represents a renewal of the Abrahamic covenant of circumcision—itself a small act of bloodshed in lieu of human sacrifice that is the sign of the covenant between the Children of Israel and God. Moses, we recall, had failed to circumcise his sons and nearly died for that failure. His wife's act of circumcision, which she described as making Moses a "bridegroom of blood," saved his life. Perhaps Moses sees himself as re-consecrating the people to the original Abrahamic agreement.

This is a plausible suggestion, but ultimately not convincing. The covenant with Abraham marked (fittingly) by circumcision—done, we must remember, at God's command—promised fertility, multiplicity, and land. The new covenant promises peoplehood, rule of law, and the goals of righteousness and holiness. A different sign and symbolic marking would be called for. And God has not (yet) called for one.

My reading is supported by one more literary fact. After Moses has thrown the blood on the people, the text immediately turns to other matters, leaving the blood-spattered people without a further word. We will not hear of them again for eight chapters. When we finally do look in on them, they will be demanding that Aaron make them other gods to replace the long-absent Moses: for the people, if not for the reader, the episode of the golden calf is *the* textual sequel to experiencing the so-called blood of the covenant. We are invited to ponder how passions

aroused by being bathed in blood (at the hand of Moses) might soon find
unruly expression—and at the first opportunity.*

"And They Saw the God of Israel"

God neither endorses nor opposes Moses's deed. He remains silent. Perhaps He is waiting for the next act, the one He had asked for. Only now do
Moses, Aaron, and the others finally obey God's charge to ascend the
mountain. Having left the "bloodied" people behind, we join the party on
the mountain, hoping thereby to discover what the Lord had intended:

> Then ascended (*vayya'al*) Moses and Aaron, Nadab and
> Abihu, and seventy of the elders of Israel; and they *saw*
> (*vayyire'u*) the God of Israel (*'elohe yisra'el*); and under His
> feet [was] like the work of paved sapphire stone, and like the
> very heaven in clearness. And [or "But"] upon the nobles
> of the Children of Israel (*'atsile bene yisra'el*) He laid not
> ("stretched not out"; *lo' shalach*) His hand; and they *beheld*
> (*vayyechezu*) God, and *they ate and they drank.* (24:9–11; em-
> phasis added)

This is, to say the least, an astonishing tale. Taken literally, it strains
credulity. Did these mere human beings literally see, with their own eyes,
a visible—corporeal—God of Israel? Did they really have a picnic in the
divine Presence? These bold and shocking claims led traditional interpreters to find alternative and apologetic readings. Ibn Ezra said the
group experienced a prophetic vision.[16] Maimonides (*Guide of the Perplexed* I. 4) insisted that they experienced a purely intellectual perception, not a real seeing with the eyes. Onkelos, in his Aramaic translation,
completely changed the text: "And they saw their sacrifices that had been
accepted, as though they had eaten and drunk."[17]

---

*Needless to say, we are not suggesting that the strewn "blood of the covenant"
was still on their faces forty days later at the golden calf. The blood can be washed
off—even in the desert—but its effects on the soul may linger.

Paradoxically, some interpreters in our more secular age appear more inclined to take the report at face value, especially since the description of what the group "saw" is confined to the platform "beneath God's feet." Robert Alter calls the "seeing" an actual "beholding" and refers to the eating and drinking as "a communion feast enjoyed by the elders at God's feet."[18] Brevard Childs, though pointing out that what they saw was "only an approximate analogy to the reality itself," sees in the account an "awe-inspiring majesty leading far beyond the human imagination"; he adds that we have here a special category of genuine perception.[19] Most commentators seem to agree that the elders on the mountain were, one way or another, vouchsafed a special revelation from the Lord.

I confess to having doubts. Several things give us pause—indeed, do so right from the start. According to God's instructions, this elite group was supposed to go up the mountain and prostrate themselves (or worship) from afar. But according to the text, they did no such thing.[20] We do not have to treat them as disobedient. Perhaps they were on their way to prostrating themselves, fully in the mood, when something else occurred.

Before trying to say what that might have been, we should consider what the Lord may have had in mind by summoning this group up the mountain. The entire picture, symbolized by their physical ascent, suggests the goal of closer communion between Israel and God. Although the people as a whole may have wanted a closer connection with the Lord, they were too frightened (and unfit) to get any closer. Any communion would have to be mediated by this elite group, a task their experience on the mountain might prepare them to assume. How would they conduct themselves? Would they exhibit the proper spirit and decorum—a mixture of awe and wonder, reverence and attraction, distance and nearness? The elders—and Aaron and sons—may be auditioning for future employment in managing the sacred things.

But the ultimate target of this experience may have been Moses (and the reader). Depending on how Aaron, his sons, and the elders perform, Moses (and we) may learn something important about how communion with the Lord should and should not take place. If he (and we) have learned something about this subject from the ordinances denouncing

Canaanite practices, and if we have learned something from the blood-strewing episode we just witnessed, we may learn something new also from seeing how the elite perform. From all these clues, Moses (and we) may be better prepared to see the need for the extensive instruction the Lord will Himself soon provide.

So what really happened to the nobles on the mountain? Imagine yourself one of the elect, a person of broader experience and (you believe) higher sensibilities than the common people. Unlike the multitude, you are moved not only by fear but also by wonder. You have a taste for beauty and a love of finery. You are honored to have been invited to ascend to the "place" of the Lord. In what frame of mind do you climb upward? What will you expect to encounter? It is the heat of the day. Your senses will be on high alert. You will be anxious but eager, looking keenly for a numinous appearance that will suddenly arrive, in answer to your hopes and longings. As you climb in the hot sun, your imagination also heats up. With each gust of wind or rush of sand or movement of dry shrubbery, you begin to "see" things before you. These sightings are at first uncertain and vague, and you strain to see more clearly. Suddenly, there it is: a glorious "vision" before you. It arrests you and overwhelms you with its beauty, exactly as you have hoped. You are having an out-of-body experience; you must be in the presence of God—the God *of Israel*. (You do not ask yourself how you are able to recognize that it is *He*.) You dare not look directly at His face; you cast down your eyes to behold the ethereal spectacle of a sapphire-paved firmament beneath what you imagine can only be the "feet of God."

Whence came this vision? Was it a "godsend"—even if it was only the product of a heightened imagination—like Abram's vision in the covenant between the sacrificial pieces (Gen. 15), or Jacob's dream-vision of the angel-filled ladder (Gen. 28)? The text lends no support to this view: it does *not* say that the Lord appeared to them or that He came to them in a vision. The agency is all theirs: "they saw." Rather than a real sighting, was this just a wish-fulfilling projection of an aestheticized notion of what the God of Israel must look like: beautiful, splendid, glorious, luminous—like the heavens above? The nobles saw nobility incarnate, and it pleased them greatly. They celebrated the happy event with a picnic lunch in the Divine Presence.[21]

The nobles' experience on the mountain is the upper-class counterpart of the people's response to the behavior of the mountain during
the pronouncement of the Decalogue. The people had a synesthetic experience, "seeing the thunder" (20:15), and it frightened the life out of
them; the nobles had a supra- (or hyper-) sensory experience, "seeing the
God of Israel," and it delighted them thoroughly.

Needless to say, this is largely speculation, based partly on well-
known ideas about how desolate landscapes are especially apt to inspire
religious visions, and partly on reasoning backward from the beautiful
picture the nobles "saw"—and they really did see something, whether
or not it was "real"—to what they might have hoped to see. But it is not
entirely speculation. Several peculiarities in the text support such a
reading.

First, two different verbs for "seeing" are used that I translated as
"saw" and "beheld": *ra'ah* and *chazah*. The first is usually the word used
to describe an ordinary act of visual sense-perception: the eye's taking
in the definite look of a visible object. The second is used, mainly in prophetic literature (as in Isa. 1:1), to describe a kind of beholding *beyond*
what can be seen in the physical present. It is used to describe what a
prophet or seer "sees" in an ecstatic state, what someone "sees" when he is
deceived by appearance, and what someone "sees" with his intellect.[22] In
our present story, what "they saw (*ra'ah*)" becomes in the very next verse,
"they beheld" (*chazah*). They very likely beheld something not physically
present, perhaps something present only in their own imaginations.

Second, and more telling, the nobles have a shockingly prosaic reaction to their astounding vision: "and they beheld God and they ate
and they drank." Unlike Moses at the burning bush, they do not hide
their eyes; they feel neither awe nor fear; they just eat and drink. This
eating and drinking are not presented as a ceremonial meal; there is no
hint that they were enjoying a "meal shared with God," in the form of
the so-called peace offering. They appear to be pleased but not overawed
by what they have "beheld." Had they really "seen" God's glory, would
they have had lunch with Him? As we will soon learn, Moses, genuinely
in the presence of God, does not eat or drink for forty days and forty
nights.

Finally, and decisively, we have not only the nobles' reaction to their "vision" but also the Lord's reaction or, rather, *non*reaction: "and upon the nobles (*'atsilim*) of the Children of Israel He laid not His hand." The usual interpretation of this remark relates it to the warning, given only later to Moses, that "man cannot see My face and live" (33:20); for such readers, it seems to express the text's amazement that the elders could behold God and not die. But even this reading need not imply that the Lord was pleased with what they "saw" and how they responded. The text, most strangely, reports an absence: it tells us only what the Lord *does not do.* It tells us of a forbearance that would make sense if the Lord were in fact displeased with what just occurred.

Why, and with whom, might He be displeased? Toward whom is He staying His hand? Toward the "*nobles*"—the word *'atsil* occurs in the Torah only here. Who are they? Certainly the seventy elders, and almost certainly also Nadab and Abihu: were they excluded, the text would have said instead "toward the *elders* (*zekenim*)." Might Aaron be a noble as well? Perhaps. Is Moses? I doubt it. The entire chapter seems to distinguish between Moses and the nobles to show Moses (and us) the difference in how they relate to the divine. The nobles "see"; Moses hears. That difference points precisely to the problem (discussed at length in Chapter Three): the uninstructed live following their eyes, whereas the Torah's way of life arrives through the ears: "we will do and we will hear."

As to the reason for His displeasure, Rashi attributes it to "their attempt to catch a glimpse of the Supreme Being," and he regards His forbearance as temporary:

> But it was only because God did not wish to disturb the joy caused by the Giving of the Torah, that He *did not punish them instantly, but* waited (postponed the punishment) for Nadab and Abihu until the day when the Tabernacle was dedicated, *when they were stricken with death,* and for the elders until *the event of which the text relates,* (Num.11:16) "And when the people complained . . . and the fire of the Lord burned among them and destroyed the edge of the camp," referring to those who were the nobles of the camp.[23]

But the reason for displeasure (and for delayed punishment, if any) may be more prosaic. The Lord does not blame the nobles for illicit desires or even for the vision they experienced. They, no less than the masses, regrettably can encounter the divine only in sensual and corporeal form. To be sure, their approach to the divine is more refined and aesthetically uplifting than the bloody communal sacrifices. But their projected vision of the God of Israel is, in a sense, a psychic or "spiritual" violation of the principle that forbids making images of the divine. To "picture" Him is to misunderstand.[24]

Whether displeased or not with the nobles, the Lord says nothing about what they saw and did. But He now breaks silence for the first time since ordering Moses to bring the party up the mountain. His remarks function as His commentary on the two episodes just concluded, as well as His introduction to the momentous events that will follow.

Moses to the Mountaintop: An Addendum to the Law

The Lord has seen enough of the "experiment" with the elders, Aaron, and his sons: the nobles have failed the test. Or perhaps they do not so much fail as act according to their all-too-human limitations. Either way, the Lord now thinks that Moses will have seen enough to be ready to accept the grand addition He must now append to His teaching:

> And the Lord said unto Moses: "Ascend [singular] to Me into the mountain and be there; and I will give you the tables of stone (*luchoth ha'even*), and the law (*torah* [singular]) and the commandment (*mitsvah* [singular]), which I have written, to teach them." (24:12)

"And": the Lord's words are to be understood as a continuation of, via a comment on, what has just occurred. To put it crudely: "Did you see that, Moses? Now get yourself up here, pronto, and prepare to stick around. I have big news for you." What big news; Tables of stone (not your book on parchment), already written by the Lord, for the purposes of teaching "them" (the people, the nobles, everyone?) *the law* and *the commandment*—new terms both and both singular. What law and what commandment? A law and a commandment that will promote the goal of helping Israel commune with the Lord, avoiding the defects of the efforts just exposed and moderating the weaknesses in the human soul from which they arise: a Dionysian taste for blood and a tendency for merging and wildness (soon to be made manifest), and an Apollonian aestheticism and love of visible beauty. Spoiler alert: what is new will be the law and commandment of the Tabernacle, where both will have a home, but under divine rule and order.

We should not get ahead of ourselves. We must first see how Moses responds to the Lord's latest charge:

> And Moses rose up, and Joshua his minister ("chief assistant"; *mesharetho*); and Moses ascended into the mountain of God. And unto the elders he said: "Abide for us here (*shevu-lanu vazeh*), until we return unto you (*nashuv 'aleykhem*); and, behold, Aaron and Hur are with you; whosoever has a cause (*devarim*), let him come near unto them." And Moses went up into the mountain, and the cloud covered the mountain. (24:13–15)

Moses obeys God's order, but not exactly. Once again he takes liberties—more precisely, he takes Joshua. This is strange on several counts. Where had Joshua been that he could be recruited for the climb? He was not mentioned among the party of nobles summoned to go up and make obeisance, and he is clearly not one of the elders. Where did he come from? Once again, as at his first entrance before the battle with Amalek, he suddenly appears out of nowhere, just when Moses wants him. There Moses told him to raise an army; here Moses takes him along for reasons known only to himself. We notice that Moses does so without instruction—nay, against instruction: the antecedent command to ascend (v. 12) was in the singular, and the original order, also singular, was emphatic: Moses *alone* shall come near unto the Lord (v. 2).

Joshua, known to us so far only as a military man, is described here as Moses's minister or chief aide-de-camp.[25] One might expect Moses would leave him behind, to serve as his eyes and ears and to govern in his absence. Not so. Moses, before ascending, turns to the elders and deputizes Aaron and Hur—another character who appears out of nowhere and who also has been seen only at the battle with Amalek, as Aaron's partner in holding up Moses's hands—and puts them jointly in charge. More precisely, he puts them in charge of the "judicial" task of resolving disputes that might break out, a task for which they have no experience and, without Joshua, for which they have no natural enforcer. Moses makes no provision for other kinds of issues that might—and do—erupt while he is gone. In language that eerily echoes Abraham's speech to the lads when he and Isaac ascended Mount Moriah—"Abide for yourselves here" (*shevu lachem poh*), and "we will return to you" (*nashuvah 'aleykhem*) (Gen. 22:5)—Moses bids the elders farewell and ascends into the mountain.

In the end, Moses does what he had been told to do: he alone goes up to the [top of the] mountain. The mountain is now covered by a cloud, anticipating the imminent arrival of the Divine Presence. We eagerly await news of what will happen to him up there. But in our concern for the missing Moses, we should not forget that someone else has disappeared. Where is Joshua? Moses presumably left him behind, somewhere below the peak—let's say, in a camp halfway up—and will encounter him when, weeks later, he descends from on high (32:17). What function Joshua could possibly play, isolated midway up, we cannot even imagine; yet we are made aware that he will not be present in the camp below, should Aaron (and Hur) have need of him. Moses's incomplete obedience to God's command, to "ascend alone," may prove costly.[26]

The True Summit Meeting

We readers of this account, like the people on the ground and like the elders, have now lost sight of Moses. We strain to see what can be seen. As the curtain comes down on this episode—and on the whole section of Exodus that presents the revelation at Sinai and the precepts of the Torah—our last view is at once elevated, awe inspiring, and terrifying:

> And dwelt (*vayyishkon*) the glory of the Lord (*kevod-Y-H-V-H*) upon Mount Sinai, and the cloud covered it six days; and the

> seventh day He called unto Moses out of the midst of the
> cloud. And the appearance of the glory of the Lord was like
> devouring fire on the top of the mountain in the eyes of the
> Children of Israel. (24:16–17)

In elevated and poetic language, we hear the preparation for the special
revelation to be given to Moses—a revelation, we have suggested, made
necessary by the large psychosocial difficulties that were exposed in the
events we just witnessed.

The glory of Y-H-V-H[27] "dwelt"—abided—upon the mountain: as
Cassuto points out,[28] the first word, *yishkon,* "dwelt," anticipates the subject of the concluding portion of Exodus, the building of the *mishkan,*
"Tabernacle," a sanctuary that will enable the Lord to *dwell* in the midst
of His people (see 25:8). Following a common biblical pattern first seen
in the story of Creation (Gen. 1–2:3), in which six days of action prepare
for its completion on the seventh, Moses is allowed six days to prepare
himself to meet the Lord.[29] On the seventh, he is summoned out of the
cloud to appear before Him. Overcome with awe as we read these words,
we hold our collective breath.

The people on the ground are also holding their breath, but more
in terror than in awe. They have not had the benefit of reading the last
verse. Unlike the last time when there were big doings on the mountain,
they do not "see the thunder" (20:15)—there is none to be "seen"—but
what they do see is even more frightening. In their eyes, the text takes
pains to emphasize, the glory of the Lord looks like a devouring fire. And
Moses has gone to meet it. We can surely forgive them for wondering
whether he will get out alive:

> And Moses entered into the midst of the cloud, and went up
> into the mountain; and Moses was in the mountain forty days
> and forty nights. (24:18)

The story concludes by setting up suspenseful expectations. We
readers know, because we are here told, that Moses will be in the mountain forty days and forty nights, living on a plane that transcends the

necessities of human life; indirectly, we also learn that he will return. But the people on the ground have no such reassurance. Days and weeks will pass, and Moses will not return to them. While they worry and we wait, and while nothing appears on the surface to be happening, a new "birth" is quietly incubating during the pregnant forty days and forty nights. At the end of this period, the world of Israel—and of humankind—will never be the same.

S • E • V • E • N • T • E • E • N

"Let Them Make Me a Sanctuary"

oses has entered into the cloud atop Mount Sinai, invited in by the Lord Himself to receive the tables of stone, which the Lord has "personally" inscribed. While the Children of Israel look up awestruck at the fiery mountain, anxious for their leader's welfare, we readers are privileged to hear the conversation taking place in the cloud. To our surprise, there is no talk of tables of stone. Indeed, there is no conversation. Instead, the Lord embarks on a (seven-chapter-long) monologue of instructions for building Him a sanctuary, the so-called Tabernacle or, in Hebrew, *mishkan*. Moses will not say a word.

Readers who were previously thrown off their narrative expectations by the three-chapter-long uninterrupted rehearsal of the ordinances (21–23) may now be completely baffled. Upon reflection, they will have come to see the ordinances as welcome elaborations of the principles enunciated in the Decalogue, and therefore as an indispensable part of the story of people formation. But this Law of the Tabernacle seems at first glance to be utterly unprecedented, both in substance and in manner of exposition. In place of the Lord's heroic deeds during the plagues, the Exodus, and at the Sea of Reeds, and in place of His majestic speeches in the giving of the Law, we now get meticulously detailed plans for a massive building project, for which the Lord plays

451

architect, furniture designer, and interior decorator. His plan for the Tabernacle also includes establishing a hereditary priesthood and instituting animal sacrifices on a massive scale, innovations we readers were not expecting.[1]

What is going on? Why the Tabernacle, and why *this* Tabernacle? Why wasn't the previous legislation sufficient? For whom, and for what, is the Tabernacle—or the sacrifices? What role do they play in the unfolding story of the text and, more important, in the formation of the Israelite people? And why is Moses speechless? In considering these questions over the next three chapters,* I hope to show that the story of the Tabernacle is an essential part of the Exodus narrative and a fitting culmination of the tale that began with the Israelites' enslavement in Egypt—indeed, of the tale that began with the Lord's Creation of the world. Moses, and we readers, must come to see that far from being an afterthought or a foreign interpolation, the Tabernacle occupies a central and indispensable place in the definition and national purpose of the Israelites, equal in importance to their deliverance from slavery in Egypt and to the Law they just received.

A few comments on how I will proceed. Rather than say up front what I think we have learned, I will allow that understanding to emerge from the text, as it unfolds for Moses and for us. Because we are committed not only to learning from the account about the structure and function of the Tabernacle but also to thinking with the account about its meaning and importance, I will not abandon the narrative approach I have followed to this point. We will continue to read as naively as possible, attending to the dramatic situation and taking nothing for granted. To appreciate something as a gift, we must be able to experience it as a surprise. Because of the detailed (not to say boring) character of the material, however, I will depart from my previous line-by-line commen-

---

*This chapter (covering Exodus 25 through all but the last two verses of Exodus 27) will deal with the instructions for the physical structure of the Tabernacle and its appurtenances. Chapter Eighteen (covering Exodus 27:19–29) will deal with the instructions for the priests (their attire and installation), the daily animal sacrifices, and the purpose of the Tent of Meeting. Chapter Nineteen (covering Exodus 30–31) will deal with the other matters connected with the Tabernacle, including the head tax that supports it, the artisans who shall produce it, and Sabbath rest that transcends it.

tary and will rely instead on summaries of various portions of the text in order to concentrate on those passages that will help us answer the larger questions. As a result, many of the finer points will surely get lost. Hoping to make sense of what is going on and why, I will leave those subtler details for another day and another author.[2]

Literary Antecedents

Although we may be surprised to run into the Tabernacle, we readers are not exactly unprepared to think about it. Our previous literary experiences and philosophical reflections are likely to be relevant to the present materials. On the literary side, first, we have encountered passages that beg further attention to how the Israelites should relate to the divine. We recall that *Y-H-V-H's* original offer of the covenant invited the Israelites to become a "kingdom of priests and a holy nation." But until now, they have received very little instruction—except about the singularly important Sabbath—that was explicitly tied to "holiness." And apart from the call for three annual pilgrimage festivals, there has been no reference to ritual observance, forms of worship, or sacrificial offerings and no mention at all of priests.[3] There have been multiple warnings against idolatry, in the Decalogue and in the ordinances, and strong anticipatory condemnations of the religious practices of the Canaanites, whom the Israelites will soon meet in the Promised Land. But they have received virtually no positive instruction about approaching and worshipping the divine.

The need for such guidance became clear in the last chapter. Without instruction, Moses built an altar and offered sacrifice unto the Lord, in a ceremony involving much strewing of blood. Then the elders (and Aaron and his sons Nadab and Abihu), summoned to "bow down from afar off" before the Lord, experienced a sensualized vision of the God of Israel, before which they sat down matter-of-factly to eat and drink. Both of these events reflected an understandable—even laudable— wish to be in contact with the divine, but neither the blood-strewn sacrifice nor the aestheticized vision was satisfactory. Accordingly, we might expect that the Lord would respond by teaching Moses exactly how He should be "approached": in what setting, when and by whom, and in what manner. To readers who have come to see the need for such guidance, the long instruction on the Tabernacle should prove timely and fitting.

Second, we have been alerted to the difference between the way Moses relates to God and the way the people relate to God: the former, steadily and on an intellectual plane; the latter, forgetfully and requiring visible signs and wonders. (When the Lord did reveal Himself to them, while giving the Ten Commandments, they were terrified and wanted no connection with Him at all.) We have just seen an attempt to create an intermediate group between Moses and the people—the elders, Aaron, and his sons—who might mediate between their two approaches to the divine, but that attempt was not successful. And for those who have not yet noticed the difficulty, we will soon have the most important literary clue of all—not an antecedent story but a parallel one, in the mirror of which we can perhaps best understand what the Lord is up to here. Even while the Lord is instructing Moses about the Tabernacle and its appurtenances, brother Aaron and the people are down below, simultaneously constructing and worshipping a golden calf.[4] To really appreciate the present scene of the Lord's instructing Moses about the Tabernacle, we should view it in "split-screen" with the scene of the golden calf. The teaching about the Tabernacle may thus be seen as an anticipatory answer and preferred alternative to the golden calf—a view that will be confirmed later when we read, immediately after the story of the golden calf, about the actual building of the Tabernacle, letter for letter according to the instructions. The narrative structure strongly suggests that the Tabernacle is being built to cabin, to house, to educate, and to elevate the impulses, needs, and passions that find uninstructed expression in the story of the calf.

Finally—still considering literary antecedents—the Tabernacle will be Israel's first big project as a newly covenanted people; yet it is hardly the Bible's first architectural or artistic venture. If we remember what we have read about the previous, often dubious projects reported in the Torah, we will be prepared to hear echoes and make comparisons. In addition to Moses's altar (Ex. 24), there have been multiple acts of building and making. The building of Pithom and Raamses, the store cities for Pharaoh, was the Israelites' only prior construction project, performed as slaves under Pharaoh's command (1:11). Before that, and especially relevant here, we recall humankind's grandiose building venture, the city and tower of Babel, an uninstructed project of the whole human race united, thwarted by the Lord Himself (Gen. 11:1–9).[5] Before that, we have the morally dubious inventor of farming and sacrifices, Cain, fratricidal founder of the first city, whose shady descendants (Lamech and sons) are the founders also of the arts (Gen. 4). Before that, we have Adam and Eve, inventors of the needle and makers of (flimsy) fig-leaf aprons to clothe their nakedness (Gen. 3:7), whose defective handicraft the Lord Himself remedied with a gift of superior coverings made of animal skins (Gen. 3:21).

In contrast to these dubious or defective human artful undertakings, we remember two highly successful divine projects, both of them very relevant here. We recall Noah's ark, the only previous "joint" building project, in which Noah's hands faithfully carry out the Lord's instructions (with detailed measurements, given—as here—in cubits) to save a living remnant from the impending watery devastation.[6] And before that, "In the [very] beginning," we have the celebratory account of the Lord's six-day Creation of the heavens and the earth, bringing order out of chaos through acts of articulate speech and providing a terrestrial home for humankind, made in His image. And as the perfection of that story, we recall that the Lord completed His creation by hallowing the seventh day, the first insertion of "holiness" into the created order; this becomes the basis for the Sabbath teaching in the Decalogue, and, as we will see, an enlarged Sabbath teaching appended to the Law of the Tabernacle.

Readers who have noticed the failings and defects of prior human projects (especially in Babel and Egypt), seen against the successes and perfections of the Creation and of Noah's ark, should be interested to see whether the new (joint) building project can correct the errors of prior human artistry and, more important, complete the Lord's own acts of making. Noah's ark, built according to a divine blueprint, was the vehicle for a re-Creation of terrestrial life. Can the Tabernacle, built according to a divine blueprint and housing the (different) Ark of the Covenant, become the vehicle for the world's second sanctification: a sacred space for the indwelling of the Lord among His people? Might the Tabernacle function somehow as a "completion" of Creation?

These three literary experiences lead us to hope that the Tabernacle may simultaneously (1) answer to deep human need and longing, (2) serve as both concession to and guidance of dangerous human impulses, and (3) function as a completion and culmination of the Lord's plans for Israel and, through it, for humankind. These hopes rest not only on literary echoes but also on philosophical reflections concerning important unresolved questions.

Lingering Questions

The literary antecedents echoed in this chapter contain several lingering questions—in contemporary terms, psychosocial, political, and theological questions—that the Tabernacle will also specifically address. Readers of this commentary should easily recognize these questions, as I have flagged them along the way. In the psychosocial realm, certain troublesome and dangerous human predilections—especially those leading to interpersonal conflict—have already been dealt with in the ordinances (*mishpatim*). But deeper and ambiguous tendencies remain unaddressed. What, for example, to think and do about the human penchant for artfulness and creativity: on one hand, a grateful expression of our God-given and Godlike capacities; on the other hand, a proud temptation (as in Babel) to human self-glorification? What to think and do about the love and imitation of visible beauty: on one hand, a celebration of order and proportion; on the other hand, an elevation of the aesthetic above the righteous and the holy, and an invitation to idolatry? What to think and do about the impulse to sacrifice: on one hand, an acknowledgment of and submission to the divine, born of a wish to know God; on the other hand, an expression of human bloody-mindedness and penchant for chaos, born of a wish to merge with the divine or manipulate it through gifts, on the proud assumption that "It" likes what we like? What to think and do about the human inclination to trust seeing over all other senses, to represent all things in visible images, and to regard "out of sight" as "out of mind"—a predilection especially problematic when the God Who calls is invisible, while even the loftiest visible things (the sun, the moon, and the stars) are mute about how to live? What to think and do about humanity's twin but opposed tendencies toward mastery and servility: thinking and acting as if we were divine (and lording it over "lesser" folk and lesser creatures), and thinking and acting as if we were no better than the beasts? What to think and do about the tendency of human beings to take comfort by banding together in large groups and the tendency of large groups to let loose wilder passions of the soul?

We wonder whether God's Way can address—and safely make room for—these deep-seated human needs, passions, and tendencies, through means that go beyond the ability of the ordinances to control specific conduct and prevent mutual wrongdoing. Might the Tabernacle speak more directly and profoundly to the deepest and most dangerous passions of the soul, giving them their place in the economy of psychic and social life but keeping them under (divinely prescribed) order and measure? Might it make a safe home for both of what the Greeks called Apollo and Dionysus: for artistic expression, the love of visible beauty and harmony, and the devotion to seeing and beholding, as well as for the urge to sacrifice, the longing to efface boundaries and merge with the divine in shared ecstasies?

Next, there are lingering political issues, primarily about the relationship between the leaders and the led. How does one mold a collection of ex-slaves (now but two months out of Egypt) into a genuine political community capable of self-governance? The covenant and the Law are, of course, central instruments in this process, as is the shared history of slavery and deliverance. But would not some common projects and practices—not only collective self-defense in war but also communal self-advancement in peace—make a big difference? Might the building of the Tabernacle—with contributions from all the people and with the collective actions needed to disassemble and reassemble it as the people move from place to place—provide the shared work that can build community more securely than words? Might the communal practice of animal sacrifice institutionalize a common longing for the divine and shared wishes to express gratitude or to atone for sin before God?

And what about the governance of the people? Is the leadership of Moses the lawgiver, backed by his judicial bureaucracy, sufficient? Can the community progress from hierarchy to equity by substituting the rule of law for the rule of Moses? When Moses goes, what will attach people to the rule of his (or rather God's) law? Is not something more than law required—namely, ritual and worship—to sustain a community, especially for a people that aspires to holiness and a connection with the divine? Even while Moses is still here, does he—in his almost superhuman virtue—have what it takes to address the people's earthier longings? Does not a "kingdom of priests" require actual priests?

The last comment about priests points to lingering theological questions. The Children of Israel have just entered into a covenant with the Lord at Mount Sinai. How can that relationship be preserved, especially after they leave the mountain and head for Canaan? Does its preservation depend upon repeated revelations and encounters—with the cloud, the fire, and the divine voice? Or are there less episodic, more permanent, less threatening ways to perpetuate the relationship: from the human side, through remembrance, ritual, and sacrifice, and from the divine side, through other forms of "being present"? Can the Tabernacle provide the needed venue for ongoing communication?

Lastly, what would be the ultimate purpose of such a "meeting house," and whom would it benefit? Would it mainly satisfy human needs and contain and regulate human weaknesses, while also promoting community solidarity and identity? Or would it—also or instead—satisfy the "desire" of the Lord that He be *known* and that He gain glory from His people, not only as a "man of war," as a liberator or lawgiver, or even as an architect but also as an abiding and familiar Presence in their lives?

Having reminded ourselves what may be at stake, we are ready to attend to the Lord's instructions for the Tabernacle. To experience them as Moses did, we will follow them in the order they were given to him, pausing in those places where we find help answering the many questions just posed. By the end, we hope to weave the various threads into a plausible picture of the Tabernacle's meaning that addresses all of our lingering questions. Two main ideas will guide our reading: the Tabernacle as a necessary concession to human need and limitation; on the other hand, the Tabernacle as a culminating fulfillment of the Creation and of God's Way for humankind.[7]

A Synopsis: The Beginning and the End

Moses expects to hear about tables of stone. The Lord speaks to him instead about stuff: fine goods that Moses is to collect from the people, gifts to the Lord that will serve as materials for a new building project:

> And the Lord spoke unto Moses, saying: "Speak unto the Children of Israel, that they take for Me a contribution ("dedicated donation"; *terumah*); of every man whose heart makes him willing you shall take ("receive") My contribution. And this is the contribution that you shall take of them: gold, and silver, and bronze; and blue, and purple, and scarlet [yarns], and fine linen, and goats' hair; and rams' skins dyed red, and sealskins, and acacia wood; oil for the light, spices for the anointing oil, and for the sweet incense; onyx stones, and stones to be set, for the ephod, and for the breastplate." (25:1–7)

The project will begin with a call for voluntary donations*—from each according to his wish and capacity—collected from everyone willing to dedicate something to the Lord. The entire people, Moses is taught, should be allowed to contribute to this project, not under compulsion as with Pharaoh's projects but freely. Fittingly, the first act of this newly covenanted people is to be a gift—an act of grace—offered out of each person's private possessions. Every Israelite will make a personal investment in the community and in its collective aspiration.

---

*Although the project does indeed begin with such a request, the seven-chapter *account* of the Lord's instructions begins with the phrase, "And the Lord spoke unto Moses, saying." That phrase will be repeated six more times in Exodus 25–31, each time to introduce a distinct subject and task into the otherwise uninterrupted account of the Lord's directives. The seventh occasion precedes the Lord's (renewed) instructions about keeping the Sabbath, in passages to which we will return in Chapter Nineteen. It is worth pointing out at the start that the seven-part instruction refers to six different pieces of work and then to the day of rest that completes it. This is the first of several ways in which the account of the Tabernacle invites comparison with the story of Creation (Gen. 1–2:3), something we shall consider explicitly at the end of our exploration (in Chapter Twenty-Two).

But the offering should also be bountiful. The gifts to be solicited are valuable and costly: precious metals (gold, silver, and bronze[8]), expensive dyed yarns, animal skins, timber, oil and spices, and precious gems. Even from the account of the mere materials, we anticipate something fine and lovely to look at—and also to smell and to feel (spices, anointing oil, incense). And where would these ex-slaves find precious metals or fabrics? Attentive readers will remember that they received gifts of silver and gold jewelry (and fine clothing) from the Egyptian people on their way out of bondage. Was this the purpose of those gifts? Is the Tabernacle the only object on which they might be lavished?

Having begun with the materials, the Lord concludes His introduction with succinct remarks about what they are for and how they will be used, in the process identifying the other aspects of the project: its form or idea, its makers, and its purpose:

> "And let *them make* (*ve'asu*) Me a sanctuary (*miqdash*), *that* I may *dwell among them* (*veshakhanti bethokham*). According to *all that I show you* [singular], the *pattern* of the tabernacle (*tavnith hamishkan*), and the *pattern* of all the furniture thereof, even so shall *you* [plural] make (*ta'asu*) it." (25:8–9; emphasis added)

Regarding this purpose, three things are noteworthy. First, the Lord wants to have a "*sanctuary*"—a place that is *qadosh* or "holy," a place that is set apart and dedicated to Him. Second, "*they*"—the Children of Israel—should make it for Him; He will not make it for Himself. Third and most significantly, He wants it in order to "dwell" among them. The purpose is simultaneously "political" and "religious." The people's first positive communal and community-forming act is to build a sacred place—dedicated to the Lord yet central to their collective being—whereby He may continue to be present in their midst. (What this means we shall consider later.)

Readers familiar with the Tabernacle—and with its later replacement by Solomon's Temple, not to speak of modern houses of worship—may not notice that this call for a humanly constructed sanctuary is a radical idea. In context, it is news to both Moses and the reader. In the

Song at the Sea (containing the Bible's only previous use of the word *miqdash*, "sanctuary," there vocalized as *miqqedash* in the Masoretic tradition), Moses had foreseen that the Lord would bring the Israelites to a sanctuary of His own devising:

> "You will bring them in, and You will plant them *in the mountain* of Your inheritance, the *place,* which, O Lord, *You have made* for Your abode (*leshivtekha*): the *sanctuary* (*miqqedash*), O Lord, that *Your hands* have established." (15:17; emphasis added)

But, perhaps correcting the Song, the Lord now makes it clear that He has in mind a different sanctified space, not high on the mountain but in the camp, made by the hands of the people. Until now, Israel had been commanded to keep a weekly Sabbath day as sanctified time unto the Lord; now, Moses learns, they must erect for Him a sanctified space—physical, visible, and tangible. Sacred time is not sufficient to attach the people to their God. The people must also be able to behold and to live always in the presence of an embodied sacred place. But there is more.

This sacred space is radical in another respect. It is not, as in some pagan cultures, to be a "house" in which God lives: the Lord does not say, "that I may *live in it*" but "that I may *dwell among them.*"[9] The sanctuary will be the locus of the Lord's Presence, of His "indwelling" among and toward His people. (Just how and why are mysteries to which we will return.) As we will later be told, the *mishkan* is to be the Tent of Meeting between the Lord and His people. Its portability is of the essence: wherever the Israelites go, the Tent of Meeting goes with them, open for a rendezvous with God.

As to who is to make the Tabernacle, the first word—but not the last—is that the people shall make it: it is to be a community project, for the Lord. Just as they shall supply the materials, so, it seems, shall they do the building: "Let *them* make me. . . ." But as we will soon learn, some among them, gifted in the arts and crafts, will be summoned to play singular parts in executing the designs: artistic genius will play a part in this creation, but only under divine direction.[10]

The materials given, the makers identified, and the purpose stated, all that is left is to address the form—the shape or pattern (*tavnith*)—for the construction and the furnishings. These patterns, the Lord tells Moses (and not for the last time), He will show him aloft. Afterward, Moses must instruct the people, in their making, to imitate the patterns precisely. Are we to understand that there is a visible and physical *mishkan*—or dwelling place of the Lord—on the mountain or in the heavens? Or is the pattern not visible but intelligible, to be conveyed in measured and measuring speech? Or—a radical thought—is the "original" celestial "pattern" not an embodied dwelling place but the arrangement and configuration of the heavenly bodies, the measures and proportions of which can then be embodied in the geometry and numerology of the earthly Tabernacle?[11] All we know is that there is a pattern to be seen above that is to serve as the model for the *mishkan* below. The plans for its construction follow immediately.

Before investigating those plans, it may be instructive to compare this (nine-verse) synopsis of the Lord's building project with the (nine-verse) story of the city and tower of Babel (Gen. 11:1–9). That human project began after the Flood, in fearful and proud defiance of God's injunction to be fruitful and multiply and *to spread out* over the whole earth. Afraid of further natural calamity and not trusting in God's providence or His new covenant with humankind through Noah, the people took matters into their own hands. They too began with the materials, man-made bricks, created by firing moistened dust of the ground, a defective parody of the Lord's creation of man. The Lord animated the ruddy dust of the ground with His breath of life; the Babel builders whitened the ruddy earth by means of fire, the principle not of life but of deadly transformation. Bricks in hand, the human builders began to build a city—an artificial and permanent dwelling comprising houses with closed doors, not a community of tents open to the world—with a tower whose top would be in heaven: either an effort to connect with the heavenly powers aloft out of fear or an effort to render them irrelevant out of pride.[12] The stated purpose: to "make us a name, lest we be scattered abroad upon the face of the whole earth." A self-made and godless home for the human race and an act of complete self-re-creation, Babel stands as a refutation of God and His creation and His covenant with humankind.[13] By contrast, the Tabernacle will be a completion of both the Creation and the Law, as God prepares to dwell among His creatures and to know and be known by them in this gifted terrestrial place for His indwelling.

The Heart of the Tabernacle

After His introductory synopsis, the Lord proceeds to describe the blueprints for the various parts of the Tabernacle. He begins not with the building itself but with the holy articles to be kept inside. The reason is obvious: their holiness exceeds that of the Tabernacle, which exists only to protect them. The objects for the Holy of Holies are dealt with first.[14]

First to be described, and first in importance, is the Ark (*'aron*), a rectangular box to be made of acacia wood, overlaid in pure gold inside and out, and adorned with golden molding all the way around.[15] Four golden rings shall be mounted, two on each side (the exact placement is unclear: either at the corners or at the feet), through which gold-covered poles shall be permanently inserted with which to transport the Ark when it must be moved. The purpose of the Ark is to house the "Testimony" ("witness"; *ha'eduth*) of the Lord: "And you shall put into the Ark the Testimony that I shall give unto you" (25:16). And what shall we understand by the "Testimony"? Moses is not yet told, but we imagine it will be the aforementioned tables of divinely inscribed stone: the (as yet unidentified) guiding words of the Lord, an eternal gift to His people and a witness to the covenant between them.

After the Ark itself, the Lord prescribes the plans for its cover (*kapporeth*), also to be made of pure gold.[16] This is no ordinary lid. Out of the same single piece of covering gold, two cherubs shall be fashioned, one on each end of the Ark cover, with outspread wings covering the lid. Although the form of the cherubim is not described,[17] they are to face each other and both are to glance downward—at once signaling the importance of the Ark (and its contents) below them while averting their gaze from what might be above them. The covering is to be placed on the Ark from above, and—the Lord repeats—into the Ark Moses shall place the Testimony that the Lord will give to him.

The golden representations of cherubim recall for us the Torah's only previous mention of these beings, at the end of the Garden of Eden story. There, upon the expulsion of Adam and Eve following their disobedience, the Lord placed (genuine) cherubim—also no description given—to guard the path to the Tree of Life (Gen. 3:24). In that story, the cherubim signaled the end of the time when human beings might live innocently in the presence of God. Might (the likenesses of) the cherubim in *this* story and on the *kapporeth* signal the possibility of atonement and a return to living with the Lord? Could the Ark and its contents be, for the people, the true "tree of life"?

Sure enough, the ark cover is not purely for adornment. It will be the site of further revelation and instruction, from God to Moses:

> "And there I will meet with you [singular], and I will speak with you from above the ark cover, from between the two cherubim that are upon the Ark of the Testimony, of all things that I will give you in commandment unto the Children of Israel." (25:22)

From above the Ark containing the Testimony of His covenant and foundational teachings, and from the "empty throne" between the cherubim, the Lord will continue to meet and speak with Moses, issuing new commands, as needed, for the people to follow. Moses and the Israelites still need revelation and prophecy. As the people travel from Sinai, the Tabernacle will replace the mountain as the place of meeting, and the Lord will not abandon them. From then on, at least throughout their wanderings in the wilderness, the word of the Lord will originate from *within* the community, from within this sanctified space, in a portion of the Tabernacle that will be called "the Holy of Holies." (Later biblical passages will refer to the wings of the cherubim as the seat of the Lord and the Ark as His footstool.)

Readers may wonder whether the crafting of the cherubim violates the Decalogue's injunction against making graven images, a question raised already by traditional commentators.[18] But the prohibition banned images of *natural* creatures, which the cherubim are not. Moreover, unlike the golden calf, which Aaron will make and the people will worship, the cherubim are clearly not objects of worship: they do not speak the words of the Lord, which are recorded in the Ark below them and will be spoken to Moses from the space above them. Yes, they appeal to the love of visible beauty and artful splendor, but they pay tribute to the Lord who ordered them made according to His specific instructions. Art and beauty are given an honored (and hidden) place at the center of the Tabernacle, but they are subordinated to the word of God.

The Table and the Lampstand: Earth and Heaven

After the Ark and its cover, the Lord gives the instructions for the Table, which is to stand outside the Holy of Holies in the (merely) Holy space. Like the Ark, the Table shall be made of acacia wood overlaid with pure gold, with a golden crown and a gold border all around. The utensils for the Table—dishes and pans, jars and bowls (suitable for pouring libations)—shall be made of pure gold—but nothing is said about their use or about what should be placed in them. At the end, the Lord states the Table's purpose:

> "And you [singular] shall set upon the Table showbread ("Bread of the Presence": *lechem panim*) before Me always." (25:30)

In the rituals of neighboring peoples, congregants brought prepared meals to feast their gods—just as they feasted their kings—assuming that the gods, like human beings, also need and delight in food and drink. But the Lord of Israel makes clear that He needs no such corporeal service.[19] The dishes, though beautiful, remain empty; the chalices are never filled. The bread, perhaps to reciprocate and remember His daily gift of manna or perhaps to express gratitude for "bread from the earth," is offered symbolically—always—to His Presence, expressing the people's desire that He should never "pass away" from them. (Later, we will learn that the showbread—twelve loaves representing the twelve tribes—is to be replaced weekly on the Sabbath and the stale loaves eaten on the Sabbath by the priests [Lev. 24:5–9].)

After the Table comes the Lampstand or Candelabra (*Menorah*), the Tabernacle's source of light. It will stand in the Holy Place opposite the Table bearing the showbread. Like the Ark cover, it too will be hammered out of a single piece of pure gold; as with the Ark cover, after reading the intricate requirements for its construction, we cannot imagine how any human being could make it. The basic idea is a structure that will bear seven oil-burning lamps, each lamp perched atop an ornate floral element that crowns one of the Candelabra's branches, which form three matched pairs symmetrically placed on either side of the central seventh branch. The lamp-bearing floral cups are compared to almond blossoms, with distinct calyces and petals; similar cups are to be placed below the crown on each of the branches, as well as along the stem below the branching. Separate utensils—snuffers or tweezers to remove the burnt wicks and trays (to dispose of the wicks and perhaps to carry out the lamps for cleaning)—were to be fashioned, also out of pure gold. As if conceding that the instructions are confusing, the Lord concludes by telling Moses that he should make these things after the pattern that is being shown to him on the mountain.

Moses is told nothing about the Candelabra's significance—why it has to be constructed this way—or about its symbolic meaning in the Tabernacle or in the life of the Israelite people. Interpreters have rushed in to fill the void, and interesting suggestions abound. Maimonides, for example, ignores the details and takes a purely functional view: the *Menorah* exists to enhance the glory and splendor of the house. Abravanel, making much of the details, takes an allegorical view. The Lampstand of the Lord is the soul of man; the seven lamps symbolize the seven degrees of wisdom to be found in the Divine Law; the cups, calyces, and flowers represent the various sciences that branch out from each other; but the single piece of gold from which all parts are made is the common divine source of all.

There is an additional possibility. Taking seriously the Lord's insistence that the pattern for the Lampstand is to be seen on (or from) the mountain, this interpretation hearkens back to the beginning of Genesis, to the account of Creation (Gen. 1–2:3). From its opening words, that story delivered the massively important news that the heavenly bodies—the sun, moon, and stars—are not gods but merely creatures of the true God. The demotion of these luminaries—especially the sun—

is a major theme in the story. Light—God's first creation (Day 1)—is created before the sun; day and night are created before the sun; and vegetation (on Day 3) is created before the sun, which appears only on Day 4. Could the seven lights of the Candelabra represent the seven visible "wandering stars"—the planets, literally, "wanderers"—that move in their own independent paths across the heavens, distinct from the revolving sphere of the so-called fixed stars: Sun, Moon, Mercury, Venus, Mars, Jupiter, and Saturn? Thought by other peoples to be animated, here the seven are arrested together in a unified image of the heavenly lights, created and ordered by the Lord and made under His direction. They exist to bear God's first creature, light; they are not themselves divine and not to be worshipped. Before them in the Holy Tabernacle stands the Table bearing bread from the earth, on which their light shines, but from which no obeisance is given. On this account, the Candelabra, a golden image of the heavenly lights, represents the rejected objects of nature worship, now seen as mere creatures; at the same time, it illuminates the antechamber to the Holy of Holies, where the true Divine, beyond and above nature, is to be encountered.

The Holy Place and the Holy of Holies

Having described the sacred furnishings of the Tabernacle, the Lord proceeds with instructions for the portable tent in which they will be housed: first, the coverings; next, the three-sided wooden frame over which the coverings will be draped, also to form the roof; and finally, two smaller curtains—one to divide the space internally into two unequal parts, the other to close it off on the fourth (eastern) side. The parts of the structure are created to enable easy assembly, disassembly, and transport. I will summarize the plan, departing from the order of presentation and ignoring many of the details,[20] to better visualize the intended structure. (The figure gives the floor plan.)

The Tabernacle's footprint will be a rectangle measuring 30 cubits (about 45 feet) by 10 cubits (about 15 feet), with the long sides facing north and south. Three wooden walls, 10 cubits tall, are erected on the northern, southern, and western sides; each wall is constructed from

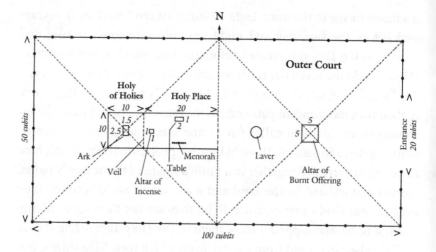

The Wilderness Tabernacle. Reprinted from *The JPS Torah Commentary: Exodus* by Nahum M. Sarna by permission of the University of Nebraska Press. Copyright 1991 by the Jewish Publication Society.

interlocking identical planks of acacia wood, overlaid in gold and seated in silver pedestals. The eastern end of the tent, which serves as the entrance, lacks a wall; it will eventually be covered by the Screen.

The tent covering comprises four layers. The inner layer, which will be seen from within as the ceiling or roof above the golden walls, will also be a feast for the eyes. It is to be made of fine twisted linen, using blue, purple, and scarlet yarns, and containing, worked into it, a design of cherubim. Ten multicolored sheets are sewn together in paired sets of five, which are then linked with gold clasps along the adjoining edges of the two large five-piece curtains. The assembled layer extends length-wise from the eastern opening to the base of the western wall. From the inside, an expanse of curtain will be visible overhead, with the gold clasps that link the two half-curtains shining like stars.

Covering the inner curtain are three more layers, made of coarser goats' hair, rams' skins, and sealskin, for insulation and pro-tection against the elements. At the end of the instructions for the coverings and the wooden walls, Moses is again told he is to erect the Tabernacle according to the plan that was shown to him on the moun-tain (26:30).

The Veil (*parokheth*) and the Screen (*masakh*) complete the Holy Place. Both are made from fine twisted linen, woven of blue, purple, and crimson yarns, as was the innermost tent covering. The Veil, like the inner tent curtain, will contain a design of cherubim worked into it; the Screen, less fancy, will be embroidered but without such emblems. The Veil partitions the space of the Tabernacle unequally into two "rooms": to the west, a cubic space (10 cubits long, wide, and high), the Holy of Holies (*qodesh haqqodashim*), which will contain the Ark and *Kapporeth*; to the east, the Holy Place (20 cubits long, 10 cubits wide and high), which will contain the Table and the Lampstand, the former set near the north wall of the Holy Place, the latter near the south wall. (The Holy Place will also contain the Altar of Incense, to be placed in front of the Veil before the Holy of Holies. Because the Lord introduces it only later (30:1–10), I will delay discussing it until Chapter Nineteen.) To the east, the Screen closes off and becomes the entrance to the Holy Place, separating it from the surrounding courtyard.

The Altar and the Courtyard

After giving instructions for the Holy Place, the Lord speaks next about the surrounding courtyard, beginning with its most important feature, the Altar:

> "And you shall make the Altar (*mizbeach*) of acacia wood, five cubits long, and five cubits broad; the Altar shall be four-square; and the height thereof shall be three cubits. And you shall make its horns upon the four corners thereof; the horns thereof shall be of one piece with it; and you shall overlay it with bronze. And you shall make its pots to take away its ashes, and its shovels, and its basins, and its flesh-hooks, and its fire-pans; all the vessels thereof you shall make of bronze. And you shall make for it a grating of network of bronze; . . . And you shall put it under the ledge round the Altar beneath, that the net may reach halfway up the Altar. . . . Hollow with planks shall you make it [the Altar]; as it has been shown you in the mountain, so shall they make it. (27:1–8)

As the Ark is to the Tabernacle proper, the Altar is to the Courtyard. From above the Ark, the Lord will (literally) communicate to the people through words spoken to His servant Moses; from above the Altar, the people will (symbolically) communicate with the Lord, through offerings brought on their behalf by the priests. The existence of an altar, we note, the Lord here takes for granted (or wants Moses to regard as unavoidable): He does not say, "You shall make *an* altar" but "You shall make *the* Altar."[21] But we readers, if we have been alert, should not take this for granted.

Instead we should remind ourselves of the most pertinent antecedents. Moses has made two altars, both without instruction. The first he built after the battle with Amalek "and called the name of it 'Y-H-V-H is my banner'" (17:15). No mention was made of any sacrifices. The second, built (last week?) as part of the ratification ceremony, was the site of burnt offerings and peace offerings of oxen, brought by the youths, followed by the blood-strewing ceremony—events that may have provoked or justified the sacrificial cult into which we are now entering. But between those two episodes involving Moses, we had the Lord's own words about altars and sacrifices, uttered in response to the people's reaction to their experience of the Decalogue:

> And the Lord said unto Moses: "Thus you shall say unto the Children of Israel: 'You yourselves have *seen* [only] that *I* have *talked* with you from heaven. [Therefore] You shall not make with Me gods of silver, or gods of gold, *you* shall not make unto *you*. [Instead] An altar of earth you shall make unto Me, and shall sacrifice thereon *your* burnt offerings, and *your* peace offerings, *your* sheep, and *your* oxen; in *every* place where I cause My *Name* to be mentioned I will come unto you and bless you.'" (20:18–20; emphasis added)

Make not unto *you* gods of silver or gods of gold. Sacrifice (instead) *your* offerings—not Mine—using *your* sheep and *your* oxen—presumably as the spirit moves you. On a simple earthen altar, nothing fancy. This is, after all, for you. Me? I will bless you where I cause My Name to be mentioned.

Does this earlier discussion of altars and sacrifices sound like what we are getting in the Tabernacle? If not, should we be taking the present Altar for granted?

Consider, further, the horns. It seems to be taken for granted that altars come with horns: "You shall make *its* horns upon the four corners." The horns should not be separately made and added to the altar; rather, they are of a piece with it. Why horns? No one knows for sure, and there is much scholarly controversy about their origin, both in the surrounding cultures and within Israel. In later rituals, blood will be daubed on the horns in ceremonies of consecration, and people seeking refuge in the sanctuary will grab hold of the altar by its horns. Practical-minded people point out that the horns would be useful for tying down a sacrificial animal; others speculate that the four horns represent the four corners of the earth, over which the Lord rules supreme.

But we cannot help associating horns with the bull, the animal notorious for strength, tenacity, potency, and virility, and widely worshipped as a god, especially among agricultural peoples like the Assyrians, Egyptians, and Canaanites. In addition, looking on celestial events, those neighboring peoples had attached special significance to the celestial Taurus, the bull, because of its connection with springtime and the earth's fertility. During the Age of Taurus (a two-millennium period ending roughly in 2140 BCE, around the time of the birth of Abraham (around 2014 BCE), which gave way to the Age of Aries, the Ram), the sun would rise in that constellation during the spring equinox, the propitious time for planting. The Age of Taurus saw the rise of the great agricultural civilizations in Mesopotamia and Egypt, along with their fertility religions, the building of megaliths and pyramids, and the cultic worship of the cow and the bull in Canaan and Egypt (as well as Crete and India).[22] Finally, Aaron will make a golden bull for the people below—even before the Lord finishes speaking these instructions to Moses on the mountain—when they demand from him "gods that will go before them."

Might the horned Altar be a rejection of the terrestrial and celestial bulls and an anticipatory refutation of the golden bull? Has the Lord grabbed Taurus by the horns, making him a mere altar on which offerings will be made, instead, to Him?

Made out of acacia wood, the Altar will be covered inside and out with bronze, to keep the wood from burning, and not with the gold or silver used throughout the Holy Place and the Holy of Holies. The substitution of bronze makes functional sense: one does not line hearths or fireplaces with precious metals. But the call for bronze in the offering of "your sacrifices" also underscores the injunction against idolizing the Lord with gold and silver images: you must make a bronze (horned altar) for sacrificing oxen, not a golden statue of a bull, mistaken for a god.

The Altar is to be a hollow—hence portable—structure, open on top and filled at each stopping place with earth or rocks, upon which the fire may be built and sacrifices offered. Five bronze utensils (accessories for the sacrifices), a bronze meshwork grating to be laid across the middle of the Altar (perhaps to receive the offerings), and bronze rings and bronze-covered poles for carrying it complete the structure.

Nothing has yet been said about the nature, timing, and manner of the offerings. This temporary omission will be corrected with seven full chapters of instructions at the beginning of Leviticus, all about the various kinds of sacrifices. (We will get a foretaste of the sacrifices in connection with the ceremony for consecrating the priests; see Chapter Nineteen.) Although Moses and the reader do not know it yet, the Altar will get plenty of use. Whether all of those sacrifices were intended here at the start, or whether they were added later in response to intervening events (the golden calf), is an interesting question I leave for the reader.

From the instructions for the Altar, the Lord moves to instructions for building the courtyard for the Tabernacle (*chatsar hammishkan*), which will enclose both the Tabernacle proper and the Altar (27:9–19). The courtyard will be a closed rectangular space, 100 cubits long (in the east–west direction), 50 cubits wide, and 5 cubits high. Its walls will be made of identically spaced hangings of fine twisted linen, each suspended between two bronze pillars spaced 5 cubits apart and mounted in bronze pedestals. The hangings on the southern, northern, and western sides are continuous and have no openings. The hangings on the eastern side are in three parts: to either side, a side-hanging, 15 cubits wide (hung between four pillars); and in the center, the entrance or gateway to the courtyard, in the form of a screen 20 cubits wide (hung between five pillars) and made of deep violet, dark red, and scarlet wool and of fine twisted linen embroidered with needlework—exactly like the Screen before the Tent inside.

Within the courtyard, it is not clear just where the Tabernacle and Altar are located. But the prevailing theory, following the principle of symmetry, holds that the (eastern) entrance to the Tabernacle lies at the midpoint of the courtyard, on the line bisecting the court into eastern and western halves, each 50 cubits square. The Tabernacle would therefore lie entirely within the western half (away from the sunrise), and if centered between the southern and northern walls of the courtyard, would be surrounded on each of three sides by a space of 20 cubits. The Holy of Holies would occupy the central 10-cubit square of the western half, and the Ark within would be at its exact center. For symmetry, the Altar might occupy the exact center of the eastern half, halfway between the eastern gate and the screened entrance to the Tabernacle—in a straight line on the east–west axis.

If these are indeed the placements inside the courtyard, the entire layout symbolically turns the Israelites' backs to the rising sun. They sacrifice sheep and oxen (the ram and the bull) to their God, Who "dwells" to the west, screened and unseen, speaking from His seat above golden cherubim and guarding an Ark—in the center of His Holy of Holies—containing His teachings as a "Tree of Life" for His people. But to repeat, there is no textual evidence for the geometrical placements that would sustain these interpretations. At the same time, however, the Lord clearly cares about the alignment of His Tabernacle in cosmic space.

The basic plan for the overall structure and chief features of the Tabernacle now complete, we pause briefly to imagine the look of the whole and the thoughts that picture arouses. Against the barren desert, we picture a (portable) structure of elegant measure and proportion, on a human scale but fit for a king. We see a large rectangular courtyard, half the size of a football field, surrounded by white linen hangings, strung between regularly spaced bronze pillars. Inside the eastern entrance is a large, gleaming bronze altar. At the far end, in line with the entrance and the altar, is the richly covered and gleaming Tent of Meeting, with gold-plated walls, a red roof of animal skins, and a richly colored curtain (the Screen) across the entrance. Hidden inside the Tent, we picture the magnificent golden *Menorah* and Table of showbread, facing each other in the antechamber to the inner sanctum. (We will later add the Altar of Incense to this picture.) Hidden behind the Veil in the Holy of Holies, we picture the gold-lined Ark, its gorgeous golden cover with the two cherubim, containing and guarding the Testimony of the covenant, the Word of the Lord.

The major impressions are of shining gold, flashing like fire in the noonday sun; royal blues, purples, and reds; order, symmetry, and precision, the marks of perfect rationality, covering over and paying homage to the deepest of mysteries; a feast for the eye and a boost to the spirit; a place of community and uplift, a place that caters to our love of beauty and our desire to offer gifts to our God: our God Who is not in heaven but Who will meet us here; Who will meet us anywhere we pitch His Tabernacle; our God—we almost forgot—to Whom we will offer animal sacrifices on the Altar; the Altar, a place of bloody slaughter in plain view of all; this Tabernacle, the mixture of the ugly and the violent with the beautiful and the ordered—like life itself—all housed and held in one microcosmic space.[23]

"That I May Dwell Among Them"

God's Prime Ministers and the Tent of Meeting

T he plans for the Tabernacle concluded, the Lord continues by instructing Moses about its officials, the priests. Although we may not realize it yet, they are going to play a dominant role in Israelite society, in keeping with the Tabernacle's critical place in the future life of the people. Theirs is a new position, tied to the sanctuary and its sacrificial practices. Their work: to mediate (by as yet undisclosed means) between the people and God. The task of leading the people in peace and war still belongs to Moses, but the priests occupy a new and privileged center of authority and power within the covenantal community. They are, by occupational definition, God's prime ministers.

The description of the priests' activities will come mostly in Leviticus. The bulk of the present instruction deals with the impressive priestly garments, describing their composition and design in considerable detail. Much of that detail we will ignore in order to concentrate on the clothing's larger significance. But we must first attend to the Lord's preface to those plans. Addressed pointedly to Moses, it carries important implications for leadership in Israel.

Brother Aaron and Sons, Priests: An Introduction

And you (*ve'attah;* [Moses]), you shall *command* the *Children of Israel*, that *they* take you pure oil of beaten olives for the light, to kindle a lamp perpetually (*leha'aloth ner tamid*). In the Tent of Meeting, outside the Veil which is before the [Ark of the] Testimony, *Aaron and his sons* shall set it in order, to burn from evening to morning before the Lord; it shall be a statute *forever throughout their generations* on behalf of the Children of Israel.

And you (*ve'attah*), you shall *bring near* unto you *Aaron your brother,* and his sons with him, from among the Children of Israel, that *they be priests unto Me*—Aaron, Nadab and Abihu, Eleazar and Ithamar, Aaron's sons. And you shall make holy garments for *Aaron your brother,* for *glory and splendor.*

And you (*ve'attah*), you shall *speak* unto all that are wise-hearted, whom I have filled with the spirit of wisdom, that they make Aaron's garments to sanctify him, that *he be a priest unto Me.* And these are the garments which they shall make: breastplate and ephod and robe and checkered tunic (*kethoneth*), turban and sash; and they shall make holy gar-ments for *Aaron your brother,* and for his sons, that *he be a priest unto Me.* (27:20–28:4; emphasis added)

The preface is divided into three parts, each beginning with the syn-tactically unusual (and nameless) invocation of Moses, "And you," and employing an unnecessary double pronoun: "And you, you shall com-mand"; "And you, you shall bring near"; "And you, you shall speak."[1] This unusual form bespeaks a difficulty with Moses, for which God seeks to provide reassurance.

Having heard the grand plans for the majestic building, Moses ea-gerly awaits word of his role in its operation: What am *I* to do here? To his surprise—perhaps to his disappointment—he learns that others will run the sanctuary. As for you, Moses, you get to command the people, you get to summon (and install) the priests in their splendor, you get to instruct the wise artisans about the priestly garments. For now, Moses, you are still in charge of everything and indispensable. But the Lord lets him know, in this indirect way, that with respect to the House of Meeting between the Lord and His people, Moses is going to be replaced by Aaron and his line. Seven times in these prefatory remarks, Moses hears Aaron's name (and never his own), three times as "Aaron your brother." We will return to this matter soon. But we proceed in order, sticking close to the text.

As with His instructions for building the Tabernacle (25:2), the Lord begins by directing Moses to command the people to bring him necessary materials—this time, pure oil from beaten (not pressed) olives—needed for a light that is to burn in the Tabernacle from evening to morning, in the Holy Place before the Lord, perpetually. Unlike the earlier one-time request for precious metals, yarns, and gems to make the building, this command to bring oil applies for all time, as the light must be lit "forever, throughout their generations." The people will supply the oil; the priests will see to it that the lamp stays lit.

As nothing is said about the meaning and purpose of the perpetual flame, commentators have offered both functional and symbolic explanations: to illuminate the otherwise dark Holy Place[2] or to serve as a symbol of God's first creation (light), of the heavenly bodies that bear that light, of the human soul, or of the fire (and cloud) associated with the Lord's presence. Whatever its meaning, the Lord wants Moses (and us) to know that lighting the perpetual flame in the Holy Place is the first priestly task, even ahead of the sacrifices. On behalf of the Children of Israel, Aaron and his sons will keep light and flame before the Lord, every day and forever.

Having been told that Aaron and his sons are to tend the perpetual light, Moses is next told to recruit them—"Aaron your brother and his sons," each mentioned by name[3]—separating them out from among the people so that they may serve as priests unto the Lord. That they come from the people—and are "closer" to the people than Moses—is part of what qualifies them to be priests. They must mediate between the people and the Lord, and crucially, they must serve the Lord on behalf of the people in ways that make sense to the people, which is to say by visible and physical means. Moses is not only to recruit them; he is told to make holy garments for his brother Aaron for glory and splendor, and a sight to behold.

Nothing is said about Moses's reaction to this news. Was he delighted for his brother? Was he sorry to have been passed over? Did he envy his brother the glory and splendor of his regalia, or was he relieved to have the sacerdotal functions, not his forte, taken off his hands? Was this a demotion or a promotion? The text is silent, and we have no basis for speculating about Moses's thoughts.[4] But as we later learn, he did not hesitate to carry out the instructions. When the priests are selected and installed, it will all indeed be Moses's doing.

Yet certain echoes prevent us from resting easily with the text's silence on Moses's reaction or with his later unhesitating compliance. "Aaron your brother" is a phrase we have heard three times before, always spoken by the Lord; the first time was as part of His angry response to Moses's refusal, at the burning bush, to accept his mission:

> And the anger of the Lord was kindled against Moses, and He said: "Is there not Aaron, your brother the Levite? I know that he can speak well. . . . And he shall be your spokesman unto the people; and it shall come to pass that he shall be to you a mouth, and you shall be to him in God's stead." (4:14–16)

In discussing that passage, we speculated that the introduction of Aaron silently raised the specter of fratricide (literal or metaphorical), the primal iniquity that loomed over the entire book of Genesis and that notoriously afflicts all political founding: the ruler *as ruler* has no brothers (equals).[5] Happily, the reunion of Moses and Aaron was more than amicable, and they cooperated well through the episodes of the plagues and the deliverance. Aaron accepted his subordinate role, and there have been, to this point, no hints of rivalry.[6] But founding time has arrived, and brotherly tension might well emerge. "Aaron your brother," thrice recited, casts a note of disquiet over the scene—please note, not because either brother feels animosity for the other, but because the circumstances may now place them in dangerous opposition or expose one or both of them to lethal danger.[7] Aaron, a man of the people, who speaks their language, is about to be elevated to the lofty but dangerous position of High Priest. Does tragedy—or iniquity—lurk behind the curtains of the Tabernacle?

Readers may wonder why I am bringing up such an unpleasant topic in the midst of this celebratory presentation of the Tabernacle and its officials. Why imagine a potential tragedy out of next to nothing, out of the seemingly innocent phrase "Aaron your brother"? Departing from my preference for suggestion over explanation, I will try to explain, for the matter is important.

Let us review the relationship between Moses and Aaron from its beginning. Moses, who angered God by refusing to undertake the mission alone, pleading that he was not a good speaker, got brother Aaron, the Levite, to be his spokesman, and Moses to be to him as a God. Their reunion was amicable and the partnership ran smoothly, without any friction—perhaps lulling us to think that brotherly rivalry, endemic to human nature and the bane of the patriarchs, had been eradicated. But careful readers will have noticed that Aaron's role in performing the plagues before Pharaoh diminished to a vanishing point, whereas the standing of "the man Moses" became very great, and that God was at pains to increase it further, both at the Sea of Reeds and at the pronouncement of the Decalogue—scenes in which Aaron played no role. But issues connected with sacrifice and worship, involving Aaron and two of his sons (Ex. 24), led to a major change in leadership structure, precisely connected to matters of sacrifice and worship: the building of the Tabernacle and the installation of the priests. Whereas before Aaron played spokesman to the people for "godlike" Moses, now Aaron is to minister to the Lord on behalf of the people—on a pathway from which Moses is excluded. And here is the clincher: at the same time that Moses is receiving these instructions for the future investiture of the priests, brother Aaron (as we will see in Chapter Twenty) is down below, facilitating iniquitous acts of idolatry and sexual license, involving a golden calf that he himself created as a replacement for the missing Moses—all this without any overt psychic enmity or rivalry. The priest and the statesman—or the populist and the aristocrat—are destined for separate tracks and, in the absence of divine instruction, tragic opposition.

Even *with* divine instruction, the consequences for Moses and Aaron are hardly cheering. Though the text will hold Aaron responsible for letting the people loose at the golden calf (32:25), he will not be punished: Moses will not even seriously rebuke him, for he knows that God has appointed Aaron to be High Priest. But Aaron's two sons, Nadab and Abihu, will be afflicted with an excess of priestly zeal; they will be killed for offering strange fire before the Lord (Lev. 10:1–2), in what looks very much like the iniquity of the father being visited on the sons. Next, when Moses purges the iniquity of the calf and reunites the camp, he will do so by ordering the Levites to kill their brothers; though Aaron is spared, 3,000 men will die (32:27–29). Finally, Aaron himself will eventually pay for what happened with the calf—and for having been compelled by Moses to join the team of leadership—as his fate is inextricably linked to that of his brother.

At the wilderness of Zin, with the people murmuring against Moses because of a lack of water, God tells Moses and Aaron to assemble the people and to speak to the rock before their eyes, so that it would give forth water. But Moses, in hot anger at the people, does not speak to the rock but *smites* it twice to bring forth water. In response, the Lord tells both Moses and Aaron that, because they did not sanctify him in the eyes of the Children of Israel, they will *both* not enter the Promised Land (Num. 20:7–12 and 20:24). Moses and Aaron are both punished (with premature death) for what Moses alone did, for "failing to honor Him before the people." Aaron dies for Moses's sin.

The problem of brothers, alas, has not been solved, and a shadow of iniquity hovers over the founding and the Tabernacle. The holy things themselves are fraught.

The Priestly Vestments

We return from these dark thoughts to the bright picture of clothing for the priests—holy garments, glorious and splendid. Moses is first charged to make them (or to have them made); he is then told to commission all the wise-hearted—those whom the Lord has filled with the spirit of wisdom—to make them for his brother Aaron and his sons. There follows the list of six major items that need making: breastplate, ephod, robe, tunic, turban, and sash. Why this emphasis on clothing and on these six articles of fancy clothing?[8]

Clothing is, to begin with, an artful improvement upon nature, an expression of reason's ability to rule over instinct, a mark of the human difference. As we learn from the Garden of Eden story, clothing is, after language and the needle, humankind's first invention, a humanizing response to the shame-filled discovery of our nakedness and insufficiency (Gen. 3:7). Sublimating *eros* and redirecting it upward, the fig-leaf girdle is the first step toward adornment and beautification, craft and custom, society and civilization. Improving on their flimsy effort, the Lord made them coats (sing., *kethoneth*; plur. *kothenoth*) of skins—His first gift to human beings as they went out into the world, away from but reminded of His presence—and He clothed them Himself (Gen. 3:21). Now, in the Tabernacle of His Presence, He welcomes back His priests by designing for them clothing suited to the purpose. Just as His edifying Laws mean to clothe and adorn His people's souls, so His dignified garments mean to adorn His ministers' bodies.

The priests' garments do more than cover them. Richly colored and ornate, they will bring glory and splendor to their wearers, and by reflection, to the Lord they serve. To meet the "King of Kings," His ministers should make themselves beautiful, dignified, elegant, fitting, tasteful. Like any uniform of office, the garments honor the wearer and summon him to display his commitment to a purpose higher than himself. And the people viewing him can tell at a glance that the wearer serves One worthy of such finery. Lovers of visible beauty, they will admire the wearer and be attracted to his cause. For it is the uniform, the mark of office, not the person wearing it, that is splendid—an acquired splendor and a gift ordained and granted by the Lord Himself.

There is more. As we shall see, the garments of the priests are not merely plush and pleasing. They will carry signs and symbols of Israel's (complicated) national history and spiritual purpose. And they will reflect the God Whom their wearer serves. The High Priest of Israel will thus be uniquely attired, in ways that point at once to the special people he represents and to the glory of the Lord God of Israel, Creator of heaven and earth, redeemer and teacher of His people.

There is, however, risk in all this splendor—and risk even in reading about it. One can get carried away and forget Whose gift one carries
or Whom one is meant to serve, as the trappings of office become ends
in themselves. External beauty invites both pride within and idolatry—
or envy and resentment—without. Once again, the language of the passage brings this difficulty to mind. After the Garden of Eden, the most
famous piece of clothing belongs to Joseph, his coat (*kethoneth*) of many
colors, a gift of his father Jacob, a source of Joseph's pride and vanity
and of his brothers' envy and hatred. It was, to exaggerate but slightly,
this beautiful coat that landed Israel in Egypt.[9] Now, in this first reference to clothing since the Exodus from Egypt, the Lord gives a *kethoneth* and much more to his priests.* Will they be able to resist pride and
vanity? Can they avoid arousing envy and enmity from would-be rivals
or illicit desires from their admirers? Joseph, we recall, had his coat of
office torn from him not once but twice, the second time while resisting
the sexual advances of his master's wife. Clothing does not always hide
the nakedness it is intended to cover and adorn—a subject to which we
will return. For now, we set these questions aside and proceed to examine the complex costume itself.

The High Priest's outfit is to comprise six woven items, which I present here from the inside out, for ease of visualization: closest to the

---

*In the entire Torah, the word *kethoneth* is used only for three coats (or tunics):
the coat of skins made by God for the departing Adam and Eve; Joseph's coat of many
colors, the pride-and-envy-producing gift of his father Jacob; and the (colorless) linen
tunic the Lord orders for the priests. Just as the coat of skins was meant as a replacement for the flimsy apron of fig leaves, so the plain linen tunic God prescribes for
Moses's brother Aaron was meant, in part, to avoid for Aaron and Moses the "(un)
brotherly" consequences of Jacob's gift to Joseph. Moreover, unlike Joseph who had
his tunic stripped (*pashat*) from him by his brothers, Aaron will (at first) have his
clothing put on him by his brother Moses—another directive of the Lord; yet later,
also at the Lord's command, Moses will indeed strip (*pashat*) Aaron of his priestly
garments in preparation for his ordained death (Num. 20:26–28). But in addition to
the tunic, God also orders the royal robe (with pomegranates and bells), the ephod,
the breastplate, and the golden crown. Avoiding the risk of brotherly rivalry may have
been on God's "mind" with this gift of a plain *kethoneth,* but that does not mean that
His attempt to avoid it made it disappear, if not as a psychic feeling, then as an ontological fact. Brotherhood and rule do not go together. Remember, please, what is happening on "the split-screen."

body, a plain linen tunic (*kethoneth*, with sleeves); a multicolored woolen-and-linen sash or girdle around the waist to hold the tunic; over the tunic, a sky-blue robe, hemmed all around its base with alternating woven pomegranates and golden bells; over the robe, the ephod, a multicolored skirt or apron, open in front but closed in back, held up by two shoulder straps attached front and back to the ephod's waistband; over the heart, and attached above and below to the ephod, a richly colored square breastplate or pouch; and on the head, a linen turban. In addition, we later learn, the priest will wear a golden crown across his forehead; below the tunic, he is to wear linen britches covering his loins and thighs to prevent exposure.[10] Several features of these articles deserve comment.

The ephod (*'ephod*) and the breastplate (*choshen*), described first and in greatest detail, are stunning multicolored pieces of weaving. Significantly, both carry attachments of precious stones, bearing similar engraved writing. Attached to the shoulder straps of the ephod will be two large onyx stones, each engraved with the names of the Children of Israel, six per stone, in the order of their birth:

> And you shall put the two stones upon the shoulder-pieces of the ephod, to be *stones of remembrance* for the Children of Israel; and Aaron shall *bear (nasa') their names* before the Lord upon his two shoulders for a *remembrance.* (28:12; emphasis added)

Across the front of the breastplate, in four rows of three stones each, are twelve different precious gems set in gold casings, each gem bearing an engraved name of one of the twelve Children (or tribes) of Israel:

> And the stones shall be according to the names of the *Children of Israel,* twelve, according to their names; like the engravings of a signet, every one according to his name, they shall be *for the twelve tribes.* . . . And Aaron shall *bear (nasa') the names* of the *Children of Israel* in the breastplate of judgment upon his heart, when he goes in unto the Holy Place, for a *remembrance* before the Lord continually. (28:21, 29; emphasis added)

Why this double presentation of the names of the Children of Israel? What does it mean for the priest to "bear the(ir) names" and to bear them "for a remembrance"? What is being remembered?

This book called "Names"—*Shemoth*—began, you will recall, listing the names of the literal Children of Israel: "And these are the names of the Children of Israel who came into Egypt with Jacob" (1:1). In its every use since then, the phrase "Children of Israel" has meant not Jacob's sons but their collective descendants, the Israelites, arranged in tribes named after the eponymous original sons-of-Israel. These names, in both their meanings, the High Priest now carries symbolically, supporting their weight on his shoulders and holding them close to his heart as he self-consciously represents them before the Lord. The names on these lustrous "memory stones"—visible to the One viewer "above" and (in their individuality) to the many viewers before them—serve primarily to remind the priest that he comes before the Lord not for his well-appointed self but as the humble representative of the entire people of Israel—and of their 400 years of national history. Although the Israelites are tribally separate (each tribe with its separate stone on the breastplate), the engraved names on the stones of the ephod imply that they are united both in their common origin—the sons of one man, Jacob/Israel—and in their devotion to the Lord, before whom the High Priest stands as their representative. Secondarily, by this symbolic means, the Lord is also to be "reminded" that the High Priest appears on behalf of the collective people in their unity and heterogeneity. Finally, perhaps the Lord also seeks to be "reminded"—by this instrument of His own devising—of the merit of the ancestors, with whose descendants He has made a covenant and who still worship the God of their fathers.

The breastplate, sometimes called (as here) the "breastplate of judgment," will have an additional, more mysterious function:

> And you [Moses] shall *put inside* the breastplate (or "pouch") of judgment (*choshen hammishpat*) *the* Urim and *the* Thummim; and they shall be upon Aaron's heart, when he goes in before the Lord; and Aaron shall *bear the judgment* (*mishpat*) *of the Children of Israel* upon his heart before the Lord continually. (28:30; emphasis added)

Aaron will bear before the Lord not only the names of the Children of Israel on the engraved gems; he also must bear upon his heart their judgment, a matter somehow connected with the *Urim* and the *Thummim*.

The Lord speaks to Moses as if *the* (not "an") Urim and *the* (not "a") Thummim, whatever they are, were already well-known "objects," which now need only to find their proper home in the pouch on the High Priest's chest. Moses is not told to "make" them, only to place them inside the (double-folded) breastplate. Nothing is said, here or anywhere else, about their use or purpose; readers for centuries have struggled to explain their character and use. A common scholarly opinion holds that they have a function in the delivery of oracles, when representatives of the people come before God to seek His judgment about important matters—for example, about guilt or innocence, the wisdom of a proposed enterprise, or the outcome of a future battle. Analyzing the few later biblical passages referring to the use of the Urim and Thummim, Cassuto suggests that (only) the leaders of the people may approach the priests for God's verdict on matters of public concern that lie beyond the realm of human knowledge (such as the outcome of some future event). The question will be put to the priest in a way that admits of only binary and opposed answers, and the answer will be given by lot—not by chance—as the Lord guides the priest's hand to extract the correct answer from the pouch. On this reading, the Urim and Thummim become two lots: one for an affirmative, one for a negative answer; or one for each of two mutually exclusive possibilities.[11]

Beneath the ephod with breastplate and over the tunic is the long priestly robe (*me'il*), dyed the aristocratic color blue (*tekheleth*), adorned all around the hem with "a golden bell and a pomegranate, a golden bell and a pomegranate" (28:34). The pomegranate, a characteristic fruit of the Promised Land, is widely celebrated as a symbol of fertility and beauty; plain on the outside, it is pregnant with sweet and shining seeds. Hannah Mandelbaum suggests that the High Priest's glorious robe declares that the true beauty resides not in appearances but in what lies within.[12] But the Lord's instructions emphasize the bells:

> And it [the robe] shall be upon Aaron to minister; and
> heard shall be its sound when he goes in unto the Holy

Place before the Lord, and when he comes out, *that he die not*. (28:35; emphasis added)

What is the importance, in the High Priest's comings to and goings from the Holy Place, of making himself heard? Why is he at risk of death?[13]

No courtier, no matter how high up at court, would presume to enter unannounced into the king's private space: it would be an arrogant and insolent act. Likewise here. Even when en route to do his priestly tasks (for example, tending the perpetual flame), the High Priest must remember before Whom he stands and act accordingly. The ringing of the bells notify the Children of Israel that the High Priest has gone into the Holy Place (or come safely out), and they symbolically notify the Lord that He is about to have priestly company. But the ringing of the bells is also a critical reminder to the High Priest that he not conduct himself as if he himself were the lord of the sanctuary, beautiful on the outside but dead to the Lord within. To traffic arrogantly in the Holy Place and in the holy things is a lethal act, literally and figuratively.

These are the high points of the six items of clothing, to be woven by the wise artisans as yet unnamed. But there are two (unwoven) additions to the original six that turn out to be very important for the meaning of the priestly function: the crown across the forehead, the britches to cover the loins—the highest and the lowest. Both have connections to iniquity and the risk of death. First, the crown:

And you [Moses] shall make a plate (*tsits*) of pure gold, and engrave upon it, like the engravings of a signet: "Holy to Y-H-V-H" (*qodesh la-Y-H-V-H*). And you shall put it on a thread of blue, and it shall be upon the turban; upon the forefront of the turban it shall be. And it shall be upon Aaron's forehead, and *Aaron shall bear (nasa') the iniquity of the holy things ('avon haqqodashim), which the Children of Israel shall hallow (yaqdishu), [even] in all their holy gifts;* and it shall be always upon his forehead, that they may be accepted before the Lord. (28:36–38; emphasis added)

The ephod straps and the breastplate of judgment over the priest's heart carry precious stones engraved with the names of the Children of Israel. But on the golden plate across his forehead—the only piece of gold[14] in his costume—he will carry an inscription that defines the purpose of the entire enterprise: the Tabernacle, the High Priest and his attire, and all the sacrifices and other activities he is to perform there are set aside for and devoted to—that is, holy to—the Lord. This shining piece of gold is engraved not with a visible image but with sacred words: sight in this case will be subservient to Holy Writ. "Holy to *Y-H-V-H*" is the motto and meaning of the entire place—a sacred space unto the Lord, the analogue of the Sabbath's sacred time.

The text does not allow us to rest with these uplifting insights. Instead it shocks us with a dark coda. No sooner are we told that this golden crown, advertising "Holy to the Lord," shall be on Aaron's forehead, than we learn that "Aaron shall *bear the iniquity of the holy things* that the Children of Israel shall hallow, even in all their holy gifts" (28:38). What has Aaron's golden crown to do with iniquity? How can there be iniquity in the holy things that the Children of Israel set apart and offer? And what does it mean that the High Priest shall *bear* them—in addition to bearing the names and the judgments of the Children of Israel before the Lord forever?

The Iniquity of the Holy Things

"Bearing iniquity" has two distinct and opposite meanings. It can be protective, meaning "to carry perversity away" in order to prevent punishment or disaster by an overt act of atonement: for example, "And the [scape-] goat shall bear upon him all their [the Israelites'] iniquities" (Lev. 16:22). Or it can be punitive, meaning "to carry perversity with you," either your own or someone else's. Cain, for example, complained after the murder of his brother that "my iniquity is more than I can bear" (Gen. 4:13); and "the iniquities of the fathers are visited on the sons" (Ex. 20:4). Much of the priests' work, it will turn out, will be of the former kind; they will serve as buffers between God and man, holding off punishment for the people's iniquities through guilt and sin offerings.[15] But here we seem to have an instance of the latter. What could it possibly mean to say that the High Priest carries with him the iniquity *of* the holy things?

Traditional commentators and scholars generally say that Aaron, because of the gold plate on his forehead and its promise of dedication, will carry with him and then atone for the transgressions made by the people in connection with the order of the services or with blemishes in the animals they offered for sacrifice. Says Cassuto, speaking for many: "The declaration engraved on the plate will prove that everything was intended to be *holy to the Lord,* and if aught was done irregularly, the intention at least was good."[16]

But an iniquity, an *'avon,* is more than a mistake or a mere error. It is not an unintentional missing of the mark but a serious act of perversity or twistedness, whether intended or not, whose consequences linger in the world perhaps for generations. Further, the Decalogue (and also the ordinances) suggested close connections between iniquity and idolatry, as if the latter led to the former—exactly what is taking place now (or soon) in the camp below. For all these reasons, "the iniquity (singular) *of* the holy things" suggests a problem deeper and more serious than a blemished sacrifice or a ritual improperly performed. What might it mean to suggest that there is something iniquitous in the holy things themselves, for which the High Priest undertakes in his person to atone?

As it happens, the text has been giving us clues for some time. We have already discussed the specter of fratricide, having to do with the appointment of "brother Aaron" and Moses's displacement from the holy things. But the theme of fratricide is subtly raised also in the account of the names written on the ephod and the breastplate. According to the Lord's instructions, the names of the twelve sons of Jacob are to be written on the stones, but they do not correspond to the twelve tribes now before Sinai. There is no tribe of Joseph, who was hated and nearly killed by his brothers and who became lost to Egypt. Joseph's bones are present in the camp at this very moment, but his descendants—split into the two tribes of Ephraim and Manasseh—do not bear his name. For the careful reader, remembering the "Children of Israel" according to their birth order, but also referring to them as "the tribes" of the current people, calls attention to that disjunction and to the problem of

Joseph and his brothers.[17] While Abraham, Isaac, and Jacob might be revered names, the remembrance of the original Children of Israel (according to their birth order) is a memory of fratricidal impulses and near (even "virtual") fratricide: thanks largely to his brothers, Joseph was "killed" as a Child of Israel. The High Priest's regalia memorialize the iniquity of fratricide.

There may be something perverse, moreover, in the impulse to sacrifice itself, a strange thought given how much sacrificing God will soon command. To see this, we need to revisit the history of sacrifice in the Torah, beginning with Cain, the human prototype—the first man born of woman, first in sacrifice, first in fratricide, first political founder. Sacrifice, according to the Torah, is of human origins. God neither commands nor requests it; we have no reason to believe that He even welcomes it. On the contrary, we have reason to suspect that the (uninstructed) human impulse to sacrifice is highly problematic, especially from God's point of view.

The human impulse to offer gifts and oblations to the divine reflects competing, deep-seated passions. First, fear and gratitude: fear that unless appeased with presents, the powers-that-be will thwart our hopes and wreck our plans; gratitude for good results and good fortune, interpreted as divine favor. Second are "the ecstatic passions," associated with bloody and orgiastic sacrifice (in ancient Greece, the province of Dionysus): the primal desire to transgress boundaries and the self-surrendering wish to merge body and soul with some larger entity. Third, rational calculation, not to say cunning manipulation: to put the gods in our debt or, more nakedly, to bribe them to deliver benefits and withhold harms. Finally and more honorably, ignorance of the divine and the wish to dispel that ignorance. Human beings intuit the presence of higher powers, experiencing awe and wonder before natural spectacles: sunrise and sunset, new and full moons, thunder and lightning, the fall of water out of the sky, the seasonal changes in the earth. Natural piety gives rise to the desire to close the gap between the human and the divine, to establish ties, to gain a close connection to the whole and its ruling forces.

But how to act on these desires? How to communicate with something so remote, unknown, or inscrutable? Curiously, in bringing offerings, human beings do not behave as if the divine were inscrutable. On the contrary, the fact of offering sacrifice and the particular gifts offered bespeak clear assumptions about the divine: that gods are beings that could care about me; that they would be more likely to care for me—do me good and not evil—if I could please them; that they are pleased by gifts. Why? Because *I* am pleased by gifts. The gods, in other words, are just like me, and they must like what I like.

The ambiguity at the heart of the human impulse to sacrifice now stands revealed: all of these underlying assumptions—even in the best case, a sacrifice from pure gratitude—are in fact expressions of perverse pride and presumption, masquerading as submission. Any deity worthy of the name must no doubt see this for what it is—and also see that it must be accommodated.

Once it becomes clear that the Children of Israel need sensuous experiences in order to come closer to God, the Lord will institute sacrifices, even on a massive scale, making room for those impulses but only under strict regulation. But that fact should not blind us to the perverse presumption implicit in the human urge to bring gifts to God.

More clearly perverse is the sacrifices' content: the slaughtering of animals and strewing of their blood. The Torah's view of this subject is found in the story of Noah's uninstructed sacrifice after the Flood. Presumably in an act of thanksgiving and perhaps also hoping to stave off further rain, Noah sacrifices some of his animal roommates, which he has rescued from the antediluvian world of violence and bloodshed. It is not difficult to imagine what moves him to do so. Overwhelmed by the destructive power of nature but even more impressed by his own salvation, he is moved by strong feelings of dread, awe, and gratitude to acknowledge the superiority of the divine. Noah's close encounters with the other animals aboard the ark would have convinced him that he is more than just the chief among the faunae. But his new awareness of divine power and providence confirms him in thinking his species is special and, simultaneously, separate from his animal relations. Noah's self-defining first act in the new world is an act of violence against his fellow creatures.

Noah's impulse to express gratitude is thoroughly intelligible, but his belief that God would like to gorge Himself on roasted meat—or, more modestly, enjoy its aroma—is utterly unfounded. Noah's animal sacrifice reveals his own preference for meat—or at least his willingness to shed blood. God's comment on Noah's sacrifice lets us know how to judge it: "I will not again curse the ground any more for man's sake; *for the imagination of man's heart is evil from his youth*" (Gen. 8:21; emphasis added). Even righteous and simple Noah, the new and better Adam, is not pure at heart and has a taste for blood. Explicitly for this reason, God now decides against blotting out and starting over: the untutored way of nature must be replaced by the tutored way of law. The covenant with Noah and the institution of Noahide law are the direct answer to animal sacrifice and to the Dionysian impulses of the human soul that lie behind it.*

Let me not be misunderstood. We are a long way from the story of Noah and the beginnings of civil society under law. The patriarchs built altars, and so have Jethro and Moses, without negative divine comment. God Himself is now giving instructions to build Him a Tabernacle, soon to be the home of massive animal sacrifice, instituted at the Lord's insistence. For various reasons that need not concern us, in the world's—and Israel's—present context, animal sacrifice is a practice whose time has come. Moreover, as I will suggest when we come to the subject, the

---

*The Noahide law made explicit, but also regulated, what was implicit in Noah's sacrifice. Noah displayed self-conscious separation from the animals; the law responded by establishing man's nearly complete alienation from the animals, embodied in a near-absolute permission to eat meat. Noah displayed a taste for shedding blood; the law responded by absolutely prohibiting the eating of animal blood and by demanding in-kind retribution for the shedding of human blood. Noah sought a new relationship with the divine through sacrifice; the law established a new relationship with God through a demand for doing justice. A divinely backed law humanly enforced and a divinely pledged covenant humanly recognized together form a precise and elevating response to the inner meaning of Noah's sacrifice, seen as a search for contact with the divine.

The present Law of the Tabernacle and its sacrifices are, we have already suggested, the exactly analogous divine response to the inner meaning of the sacrifices of Exodus 24 and, in anticipation, of the worship of the golden calf.

institution of sacrifices at the Tabernacle's Altar should be seen not only as concessions to human weakness, wildness, need, and limitation but also as something important for the Lord. Yet even granting the necessity and desirability of animal sacrifice in Israel, there remains something irreducibly unsavory about it—and the Lord makes Moses and the reader know it. Because of the sacrifices, there is iniquity—unavoidable and intrinsic—in the holy things. Thus speaks not just a modern sensibility but also the Lord Himself. We have it on the highest authority.

Even where animal sacrifice is conducted under strict regulation, its iniquitous aspects are very much in play. The practice always runs the risk of exciting the wilder passions in the presence of so much blood and gore. On the other hand, should desensitization set in—as it usually does, for example, for butchers and surgeons—the practice will depend on willful blindness to the perversity of watering the earth with blood and of destroying life in praise of its Creator.

There is also, arguably, a stain of perversity in the story we have ourselves been reading. The Israelites were enslaved in Egypt as an indirect consequence of the near-fratricide committed by the Children of Israel against their brother Joseph, who instituted the practice of slavery that would later be directed against them after his death. The Lord's redemption of the Israelites from bondage was accomplished finally by slaying all the firstborn sons of Egypt, a punishment we tried to justify on grounds of collective guilt, but which surely involved the deaths of innocent newborn babies. The killing was ultimately on Pharaoh's head and was absolutely necessary, but there was also something unsavory about God's "sacrifice" of innocent life for Israel's sake, never to be forgotten. In consequence, we have argued that the Lord's subsequent insistence on redeeming Israel's firstborn sons by means of animal sacrifice is at least partly a remembrance of that perverse though necessary deed.[18] Is it possible that when the High Priest appears before the Lord bearing the inscribed names over his heart and on his shoulders, he is confessing silently to all these remembered iniquities?

Finally, there is the perversity of sexual wildness and forbidden unions often associated with religious practice.[19] This suggestion gains support from the final article of clothing, the britches, where the danger of the priests' own iniquity is explicitly mentioned:

> And you shall make them [Aaron and sons] linen breeches to cover the flesh of their nakedness; from the loins even unto the thighs they shall reach. And they shall be upon Aaron, and upon his sons, when they go in unto the Tent of Meeting, or when they come near unto the Altar to minister in the Holy place; that they bear not iniquity, and die; it shall be a statute forever unto him and unto his seed after him. (28:42–43)

Were it not for the previous passage about iniquity, the mention of britches—undergarments, from the loins to the knees—would appear to be simply an afterthought. As it is, they are quite a comedown from the golden plate proclaiming "Holy to the Lord" that crowns the High Priest's forehead: from the sublime to the ridiculous. Yet there seems to be a connection between the high and the low, especially among the priests. The term for britches, *mikhnasayim,* occurs in the Bible only in connection with the priestly garb.[20] We know from outside sources that underwear was not everyday apparel for anyone but the priests, and yet underwear was not previously mentioned as part of their glorious and beautiful trousseau. (Unlike their other garments, into which the priests are helped by others, the britches they must put on by themselves.) Yet with thoughts of iniquity nearby, the Lord makes sure to add that the britches are "to cover the flesh of their nakedness." From the splendid coats of many colors, we are taken back to the Garden of Eden and the concern with covering up. The danger is sexual and not trivial.

Already in Exodus 20, in connection with the earthen altar He mentioned to Moses, the Lord had shown concern about indecent exposure connected with sacrifices:

> "Neither shall you go up by steps unto My altar, that your nakedness be not uncovered (*lo'-thiggaleh 'ervathekha*) thereon." (20:23)

Priests, not having yet been appointed, were not mentioned; neither were britches. But an implicit concern was expressed that the activity of sacrifice would release inhibitions and arouse primal sexual passions. As scholars have noted, priests in neighboring cultures used to perform the sacred rituals in a state of nakedness (and arousal), and artwork shows that Egyptian priests wore only a short apron. Neighboring peoples employed temple prostitutes, and sex with animals was also incorporated into pagan religious rituals[21]—targets of some of the apodictic (and capital) ordinances discussed in Chapter Fifteen. Finally, as we will see in the episode with the golden calf, the impulses to idolatrous worship and orgiastic sexuality keep company with one another. For good reasons, even the High Priest of Israel must be protected from his own iniquitous propensities. Reminding the reader of the proper procreative direction of sexuality, the Lord concludes by telling Moses that the covering of the priest's nakedness shall be a statute forever, for him and for his seed after him.

Installing the Priests

Having described the priests' clothing, the Lord next instructs Moses about the rituals required for their installation. Moses himself is to do the honors, transferring the priestly functions from himself to Aaron and his sons. The ceremonies, to be repeated daily for seven days, comprise ritual bathing, robing, and anointing of Aaron, and bathing and robing of his sons; several different sacrifices of animals and offerings of grain; and a sacrificial meal for the priests. The animal sacrifices include a young bull offered in expiation of sin, a ram burnt whole as a gift for the Lord, and a second ram used in the consecration ceremony itself. The grain offerings include flatbread baked from plain flour, flatbread baked from flour mixed with oil, and flatbread spread with oil after baking. These offerings provide a small foretaste of the extensive sacrificial cult that will be prescribed in great detail in the opening chapters of Leviticus, which also contains an account of the actual installation of the priests, virtually identical letter for letter to these instructions (Lev. 8-9). We will attend only to those high points of the ceremonial plans that help us think about the larger purposes involved.

For the first time in Israel, Moses will institutionalize a division of authority. Although acting under divine instruction, he is to do almost everything himself. He is to take the animals and the flatbreads and present them before the Altar; he is to lead Aaron and his sons to the Tent of Meeting and bathe them thoroughly; he is to gather their garments and personally clothe Aaron, bottom to top—omitting only the britches, which Aaron dons himself; he is to anoint Aaron's head with oil; he is to present and clothe Aaron's sons (without anointing them). This ceremonial delegation of priestly authority God places entirely in Moses's hands to make it clear to everyone that (whatever Moses may privately think) these new offices have his full support and blessing.

The Lord concludes the instruction about robing the priests with the following comment:

> "And *they* shall have the priesthood by a statute *forever* (*le-huqqath 'olam*); and *you* shall *install* ("consecrate," literally, "fill the hand of"; *mille'tha yad*) Aaron and his sons." (29:9; emphasis added)

By an investiture in divinely designed clothes, an otherwise ordinary man becomes a High Priest, an office he retains so long as he wears the official vestments: the clothes make the officer. The office, like its attire, is a family heritage and obligation forever; the priest serves not because of merit or talent but because of law and lineage. Moses, for his part, shall figuratively "fill their hands" with the tasks of office and the instruments needed to accomplish them.[22]

The very next sentence speaks about the hands of the priests and the first act they must perform on the road to attaining office—the presentation of the sin offering:

> "And you shall bring the bullock before the Tent of Meeting; and Aaron and his sons shall lay their hands upon the head of the bullock. And you shall kill the bullock before the Lord, at the door of the Tent of Meeting." (29:10–11)

The laying on of hands—an act that will become standard practice for every person who brings an offering—is here unexplained. But it seems as if the priests are completing their purification by symbolically making the bullock their substitutes—perhaps it also carries, by symbolic transfer, their sins and iniquities to be slaughtered in their stead as expiation.[23] Moses is instructed to perform the slaughter and is told what to do with the various parts. Two items are of special interest. First is the instruction about the animal's blood: Moses is to apply a small amount of the blood—using his finger—to each horn of the Altar and to pour (*shafakh*)—not throw (*zaraq*)—the rest of the blood around the Altar's base (29:12); perhaps this is a correction of his uninstructed ways with blood in the recent sacrifice of ratification. This carefully prescribed use of blood will become standard practice for all sin offerings.

Second, and peculiar to this original sin offering, although the innards will be burned upon the Altar, the flesh will not be eaten by the priests but will instead be burned outside the camp—a practice that will later be followed only when either the High Priest or the entire people commit an inadvertent transgression (Lev. 4:1–21) or on the annual Day of Atonement, Yom Kippur (Lev. 16:27). The consecration of the priests begins with atonement for their—and the whole community's—prior transgressions. Or, on a second reading, it begins by treating the consecration ceremony as if it were, for the reasons we discussed earlier, itself an unintentional transgression.

The practice of throwing blood on the Altar reappears with the second sacrifice, the burnt offering of an unblemished ram. After the priests lay their hands upon its head, the animal is to be slaughtered, its blood dashed on the sides of the Altar itself, and the body burned in its entirety as a gift for the Lord. Its corporeality vaporized, all that will remain of the meat is the aroma—a way of making clear that the offering is not about eating and must not be regarded as food for the Lord's "body." The Lord says only that He will find the savor sweet—perhaps a metaphor for His delight in the wholeheartedness of the human gift giver.

The final animal sacrifice, the so-called ram of consecration, is the most elaborate. After the priestly laying on of hands, Moses is to slaughter the animal and place small bits of its blood on the right earlobe, right thumb, and right big toe of Aaron and his sons, dashing most of the rest against every side of the Altar. He is to mix some of it with anointing oil and sprinkle (*hizzah;* 29:21)[24] it on Aaron and his garments, and his sons and their garments, rendering them all "holy." The ram's innards are then burned on the Altar, intermixed with portions of the three offerings of flatbread. Portions of the flesh are offered to the Lord—including a designated portion assigned as coming from Moses himself, to indicate his willing participation—while the rest is consumed by the priests in the shared sacrificial meal.

As in Moses's earlier uninstructed sacrifice, blood is offered as a sign of devotion and dedication. Its division between two recipients—for example, the priests and the Altar, representing God—is again meant to ratify the bond between them. What is different here is that Moses is being taught how to do it without risk of Dionysian excess. Of particular interest is the delicate application of small amounts of sacrificial blood to (only) the right ear, right thumb, and right big toe of each priest. In rising to the sacred office, the priests symbolically agree that they will henceforth bend the best (the right side) of their attention, their deeds, and their ways on earth to the call of the Lord: they will heed the words, they will hold fast to the deeds, they will walk rightly in His ways. The same meaning attaches to the gentle sprinkling of their holy vestments with a mixture of blood and anointing oil: although the clothes "make" the priests, a dedication of life's blood sanctifies the clothing for that purpose. God agrees with you, Moses: blood is of the essence. But it must be used with care and under strict instruction, lest wildness and bloodymindedness ensue. Only some may handle it and only in prescribed ways. We imagine that Moses gets the message.

If the rules of sacrifice may be said to correct Moses's previous practice in the camp, so the teaching about eating may be said to correct the picnic lunch the elders enjoyed after their ecstatic vision of the God of Israel. Moses gets strict instructions about preparing the flesh of ordination and eating the flatbread. Only those who made expiation when they were consecrated may eat of the meal, for the meal itself is holy. Whatever is uneaten must be put into the fire; again, it is holy and must not be eaten by others. The elders (and Aaron and sons) on the mountain ate and drank in (what they believed to be) the Divine Presence, but they did so without prior acts of expiation or dedication. They just ate like hungry folks. Not so the priests in the Tabernacle, who are genuinely in God's Presence. There is another big difference. Unlike the picnic on the mountain, the meal of consecration pointedly will not include drinking. Sanctification in Israel is to be sober.

The Lord concludes the directions about the installation of the priests with instructions about the Altar, which must also be purified:

> "And thus shall you do unto Aaron, and to his sons, according to all that I have commanded you; seven days shall you consecrate them. And the bullock of sin [offering] (*par chatta'th*) you shall offer each day, beside the other offerings of atonement; and you shall *purge* [that is, remove the *sin* of; *chitte'tha*] the Altar when you make atonement for *it*; and you shall *anoint* it to *sanctify* it. Seven days you shall make *atonement for the Altar,* and sanctify it; thus shall the Altar be *holiest holiness* (*qodesh qodashim*); whatsoever touches the Altar shall be holy (*yiqdash*)." (29:35–37; emphasis added)

What is said about the Altar is most surprising: the place of sacrifices, including the sacrifice to atone for sin, is itself in need of atonement for its own "sinfulness." What is it about the Altar that needs constant atonement and purging, if not the very fact of sacrifice itself?[25] The sacrifices may dirty the Altar physically, with gore, fat, and ashes; yet the call for atonement asks for more than swabbing it clean. One must atone for the iniquity of animal sacrifice itself and for the violent and chaotic impulses it entails and stimulates; and one must do so with another (carefully specified) sacrifice—a thought that is not as contradictory as it seems. The sin-cleansing sacrifice amounts to a confession of the very sin being expiated.

There is more. After atoning for the Altar, one must next anoint it to sanctify it. Wonder of wonders, the place of sacrifice, blood and guts and all, attains holiest holiness—having virtually the same status as the inner sanctum of the Tabernacle, the Holy of Holies, the place of the Ark, and the cherubim-bearing Ark cover.[26] The purity of the practice depends, to be sure, on the spirit with which one approaches it. But it depends also on adhering to the bodily rituals that pay homage to our embodied life—this mélange of the beautiful and the ugly, the pure and the sinful—that comes willingly and knowingly to atone for its failings, to express gratitude before the Lord for the gift of life, and to commit to a God-seeking way of life.

The Daily Sacrifices and the Tent of Meeting

These reflections should leave us unsurprised that the Lord's next words extend the subject of sacrifices to those that are to be offered daily and publicly, in perpetuity. The daily sacrifices will be the fundamental activity that the priests perform on behalf of the entire community:

> "Now this is what you [singular] shall offer upon the Altar: two yearling lambs day by day, perpetually (*tamid*). The one lamb you shall offer in the morning; and the other lamb you shall offer at dusk. And with the one lamb a tenth part of an *efah* of fine flour mingled with the fourth part of a *hin* of beaten oil; and the fourth part of a *hin* of wine for a drink offering. And the other lamb you shall offer at dusk, and shall do thereto according to the meal offering of the morning, and according to the drink offering thereof, for a sweet savor, an offering made by fire unto the Lord. It shall be a perpetual burnt offering (*'olath tamid*) throughout your generations at the door of the Tent of Meeting (*'ohel-mo'ed*) before the Lord, *where I will meet with you, to speak unto you there.*" (29:38–42; emphasis added)

Each day, at its beginning and at its end, a young lamb is to be wholly burned on the Altar, a gift of gratitude or atonement to the Lord: these offerings become the core of the entire sacrificial practice.[27] The lamb, the embodiment of young and innocent life, is joined by small portions of three other primary foods—flour, olive oil, wine—all of which, though humanly altered, are, like life, gifts of God's bountiful creation: grain, olives, and grapes.

But why, we need finally to ask, does the Lord require these daily sacrifices, imitations of a human meal but burnt to smoke, and offered up to Him twice a day? Surely He has no ordinary need for nourishment. Are the offerings then solely for our sake, to remind us daily—when we rise up and when we lie down—of what we owe for our existence, given us not for our merit but as an act of grace? Are these offerings of gratitude intended to introduce a similar gracious disposition into our souls?

Or, regarding them as offerings of expiation, are they intended to inculcate the habit of owning up to our misdeeds and rectifying even unknown claims against us? Is such discipline of expressing gratitude and assuming moral responsibility not only good for the soul but also indispensable for any human community, especially one that is called to be a kingdom of priests and a holy nation? Are not gratitude and contrition the only truthful responses to the existence of life in an ordered world and to the harm that life necessarily does in pursuit of its own ends?

All to the good. Before daily partaking of the bounties of life, and after consuming them throughout each day, it is fitting and salutary—both for individuals and communities—to acknowledge our indebtedness to the Power that makes it all possible and to express our remorse for the transgressions we commit against the world and its Source. But the context suggests something more. The sacrifices are not only for the human beings; they are important also for Him. Strange though it is to say, the Lord needs the sacrifices, not to eat, but analogously to our need for food: in order to live in our world. He "needs" for human beings to recognize His presence in order to be Himself fully present in His world. The purpose of the daily sacrifices, He comes close to saying, is to keep the association alive: [if] you bring the daily sacrifices to the door of the Tent of Meeting before the Lord, [then] "*I will meet with you and speak unto you there.*" If there are no sacrifices, there can be no meeting. The Lord will go into eclipse—not as an act of will or as punishment to us, but as an unavoidable consequence of being ignored. If God's Presence is unnoticed, unknown, or unacknowledged, He is not Present.[28] Not to be known is, in a very real sense, to cease to be. I-Will-Be-What-I-Will-Be depends on His creatures for "Being-What-He-Is."

"That I Might Dwell Among Them"

The point is made more explicit in the immediate sequel, which provides a ringing conclusion to the instructions for the Tabernacle. It offers a surprising revelation about the purpose of the Tabernacle and of the whole story that we have been reading from the beginning of Exodus—even of the entire Torah:

"And there I will meet with the Children of Israel; and [the Tent] shall be sanctified *by My glory* (*bikhevodi* [the basic form of the noun is *kavod*]). And *I* will sanctify the Tent of Meeting (*'ohel mo'ed*), and the Altar; Aaron also and his sons will I sanctify, to be priests to Me. *And I will dwell among the Children of Israel (veshakhanti bethokh bene yisra'el), and will be for them a God.* And they shall *know* that I am *Y-H-V-H* their God, that brought them forth out of the land of Egypt, [so] *that I may dwell among them (le-shokhni bethokham).* I am *Y-H-V-H* their God." (29:43–46; emphasis added)

In these summarizing words, the Lord makes it clear that when He meets with the Israelites "there," in the Tabernacle—when He reveals Himself to His people through Moses—the place will be sanctified *by His glory*. It is, finally, not the clothing or the sacrifices or the sprinkling of blood, but only His Presence that will sanctify—make holy—the Tent and the Altar and the priests who serve Him. The people and their priestly representatives must properly perform the rituals to "deserve" the Presence, but it is the Presence alone that sanctifies.[29]

There is more good news. Back in Egypt, when the Lord revealed himself to Moses as *Y-H-V-H* and gave the Israelites His sevenfold promise, He predicted that one day "you shall *know* that *I am Y-H-V-H* your God who brought you out from under the burdens of the Egyptians" (6:2–8). The dispirited people turned a deaf ear (6:9), and since then there has been no explicit mention that they attained any knowledge of God. Here, Moses (also the reader) learns for the first time that, through the Tabernacle, the Lord's goal of being known by His people will be fulfilled. Even better, that knowledge will not be abstract and remote, but up close and personal.

The Lord ends with a statement of His ultimate purpose: "that I may dwell among them"—*shakhanti bethokham*. We have heard these words before, in the brief statement of purpose the Lord offered at the start of His instructions for the Tabernacle (25:8). But now they are fit into a larger context. Through the Tabernacle, the people will come to know something altogether new and decisive about their God. They will not only know Him, *Y-H-V-H*, as the God Who led them out of Egypt; but they will also know why He did it: so that He might forever after dwell among them. He wants to be known not only as their deliverer from bondage but also as an immediate and permanent Presence in their lives. He wants to be known not as the God of the Mount Sinai experience or as a remote God in heaven but as a Presence in their midst, here and now: as a God—an awesome protector, guide, friend, and judge—in their daily lives.*

This self-revelation of Divine intent casts powerful light on all of God's dealings with the Israelites—and, dare we suggest, on God's hopes and plans for humankind almost from the Beginning. We understand more clearly why Israel becomes a people here in the desert, with a high sacral calling even before they acquire land, economy, or political institutions. God's purpose—for them and, through them, for humankind—is more than national liberation, political founding, and decent interpersonal morality (though He surely cares about these moral-political goals). It is more even than righteous and holy conduct. It is, in the end, to make Himself known by His human creatures and to be *known in the right way*—not only as a mighty power or a wise lawgiver but also as a "Presence." The benefits of this relationship, strange to say, flow not to humankind alone.[30]

Long ago I pointed out that, uniquely in the history of the world, the Children of Israel become a people before they become a political entity proper—before they have land, an economy, an army, or the institutions of government. Their formation as a people is legal, moral, and spiritual. The Decalogue and the ordinances are to shape their legal-moral character and, to some extent, their spiritual one. But it is only in and through the Tabernacle that their sacral mission is to be fostered and pursued. Paradoxically, it is these concrete rituals, presided over by a priestly technocracy that performs them for the community, that bring

---

*Readers will, we hope, recall the great emphasis placed on *knowing* during the contest with Egypt and the Lord's repeated concern "that you shall know that I am *Y-H-V-H*." We have here a culmination of that concern, with something new added to what can now be known about Him: His desire to be—and to be known to be—a Presence in the everyday life of His people.

Israel to realize the Lord's ultimate purpose with humankind: not only that human beings shall know about the Lord, but also that they shall know Him intimately as a living Presence in their—our—everyday lives, for our sakes but also for His.

Theological Musings

We have wandered into the thicket of theology, against our own strictures and against what we learned from the Lord's rejection of Moses's attempt to gain knowledge of Him by trying to learn His name. Until now, we have been content to allow the Lord to be a leading character in the story we are reading, attending eagerly to what He says and does, and hoping thereby to learn something of What-He-Will-Be. We have been comfortable doing so: we are not bothered by the (alien) philosophical question about the "existence" of God, a question that presupposes enough knowledge of God's "nature"—not to speak about the meaning of "existing"—to make the question at all meaningful. But mindful that the present passage cries out for theological reflection, let us briefly put our toe in the water.

What piques wonder and curiosity is the phrase, "I will dwell among them." What in the world could it mean that "God dwells" among human beings and that He dwells in the Tabernacle—that His glory is present in the Tent?[31] To this reader, it is a complete mystery, perhaps better left without comment. Still, because the difficulty I face is surely not mine alone, I will venture a few halting observations.

The source of our perplexity seems to be this: God is presented as person-like in His doings, but as One who does these things without the bodily instruments through which human persons act. What can *dwelling* mean for such as "He"?

As noted before, the verb translated "dwell"—*sh-k-n*—implies transience, a temporary settling into an impermanent residence; He is going to dwell among them, not abide *in it*. To dwell among them, temporarily occupying the sanctuary, implies that the Lord is not remote but near, or at least capable of being near, and that unlike the so-called gods of nature, including the eternally silent heavenly bodies, He is not indifferent to human beings. That He can dwell in a movable sanctuary implies also that He is (or can be) everywhere. He is not confined to place: wherever the Israelites are on their journey, if they build it, He will come.

Still, what is it that "comes" and "dwells"? How to even begin to imagine the indwelling of an invisible deity? One temptation, to be resisted, is to imagine a quasi-physical being, invisible and ghostlike, somehow taking up space despite lacking extension and corporeality. This temptation lies with imagination itself, and anyone who tries to *imagine* God will likely succumb. Because the faculty of imagination rests largely on the sense of sight, it cannot avoid working in spatial and physical terms. When we then mentally try to correct the error by deciding to "suck out" all materiality, we get only contradiction and confusion. As the Torah has already told us, the God of Israel cannot be imaged or imagined.

But the opposite temptation, that the Presence is a pure spirit or disembodied intellect available to those who approach in the proper frame of mind, should also be resisted. It is true that minds can take inspiration from other minds and that major insight is generally experienced as something "flying in from the outside"—what Aristotle called the "agent intellect" or (divine) *nous* that grasps and fills our receptive minds. (In less high-falutin' terms, the phenomenon is captured in the expression, "It hit me," or, in the comic strips, by a light bulb going on over the head.) But if the previous suggestion was too corporeal and crude, this one is not corporeal enough, yet equally crude. For one thing, disembodied intellects do not care a fig for human beings and surely do not bring them forth from bondage. For another, the presence of the Lord is very often accompanied in the text by cloud or fire, out of which He may be heard to speak. When the Presence "chooses" to Appear— or, better, when the Presence becomes Apparent to us—it sometimes Appears also in physical ways. Fidelity to the text means not ignoring the physicality of the matrix for the Divine Voice. Both alternatives, the pseudo-physical and the purely spiritual, seem to suffer the distorting effects of philosophy and its alien categories.

Sophisticated readers may try to avoid thinking about "what exactly is present, if anything." They believe that the anthropomorphic suggestions—"dwelling among them"—are unavoidable ways in which human beings try to deal with the mysteries of ultimate reality, which is beyond our sensory experience. (Torah, says Maimonides, speaks the language of human beings.) The fact of insight they accept; inspiration they acknowledge; they may even admit that prophecy, a spiritual kind of genius, is possible when a "divine voice" like Homer's Muse arrives unbidden within the prepared mind. They may even be prepared to believe that the word of the Lord came to Moses—God only knows how—with teachings of law and morality and even with blueprints for the Tabernacle—and that the Lord could be "found" in the Tent of Meeting in the form of His teachings inscribed on the stone tables in the Ark and in His architectural instructions embodied in the building itself and its appurtenances. A symbolic presence, perhaps, or the presence of His works, but not the Divine Presence itself.

Still other readers, psychologically and existentially inclined, ingeniously suggest that the Divine Presence is experienced by those who seek it, through the sacrificial offerings that are intended to evoke it. Put in a frame of mind that is open to the Lord, quite wonderfully the worshippers "find" what they are seeking—in inspiration or elevation of soul or peace of mind, something that is "given" to them in response to their search: seek and ye will find.

Such efforts to ease the perplexity are not without force and appeal. But if I wish to remain a faithful and sympathetic reader of the text before me, without importing personal beliefs or imposing alien notions, I cannot follow them. I cannot discount the text's statements that, although the Voice generally speaks to Moses without accompanying visible phenomena, He also comes to Moses and the people with a cloud or with fire, which, when they appear, are seen by many. I cannot explain away (later) passages that say that the glory of the Lord *filled* the Tabernacle and that at such times, even Moses could not enter. I am quite sure that I do not know what this "filling" means. But unlike many readers, I am becoming comfortable with the idea that I am not supposed to know what this means. I see in the insistence on explaining the inexplicable a faulty desire to reduce the Divine into human or intellectual terms, to render the Lord into a new and better Pharaoh or into the so-called god of the philosophers.

The text being what it is, and Moses being who he is, this is hardly the last word on the subject. We will revisit it in Chapter Twenty-One, when Moses pleads with God to let him see His glory and receives an astonishing answer. For now, we are grateful for this new addition to our "understanding" of the One who signs off by calling Himself, "*Y-H-V-H*, your God."

Beyond Animal Sacrifice

Human Art, Divine Rest

In His last remarks, with their ringing statement of purpose and with His final "sign off" ("I am *Y-H-V-H* their God"), it would appear the Lord has concluded His instructions for the Tabernacle. Moses has received the blueprints for the building and its furnishings; he has gotten his orders for outfitting and installing its priestly officers. And now, with the Lord's directives for the daily sacrifices and especially with the revelation of His intentions for the sanctuary, the account of the Tabernacle seems complete. A permanent and living connection between Israel and the Lord is to emerge through twice-daily offerings of gratitude and contrition before the Tent of Meeting, within which Moses and the people will not only encounter the repository of God's Law but will also experience His Divine Presence.

To our surprise, however, and perhaps also to Moses's, the account is not finished. The Lord continues for two more chapters (30–31) with instructions for daily offerings of incense, periodic collections of taxes to support the sanctuary, appointment of craftsmen to make the Tabernacle and its furnishings, and renewed injunctions about Sabbath rest. These are not simply afterthoughts, though at first glance it is difficult to see why they have been postponed or what they have in common. But careful attention to each of the topics and to their interconnections leads to an interesting suggestion, which—again in violation of my strictures—I offer in advance, hoping thereby to let readers test the hypothesis as they read the seemingly unrelated sections that follow.

The design of the Tabernacle and the animal sacrifices speak to the anarchic passions of the human soul, making room for them in the people's daily lives but regulating them under strict rule and measure. Number and ratio, order and form, hierarchy and ceremony are used to restrain and elevate the Dionysian impulses to bloodshed, wildness, and chaos. The new topics, by contrast, will speak increasingly to the opposite dangers: the excesses of formality and control and, indeed, of proud rationality itself. If the previous instructions addressed the proclivities of the populace, the present ones address the proclivities of the elite, especially the priests and artists. Their superior talents and refined tastes can help satisfy, control, and elevate the people's inclinations, but the elite's own inclinations—and the pride incident to their status and work—must also be addressed, regulated, and properly subordinated to the divine.

An Altar of Incense: To Humble the Priests

Needless to say, the Lord does not announce His larger intention for these new instructions. He descends without pause from the sublime to the pedestrian, prescribing another item of furniture not previously mentioned: "And you shall make an altar (*mizbeach*) to burn incense [upon] (*miqtar qetoreth*)" (30:1). This is no mere addendum; neither is the late placement of these instructions an accident.[1] To understand its purpose and delayed introduction, we must follow the account of the new altar itself.

The Altar of Incense is, in outline, a smaller version of the Altar of Burnt Offering:* a square-topped wooden structure (one cubit per side and two cubits high), terminating in horns at the four corners. But

---

*To avoid possible confusion, I note here the several names used for the two altars. The altar for offering animal sacrifices, located in the courtyard (previously described in Chapter Seventeen), is referred to as the Altar of Burnt Offering (*mizbach ha'olah*), the Bronze Altar (*mizbach hannechosheth*), or (just) the Altar (*hamizbeach*). The altar discussed here, to be located in the Holy Place (in front of the Holy of Holies), is referred to as the Altar of Incense (*mizbach haqqetoreth*) or the Golden Altar (*mizbach hazzahav*).

whereas the Altar of Burnt Offering will be covered in bronze, this one is to be covered all over—roof, walls, and horns—with pure gold; it is to be decorated around its sides with gold moldings and crowns and equipped with golden rings and poles for carrying—exactly like the holy Ark near which it will reside. It is to be placed inside the Holy Place just before the Veil that covers the entrance to the Holy of Holies, home of the Ark of Testimony "where I shall meet you" (30:6).

To the description of the Golden Altar and its placement, the Lord appends instructions regarding its use—something He did not do when He gave the blueprint for the Altar of Burnt Offering. More important than this altar is what will be offered upon it:

> "And Aaron shall burn thereon incense of sweet spices (*qetoreth sammim*); every morning, when he dresses the lamps, he shall burn it. And when Aaron lights the lamps at dusk, he shall burn it, a Perpetual Incense (*qetoreth tamid*) before the Lord throughout your generations." (30:7–8)

Although the Altar of Incense resembles the Altar of Burnt Offering, its use is connected instead with the Lampstand. Twice a day, morning and evening when he attends the lamps of the Candelabra, Aaron the High Priest shall burn incense of sweet-smelling spices before the Lord on the Golden Altar. To his keeping a Perpetual Light going is added the task of maintaining the Perpetual Incense. Moreover, he must offer a particular incense and nothing else:[2]

> "You shall offer no strange (*zarah*) incense thereon, nor burnt offering, nor meal offering; and you shall pour no drink offering thereon. But [the one exception], Aaron shall make atonement upon the horns of it once in the year; with the blood of the sin offering of atonement once in the year shall he make atonement for it throughout your generations; it is Holiest Holiness (*qodesh qodashim*) unto the Lord." (30:9–10)

Several questions suggest themselves. Why are the daily sacrifices not sufficient? Why must the High Priest bring additional offerings, but only of incense? For whose benefit does he bring them? For what does the altar require annual atonement? In a word, what is the point of the Altar of Incense?

The word for "incense," *qethoreth,* like the cognate word for "burn," *miqtar,* comes from the Hebrew root *q-t-r.* The noun derived from this root means "smoke," and the verb *hiqtir* from this root means "burning incense in an act of worship." Maimonides suggests that the purpose of burning the incense is to drive out the noxious smells coming from the Altar of Burnt Offering in the courtyard and keep them from befouling the Tent of Meeting. But the golden magnificence of the Altar of Incense and the timing of incense burning to coincide with the care of the Candelabra suggest a more significant purpose than the application of air freshener. So too does the refined character of the perfumed spices.

The clue comes, ironically, from the Hebrew word for "altar," *mizbeach,* which derives from the verb *zavach,* "to slaughter; to slaughter especially for sacrifice." An altar—*the* Altar—is, in essence and by definition, a place of animal killing and sacrifice. Because it is similar in shape and because it also will be used for sacred offerings, the Altar of Incense gets called an "altar," but only to differentiate it from the one in the courtyard: "You shall make a [second] *mizbeach,* [but only] to burn incense on" (30:1). This carefully designed altar will not be an altar at all, a message underscored by the explicit injunction not to offer on it sin offerings or meal offerings or wine libations. As gold is to bronze, as the Tent of Meeting is to the courtyard, as the High Priest is to the people, so the sweet-smelling spices are to slaughtered animals: incense is literally the *anti-*sacrifice.

The offerings on the Altar of Incense are more elevated and refined, not only literally but also symbolically. Because of his grand office, the High Priest needs to bring a unique and superior offering that reflects the privileges and liabilities of his station and its lofty activities. In the daily animal sacrifices on the Bronze Altar, the priests—on behalf of the entire people and in the publicity of the courtyard—will offer up before the Tent of Meeting substitutes for our embodied life, in flesh and blood; the Lord will receive this sacrifice as a "sweet savor," a sublimation of "taste." In his daily burning of incense, the High Priest—largely on behalf of himself and in the privacy of the Holy Place (and in the company of the Perpetual Light)—will offer up before the Holy of Holies an aromatic cloud produced from vaporized burnt spices; the Lord will receive this as a sweet smell even as He sees the light. Most significantly, the cloud of incense serves as an emblem of—and response to—the invisible Presence of the Lord, who sometimes appears as a Voice within a cloud; the High Priest in turn prepares his own cloud through which to meet Him. Approaching the divine demands reticence and awe. Those encountering the divine must acknowledge its irreducible mystery.

Why is this extra offering necessary? To remind the High Priest before Whom he stands and to expunge the unseemly feelings that are occupational hazards of the priesthood. His activities on behalf of the people at the Altar of Burnt Offering might swell his pride, as might his privileged access to the Holy Place and its golden furnishings, which he is alone to manage. Or the sacrifices may stir up coarser passions, for which he needs to make atonement and to obtain purification. The fragrant incense sweetens and atones for his soul, even as he offers it to the Lord.

We shall later learn that, in addition to the daily burnings of incense, the Golden Altar is to have special uses during the annual day of atonement, when there will be a minimal mixing of the two kinds of offerings. Animal blood from the sin offering sacrificed on the Bronze Altar will be applied to the Golden Altar's horns, a ceremonial act to atone not only for any errors or misuses of the altar or its incense during the past year but also especially—as we saw with the Bronze Altar—for the act of offering itself. The Altar of Incense, once purified, reacquires the status of *qodesh qodashim*, Holiest Holiness. Then, as the High Priest enters the Holy of Holies for the only time during the year, he will carry with him live coals and handfuls of sweet spices. Burning the spices upon the coals, he will produce behind the Veil a cloud of incense that will screen him from the Divine Presence, now "resident" above the Ark of Testimony, so that he not look on God and die.[3] The cloud of incense both imitates and hides the Divine Presence: man, in the exemplary figure of the High Priest, approaches God eagerly, but through a cloud, humbly and cautiously, with awe-fear-reverence.[4]

Counting the Men, Ransoming Their Souls

With His final remarks about the atonement for, and the supreme holiness of, the Altar of Incense, the Lord stops. He has spoken without pause or interruption for a very long time—in the text, since the beginning of Exodus 25. Moses does not respond: perhaps he is astonished or overwhelmed by this ceremonial abundance and also uncertain why it is necessary; perhaps he is just taking it all in, trying to remember what needs doing. Moses being silent, the Lord speaks once more, once again on a surprising subject: the half-shekel and the census.[5] Scholars suggest that the link to the previous topic is the theme of atonement, there of the Altar, here of the entire population, one person at a time. But the census and half-shekel assessment also have important political implications:

> And the Lord spoke unto Moses, saying: "Whenever you take the sum [literally, "lift up the head"; *thissa' 'eth-ro'sh*] of the Children of Israel, according to their number, then shall they give every man a ransom for his life (*kofer nafsho*) unto the Lord, when you number them (or, "for numbering them"; *bifqod 'otham*); that there be no plague among them, when (or "because") you number them. This they shall give, every one that passes among them that are numbered . . . half a shekel for an offering to the Lord. Every one that passes among them that are numbered, from twenty years old and upward, shall give the offering of the Lord. *The rich shall not give more, and the poor shall not give less, than the half-shekel*, when they give the offering of the Lord, *to make atonement* (*lekhapper*) *for your lives*. And you shall take the atonement (*hakkippurim*) money from the Children of Israel, and shall appoint it for the service of the Tent of Meeting, that it may be a memorial for the Children of Israel before the Lord, to make atonement for your lives." (30:11–16; emphasis added)

The collection of half-shekels—a shekel here is not a coin, but a weight of solid silver—clearly functions as a tax, to be used to support the construction and activities of the sanctuary. But the assessment also carries several impressive communal and political implications. Like the previous nation-building activities in which everyone, without exception, took part—offering the Paschal lamb on Exodus eve, crossing the Sea of Reeds, giving consent to the covenant—every member of the community again gets to say "Yes" to this new relation to God through the Tabernacle. Assent is not exactly voluntary this time; the half-shekel contribution is compulsory. But everyone makes an equal investment and gets an equal share in the relationship with God.[6] No poor man can opt out, but neither can any rich man buy himself a larger place before God by endowing a named plaque for the Candelabra or a memorial inscription on the Veil. Materially and symbolically, no one is closer to—or farther from—God than anyone else. Moreover, the gift of a half-shekel, rather than a whole one, implies that each person's gift is by definition partial and that mutual interdependence in relation to God and to each other is the founding truth of Israel as a political community.[7]

All to the good, but that is not the main thread of the story. The half-shekel assessment is described first not as a tax for the community but as a ransom for one's life unto the Lord and a protection against plague, required because of the act of census taking. What is the problem with counting your people and with being counted? What needs atonement or ransoming?[8]

Three possibilities come to mind. The enumeration of the male population—mustering men and taking a head count—is often a prelude to war: what then needs expiation is not the counting but the impending killing, and what needs ransoming is one's own life against the risk of death of battle.[9] Second, as a preparation for war, by relying chiefly on one's own numbers and force of arms, census taking implies a lack of trust in the Lord. Third, the census, like all acts of counting, homogenizes the counted: to enumerate human beings is to treat each person as the same as the next, not only interchangeable but also soulless. All three implications trigger a need for expiation, beginning with the last, for the ransom is for one's life or soul. Each person's soul is symbolically lost in submitting to the count, is spiritually lost in relying only on one's own arms, and is physically and morally at risk in the war for which census taking is preparation.[10]

Beneath the surface, there may be a larger target: the pride of reason and the hubris of reckoning. To this point, we have seen how the Lord brings number and measure, precision and proportion, to create a safe and regulated home for the ecstatic human passions: to bring Apollonian clarity and distinction to Dionysian ambiguity and chaos. Sacrifices are allowed, but only under the rule of reason and reckoning. But rationality—especially quantifying rationality—carries its own dangers: it abstracts from everything nonquantifiable or ineffable; it reduces richly complicated subjects to their measurable aspects; it homogenizes the world in the service of managing it better. Counting your troops and taking pride in the sum allow you to overlook the profound truth that unique individual lives are on the line, lives whose disappearance will later be reckoned only as a dip in the census.

Even less-mathematical reason is not without risks: to name and to count are to act as if one knows through and through the thing named or counted. Counting heads for a census, like mustering bodies for war, pretends to such knowledge: what is seen are heads bearing arms, men reduced to potential warriors. What is overlooked are men as individual, ensouled creatures capable of a relationship with their Creator. A measured amount of silver is donated to ransom one's non-measurable soul from both physical and intellectual disappearance.

The donation of the half-shekel, while universally required of each person, rich or poor, is in fact the opposite of homogenization: donating is an activity of soul, unlike being counted in body, which is passive. Moreover, each soul is equally worth redeeming; whatever other distinctions exist among people, in the need for expiation before the Lord—as in the need to give consent—all are equal. Although the silver functions as a tax and an inoculation against plague, it also becomes an equal contribution to the Tabernacle; the donated silver becomes material for the silver sockets for the tent posts. With his half-shekel, each person gets to make an equal investment in the Tent of Meeting, serving at once as a memorial to the Lord and as atonement for his soul.

The Human Makers

The elaborate plans now complete, from blueprints for the Tent and its Ark down to formulas for the oils of anointment and the spices for incense (not discussed here), the Lord turns to implementing the plans and hence to the need for human makers. Who among this collection of ex-slaves, experienced only in making and laying brick and mortar for Pharaoh, can execute these elaborate instructions for an edifice of such beauty and elegance? How can these craftsmen be found, and who will find them? And how will they be able to do the necessary work?

In addition to providing answers to these questions, we also expect that the Lord's account will address, at least indirectly, the place of art and artists in the way of life He is initiating in Israel, as well as our lingering questions about human making. Can artistic genius flourish in Israel without giving free rein to the artists' pride-filled and glory-seeking propensities? Can the artist of the beautiful lead people to the divine, or will he instead encourage the deification of his art—and himself? How do the reasoning and know-how of the craftsman relate to biblical wisdom and to knowledge of law, morals, and God?

The answers to the first set of questions come straightaway:

And the Lord spoke unto Moses, saying: "*See* (*re'eh*), I have called by *name* (*shem*) [that is, "I have appointed"] Bezalel the son of Uri, the son of Hur, of the tribe of Judah; and *I have filled him* [with] a divine spirit (*ruach 'elohim*), in wisdom (*chokhmah*) and in understanding (*tevunah*) and in knowledge (*da'ath*), and in [that is, "regarding"] all manner of workmanship (*mela'khah*), to invent cunning works (*la-chashov machashavoth*), to work in gold, and in silver, and in bronze, and in cutting of stones for setting, and in carving of wood, to work in all manner of workmanship (*mela'khah*). And *I*, behold, *I* have appointed with him Oholiab, the son of Ahisamach, of the tribe of Dan; and *into the hearts of all that are wise-hearted I have put wisdom* (*chokhmah*), that they may make all that I have commanded you." (31:1–6; emphasis added)

The Lord Himself has undertaken the task of finding and appointing the appropriate talent, and here He tells Moses the result. The overall responsibility for the project and the people will still belong to you, Moses, but the division of functions and responsibilities continues. Just as Aaron and his descendants are appointed as priests to manage the Tabernacle and the sacrificial cult (the domain of Dionysus), so a group of talented artisans are appointed, also by God, to build the beautiful structure and its spectacular furnishings (the domain of Apollo). "*See*" (not "Hear"), He says to Moses, "I have called *by name*" the following: Bezalel ("in God's shadow") will be the master craftsman and chief contractor; Oholiab ("father of tents") will be his second in command, assisted by a large number of skilled workmen. Divinely inspired knowhow will guide their hands: the artists are not the source of their ingenuity. This is the big picture, but the details are pregnant with treasured teachings, beginning with the matter of names—of the artists and of their tribes.

From this huge horde of undistinguished Israelites, the Lord—He of The Name (*HaShem*)—singles out by name (*shem*) a man previously unknown to the text and perhaps also to Moses. Bezalel is divinely appointed to lead the construction. His name, from *tsel*, "shadow," and "*el*," "god," means "in the shadow of God"—under His protective shade. Readers who listen for such things may also hear a pun on *betselem 'elohim*, "in the image of God," the primordial descriptor of humankind (*'adam*) as it was called by name into existence in the Creation (Gen. 1:26–27). We are invited to wonder whether Bezalel, under God's protective shade, is poised to fulfill the universal human potential of being in God's image by imitating His creative powers, yet in his case (only) in accordance with His wisdom and His plans.[11]

Bezalel, like Joshua with Amalek, appears in the text precisely when he is needed. Unlike Joshua, however, he does not just appear. He is called forth by the Lord and summoned also with his patronymics: he is named as a mortal member of the covenantal community, the son of Uri (from *'ur*, "flame"; perhaps a shortened form of *'uriah*, "flame of God") and grandson of Hur (whether the Hur we met before, we know not). But thanks to his divine summons, Bezalel will gain a deathless name for his work on the Tabernacle. In this book of names, Bezalel is "named" forth for glory, but by the Lord. Like Noah's ark, the building he will construct with his own hands will not bear his signature: were there a cornerstone, it would not read "Bezalel, son of Uri, Architect," but "Y-H-V-H, Creator of Heaven and Earth."

In identifying the tribal origins of the two leading artists, the Lord seems also to be making a political point. Bezalel is not only the son of Uri and the grandson of Hur but he also belongs to the tribe of Judah—destined from the beginning for political leadership and descended from Jacob's most prudent and politic son, born to his wife Leah. Oholiab, Bezalel's partner, belongs to the tribe of Dan, until now an undistinguished tribe descended from an unremarkable son of Jacob born to Bilhah, the (mere) handmaid of his wife Rachel. Unlike the priests, whom God appointed not by merit but by lineal descent from a certain branch of the tribe of Levi, the artists are chosen without regard to their families of origin or their social standing. From this we learn that in matters of art—and other wisdoms—it matters not who your father is or what your political standing. Excellence should hold sway.

Thoughts of the similarity to Noah's ark bring us back also to the contrast with Babel, whose builders sought to make for themselves a name. Unprotected in the postdiluvian world, they sought to create a permanent home for the human race, thereby re-creating also the meaning of their own existence. The name they earned for doing so was Babel, "unintelligibility" or "meaninglessness." But here, in God's protective shade, Bezalel will earn his artistic fame by hearkening to the words of the Creator-in-Chief and giving them physical reality in the midst of the Lord's people.

Bezalel is the Lord's partner not only because he follows His instructions, as a contractor follows an architect: he is, like and with the Lord, a co-creator. His ability to create is itself a divine gift and spark, a manifestation of what the Lord calls the "divine spirit" (*ruach 'elohim*).[12] This spirit takes the form of wisdom, understanding, and knowledge. Wisdom in the arts and crafts does not, at first glance, seem to have much to do with *sophia*, the wisdom of philosophers, which according to Aristotle is the most complete knowledge of the whole, capped by knowledge of the highest things. Neither does it, again at first glance, seem to have much to do with practical wisdom or prudence (*phronēsis*), the ability to deliberate well about what is to be done, in light both of the goodness of the end and of what circumstances will permit. And yet this artisan "wisdom"—in pre-philosophic cultures, widely attributed to poets and the other makers—is in fact analogous: embodying know-how needed to guide acts of bringing-into-being, intuitive clarity about the wholeness and goodness of what is being created, insight into its contributions to human well-being, and perspicacity about the circumstances and concrete details that constrain all actual doings and makings. In the present context, wisdom is a virtue of both heart and mind, guiding technical skill morally and spiritually.

To that overarching wisdom are added "understanding" (*tevunah*), glossed by Cassuto as "the capacity to deduce one thing from another and to find a way of solving any problem that may arise in the course of the work," and "knowledge" (*da'ath*), "the store of expertness that continues to grow relative to basic skill as a result of practical experience."[13] These are all divine gifts.

These gifts have until now been dormant, completely unknown to their recipients, who have toiled arduously and namelessly for Pharaoh, slavishly placing one brick atop another like the builders of Babel. How can these gifts be put to work? It is a profound mystery, about which the text says only this: "into the hearts of all that are [already] wise-hearted, I [the Lord] have put wisdom (*chokhmah*)" (31:6). We have here a perfect analogue of God's strengthening Pharaoh's heart—complete with an identical reference to the "heart." Just as something mysterious "flew in" to encourage Pharaoh's flagging spirit in the contest with God and Moses, so something mysterious "flies in" to activate the sleeping wisdom in those who are innately wise-hearted. Their wisdom awakened, they are able to execute the project the Lord has just prescribed to Moses.

Although divinely assisted, however, the work must be accomplished entirely by human agency, acting with intelligence and dexterity. The gifts the Lord has given Bezalel he will use to invent cunning devices with which to carry out the needed work in gold, silver, and bronze—the cutting of stone, the carving of wood, and every needed handicraft. In contrast not only to the god-forgetting project of Babel but also to the Canaanite temples, which were, according to legend, made miraculously by the gods that would then inhabit them, the Tabernacle is from beginning to end a model of the ideal relationship between God and man: a cooperative project, jointly created for their mutual benefit. An expression neither of human self-surrender nor of human self-deification, the artistic construction of the Tabernacle is an act of human self-realization, following a divinely inspired plan that will make the Lord's Presence known and felt in our art and everyday life.

This analysis of the surface teachings of the text returns us to the deeper questions about the place of art and artists under God's Way. Cleverness and creativity are invited in, but in the service of more than aesthetic purposes, both moral and spiritual. The true artist is God's divinely inspired co-creator, not a freelancer seeking fame for himself. The artists are God's prophets for the eyes. The beauty they cultivate becomes the skin of the good and the holy. And they help complete God's Creation by producing for it the hallowed place where man and God may meet and know each other.

Making Sacred Time

The instructions for the Tabernacle are not quite complete. As in God's Creation of the world, so in the joint creation of its "microcosmic" artifact, the work is perfected by its cessation. Having given Moses His instructions for the building, having named and set forth directives for the priests and the builders, the Lord concludes by giving Moses his own assignment. In doing so, He turns away from the sacred space of the Tabernacle and returns—yet again—to the sacred time of the Sabbath:

> And the Lord spoke unto Moses, saying: "*As for you* (*ve'attah*), you *speak* unto the Children of Israel, saying: '*Nevertheless* (or "verily"; *'akh*), My Sabbaths you shall keep (or "guard"; *shomer*), for it is a *sign* between Me and you throughout your generations, *to know* that it is I *Y-H-V-H* Who sanctifies you.'" (31:12–13; emphasis added)

The Priests will tend the lamps and perform the sacrifices; the artisans will design and build the Sanctuary. But you (*ve'attah*),[14] Moses, must continue to speak to—to lead and instruct—the Children of Israel, this time about their duties and about the things that matter most. You will speak not about sacred buildings or holy sacrifices; you will not speak about work. You will speak to them instead about Sabbath rest and the sanctification of the time of their lives.

Moses has dealt with instructions about sabbatical rest three times before. He delivered them in connection with the gift of manna (16:23–29); he received them, along with the people, as part of the Decalogue (20:7–10); and God renewed them in the ordinances, in connection with the sabbatical year (23:12). But the instruction here, in the context of the Tabernacle, coincides with the first opportunity to institutionalize the cycle of work and rest and to teach about the supreme priority of the Sabbath. Yes, you Children of Israel now have this massive building project, a Holy Sanctuary for Me, Y-H-V-H your God, and it will no doubt take weeks, even months to erect. But please know—"nevertheless"—all work on My Tabernacle stops on the Sabbath. Your work for Me does not take precedence over My prescribed rest for you. Serving God is nothing like serving the self-serving Pharaoh.[15]

The point is not only personal but also very much political. The Egyptian alternative is once again (along with Babel) the implicit target. Caught up in the project of work and building, most of the Israelites—who often express a hankering to return to Egypt—would be in danger of lapsing into the slavish mentality of men who never cease from toil or lift their gaze. Others, especially the masterminds and master craftsmen, would be in danger of lapsing into the mentality of masters, who through their creativity and their control over the workers imagine themselves to rival the gods. The Sabbath teaches that human beings are neither slaves nor masters but children of the Lord. A world lacking the Sabbath, even if it contained the Holy Tabernacle, would be a world of slaves, whose more zealous builders would paradoxically feel as if they were making themselves divine.

The Sabbath is therefore more than just a day of rest, and the benefit flows not only to the Israelites. Keeping it faithfully, God says, is a sign of the covenant "between Me and you, throughout your generations." I gave it to you; you keep it for Me. Why? In order "[for you] to know[16] that it is I, Y-H-V-H, Who sanctifies you"—an echo of God's desire to be known as the Benefactor and Sanctifier of His people.

The message is not just edifying. It is also threatening. Precisely because it is the preeminent sign of the new covenant between God and Israel, Sabbath keeping is a serious matter, holy to the people, holy unto the Lord. Violating it will not be tolerated:

> "But you shall keep the Sabbath, for it is *holy unto you;* every one that profanes it shall surely be put to death (*moth yumath*); for whosoever does any work (*mela'khah*) therein, that soul (*hannefesh*) shall be cut off (*karath*) from among his people. Six days shall work (*mela'khah*) be done; but on the seventh day is a Sabbath of solemn rest (*shabbath shabbathon*), *holy to the Lord;* whosoever does any work (*mela'khah*) in the Sabbath day, he shall surely be put to death (*moth yumath*)." (31:14–15; emphasis added)

"Shall surely be put to death . . . Shall be cut off from among his people . . . Shall surely be put to death." In case you did not get it the first time, I give it to you three times for emphasis.

Tough talk and totally unacceptable to modern ears. The death penalty for working on the Sabbath? Even the most sympathetic reader will recoil and possibly rebel. Had the Lord confined Himself to saying that a Sabbath violator "shall be cut off from his people," we could readily find a congenial way to interpret this. If Sabbath observance is the essential bond that links Israel and the Lord, then desecration of the Sabbath breaks that bond and leaves the violator outside the covenant. The punishment of ex-communication merely ratifies the violator's willing deed: he gets from the community what, in effect, he asked for.

We cannot easily make a similar case for the death penalty, and we are in good company. The severity of the punishment bothered the talmudic sages. Sharing our abhorrence at taking a life, they added so many procedural constraints and prerequisites to the death sentence (and not only for this offense) as to make carrying it out virtually impossible. Apart from one case of a man who collected wood on the Sabbath (Num. 15:32–36)—introduced as if to let everyone know that God meant what He said—we have no evidence that anyone was ever executed for desecrating the Sabbath.

For us readers, however, such a humane practical solution to the dilemma is a coward's way out. Fidelity to the text requires that we make the effort to take the words of Exodus—and the word of the Lord—on their own terms. We should at least try to understand the thinking that might inform this heavy punishment for profaning the Sabbath—not merely that it provides powerful deterrence, but that it might even be just.

One plausible approach is to collect the other deeds for which the Lord has already decreed the ultimate punishment and where He used the identical words, "you shall surely be put to death" (*moth yumath*). These matters we have previously seen fit to accept as justly capital offenses: premeditated murder, kidnapping with an intent to sell into slavery, striking or cursing one's father and mother, and lying with animals (bestiality). A community that esteems every human life, freedom from bondage, family life, and the dignity of the human difference will have no room in it for people who willfully attack these foundational principles. An honorable reader—even a modern one—who appreciates the righteous and holy way of life that the Lord seeks to establish for humankind would, we dare to suggest, not only see why these particular crimes and iniquities render one unfit for membership in Israel; he might even declare the death penalty appropriate for himself, should he be found guilty of such an offense. Can an honorable reader of the present passages say the same thing? Can he see how the profanation of the holy Sabbath might belong in the same class of offenses?[17]

In discussing the Decalogue (Chapter Thirteen), I argued that the central and distinctive principles of God's Way for humankind are its two positive injunctions: to keep the Sabbath holy and to honor one's father and mother. The societal proscriptions of murder, adultery, theft, false witnessing, and coveting are also, to be sure, foundational. But the decisive difference embodied in an aspiring kingdom of priests and holy nation—later explicitly identified with the charge, "Be you Holy, as I the Lord am Holy" (Lev. 19:2–3)—resides in the demands for Sabbath observance and filial piety. These two requirements, taken together, announce a way of life in which duties to God and duties to man are fully integrated. They pay tribute to the distinctiveness of man as the one creature who can celebrate and imitate his Creator, but who must also honor the human beings who gave him bodily life, and who must refrain from the iniquitous practices of incest, patricide, and bestiality.

Thus says the Decalogue, read in a wisdom-seeking spirit. But in the present context of building the Tabernacle, a sacred place of Meeting between God and Israel, the singular importance of the Sabbath receives an additional valence. The Tabernacle moves from place to place; being made of stuff and made by men, it is vulnerable to decay and eventual destruction. But the God-given seven-day rhythm of life inheres in the world and endures forever, provided that one remembers to keep it. Not the Tabernacle but the Sabbath stands revealed as the eternal sign of the covenantal relation between each Israelite (and all Israel) and the Lord. To willfully violate the Sabbath means to reject that covenantal connection. It is arguably a capital offense because it not only attacks the Head and Source not only of life and the Creation—and therewith the ground of one's own existence—but also rejects every Israelite's special calling and purpose in the world. It is a renunciation of the covenant and one's place within the covenantal community and also, in effect, a betrayal of a "marriage" or, if you will, an act of patricide against God.

Again, let me not be misunderstood. I am not endorsing the practice of killing people who gather wood or drive a car on the Sabbath. I applaud the successful attempts of the Rabbis to nullify the punishment—without, however, nullifying the principle. But one can learn something important about a people by trying to understand what they regard as higher than life itself and what they will destroy a life in order to uphold.* If I have not succeeded in making the case, I invite the reader to improve upon it—and let me know.

---

*For the Bible, human life—*every* human life—is precious, and generally speaking, its violation is a great evil. Even so, it is not the highest good, for there are things more precious than life, things for which life may be sacrificed. Readers for whom nothing is higher than human life will of course not be able to accept *any* capital punishment or the ultimate sacrifice, never mind for safeguarding the Sabbath.

Happily, the teaching about the Sabbath does not end with the penalties for its violation, but with a repetition and renewal of the charge and purpose:

> "And the Children of Israel shall keep the Sabbath, to observe [literally, "to do or *to make*"; *la'asoth*] the Sabbath throughout their generations, for a perpetual covenant. Between Me and the Children of Israel it is a sign forever; for in six days the Lord made (*'asah*) heaven and earth, and on the seventh day He refrained [from work] and was refreshed (*shavath vayyinnafash*)." (31:16–17)

Something new has been added to the charge. The Children of Israel are not only to keep or guard the Sabbath; they are also supposed to observe or, literally, *make* the Sabbath throughout their generations. The seventh day has been blessed from time immemorial; knowledge of that fact was introduced into human consciousness only with the Decalogue. Yet, acting on that knowledge—to make something of that fact in one's everyday life—is a novel and transformational deed. The multiple "makings" involved in the building of the Tabernacle (the same verb, *'asah*, appears in the instructions, in one form or another, more than 120 times) give way to and are outweighed by the singular making of the Sabbath, forevermore. And it is this singular spiritual making—observing the sabbatical cessation from physical making—that is the heart of the perpetual covenant between Israel and God.[18]

At the end of God's speech—at the very end of His entire speech of instructions for the Tabernacle—God repeats the universal ground of Sabbath observance: the Lord's activity in the Creation. But it now and forevermore keeps company with the Sabbath's significance only to the Children of Israel. All peoples can in principle know the Creator and the Creation, but only Israel enjoys an intimate "marriage" with the Lord, which has the Sabbath as its preeminent and enduring marital sign.[19]

As just mentioned, the teaching ends by repeating the Decalogue's reason for the Sabbath: the story of Creation. At the end of the six days of making the heaven and the earth, the Lord desisted from further work. But with the very last word comes a new addition to the teaching:

the Lord not only refrained or abstained from His creative work but He was also "refreshed" or, as Alter translates *yinnafash,* "He caught His breath."[20] To be "refreshed" goes beyond resting, and it achieves more than the banishment of fatigue. It is a matter of being re-in-spirited, of having one's soul restored to its uncorrupted state—open to the marvels of the world, grateful for its existence and our own, moved to live a life worthy of these unmerited gifts.

What "re-inspiration" could possibly mean for God, God only knows. But we have had one prior encounter with the idea of "refreshment"—in the only other use of the verb *nafash* in the entire Torah: the passage in the ordinances about the Sabbath:

> "Six days you shall do your work, but on the seventh day you shall rest; that your ox and your ass may have rest, and the son of your handmaid [that is, "your servant"] and the stranger may be refreshed (*veyinnafesh*)." (23:12)

Sabbath observance, we are reminded, liberates our animals from arduous toil and allows them to rest. But it also allows human beings, even our servants and resident aliens, those most at risk of discouragement, to "catch their breath" and be "inspirited." God Himself took inspiration from the primordial Sabbath. In making the Sabbath for ourselves, we not only rest from toil. We reinvigorate ourselves in soul, *in imitatio dei.*

The long speech ended, Moses once again does not say a word. We must wonder why.[21] But the text does not give us time to do so:

> And He gave unto Moses, when He had made an end of speaking with him upon Mount Sinai, the two tables of the Testimony, tables of stone, written with the finger of God. (31:18)

Moses finally gets what he was promised, the divinely constructed tables containing the law (*torah*) and the commandment (*mitsvah*), carved in stone by the finger of God.[22] With this final gift, the story comes full circle: God's tables of the Testimony, the story's last word, are to be placed in the Ark, the story's—and man's—first "creature." The giving of the law is over. It now passes into human hands. Astounding. Glorious. And oh, so promising.

Taking Stock

With the Law of the Tabernacle behind us, and before turning to the dramatic narrative before us, let us pause to take stock of what has been accomplished. Three chapters ago, at the start of our discussion of the Tabernacle, we wondered whether and how this part of the Sinai legislation would address the psychosocial, political, and theological questions left unattended by the Decalogue and the ordinances. Here and there throughout the discussion, I have explicitly noted points of contact between those questions and the plans for the Tabernacle. It remains here at the end to gather those points into a coherent outline of an answer.

Whatever else it accomplishes, the Tabernacle surely addresses the anthropological issues we visited at the beginning. It provides a home for human artfulness, creativity, and the love of splendor, but it does so without encouraging hubris or popular idolatry. It provides a home for the impulse to sacrifice and the search for ecstatic experience, but without encouraging bloody wildness or abject self-surrender. It embraces work and service without encouraging either the pride of mastery or the abasement of servitude. These things it accomplishes—or seeks to accomplish—by having the entire enterprise governed by God's rules and devoted to His purposes for Israel.

Politically, the Tabernacle helps unify the people by engaging them in a common building project—one they must repeat each time they arrive at a new location. The plans for its construction and operation moderate the singular rule of Moses by an authorized delegation of function and authority to the artists and priests. To the unity promoted by living under a common law, the Tabernacle adds daily religious rituals, which provide unifying experiences that give concrete meaning to the call to become a kingdom of priests and a holy nation.

Theologically, it precisely answers inchoate human longings for a relationship with the divine, regularizing the time, place, and forms for communication and bringing the divine down to earth and into the everyday life of the people. It promotes a healthy mixture of awe and wonder, fear and gratitude, respectful distance and attached nearness that elevates the human being without encouraging a desire for apotheosis.

Exactly as hoped, the Tabernacle will cabin, house, educate, and elevate the needs, passions, and longings of people seeking God, guiding their aspirations and controlling their excesses. In addition, it will fulfill the Lord's desire to be known and be close to His people by fulfilling His plans for humankind and the world He created.

We are, of course, not suggesting that the Tabernacle will actually succeed in meeting these fundamental human needs and constraining these dangerous human tendencies. Whether it will do so is an empirical question, to be answered only by future events. For now, the Tabernacle does not even exist save in the Lord's instructions. Yet we have seen enough to discern its overall intent—an intimate relationship between Israel and the Lord, evident in Israel's everyday life—and to see how the ideas and practices for building and using the Tabernacle provide guidance for those deeper dimensions of human life that are beyond the reach of the (merely) ethical ordinances. If a sound political community rests not only on a shared narrative of its past and on formative civil law and custom to guide its present but also on a shared striving to be in touch, for the enduring future, with something higher than itself, the People of Israel have been given all three legs on which to found their national edifice.

One more matter detains us briefly. In various places in the last three chapters, we have seen echoes of the story of Creation with which the Torah begins. At the start of the story, the Glory of the Lord was on the mountain, covered in cloud for six days; then, on the seventh day, He called Moses to Him out of the midst of the cloud, into which Moses entered to receive His instructions for the Tabernacle (24:16–18). Those instructions, presented in Exodus 25–31, come in seven distinct speeches: the sixth is about (wise) human beings who will do all manner of creative work, and the seventh calls for desisting from work and keeping the Sabbath. Like the Lord in creating the world according to His speech, the human makers, acting under the Lord's verbal orders, bring into being a visibly splendid whole that will allow the Lord of all to dwell within. Also like the Lord in Creating the world, the divinely endowed human makers will stand down from their work to hallow the seventh day. As with the injunction to remember the Sabbath day, the creature made in the image of God is once again called to imitate its Creator.

It is beginning to look as though the project of Creation through which the Lord brought the natural world and the human race into being is here to be completed in a joint building project through which human beings, following the Lord's instructions, create a place where the Lord and His "image" may meet and know one another—like groom and bride, like neighbors, or, dare I say, like friends. To make this case more persuasively, we will need evidence that awaits us toward the end of Exodus, where we will learn of the actual building of the Tabernacle according to the plans outlined here. For now, we go forward filled with good hope, ready to look in on the Children of Israel assembled at the foot of the mountain, while their leader lingers above.

The Covenant on Trial

The Golden Calf

An optimistic reader of the Sinai narrative may have been lulled—with my encouragement—into a hopeful view of the emerging formation of the Israelite people. The Israelites were long enslaved in Egypt; God delivered them, destroyed their pursuers, and nurtured them in the wilderness. God then proposed a covenant, and the people accepted it. God pronounced His principles of law (the Ten Commandments) and, through Moses, set forth His specific ordinances; the people agreed to abide by them. To secure for the people a more intimate relationship to their God, Moses is up on the mountain receiving instructions for building the Tabernacle, a sanctuary that will enable the Lord to abide among them forever.

Yet a careful reader, looking beneath the cheery surface, will be aware of several problems, all potentially serious: for the people, for the covenant, for God, and especially for Moses—and also, therefore, for their several interrelationships.

Political and Theological Problems

Although emancipated from bondage in Egypt, the people remain slavish in soul. Restive, fearful, and quarrelsome, they have no experience of personal or political self-rule. They were technically free to reject the proposed relationship with the Lord, but their habit of submitting to authority made them view His proposal as an offer (from a "super-Pharaoh") that they could not refuse. And while they gave their consent to the proposed covenant, it was hardly informed consent: they first did so even before they had any idea of what it would require of them. In approving it the second time, they said, "We will do, and [then] we will hear"—a promise of obedience preceding understanding that does not bespeak a psychically free people.[1] The people are pleased to have the care and protection of the Lord, victor over Pharaoh and unrivaled among the mighty; they might even harbor some longing for a relationship with Him, of the sort He promised them (19:5). But when the Lord addresses them directly, they are overawed and terrified: as they know Him so far, the Lord is dreadful, perhaps a little loving and gracious, but certainly not merciful. They prefer a visible and less threatening human leader (20:15–16), unaware that such a leader comes with risks of despotism on his part and of abject dependency and even idolatrous worship on theirs.

The covenant, though very demanding, was accepted by the people not once but twice. But since the Law is given to a free (or free enough) people, they are free to fail in adhering to it. And given the demands, failure is virtually inevitable.* But whereas the Israelites (and we) were told the happy results of keeping the covenant—they will become the Lord's treasure among the peoples of the earth, a kingdom of priests, and a holy nation—nothing has yet been said about the consequences of violating it.[2] What will happen if the people disobey, frequently or fundamentally? Will the covenant be destroyed? If not, may it then be violated with impunity? Can there be forgiveness and renewal? If not, what alternative but despair? Who should enforce the covenant and how?

---

*The given civil law itself makes this clear. The ordinances explicitly assume that the people will continue to murder, injure, and steal from one another. God's law does not naively imagine the transformation of human beings into angels. Furthermore, the repeated exhortations against idol worship alert the careful reader that acts of apostasy are probable. The likelihood of idolatry invites a still more radical suggestion: it may not only be virtually inevitable but it may also be necessary. This suggestion will be filled in shortly.

Even God faces a difficulty. The people have freedom that, as noted, includes the freedom to fail. If they fail too often, and especially if they commit idolatry, the whole relationship will be in doubt—just as marriage is befouled by a spouse's adultery. Will God then be forced to destroy them and start over, as He threatened He would? Or will He forgive them and allow them to try again? Knowing that the likelihood of failure is built into the law, God will require a human agent willing and able to enforce it on His behalf and to show the people a way forward despite their transgression. He needs someone whom the people will trust and respect above all others, someone who will lead them without their ceasing to be *His* people, someone who will lead the people without appearing—either to them or to himself—to be divine. In addition, God must look forward to the law's passing fully into human hands, when the people are ready to accept it freely and knowingly, so that He can recede from the scene and leave the Israelites to govern themselves under the law He has given them.

All of these problems point heavily to Moses, who is caught in the middle. Can he accept and defend this wayward, still-slavish people? Will he lead them willingly, despite their stiff-necked and backsliding ways, and will he take the initiative when bold leadership is needed? If he becomes the sole interpreter and enforcer of the law, will he not become for the people another Pharaoh, even another "god"? Can Moses, who was for many years willing to herd Jethro's sheep, now be content to lead a human flock and one that is also not his own? Most important, how much of his own personal flourishing will Moses willingly sacrifice to do so? Nothing he has said or done to this point enables a careful reader to put these questions to rest.[3]

All of these difficulties rise to the surface in the story of the golden calf. I am tempted to say that this episode occurs where it does in the narrative specifically to address these issues. If the people are servile and prone to idolatry, if the covenant is fundamentally at risk, if it is uncertain whether God can find the proper human champion of His wayward people, if we do not know whether Moses will finally and fully embrace the nation-founding mission and its people—then we would like to find this out sooner rather than later.

All these matters are promptly put to the test. The episode with the golden calf represents the essential and unforgivable violation of the covenant: mass idolatry—an act that undermines the covenant's very foundation and that has been declared several times over to be deserving of death. The crisis comes quickly, almost before the covenant-ratifying blood has dried on the people.

Addressing the Problem: The Golden Calf

Most readers, ignoring the theological-political context and the practical problems, treat the episode of the golden calf simply as a shameful blot on the nation of Israel, a mark of the people's inconstancy, ingratitude, and servility. And so it surely seems to be. But read in context, we see even more its function in the process of people formation. After reflection, we can even imagine it as a necessary—or almost necessary—part of God's plan. Was it not God Himself Who arranged to get the gold and silver into the hands of the Israelites, solicited from the Egyptians when the Israelites left Egypt? Many interpreters regard these gifts as partial—or at least symbolic—reparations for the years of Israelite servitude in Egypt. Even so, their presence among the people sets up a crucial test. Like so many other things in human life, precious metals can be used for good or ill, in the service of the Lord or in the service of false gods. As our text has made clear, the gold the Israelites received from the Egyptians might be used—logically, must be used—either in constructing the Lord's Tabernacle or in fashioning a molten idol, the two alternative ways of connecting people to the divine by artistic means. By providing these materials while removing Moses from the people's midst, God creates the conditions for testing them, and eventually and especially their leader. Either the people will not turn to idolatry, in which case Moses's authoritative leadership is not urgently required—or they will fall into idolatry, in which case Moses must be pressed into fully taking charge. Surprisingly, Moses's and the people's (and also the reader's) experience of the Lord will also undergo alteration. As it turns out, the Lord Himself is pressed into revealing (more of) Himself and exposing the softer sides of His "character." Stretching the point to the nearly unbelievable, we may even wonder whether God's new self-revelation, here in the desert, was an indispensable part of His overall plan.

Having broached this idea about God's deliberate self-revelation, let us consider a matching radical suggestion: the people's act of idolatry was not only all but inevitable; it was in fact also necessary—yes, even desirable—for executing the divine plan for their peoplehood. On this radical reading, God was not so much testing the people as providing them the opportunity to sin massively. Why? Because a properly executed covenant between God and Israel requires an informed and free choice on the part of the people. They must choose God as much as God has chosen them. Until now, their frightened, slavish souls were incapable of such a free choice; it was only in sinning that they gained the freedom to choose God. Just as Adam and Eve's first act of human freedom was an act of disobedience,[4] so the Israelites' first true act of national freedom was their disobedient demand that Aaron make them gods. Through acting freely on their own, they were able to experience responsibility, sin, and guilt; suffer estrangement from God; and feel the need for repentance and forgiveness. These experiences made them eager for and receptive to a merciful and forgiving God, a ruler Who is, in this crucial respect, utterly different from Pharaoh. Only after falling away and being forgiven can the people freely and knowingly return to embrace the (renewed) covenant with the Lord. Only then can they choose to have God dwell in their midst.

Obtaining for the Israelites such a redemptive opportunity will require new exertions from Moses, whose understanding of his mission must also change. He will have to re-center himself in relation to both God and the people. He will have to make the people's cause his own, while ruling over their worldly affairs and enforcing God's law. He must also accept the people's need for an institutionalized, ritualized relationship with the Lord (via the Tabernacle), as well as accept that not he but Aaron and the priests will mediate between them and the Lord. Moses, in short, must rise to the occasion, gaining glory while leading and ruling the people, yet all the while—wittingly or not—preparing the ground for his own disappearance.

Making the Golden Calf

Whatever the merit of these speculations, they convey the momentous political and theological importance of this story. Here is how it begins:

> And when the people saw that Moses delayed to come down from the mountain, the people gathered themselves together to [or "against"] Aaron, and they said to him: "*Up! Make* for us gods (or "a god"; *'elohim*) who *shall go* [the verb is plural] before us; for as for this Moses, the *man* who brought us up from the land of Egypt, we do not know *what has become of him*." (32:1; emphasis added)

The people are more than restive; they are rebellious. They set themselves against Aaron; they do not ask politely but command imperiously. Yet we cannot altogether blame them.

Stuck at the base of the mountain without their great leader, the people are afraid. They want to move, but they need someone to go before them and show the way. Moreover, they have never been told how long Moses will be gone on the mountain, and after he is absent for forty days and nights,[5] they have legitimate cause to worry that he is never coming back. Perhaps he has abandoned them, or for all they know, the awesome fiery God might have consumed him. True, the people seem to forget that it was the (ever-invisible) Lord, not the man Moses, who took them out of Egypt. From where they stood, it was Moses, wielding his staff, who was the visible agent whenever crucial deeds were needed—exiting Egypt, at the Sea of Reeds, and in the battle against Amalek. Although the people request that Aaron make them "gods" who will go before them, they are in fact seeking a replacement for Moses, not exactly for the Lord. With Moses the mediator gone, they quite reasonably conclude that they no longer have access to the Lord and His power.[6]

Faced with a rebellious mob, Aaron is in a tough spot. It is too easy to say that he should simply resist their demands and urge them to be patient. He has very likely been doing that for days. Forced now to step into Moses's shoes yet lacking Moses's toughness or moral authority, Aaron tries to pacify the people by seeming to accede to their request. Seeking to gain the upper hand, he stalls for time; he asks the people for a personal sacrifice that he hopes they will refuse:

> And Aaron said to them, "Break off your gold rings that are
> in the ears of your wives, your sons, and your daughters, and
> bring them to me." (32:2)

But Aaron's strategy fails. To his likely amazement, all the people unhesitatingly deliver up their golden earrings. Feeling their urgency and seeing no way out, Aaron melts the gold, plates it upon a wooden model, and, with an engraving tool, fashions the details of the golden calf ('egel).* He may have intended the calf to serve merely as a symbol or as an empty throne for the absent Lord (like the cherubim proposed for the cover of the Ark in the Tabernacle; 25:17–22). But the people, once let loose, take the statue itself for a deity. "And *they* said, '*These* are your *gods*, Israel, which brought you up [again, plural verb] out of the land of Egypt'" (32:4; emphasis added).[7] Far easier for them to credit something like bull power than the unimaginable (because un-image-able) power of Whom Moses speaks.

Aaron, rapidly losing ground, tries desperately to turn the people back to the worship of the Lord. He builds an altar before the calf and proclaims, "Tomorrow shall be a feast (*chag*) unto *the Lord*" (32:5; emphasis added). But it is too late. Having had their passions fed in the

---

*The "calf," imaged in gold, is not really what we ordinarily imagine a calf to be: soft, tender, and edible. 'Egel rather denotes a young ox, an ox in the full vigor of its youth. It is an image of natural potency and virility. A sacred bull worshipped by the Egyptians, Apis, was among the oldest of their gods, at first linked with agriculture and later also a mediator between human beings and the other gods, Ptah and Osiris. Needless to say, Aaron's making this likeness violates the second injunction of the Decalogue, which proscribes the making (and worship) of graven images of natural beings. And, in context, as a project of artful making, it stands as the antithesis of the Tabernacle and its golden furnishings, the plans for which Moses has just finished receiving.

foolish hope that feeding would moderate them, the people are not appeased but all the more excited:

> And they rose up early on the morrow, and offered up burnt offerings and brought peace offerings, and the people sat down to eat and drink, and rose up to play (*letsacheq*). (32:6)

Having broken the central bond of law, the people fall into full debauchery, sacrificing to the calf and engaging in orgiastic "play"[8]—a common practice, among the neighboring pagans, of celebrating their gods of virility and fertility.

We should not be surprised that Aaron, in his only chance to lead on his own, has hardly covered himself with glory. We recall that he was appointed to the mission only because Moses insisted that he himself did not know how to speak effectively to the people (4:10–17). But partly because Aaron is a more representative leader, whose compliant character brings him closer to the people, he lacks the elevated standing and moral authority to control them and keep them on course, especially in critical times. Ever at risk of being overthrown—as he nearly was here—Aaron must govern by flattery and appeasement. Such measures, however, rarely work with a multitude; on the contrary, they tend to be corrupting. In a word, "representative leadership" does not lead but follows. It only enables the people to go more readily wherever they would have gone without it.[9]

Moses Takes the Case

The covenant has been broken and in the most fundamental way. The exclusive fidelity of the intimate "I-Thou" relation between the Lord and His people, the very foundation of the entire agreement, is shattered. Moreover, as predicted in the Decalogue, the forbidden "taking of other gods before Me" and the proscribed worshipping of graven images have led to further iniquities: sexual debauchery and licentiousness. Test or no test, the people have failed miserably. What is to happen now?

The scene shifts back to the top of the mountain, where the Lord delivers the bad news to Moses:[10]

And the Lord spoke unto Moses: "*Go*, get you *down*; for *your* people, that *you* brought up out of the land of Egypt, have corrupted (*shicheth*) themselves. They have turned aside quickly from the Way (*derekh*) that I have commanded them; they have made them a molten calf and they have worshipped it and sacrificed to it; and they have said, 'These are your gods, Israel, which brought you up out of the land of Egypt.'" (32:7–8; emphasis added)

In response to Moses's stunned silence, the Lord continues:

"I have seen this people, and behold, it is a stiff-necked[11] people. And now, let Me alone, that My wrath may burn hot against them and I may consume them (*va'achallem*; the root is *kalah*, "to put an end to"); and I will make of you a great nation." (32:9–10)

Several things in the Lord's speech are noteworthy. He first commands Moses to end his long stay on the mountain: to go down to his people—to the people whom not He but Moses delivered from bondage in Egypt, to the people who, the Lord informs Moses, have corrupted themselves. Presenting the indictment against them (that is, against Moses's people), the Lord next accurately describes their deeds of idol worship, making clear for Moses the problem he is to go down and fix. But when Moses neither speaks nor moves, the Lord—whether speaking sincerely or not—orders Moses to leave Him (or get out of His way), so that He might consume the people. In a coda to the threatened destruction, the Lord tempts Moses with an offer to make of *him* a great nation—the same promise God made when He first called Abraham (Gen. 12:2). Let Me destroy these people. We can then start over with you.

How will Moses react? He surely knows that the people deserve destruction for their idolatry; in the ordinances that he himself presented to them, God made it abundantly clear that the wage for worshipping other "gods" was death. Yet in openly threatening to deliver the expected punishment, the Lord is also, we suspect, testing Moses's attitude toward the people. Will he finally take responsibility for them? Will he come to their defense, or will he abandon them to their fate and opt instead for personal grandeur?

To his great credit, Moses rises to the occasion. Refusing to do as he is told, Moses treats the Lord's order to leave Him alone as an invitation to do the opposite, and he immediately takes up the people's defense.[12] Moreover, he totally ignores God's offer to start over again with him alone:

> And Moses besought to calm [literally, "besought the face of"] the Lord *his* God, and he said: "Why, Lord, does Your wrath burn hot against *Your* people, that *You* brought forth out of the land of Egypt, with great power and with a mighty hand?
>
> Why should the Egyptians speak saying, 'For *evil* did He bring them forth, to kill them in the mountains and to consume (*ulekhallothem*) them from the face of the earth'? Turn from Your fierce wrath, and *repent* (*vehinnachem*) from the *evil* against *Your* people. Remember Abraham, Isaac, and Israel, Your servants, to whom *You did swear* by *Your own self,* and said to them: 'I will multiply your seed as the stars of heaven, and all this land that I have spoken of will I give unto your seed, and they shall inherit it forever.'" (32:11–13; emphasis added)

Moses begins by addressing the Lord as *his* God, denying any suggestion of distance between them; he takes God's side but refuses to cut loose the people. He next makes three arguments against God's threatened destruction, using God's own words against Him. He reminds the Lord of His devotion and service to His own people—they are *Your* people; note that he does not say "*my* people"—in whom You have invested so much. He invokes the shame that destroying His people would heap upon the Lord in the eyes of the Egyptians. And he reminds the Lord of His past sworn promises to the patriarchs, promises of enormous future fertility and a promised land. Love Your people; avoid disgrace; keep Your past promise for the sake of Your people's future. In addition, by reminding God of His irrevocable promise to the patriarchs, Moses implicitly rejects the offer to overturn his ancestors and to become a second Father Abraham.

Why does Moses say this? Why does he refuse God's offer and so vigorously seek to save the people from destruction? So pleased are we with Moses's seeming concern for the people, and so impressed with his boldness and newly revealed rhetorical gifts (giving the lie to his earlier protestation, "I am not a man of words"), that we readers generally fail to ask ourselves these fundamental questions. Yet if Moses's attitude toward the people is on trial here, we should pause to consider what he might have said instead.

Because Moses has pleaded for clemency, it is natural to consider that he is moved by compassion, perhaps also by personal guilt for having left the Israelites in poor hands while he lingered in the company of the divine. More generally, Moses may feel responsible for failing to appreciate their neediness, for neglecting to allow for their present slavishness and past servitude, and for being impatient with their bumbling and recalcitrance. In this view of his motives, Moses, hearing the people threatened with destruction, gives voice to a long-buried compassion, seen when he first emerged from Pharaoh's palace and three times took up the cause of underdogs. Although a spirited Levite, with a strong sense of manly righteous anger at injustice, Moses also retains—even in his very name—the marks of the maternal tenderness to which he owes his life. His long experience of exile and estrangement may also have disposed him toward clemency and care for lost and wayward souls.

Attractive though this account may be, I think it misses the mark. No question, Moses has a compassionate side. But it will come into play only later in this episode, after he descends to the camp, sees the people at their worst, and, as it were, joins them in their sin by destroying the tables and literally annulling the covenant. When he confronts God here, different motives seem to be at work. The clues may be found in the very arguments that he makes to the Lord. The matters to which he calls the Lord's attention are important also to himself: previous investment, avoiding disgrace, and keeping promises.

First of all, Moses—like the Lord—has invested a great deal in the people and in the project of delivering them from bondage and bringing them to God. Like the Lord, Moses too "brought [the people] forth out of the land of Egypt, with great power and with a mighty [staff in his] hand." He worked hard to emancipate them; he rejoiced with them in song at the Sea of Reeds; he dealt with their murmurings in the desert; he secured them a victory over Amalek; he brought them to Sinai and mediated for them a covenant with the Lord. Any ambition that Moses might have entertained for honor and glory—and who can confidently deny that he has such aspirations?—are bound up with their successful transformation into a people special unto the Lord.

Second, Moses's reputation is also at risk should the Israelites be destroyed. The argument he makes to the Lord applies also to himself: Why should the Egyptians be able to say (also) of me, Moses, "For evil did he bring them forth"? It was Moses who made a spectacle of himself in Pharaoh's palace, returning from exile to the home of his youth, confronting the mighty monarch, and sacrificing his high standing for the sake of these lowly Hebrew slaves. If the people are destroyed, he will be a laughingstock.

Finally, Moses recognizes the senselessness of the alternative plan that God offers to his ambition. His life project is to be the founder of a special people, here and now, not to be, like Abraham, the father of a family[13] that only later might grow into a nation, which would then require its own experience of servitude before someone else would deliver it to enter a covenant with the Lord. Nor is there any reason to assume that this future people would be any less stiff-necked or wayward than the present Israelites. In reminding God of His promise to the patriarchs, Moses has found a subtle way of telling God that starting over again with Moses makes no sense: for Him, it can only be these people or none at all.[14] Recognizing this, Moses speaks up for the people as they are, despite their failings. Having earlier bought into the project but not into the people, he now sees not only that they need him but also that *he needs them*—and that he belongs with them. Faced with the threat of their disappearance, Moses understands for the first time why God has spoken of them to him as "*your* people." No wonder he argues against their destruction.

Moses's argument works. Whether the Lord is persuaded by Moses's arguments or moved by his impulse to save the sinful people, the result is the first (of six) moments of increasing forgiveness[15]: "The Lord repented (*vayinnachem*) of the evil that He said that He would do unto *His* people" (32:14; emphasis added). Thanks to Moses's forceful intercession, the Lord reclaims His people and promises to forgo their deserved destruction. The people have been spared, for now.

Other parts of Moses's appeal, however, remain unaddressed. The Lord does not renew His commitment regarding the land once promised to the patriarchs, and He says nothing about restoring His covenant or His relationship with the present Israelites. Moses still has much more work to do. But he has accomplished his primary purpose: to save God's people—*his* people—from destruction.

Yet Moses's success in this appeal has unforeseen consequences. Having embraced God's people as his own and having secured an annulment of their punishment, Moses is now responsible for them, willy-nilly. Like someone who pulls a drowning man from a river, Moses finds that this "drowning people" are now his forever. And having put their welfare ahead of his own, he is compelled to take their matters into his own hands. He now heeds God's order: "Go! Get you down" to "your people." Although he does not know it yet, it will be up to him to straighten them out, without further instruction.

Moses Takes Charge

If it was part of God's plan to get Moses to take charge of the people and clean up their mess without having to return to Him for guidance, the plan works perfectly. We accompany Moses down the mountain to the iniquitous camp:

> And Moses turned and went down from the mountain, with the two tables of the Testimony in his hand; tables that were written on both their sides, on the one side and on the other were they written. And the tables were the work of God, and the writing was the writing of God, graven upon the tables. (32:15–16)

The descent begins majestically, as Moses carries the divinely made and divinely inscribed tables of the Testimony in his hand. Although he descends with an anxious heart, he still bears God's gift to the people. Perhaps things are not as bad as the Lord said they were.

But partway down, after Moses picks up Joshua, the picture darkens. They hear noises rising from the camp:

> And when Joshua heard the noise of the people as they shouted, he said unto Moses: "There is a noise of war in the camp." But he [Moses] said: "It is not the sound of the answering of might, neither is it the sound of the answering of weakness, but the sound of answering in song do I hear."[16] (32:17–18)

The Lord had said that the people "have made them a golden calf and have worshipped it and have sacrificed to it"—in the past, perhaps only once. Moses was not prepared to find them still at it. And the Lord had said nothing about dancing[17]:

> And it came to pass, as soon as he came near unto the camp, and he saw the calf and the dancing, that Moses's anger waxed hot, and he cast the tables out of his hands, and he shattered them at the foot of the mountain. (32:19)

Despite having been forewarned by the Lord, Moses, seeing with his own eyes what the people are doing, seethes with the same anger he had just protested against in the Lord. At the very site at which, forty days earlier, he and the people had ratified the covenant,[18] he now ratifies its annulment by casting away the Testimony—pointedly noted to be written by God on tables that were the work of God—and smashing it with his own hands.

Why is Moses so angry? Why does he shatter the tables? Even though the Lord has told him about the calf, the wild and chaotic scene he sees with his own eyes is beyond what he could have imagined. Accordingly, his solicitude for their lives, which he now regrets, turns into rage at their unworthiness and sinfulness. Having calmed the Lord but now compelled to act in His stead, Moses is outraged on the Lord's behalf: I now feel what He was feeling. In addition, given his own efforts on their behalf, and given that he has made them his people by rescuing them from destruction, Moses has reason to take the people's betrayal personally; he may be outraged also for the insult to himself. He may also be angry at himself for his part in their transgression: his long absence without adequate notice, his failure to leave behind proper leaders. But there is a fourth and intriguing possibility, suggested by Robert Sacks: Moses, who just spent forty days and forty nights in unmediated conversation with God, receiving elaborate instructions for building a Tabernacle, is incensed because he now realizes that the proposed Tabernacle is, at bottom, just another golden calf, a concession to the people's need for visual representation of the divine and a focus for their Dionysian impulses.[19]

But whatever the reason(s) for Moses's anger—the possibilities are not mutually exclusive—his shattering of the tables carries an additional implicit meaning. Not only does Moses officially confirm by this deed the annulment of the spiritually broken covenant, concretizing for the visual-learning Israelites, via the shattered tables, the metaphysical meaning of their misconduct.[20] He also joins the people in their guilt, in effect taking responsibility for their apostasy. The people's idolatry violated the covenant, but it was Moses's act with the tables that literally destroyed it. Instead of abandoning or repudiating his charges, he links his fate with theirs. Even as he pronounces judgment upon their actions, Moses shows himself to be that most rare and noble kind of leader, a person who willingly accepts full responsibility for all sins and errors committed by those under his command, even when they are done without his knowledge or against his orders.[21]

With the breaking of the tables, the community—Moses included—reverts to the condition of anarchy that preceded the giving of the law from on high. In this way, the text clearly exposes the tension between law and leadership, a latent theme of this entire episode, indeed of the whole Exodus story: getting, and giving, the law is one thing, personally ruling the people is another. The people have demonstrated their inability to live under law in the absence of a visible leader. Their leader Moses, confirming that fact by shattering the law, must now try to regain command in the face of total anarchy. His rebellious people need to be dealt with, promptly and dramatically, from within the community but outside the law.

Moses Restores Order

Although the covenant and the law are now annulled, the idolatry that destroyed them cannot go unpunished, and the riotous people must be brought back into line and into contrition. Moses immediately takes drastic action. He first destroys the idol and makes the people drink its powdered remains; he remonstrates with brother Aaron about leadership and responsibility; finally and most impressively, he divides the camp and violently restores order.

First things first: getting rid of the calf:

> And he took the calf that they had made, and burned it with fire, and ground [it] to powder, and strewed [the ash] upon the water, and made the Children of Israel drink [that water]. (32:20)

These simple deeds not only expose the impotence of the statue that the people had been worshipping as divine. They also symbolically force the people to acknowledge their sinful faithlessness by incorporating the statue into their very being.[22] Their ersatz "god" is pulverized, never to be reconstituted, but their sin is embodied forever, becoming part of their cultural DNA.[23] In addition, these actions may also have a practical significance, as an aid in determining individual guilt: as both talmudic and modern scholars suggest, the drinking of the powders may function like the ordeal of drinking that will later be imposed on a wife suspected of adultery, where the psychological stress could somehow reveal who was guilty and who was not.[24]

Having dealt first with the idol and its worshippers, Moses next turns to Aaron, their erstwhile leader. The conversation deals explicitly with who was responsible for what happened; it also deals, implicitly, with the relationship between the two brothers and their styles of leadership. Moses begins—speaking, we suspect, in a vexed tone—by blaming Aaron for the people's sin and challenging him to justify himself:

> And Moses said unto Aaron: "What did this people *do* to *you* that *you* have brought a great sin upon them?" (32:21; emphasis added)

Aaron tries to calm Moses down, rejecting the charge and shifting the blame elsewhere:

And Aaron said: "Let not the anger of *my lord* burn hot; you *know* the *people,* that *they* are set upon evil. So *they* said unto me: 'Make us gods, which shall go before us; for as for this Moses, the man who brought us up out the land of Egypt, we do not know what has become of him.'[25] And I said to them: 'Whosoever has any gold, let them break it off; so they gave it to me; and I cast it into the fire, and *there came out this calf.'"* (32:22–24; emphasis added)

Aaron's response does him little credit, as he vacillates between supine pleading and brazen (and false) denial of responsibility: 'Do not get angry with me, your lordship,[26] when you know how wicked these people are. And, if you really want to know, it was *your* protracted absence that was ultimately responsible. Me, I merely threw the gold into the fire, and presto, *out came the calf!'*

Moses almost certainly takes Aaron's protestation of innocence and his tall tale of the calf's spontaneous birth as tantamount to a confession. Yet although he recognizes his brother's culpable weakness, Moses says nothing further to Aaron. Among other reasons for his restraint, he remembers God's words that Aaron would become High Priest in the Tabernacle. He also knows Aaron's weakness as a ruler of men, as well as the truth of Aaron's assessment of the people. Gauging accurately the anarchic state of the camp, Moses takes quick and decisive action. The past cannot be undone, but the present political problem must be addressed at once.

Imagine the scene, and consider the political and theological situation from Moses's point of view. He is alone and, except for Joshua, without obvious allies. Aaron is useless to him; Hur has disappeared into the crowd. There are more than 600,000 men in the camp, stirred up and disorderly, and annoyed with him over his disappearance. He cannot appeal to God for help: having saved the people from His destruction, they are now his to manage. Unless he punishes the people himself, Moses cannot be sure that the Lord won't change His mind and consume them entirely. For everyone's sake, he needs to punish the sin, purge the stain of idolatry, and establish a precedent. He needs reliable allies, now and for the future. He needs to reunite the camp under his authority and turn it again to the Lord. Watch how he proceeds. Whether or not you like what he did, see if you have a better idea:

> And when Moses saw that the people were broken loose—for Aaron had let them loose as a shameful thing among their adversaries—then Moses stood, in the gate of the camp, and said: "Who is for the Lord? To me!" And all the sons of Levi gathered themselves together to him. And he said to them: "Thus says the Lord, the God of Israel: 'Put every man his sword upon his thigh, and go to and fro from gate to gate throughout the camp, and slay every man his brother, and every man his companion, and every man his neighbor.'" And the sons of Levi did according to the word of Moses, and there fell of the people that day three thousand men. And Moses said [to the Levites]: "They filled your hands [or, "Fill you hands"; *mile'u yedekhem*] today to the Lord, for every man has been against his son and against his brother; that He may also bestow upon you a blessing this day." (32:25–29)

The heart of the action is the division of the camp on the basis of professed loyalty to the Lord. Accomplishing several goals at once, Moses, standing alone in the gate of the camp, recruits allies who want to fight for God: "Who is for the Lord? To me!" Strikingly, only Moses's fellow Levites—descendants of Levi, the spirited son of Jacob, who (along with Simeon) violently avenged the rape of their sister Dinah—answer the call. The Levites alone declare themselves "for the Lord"; the other tribes keep their distance—perhaps by itself a declaration of their continued apostasy.

We must not conclude that the Levites had abstained from worshiping the calf. According to the text, *all* the people brought their gold earrings to Aaron, and there is no reason to believe that there was less than full participation in the wild festival the next day. The spirited Levites—perhaps fearful of Moses's wrath and grasping at the chance to become allies in his cause, perhaps also feeling remorse for their complicity in the transgression now that the deed has been exposed as sinful—quickly enlist on Moses's and the Lord's side when given a chance of redemption. Violence in defense of their own, we may say, is in their Levite DNA. But here, they shed blood not in defense of their own kin but in defense of the Lord. In His name, they prove themselves perfectly willing to kill their own brothers.[27] Remarkably, their fratricidal conduct on God's behalf later entitles them as priests to mediate between the people and the Lord.

Moses's instruction to the Levite volunteers is chilling. He puts the death-dealing words, which are surely of his own devising, into the mouth of "the Lord, the God of Israel."[28] In God's name, he orders them to engage in wholesale (and, it seems, random) slaughter throughout the camp, "to and fro from gate to gate." When specifying whom to slay, he does not speak about the guilty but about brothers, companions, neighbors. He orders every Levite to practice fratricide.

At the end of the day, three thousand men lie slain.[29] Who were they? Traditional exegetes, eager to see only justice at work, have taught that the righteous Levites killed only the guiltiest Israelites, the ringleaders of the rebellion—people whom they would have identified during the celebrations or perhaps those whose guilt was "revealed" by their response to the "ordeal" of drinking the ashes of the idol. But this distinction is nowhere in the text. There is no reason to believe, from the description of the licentious celebration, that there were *any* innocent among the guilty. And Moses, in instructing the Levites about the killing, does not distinguish between "guilty" and "innocent." Neither does he—either in his own name or in the words he attributes to the Lord—speak at all about doing justice. It is possible that the Levites did know from the start who most deserved to die; it is also possible, once the fighting began, that they might fairly ascribe guilt—and continued opposition to the Lord—to any persons who took up arms against them; it is even possible to ascribe guilt to everyone who did not answer Moses's call, "Who is for the Lord?"

Such speculations aside, the plain text makes it appear that the killings by the Levites are less a matter of justice and more a matter of cleansing and purgation—requiring sacrificial victims as the necessary means of purification—and of frightening the many into obedience by making an example of the few. Moses and the Levites administer shock therapy to the body politic, excising a diseased part to save the whole, allowing the "patient" to go into remission (but, alas, never to be cured).[30]

At the end of the day, the killing over, Moses speaks words of comfort to the Levites who have kindred blood on their hands. The enigmatic expression he uses—"They filled your hands to the Lord"—echoes the phrase for installing the priests in the plan God gave Moses for the Tabernacle ("and you shall fill their hand," *umille'tha 'eth-yadam;* 28:41). Your sacrificial deeds, Moses may be telling them, have consecrated you unto the Lord; they have installed you as His priests (in place of the first-born). Or, if the translation should be read as imperative, "Fill your hands to the Lord,"[31] perhaps Moses is encouraging them now to give new sacrifices to the Lord, to install themselves by making atonement for their fratricide and child slaughter. Either way, Moses holds out to the Levites the prospect that the Lord will bless them for their deeds this day.

Despite all these ambiguities, the big picture is clear: Moses's action, with the help of the Levites, is a most impressive and successful—albeit horrifying—act of leadership in perilous times. By dividing and purging the people via a small civil war, he reunites them, all in the name of the Lord. He clearly establishes the sin of idolatry and makes visible its terrible consequences. Acting as the Lord's (self-appointed) fury, he not only reinstitutes his own command over the newly contrite people. As a result of the manner in which he reconstituted the community, he now also "owns" these people, even as they continue to be the Lord's: having spared and purified them by bloodshed, Moses acquires and accepts full responsibility for their future well-being—exactly as the Lord hoped he would. He also has gained bold and effective fighters who can help him keep order in the future, especially when he again ascends the mountain to speak with God. By making sure that the Levites remember for Whom they have been fighting, Moses redirects them toward the Lord, explicitly affirming the principle that zeal for the Lord's honor is higher than the love of one's own kith and kin. A remarkable set of accomplishments for a man who, for the first time, is not merely carrying out divine orders but giving them.

And yet, disquiet hovers over this story. The division of the camp and the selective (or random) killings may have been necessary, if there was to be any hope of preserving the entire people and bringing them back into alignment with the Lord. The reestablishment of Moses's authority through force may have been equally necessary. But in the renewal of the people as a people, the long-dreaded political iniquity of fratricide is not avoided; on the contrary, Moses pointedly insisted on it in his instructions, which he even attributes (without warrant) to the Lord. He incurs no blame for his deeds here, and his strategy proves successful: when he next goes up the mountain, there will be no rebellion, no orgies, no idolatry. Nevertheless, Moses's deeds cast a lingering stain of iniquity—the original iniquity, Cain's slaying of brother Abel—over the entire people and over his own new regime. It is to the Torah's enormous credit that, unlike Machiavelli, it refuses to treat ugly political deeds as if their necessity could whitewash their ugliness: in somber tones we are told, "And there fell of the people that day three thousand men." The fratricidal iniquities of Moses's re-founding will have to be answered for. Fittingly, they will be answered by evils that are unleashed on Moses's own brother Aaron and his sons, Nadab and Abihu, evils not only linked thematically to the present story but also caused ultimately by the fratricidal implications of Moses's original unwillingness, at the burning bush, to undertake God's mission alone.[32]

Thanks to Moses's action, the political situation in Israel was again, for now, corrected, but in strictly human terms. Yet more is required. The Israelites must now make their peace with God and reknit with Him their fractured relationship.

The Forgiving God and the
Glorious Moses

With order restored among the people, Moses must turn next to rectifying matters with God—on their behalf and also his own. Thanks to his previous pleas, God has already agreed not to destroy the people. But He has said nothing about the Promised Land, about a renewal of the covenant, or about His Presence in the Tabernacle among the people. Moses, with his work cut out for him, goes to it immediately and eagerly.

Moses for the Defense: Seeking
Forgiveness on High

After the day of slaughter, night passes eerily in the camp. We imagine the frightened people anxiously murmuring to themselves: "What now?" "Who is next?" "What will become of us?" When day breaks, Moses immediately addresses their concerns:

> And it came to pass on the morrow, that Moses said unto the people: "*You* have sinned a great sin; and now *I* will go up unto the Lord, perhaps *I* shall make atonement for *your* sin." (32:30; emphasis added)

Though holding himself apart from the people, who have "sinned a great sin," Moses promises to plead their case before the Lord, nobly taking it upon himself to try to atone for them. Although their anxiety no doubt persists, they are grateful that Moses will take their case before the Lord:

> And Moses returned unto the Lord, and said: "Ah now, *this people* [N.B.: not "Your people" or "my people"] have sinned a great sin, and have made them gods of gold. Yet now, if You will forgive *their* sin—; and if not, blot *me*, I pray You, out of Your book which You have written." (32:31–32; emphasis added)

Boldly taking the initiative with the Lord, Moses confirms the people's sin and starts to enter a plea for divine forgiveness. But he interrupts himself mid-sentence, as if recognizing that his request is unreasonable and that it would be refused. He tries instead a different approach. Should the Lord *not* be willing to forgive the people, Moses asks to be added to the ranks of the guilty and blotted out from the Lord's book[1]—erased with them or perhaps even instead of them. As he has said, "Perhaps *I* shall make atonement for *your* sin." Far from accepting the Lord's earlier offer to make him a second Abraham, Moses asks to be written out of the story if He refuses to forgive the people.*

The Lord rejects outright Moses's offer of martyrdom. But Moses nevertheless succeeds in moving Him a step or two toward his goal of forgiveness:

> And the Lord said unto Moses: "Whosoever has sinned against Me, [only] him will I blot out of My book. And now

---

*Although Moses asks to share the fate of the sinning people, he still distinguishes between "*their* sin" and "*me*." We must therefore consider that Moses, in asking to be blotted out from the Lord's book, is (honestly or rhetorically) speaking also or even mainly about his *own* interests: If You don't forgive *them*, I will have no reason to live, and Your great promise to me about my mission in life will be null and void. At a later stage of Moses's pleading, he will efface the distance between them and him: in his final and successful plea, he will entreat the Lord to "pardon *our* iniquity and *our* sin, and take *us* for Your inheritance" (34:9; emphasis added). See the later discussion.

> go, lead the people unto the place of which I have spoken unto
> you; behold, My angel (mal'akh) shall go before you; never-
> theless in the day when I visit, I will visit their sin upon them."
> (32:33–34)

Speaking first about Himself, the Lord talks not about mercy but
about justice. Only those who have sinned against Me will be erased;
punishment—at least such severe punishment—must be earned. Yet
the Lord can only be pleased by what appears to be new evidence of
Moses's growing care for the people and his apparent willingness to
take their punishment upon himself. Thus He is moved to exhort Moses
to resume his aborted mission and to lead the people to the Promised
Land—a sign of His softening toward the people. What is more, He
promises Moses the accompanying presence and guidance of His angel—
not Himself, to be sure, but His messenger.

Yet despite this encouraging revelation—a second moment toward
an eventual reconciliation—the Lord is in no mood for forgiveness.
When He Himself next visits the people (at some unspecified time),
they will pay for their sin: "And the Lord smote the people for what
they had done in connection with the calf that Aaron had made"
(32:35).[2]

Stepping back momentarily from the text, we observe that we have
arrived on the threshold of an astonishing turn of events that will provide an answer to the big question: How to recommit God to Israel—
and Israel to God—when God has refused Israel His Presence? Here we
are told that the Lord intends to smite the people for their sin, but just
two chapters later, the people begin building the Tabernacle according
to the Lord's previously given instructions, so that He, newly forgiving,
may dwell among them. This transformation is almost completely the
work of Moses, who as a consequence is also utterly transformed. Furthermore, the Lord's ready receptiveness to Moses's pleading makes us
suspect that this transformation of Moses may be the Lord's primary goal in these negotiations. Moses wants God's forgiveness; God
wants Moses's transformation. We must watch carefully to see how
this works.

For the moment, Moses, although dissatisfied, holds his peace. The Lord, continuing to explain His last remarks, also gives Moses his new orders:

> And the Lord spoke unto Moses: "Depart, go up from here— you and the people whom you have brought up out of the land of Egypt, unto the land that I swore unto Abraham, unto Isaac, and unto Jacob, saying, 'Unto your seed will I give it.' And I will send an angel before you; and I will drive out the Canaanite, the Amorite, and the Hittite and the Perizzite, the Hivite, and the Jebusite—unto a land flowing with milk and honey; but I will not go up in your midst, for you are a stiff-necked people; lest I consume (*kalah*) you in the way." (33:1–3)

God orders Moses and the people to head for the Promised Land in accordance with His promise to the patriarchs. He offers an angel to guide their journey and even promises to drive out the six nations currently occupying the land. He will not, as Moses had reason to fear, abandon the people. But annulling the plan for the Tabernacle, He refuses to go in their midst, lest He consume the people on the way. How, we wonder, can Moses reclaim God's Presence and in a way that will not harm the people?

When the people learn from Moses (in the next verse) that the Lord now refuses to go with them, they fall into mourning, and "no man put on his ornaments"—a fitting gesture, given that their idolatry began with their gold earrings. God attempts to console the people, having Moses tell them that He is staying away for their own good: "If I went up in your midst for a single moment, I would consume you" (33:5). He instructs them to keep off their jewelry, as befits their lapsed condition, but adds, only slightly more promisingly, that He will see later what response from Him they have come to deserve: "And I shall know what to do with you" (33:5). Responding contritely, "the Children of Israel stripped themselves of their ornaments from Mount Horeb" (33:6).[3]

But while the people mourn, Moses goes hopefully to work. He moves his own tent far outside the defiled camp and calls it the Tent of Meeting—clearly a substitute for the Tabernacle—where he hopes to continue his and the people's relationship with the Lord. He is not disappointed. Whenever Moses goes out to the Tent, all the people, filled with contrition, watch him anxiously from the openings of their own tents. And whenever Moses enters the Tent, a pillar of cloud descends to its doorway from which "the Lord spoke with Moses." The effect on the people is most salutary. On seeing from afar the pillar of cloud before the Tent, the people prostrate themselves in awe-filled worship, each at his own tent opening, "communing" with the Lord in the only way they now know how. But the relationship between God and man that unfolds at the Tent involves no such subservience or self-effacement:

And the Lord spoke to Moses face to face, as a man speaks to his friend. (33:11)

How are we to understand this astonishing image? What is meant by "speaking face to face"? We note, first, that nothing is said about *seeing* each other. The intimacy is not of looking but of speaking; it is not sensible but (primarily) noetic. The communication takes place "mind to mind," without the need for images or visions or trances—exactly to Moses's taste. But the encounter is not coldly noetic. As in a face-to-face conversation of friends, each is altogether present and warmly open to the other—in honest, direct, guileless speech. Hierarchy and awe-inspiring distance all but disappear. Fully answering Moses's desire for communion with the divine, the Lord descends yet does not condescend to His "friend," "this man Moses."[4] In addition, by visiting him in his tent, the Lord accepts Moses's hospitality and at the same time teaches Moses to appreciate what the people need and want: a designated, sanctified, terrestrial place for communing with and worshipping the divine, a place where they too might experience its presence.

Encouraged by the Lord's solicitude and taking advantage of His intimate speech (as well as the evident penitence of the people), Moses presses his case. He appeals for greater knowledge of the Lord and urges the Lord to personally accompany the people. His boldness and rhetorical genius are stunning:

> And Moses said to the Lord: "*Look: You* say to *me,* 'Bring up *this* people.' But *You* have not let me *know whom* You will send with me. And *You* have said, 'I know you by name and you have found favor in My eyes.' So now, therefore, please, *if* I have [indeed] found favor in Your eyes, please let *me know Your ways* (*derakhekha*), that *I* may *know You,* to the end that I may find [real] favor in Your eyes—and *see,* that *this* nation is *Your people.*" (33:12–13; emphasis added)

Moses begins by expressing dissatisfaction with the Lord's offer to send His messenger to lead the people on their journey. What sort of messenger, and of what disposition? Will he be forgiving and kind to the people, or will he be, as Moses has reason to fear, punitive and harsh?[5] But Moses promptly moves from complaining that he does not know the messenger to pleading for greater knowledge of the Lord Himself: "Let me know *Your ways.*" We are reminded of Moses's bold request at the burning bush to know the Lord. But the context here is different, and so are the nature of Moses's question and the reason he is asking it.

At the burning bush, seeking to know God's name, Moses asked to know God's nature or essence. He was no doubt motivated partly by a need to learn whether God's powers were adequate to the mission He proposed for him, as well as by his anticipated need to inform the people Who it was Who had sent him to them. But Moses was, I believe, primarily motivated by an intellectual desire to learn the truth about the divine, knowledge sought for its own sake. Here, although Moses's philosophical interest is clearly still present, he feels strongly his political responsibility for the Israelite people. God has just favored Moses with unprecedented "friendship," coming down to join him in the Tent of Meeting. Moses, his personal thirst for God now partially quenched, seeks to extend that intimacy, but no longer for himself alone. He now wants to know not the Lord's essence but His *ways* in the world—His direction or path, His intention or purpose, but especially His "flexibility": whether, and on what basis, He is capable of forgiveness.[6] By thus increasing his knowledge of the Lord, Moses seeks to find even greater favor in His eyes, favor that can be used to benefit His people. He concludes by alluding precisely to this practical point: consider, Lord, that "*this*" nation is in fact *Your people*.

Moses's plea succeeds. In a third moment of softening, the Lord appears to accede to the first part of his request, the part concerning who will go with him: "My Presence [literally, 'My face,' *panay*] will go, and I will give you rest (*vahanichothi lakh*)" (33:14)—in other words, Not to worry, Moses, I will put your mind at ease.[7] But Moses is still not satisfied, for two reasons. Although the Lord has said that He Himself will go, He has not specified with whom: only with Moses or also with the people? Second, He has ignored Moses's request to know His ways. Moses, speaking boldly and frankly—as a man might speak with a friend—presses for clarification and urges the Lord to go with the people, not only with him. At long last and for the first time, Moses speaks not of "me" and "them" but of "us" and "we":

> And he said unto Him: "If Your Presence ('Your face,' *pan-ekha*) will not go, carry *us* not up hence. For wherein now shall it be known that I have found grace in Your sight, I *and Your people*? Is it not in that *You* go with *us*, so that *we* are distinguished, I *and Your people*, from *all the people* that are upon the face of the earth?" (33:15–16; emphasis added)

Moses's argument is powerful. He exploits God's response to his urgent question at the burning bush. To Moses's "Who am I?" the Lord had answered, "I will be with you (*'Ehyeh 'imach*)"—meaning, among other things: Who are You? You are the one *with whom I will be*. Now, hammering away at "I and *Your People*," Moses quite properly insists: Who am I, and *who are the Israelites*, if God is not with *us*? How can *we* Israelites become the holy nation God wants us to be, and how can I, Moses, be their leader on their path toward holiness, if the Lord (Himself) is not *with us*?

Once again Moses is successful, but once again only in part. The Lord, in a fourth moment of softening, accepts Moses's plea because it comes from Moses:

And the Lord said unto Moses: "Also this thing that you have spoken I will do, for *you* have found grace in My sight, and I know *you* by name." (33:17; emphasis added)

The Lord agrees to go with Moses and (by implication) with the people. He will, as promised, distinguish this people from all the other peoples of the earth. But He does so only because Moses—and only Moses—has found favor in His eyes. His relationship with the people is not yet repaired.

Moses, still not satisfied, now makes his boldest request:

And he said, "Let me see [or 'Show me'; *har'eni, from ra'ah*, "to see"], please, Your glory [*kavod*]." (33:18)

Why this plea for a theophany? And why now?

Moses's reasons are, once again, probably mixed. God simply ignored his earlier request to "know Your ways," and Moses renews a version of the same entreaty. He still wants to know God, as a man might want to better know his friend or as a god-thirsty mortal his deity. But that personal reason is subordinate to the political one: the fate of the people to whom Moses has now attached himself. So far, God has softened four times in response to his requests, because Moses has found favor in His eyes—including the additional favor Moses earns here by pleading so selflessly for the people. But the Lord has said nothing about forgiving the people or about *their* having a chance once again to find favor in His eyes. On their behalf, Moses needs to know whether God is a god of mercy and forgiveness or whether He insists on strict justice and punishment. Will he later avenge the people's idolatry, perhaps when Moses is no longer present to redeem them? Moses needs to know, yes or no: Will you forgive the people? And if not now, how can they (we) earn your forgiveness?

This request differs from all Moses's previous efforts to know the divine. Here, he does not seek to know God's ways (or to learn His name) but to be shown (or *to see*) His glory (*kavod*). Moses wants God to appear to him fully, intimately, visibly face to face. He asks for unmediated, direct insight into the deity. It is a most audacious request, delivered politely but without fear or even awe.

Astonishingly, the Lord's answer is, yet again, a partial concession to Moses's petition—the fifth softening in this remarkable series of conversations. The Lord will grant Moses a passing glance at Himself, albeit not a full revelation. But He does not yield on the question of pardon and forgiveness:

> And He said: "I will make all My goodness (*kol-tuvi*) pass before you [literally, 'before your face'; *'al-panekha*], and I will proclaim the Name of the Lord before you; but I will be gracious to whom I will be gracious, and will show mercy on whom I will show mercy." And He said: "You cannot see My face, for man shall not see Me and live." (33:19–20)

Neither His glory nor His face, but only His goodness—what we might call His "moral" attributes—will the Lord show to Moses. He will also proclaim before Moses His personal Name—presumably something more revealing than the enigmatic "I Will Be What I Will Be." But as for His grace and His mercy, these are not under man's command or control: once again God answers with a disarming version of "I Will Be What I Will Be."

But in what must seem an evasive reply to Moses's entreaty that God show grace to His people, the Lord has in fact delivered a profound teaching (and not only about Himself): punishment must be earned, but grace and mercy are gifts. Even to the repentant, they come unbidden and uncompelled; their arrival seems—correctly—to be from "out of this world." By this teaching, God also corrects Moses's assumption that knowledge of God may be used to influence His conduct: even knowing God's ways or goodness will not enable Moses to restore Israel to favor in God's eyes. Knowledge does not command grace. Philosophizing is ultimately unendowed.

And as for the possibility of knowing God fully and thoroughly—of knowing His "face," that is, His being or essence or person—the Lord delivers a definitively negative verdict. Such knowledge is impossible for a human being: "Man shall not see Me and live." This pronouncement does not mean, as is often thought, that the sight of God would kill one instantly. Nor does it imply that one *can* see God but only in the afterlife. The idea seems rather to be that the human mind—even the very best human mind—cannot comprehend—"see"—what is indefinable, unlimited, unfathomable, and incomprehensible. Although Moses and God may speak as if face to face—without intermediation, with full openness, and with mutual intelligibility—God cannot be known or seen completely.

Yet Moses, like no man before him or since, has uniquely earned and will receive a (partial) theophany. God Himself offers to arrange for Moses a second-best—and the only possible—revelation of the divine. It will be the only such revelation ever given to a human being:

> And the Lord said: "Behold, there is a place by Me, and you shall stand upon the rock. And it shall come to pass, while My glory (kavod) passes by, that I will put you in a cleft of the rock, and will cover you with My hand until I have passed by. And I will take away My hand, and you shall see My back; but My face shall not be seen." (33:21–23)

Moses, who at the burning bush had to hide his own face so as not to look upon God, will here be shielded by the hand of God from seeing all but His "back."[8] Along with Moses, we too will soon learn what it is that he alone was allowed to "see."

On the threshold of the revelation Moses is about to receive, let us observe that it will have profound, albeit temporary, theologico-political implications. One man, and one man only, gets privileged access to secret knowledge of the divine (limited though it must necessarily be). The rest of the people, the "ignorant many," will have to trust that the "Enlightened One" truly knows what he is doing. At least for now, the desired political condition of equity—equal status for all adult members of the community, equally called to be holy men unto the Lord—is on hold, especially as the whole people have yet to be forgiven. But there is good news. In Israel, in contrast to ancient aristocratic societies, the distinction between "the one" (or "the few") and "the many" is not permanent. As I just pointed out, thanks to the Torah in which we are reading about it, the revelation that Moses received of the Lord's "backside" is now accessible also to us, owing both to God's "turning His back" on Moses and Moses's subsequent disappearance into the Law. Hierarchy for now, equity forever. The immediate sequel shows how it is to happen.

A New Revelation, a Renewed Covenant

Before Moses can receive his personal theophany, he must make preparations that have more than personal import. In keeping with the communal emphasis of Moses's appeal, the new revelation will be given to him only in the context of a renewed covenant between God and Israel. The momentous conversation at the Tent of Meeting ends with these divine instructions:

> And the Lord said unto Moses: "Hew yourself two tables of stone like unto the first; and I will write upon the tables the words that were on the first tables, which you did break. And be ready by the morning, and come up in the morning unto Mount Sinai, and present yourself there to Me on the top of the mountain. And no man shall come up with you, neither let any man be seen throughout all the mountain; neither let the flocks nor herds feed before that mountain."
> (34:1–3)

The new covenant, although identical in its requirements to the first one, will be reestablished on a different basis. This time Moses will make the tables,[9] and the Lord will write on these man-made stones the binding divine words, "those that were on the first tables."* The law is passing more fully into human hands. When the text later reports how the tables were inscribed, it will be unclear whether God or Moses did the writing.

---

*Since it has been throughout unclear what was written on the first tables, we are no wiser about what is written on the second. The so-called Ten Commandments? The ordinances? The instructions for the Tabernacle? All of the above? We will return to this matter.

The rest of the instruction anticipates the special revelation vouchsafed to Moses: only he is to be on the mountain. He alone must present himself to the Lord at the top of Mount Sinai. Moses, no surprise, does exactly as he was told:

> And he hewed two tables of stone like unto the first; and Moses rose up early in the morning, and went up unto Mount Sinai, as the Lord had commanded him, and took in his hand two tables of stone. (34:4)

Up early, and eager for the encounter, Moses stands ready for both the revelation and the renewal of the covenant. We readers are privileged to hear—and allowed to imagine—what happened next:

> And the Lord descended in the cloud, and stood with him there, and proclaimed the Name of the Lord. And the Lord passed by before him, and proclaimed: "The Lord, The Lord (*Y-H-V-H*, *Y-H-V-H*), god merciful and gracious (*'el rachum vechannun*), slow to anger [literally, "long of anger"; *'erech 'appayim*], and abundant in loving-kindness (*chesed*) and truth (*'emeth*); keeping loving-kindness unto the thousandth generation, forgiving iniquity (*'avon*) and transgression (*pesha'*) and sin (*chatta'ah*); but who will by no means clear the guilty, visiting the iniquity of the fathers upon the children, and upon the children's children, unto the third and unto the fourth generation." (34:5–7)

The first sentence gives the summary; the rest gives the specific content of the Lord's proclamation: His name and His so-called moral attributes. Regarding the Name of the Lord, uttered twice in succession, we are none the wiser. Indeed, one way to understand the repetition of the divine name is as a denominative sentence that again declares, tautologically, the mystery of the divine: "The Lord, He is the Lord" or (literally), "'He-Will-Be,' He is 'He-Will-Be.'" We cannot "see" His "face"; we cannot know His being or essence. But because we have been able to "see" Him in action—displaying something of what He-will-be in the affairs of His people—it is possible to see evidence of the attributes He here attributes to Himself: the goodness that constitutes what Moses "sees" as His "back."

Jewish tradition derives from this self-revealing description the so-called Thirteen Attributes (*middoth*) of God, which play a significant role in traditional liturgy.[10] Because of the singular character of this theophany, I can understand why it invites separation from its context, to be treated as a freestanding account of the divine character. But I am interested, here, to see how this revelation functions in our unfolding story of the renewal of the covenant and the preparation of Moses for his new role with the people—and, especially, to learn whether God's character admits of an enduring relationship with wayward, stiff-necked, and sinful human beings who fall short of what is required of them. In other words, people like us.

We see immediately how God's revelation addresses Moses's major concern head-on. Are you a God capable of forgiveness? Can you show mercy; can you pardon these people? Or are you a strict and exacting God Who cares only for justice and Who means what He says when He announces severe punishments for disobedience and betrayal? Is our failure necessarily deadly?

The answers to these questions are of existential importance to the Children of Israel and to Moses as their leader—and to us, the readers. To put it starkly: Is the world the kind of place in which we human beings can readily accept an invitation to aim for the highest, despite knowing that we are likely to fail, because there can be mercy and forgiveness if we repent our failures and renew our efforts to succeed? Only in such a world can a person or a people eagerly aim for moral and spiritual perfection.

The news Moses receives is most heartening: the revelation stresses God's "softer" side, as we have seen it slowly emerge in this conversation under Moses's prodding. For the first time in the Torah, the Lord presents Himself not as God Almighty, or as the God of Battles Who will defend Israel His firstborn, or as the God Who seeks glory by meting out harsh justice to the Egyptians. He supplements the picture of the powerful and dreadful Lord of Hosts, about Whom Moses and the people sang in the Song of the Sea, and He qualifies His own self-description, offered in the Ten Commandments exactly in connection with the issue of idol worship, as "a jealous [or "impassioned"] God." What He reveals here is, one might say, a more maternal deity, a God full of mercy[11] and grace Who does not rush to exact punishment when angered ("long of anger"), Who overflows with loving-kindness and keeps it to the thousandth generation, and Who forgives iniquity, transgression, and sin.

This new picture of the Lord is encouraging also for the reader. It is the first clear instance in the Torah in which God discloses His loving side, foreshadowing His reputation as "father"—or "parent"—to His people. A careful reader may wonder, Was this always part of God's character, or was it evoked or elicited only by Moses's persistent pleading? More radically, was it evoked only once it was needed, as a result of the people's sinfulness? The Lord was not always merciful in the face of massive evil. We recall how, even before there was any law whose violation called for punishment, He was perfectly willing to drown almost all terrestrial life (save for Noah and his ark-mates) in response to mankind's wicked and violent ways. Was this episode with the golden calf necessary not only for the people to learn the devastating meaning of sin and the beauty of repentance, or for Moses finally to shoulder responsibility for the people, but also for God to emerge in human experience as a God of forgiveness?

Regardless of whether God was always a God of mercy and grace, one thing is clear: the new revelation of this side of His nature is the indispensable condition for the renewal of the covenant and for the Israelite future as a holiness-seeking people. But this good news comes only through Moses's persistent and insistent pleading on behalf of the people. Now that the justice-loving Moses has discovered for himself the need for compassion and mercy, the Lord is prepared to let him know that they are available.

Yet the Lord, by His own account, is not simply a softie: He will temper His mercy with justice. In concluding the theophany, He reminds Moses that He "will by no means clear the guilty" and that He will "visit the iniquity of the fathers upon the children, and upon the children's children, unto the third and unto the fourth generation."[12] For many readers, this conclusion entirely vitiates the humane picture of the rest of the revelation. Far from attesting to God's justice, this aspect of the Lord's self-proclaimed character seems, to many readers, grossly unfair.

How can it be just for the children and the children's children to suffer iniquity on account of their iniquitous forebears? But as we noted when discussing the Ten Commandments, iniquity differs from sin, for which only the sinner gets punished. The twisted effects of iniquity linger in the world as the stain of pollution. The residues of iniquitous conduct are less a matter of just punishment and more of their intergenerational consequence.

A word about the attribute translated as "abundant in truth," for there is more here than meets the eye. The word for truth, 'emeth, may better be translated as "firmness" or "faithfulness." It carries connotations of steadfastness and reliability or of honoring one's word or keeping one's promises—and, therefore also of "justice." And while it is comforting to know that the Lord will keep faith with His promises of reward, it can be distressing to remember that the Lord will be equally steadfast in His promise of punishment. His remaining true to Himself can be a mixed blessing, depending on how true one is to Him—and whether one prefers mercy to justice, or the reverse.[13]

The revelation complete, Moses responds most appropriately, first with reverential deference, then with bold supplication:

> And Moses made haste, and bowed his head toward the earth, and worshipped. And he said: "If now I have found grace in Your sight, O Lord, let the Lord, I pray You, go in the midst of *us*; for it is a stiff-necked people; and pardon *our* iniquity and *our* sin, and take *us* for Your inheritance." (34:8–9; emphasis added)

Taking advantage of the gift of personal theophany—an expression of the Lord's favor and of His self-declared goodness—Moses asks directly for the ultimate goal of his pleadings: a full pardon of "*our* iniquity and *our* sin," a renewal of the covenant, and the Lord's once-promised Presence amidst the people. Moses ignores the Lord's prior declaration that His mercy and grace cannot be commanded or earned by human doings. He simply asks that God's grace, so wondrously bestowed upon him in this theophany, now be given to the entire people, his "fellow sinners." Moses, who went up the mountain seeking atonement for their great sin

(32:30), now, in his final appeal, unequivocally identifies himself as one among them, a full partner in *our* sin.

The appeal succeeds, even beyond Moses's hopes. In relenting for the sixth and final time, the Lord—moved by Moses's expression of solidarity with the sinners—renews and expands His prior commitment to the people:

> And He said: "Behold, I make a covenant; before all your people I will do marvels, such as have not been wrought in all the earth, nor in any nation; and all the people among which you are shall see the work of the Lord that I am about to do with you, that it is tremendous. Observe you [singular] that which I am commanding you [plural] this day; behold, I am driving out before you the Amorite, and the Canaanite, and the Hittite, and the Perizzite, and the Hivite, and the Jebusite. (34:10–11)

The covenant is more than renewed. Looking ahead to the Promised Land, this new agreement promises unprecedented marvels—in particular, the expulsion of the present pagan occupants of the land to make way for the Israelite nation, entering upon its true home. God gives Moses everything he wanted, missing only the words, "I forgive you."[14]

Conditions of the New Covenant

But the new covenant, like the first, is not one-sided. The Lord alerts Moses to a coming series of commands that the people will have to follow: "Observe you [Moses] that which I am commanding you [the people] this day." The commands follow immediately. Most of them revisit ordinances previously given (in Exodus 23) regarding the calendar for ritual observance and, especially, the avoidance of idolatry. This time, for obvious reasons, they are delivered in sterner speech. For easy reference, I number ten separable commands:

> (1) "Take heed to yourself, lest you make a covenant with the inhabitants of the land whither you go, lest they be for a snare

in the midst of you. But you shall break down their altars, and dash in pieces their pillars, and you shall cut down their cultic poles.[15] For [*ki*; "here's the reason:"] you shall bow down to no other god; for the Lord, whose name is Jealous [*qanna'*; "Impassioned"], is a jealous ["impassioned"] God; lest you make a covenant with the inhabitants of the land, and they *whore* [*zanah*; "play the harlot"] after their gods, and *slaughter* sacrifices unto their gods, and one of them *calls* you, and you *eat* of his sacrifice; and you *take* of their daughters unto your sons, and their daughters *whore* after their gods, and *make* your sons *whore* after their gods. (2) You shall make you no molten gods. (3) The Feast of Unleavened Bread shall you keep. Seven days you shall eat unleavened bread, as I commanded you, at the time appointed in the month Aviv, for in the month Aviv you came out from Egypt. (4) All that opens the womb is Mine; and of all your cattle you shall sanctify the males, the firstlings of ox and sheep. And the firstling of an ass you shall redeem with a lamb; and if you will not redeem it, then you shall break its neck. All the firstborn of your sons you shall redeem. And none shall appear before Me empty. (5) Six days you shall work, but on the seventh day you shall rest; in plowing time and in harvest you shall rest. (6) And you shall observe the Feast of Weeks, even of the first fruits of wheat harvest, and the Feast of Ingathering at the turn of the year. (7) Three times in the year shall all your males appear before the Lord God, the God of Israel. For I will cast out nations before you, and enlarge your borders; neither shall any man covet your land, when you go up to appear before the Lord your God three times in the year. (8) (a) You shall not offer the blood of My sacrifice with leavened bread; (b) neither shall the sacrifice of the Feast of the Passover be left unto the morning. (9) The choicest first fruits of your land you shall bring unto the house of the Lord your God. (10) You shall not seethe a kid in its mother's milk." (34:12–26; emphasis added)

We discussed many of these matters in dealing with the ordinances, as presented (somewhat differently) in the first covenant. As we are focusing here not on specific commandments but on the changing relationships among God, Moses, and the people, I will confine my comments to a few essential points.

First, the entire list anticipates the future encounter with the Canaanites, whose earthy and earth-worshipping ways are very seductive and whose practices are worlds apart from the way of Israel. The warnings against yielding to their blandishments are conveyed in seven verbs that highlight the problem—*whore, slaughter, calls, eat, take, whore, make whore*—at the center of which is the seemingly innocent practice of sharing a meal and partaking of the sacrificial offering.[16]

Second, in keeping with the caveat about nature worship, the renewed emphasis on the seasonal festivals and on the injunctions regarding firstborn and first fruits is intended to direct the people's attention away from "Mother Earth" and the so-called gods of fertility and toward the Lord, Creator of heaven and earth.

Finally, the ubiquitous and essential principle of the Sabbath, originally introduced as a way of sanctifying time away from the motion of the heavenly bodies, is here presented as liberating the people from the demands of planting and harvesting—other aspects of being tied to "Mother Earth" and deferring to her rhythms and turnings. Israel, once again, is to be a people with a spiritual purpose, defined even before it has a land and is tethered to its soil.

With the conditions for the renewal of the covenant stated, the Lord moves to have them preserved in writing. Fittingly, the written story of Moses on the mountain concludes with a report of writing on the tables of stone:

> And the Lord said unto Moses: "Write for you *these* words, for in accordance with these words I have made a covenant *with you and with Israel*." And he was there with the Lord forty days and forty nights; he did neither eat bread, nor drink water. And he wrote upon the tables the words of the covenant, the ten words. (34:27–28; emphasis added).

There is plenty of ambiguity in these remarks. Are the conditions for renewing the covenant, to be written by Moses on some unspecified object, the same as the "ten words" that we are told are written on the tables? If not, are the ten words the same as the "ten commandments"? If so, what about the rest of the commandments, ordinances, and instructions for the Tabernacle, each or all of which were presumably written on the first set of tables? And who is the "he" that wrote upon the tables: God or Moses? God had said that He would write on the tables that Moses would make (34:1); yet in the context here, which celebrates for us (only) the elevated and superhuman doings of Moses (neither eating nor drinking for forty days), there is reason to suspect that *he* did the engraving—whatever was engraved.

We can do little to resolve these ambiguities. But the last one, I suspect, is deliberate. With the law about to pass into human hands, on tables pointedly prepared by Moses, and with the intimate conversation and association of Moses and the Lord for forty days and forty nights,[17] it seems right that we should not have to decide whether the writing was done by the Lord or Moses. A coauthorship of the new dispensation, reflecting the agreement miraculously achieved between them, could not be more fitting.

The Glorious Moses

The forty-day summit meeting between Moses and God is over. Both have reason to rejoice. Moses has won a pardon for the Israelites and negotiated the Lord's return to His people; his desire to know God has been partially satisfied, through the most welcome revelation of His attributes—most notably, mercy, grace, and loving-kindness. The Lord, meanwhile, has used His anger and His threat to destroy the Israelites to provoke Moses not only to come to their defense but also to assume full leadership of the people and responsibility for their future well-being. The "happy ending" of the story of the golden calf lacks only an account of Moses's return to level ground, where, after this second forty-day absence, the people await him, this time in a different mood.

Once again, Moses descends the mountain carrying tables of stone, but everything else is different:

And it came to pass, when Moses came down from Mount Sinai with the two tables of the testimony in Moses's hand, when he came down from the mountain, that Moses *knew not* that the *skin of his face sent forth beams* [or "shone"; *qaran*], while He talked with him. And when Aaron and all the Children of Israel *saw* Moses, behold, the skin of his face sent forth beams; and they were *afraid* (*yare'*) to come near him. And Moses called unto them; and Aaron and all the chieftains of the congregation returned unto him; and Moses spoke to them. And afterward *all* the Children of Israel came near, and he gave them in commandment all that the Lord had spoken with him in Mount Sinai. And when Moses had done speaking with them, he put a veil on his face. But when Moses went in before the Lord that He might speak with him, *he took the veil off,* until he came out; and he came out; and spoke unto the Children of Israel that which he was commanded. And the Children of Israel saw the face of Moses, that the skin of Moses's face sent forth beams; and Moses put the veil back upon his face, until he went in to speak with Him. (34:29–35; emphasis added)

This passage is, as scholars have noted, written in an elevated style perfectly suited to the grandeur of the subject. Although it begins by focusing on the tables Moses is carrying—itself a subject worthy of elevated speech—the rest of the story deals with Moses's shining (or glowing or radiant) face, an unexpected effect of his intimate encounters with the Lord. Something of divine glory remains with Moses—and, it seems, will remain with him permanently—as he reenters the community of Israelites.

Over the centuries, there has been controversy over what exactly was altered in Moses's appearance, and the text is admittedly not clear. Because the Hebrew word, here translated as "sent forth beams" (or "shone"), *qaran*, is a denominative verb (used nowhere else in the Torah) of *qeren*, "horns," interpreters (beginning with Aquila's—Onkelos's—translation of the Torah into Greek in the second century CE) have claimed that Moses had sprouted horns on his head. Given the historical context, the idea may even seem plausible: the horns of bulls and rams were widely used as symbols of nature's majesty and over-whelming power, and horned deities played a significant role in the An-cient Near East. Several Egyptian deities of the Mosaic period (among them, Bat and Hathor) were represented with human faces topped by the horns of a bull or a ram. Following this interpretation of the text, Western art—most famously in Michelangelo's renowned statue—often showed Moses with horns atop his head.

But given the textual context, this interpretation cannot be sus-tained: the subject of the verb, *qaran*, is "the skin of his face," not the "top of his head." In the Torah—precisely in opposition to the horns on Egyptian deities' heads or on the golden calf, and to the veneration of nature altogether—the representation of Moses's divine-like potency ap-pears not as horns but as (horn-shaped) *shafts* (or "rays" or "beams" or "projections") *of light* (or "radiance" or "glow"). It is God's first crea-ture, light, that reflects its supernatural source and projects it from the mediator's face outward toward the faces of the people. In the Torah, not bull-headed strength but open-faced intellect and care are the reflections of the divine.

Whatever the meaning of *qaran*, Moses's encounter with God cer-tainly altered his appearance in a way that radically changes his rela-tion to the people. The face is the face of Moses, but the light it radiates comes from the Lord. As Ruth Martin has put it, "God's 'I-am with you (*'ehyeh 'imach*)' is now stamped across his face"[18]—a sign not only of his elevated authority with the people but also of the renewal of God's so-licitude and care for them. Most wonderfully, humble Moses—despite his elevation—is completely unaware of his new godlike radiance. He has come simply to bring the good news and the replaced covenant.

Yet the people, seeing Moses's beaming face, are awestruck and afraid: Who, exactly, has come back to them and in what spirit? They remember his violent purging of the camp on the Lord's behalf, before he left them to return up the mountain. Does this radiance bode fur-ther evils for the camp? Playing it safe, they stand far off.[19]

But Moses calls out to them and invites their approach. Their fear dissolved, first Aaron and the heads of the tribes, and afterward all the Children of Israel, come near and listen attentively—face to face with his godlike countenance—as he transmits all the Lord's commandments. Marvelously, although no man can see God's face while they live, the people are enlivened by seeing God's reflected glory on the face of His divine messenger.

Having brought the news from on high to the people, Moses, still aglow, veils his face—we do not know why. Perhaps he wishes to remain hidden, like the Lord an unseen but seeing ruler, who paradoxically keeps his elevated standing by dissembling his superiority. Conversely— and I think more likely—perhaps he does not want, in everyday life, to traffic in or desacralize his spiritual elevation, so he reserves his reflected radiance for those occasions when he is functioning as mediator between God and the people.[20] He removes the veil whenever he goes to speak with the Lord, and he keeps it off when he reemerges to communicate God's messages and commandments to the people. Moses, coming out of hiding to face both the Lord and the people on the Lord's behalf, is now able to bind them together with an unbreakable bond.

What Has Been Accomplished?

Our story completed, we again step back to take stock. At first glance, the difficulties with which we began our exploration appear to have been solved or at least ameliorated. The people now have both the law and the leader they require, and they can aspire anew with the knowledge that they may be forgiven by a gracious and merciful God. The covenant, once shattered but now permanently renewed, has survived its existential threat. The Lord has His proper champion, ready and eager to rule in His name. And Moses has gained not only his needed authority but also a more intimate knowledge of God and His gracious and merciful ways. And—as we learn only much later—thanks to his pleading with the Lord on their behalf, Moses acquires a glorious place in the hearts of the people, who will continue to tell his deathless story—and, in large part thanks to him, their deathless story as well.

And yet. And yet. On further reflection, the thoughtful reader finds the current scene disquieting. Veiling or no veiling, humility or no humility, Moses has become a godlike figure, towering above the people, an object of awe and reverence. Can this be what the Lord intended? Has not the solution to the first set of problems left a new one in their place?

The situation is complicated and needs to be placed in context. We must recall that Moses's present standing is the culmination of a series of events whose major purpose was to elevate him in the eyes of the people. First, at the end of the miraculous episode at the Sea of Reeds, we were told that "the people feared the Lord, and they *trusted* in the Lord and [for the first time, also] *in his servant Moses*" (14:31; emphasis added). Later, at Mount Sinai, before the revelation of the Ten Commandments, the Lord tells Moses that He will produce a stunning display on the mountain so that the people thereafter "will trust also in you forever" (19:9). That plan seems to work almost immediately. After the Lord finishes speaking and the pyrotechnics cease, the people express their fear of the Lord and demand that Moses speak with them instead; as anticipated, their increased fear of God increased their attachment to Moses (20:16). Yet so successful was this elevation of Moses that, when he went up the mountain the first time, the Israelites forgot about God and demanded a replacement for Moses. The regrettable result of Moses's previous elevation was the sin of the golden calf.

Yet here, having resolved the problems revealed in the story of the golden calf, Moses is at his zenith, standing higher than ever before. His face shining with reflected divine light, he exudes more than mere personal charisma. Among the people, who see that he has been touched by the divine fire, Moses—exhibiting a radiance of reflected divinity—has acquired an even more godlike status.

What are we meant to think of Moses's near apotheosis? On one hand, he will need (and will keep) this elevated status to deal with the terrestrial and political challenges that the people will face, both internally and externally. But on the other hand, we sense an even greater danger that the people will mistake Moses for God and worship him. And we worry lest Moses himself, although humble for now, fall prey to this error and rule as Pharaoh did, assigning himself divine standing.

As if to acknowledge these dangers, the Torah presents their remedy in the immediate sequel, at least with respect to worship. Moses will immediately use his elevated status to build the Tabernacle, to redirect the people's awe and reverence to the Lord. He will summon the people to their first communal project; he will direct the building of a sanctuary where they can satisfy their longings for a relationship to the divine—and, hereafter, in a manner that has no need for Moses's mediation. In all spiritual matters, it is to be Aaron and his sons, not Moses (or his irrelevant descendants), who will play the mediating role in handling the divine or holy things. Soon after the end of Exodus, Aaron, the people's guide to golden calf, will stand established as the High Priest. But this time, and from now on, he will in all respects obey instructions given by the Lord. The people acquire an institutionalized route to the divine that completely bypasses Moses, their godlike mediator. The chance of worshipping Moses in place of God becomes vanishingly small.

In political matters, however, Moses's ongoing elevation creates another difficulty. His supreme authority still seems necessary, as the people are far from ready to govern themselves under the law they have received. There remain many external threats and internal conflicts that must be countered before the Israelites are ready to enter the Promised Land; for such matters, Moses's singular leadership, backed by divine authority, remains indispensable. Eventually, his work complete, Moses will exit the scene, leaving his law in charge. But the path to that point will be fraught with difficulties. Rivals among the people—for example, Korah—will rise to oppose him, objecting precisely to his elevated standing ("the whole congregation is holy"), and Moses himself will be in danger of acting with hubris, failing to trust in the Lord. Although much progress has been made, the vexed questions of the leader and the led have not been permanently settled. We are beginning to suspect they never will be.

The Completion(s) of the Tabernacle

T he episode of the golden calf is over. The crisis is past. Moses, through his political skills, has restored order to the camp. Through his rhetorical skills, the Lord has been appeased, and the people are (all but) forgiven. The covenant is renewed; the stone tables have been replaced; the cloud of the Lord again visits the camp. The people are contrite but apprehensive, aware of how close they came to catastrophe. And Moses, reflecting God's glory on his face, has authority with the people as never before. Dutiful servant that he is, he uses this authority straightaway to turn the people toward the Lord. He promptly gathers them together in order to present the plans for building the Tabernacle—plans that we previously heard, but they did not.

The construction of the Tabernacle occupies the final six chapters of Exodus. Much of it involves verbatim repetitions of the instructions we reviewed in Chapters Seventeen through Nineteen, with only mood or tense changes in the verbs (for example, from the imperative, "they shall make," to the indicative, "they made") and other trivial variations. Not very exciting the first time, on second reading the details of architectural and furniture design test the attention span of many a reader. But the extensive literal duplication, a favorite technique of epic, lends gravity to the work, slowly building up the grandeur and intricacy of the finished product. More important, it is a superb way to drive home the extraordinary fidelity of the Israelite workmen to the Lord's instructions.

But the repetition also hides from the casual reader some crucial questions. Should we read about the obedient construction of the Tabernacle as if the golden calf never happened? Or, less radically, as if it were but an insignificant interruption? Or should we instead understand the Tabernacle, now under construction, precisely in relation to that idolatrous and rebellious incident? Might not the people relate to the project and the Tabernacle in the light of their lapse and their brush with extermination? More important, might not Moses—the only person to have heard the plans beforehand, and himself no enthusiast for such ritual extravagance—now look on the entire venture with new understanding? What should we readers make of the fact that this account of building the Tabernacle, by adhering verbatim to the Lord's previously given instructions, forms a closing bookend for the story of the golden calf, containing that story just as the Tabernacle will contain the impulses that caused it? Finally, how does this account relate to God's previous "building project"—His Creation of the world, reported at the beginning of Genesis—for which instructions to bring something into being were repeated (almost never verbatim) in reports of their actualization—another matter to which we will return?

These questions remind us that this building project belongs to the unfolding account of the formation of the Israelite nation, in its relation to the Lord and His Way for humankind. On display will be not only the Tabernacle but also the various actors in the story, in their evolving place in the national project: Moses, the people, the artists, the priests, the Lord. What is being created is more than a building.

With these thoughts in mind, I will tread very lightly over this account, emphasizing only what is new and what seems important. At the end, I will say what I think it means.

Time Matters Most

The first novelty occurs right at the beginning:

> And Moses assembled all the congregation of the Children
> of Israel (*kol-'adath bene yisra'el*), and said unto them. "These
> are the things (*haddevarim*) which the Lord has commanded,
> that you should do them. Six days shall work (*mela'khah*) be
> done, but on the seventh day there shall be to you a holy [day],
> a Sabbath of solemn rest (*shabbath shabbathon*) to the Lord;
> whosoever does any work (*mela'khah*) therein shall be put to
> death. You shall kindle no fire throughout your habitations
> upon the Sabbath day." (35:1–3)

Moses assembles the Children of Israel as a congregation, *'edah*.[1]
He begins by telling them why he has convened them: to convey the tasks
that the Lord has commanded them to do. But he prefaces his comments
with an admonition.

Whereas God concluded His plans for the Tabernacle with renewed
instruction about Sabbath keeping (31:12–17), Moses opens with it. Before he says a word to them about the necessary work, Moses teaches
the Children of Israel the primacy of Sabbath *rest*. Lest they become too
eager to throw themselves into the project, they are put on notice: at the
risk of their lives, they must keep the Sabbath. More important than
building this beautiful sacred space for the Lord is their internal devotion to His sacred time, now theirs as well. Honoring the rhythm of Creation has become the framework not only for creating the Tabernacle
but also for their very lives. In his own addition to God's instruction,
Moses insists that fire—essential to work, as source of energy and principle of transformation—may not be kindled on the Sabbath, neither on
the construction site nor in their dwelling places. The first order of business for the repentant people is the business of Sabbath keeping.

While this teaching makes sense in its own terms, it is especially
fitting under the present circumstances. The people just demonstrated
their love of visible objects and glittering surfaces; they rushed toward
tangible beauty and evident grandeur. They want a material object for

their god; they want their god to be a thing. Like most of the world, they think material objects give meaning to the moment, and they do not understand that it is the moment that gives meaning to things.[2] It is not only their zeal for work that needs to be moderated but also their preference for the things of the world over the ordering of their souls. Before they get started upon fashioning architectural splendor, even for God, they need to be reminded that the original and enduring presence of holiness in the world is the Sabbath, set apart by God beyond the heavens and the earth, as the crown of His Creation.

Willing Contributions

Turning next to the project, Moses first conveys the Lord's request for voluntary contributions of materials, listing them all, and for the wise-hearted men to come forward to make the Tabernacle, all its parts and appurtenances, as the Lord commanded—again, listing them all in concise summary. So instructed, the people depart from Moses's presence, only to return bringing abundant gifts of the wanted materials. The description of their offerings is long and detailed, expressing their keen enthusiasm for the project and their eagerness to comply with the Lord's request—and perhaps their having taken Moses's hint about attachments to material things. Both men and women contribute gladly, as do both ordinary folk and nobles (35:4–28). Energetic generosity is everywhere. The text concludes:

> Every man and woman whose heart urged them to bring [stuff] for all the work (*hammela'khah*) that the Lord had commanded to be made by the hand of Moses—[through these,] the Children of Israel brought a freewill gift (*nadav*) unto the Lord. (35:29)

Moses then tells the people that the Lord has appointed Bezalel and Oholiab to preside over the creation of the Tabernacle and He has implanted in them the spirit of God (*ruach 'elohim*) and wisdom of heart to enable them to do the work and teach others how to help them. Next, he summons these artists, not only Bezalel and Oholiab but "every one whose heart stirred him up to come unto the work to do it" (36:2). As the artists begin their work, materials continue to pour in, more than are needed—so zealous are the people for the project and so little do they know limits.[3] Atoning for their ill-advised contributions for the golden calf and pleased to be accepted again into the Lord's covenant, they are eager to get and stay on the right side of God.[4] The artisans—the people who know measure—complain to Moses of the excess, and he orders the people to cease their offerings. Only then are they restrained from their prodigality. The stuff they have contributed is enough for the work; in fact, it is too much (36:7). Moses's authority is the remedy for "too much."

The people's gifts now in hand, the artists get to work. We are told, in great and repetitive detail, of all their makings: the curtains, the wooden framework, the Veil and the Screen, the Ark and the Ark Cover (with the cherubim), the Table, the Lampstand (with the lamps), the Altar of Incense and the holy oil, the Altar of Burnt Offering and the Laver, and the courtyard enclosure. (The order of making differs from the order prescribed in the instructions, where the most important items— the Ark and Ark Cover, the Table, the Lampstand—came first; in the making, the containing structures come first, to provide the place where the treasured objects can be housed.) Bezalel is in charge of design and execution, especially of the holiest and most complicated items, beginning with the Ark and the Ark Cover, the Table, and the Lampstand. There is only one new wrinkle worth mentioning. In discussing the making of the bronze Laver and its bronze stand, the text tells us that they were made from the (bronze) mirrors of the women who stood in array at the entrance of the Tent of Meeting (38:8). Even these instruments of vanity and adornment—serving sexual attractiveness—are surrendered to the service of the Lord.[5]

Completing the Work

After describing the making of each part of the Tabernacle, the text gives us the "reckonings [or 'accounts'] of the Tabernacle" (*pequde hammishkan*), as these were ordered by Moses (N.B.: not by God), kept by the Levites, and written down "in the hand of Ithamar, son of Aaron the priest" (38:21ff). Among reasons he might have for ordering an accounting,

Moses clearly wants all transactions to be transparent so that no one could accuse him of enriching himself from the people's donations.[6] The record memorializes the separate contributions of Bezalel and Oholiab and notes the exact (large) amounts of gold, silver, and bronze used in the building. The silver, the text notes, comes from the head tax of a half-shekel of silver (see 30:12–16, discussed in Chapter Nineteen), here obtained from each of 603,550 men over the age of twenty. After the inventory, a final section (39:1–31) describes the making of the priest's elegant attire, again almost verbatim after the previously given instructions: ephod, breastplate, robe, tunic, turban, girdle, and finally the golden crown, inscribed "Holy to the Lord."

Each of the Tabernacle's parts having been finished, the text then sums up the work. It begins with a synoptic conclusion:

> *Thus was finished all the work* ('avodah; [not *mela'khah*]) of the Tabernacle, [of the] Tent of Meeting; and the *Children of Israel did*—according to all that the Lord commanded Moses, so they did. (39:32; emphasis added)

"Thus was finished . . . all the work . . . of the Tabernacle, Tent of Meeting." The words and the cadence awaken a memory of the completion of the first successful building venture, God's "project" through which it all began: "Thus were finished . . . the heaven and the earth . . . and all their array" (Gen. 2:1). Such verbal echoes of the Creation story will increasingly recur as we approach the end of the story of the Tabernacle and with it the end of the book of Exodus. We will wait until we have collected them all before discussing what they mean. For now we note the chain of command: the Lord commanded Moses, and the Children of Israel—not just the artisans—did it all, according to the Lord's command. Perhaps that is why their obedient doings are here called 'avodah (not *mela'khah*), a word known from our discussion of Egypt that means both "work" and "service." Even commanded work, if willingly done for a higher purpose, is service, not mere servitude.

Now near the end of our inquiry, we can see more clearly how being a servant of *Y-H-V-H* differs from being a servant to Pharaoh. In some respects, the Israelites appear to have merely exchanged one form of service (*'avodah*) for another. In neither case are they free to give the law to themselves. They still owe obedience and submission to an external and superior authority, and there are serious penalties for failing to comply. But there the similarities end. The way of Pharaoh and the Way of the Lord differ massively in the form, purpose, and content of their respective laws. In Egypt, Pharaoh rules by arbitrary will and imposed edict, and the laws need not apply to him; in Israel, the people agree to accept God's ordinances, and the rule of law applies equally to all. In Egypt, the people's service advances Pharaoh's interests and control; in Israel, the people's service promotes their own elevation and perfection. God's Law counters the enslaving passions of fear and despair, greed and lust, pride and envy; it inculcates virtuous habits of courage, moderation, self-command, empathy, and righteousness; and it invites all members of the community to seek and imitate the divine. The commandments about the Sabbath and honoring father and mother teach gratitude rather than grasping, reverence rather than insolence; the commandments about coveting teach contentment and civil harmony; and the commandments about the stranger and the poor—and the experience of slavery in Egypt—teach compassion and generosity. The Tabernacle feeds human longings to be in touch with the divine. Taken as a whole, God's covenant directs human beings to fulfill the promise implied in being the earth's only creature made in the image of God.

The various parts of the Tabernacle now complete, the time has arrived to erect the building. The first step is to bring everything to headquarters, to Moses: "And they [the Children of Israel] brought the Tabernacle unto Moses, the Tent, and all its furniture" (39:33). There follows yet another complete inventory, this time of the items as brought to Moses: clasps, boards, bars, pillars, sockets, and coverings; the Veil, the Ark of the Testimony with its staves and Ark Cover; the Table with its vessels and showbread; the Lampstand with its lamps, vessels, and oil; the Golden Altar with its oil and incense; the Screen; the Bronze Altar with its grating, staves, and vessels; the Laver and its base; the hangings, pillars, sockets, and gate screens (with their cords and pins) for the courtyard; and the garments for Aaron and his sons, to minister in the priest's office in the sanctuary (39:33–41). The delivery complete, the text summarizes in lofty terms the people's deeds: "According to all that the Lord commanded Moses, so did the Children of Israel all the work (*'avodah*)" (39:42).

Moses, viewing the arriving inventory, also takes careful notice and is duly impressed. The people have performed admirably, better than he expected. But Moses too is on display:

> And *Moses saw all-the-work* (*kol-hammela'khah*), and, *behold* (*hinneh*), they [the Children of Israel] had done it, *as the Lord had commanded*; even so had they done it. And *he blessed them, [did] Moses*. (39:43; emphasis added)

Moses *saw*. He saw *all the work*. All the work that *they* had done. And, *mirabile dictu*, it was done exactly as the Lord had commanded—that is, as Moses, following God's orders, had decreed. Spontaneously and enthusiastically, he pronounces his own blessing upon them, this Moses.

Once again, the language recalls—no doubt deliberately—the story of the Creation, and the way it ended:

> And *God saw all*-that-He-had-made (*kol-'asher 'asah*), and, *behold* (*hinneh*), *it was very good*. . . . And on the seventh day God finished His work (*mela'khto*), which He had made; and He ceased on the seventh day from all His work (*mela'khto*), which He had made. *And God blessed the seventh day*, and hallowed it; because on it He ceased from all His work (*mela'khto*), which God in creating had made. (Gen. 1:31–2:3; emphasis added).

God *saw*. He saw *all*. All that *He had made*. And, *mirabile dictu*, "it ['the all'] was very good"—an expression that in context means: it was complete and done exactly as He had ordered it in speech.* The work fin-

---

*In every one of the separate acts of Creation, God first announces what He wants to do or happen next, after which we get a report of the deed. For example, "And God said, 'Let the earth bring forth the living animal after its kind'"; "And God made

ished in six days, God sets aside a seventh day, a day of cessation or "rest." His Creation He completes with a blessing, a blessing He pronounces not on His work—the created world—but on the separated time of rest.

What are we to make of these echoes between Moses-and-the-Tabernacle and God-and-the-Creation? A general discussion must await the end of the account. For now, we notice these new features about the principals: God, judging according to His own (unstated) standards, pronounces the created world "very good." But He blesses not His work but something "out-of-this-world": the set-apart time of His cessation from work. Moses, judging according to God's instructions for the Tabernacle, pronounces not so much on the work but on the people's obedience. He bestows his blessing not on the Tabernacle but on the Children of Israel. They have created a beautiful building that will serve as the Lord's dwelling, but they deserve a blessing not only or mainly for their artistry but also for heeding the word of the Lord. Their willingness and ability to do so, in contrast to their conduct in creating the golden calf, elicits Moses's enthusiasm, for it also matters greatly to him personally.

As we noted in reviewing his pleading for the people after the episode of the golden calf, Moses has not only just embraced the Children of Israel as his own, speaking of them to God as "we." He has staked everything on their worthiness for a second chance, and here is the first test of that wager. Their willingness to hearken to God's commands, as he relayed them, no longer depends on his charisma, for the people have discerned the difference between Moses and God and experienced the Lord's grace in forgiveness. In creating a sanctuary where they will commune with Him, they have hearkened to the instructions knowing that they come from the Lord. Moses's attempt to connect the people to God

---

the animals of the earth after their kind" (Gen. 1:24–25). Only in the case of light, God's first creature, is the deed letter-for-letter identical to the commanding speech. Each time, God must *look* to see whether what was made was (sufficiently) in accord with His instructions. His judgment on that score is always, and repeatedly, rendered, "And God saw that it was good." There are two exceptions to that pattern: two creatures are not said to be good, heaven and man. We shall look at them toward the end of this chapter.

through obedience has, in this instance, succeeded. This success anticipates a time when the lawgiver must disappear into his law. No wonder Moses is moved to pronounce his blessing on the people.

His work, needless to say, is hardly finished. His leadership will be needed for nearly forty more years of wandering in the desert. And as soon as the Tabernacle is consecrated, God will continue to speak with him from above the Ark and between the cherubim, pronouncing new commandments for the people to follow. Yet in the creation of the Tabernacle, Moses, following God's directives, has diffused his singular control of the relationship between God and the Israelites. He has brought the people into the activity of co-creation, as partners with God; he has brought them from terror before the Lord (and terror in His absence) to joyful builders of a Tent in which to meet Him; and in the persons of the priests, he has willingly surrendered the exclusive role of mediating between the people and God. Through the Tabernacle, a new dynamic is being created that will permit new forms of relations between God and the distinct principals: Moses, the priests, and the people.[7]

Although the time is still far off, the Tabernacle may also be seen as an early harbinger of a post-Mosaic age. It will be the province of brother Aaron and his descendants, indefinitely. Moses still has the mantle of political and military leadership—as will his replacement Joshua—and the Lord will still speak to Moses from the Holy of Holies. But the Tabernacle will become the center of the Israelite community, and what goes on there will be the domain of the priests. Whether he knows it or not, Moses, God's temporary middleman with the people, is pronouncing his blessing on an arrangement that will outlast him. He can do so gladly only on the condition that the people will hearken to the Lord's instruction, as they have done here.

The Sabbath is permanently blessed, and blessed by the Lord. But the people will need all the help they can get if they are to live up to their sacred calling, especially when Moses disappears. On this occasion, they have shown themselves eminently worthy, a fact Moses graciously acknowledges with his blessing. The text, as it fades out on the scene, acknowledges Moses's nobility (and his eventual disappearance) by making his name the last word: "And he blessed them, [did] Moses."

Raising the Tabernacle

Moses's blessing of the people—his last reported speech in Exodus, analogous to God's last reported speech in the Creation—brings the Lord promptly to his ear, with orders to erect the Tabernacle:

> And the Lord spoke unto Moses, saying: "On the first day of the first month you [singular] shall rear up the Tabernacle, the Tent of Meeting." (40:1–2)

The timing is highly significant. On the first day of Aviv, the vernal New Year, a little less than a year after the moonlit mid-month night of the Exodus, the Lord wants Moses to erect the Tabernacle, the Tent in which He intends in perpetuity to Meet with his people. Against a calendric background in which nature and the earth stand on the threshold of another annual cycle of renewal, the Israelites are to raise up a memorial of their once-in-history divine encounter at Sinai, both a permanent— noncyclical—abode for future prophecy and revelation and a permanent abode for the Divine Presence. As with the three annual festivals, the cycles of nature are subordinated to the historical doings of man in relation to the One Who says of Himself, "I Will Be What I Will Be."

There follow thirteen more imperatives (40:3–15), all second-person singular ("You shall"), all directed at Moses. The first six detail the order in which the Lord wishes the furnishings of the Tabernacle to be placed inside and the positions of their placement. Once again, an inventory, this time for moving in and setting up: Ark of the Testimony, Veil, Table (with showbread), Lampstand (with lamps), Golden Altar of Incense (before the Ark), Screen to the door of the Tabernacle, the Altar of Burnt Offering, and the Laver (between the Altar and the Tent of Meeting), with its water. When the furnishings are in place, Moses is to set up the courtyard round about and to hang the screen for its gate (40:3–8). Next, Moses is to anoint with oil the Tabernacle and its furnishings, the Altar of Burnt Offering, and the Laver, rendering them holy (40:9–11). Finally, he is directed to bring Aaron and sons to the Tent of Meeting, wash them, clothe them, and anoint them "that they may minister unto Me in the priest's office; and their anointing shall be to them

for an everlasting priesthood throughout their generations" (40:12–15).[8]
The last of these instructions underscores the permanence of the priesthood while silently reaffirming the passing importance of Moses, who—
as we often noted—has no relevant descendants. He is to usher in his
brotherly alternative.

No matter. Moses hesitates not a whit: "Thus did Moses; according
to all that the Lord commanded him, so did he" (40:16). This summary
statement of compliance is followed by a detailed report of Moses's
deeds, which (just this once) I will spare the reader (40:17–33). Yet here
again, there are two more echoes of the Creation story. First, the account of Moses's deeds is divided into seven parts, each of which ends
with "as the Lord commanded Moses."[9] In the story of Creation, seven
times the Lord looks at what He did and sees "that it was good"—meaning
that it was as He commanded. Second, the account of the Tabernacle's
raising ends, "And Moses finished the work (*vayekhal Mosheh 'eth-
hammela'khah*)" (40:33), a reverberation of "*And God* on the seventh day
finished His work, which He had made (*vayekhal 'Elohim . . . mela'khto
'asher 'asah*) " (Gen. 2:2; emphasis added). The people made the parts,
adhering faithfully to the Lord's instructions as delivered to them by
Moses. But Moses, no doubt with help from the people, erects the
whole, also adhering faithfully to the Lord's instructions.

When the people finish their work, they receive Moses's blessing.
When "God . . . finished His work," He separated out a seventh day to
which He gave a blessing. When "Moses finished the work," not a word
is said. What happens instead is beyond blessing.

The Presence of the Lord: Glory, Cloud, and Fire

Then [or "And"; *ve-*] the cloud covered the Tent of Meeting,
and the glory of the Lord (*kevod Y-H-V-H*) filled the Tabernacle. And Moses was not able to enter into the Tent of Meeting, because the cloud abode thereon, and the glory of the
Lord filled the Tabernacle. (40:34–35)

No sooner is the Tabernacle complete—"And Moses finished the work"—
than the Lord descends to occupy it, like a monarch in a newly built

palace. His Presence is manifested in the form of a cloud covering the Tent and—impossible to describe—in the appearance of His glory (*kavod*) filling the sanctuary. This re-creates exactly the scene atop cloud-covered Mount Sinai when the glory of the Lord dwelt upon it and Moses ascended to receive the instructions for the sanctuary.[10] The Lord has indeed come down to dwell with His people, where they live. No longer remote, He is in their midst.

But He is not simply accessible, even to Moses. Moses cannot enter the Tabernacle to meet or speak with the Lord, to be with "I-Will-Be-With-You," as he was "face to face" with Him on the mountain. Along with the people, Moses too must now keep an awe-filled distance. Thanks to his efforts with the Tabernacle, God is now near, but Moses's privileged access is no more. The last thing we hear about Moses in the book of Exodus is the denial of his former level of intimacy: "And Moses was not able to enter into the Tent of Meeting." On the mountaintop, the Lord had invited Moses into the cloud on the seventh day. Here, when He next speaks with Moses (reported in the first verse of Leviticus[11]), He will do so from out of the Tent of Meeting. Moses is still very much in charge, and God will continue to speak with and instruct him. But with respect to the Lord's Presence, Moses is but a mortal subject like the rest of us.

Exodus concludes with remarks not about God and Moses but about the cloud, the people, and their movements:

> And whenever the cloud was taken up from over the Tabernacle, the Children of Israel went onward, *throughout all their journeys*. But if the cloud was not taken up, then they journeyed not till the day that it was taken up. For the cloud of the Lord was upon the Tabernacle by day, and there was fire therein by night—in the *sight* of all the house of Israel, *throughout all their journeys*. (40:34–38; emphasis added)

These final verses are written in high poetic style, fitting the grandeur of their content and their place at the book's conclusion.

Whatever else it might mean to Moses and the priests, the Divine Presence amidst His people, manifested in the cloud over the Tabernacle, has special significance for them and for their travels. Even though they will depart the "holy" mountain, the Children of Israel will bring with them a portable Sinai in miniature. They will continue to have His leadership and protection as they head for the Promised Land and "throughout *all* their journeys." While the cloud remains on the Tabernacle, the people will stay put, and when the cloud lifts, it is time to move on: the people move as followers of the Lord. At each new stopping point, the Tabernacle will be reassembled, and the cloud will reappear and settle above it. In full view of the house of Israel, the Lord's cloud by day and His fire within by night will demonstrate that He is always with them. The God of mercy, grace, and compassion has taken them back in full.

These last verses, on the subject of journeying, carry more profound teachings. Unlike the fixed palace of an earthly monarch, the portable Tent of Meeting moves as the Lord directs. As He is not bound to a natural place or to a manufactured residence, so His dwelling place, like the people who built it, moves after Him. Moreover, unlike the so-called divinities of nature, He moves not in circles but toward a goal. The people who follow Him do likewise. Throughout all their journeys— and not only their spatial journeys—they are blessed to be able to follow the path He leads them on. The end of Exodus invites us to accompany the Children of Israel on their future journeys—journeys still unfinished, and still following the Lord.

The Tabernacle and People Formation

Throughout this discussion of the Tabernacle, I have emphasized its spiritual aspects, focusing on the opportunities it will create for new relationships between God and the people, the priests, and Moses. But we should not overlook the indispensable contributions that the Tabernacle makes to the formation and solidarity of the Israelite people. We need to appreciate how God and Moses are laying foundations for national self-definition that will persist long after Moses is gone.

First, the people have become agents. At the beginning of Genesis, God was the only actor. At the beginning of Exodus, the Children of Israel were passive slaves in Egypt, incapable even of crying out. Their deliverance from bondage was the work of God, aided by Moses and Aaron, his ministers and servants. The people marked their doors on the night of exodus, and they willingly entered the water at the Sea of Reeds, but the real work was done by others. When attacked, they defended themselves against the Amalekites. But only now do the people—all of them, not just the leaders—freely undertake a major project in a time of peace, not as passive beneficiaries of the Lord's largesse but as His partners.

Second, what they build they build in obedience to God's commands. For the first time since the Law was given, they demonstrate their capacity to live under its rule. Unlike at the golden calf, where they abandoned the law during their leader's absence, here they zealously adhere to its letter and its spirit. God through Moses commands; the people obey—all of them, gladly, without murmuring. Each one's obedience to this law involved sacrifice of private treasure for the common good; they were not told just to avoid wrongdoing, they were asked instead to contribute, at personal cost, to a positive venture. For their remarkable compliance, they earned Moses's blessing.

Third, they created a national center around which to rally and through which to define themselves. Never before had the Israelites had a center of their own. The patriarchs, wandering shepherds, had none at all. As Hebrews in Egypt, they lived in Goshen, ghettoized away from the national center, until they were forcibly moved to build storage cities—not for themselves but for Pharaoh. From now on, the Tabernacle, built by their own hands, will be their permanent center. Because it is portable, it will travel with them—indeed, it will lead them. Wherever they are, the Tabernacle will define the national community. They will never again be uncentered.

Finally, as the national center, the Tabernacle is less a building than a crossroads for communion with *Y-H-V-H*. Throughout Exodus, the connection between the Israelites and God has been difficult and unsatisfying, partly because they were unready, partly because it was mediated only through Moses and then unpredictably. Now, educated by the experience of the golden calf, they want a more direct avenue to the divine and possess the means for having it. No longer is Moses needed as a go-between. They can bring their sacrifices to the Tabernacle, and the functionaries of the sanctuary will mediate for them. All will have equal access to make their offerings of atonement and gratitude. The shared practices in relation to God are a major step to the condition of equality under God and the Law that is God's political ideal for humankind.

Yet these transformations toward peoplehood are not without difficulty. The risk of mistaking Moses for a god, inherent in the original charismatic leadership, no longer exists, but an institutionalized priesthood carries risks of its own. Accession to the priesthood, being hereditary, does not require virtue, either moral or intellectual. The trappings of priestly office invite self-importance and jealousy. Presiding over the "iniquities of the sacred things" risks excessive zeal. Through familiarity, the routinized rituals can become lifeless and dull. Devotion to the minutiae of sacrifices and anointments can swamp concerns for righteousness and humanity. The priest may be—and later will be—at odds with the prophet (and with the king),[12] and the people will suffer. Later history will show that like the moral law, the Tabernacle and the priesthood, though necessary, are hardly sufficient to ensure the people's fulfillment of their covenantal mission.

Yet at this early stage in the birth of God's nation, there is no doubt that the Tabernacle and the relationships it fosters constitute a giant step forward on the path to peoplehood under God's Way. Inspired by their own agency and accomplishments, attached to a central sanctuary they build and rebuild with their own hands, practicing the rule of law, and enjoying a new, equal, and less-threatening relationship with the God in their midst, the Israelites are united and ready, as never before, for "all their journeys"—open-ended but aspiring. Encouraged and fortified, they go forward as followers and servants of Y-H-V-H their God, Creator of Heaven and Earth, Who brought them out of the land of Egypt, out of the house of bondage.

Tabernacle and Creation: Microcosm or Completion?

From the beginning of our discussion of the plans for the Tabernacle, we have seen many passages and formulations that invite or even require us to think about the Tabernacle in relation to God's Creation of the world. We noted that Moses was summoned into the cloud to get the instructions for the Tabernacle on the seventh day, after waiting six days on the mountain. We saw that the instructions had seven parts, with the seventh devoted to keeping the Sabbath. We heard about "the spirit of God (*ruach 'elohim*)," which in the Beginning of Time "hovered over the face of the waters" when He undertook to bring order to chaos (Gen. 1:2), but which—never mentioned since—the Lord now infuses into Bezalel, the Tabernacle's chief artificer. We noted Moses's explicit reference to the Creation's six days of work followed by one day of rest in his exhortation about the Sabbath. We picked up the several allusions, at the end of the project, regarding "seeing all the work" and "finishing the work"— in which Moses (not Bezalel) and his Tabernacle are compared to God and His Creation. And we noted Moses's blessing of the people, echoing but transforming the Lord's blessing of the Sabbath day.

These allusions have long been noted and commented on, by both the Tradition and contemporary scholars.[13] Jon Levenson, for instance, presents a sustained argument that the *mishkan* is a microcosm of the whole:

> The function of these [textual] correspondences is to underscore the depiction of the sanctuary as a world, that is, an ordered, supportive, and obedient environment, and the picture of the world as a sanctuary, that is, a place in which the reign of God is visible and unchallenged, and his holiness is palpable, unthreatened, and pervasive. . . . As in many cultures, the Temple was conceived as a microcosm, a miniature world. But it is equally the case that in Israel (and probably also in other cultures), the world . . . was conceived . . . as a macro-temple, the palace of God in which all are obedient to His commands.[14]

Levenson argues further that the world and the sanctuary are not just homologous or parallel "buildings." Quoting a midrash (*Pesiqta Rabbati* 6) that presents the sanctuary as the "completion, the consummation of the primordial cosmogony," he concludes that

> they implicate each other, and neither is complete alone. The microcosm is the idealized cosmos, the world contemplated *sub specie creationis*, the world as it was meant to be, a power-

ful piece of testimony to God the creator, a palace for the victorious king. To view creation within the precincts of the Temple is to summon up an *ideal world* that is far from the mundane reality of profane life and its persistent evil. It is that ideal world which is the result of God's creative labors.[15]

The Tabernacle/Temple, as microcosm, parallels the cosmic order, itself a project against chaos, darkness, and evil.

I am drawn to a different alternative, in which the Tabernacle serves as the completion not of cosmogony but of a long historical process, intended from the start to correct for certain unavoidable *deficiencies* of the Creation: the natural incompleteness of the human being and the impossibility of his gaining completion on his own by looking to "the cosmos." Far from serving as a microcosm, the Tabernacle is an *"anti*-cosmos"—a replacement for, and a rejection of, looking with reverence on the heavens and the earth. This alternative derives not from scholarly arguments or imported theological or philosophical concepts (including "cosmos," itself not a biblical term) but from clues within the text itself. To find our way, we need to revisit the Beginning for its account of the creation of man[16]:

And God created the human being (*ha'adam*) in His image (*betsalmo*), in the image of God (*betselem 'elohim*) created He him, male and female created He them. (Gen. 1:27)

Man is the ultimate work of creation: he is the last of the creatures listed in hierarchic order, and once he appears at the end of the sixth day, creation is finished. Although man himself is not said by God to be good—a point to which we shall return—once he is present (and blessed), "God saw *all* that He had made, and, behold, it was *very* good" (1:31; emphasis added). I take this to mean that "all"—heaven and earth—was now complete and lacking nothing in its cast of characters. Blessed with dominion or rule over the other animals, man is the most godlike of the creatures: man alone is said to be in the image of God.*

---

*Any image, insofar as it is an image, has a most peculiar manner of being: it both *is* and *is not* what it resembles. The image of my granddaughter that smiles at me

To see how man might be godlike, we look at the text of the Creation story to see what *God* is "like." From reading about His activities and powers, we learn that God speaks, commands, names, blesses, and hallows; makes and makes freely; looks at and beholds the world; cares about the goodness or perfection of things; and addresses solicitously the living creatures and provides for their sustenance. In short, God exercises speech and reason, freedom in doing and making, and the powers of contemplation, judgment, and care. Doubters may wonder whether this is true of God. But it is indubitably clear—even to atheists—that we human beings have these qualities and powers and that they lift us above the plane of a merely animal existence. Human beings, alone among the creatures, speak, plan, create, contemplate, and judge—and bless. Human beings, alone among the creatures, can articulate a future goal and use that articulation to guide them in bringing it into being by their own purposive conduct. Human beings, alone among the creatures, can think about the universe, marvel at its many-splendored forms and articulated order, wonder about its beginning, and feel awe in beholding its grandeur and in pondering the mystery of its Source.

But the text does not exaggerate our standing. Man may be, of all the creatures, the most intelligent, resourceful, conscious, and free—and in these respects the most godlike—but he is also the most questionable. Man may have powers that resemble divinity, but he is also at most merely an image; man, who, quite on his own, is prone to think of himself as a god on earth and to lord it over the animals, is reminded by the biblical text that he is, like the other creatures, not divine. Though brought into being by a special creative act, man appears on the same day as the terrestrial animals; though in some respects godlike, man belongs emphatically to the world of animals, whose protective ruler he is told to be. As later verses about food remind us, we are, like the animals,

---

out of the picture frame on my desk is my granddaughter—not yours. But it is not really she—just a mere image. Yet an image not only resembles the original. It also points to and depends for its very being on that of which it is an image. Man, like any other creature, is simply what he is. But, according to the text, man is—in addition— also something more, insofar as he resembles the divine. Whether man comes to appreciate his special status—and especially what it means to be dependent on the "Original"—is one of the main concerns of the rest of the Torah.

needy and vulnerable. Man is the ambiguous being, in-between, more than an animal, less than a god. This fact makes him a problem.

The text subtly makes the problem visible. After nearly every act of creation, God looked at the creature and "saw that it was good." He does not do so with man. Man alone among the earthly creatures is not said to be good. Why?

"Good" as used throughout Genesis 1 cannot mean *morally* good; when "God saw the light that it was good" (Gen. 1:4), He could not have seen that the light was honest or just or moderate. "Good" seems rather to mean fit to the intention and plan, fit to itself and its work, and, especially, complete, perfect, fully formed, and fully what it is. A being is "good" insofar as it is fully formed and fully fit to do its proper work.

A moment's reflection shows that man as he comes into the world is not (yet) good. Precisely because he is a free being, he is also incomplete or indeterminate; what he becomes depends always (in part) on what he freely chooses to be. To put it more pointedly: precisely in the sense that man is in the image of God, man is not good—not determinate, finished, complete, or perfect.[17] It remains to be seen whether man will *become* good, whether he will be able to complete himself (or be completed).

This lack of completeness, metaphysically identical with his freedom, is, of course, the basis of man's moral ambiguity. As the being with the greatest freedom of motion, able to change not only his path but also his ways, man is capable of sin and iniquity, of missing the mark, of twisted perversity, of deviating widely from the way by which he and the world around him would most flourish. The question becomes: From where will man gain the necessary knowledge for living well, both for himself and for his neighbor, both alone and in community? To what will he look for guidance? And even with that knowledge, what will keep him in line?

Absent outside instruction (to wit, the Torah) and left to their own devices, human beings will most likely look first to nature, and in particular to those elements that seem to display the greatest beauty, perfection, and permanence or that have the greatest influence over human life. They will look up to the stars, shining steadily, fixed in constellations that circle uniformly and endlessly. They will look to the earth, the ever-renewable source of life's necessities. They will look to the sky, the source of precious rain (or, in Egypt, to the Nile). They will look especially to the sun, source of light, warmth, and the growth of crops. Because of its permanence, its ceaseless and perfect circular "motion," its power and beauty, and above all its importance for human life, the sun is always and everywhere the prime candidate for natural divinity. In addition, human beings will look to certain terrestrial beings that seem to embody fertility, virility, power, longevity, mystery, or cunning: the frog, the bull, the sea monster, the scarab, the crocodile, and the snake are emblems of these extraordinary capacities. As human beings will seek to use astrological knowledge of the heavens to guide their affairs, so they will seek to harness the powers of these awesome creatures to improve their own condition. They will offer gifts to these "natural divinities" in hope of making them more hospitable to human needs and wants.[18]

The Bible takes a dim view of all this and of veneration for nature in all its forms. From the very start, it (silently) polemicizes against the worship of heaven and the heavenly bodies. Perhaps the main teaching of Genesis 1 is the nondivinity of nature, and in particular of the sun, the moon, the stars—in short, of everything connected with heaven. The sun is the chief target for demotion: light, time, and even vegetation are presented as not requiring the sun. Not heaven but man has the closest relation to God; heaven, like man, is not said to be good.

There is a connection between the two creatures not said to be "good": the "nongoodness" or incompleteness of man cannot be fixed by worshipping nature or by looking to the indifferent heaven for guidance. The heavens may, as the psalmist sings, declare the glory of God (Psalms 19:1), but they say not a peep about righteousness. Absolutely no moral rules can be deduced from even the fullest understanding of nature. The most basic prohibitions against cannibalism, incest, murder, and adultery—constitutive for all decent human communities—cannot be supported by or deduced from the natural world. From the point of view of righteousness, indeed for all practical human purposes, cosmic gods are about as helpful as no gods at all. Knowing even that man is the highest creature, because free, does not lead to any clear guidance about how his freedom is to be used. Indeed, man's eventual awareness of nature's cosmic indifference will only worsen his natural restlessness: I may be the most godlike and freest of creatures, but I am not at home in the world. Such thoughts will ultimately lead him into fatalism and despair, or, what is equally dangerous, into the arms of powerful but amoral human masters or magicians who promise him the moon—and, ultimately, victory over death.[19]

The story of the Creation is, however, not mute on where man should ultimately turn, and it does not end with the creation of the "cosmic" beings. Not only does the Bible teach from the first sentence the primacy of God as the *Creator* of heaven and earth. Happily, unlike the nature "gods," this Lord of Creation is not indifferent to how His "image" will turn out, how he might become "whole" or complete, and how he might feel at home. He follows the creation of the so-called cosmos and of mobile man in His own image by setting aside a sanctified Sabbath day beyond the mobile universe, which will become the lodestar of His plan to shape the souls and guide the lives of His favorite but problematic creature. Sacred time, like God, beyond nature and present from the Creation,* will become the balm for the soul and the cure for its restlessness.

After the story of the Creation, the remaining tales of Genesis (and the narrative first section of Exodus) reveal in greater detail the many aspects of man's moral ambiguity and God's early efforts to address it, all in the service of making man "good"—complete, whole, holy. The Garden of Eden story shows the tragic meaning of lost innocence yielding to human choice—non-obedience—exercised by looking to nature (the tree) for wisdom about how to live. The paradigmatic story of the first man born of woman, Cain, shows that brotherhood uninstructed means rivalry to the point of fratricide—over a matter of sacrifices. After Adam dies and the earth degenerates into violent chaos, the Lord washes out most of the Creation and starts over with Noah. He preserves life against the watery chaos through the rational artifice of the ark, and for

---

*Here we see the error of those who treat the story of Creation (only) as a cosmogony and the result as a "cosmos." The so-called cosmos was the product of God's six days of work, but the completed Creation embraces also the seventh day, where no *thing* is created. God is prior to the heavens and the earth, and His Sabbath is likewise "out of this world."

the first time, He establishes a covenant with the earth and prescribes a foundational Law for humankind, the Noahide code, in defense of life. But after a metaphorical patricide in Noah's house and the hyper-rational—godless and amoral—project of Babel (a technological refuge against nature's cruelty and indifference, but not a true home for mankind), the Lord ceases to work with the whole human race. He tries more modestly with one follower, Abraham, to get a foothold on earth for His Way. Forming a covenant with Abraham and teaching him something about justice, He succeeds, not without difficulty, in keeping something alive within the patriarchal families for three generations, avoiding fratricide, patricide, and incest. His people come down into Egypt, the watery fertile place, where they are fruitful and multiply and swarm like fish. But it is only in Exodus that His full plan takes shape on a *national* plane, a plan that we have been following from the beginning of this book.

In its essentials, the plan for people formation comprises separation and deliverance, law, and worship in the Tabernacle. Human nature in community is to be completed—made good—through culture: through story and song, through law and custom, and through ritual. The first attaches people to something larger than themselves through shared tales of their past history and experience, their suffering and persistence. The second guides their day-to-day lives toward personal fulfillment and the common good, according to acknowledged ethical and moral principles. The third gives expression and direction to the deepest longings of their souls: to be in touch with what is highest and best.

At the center of this plan is the giving of the Law at Mount Sinai. But before they can receive the law, the people must come to appreciate its necessity. They first have to be shown what is wrong with nature worship. Through the contest with Pharaoh and through the plagues, the Lord demonstrates how inhospitable the waters below and the heavens above are to human need and aspiration. He shows how reliance on those powers, and on the human agents that seek to manipulate them, brings the despotic rule of man playing god—which the Israelites experience firsthand—and the enslavement and eventual destruction of the rest. He shows His people that He is mightier than nature, and mightier too than the mightiest king and the strongest civilization that have taken their bearings from nature and from altering nature for human benefit.

The second stage, anarchic life in the dry wilderness, prepares the people to discover the need for Law. They learn to moderate their appetites through the rules about manna; they get their first lesson in courage in the battle against Amalek; the visit from Jethro introduces some measures for the institution of justice and points toward the need for divinely given law. The people learn that the Lord is not only powerful but also solicitous of their daily welfare. These experiences prepare the people to see the necessity of Law. After the deliverance from Egypt and their early wilderness experience, they readily accept a covenant with the Lord. The Lord and His commandments will provide what neither nature nor Pharaoh can give them: the principles and guidelines for self-rule and human flourishing. Serving God, unlike serving Pharaoh, is the very opposite of servility.

When the Law comes, it comes first as divine speech backed by lightning and thunder: a logos with teeth. The beginning of the Law mainly addresses the mutual wrongdoings of human beings that result in oppressive slavery, bodily harm, damage to property, and loss of reputation. Not content, however, with punishing crime and rectifying tort, the law moves gradually into moral and spiritual domains. It encourages compassion for the stranger and humaneness toward the widow, the orphan, and the poor; it teaches truthfulness and fairness in judging; it institutes Sabbath observance, giving the more-than-natural, out-of-this-world seventh day a central place in the moral-political order of human things; it institutes sacred festivals for the Lord and a sabbatical year for the Land.

So far so good. The Lord has disclosed Himself to be mightier than either nature or Pharaonic Egypt. He has shown Himself to be solicitous of His people and a teacher of law and morals. But something is missing, an answer to the longings of human beings to be in touch with what is highest and best, longings expressed in the text beginning with the sacrifices of Cain and Noah and continuing to the episode of the golden calf. Once they have experienced His power and beneficence, the people seek communion with the Lord.

In the past, they did so ambivalently. They stood apart in fear and trembling during the Decalogue, but once Moses disappeared on the mountain, they feared the Lord's absence. They feared His power and shuddered at His judgment, but they wanted His protection and His guidance. When God seemed to have abandoned them, they made in His place an idol.

Yet after the golden calf, something wondrous happens. The people learn, through the worst sort of disobedience, that the Lord is not only powerful and judgmental but also merciful and full of compassion. In the presence of repentance and return—thanks to "the man Moses," whose mother looked on him as an infant and "saw that he was good"—He is willing to forgive. Reassured by this discovery, the people are more than prepared to allow Him into their everyday lives. The Tabernacle—not a microcosm of nature but a divinely instructed, humanly built alternative to nature—is the perfect vehicle to satisfy their longings for the Divine Presence near at hand, and they go to creating it eagerly, with the *ruach 'elohim*, and earn Moses's blessing.

In the Creation, God gives the orders and carries them out Himself. In building the Tabernacle, He gives the orders, but the people carry them out. As a cooperative project between Creature and Creator, the Tabernacle stands as a completion of Creation—not as a summary or microcosm but as the culmination. God's Creation produced a hospitable world in which human beings can live. God's Law sets forth a Way under which they can live well. God's Tabernacle, built for Him by human beings, offers rituals by which they can aspire to be holy, as the Lord their God is holy.

The Tabernacle is the capstone of God's cultural project to remedy man's incompleteness and restlessness. Human beings can be complete and at home only when they acknowledge their dependence on their Creator, and even more when they come intimately to know their Creator and He them. The Creation itself will be complete only when the Creator is known and intimately Present in the life of His godlike creature. It was, we recall, for their *mutual* benefit that *Y-H-V-H* took up with Israel in the first place: that they may come to know Him, and that He may be part of their lives forever. "I am the Lord their God, that brought them forth out of the land of Egypt, *that I may dwell among them. I am the Lord their God*" (29:46; emphasis added).

Epilogue

We have arrived, at long last, at the end of the book called "Names." It began with the sons of Israel descending into fertile Egypt, where they were fruitful and multiplied, only to be enslaved and forced to build cities to store Pharaoh's surplus grain. We finished with the Children of Israel in the Sinai desert raising a portable Tabernacle for *Y-H-V-H* their God, Who had delivered them from bondage so that He might dwell among them. It is impossible in few words to review what we have seen or learned along the way. Yet a brief return to the concerns that guided our reading seems a fitting way to conclude.

I undertook this study mainly to explore basic questions of people formation: What makes a people a people? What forms their communal identity, holds them together, guides their lives? To what do they look up? For what should they strive? Exodus speaks to these questions through two unfolding and intersecting stories: the founding of the Israelite nation via deliverance and command, and the growing knowledge of God via divine revelation.

To counter the dangerous and degrading ways of humankind uninstructed, God sets out to establish an enduring communal outpost for justice and holiness. His national alternative is built on three pillars: first, the Israelites' shared experience and lasting memory of oppressive slavery in prosperous Egypt, and their astonishing deliverance and miraculous sustenance in the wilderness; second, a covenantal comprehensive law governing all aspects of life through constraint, encouragement, and uplift; and finally, the Tabernacle, an embodiment of their aspiration to remain in contact with what is highest. In each case, God provides initiative and direction. But the people increasingly become co-partners in the venture. They mark their doors to choose deliverance; they enter the Sea of Reeds; they twice consent to the covenant and its demanding obligations; and they eagerly build the sanctuary and embrace a national future under God. Although their story has just begun, and many trials—and failures—lie ahead, God and the Israelites have accomplished an impressive amount in the forty chapters of Exodus. We are left with the grand vision of a kingdom of priests and a holy nation who bear God's Way to a better life before all humankind.

Indispensable to this story is the self-revelation of *Y-H-V-H,* Israel's mysterious God, Who makes clear at the outset His desire to be known by human beings. In the book of Exodus, we discover that He is compassionate, loyal, awe-inspiring, powerful, righteous, solicitous, philanthropic, merciful, and present. He is moved by pity for His suffering people and recalls His promise to Abraham, Isaac, and Jacob. He answers Moses's request for His name with an enigma, to be clarified by watching what He says and does. He is stronger than nature gods or human magicians. He is true to His word and executes judgment on evildoers. In the wilderness, He sustains His people with water and manna; His world is hospitable to human need. Unlike indifferent natural powers, He enters into a covenant with human beings that ultimately aims to make them holy as He is holy. Unlike the edicts of despotic human rulers, His Law applies equally to all and is intended for everyone's benefit. Israel may be the Lord's firstborn, but He cares also for the stranger, as well as the widow, the orphan, and the poor, and, through the example of His Law, for all humanity. Most impressively, He is merciful and gracious, slow to anger, full of loving-kindness, and willing to forgive in the presence of repentance. Against the tragic view, His world encourages high striving despite the recurring likelihood of failure. He speaks with Moses face to face, as a man speaks with a friend. And although He grants Moses (only) partial knowledge of Him, He seeks to be known throughout the world and begins an intimate relationship with His people—all of them—through the Tabernacle. Though *Y-H-V-H* is still mysterious, the Israelites (and the reader) know Him much better at the end of Exodus than they did at the beginning.

The stories of people formation and divine revelation are, of course, intimately connected. God has His hand in all aspects of Israel's national emergence. And Israel's progress toward peoplehood is required for humanity's growing knowledge of the Lord. No God, no Law; no Law, no people. Conversely, no people of Israel, no knowledge of God. He is known from His deeds, His Law, and ultimately from His Presence among His people.

These stories are linked by a third: the story of Moses, God's champion and the people's teacher. A goodly child, given an Egyptian education, he shows exquisite fellow feeling as a spirited defender of underdogs. Caught by wonder at the burning bush but transformed by awe and eager to know God, he reluctantly accepts his political assignment. He courageously holds his own with Pharaoh, leads the Israelites out of Egypt, and sings out God's glory at the Sea of Reeds. Gaining confidence and acquiring prudence, he is alternately judge, lawgiver, prophet, advocate, scourge, and pleader for God's people, eventually embracing their fate as his own. Throughout, he is guided by a divine Voice in his head, doing as he is told but increasingly able to advance the mission on his own. Granted an intimate but necessarily partial revelation of God, Moses lives thereafter bearing God's reflected glory on his face. Unlike Plato's philosopher-king, who rules only a city in speech, Moses founds and rules God's nation, teaching it the revealed Way of the Lord.

So much for Exodus's account of the founding of God's nation. But gaining this knowledge is not the most important part of what reading Exodus can do for the wisdom-seeking reader. As in any philosophical quest, the most significant accomplishments take place in the mind and heart of the inquirer. What, then, can today's searching reader carry away from this old story? Does it have for us any universal or contemporary significance? Rousseau, in the epigraph to this book, marvels at the durability of Moses's laws, "capable of surviving the customs, laws, empire of all the nations . . . to last as long as the world." The causes of this permanence, he says, "deserve the study and admiration of the sages, in preference to all that Greece and Rome offer." What, then, might we have learned from this text about our own lives and nations, as human beings or as citizens? We must each answer for ourselves. To encourage your reflections, I offer a few of mine.

One general point emerges simply from the three-pillared structure of Israel's founding. Can a people endure and flourish if it lacks a shared national story, accepted law and morals, and an aspiration to something higher than its own comfort and safety? Can a devotion to technological progress, economic prosperity, and private pursuits of happiness sustain us when our story is contested, our morals weakened, and our national dedication abandoned? I doubt it. Living increasingly between technocracy and hedonism, defined not by our duties or callings but by our devices and whims, we are feasted in body but famished in soul, and our national fabric is unraveling.

Biblical Israel is for deeper reasons a paradigm of worthy nationhood: it is a particular people but with a universal law. The bonds of kinship and shared history create attachments that induce people to care concretely for one another, while the universal law recognizes and advances the dignity of all human beings. Certain particularities of Israel's founding experience seem to me universally relevant for national character. People who have suffered estrangement and deprivation are more likely to feel sympathy for strangers and compassion for the needy than are those who have known only prosperity. People who have experienced tyranny are more likely to treasure freedom, especially if they have struggled to attain it, than are those who have never known anything else. People nourished collectively in the wilderness are more likely to be grateful for the blessings of existence than are those who regard human life as a zero-sum game and grasp all they can for themselves.

As for the Law, I have argued throughout for the abiding wisdom of the Decalogue and the ordinances: the importance of honoring father and mother for decent family life and cultural transmission; the human dignity and equality promoted by Sabbath remembrance; the reorienting of the heart toward shareable goods in the injunction against coveting; the high valuing of human—and animal—life and limb; the special regard for a pregnant woman and the child she carries; the humane treatment of the stranger; the compassionate protection of widows, orphans, and the poor; the devotion to truth and justice in disputes at law, indeed, in all human interactions; the teaching of communal gratitude through the sacred festivals; the inspiring call to imitate God in His holiness. Against degrading human proclivities, the Law teaches service rather than servility or mastery, reverence rather than idolatry or insolence, aspiration to communal perfection rather than complacency or despair. It is at once a yoke and a tree of life, and a tree of life because it is a yoke, voluntarily shouldered. It not only delimits wrongful conduct that threatens civil peace and order; it also promotes human excellence and directs the soul toward the divine source of all blessings.

And what about this "Source"? What can a philosophical reader, not already an adherent of biblical religion, learn about God—not only as a character in this book? For such a reader, can reading this text fulfill His wish to be known? It seems a tall order, not least because according to the text itself, even Moses, who was granted a personal theophany, could not really see God, only his back side. Moreover, according to Maimonides—a supremely philosophical reader—anyone wishing to truly appreciate the glory of God must take up natural science, a view at odds with my anti-cosmological reading of the Bible. Still, my reading of Exodus would be incomplete were I not open to the possibility of encountering God in a direct and personal way—not just intellectually but also experientially—with awe and fear, with joy and praise.

Parts of my answer to this question have already been given in the several places where the theological question has compelled my attention. The improbable emergence and astonishing endurance of God's nation—possible only through its adherence to His Torah—and the spread and persistence of much of His teaching throughout the West are impressive facts. Moses's prophetic genius is, I submit, nothing less than a godsend. Even more so, the book of Exodus and the Law, which illuminate our human limitations and inspire our higher possibilities. The unity of Creator, Redeemer, and Lawgiver is a compelling and deeply moving idea. But on my most recent readings, the Tabernacle has been for me a new source of insight and reverent awe.

God, says the text, took up with the Israelites in order to dwell among them and be known, not just by the likes of Moses or Moses Maimonides but also by ordinary human beings. Their—our—aspiration to be in contact with what is highest, expressed first in the pagan error with the calf, He addresses with the Tabernacle, where people gather in His service and where His Presence can accordingly be felt. Having witnessed the Tabernacle's raising, I try to imagine it occupied, myself among the assembled.

They—we—congregate in a place whose design is His, containing a Holy of Holies housing the Law that He gave, and look longingly together in His direction offering sacrifice and praise. Many come offering contrition, seeking self-purification and spiritual renewal. Others are expressing gratitude for redemption or the sheer glory of existence. None will see Him, but all have heard and will flourish under His Word. We have no knowledge of His nature, but we bear collective witness to His awesome Presence. When performing the prescribed rituals or raising our voices in worship and song, we may on occasion be lifted up to otherworldly states of feeling and awareness, sensing for a moment that attachment to God is the core and peak of existence. Could this be what is meant by knowing His Spirit and feeling His Presence?

Politically, we twenty-first-century Americans still have much to learn from the book of Exodus, precisely because we are not theocrats but loyal yet worried members of a modern liberal democracy. History shows us that inflammatory mixtures of religion and politics can have deadly consequences—from the Crusades, the Inquisition, and the Thirty Years' War to today's Islamist jihad against the infidels. But we also know the twentieth century's godless politics associated with Hitler, Stalin, and Mao that, rejecting biblical morality, slaughtered more people than all previous religious wars combined and crushed the spirit of millions more. As G. K. Chesterton put it, "when men choose not to believe in God, they do not thereafter believe in nothing, they then become capable of believing in anything." With atheism on the rise in Western societies, we may soon discover what happens should humanity return to the dehumanizing conditions that prevailed before biblical times: the techno-despotic ways of the Egyptians, the earth-worshipping and licentious ways of the Canaanites, or the cosmopolitan and soulless dream of the Babel builders that man will be a god to man.

In these confused and dangerous times, with most Western nations struggling to articulate why they should exist at all and with the human future in the balance, we can ill afford to neglect any possible sources of wisdom about human affairs. As Rousseau argued 250 years ago, the timeless book of Exodus remains an indispensable resource for thinking about the good life and the good community, freedom and law, justice and holiness, and the meaning and purpose of our existence. It deserves—and rewards—our most serious attention.

Notes

Introduction

1. These permanent questions have risen to the surface of our turbulent times, as controversy swirls about the meaning and goodness of the nation-state and the idea of "peoplehood." We live evermore in a globalized age, thanks to instant communication, easy travel and open borders, and unprecedented worldwide commerce and economic interdependence; throughout the West, cosmopolitan elites increasingly regard themselves as "citizens of the world." Yet we live also in an age of resurgent nationalism, roiling the polities of Europe and the United States; rallying around the national flag, citizens who love their own ways increasingly resent seeing them diluted by what they perceive to be non-assimilating immigrants or threatened by global conglomerates, foreign ideologies, and transnational bureaucracies. Today, within the United States and other countries that have for decades celebrated "multiculturalism," ethnic and racial divisions and the use of hyphenated-identities have increased, raising for thoughtful citizens questions of what unites us and what can hold the nation together. Even in long-established polities, what makes a people a people is again a live—indeed, an urgent—question.

ONE Into the House of Bondage

1. *Bereshith* ("In Beginning," rather than Genesis, "coming-into-being") is famously a book about beginnings; *Bemidbar* ("In the Wilderness," rather than Numbers) gives the full experience of the desert wanderings; and *Devarim* ("Words," rather than Deuteronomy, "the second law") is largely devoted to the final speeches and songs of Moses. Not obvious to me is any thematic keynote being struck by *Vayiqra* ("And He [Y-H-V-H] Called," rather than Leviticus, "Levitical or Priestly Matters").

2. "Egypt" is the very last word of Genesis: "and they embalmed him [Joseph] and he was put into a coffin in Egypt" (Gen. 50:26). The end of Genesis anticipates an Egyptian world that literally knew not Joseph, and with it the deadly outcome that awaits the Children of Israel in Egypt. Joseph's mummification, which coveys his full Egyptianization, also hints at the risk of Israelite assimilation.

The Hebrew name for Egypt, *mitsrayim*, is the dual form of the noun, *matsor*, meaning "siege" or "entrenchment," as well as the dual form of the noun, *metsar*, meaning "tight straits" or "distress." *Mitsrayim* to an ancient Hebrew speaker could therefore mean both "double fortress" and "double distress." *Mitsrayim* also contains the word for water, *mayim*, a fitting pun for the watery nation. Finally, the combination of entrenchment, tight straits, and water points also to the process of childbirth: Egypt is *the* fertile place, and childbirth is a big theme in the first two chapters of Exodus. (I have much more to say about the meaning of Egypt in Chapter Six.)

3. Only the names of the sons are mentioned. The unnamed yet "absent presence" of their mothers becomes all the more striking when, by chapter's end, we learn of the crucial importance of two women, the Hebrew midwives Shifrah and Puah, the only other persons of this generation whose names we learn. The memorable male-centered beginnings need to be corrected and rescued by heroic women. As we will see, women and their relation to birth and children provide the first crucial lesson about the difference between mighty Egypt and nascent Israel.

4. In fairness, one should add that the same verb is used also in God's twofold injunction to Noah and his sons after the flood: "Be fruitful and multiply and fill the earth (*umil'u 'eth-ha'arets*). . . . And you, be fruitful and multiply, and swarm (*shirtsu*) in the earth and multiply there" (Gen. 9:1, 7). After the flood, the earth was to be filled with life, not with water. The Children of Israel, ensconced in Egypt and doing what comes naturally, are accomplishing the same result: "and the land was filled with them" (*vattimmale' ha'arets 'otham*).

5. There is a further ambiguity concerning this description of Israelite proliferation. Is it a true or "objective" account, disclosed by the neutral and nameless voice of the text? Does it represent the way the Children of Israel saw themselves? Or does it rather reflect the way that the *Egyptians* perceived them? Although I am inclined to take the account at face value, the fact that the next verse introduces the Pharaoh who looks upon them with fear and revulsion may suggest that this hyperbolic description is something of an exaggeration, reflecting Egyptian concerns and prejudices. If this is the picture that will strike the new Pharaoh, it is perhaps more understandable why "he knew not Joseph" and why he did what he did (see below).

6. The text's silence on what the Israelites were thinking can be explained in another way: it is giving us (only) the *Egyptian* point of view, in relation to which the Israelite point of view is irrelevant. (I owe this suggestion to Amiad Cohen.)

7. The great twelfth-century Jewish commentator, Ibn Ezra, treats *vayaqam*, "rose up," as signifying political revolution. As evidence, he cites Saul's charge of political rebellion in 1 Samuel 22:8. In other places, the phrase *qum 'al* means to "rise up against"

or "rebel against." Here, that phrasing is used, but the clear meaning is that the new Pharaoh rose up to rule over Egypt, not to rebel against it.

8. Could Pharaoh's lack of memory of the past and his attendant ingratitude be the mirror image of similar forgetfulness and ingratitude on the part of the Israelites? Once again, we are invited to wonder about *their* collective memory at the time of the new Pharaoh. Do the Children of Israel at this *later* date still know Joseph? Do they know their ancestor Jacob/Israel? More importantly, do they still know the God of Jacob? Once again, we do not know, but I continue to doubt it. Although the text's silence on their subjective reality and self-understanding is not necessarily evidence, the aura of the first two chapters seems to bespeak God-forgetting and lapsed cultural memory. *They* never refer to themselves as "Children of Israel" (or anything else for that matter). And a good case can be made—and I will do so in subsequent chapters—that the Israelites come to know the Lord only *after* and *because* the Egyptians were compelled to recognize Him first. This does not, however, mean that the Children of Israel do not have *some* externally recognizable cultural identity (manifested, say, in physical appearance and dress, diet, family structure, and work): otherwise, how would the new Pharaoh have been able to recognize them? See the later discussion and Note 10.

9. Given our interest in people formation, let us pause, at its first mention in Exodus, to notice the word *'am*, which I always translate as "people." It is to be distinguished from the word *goy*, which I translate as "nation." Although the terms are often used interchangeably as synonyms (and I will do so too), the basic ideas are significantly different. A nation (as the Latin root, *natio*, implies) is a group of people defined "naturally," by birth or nativity, by shared descent from common ancestors. A people, by contrast, is a group of human beings defined culturally and politically—by their language, mores, laws, projects, and way of life. The terms first appear in Genesis's two stories of human division and the multiplication of languages. In Genesis 10, we learn the genealogies of the nations (*goyim*) of the world, spread abroad in their branching descent from the three sons of Noah, each nation "after his tongue, after their families" (10:5). (*Mitsrayim*, the eponymous forbear of venerable Egypt, is one of the sons of Ham, Noah's irreverent and hotheaded son.) In Genesis 11, when the whole human race, resisting dispersion, gathers to build the city and tower of Babel, God comments that they are one people (*'am*), with one language and a bold and impious project; he confounds their languages and scatters them across the face of the earth. In addition to *goy* and *'am*, we later encounter a special third term for the collectivity that is the Children of Israel: *'edah*, translated as "community." It occurs in three places where the Israelites are called to special encounters with the Lord: the Paschal sacrifice (12:3), the gathering of the manna (16:1–2, 9–10; 17:1), and the beginning of their construction of the Tabernacle (35:1, 4). (I am indebted to Alexander Orwin, then a graduate student in the Committee on Social Thought, from whose term paper "A Community Before the Lord: *Goy, 'Am,* or *'Edah*?" I learned much on this subject.)

10. From Genesis, we know, for example, that there were differences in diet (43:32); that the Israelites were shepherds, whereas the Egyptians abominated shepherds

(46:32–34); that the Egyptians shaved, whereas the Israelites (probably) did not (41:14); that the Israelites buried their dead, whereas the Egyptians embalmed them (50); and that the Egyptians practiced worship of the sun, whereas the Israelites surely did not (41:45).

11. The prophecy given to Abram, during the covenant between the sacrificial pieces, foretells of a bondage that goes beyond mere servitude to include the afflictions of abasement and humiliation: "Know for sure that your seed shall be a stranger in a land that is not theirs, and shall serve them; and they shall afflict (or "abase"; 'inna) them for four hundred years" (Gen. 15:13). They will be strangers; they will be servants; they will be abased and humbled for four hundred years. The same verb, 'inna, is also used to describe what the prince of Shechem did to Dinah: he not only took her and lay with her but he also humbled her (Gen. 34:2). In light of this usage in the Dinah story, the Rabbis saw a possible sexual meaning in the abasement of the Egyptians: not, as with Dinah, unwanted intercourse, but its opposite—enforced separation of husband and wife—a perfect strategy for blocking Israelite reproduction. That is in fact the way the Passover *Haggadah,* glossing a Hebrew noun of the same root ('oni) in Deut. 26:7, presents what the Egyptians did to the Israelites.

12. Building on the sexual understanding of 'inna presented in the previous note, a famous rabbinic statement in the Talmud says that "the Jewish People were redeemed from Egypt because of the merit of the righteous Jewish women" (Babylonian Talmud, Tractate Sotah 11b). The midrash goes on to explain that the women would go to visit their husbands in the fields after work and would playfully seduce them so that they would have sexual relations and continue to proliferate as a people. (My thanks to Nathan Laufer for this suggestion and reference. This idea will return in the last chapter in connection with the bronze mirrors that the women donate to build the Laver for the Tabernacle.)

13. If one reads *la-meyalledoth ha'ivriyyoth* as a noun with its adjective, then the words mean "the Hebrew midwives." But if one reads the words as a verb with its direct object, then they mean "the women who birthed the Hebrews"; thus, "the midwives *to* the Hebrews."

14. Pharaoh asks the first question in Exodus. His "why" is not, however, a disinterested quest for knowledge of cause or reason, but rather a rebuke, issued in an accusing spirit. We will want to compare this with Moses's questions in Exodus 2 and especially in Exodus 3 (v. 3).

15. See for example Genesis 20:11, where Abraham explains to Abimelech that he passed off Sarah as his sister because, he thought, "surely, the fear of God (*yir'ath 'elohim*) was not in this place."

16. In going forward, especially in the plague narratives and the contest between Pharaoh and the Lord, let us watch carefully for any signs of similar natural reverence, piety, or "fear of Heaven." Can this germ of natural piety mature enough to lead—a few, some, many, all?—people to the Lord?

17. This is not merely my opinion. "And God dealt well with the midwives; and the people multiplied and waxed mighty. And it came to pass, because the midwives

feared God (or "the gods"; *ha'elohim*), that He made them houses" (1:20–21). That God rewards the midwives does not, of course, require that they were Israelites; on the contrary, their deed is all the more praiseworthy if they were not. At the same time, we should note that, if they were indeed Egyptians, it would be the first occasion (since Noah) on which the God of Israel bestows favor on non-Israelites. (I owe the last observation to Yehoshua Pfeffer.)

18. We are not told whether the Egyptians—all, some, or any—obeyed his edict.

19. Literalist readers will take issue with my claim, pointing out that it is an exaggeration—which, as a *purely factual* matter, it is. What Pharaoh's intransigence and God's retribution will later produce is "merely" the deaths of the *firstborn*, human and animal, followed by the destruction of the Egyptian army by drowning in the Sea of Reeds. But at least symbolically, the slaying of the firstborn means the death of the national future. After the episode at the Sea of Reeds, Egypt dies in the text, never to be mentioned again until the Book of Chronicles.

20. As we learn from Sophocles's *Oedipus Tyrannos,* patricide and incest are the paradigmatic crimes of the tyrant. By thus denying one's contingent and dependent beginnings, these deeds of the overmastering man bespeak his desire to become his own source and to attain self-sufficiency. I hasten to add that Sophocles has the chorus call Oedipus "a paradigm of man," suggesting that his aspirations are not idiosyncratic but endemic to being human.

21. Actually, the Children of Israel may have a double experience of changing and losing their cultural ways. At the beginning of our story, they are prospering in Egypt, growing in number, and inhabiting a most fertile part of the country. Very likely, they have loosened their ancestral ties to the patriarchs; they may have assimilated to certain Egyptian ways and teachings; they may even have forgotten God. Then, when they fall into slavery, they will lose their independent status and whatever Egyptian notions and leanings they may have acquired. They will be left with nothing.

TWO   The Birth and Youth of the Liberator

1. A truly naïve reader, reading Exodus for the first time and without foreknowledge of the overarching story, will of course not know from reading Exodus 2 why he is reading about this fellow Moses: Who is he? And what is his connection to the enslaved Israelites? Such a reader would probably be better suited than we to enter into Moses's experiences in this chapter, for Moses, as we shall see, also does not know who he really is or what his future holds. It is thus improper of me to tip my readers off about Moses's destiny: better to experience vicariously his birth and youth without anticipating his later importance. Still, because I am reading Exodus with a view to questions of people formation, leadership, and law, I cannot help focusing attention on those aspects of the story that I believe shed light on those themes. Thus, we will read the story of Moses's birth and youth not only for its own sake but also to discover what made him eligible to receive God's call, what made him suitable to become Israel's liberator. (Let me immediately acknowledge the difficulty of referring to Moses as the

future "liberator" or "redeemer" of Israel: according to the text, as we shall see, that honor belongs to God. We will want to explore the relation between the divine redeemer and His human champion.)

Two more introductory observations about Exodus 2. More than many other biblical chapters, it is from start to finish open to multiple possible readings and interpretations—I think self-consciously so, in keeping with the ambiguities of Moses's identity and subjective experience. Also, in contrast with the first chapter of a book called "Names," many of the characters in this chapter are unnamed, and Moses's name, as we shall see, has its own ambiguity. When, only late in the chapter, a few names start to appear, we should consider why.

2. The opening of this chapter is logically linked to Pharaoh's command, which concluded the previous one: the first word is "and" (or "but"), translating the first letter *vav*. (Chapter divisions were not present in the original text.)

3. *'innah*. As noted earlier, the same verb is used to describe what the Egyptian taskmasters did to the Hebrew slaves (1:11).

4. The description in the text, following a standard pattern, makes it seem as if this were the first union of this Levite man and this Levite woman and that Moses is a firstborn. Why does the text convey this mistaken impression? Most likely, to encourage us from the start to consider Moses as a child of the first rank and to regard his birth as the beginning of a new era—both of which suggestions turn out to be true.

5. We later learn for sure that he was not the youngest: for one thing, Joshua was much younger. For another, when the Exodus finally occurs decades later, thousands of Israelite children are among those who go out; they would have been born when Moses was in Midian. The most likely explanation for this glut of Israelite children is that the edict was soon abandoned or not successfully enforced.

6. We also do not know whether Moses was circumcised. This issue will explicitly arise in Exodus 4 (see Chapter Three in this book).

7. It is a judgment we have not heard anyone make about anything since Genesis 1, where God saw that (almost) everything He had made was good, and since Genesis 3, where the woman "saw that the [forbidden] tree [of knowledge of good and bad] was good for food." We will return to this point in the last chapter.

8. The Tradition makes something concrete out of the parallel. Says Rashi, commenting on this verse, citing the sages, "When he was born, the whole house was filled with light (*Sota 12a*)." *Pentateuch with Targum Onkelos, Haphtaroth and Rashi's Commentary: Exodus*, trans. Rev. M. Rosenbaum and Dr. A. M. Silberman (New York: Hebrew Publishing Company), 6. Nathan Laufer (in a private communication) suggests that "this comment is a premonition of the light that Moses will radiate when he comes down with the second tables from Mount Sinai, after God revealed His glory to him [in Exod. 34], undoubtedly, the high point of his prophetic experience with God." We will revisit this idea when we examine that scene in Chapter Twenty-One.

9. I owe this suggestion to a shrewd mother, Amy Kass.

10. The Hebrew word here translated "to him," *lo*, could also be translated "for him."

11. Later, Moses will claim not to be a good speaker. He is an assertive fellow whose forte is not making assertions.

12. In an inverted echo of the Dinah story, where angry Levi (with Simeon) kills all the men of Shechem to avenge the rape of his sister, here a clever (nameless) Levite sister asserts herself to save her brother.

13. Not everyone reads her comment as explaining the *name*. Rabbi Naftali Zvi Yehuda Berlin (aka Netziv) has an ingenious alternative reading, in which her comment explains rather her decision to *call him her son*: "'And he became a son to her'— Since she saved him from death and also raised him, it was considered as though she had given birth to him, as she says: 'And she called his name Moshe.' . . . In the Egyptian language, this word in this form means 'son.' Thus she explains the reason why the child is hers: 'for I drew him out of the water.' For it is as if he drowned in the river, and so his father and his mother have no portion in him, and I am the mother of the child. This is truly called acquiring a person. . . . According to our words, the word '*meshitihu*' (I drew him out) is not related to the name Moshe, but rather is the explanation that she called him ['son'] Moshe" (Ha'amek Davar, Shemoth 2:10; emphasis added). Netziv adds in conclusion, "In any event, this is the way of the holy language— to present a play on words."

14. Many people have noted the further irony in the lexical error of the explanation of the name. The verb *mashah* means not (passively) "drawn out of the water," but (actively) "*to* draw (something) out of the water." Named as if anticipating his later deeds, *Mosheh* is "one who draws out"; "one who is drawn out" would be called *mashui*.

15. I am indebted to Amiad Cohen for the ideas in this paragraph. As we will see in the next chapter, Moses will gain his personal and cultural identity largely in relation to the Lord, starting at the burning bush.

16. According to one midrash, Pharaoh anticipated the birth of a child who would overthrow his rule and save the Egyptian people—thus, perhaps, explaining his peculiarly stated decree to kill *all* male infants. Pharaoh's daughter plays her part in saving a child who just might be this savior.

17. Picking up on this "feminine" aspect of Moses's character, Aaron Wildavsky titled his masterful study, *The Nursing Father: Moses as Political Leader* (Tuscaloosa: University of Alabama Press, 1984); it was reprinted posthumously as *Moses as Political Leader* (Jerusalem: Shalem Press, 2005).

18. See the book of this title, *Secrets of the Great Pyramid,* by Peter Tompkins (New York: Harper Collins, 1978).

19. We gladly acknowledge, however, that the text, in its silence about Moses's education, is apparently not eager to have us reach such a conclusion. The text apparently means for us to see that Moses's stature and capacity as a leader in Israel are owed neither to his native gifts nor to his princely rearing, but entirely to his serving as the Lord's loyal deputy and obedient minister.

20. The examination of mummies reveals that some Egyptians were circumcised, but this practice did not take place at birth and was, of course, unrelated to any covenant with the Lord. It appears rather to have been an initiation rite, practiced around

the time of puberty or later, that introduced the young man into the society of males (warriors).

21. Philo, in his biography of Moses, engages in extensive speculation on Moses's education in Pharaoh's house and on the connection between that education and the way God catches Moses's attention. (*Moses I*, in *Philo*, vol. 6, trans. F. H. Colson [Loeb Classical Library, Harvard University Press, 1935], sections 5–7. My thanks to Judah Mandelbaum for calling this to my attention.)

22. It is instructive to compare this maiden appearance of Moses with that of Joseph, about whom we first hear when he is seventeen years old. Joseph is his father's pet, bedecked in the cloak of rule, but given over to self-glorifying dreams and annoying bragging about them. He does not go out to his brethren, save to spy on them and to report their misconduct to their father Jacob. Later, when sent by Jacob to his brethren, fratricide is narrowly avoided.

23. Whose point of view do we have here? We do not know whether this entire description, including the ethnic identity of the two men and the identification "one of his brethren," is seen and known by Moses himself or only by the text (and therefore us), a question underscored by the fact that the Israelites (including Moses, were he thinking like an Israelite) would not have referred to themselves as "Hebrews."

24. These questions about the *factual* state of Moses's prior knowledge may deflect us from the main point. If, as I believe, we are given this story mainly as a *paradigm*—to show us young man Moses's natural reaction to the text's one crucial fact, namely, the brutal oppression of Israel in Egypt—we should probably read this story *as if* Moses is here encountering an Israelite and his oppression *for the first time*.

25. As with everyone else at this stage in the story, Israelite as well as Egyptian, the existence of the divine appears to be utterly neglected. From the beginning of Exodus until this point, we readers, like the participants in the story, are being lulled into believing that God is, at best, on vacation. Because He is out of our sight, we may be inclined to forget that He is watching.

26. Amiad Cohen supports this view by suggesting that, in killing the Egyptian, Moses is also "killing" or abandoning—wittingly or unwittingly—his own Egyptian identity. In the next episode, according to Cohen, he will approach the brawling Hebrews as one of them.

27. The word "man," *'ish*, occurs three times in these two verses: "Egyptian man," "Hebrew man," "no man." Moses, although both Egyptian and Hebrew, functions in the story as the opposite of "no man."

28. In this respect, he resembles somewhat his adoptive mother, Pharaoh's daughter, who likewise took the side of the underdog. But where she was moved by soft-hearted compassion, Moses is moved by Levite spiritedness and righteous indignation.

29. This formulation reminds the reader of the deeds of his ancestor Levi in avenging the rape of Dinah. We might therefore say that this encounter awakens the Levite spiritedness in Moses and perhaps also increases his awareness of his hitherto dormant Israelite identity.

30. I have been surprised over the years to discover that none—and I mean none—of my students is as impressed with Moses in this episode as I am (and have been all my life). Indeed, most condemn him for his homicide, a deed that many of them will *never* countenance. In deference to their views, I invite readers to make their own evaluations, after taking seriously my own. I will return to Moses's homicide in the next chapter in the context of the "Bridegroom of Blood" episode.

31. The use of the expression "the second day," rather than "on another day," indicates that the second episode is to be seen as the continuation of the first: they are two conjoined aspects of the debut of young man Moses.

32. The word translated "neighbor," *re'a*, means "associate," who can be more or less close. It can be used to mean everything from "brother" or "friend" to "companion" or "fellow."

33. These lovely uncertainties accurately reflect the mysterious ways in which "things become known."

34. The story, as presented, reads as though the episode at the well occurs immediately upon his arrival in Midian, but the text clearly tells us that he "dwelt" (or "stayed") there. Still, because we are interested not in the historical but in the paradigmatic facts, the story at the well presents the first *essential* facts about Moses in Midian. Later, we will have reason to believe that many years may have elapsed between his arrival in Midian and this episode at the well. (See Chapter Three, Note 29.)

35. Abraham's servant had stopped at a well to find a wife for Isaac and was rewarded by the arrival of Rebekah, who kindly brought him water and who heroically drew huge amounts of water to graciously water his camels (Gen. 24). Jacob, fleeing his brother Esau and sent away to find a wife at the home of his mother's brother, arrives in Paddan-aram, where he immediately meets and falls in love with beautiful Rachel at a well, defying the gathered crowd of shepherds by lifting a massive boulder from the well's mouth and watering her flock (Gen. 29).

36. If one were reading the three stories *developmentally*, one might say that Moses has come to this sense of himself only as a result of the previous two episodes. After the first, he was no more an Egyptian; after the second, he was alienated from the Israelites. Here in Midian, he is stripped of all previous identities save for his humanity. We wonder whether the "universality" of his beneficence is important to his eligibility for God's mission, disclosed in the next chapter.

37. There is no evidence, either here or later, that Moses is, like Jacob at the well or with Rachel throughout, a lover of women. Unlike Jacob at the well, he says not one word to the women. At the same time, however, he may well be moved by their sisterly comity—the three Hebrew verbs for "they came," "they drew water," and "they filled" [the troughs] all end with the same feminine plural ending "-*enah*," which creates an encouraging picture of harmonious (Midianite) sisterhood that is the opposite of contentious and murderous (Egyptian and Israelite) men. It is striking that, after this experience at the well, the text overflows with proper names, and personal life begins anew for Moses. (I am grateful to Amiad Cohen for the linguistic point and to Dan Polisar for the observation about sisterhood and names.)

38. Hannah Mandelbaum offers an additional—literary—reason why the text turns now to the Israelites. In the prophecy given to Abram during the covenant between the sacrificial pieces, he was told that "your seed shall be a stranger (*ger*) in a land that is not theirs, and they shall serve them (*'avad*), and they shall afflict (*'innah*) them four hundred years" (Gen. 15:13). In Exodus 1, we were told that the Egyptians afflicted (*'innah*) the Children of Israel and that they made them serve (*'avad*) with rigor. Only when Moses, in a way speaking for all the Israelites, affirms that he has been a stranger (*ger*) in a strange land is the prophecy *literally* complete. It is therefore time for the deliverance to begin.

39. In this chapter, the story of baby Moses begins with his weeping and ends with his naming his son after his estrangement; the story of the Israelites begins and ends with their crying out.

THREE Moses Finds God and (Reluctantly) Accepts His Mission

1. This we learn soon afterward, when the text tells us, "Moses was eighty years old, and Aaron eighty-three years old, when they spoke unto Pharaoh" (7:7). (See also Note 29.)

2. Readers have long been puzzled by the change in the name of Moses's father-in-law from Reuel to Jethro. I cannot explain the change and have no idea about its significance. My perplexity grows when, in Numbers, Moses's father-in-law is called "Hobab, the son of Raguel (= Reuel) the Midianite" (10:29), and when I learn that the Rabbis consider that he has in fact seven names (http://jewishencyclopedia.com/articles /8620-jethro).

3. We think of God's first message to Jacob, the dream he experienced when he was alone, at night, near the border between Canaan and Paddan-aram (Gen. 28:10ff).

4. We assume that God generally knows how to appeal to His customers. A perfect example is the call of Abram. When God called him in Genesis 12, Abram "is a childless, rootless, homeland-less, perhaps godless, devoted firstborn son of an old wanderer and radical, a man who has grown out of, but who may have outgrown, the Babylonian ways and gods. He is very far from the self-satisfied and secure condition of the builders of Babel whose story immediately precedes his own. We surmise that Abram may long for roots, land, home, settled ways, children, and something great, perhaps even for the divine." Leon R. Kass, *The Beginning of Wisdom: Reading Genesis* (New York: Free Press, 2003), 255. God's sevenfold promise to Abram—including a homeland, prosperity, fame, and national-scale descendants—spoke precisely to Abram's longings. We thus expect to learn more about Moses's longings from the appeal that God will soon make to him.

5. There are seven uses of the verb "to see" (*ra'ah*) or its cognates ("looked," "appear," "sight"); the seventh use is a negation of seeing: "for he feared to look upon God." These linguistic facts herald the big themes of this theophany: the visible versus the invisible, and the limits of seeing for yourself. See the following discussion.

6. There are two Hebrew words translatable as "why." The first is a nonspecific, primitive particle, *mah*, which can mean (either as a question or as an exclamation), "what?" ("what!"), "how?" ("how!"), "when?" ("when!"), or "why?" ("why!"). The second, *maddu'a*—formed from *mah* plus the passive participle of the verb *yada'*, "to know"—means literally, "What is known?" and, therefore, adverbially, "Why?" in the sense of "what is the cause or the reason." This is only the third utterance of *maddu'a* in Exodus and the first by an Israelite. Pharaoh asked it of the midwives (1:18), angrily seeking an explanation for their failure to heed his command to perform male infanticide. Reuel used the word in the sense of "How come" when his daughters return so early from the well (2:18). Moses, in contrast, seeks to know a causal explanation for its own sake. The difference strikes us as revelatory. (In Genesis, *maddu'a* is used only twice, once by Isaac to ask Abimelech and his people *wherefore* they had come to him, seeing as they hate him [26:27], and once by Joseph to ask his jail mates *why* they looked so sad today [40:7].)

7. When I first began to study Exodus twenty years ago, I inclined to the latter view: piety and obedience, I thought, require suppressing the desire to see for yourself. Thanks to further study, I have changed my mind. Only someone with a mind like Moses's is fit to be God's champion, and his desire to know the highest is not condemned. On the contrary, for leadership in God's Way, interest in the universal truth of things is every bit as important as fellow feeling, concern for justice, and the love of your own people. Moreover, the teachings of the Torah are neither opaque to reason nor hostile to inquiry, reflection, and speculation, even as the Torah may reject other forms of "philosophizing." This is good news not only for Moses but also for the wisdom-seeking reader.

8. This is only the third—and also the last time—in the Torah that God summons anyone by calling his name *twice*. The other two: Abraham is called twice by God's angel to keep him from sacrificing Isaac (Gen. 22:11) and Jacob is called twice by God in a night vision to encourage him to go down to Egypt (Gen. 46:2). In both previous cases, as here, the addressee answered *"Hinneni"* (see the next note). In both previous cases, a dreaded event turned out well. Do those cases provide precedent for the present twice-named calling of Moses?

9. *Hinneni*, "here I am" (or "behold me"), is used as an answer but eight times in the Torah: seven times in Genesis and once here. It occurs most notably in the story of the binding of Isaac, where three times Abraham gives this one-word-answer to someone who calls him by name, each time for the weightiest of reasons: once to God, once to his son, and once to the angel of the Lord who stays his hand (Gen. 22). It is also spoken once each by Esau (to Isaac, who calls him to go hunting for him; Gen. 27:1); Isaac (to Jacob, who is pretending to be Esau in order to get the blessing; Gen. 27:18); Joseph (to Jacob, when his father sends him to his brothers, on a mission from which he never returns; Gen. 37:13); and, lastly, Jacob (to God in the night vision telling him not to fear going down to Egypt; Gen. 46:2). Moses's answer, *Hinneni*, immediately places this mixed-identity fellow in the company of the Israelite patriarchs. And while Joseph's *"Hinneni"* led to Israel's descent into Egyptian bondage, Moses's *"Hinneni"*

will lead to their deliverance from Egypt. (My thanks to Hannah Mandelbaum for these last two observations.)

10. This is the first appearance in Exodus of the crucial term *qadosh*, "holy," central to the entire book and the mission of the Children of Israel. (It was used only once in Genesis, in the story of Creation, to refer to God's hallowing of the Seventh Day [Gen. 2:3].) Joshua Berman anticipates the pregnant significance of its current use: "This is precisely the site at which we would expect the introduction of the concept of *kedushah* ['holiness'], for at that very moment Moses was informed that the Children of Israel would come to Sinai to worship God (Exodus 3:12), and it is at Sinai, of course, that the Torah was given to the Jewish people and the covenant with God was consecrated. The midrash is sensitive to this point as well: "'For the place on which you stand is holy ground'—The Holy One Blessed be He said to him, "Moses, Moses! hold your place, for at this site I will give the Torah to Israel," as it says, "do not come closer. Remove your sandals from your feet, for the place on which you stand is holy ground."'" Joshua Berman, *The Temple: Its Symbolism and Meaning Then and Now* (Eugene, OR: Wipf & Stock, 2010), 9.

11. In his encounter with the nearby Divine Presence, Moses experiences in advance the remedy for restlessness and homelessness that the Tabernacle will provide for the wandering and homeless Children of Israel. (I will discuss this at the end of Chapter Twenty-Two.)

12. When Moses, much later, tells the Israelites of the nations that they must conquer on entering Promised Land, he mentions seven: the six listed here plus the Girgashites. (Deut. 7:1; I cannot explain the discrepancy.)

13. Although I share this prevalent interpretation of Moses's questions and doubts, it is certainly possible that Moses is *not* reluctant but rather *eager* for the mission and that he is exploring what he needs to know before he can accept it. In following the ensuing conversation, the reader is encouraged to see what it might betoken under this interpretation.

We should also consider an opposite possibility: God did not expect Moses to immediately embrace the assignment and deliberately used the way He presented it to provoke exactly the conversation that ensues. God may want the inquisitive Moses to ask the very questions he asks in order to advance the transformation that has just begun with Moses's conversion from wonder to awe and from seeing to hearing.

14. *'Ehyeh* is the first-person singular of the verb "to be," *hayah*, in its imperfect aspect—not perfected or completed, but continuing or incomplete. Its English translation has difficulty capturing this aspect: I am [being], or I will be [being]—with you. This word recurs in the immediate sequel as part of the mysterious answer to the question about the divine name.

15. Ruth Martin (now Ruth Martin Curry) suggests an opposite meaning of God's answer to the question of Moses's identity: "No one, not even God, can 'speak' Moses's identity to him; ultimately self-identity must be internally constituted, and constituted through deeds, rather than in words." Ms. Martin develops the point most powerfully, as follows:

This is revealed through Moses's persistent reluctance to internalize God's role for (and therefore confidence in) him. . . . A margin of doubt intercedes between what Moses hears and what Moses accepts as achievable. This doubt negotiates with God until it wins Moses a number of reassuring accessories: the power to produce wonders (the staff), and the addition of Aaron as his mouthpiece. Like the sign God offers in response to Moses's query, these tangible accouterments allow Moses to transfer his revelation to the mortal world, for it is in human terms that his success—and his identity—must pronounce themselves.

Also striking, God defines Moses in relation to Himself. . . . Perhaps in a way, "you are the man I will be with" is not only reasonable, but the most satisfying response to Moses's question: If only his own successful action will ensure Moses's confidence in his abilities and purpose, God's promise of allegiance (but importantly, not *control*) is the best reassurance. If God had answered, uncharacteristically, "I will make these things happen," rather than "I will be with you," Moses would be guaranteed success, but the significance of his agency and individuality would be denied.

(These remarks are from a remarkable essay on Moses's coming into self-understanding, written by Ms. Martin during her Senior "Fundamentals" qualifying examination for her BA in "Fundamentals: Issues and Texts," University of Chicago, Spring 2005. Quoted with permission.)

16. Using "The Infinite" as a *name* for the divine is to speak unintelligibly.

17. According to the Garden of Eden story, naming the animals was the first human act, and their names were the first human inventions. Although we are not told any of the names that the human being gave to the animals, their different names were solicited by the perceived real differences among them. God may have created them, and created them after their kinds, but their ability to be known was actualized only thanks to human speech and reason. Thus, this act of naming was the first display of our humanity, which also made the man conscious for the first time of his human difference. Yet the names he gave them may not have accurately grasped the essences of the animals, but rather expressed his feelings for or his interests in them. A poignant nonbiblical example: the elephant got a name that (in Greek) means "ivory" (*elephas*), rather than, say, "thick-skin" (pachyderm) or "rememberer" or "soulful."

18. It may be objected that to speak of "philosophy" in Egypt in the time of Moses is an anachronism, as philosophy properly understood is a later development of Greek origin. The point is well taken. Yet the seeds of philosophy—the desire to know and represent the truth about the world and its highest powers—are present implicitly in Egyptian writing and statuary. Plato is said to have traveled to Egypt, and Egypt is in many sources regarded as the place of ancient wisdom.

A second, and opposite, objection holds that philosophy—the search for wisdom—is very much present here in the person of Moses, but that its aspiration is not being rejected but rather encouraged, even if temporarily deflected and directed into more fruitful channels. Not for nothing did God choose a man interested in the cause of things to be His lawgiver, His philosopher-king.

A final objection to this suggestion holds that Moses's interest in God's name, here and later, is not really philosophical, motivated by a disinterested desire for the truth, but rather an interested request for knowledge that will either be helpful in caring for His people or that will allow him to enter more fully into an intimate relation to the divine, akin to a relationship between friends or lovers.

We shall keep these objections in mind, although the third strikes us, at first glance, as taking too literally the anthropomorphic imagery of God: What would intimacy mean between Moses and an invisible God? Much later in Exodus, however, when Moses asks to know God's glory, we will have occasion to reconsider this in a more positive light.

19. It is worth recalling how the Israelites had previously known of God and by what name. Even to the patriarchs, God had rarely identified himself other than as the God of earlier patriarchs. On two occasions, He announces that He is 'El Shaddai, "the most mighty god" or "God Almighty": once when addressing Abraham before the covenant marked by circumcision (Gen. 17:1) and once when addressing Jacob after his return to Beth El from Paddan-aram (35:11). Only in the dream He sent to Jacob (Gen. 28:13) does He identify Himself by the Tetragrammaton, Y-H-V-H, as well as "the god of Abraham your father [!] and the god of Isaac." Abraham several times uses the four-letter name, perhaps divining in this way the solicitude and closeness of the Lord. And the other patriarchs are said to "turn to the Lord." But before Moses, God had only once revealed His four-letter "name" to anyone who was wide awake—to Abram just before the covenant between the sacrificial pieces: "I am Y-H-V-H that brought you out of Ur of the Chaldees, to give you this land to inherit it" (Gen. 15:7). These facts will become thematically important in Exodus 6 when the Lord speaks of how His name was known to the patriarchs (see Chapter Four).

20. But Jacob himself receives a new name from his adversary: "Israel," meaning "God rules" or "God prevails." It is given to him as "one who struggles with God and man" (Gen. 32:29).

21. Readers probably already know that whole libraries have been written to explore the meaning and import of this "divine name," and scholars continue to ponder it as containing "the metaphysics of the Hebrew Bible." I have great respect for these efforts, but in the context of the unfolding narrative I have been more impressed by the way that the Lord's answer to Moses's question appears to curtail such metaphysical preoccupations. Yet an outstanding term paper for my 2010 Exodus class, written by John Ellison, a graduate student in the Committee on Social Thought, has given me pause:

> For these words [I Am That I Am] touch on the very aim of philosophy according to Aristotle, which is the investigation of "Being qua Being" (on hē on): "What of old and even now is always to be sought for and always

out-of-the way, What is Being?" Has our philosophical reading of Exodus brought us to the very theme of philosophy? . . .

As the Lord's words suggest, the Name of God, the Tetragrammaton Y-H-V-H derives from the Hebrew verb "*hayah, haveh,*" which . . . denotes "to be" or "to become." . . . It is most striking and not to be explained away that both Hebrews and Greeks agreed that the name of the highest principle was in one way or another Being.

Ellison explores what it means to connect God with Being (as distinguished from "*a* being") and argues that the Lord stands beyond Being and Nothing, insofar as He creates beings by acts of separation, which is to say, by means of otherness or not-Being. By then gathering the biblical evidence showing how God's relation to man goes beyond creation to embrace His beneficence, care, and justice, Ellison concludes, "He is not only the One beyond nature, but He is the True, to Whom all men should order their thoughts and deeds, the Good Who is beyond Being." The similarity to certain Platonic teachings is very suggestive. (John Ellison, "Law, Nature, and the Name of God in *Exodus.*" Quoted with permission.)

22. See Genesis 15:14, where this outcome was prophesied by God to Abram, as God told him of the future enslavement of his descendants and of their divine deliverance after four hundred years.

23. Correlatively, the signs bespeak the vulnerability and danger of unsupported human powers, and their capacity for harm, to oneself as well as to others. They seem to say that, absent the Lord's benevolence and sustaining power, human agency (represented by the rod and hand) is likely to be deadly—as it is under Pharaoh.

24. The Pharaohs wore a stylized upright cobra (Uraeus) as part of their headdress, a symbol of sovereignty and divine authority. At the same time, the conversion of the shepherd's staff (the symbol and instrument of rule) into the fearsome *nachash* may be a warning to Moses of the dangers of ruling, both to the ruler and the ruled. It also echoes the tale of the corrupting serpent (also, *nachash*) in the Garden of Eden.

25. It is of course possible that Moses's reluctance is based on the fact that he is perfectly happy in his pastoral existence, a possibility we have not considered before. Jerome Marcus (in a personal communication) suggests that Moses may resemble the hero Cincinnatus, who in old age was prevailed upon to abandon his farm to save the Roman Republic from invasion. Perhaps. But there is little to suggest that Moses is moved to accept his mission by anything resembling Cincinnatus's patriotism and love of his own people or that he was simply happy living an obscure, private life in Midian. Not ruled out, however, is the possibility that Moses is like the philosopher in Plato's *Republic,* who must be compelled to abandon his happy contemplation in order to serve his city by ruling it.

26. The discussion in this section owes much to my friend Robert Sacks's essay, "The Life and Death of Aaron the Priest." Only recently published (in Paul Wilford and Kate Havard, eds., *Athens, Arden, Jerusalem: Essays in Honor of Mera Flaumenhaft* [Lanham, MD: Lexington Books, 2017], 245–264), the author had kindly shared it with

me two decades ago in an earlier form. We will revisit the issue of brothers and fratricide in Chapter Eighteen, when God tells Moses that "Aaron your brother" will be appointed High Priest.

27. Given the ambiguity of the idea of Moses's "brethren" in Chapter Two, it is worth noting its return here: Is what Jethro understands by "brethren" the same as what Moses intended?

28. We note again the difference between the father-in-law Jethro and the father-in-law Laban, another instance of the much more harmonious family life that Moses enjoys in Midian. Could this have prepared Moses to seek such harmony in the Israelite community?

29. We had previously heard only about the birth of Moses's firstborn son, Gershom (2:22). The second son, Eliezer, may have been a baby at the time of this episode; it is probably his circumcision that will be reported later in this chapter. We will hear again of both sons only once, after the Exodus from Egypt, when Jethro comes to visit Moses at the foot of Mount Sinai (18:3). We note also that God's mission for Moses did not mention taking his wife and children. Moses is improvising, albeit understandably.

We note that we are not told the current ages of Moses's children. This is no trivial matter. Ignorance of their ages leads in turn to perplexity about Moses's age when he became a father. The earlier narrative, in Exodus 2, seemed to imply that he married and became a father soon after arriving in Midian, presumably in his twenties, and then lived decades with his father-in-law, Jethro. But as we will learn, Moses is eighty years old when he (soon) appears before Pharaoh to demand the release of the Israelites. If this octogenarian now has an infant son (or sons), when exactly was he married? And how long has he dwelt with Jethro?

30. Earlier the "wonders" were called "signs." The difference in meaning between a "wonder," *mofeth*, and a "sign," *'oth*, is worth noting. Although the first word is often understood to be a "miracle," something produced by a god, its primary sense is "conspicuous," taken from the verb *yafah*, "to be beautiful." Not every *mofeth* need be a miracle, nor need it be an *'oth*. An *'oth* is a "signal" or a "sign," pointing to a meaning beyond its visible self. The so-called voice of a sign would "speak" that meaning or signification. We will want to see whether Pharaoh is able to read the *meaning* of the wonders (the so-called plagues); for example, whether he sees them as splendid works of magic, but with no meaning beyond themselves.

31. The actual episodes of hardening or strengthening of Pharaoh's heart occur only later in the text, during the account of the ten plagues that precede the Israelite Exodus from Egypt. I have chosen to discuss this matter thematically here, where it first appears (as prophetic announcement), so that the reader will be prepared for the specific instances of Pharaoh's "re-heartening" when they arise (see Chapter Six). Readers should keep this discussion in mind when we come to the plagues.

32. See, for example, U. Cassuto, *A Commentary on the Book of Exodus,* trans. Israel Abrahams (Jerusalem: Magnes Press, 1967), 56.

33. In the forthcoming account of the plagues that God unleashes against Egypt, Pharaoh is able to rally himself for the first five plagues; it is only after the sixth plague,

boils, that the text uses for the first time the formula, "And the Lord strengthened the heart of Pharaoh." After the seventh plague, hail, Pharaoh strengthens his own heart, but after the eighth and ninth plagues, locusts and darkness, the Lord is said to strengthen it for him. (see 7:13, 14, and 22; 8:11, 15, and 28; 9:7, 12, 34, and 35; and 10:1, 20, and 27).

34. Recall Eve's boastful naming of her firstborn Cain: "I have gotten a man [equally] with the Lord" (Gen. 4:1). See my *The Beginning of Wisdom,* 125–128.

35. With this understanding of the Lord's "firstborn," we see that Pharaoh's drowning of the male babies, whether firstborn or not, was a killing of God's covenantal firstborn. Thus, the slaying of the Egyptian firstborn sons avenges, tit for tat, the enslavement and drowning of the Israelite males. Even better, it creates for Pharaoh the meaning of his own tyranny: his anti-natal policy was the perfect expression of his desire to live and rule forever, to be his own source and his own replacement.

36. It is also possible that God is teaching Moses in advance the political necessity of making an example of someone.

37. Jules Gleicher, "Moses *Politikos* [= Statesman]," *Interpretation: A Journal of Political Philosophy* 26, no. 2 (1999): 1149–1181.

38. Yet as we have already noted and shall later see, the problem of fratricide in the relationship between Aaron and Moses (and among the nascent people of Israel) is not altogether solved by the happy reunion.

39. Dan Polisar (in a personal communication) suggests that I have unnecessarily complicated a simple situation, which he would rather parse as follows: "Moses, as he was coming to Egypt to liberate the Israelites on behalf of the God of Abraham, Isaac, and Jacob, had to re-enter the covenant of that God. Otherwise he would be coming as a stranger and not as a brother. He should have performed the circumcision himself at this point but, as he demonstrates throughout, he was never focused on his family and certainly not on his children; so his wife, a more normal person, blessed with a caring father and six sisters with whom she grew up in harmony, steps into this void. Moreover, Zipporah, as the 'foreigner' and hence something of an impediment to Moses's being an Israelite leader, had to do something to prove that she was embracing the Israelite way of life, for her son and her husband if not for herself. Finally, God needed to show Moses that the path he was setting on was a risky one, potentially deadly, and he would have to take great care in all that he did (a lesson driven home later by the death of Aaron's sons)."

40. The first conversation between God and Moses, including the charge to Moses, is, as already noted, the longest conversation in the Torah. This one-sided conversation, comprising the four-word charge to Aaron, is the shortest. Moses, who protests that he is not a good speaker, speaks at length; Aaron, the good speaker, is silent.

41. The analysis that follows relies heavily on the splendid essay by Hans Jonas, "The Nobility of Sight," in *The Phenomenon of Life: Toward a Philosophical Biology* (Evanston, IL: Northwestern University Press, 2001). See also my discussion of freedom and reason in *The Beginning of Wisdom,* Chapter Two, "The Follies of Freedom and Reason: The Story of the Garden of Eden (I)."

42. Compare the prominence of "seeing" in the story of man's primal disobedience in the Garden of Eden story (Gen. 3:1–7)—following our imagination rather than divine command—with its correlated desire "to be as God." Her imagination liberated as a result of the conversation with the seductively antinomian serpent, the woman "*saw* that the [forbidden] tree [of knowledge of good and bad] was good for food, and that is was a delight to the eyes, and that the tree was to be desired to make one wise" (Gen. 3:6).

FOUR Egyptian Overtures

1. Let me suggest two possible explanations for the absence of the elders. First, Moses and Aaron did not trust the people in Pharaoh's presence and never invited them to come. Second, they asked the elders to come, but the elders, being frightened, refused. There is a lovely midrash along these lines: Moses and Aaron started out leading the elders to the palace, but on the way the frightened elders peeled off one by one, without anyone noticing. When Moses and Aaron finally arrive at the palace, they turn around only to discover that all their followers had run away.

2. I have attributed the boldness of Moses and Aaron, and their departure from the Lord's explicit instructions, to an excess of confidence, born of their prior success with the Israelites and of their belief that the Lord was with them. But it is very possible that they were instead frightened of Pharaoh and intimidated while in his presence, needing to make requests. Finding themselves alone before Pharaoh, Moses and Aaron try to brazen it out, hiding their fear behind overbold and overconfident speech. On this reading, it was their nervousness, not their overconfidence, which led them to forget the Lord's precise instructions. (I owe these suggestions to Amy Kass.)

3. This point will return very prominently at the start of the so-called Ten Commandments, in the opening verse: "I Y-H-V-H am your God who brought you out of the land of Egypt, out of the house of bondage." Suggestion: in the end, human beings face basically two mutually exclusive alternatives: either a relation to the Lord or slavery under Pharaoh. See my discussion in Chapter Thirteen.

4. It is worth emphasizing that the Israelites must leave Egypt to perform their sacrifices; they cannot perform them in Egypt. We are not told why. Perhaps, as will be suggested later, the animals that they need to sacrifice are abominations to the Egyptians. But more important than the why is this very need for separation: the Israelites cannot sacrifice to their god *in Egypt*. This means that peaceful coexistence was never a possibility here: they cannot remain God-worshipping Israelites in Egypt. A further implication: before this time, the Israelites were not offering any sacrifices to the Lord. Perhaps they had forgotten Him altogether. For four hundred years, it seemed to them that *He* has forgotten them. (I owe these thoughts to Yuval Levin.)

5. Unlike the Egyptian taskmasters (or "slave drivers," *nogesim;* from a root meaning "driver," whether of animals or of human workers), the officers (*shoterim*) were Hebrew underlings, appointed by the taskmasters to oversee the work of their Israelite brethren.

6. Moses may have a genuine ground for complaint. Yes, you told me that Pharaoh would resist your demands. But you never told me that *things would get worse* for the people and because of what I was saying and doing.

7. For an elegant and fully persuasive structural analysis of this speech, with a close explication of its chiastic structure, see Rav Elchanan Samet, "God's Speech of Salvation," a commentary on the weekly Torah portion, Vayera: https://www.etzion.org.il/en/gods-speech-salvation.

8. Commentators have noted the change from the formulation "And the Lord said" to "And God spoke," and suggest that it betokens greater distance between God and Moses: from the more intimate *Y-H-V-H* to the more judgmental *'elohim*, and from the more personal "saying" to the more remote "speaking." Therefore, in disagreement with our interpretation, some interpret this to mean that the Lord is a little miffed with Moses because of his complaining. Perhaps so. But reading what the Lord *then says to him* strongly suggests to us that Moses is being rewarded here with a new revelation and new insights into the Lord's plan. We see this as a major moment in Moses's education, a moment that is made possible by Moses's feeling his own incompetence.

9. Cassuto, *A Commentary on the Book of Exodus*, 76–77. He goes on to refute scholars who claim that the next verse (6:3) must come from a different document according to which the patriarchs knew God under a different Name. That verse, read in that way, is regarded as a central piece of evidence for the "documentary hypothesis."

10. Cassuto, *A Commentary on the Book of Exodus*, 77.

11. Genesis 17:1, spoken to Abraham at the start of making the covenant, and 35:11, spoken to Jacob, when He blesses him at Beth-El on his return from Paddan-aram.

12. Genesis 28:3, Isaac giving Jacob the Abrahamic blessing; Gen. 43:14, Jacob to his sons, praying for mercy before Joseph, as the brothers set off for Egypt with Benjamin; Gen. 48:3, Jacob to Joseph, recalling God's revelation and blessing at Luz, when Joseph brings his two sons to receive Jacob's blessing; and Gen. 49:25, as part of Jacob's final blessing of Joseph (only "*Shaddai*" is mentioned), here for the "blessings of heaven above, blessings of the deep that couches beneath, blessings of the breast and the womb"—that is, for fertility of soil and fruitfulness of family.

13. Hearing these promises, Abraham and the reader recall God's first promise to him, when He first called him: "I will make of you a great nation" (Gen. 12:2).

14. For example, "bring out" in 3:10–12; "burdens" in 1:11, 2:11, and 5:4–5; "deliver" in 3:8 and 5:23); and "service" or "bondage" in 2:23, 5:9, and 6:5.

15. Except for a small hint in the remarks the Lord made to Abram in his sleep, in the covenant between the sacrificial pieces: "Know of a surety that your seed shall be a stranger in a land that is not theirs, and shall serve them; and they shall afflict them four hundred years; and also that nation, whom they shall serve, *will I judge* (*dan*); and afterward shall they come out with great substance" (Gen. 15:13–14; emphasis added).

16. The term "free" does occur later, at Sinai, in the ordinances that describe conditions for the manumission of the Hebrew slave (21:2, 5, 11). The fact that the text

knows how to speak of slaves "going free" makes it all the more striking that the language of freedom is nowhere associated with the Israelites' earlier redemption from Egypt.

17. Not all readers agree, to say the least. Many Jews through the ages have regarded the new relationship with the Lord, just announced for the first time (in 6:7) and later spelled out in the teachings and commandments given at Sinai, as the heart of the Jewish way. As Rabbi Nathan Laufer explains (in a personal communication), there is a lot riding on these differences of interpretation: "Rabbinic Judaism, which was developed in the diaspora, saw this verse [Ex. 6:7]—and Chapters 19–24 that flesh it out—as the key to Judaism, a way of life for the individual and community in relationship to God *regardless of place*. The very purpose of the Exodus was for the Jewish people to receive God's Torah, keep its laws, and become a people holy to God. [But] the Biblical text and the 'Zionist' reading of that text see this verse not as the purpose, but as the necessary *means*, of coming and staying in the land that God promised our ancestors—of being a nation, living a life of dignity in its own land (hence verse 7 is followed by verse 8). Spinoza read the Bible, I think correctly, as a political system for the Jewish nation in their land. . . . [Yet] for nearly 2,000 years, the Torah's legal system was mostly understood on its own terms, as forming a religion, a civilization disconnected from the land (Nachmanides and a few others being notable exceptions). Not surprisingly, Diaspora Jewry continues to read that verse that way. Reinserting that legal system within its original Biblical context—as a way of life for the people to form a just and moral society, so that they can merit to stay in the land—is relatively a new, or rather, renewed, way of viewing Judaism and the significance of verse 7. That is how Religious Zionists . . . read that verse."

FIVE To Go Against Pharaoh

1. The beginning with "and" indicates continuity with what came immediately before.

2. In place of the expected imperative, "Go" (*lekh*) speak to Pharaoh, God says, "Come" (*bo'*) speak to Pharaoh. While *bo'* may have the sense of "Come on," if taken literally it would seem to mean "Come *with* Me" or even "Come *to* Me." Given God's earlier promise, "I will be with you," His opening with "Come" may be suggesting that Moses will have divine company in confronting Pharaoh or even that the Lord is already waiting for him in the palace.

3. *The Five Books of Moses: A Translation with Commentary,* trans. and ed. Robert Alter (New York: W. W. Norton, 2004), 341.

4. Sacks, "The Life and Death of Aaron the Priest," 260.

5. The analogy with circumcision of the male genitalia now makes more sense. The point is not that the foreskin has literally been removed, but that the (future) sexual power is being dedicated to and sanctified by a higher purpose: the covenantal relationship with the Lord that emphasizes paternal transmission of a righteous way of life rather than virility and manly prowess.

6. This is only the second instance of "charge" or "command" in Exodus. Earlier Pharaoh had issued a charge to all his people to drown all the newborn sons (1:22). God answers that charge with this one.

7. Levi, we are told earlier in the genealogy, also lived to age 137. In this subtle way, the text may be hinting that Amram is the Levite closest to the original one: it is through Amram especially that the spirit of Levi—spirited defender of his own—lives on in Moses and Aaron.

8. Although mentioned only here in the Torah, Elisheva brings her own impressive (political) lineage into the (priestly) line of Aaron. Her father, Amminadab, is Judah's great-great-grandson and a member of the ruling tribe. Her brother, Nachshon, Moses will later appoint as the chieftain of Judah, to stand with him in leading the people (Num. 1:7). Amminadab and Nachshon appear in the genealogy leading from Judah's son Perez to King David (Ruth 4:18–22). The Talmud reports that on the day of the consecration of the Tabernacle, "Elisheva had five additional joys over other daughters of Israel. She was the sister-in-law of the king [Moses], the wife of the High Priest [Aaron], her son [Eleazar] was the *segan* [deputy high priest], her grandson [Pinchas] was anointed for war, and her brother [Nachshon] was a prince of the tribe of Judah" (Babylonian Talmud, Tractate Zevachim 102a). According to Midrash, Nachshon was the first person to jump into the Sea of Reeds, after which all the other Israelites followed.

9. Joseph, in this and other ways a foil for Moses, was lost to Egypt, but Jacob reclaimed his Egyptian-born sons for Israel. Moses was reclaimed for Israel by God from Egypt and Midian, but his Midianite-born sons, it seems, may be lost to the covenant. Joseph, believing that affairs were now settled, promoted his firstborn son to inherit his father's blessing (a move reversed by Jacob, who did not accept the Egyptian character of Joseph's "settlement"); Moses, the man who will settle things in Israel once and for all, takes no pains on behalf of his sons. (He also did not seek a wife, showed little if any interest in his sons, and did not circumcise them.) His unique life amounts to a sacrifice of his biological legacy to "father" the Children of Israel.

10. Later, we will learn that Aaron dwells with his sons at the opening of the Tent of Meeting (Lev. 8, concluding verses) in a father-son cooperative learning of the tasks of priests. There will never be a comparable report of *any* father-son interactions between Moses and his boys.

11. Richie Lewis has raised doubts about my tendency to identify Moses's mind and speech with that of (Greek) philosophy ("rational speech"), which, of course, would be an anachronism. (We met this question in Chapter Three concerning Moses's interest in knowing the Divine Name.) For Lewis, the contrast should not be between philosopher and priest, but between prophet and priest. I am glad to have the issue joined and to leave the question open. Moses's past and future interest in knowing God's name may reflect either a "philosophical"—wisdom-seeking—interest in the nature of the divine or a personal interest in greater intimacy with his divine "friend." In either case, there is a gap between the way Moses thinks and speaks about things and the way the people do; that is at least partly why he has trouble persuading them.

12. Cassuto, *A Commentary on the Book of Exodus,* 89 (emphasis in original).

13. I assume that this is the tenth plague, the slaying of the firstborn, and perhaps also the action at the Sea of Reeds.

14. Indispensable but not sufficient. The Israelites will also need practical evidence of His reliability and of His ability to fulfill His promises and, ultimately, also of His loving-kindness toward them.

15. The Lord will later make this point explicit, just before the eighth plague, locusts: "And the Lord said unto Moses: 'Go in unto Pharaoh; for I have strengthened his heart, and the heart of his servants, that I might show these My signs in the midst of them; and so that you [singular] may tell in the ears of your son, and of your son's son, what I have wrought upon Egypt; and *that you [plural] may know that I am Y-H-V-H'"* (10:1–2; emphasis added).

SIX The Contest with Egypt

1. Actually, it would be better to describe this as a civilizational contest, pitting Pharaoh, his gods, his magicians, his army, and the enormous economic and political might of Egypt against Moses, his brother Aaron, the staffs in their hands, and their (invisible) God. This is no doubt how Pharaoh and the Egyptians saw it, and probably how the Israelites came to see it as well. For ease of expression, however, I will use the less accurate formulations, "contest between Moses and Pharaoh" or "contest between God and Pharaoh."

2. The Lord will later expressly say that He seeks to be known universally. In the warning given before the seventh plague of hail, Moses, speaking for God, tells Pharaoh, "For this purpose have I maintained you alive, to show you My power, *so that My name may be declared in all the earth"* (9:16; emphasis added).

3. The connection will later be powerfully made in the Book of Ezekiel, where Pharaoh himself is called a *tannin:* "The word of the Lord came unto me, saying: 'Son of man, set your face against Pharaoh king of Egypt, and prophesy against him, and against all Egypt; speak, and say: "Thus says the Lord God: 'Behold, I am against *you, Pharaoh King of Egypt, the* tannin *that lies in the midst of his rivers, that has said: "My river is mine own, and I made it myself* [or, *'I made myself'*]." And I will put hooks in your jaws, and I will cause the fish of your rivers to stick unto your scales; and I will bring you up out of the midst of your rivers, and all the fish of your rivers shall stick unto your scales. And I will cast you into the wilderness, you and all the fish of your rivers; you shall fall upon the open field; you shall not be brought together, nor gathered; to the beasts of the earth and to the fowls of the heaven have I given you for food. *And all the inhabitants of Egypt shall know that I am Y-H-V-H, because they have been* a staff of reed to the house of Israel'"'" (Ezek. 29:1–6; emphasis added).

4. Much later in Israel's history, the Psalmist, appealing to the Lord for help against Israel's current enemies, will remind Him: "You did break the sea in pieces by Your strength; You did shatter the heads of the *tanninim* in the waters" (Psalm 74:13).

5. In most of Egypt, except along the Mediterranean coast, it does not rain at all. This lack of dependence on heavenly water likely played a large role in Egyptian theology.

6. "So Joseph died, being a hundred and ten years old. And they embalmed him and he was put into a coffin (*ba'aron*) in Egypt" (Gen. 50:26). The difference between the Israelite and Egyptian stances toward death were heavily foreshadowed in the last chapter of Genesis, which contrasts the long funeral procession to bury Jacob in the cave at Machpelah with the embalming of Joseph. It is the difference between accepting death and denying or defying it. (It is true that, when Jacob died, Joseph immediately ordered the Egyptian physicians to embalm his father, but perhaps only to preserve it for burial; he later carried out his father's deathbed wish to be buried with his people.) See my *The Beginning of Wisdom*, 648–659.

7. Akhenaten, an Egyptian pharaoh of the eighteenth dynasty, who reigned in the mid-fourteenth century BCE, tried to do away with polytheism. He instituted a short-lived theological reform in the direction of monotheism, looking to the sun as singularly above the other so-called gods of the Egyptian pantheon.

8. The ideograms are therefore the forerunners of the eternal "*ideas*" (the *eidê*, the unchanging "invisible looks"), central notions in the philosophy of both Plato (who was known to have visited Egypt) and Aristotle.

9. This tendency is, of course, not peculiar to the Egyptians. It is, as I noted in the discussion of seeing and hearing in Chapter Three on the burning bush, an altogether *human* predisposition. In this respect the Egyptians are paradigmatically human, and the contest with Egypt is thus a contest with human predilections altogether, taken at their highest expression.

10. As we will see during the sequence of the plagues, various people tell Pharaoh to quit resisting; strong-willed and autonomous, he does not listen. What "god" would?

11. Ancient Egypt thus anticipates the dream of Karl Marx and Friedrich Engels, who looked forward to the end of politics and the withering away of the state, when the rule of men would be replaced by the administration of things. In Egypt, as in our own lifetime, that dream turned into a political nightmare, producing not liberation but despotism and massive human suffering.

12. The average person even lacks direct access to the divine, save by going through Pharaoh and the priests. (My thanks to Shawn Zelig Aster for this observation.)

13. Jewish sages have suggested that, before God delivered them, no slave had ever escaped from Egypt. Given that there were no physical barriers to getting out of Egypt, the implication is that they could not even imagine themselves as free. The enslavement of mind, heart, and soul kept them confined in Egypt; getting rid of *that* slavishness will take much more than their physical extraction.

14. Both to streamline expression and to respect traditional usage, I will use the word "plagues" to refer to all the wonders/signs/judgments. But it is worth noting that the Torah only once refers to them as "plagues." Referring to the *tenth* plague, the Lord

says "I will bring one more *plague* upon Pharaoh" (11:1). The term for "plague" is *nega'*, meaning "a blow, a hit," from the verbal root *naga'*, "to touch, to strike, to lay the hand upon." Fittingly, it is the tenth "hit" to which the Lord refers when He speaks of taking Israel out of Egypt with *His own hand,* that is, by smiting all the firstborn in Egypt.

15. Having left the Children of Israel to their bondage in Goshen, the text will be completely silent about their reactions to the plagues. Still, we suspect that they will have discovered, at least by hearsay, what is going on. For as we shall see in the next chapter, when Moses and Aaron return to them after the first nine plagues, they are entirely receptive to Moses's instructions to prepare for departure.

16. Readers who want a close line-by-line analysis should consult Cassuto's splendid treatment on which my discussion here partly depends. *A Commentary on the Book of Exodus,* 92–135. There is admitted uncertainty about what the third, fourth, and fifth plagues actually were, since we are not sure what the biblical terms for them refer to.

17. Traditional commentators disagree about this plague, some holding instead that *'arov* was a mixed assortment of wild beasts—lions, tigers, and so on.

18. This distinction was instituted, among other things, to serve an educative purpose: "that you [Pharaoh] may know that I am Y-H-V-H in the midst of the earth. And I will put a division between My people and your people" (8:18–19).

19. If we recall the earlier discussion of the *tannin,* the crocodile, and its identification with Pharaoh, Moses is told to deliver the warnings to Pharaoh ("the crocodile") when he is going to bathe in his river. The keynote plague, turning the Nile into blood, telegraphs the whole story: the home of the crocodilian sovereign will soon become uninhabitable.

20. *The JPS Torah Commentary: Exodus,* translation and commentary by Nahum M. Sarna (New York: Jewish Publication Society, 1991), 38.

21. The phrase reminds us of, but also differs from, the phrase used in describing God's creation of man in the so-called second creation story: "And the Lord God formed man (*'adam*) out of the dust of the ground (*'afar min-ha'adamah*), and breathed into his nostrils the breath of life; and man became a living soul (*nefesh chayah*)" (Gen. 2:7). The comparison leads to this suggestion: absent the gift of divine breath, human attempts to animate the dust of the ground—to revive the dead—can only produce pestilence. The same thought is suggested by the conversion of ash in the furnace into boils, the sixth plague.

22. To repeat, at the end of the nine plagues, the only member of the Egyptian pantheon still untouched is Pharaoh himself.

23. I am aware that there is no biblical Hebrew word for "nature" and that ancient Egypt probably did not have such an idea or even a concept of "world" or "cosmos." The Torah does not use latter-day philosophical categories, and neither did ancient Egypt. With apology, I use the terms throughout—as I do here—only for ease of expression in trying to convey the meaning and implications of the stories in the text. (It is, of course, possible that the Bible lacks a word for "nature" not because its author lacks such a concept, but rather because he is polemicizing against it.)

24. After the hail, Pharaoh says, "I have sinned [only] this time. The Lord is in the right and I and my people are in the wrong" (9:27; he uses judicial rather than moral language). And after the locusts, he says, "I have sinned against the Lord your God and against you. Forgive, please, my sin only this once and entreat the Lord your God only to remove this death upon me" (10:16–17).

25. Even so, as we shall see, by the next morning he is back on the attack, pursuing the departing Israelites into the Sea of Reeds, once again leading his people into destruction.

26. In response to this assertion, Dan Polisar has reminded me that a previous Pharaoh had admitted that he did not know the meaning of his own dream, subsequently showed himself willing to take advice from Joseph about how to prevent famine, and thus succeeded in his Pharaonic role of preserving the life of his people. Perhaps, Polisar suggests, what is wrong with the present Pharaoh is that, with the system having sunk further into despotism due to the introduction of wholesale slavery, he can no longer admit that there is anything he doesn't know nor can he ever take advice from anyone. I accept this possible reading, but I would point out that Joseph's Pharaoh accepted Joseph's dream interpretation only because it came with a plan that offered him the opportunity to consolidate his power, and the land management policy that Joseph suggested and instituted for Pharaoh led to the enslavement of his own people: they were compelled to give up their bodies and their freedom for food. It was precisely Joseph's advice that enabled Pharaoh to become the despot that he was meant to be. See my *The Beginning of Wisdom*, 561–569 and 629–634.

27. On Moses's first visit, Pharaoh had previously said, "Who is *Y-H-V-H* that I should hearken unto his voice to let Israel go? I do not know *Y-H-V-H*" (5:1–2). It is, of course, entirely possible that Pharaoh is not in fact acknowledging the Lord, but is playing along with what he believes to be Moses's charade of being an agent of some new god. Pharaoh would have every reason not to appear beholden to these mere Hebrews, these mere mortals.

28. Cassuto, *A Commentary on the Book of Exodus*, 103.

29. Dan Polisar (personal communication) sees a more profound meaning in Moses's insistence on the details of his request to allow the Children of Israel to leave town for sacrifices: they tacitly make clear that Israelite worship is a complete negation of Egyptian state religion: "You Egyptians believe in total subjugation of the individual to the demands of work; we Israelites will take a full week in 'idleness' (three days to journey out, a day to sacrifice, and three days to journey back)—an eternity in a country where work for Pharaoh is 24/7. You Egyptians believe in the supremacy and divinity of certain animals. We consider these 'gods' merely a vehicle for us to serve our much higher God. You Egyptians tried to separate man and wife, and to separate us from our children (whom you commanded be thrown into the river). We reject your sovereignty over the family unit, which is sacred to us; and so we will stay together."

30. Cassuto does not regard these three verses (11:1–3) as a new communication from the Lord, but rather as a flashback memory in Moses's mind, triggered by the exigencies of the moment. Cassuto points out that the Lord never communicates with

Moses save when he is alone (he is here still before Pharaoh) and that there is nothing new revealed in these few verses. Instead, Cassuto suggests that Moses suddenly remembers that there is still one more act to follow: "He recalled the directives that were given him long ago concerning the tenth and decisive plague, and he felt that the time for their implementation had now arrived. It seemed to him as if that Divine announcement was reiterated at that moment, and as if the Lord reminded him then that the plague that was soon to come would be the last." Cassuto, *A Commentary on the Book of Exodus*, 132. For myself, I see no way to choose—and no *need* to choose—between Cassuto's suggestion of a flashback memory and a fresh divine message: Who can explain the mysterious appearance of a so-called flashback memory, especially when it arrives just when it is needed? And just how does Moses—or anyone—receive ("hear") the Divine Voice, when no one else can hear it? Not in his "mind"?

31. An important question for modern readers: Will this, then, also be true about our latter-day "Egypts," our technocratic and bureaucratic societies that revere only human power and know not *Y-H-V-H*?

32. On the subject of *national* collective guilt, also regarding the matter of slavery, see Abraham Lincoln's *Second Inaugural*, echoing a Hebrew biblical sense of justice: "Woe unto the world because of offenses; for it must needs be that offenses come, but woe to that man by whom the offense cometh. If we shall suppose that American slavery is one of those offenses which, in the providence of God, must needs come, but which, having continued through His appointed time, He now wills to remove, and that He gives to *both North and South* this terrible war as the woe due to those by whom the offense came, shall we discern therein any departure from those divine attributes which the believers in a living God always ascribe to Him? Fondly do we hope, fervently do we pray, that this mighty scourge of war may speedily pass away. Yet, if God wills that it continue until *all the wealth piled by the bondsman's two hundred and fifty years of unrequited toil* shall be sunk, and until every drop of blood drawn with the lash shall be paid by another drawn with the sword, as was said three thousand years ago, so still it must be said '*the judgments of the Lord are true and righteous altogether*'" (emphasis added).

33. This, I have argued, is exactly the lesson that Abraham was taught by God in the famous conversation about Sodom. See my *The Beginning of Wisdom*, 318–325.

34. We must add one qualification, by way of anticipation. Even if we say, as I have, that God's judgments against Egypt were fitting and just, the text's account of the impending tenth plague will (quietly) treat the slaughter of the firstborn as problematic, even as it regards it as necessary, and even if can be justified as payment for collective guilt or as displaying the meaning of Pharaoh's anti-natal principles and practices. To mention only one troubling fact: innocent *newborn* first sons will be included in the carnage. In my view to its great credit, the text does not run from the iniquitousness of this fact. The Israelites may not have to atone for this slaughter, but they will be forced to remember that they obtained their deliverance at the price of these killings. Part of the meaning of their later obligation to redeem their firstborn sons—

perhaps even of marking their doors with the blood of the Paschal lamb—is a symbolic acknowledgment of this fact.

SEVEN Exodus

1. These rituals touch everything but how we relate to our fellow human beings. Those relationships are the business of law and *justice;* the ones dealt with here are the business of what will come to be the core of *holiness.*

2. "Never again will I curse the ground for man's sake, *for the imagination of his heart is evil from his youth*" (Gen. 8:21; emphasis added). To address man's bloody-mindedness, the Noahide code and covenant follow immediately. For an extended discussion of this episode, see my *The Beginning of Wisdom*, Chapter Six, "Elementary Justice: Man, Animals, and the Coming of Law and Covenant." For an extended discussion of Cain's sacrifice and of the general human impulse to sacrifice, see Chapter Four, "Fratricide and Founding: The Twisted Roots of Civilization."

3. See my *The Hungry Soul: Eating and the Perfecting of Our Nature*, 2nd ed. (Chicago: University of Chicago Press, 1999), Chapter Two, "*Omnivorosus Erectus:* The Human Form." The connection between human reason and human voraciousness was noted long ago in Aristotle's *Politics* (at 1253a): within a few lines of arguing that man alone among the animals has reasoned speech (*logos*), he adds that, separated from law and justice, man is the worst among the animals, especially with respect to sex and eating—by which I think he means incest and cannibalism.

4. See Exodus 1:22: "And Pharaoh charged all his people, saying: 'Every son that is born you shall cast into the river, and every daughter you shall save alive.'" According to legend, but not the text, Pharaoh was responding to an interpretation of one of his dreams: his court seers predicted that a baby boy born to Hebrew slaves would one day dethrone him. In fear and exasperation, Pharaoh's final anti-birth decree neglects to restrict his edict to the sons of Hebrews, thus revealing every tyrant's wish to deny that *anyone* will replace him. For a discussion of the paradigmatic story of the natural (or uninstructed) relations of fathers and sons, see my *The Beginning of Wisdom*, Chapter Seven, "Paternity and Piety: Noah and His Sons."

5. Strictly speaking, we should not call the killing of the lamb a sacrifice to the Lord. The word for sacrifice, *zevach* (literally, "feast" or "shared meal"; related to *mizbeach,* "altar"), does not occur until late in the story and then only once: "And should your sons ask you [when you have come to the Promised Land and are performing the Passover service there], 'What is this service to you?' you shall say, 'A Passover *sacrifice* to the Lord, who passed over the houses of the Israelites in Egypt when he scourged Egypt and our households he rescued'" (12:27; emphasis added). What is prescribed for the original night of Exodus was more a feast than a sacrifice, albeit a feast consecrated to the Lord, especially through the use made of blood.

6. We readers are, of course, aware that it is the earth, not the sun, that revolves. However, our usage reflects accurately humankind's lived experience, and certainly that of these ancient peoples.

7. To this point in the text, only the reader of the Torah knows about this. The first people *in* the text to learn about the Sabbath and its meaning are the Children of Israel at Sinai. It will have momentous consequences for the life of Israel, then and thereafter (see Chapter Thirteen on the Ten Commandments). For an extended discussion of Genesis 1 and the (first) creation story, see also my *The Beginnings of Wisdom*, Chapter One, "Awesome Beginnings: Man, Heaven, and the Created Order."

8. We should be careful not to overstate the change in the Israelite calendar. As we shall see later in Exodus, the seasonal festivals will be treated sometimes as agricultural and sometimes as "religious" holidays. Israel will still mark the agricultural turnings of the year, and it will reckon its monthly calendar according to the phases of the moon. When its seasonal and monthly calendar becomes fully articulated, we will see that Israel makes use of a combination of solar and lunar cycles, as do the surrounding pagan nations. However, in Israel, there is also a *transforming* overlay of *historical* time, as time gets new meaning from critical events in the national founding, each event involving an intimate rendezvous with God. The paradigmatic example of this transformation is celebrated in the annual holiday of Passover. For a superb account of the Jewish calendar, see Rabbi Nathan Laufer, *Rendezvous with God: Revealing the Meaning of the Jewish Holidays and Their Mysterious Rituals* (Jerusalem: Maggid Books, 2016).

9. My thanks to Hannah Mandelbaum for this observation and formulation.

10. Recall that it was the new Pharaoh (who knew not Joseph) who first identified the Children of Israel as a *people* (*'am*), marking them out in fear because of their great multiplicity (1:9). Here, the Lord announces in advance their becoming for the first time a *congregation* (*'edah;* perhaps not yet an *'am*), as a result of a collective act undertaken at His behest and in His direction. For the special uses of *'edah,* see Chapter One, Note 9.

11. In those lunar calendars that begin each month on the day of the new moon, the full moon will appear on either day 14 or day 15 of the lunar month.

12. Recall Moses's comment to Pharaoh regarding why the Israelites must leave Egypt to perform their sacrifices: "We shall sacrifice the abomination of the Egyptians before their eyes: will they not stone us?" (8:22; see my comment on this passage in Chapter Six). Here they will perform such a sacrifice *while still in Egypt,* and they will do it fearlessly.

13. See Jan Assmann and Zev Farber, "Sacrificing a Lamb in Egypt," http://www.thetorah.com/sacrificing-a-lamb-in-Egypt.

14. I am grateful to Judah Mandelbaum for this last insight.

15. Cassuto suggests that the Paschal meal, in keeping with the transformation of a spring agricultural festival into the theological-political one of Passover, "gives a new form and meaning to an ancient observance." Likewise, he points out, the expression "it is the Lord's passover," strongly suggests that there was already some passover-like festival, which is here given a new meaning connected with the Lord's passing over the houses. Cassuto, *A Commentary on the Book of Exodus,* 138. Although there is

no independent evidence of a pre-Israelite Paschal meal, a spring festival in Nisan is well attested from ancient Babylon.

16. The root cause of that bitter enslavement might well be said to be the incompatibility of the ways of life of Israel and Egypt: the Israelites came to agricultural Egypt as shepherds, whom the Egyptians abominated (Gen. 43:32, 46:34) As an adjunct to lamb and bread, the bitter herbs both point to their opposition and also serve to unite them here.

17. Later, when the Israelites murmur against Moses because of lack of savory food, they express nostalgia for the "*flesh pots* of Egypt."

18. I am indebted to Yuval Levin for this last insight about changing times.

19. This last formulation I owe to Yuval Levin.

20. Why seven days? No one knows. A formalist suggestion: the number seven is a number of perfection or completion. A substantive suggestion: since the Egyptian campaign still has one more episode—the pursuit and defeat at the Sea of Reeds, not too long after the exodus—the seventh day could have been the date of the parting of the Sea (see Chapter Eight). This last suggestion is nicely developed in Rabbi Nathan Laufer's *Rendezvous with God* (see Note 8).

21. As the holiday evolved, bitter herbs (*marror*), in addition to the *matsah*, were also made obligatory.

22. Later, when Moses renews the instructions immediately after the exodus, he emphasizes the need to *personalize* the enduring meaning of the deliverance: "And you shall tell your son in that day, saying: 'It is because of that which the Lord did for *me* when *I* came forth out of Egypt'" (13:8; emphasis added).

23. When Moses and Aaron first came to deliver God's promise to the elders and performed the signs before them, the result was that "the people believed . . . and bowed their heads and prostrated themselves" (4:31). But the elders did not, as was planned, accompany Moses and Aaron on their first (disastrous) visit to Pharaoh (5:1). So when Moses, armed with the good news of the Lord's new revelation, came to tell the Children of Israel, he did not start with the elders, but went directly to the people. They refused to listen to him (6:9). This time, Moses is ready and eager to work through the elders, hoping that, as they did the first time, the people will fall in line.

24. There is also no reference to a limitation of three days or to staying close by. Pharaoh's surrender is total.

25. Cassuto comments: "At the very end there is a word of blessing. The first meeting of the old patriarch Israel with the king of Egypt was marked by benison (Gen. 47:7, 10: 'and Jacob blessed Pharaoh'), and the last encounter of the leaders of Israel with the king of Egypt concludes with blessing. Possibly the Bible wished to allude thereby to what God had said to Abraham when he was first chosen (Gen. 12:3): 'and in you will be blessed all the families of the earth.'" Cassuto, *A Commentary on the Book of Exodus*, 145–146. Cassuto makes a fine literary point, but I doubt that Moses acceded to Pharaoh's request. What we have here is closer to the rest of the remark God made to Abraham when he was first chosen: "and him that curses you I will curse."

26. Some scholars, discomfited by what looks like an act of exploitation, go to great lengths to alter the meaning of the conclusion. They point out, for example, that the verb *nitsel*, a primitive root meaning "to snatch away," is often used in the Bible to mean "to snatch (from danger)" or "to rescue (from wild animal)," and not only as "to plunder." They then read the present verse not as "stripping" or "spoiling" the Egyptians, but as "rescuing" or "saving" them: the gifts the Egyptians give the Israelites clear their name and vindicate their humanity. The story of Israel in Egypt, according to these interpreters, ends in beautiful harmony, at least between the common people. I find this interpretation unlikely. As Robert Alter points out, "from beginning to end, it is a tale of Israelite triumphalism." *The Five Books of Moses*, 324. And, I would add, also of divine justice.

27. This third alternative is a combination of suggestions made to me by Nathan Laufer and Daniel Polisar.

28. Alter translates this as "motley throng," pointing out the pejorative implication of the Hebrew *'erev rav*. He suggests that the English "riffraff" would be a close approximation to the intended meaning. *The Five Books of Moses*, 382. I take liberty to note that before the large emigration from the former Soviet Union to Israel in the 1980s and 1990s, this mixed exodus may have been the only time in recorded history that non-Israelites stood to benefit by pretending to be members of the tribe.

29. Scholars try to square the difference between the prophesied four hundred years of slavery and the reported four hundred and thirty years that Israel dwelt in Egypt; one simple way to try to do this is to say that Children of Israel at first lived freely in Egypt (for thirty years?) before their enslavement began. Others trouble themselves with a more difficult problem: trying to reconcile this number with what we earlier learned about the lengths of life in the generations of Levi (6:16–25); these numbers do not add up to four hundred and thirty. Cassuto offers an ingenious solution, which depends on the sexagesimal system and on treating the numbers as symbolic. *A Commentary on the Book of Exodus*, 85–87.

30. I owe the recognition of Moses's turn from leading to teaching to Daniel Polisar. This is the first of many times that Moses offers interpretations of the meanings and future implications of important events. The next occasion will be at the Sea of Reeds, discussed in the next chapter.

31. Verse 13:8—"And you shall tell your son on that day, saying: 'It is because of that which the Lord did for *me* when *I* came forth out of Egypt"—provides the roadmap for the central *Maggid* ("narrator") section of the Passover *Haggadah*. For a full elaboration of this idea, see Nathan Laufer, *Leading the Passover Journey: The Seder's Meaning Revealed and the Haggadah's Story Retold* (Woodstock, VT: Jewish Lights Publishing, 2005).

32. Later, in Exodus 13:16, the later sign is identified with a "circlet" or "frontlet" (*totafoth*) between the eyes, suggesting a physical object. Jewish tradition has used this passage to enjoin wearing small leather boxes (*tefillin*, from *tefilla*, "prayer," in English, phylacteries) containing four scriptural passages—including this section, 13:1–10)—to be worn on the arm/hand and forehead during morning prayers.

33. The point has already been anticipated in 13:8.

EIGHT "Who Is Like You Among the Gods?"

1. This translation of *chamushim* is not without its difficulties. For one thing, what sort of arms could they have had, and where might they have gotten them, given their hasty departure? At most, they might have had wooden sticks or "lances," which, however, we never hear of them using. Second, some scholars have suggested that the word *chamushim* could be derived from *chamesh*, the number five, in which case *chamushim* might mean "being divided into groups or columns divisible by the number five" (50? 500? 5000?). The case for such a reading is said to be supported by the proximate mention of Joseph, who several times divided or multiplied things by five (see Gen. 41:34; 43:34; 45:6, 11, 22; 47:2, 24, 26). My thanks to Nathan Laufer for pointing this out.

2. Their promise is the almost-last word of Genesis: "And Joseph said unto his brethren: 'I die; but God will surely remember (*paqod yifqod*) you, and bring you up out of this land unto the land which He swore to Abraham, to Isaac, and to Jacob.' And Joseph took an oath of the Children of Israel, saying: 'God will surely remember (*paqod yifqod*) you, and you shall carry up my bones from hence.' So Joseph died, being a hundred and ten years old. And they embalmed him, and he was put in a coffin in Egypt" (Gen. 50:24–26).

3. Two possibilities suggest themselves to us. First, the Israelites, despite their miserable bondage, managed to keep alive from generation to generation the sacred memory of the great Joseph's deathbed wish and his brothers' sworn promise. They (or at least the elders) transmitted this knowledge to Moses, who—magnificently, in the midst of the Exodus—remembered to fulfill the obligation. In elegant support of this alternative, Nathan Laufer (in a personal communication) points out that the formulaic expression, *pakod yifkod*, "surely remember," occurs only four times in the Torah: twice in the speech in which Joseph first exacted the promise from his brothers (see Note 2); once here (13:19), where that speech is repeated verbatim; and once earlier, when, at the very start of his mission, God tells Moses to gather the *elders* and to tell them that "I have surely remembered you" (3:16). Laufer (following Rashi on Ex. 3:16) suggests that it is Moses's use of this well-known formula that persuades the elders that Moses is indeed speaking for God and that it is the elders who then tell Moses of the promise to take out Joseph's bones. Against this possibility, we find it highly improbable that the Israelites who, mired in their misery, seem to have forgotten their God, should have remembered Joseph and promises made to him. Hence, a second possibility: Moses gets the idea at the last minute—God only knows how—in a flash of "divine inspiration" that enables the departing Israelites to fulfill the ancient promise to Joseph just as the Lord is fulfilling His to them.

4. Although God had told him at the burning bush that He was the God of Abraham, Isaac, and Jacob, Moses probably does not know that, in removing Joseph's bones, he may also be fulfilling God's promise to Abra(ha)m, in the covenant between the sacrificial pieces: that, after 400 years of slavery, the Israelites shall return to the Promised Land "in the fourth generation" (Gen. 15:16). Joseph belongs to the fourth

generation, beginning the count with Abraham. (I owe this suggestion to Hannah Mandelbaum.)

5. See Genesis 50, which pointedly contrasts the funeral procession to bury Jacob with his ancestors at Machpelah and the mummification of Joseph in Egypt. Joseph's participation in the former may very well have awakened the Israelite in him and led him to make his final request to his brothers. For an expansive discussion of these two responses to death and their importance for understanding the difference between Egypt and Israel, see my *The Beginning of Wisdom*, Chapter Twenty-One, "Losing Joseph, Saving Israel: Jacob Preserves the Way," especially the sections titled "The Death and Funeral of Jacob" and "The End of Joseph: Mummification and Memory."

6. Even though the locations of these ancient sites are today unknown, it is clear that the sea in question could not be the Red Sea. True, the biblical name, *Yam Suf,* frequently denotes the Red Sea; yet since "*suf,*" according to Rashi, means "a marsh in which reeds grow," scholars now think that the body of water in question might be one of the Bitter Lakes that lay north of present-day Suez. Given the rest of the story, we imagine that the Israelites will be encamped on the western—that is, the Egyptian—side of this body of water, where they will soon be trapped between it and the invading Egyptian forces.

7. The same verb, *kaved,* was often used before as one of the three ways of describing what was done to "stiffen" Pharaoh's heart (either by the Lord or by Pharaoh himself): there it meant giving gravity or strength to his heart and mind or making heavy his resolve. The word will soon be used again, in an inverted meaning, to describe how the Egyptian chariots got stuck in the mud: "He took off their chariot wheels and made them drive heavily (*bikhveduth*)" (14:25). The Lord here gains (positive) "weight" by "burdening" (negative) the Egyptian war machine.

8. Could these be the same people who had sent them off with gifts of gold and silver jewelry a few days earlier? Recognizing afterward what they have lost, they may now regret their generosity.

9. Cassuto comments, "The psychological reaction of the Israelites was typical of the usual fickleness of the masses who willingly obey their leaders when things go well, but who are quick to rise up against them in time of calamity and danger." *A Commentary on the Book of Exodus,* 163.

10. We will revisit Moses's prophecy, with its emphasis on seeing, at the end of this episode.

11. These three alternatives are, in fact, typical human responses to desperate situations. The path the Lord recommends for the Israelites has more than merely local application. All dignified human action presupposes hope.

12. The instruction, "Speak to the Children of Israel that they should go forward" (14:15), parallels and answers the previous instruction, "Speak to the Children of Israel that they turn back" (14:2). As much as this episode is about destroying the overconfident and forward-charging Egyptians, it is equally about inspiriting the terrified and backward-glancing Israelites.

13. Alter, *The Five Books of Moses,* 395.

14. With their last words, the drowning Egyptians unwittingly confirm the accuracy of Moses's prophetic words to the terrified Israelites: "Y-H-V-H will fight for you" (14:14).

15. Although the Egyptians will never be heard from, the prospect of a return to Egyptian servitude is invoked by Moses in Deuteronomy, at the conclusion of the list of national curses, as the ultimate penalty Israel will pay for violating its covenant with the Lord: "And the Lord shall bring you back into Egypt *in ships,* in the way that I said to you: 'You shall not see it again.' And you will put yourselves up for sale to your enemies as bondsmen and bondswomen, and there will be no buyer" (Deut. 28:68; emphasis added).

16. The use of the verb *yasha'*, "saved," echoes and confirms Moses's prophetic speech to the terrified Israelites: "Fear not, stand still, and you will see *yeshu'ath Y-H-V-H,* the *salvation* of the Lord" (14:13; emphasis added). Moses perhaps spoke better than he knew, but his trust in the Lord was rewarded by the fulfillment of his words.

17. We note the difference between Moses and the people in what it took to induce awe-fear-reverence: for the people, it was (the sight of) dead bodies killed by the Lord's "mighty hand"; for Moses, it was (the intimate speech by, with, and about) the God of his ancestors. This difference speaks volumes about the gap between the leader and the led.

18. Alter translates *ga'oh ga'ah* as "He surged, O surged," pointing out that the verb not only means something like "to triumph," "to be exalted" but is also used to describe the rising tide of the sea. *The Five Books of Moses,* 397. The root, *ga'ah,* means "to *rise* up," as a horse rises, majestically.

19. "And Lamech said unto his wives: 'Adah and Zillah, hear my voice; you wives of Lamech, hearken unto my speech; for I have slain a man for wounding me, and a young man for bruising me; If Cain shall be avenged sevenfold, truly Lamech seventy and sevenfold'" (Gen. 4:23–24). In the preceding verses, we had learned that Lamech's sons included the father of those who played musical instruments and the forger of cutting instruments of bronze and iron; that is, the tools of song and the tools of war.

20. The verb is also in the imperfect aspect, indicating an incomplete or even ongoing activity: "was singing" and "will sing" are both possible translations. On the basis of this grammatical point, we may suggest that the act of singing this song—or at least the *need* for it—was both incomplete and unending.

21. Cassuto, *A Commentary on the Book of Exodus,* 174.

22. Among the literary clues to the structure, scholars point out that the last verse in each strophe contains repeated words: "Your right hand, O Lord . . . Your right hand" (15:6); "Who is like You? . . . Who is like You?" (15:11); "till . . . pass by . . . till . . . pass by" (15:16). And the penultimate verses contain similes of sinking: "like a stone," "as lead," "as a stone" (verses 5, 10, and 16, respectively).

23. A contraction for *Y-H-V-H,* with the same meaning.

24. It is this passage among others that led Cassuto to speculate that the Song of the Sea also cryptically celebrates the Lord's victory, told in ancient myths, over the rebellion of Rahab, the prince of the sea, and the sea monsters—the forces of watery

chaos—against the Creator of order, a tale picked up by prophets and poets, and later by the rabbinic tradition; Cassuto, *A Commentary on the Book of Exodus*, 177–181. Given what we have previously said about the anti-creation meaning of Egypt, we again find it fitting that Egypt should be defeated in a manner that also demonstrates the Lord's control over the forces of primordial chaos (represented among the Greeks by Poseidon, god of the seas).

25. This is the first time the Torah—or anyone *in* the Torah—speaks of the Lord's holiness. Much later, in prescribing the so-called holiness code, the Lord will speak of His own holiness and summon Israel to imitate Him: "Be you holy for I *Y-H-V-H* your God am holy" (Lev. 19:2; see also Lev. 11:44–45 and 20:7).

26. There is even a midrash on this subject: "The ministering angels sought to say the Song. Said the Holy Blessed One: The works of My hands are drowning in the sea, and you are saying the Song?" (Talmud Megillah 10b). But it also says that humans, because mortal, should get a chance to celebrate first. To which we would add, in our own name, that it is absolutely necessary at this stage for the slavish Israelites to see and celebrate the crushing of their oppressors and the elimination of the chief alternative, symbolized here perfectly by horses, wheels, raw power, and water. Later, once the Law is given, the people's sentiment can and will be moderated. And they will learn that "the Lord is a Man-of-War" is far from the whole truth about God.

27. Alter, *The Five Books of Moses*, 402.

28. This examination is encouraged by the fact that this is the Bible's first instance of dancing. First instances are often paradigmatic; they invite phenomenological inquiry.

29. To be clear, I am presenting these imagined scenes without moral judgment or even an adverse spin. Rhythmic bodily movements by ecstatic women, in the presence of men, cannot help but have sexual overtones. It comes with the territory of our being sexual beings.

30. A possible connection of dancing and the profane is contained in word play: the word for dancing, *mecholoth* (from *chul*, twirling), contains the word for profane, *chol*. My thanks to Assaf Inbari for this observation.

31. Moses had simply begun to sing, without the need for orders: "I will sing"; Miriam must command the women to sing.

32. There may be another (subtler) clue to the effect of Miriam's dancing on the people. The very next verses report that the Children of Israel arrived three days later at a place called Marah ("bitter waters"), so called because its waters were bitter and hence undrinkable. It is here that the people first murmur against Moses, precisely over the life-sustaining matter of water (15:22–24). (My thanks to Yehuda Taragin for this suggestion.)

33. A large part of the rest of the book of Exodus and much of the book of Leviticus are devoted precisely to these matters. As we shall see, that is what the Tabernacle and the sacrifices are in part about.

34. I owe these insights to an unpublished paper written by Avia Sandak, a student in my class on Exodus at Shalem College, Jerusalem, 2016–2017.

NINE The Murmurings of Necessity

1. The original plan called for a much shorter interval in the desert, with a direct trip from Egypt to the Promised Land lasting roughly a year. That plan was not changed until after the episode with the spies (reported in the middle of Numbers), after which God decided to keep Israel in the desert for forty years, so that the slavish generation of Israelites could be replaced. That change in the plans is, however, foretold in the narrative that we shall discuss in this chapter: "And the Children of Israel did eat the manna forty years, until they came to a land inhabited; they did eat the manna until they came to the borders of the land of Canaan" (16:35).

2. But see Deuteronomy 8:3, where Moses reviews the episode of the manna: "And He afflicted you, and suffered you to hunger, and fed you with manna, which you knew not and neither did your fathers know; that He might make you know that man does not live by bread alone, but by every thing that proceeds out the mouth of the Lord does man live."

3. We should therefore expect that the answers the text gives to these questions will be tailored to the (still) "slavish" mentality of the people.

4. In his wise and penetrating book, political scientist Aaron Wildavsky analyzes the four different political "regimes" he finds in the Torah: slavery, anarchy, hierarchy, and equity. Wildavsky, *Moses as Political Leader*. Exodus shows us the first three and points toward the fourth.

5. According to a midrash that highlights the issue of acquisitiveness and the need for moderation, Moses, after the Egyptians had drowned, had to forcefully move the people away from the Sea of Reeds where they were still gathering the decorative armor of the dead Egyptians and their chariots. The midrash is triggered by the fact that an unusual verb is used for "led," *vayyassaʿ* (15:22), which implies force in the leading and journeying. (My thanks to Nathan Laufer for this reference and insight.)

6. Robert Alter shows how this passage links the tribulations of the Israelites in the wilderness with the Plagues narrative: "There is an explicit echo of the first plague when the Egyptians 'could not drink water from the Nile.'" *The Five Books of Moses*, 403. There is also a more immediate verbal echo: the bitter waters of Marah echo the name of Miriam, "bitter water," whose name we just encountered for the first time and whom we just left behind, two verses earlier. We are free to speculate on what, if anything, the Torah means to suggest by this literary juxtaposition.

7. As with the plagues, some scholars are at pains to try to find naturalistic explanations for God's "miracles." Thus, for example, Cassuto speculates that the bitterness of the water was due to an abundance of salts (like the Dead Sea today). He then alludes to testimony of travelers who report that a local desert briar can absorb the salts and sweeten the water. *A Commentary on the Book of Exodus*, 184. I understand the temptation of such attempts to appeal to readers who deny the possibility of miracles, but, as we will see more clearly in the discussion of the manna, I think that they are fundamentally misguided.

8. Perhaps by way of anticipation, the Lord uses here the exact phrase, "hearkening you will hearken"—a emphatic combination of verb with its own participle—that he will use again when proposing His covenant to the Israelites assembled at Sinai (19:5). The mention in this passage of statutes, ordinances, and commandments also anticipates the Law given at Sinai. But what specific statute or ordinance the Lord may have communicated to the people "*there*" at Marah (15:25) is a complete mystery to me. Some people suggest that He gave them here the statutes of Sabbath cessation, later at issue in the episode with the manna. But such instruction would bear no relation to the present matter of water. Better, it seems to me, to leave unknowns unknown.

9. My thanks to Nathan Laufer for the gloss on the numbers. Twelve and seventy are, on other grounds, significant numbers of fullness: seventy is ten times the number connected with completion or perfection (as in the seven days of creation); twelve is a complete set (like ten in the decimal system) in the sexagesimal system of counting that was developed in Mesopotamia: instead of counting the ten fingers, people counted the twelve finger bones in the four (non-thumb) fingers.

10. This episode echoes the story of Hagar the Egyptian and her (and Abraham's) son Ishmael, whom Abraham had banished on Sarah's insistence. Hagar too was in the desert with Abraham's firstborn; her supply of water exhausted, she too despaired. She too cried out. God called to her out of heaven, with a great promise for her son. And when God opened her eyes, she saw a well of water near at hand (Gen. 21:15–19). Hope is the necessary condition of deliverance.

11. Many have wondered about the people's claim to be starving, especially since, as we were frequently told and will later be told again, they had much livestock with them. Did they not have milk? Could they not have killed their animals for meat? But cows without pasture will not thrive and give no milk; sheep and goats, although they can be herded in the desert, especially during the winter months, often have trouble surviving the parched summers. But these attempts at rational explanation again seem to miss the point: the text is not interested in *how* they became hungry, but only in the *fact* of their hunger and (especially) in God's response to it.

12. At first glance, the instructions given throughout this episode seem to imply that the concept of a distinctive seventh day, of a "sabbath," was already known to the Israelites, even though there has been no mention of it previously and even though the commandment to keep the Sabbath, one of the Ten Commandments, has yet to be given. (Readers of the Bible will, of course, have heard about a hallowed seventh day in the story of Creation that opens the book of Genesis, but human beings *in* the story hear about creation for the first time only at Sinai, during the enunciation of the Ten Commandments [Ex. 20].) However, on closer inspection, as I hope to demonstrate later in this chapter, I come to the opposite conclusion: this episode provides the people's first inkling of "sabbath," one that will become the point of reference for the teaching about Sabbath remembrance in the Ten Commandments.

13. Aaron has been inactive for a long time, as Moses increasingly took over the initiation of the plagues. Aaron's last solo performance was during the third plague, and his last joint action was with the sixth one. His function here may reflect his greater

closeness to the people, especially in matters of approaching God—a foretaste of what will become the duties of priests. Aaron will become Israel's first priest.

We also notice in this passage the use of the word 'edah, "community," reserved for places where the Children of Israel are to have a special encounter with the Divine Presence (see Chapter One, Note 9).

14. Later, at Sinai, we will be told that "the appearance of *the glory of the Lord* was like a devouring fire on the top of the [cloud-covered] mountain" (24:17; emphasis added).

15. Robert Alter puts it convincingly: "No migration of quail, after all, would repeat itself every evening, and no edible granules secreted by aphids would mysteriously cease every seventh day." *The Five Books of Moses*, 408. Better to regard the manna as "miracle food," a divine "cotton candy" that disappears on your tongue, but can sustain you all by itself for forty years.

16. At least according to the Torah's "folk etymology," where *man* is an earlier form of the word *mah*, meaning "what." There is another source for the name *manna*: the Arabs called the aphid droplets *mann* or even *mann as-samâ*, "manna of heaven." The Torah in many places provides its own etymology for already existing names (as with the name of Moses), very likely to make a serious point: to give known things a new and biblically significant meaning. A further lovely point: in this book of "Names," it is the people, gaining a newfound dignity, who give the flaky stuff its name after their own expression of wonder: "And the house of Israel called the name thereof *manna*" (16:31).

17. We depart here from our usual practice of not attributing to anyone knowledge about God's words or teachings—or about anything else—that we readers did not hear him being told. In that spirit, we could plausibly say that Moses has, without being told, *intuited*—from the Lord's remarks about gathering "a day's portion every day" and about a double portion on the sixth day—exactly what the Lord had in mind for the use of the manna; later in this chapter we will in fact make such a suggestion. But here, where Moses explicitly says, "this is the thing *which the Lord has commanded*," we feel constrained to accept that remark as the literal truth, even though we readers never heard Him command it.

18. The ideas and formulations of this paragraph I owe to Dan Polisar.

19. But not the Lord's. This is one piece of evidence for thinking that it was Moses, not the Lord, who authored the rule against overnight storage, intuiting it from the idea that "a day's portion every day" should be completely consumed in a day. As we will see shortly, the Lord gets angry only about something else: gathering on the seventh day.

20. Perhaps the chiefs are worried that any excess gathered will encourage hoarding or, more likely, will lead as before to spoilage. Moses speaks, at least at first, only to the chiefs who have come to report the excess gathering. The instructions he gives them they presumably relayed to the people, for the instructions were followed and there was no rot. The audience for Moses's remarks on the next morning is unstated. It could have been the same "chiefs," or it could have been the people.

21. The text plays with the assonance among *shabbath* ("sabbath" or "cessation"), *shevu* ("sit" or "remain"), *shevi'i* ("seventh"), and *yishbethu* ("ceased") to convey the deep link between cessation, staying put, and the idea of completion conveyed by the number seven.

22. This may be an anachronistic anticipation of where the manna would later be stored, namely, before the Ark of Testimony, in which the tables of Testimony are kept. However, when we read later about the building of the Tabernacle, there is no mention of the deposit of manna in the Ark. Neither will it be referred to in later books of the Torah. But there will later be other commandments to commemorate God's gift of heaven-sent manna: once the people enter the Promised Land, each person must annually bring from his new harvest an *'omer* of barley, as a wave offering to God—an offering literally *waved in the air* before the Lord as a symbolic gift, before being released for use by those bringing the sacrifice. Before he feeds himself and his family from his fertile land, the Israelite must recall God's providence with the manna in the desert. For an excellent discussion of the several rituals involving the *'omer* in relation to the manna, see the chapter on Shavuot in Laufer, *Rendezvous with God,* especially 53–66.

23. Dan Polisar wonders whether part of the reason God provides manna is to give the ex-slaves a daily routine of work, reminiscent of their time in Egypt, to prevent anomie. "Ex-slaves or ex-concentration-camp inhabitants who have no routine and are recovering psychologically from their abuse, will in the absence of routine, lead dissolute lives" (personal communication). I take his point, but would add that the routine of gathering food for yourself, rather than straw for Pharaoh's bricks, turns slavish toil into uplifting, because meaningful, work.

24. Most of the arguments of this paragraph were forcefully made by Yuval Levin in a seminar I led on Exodus in Washington, DC, in 2007–2008. Levin sees here the germ of the long-term problems of Israelite politics: "Biblical Israel will offer the world a great model for moral and spiritual living, but a very poor model for political living, for governing and self-government. Inculcating the desired attitude of gratitude is welcome. On the other hand, it is not simply true that God will always provide. The community will have to provide for itself, and it is being kept from learning that in the desert. Perhaps they are meant to be less a nation, more a light unto the nations; for they are being taught not how to govern themselves, but how to live morally." We will return to this question in Chapter Twelve, when Israel will be summoned by the Lord to become "a kingdom of priests and a holy nation" (19:6).

25. Alter, *The Five Books of Moses,* 411–412.

26. To be sure, Moses needs water just like everyone else. But unlike the ex-slaves who lived their entire lives in Egypt, the well-watered land of good and plenty, Moses had extensive experience of the desert from his years of shepherding with Jethro. As Dan Polisar puts it, "Moses knows from experience that if you're wily and patient, you'll survive [in the desert]. Having the experience only of life in agricultural, Nile-fed Egypt, the other Israelites find each experience of a lack of water to be terrifying" (personal communication).

TEN "Is the Lord Among Us or Not?"

1. Having gone this far, we cannot suppress the thought that He was in fact "behind" the Amalekite attack. Had He not used the Israelites to bait a trap for Egypt before the Sea of Reeds, precisely to teach everyone Who He Was? Might He now be interested to see just how well Israel will defend itself after having learned from that previous episode that the Lord fights on her side?

2. Amalek was the only son of Esau's son, Eliphaz, by his concubine Timna.

3. As Nathan Laufer pointed out (in a private communication), also relevant for the present story is the "leftover" blessing that Isaac gave Esau, after his had been given away by mistake to Jacob: "*And by the sword shall you live,* and you shall serve your brother. And it shall come to pass, when you break loose, that *you shall shake his yoke from off your neck*" (Gen. 27:40; emphasis added). This prophecy, containing the Bible's first mention of a sword in human hands, may be what is going on in this chapter. Says Laufer: "Perhaps that is why Amalek attacks, hoping once and for all to free themselves via the sword from the humiliating yoke of their ancestor, Esau, being duped by his brother, Jacob." If so, it will receive an ironic twist at the end: the sword mentioned will reside with Joshua, to a different outcome. For a fuller discussion of the reunion of Jacob/Israel and Esau, and of the unresolved tensions between them, see my *The Beginning of Wisdom: Reading Genesis*, Chapter Fifteen, "Brotherhood and Piety: Facing Esau, Seeing God," 466–472.

4. We may also add the prophecy of Isaac's blessing of Esau. See the previous note.

5. When Moses retells this story in Deuteronomy, offering his interpretation, he adds a detail about the attack that, although not present in our account, fits with our suggestions: "Remember what Amalek did unto you by the way as you came forth out of Egypt; how he met you by the way, and smote your hindmost, all that were enfeebled in your rear (*hannecheshalim*), when you were *faint and weary* ('*ayeph veyagea*'); *and he feared not God (velo' yare' 'elohim)*" (Deut. 25:17–18; emphasis added). The Amalekites not only attacked the ex-slaves unprovoked; they went after the weakest members of the party, lacking all decency and humanity (*no fear of heaven*). Nathan Laufer notices another lovely clue that indicates that Moses sees Amalek's attack in relation to the Jacob-Esau story, this time to Esau's sale of the birthright for a bowl of pottage. When Esau came in hungry from the field, he is twice said to be faint ('*ayeph*) (Gen. 25: 29–30). Because Jacob took advantage of Esau when he was faint, Amalek, getting even, attacked Israel when she was faint (personal communication). Yet, welcome though these additions are, we must resist allowing Moses's later interpretations of this event to decide for us what to make of it here, when it happened.

6. Whatever the reason, we have here the beginning of a division of responsibility and authority, and the separation of military from (what will soon become) legislative power; the next chapter will add the separation of sacerdotal and judicial responsibilities.

7. Some scholars suggest that the name may be related to the Hebrew word, *chiver*, meaning "pale" and, derivatively, "pure." Others relate it to *cheruth*, meaning

"liberty" or "freedom." The most probable derivation, however, is from the term *chor*, which is used in 1 Kings 21:8 to mean "noble."

According to the Tradition, Hur is the son of Miriam; according to 1 Chron. 2:19, his father is Caleb. If so, like Joshua, he belongs to the younger generation. Also if so, Moses's choice of Hur, like his choice of Joshua, may suggest that Moses, in introducing a "division of labor," may be thinking already about who might someday replace him. But, as Nathan Laufer has pointed out to me, Josephus in his *Antiquities* had a different tradition regarding Hur: he was Miriam's husband, not her son. Says Laufer: "This would make him a contemporary of Moses and Aaron and would better explain why Moses will later delegate the responsibility of dealing with the Israelites to Aaron and Hur when he goes up to be with God on Mount Sinai" (personal communication). At the end of the day, Hur and the reason he was chosen remain a mystery.

8. In watching and assessing Moses's actions, we readers are in the same boat as the people. But we have the privileged position of watching and assessing their actions as well.

9. I owe this argument and interpretation to Judah Mandelbaum.

10. This is only the second human use of swords in the Bible. Simeon and Levi used them to slay all the males in Shechem, as well as the king Hamor and his rapist son Shechem (with their sword's edge), to avenge the rape of their sister Dinah (Gen. 34:25–26). No one had told them to do this. God makes no comments on their deed; He is not even mentioned in that bloody chapter. Also perhaps relevant, as we noted earlier, Esau had been told, in Isaac's blessing, that *he* would live by the sword. The sword that was to have been Esau's winds up in Joshua's hand. See Note 3.

11. Likely paying attention to the sword's sharp edges, Rashi suggests: "He [Joshua] decapitated their [the Amalekites'] strongest warriors, and he left over only the weak among them, but he did not slay them all" (*Pentateuch: Exodus,* commenting on Ex. 17:13). If true, Joshua's action would be the opposite of what the Amalekites did, according to Moses's later retelling: they attacked the faint and weary, having no fear of God (Deut. 25:17–18). See Note 5. It is, of course, very possible that "Joshua" in this verse is a synecdoche, a stand-in for the whole army of Israel.

12. My thanks to Richie Lewis for suggesting the parallel to the Homeric heroes. That the divine power passes through Moses's *hands*—that Moses is the mediator between God and man—will later be underscored in two episodes involving the future of Joshua. First, the Lord tells Moses to appoint Joshua his successor: "And the Lord said unto Moses: 'Take you Joshua the son of Nun, a man in whom is spirit (*ruach*), and *lay your hand upon him*'" (Num. 27:18; emphasis added). Last, in the almost final verse of the Torah, we hear of the succession of Joshua after the death of Moses: "And Joshua the son of Nun was full of the spirit of wisdom; for Moses *had laid his hands upon him;* and the Children of Israel hearkened unto him, and did as the Lord commanded Moses" (Deut. 34:9; emphasis added). My thanks to Nathan Laufer for pointing this out.

13. Some readers may be uncomfortable with these and earlier suggestions that seem to reduce the Divine Presence and Power to a merely psychological—and there-

fore "subjective"—state of the human mind. But that is not what I mean and not what I think. In speaking about the Divine Presence, I am less focused on the efficient cause of the phenomenon in question, but rather on its internal content and meaning. Anyone who believes in the existence of *in-spira-*tion—of the fact of "spirit" coming "in"—and who thinks about it for more than five minutes, will recognize that *what* it *is,* no less than "where" it comes from, bespeaks the "presence" of something beyond our ordinary way of living and acting. We return briefly to this topic at the end of this chapter.

14. There is another question, about agency: God says that "*I*" will blot out their remembrance. Does this mean that He will do it by His own "hand" alone, the way He smote the firstborn in Egypt? If so, could this be expressing a *negative* judgment about the recent battle, and more generally, about the insufficiency of human hands to do what needs to be done? Or is it, conversely, a suggestion that, in the future just as here, God will work His will through human hands (beginning with Joshua)? I incline to the latter view.

15. Robert Alter comments, "In all this, as in the Plagues narrative, history is transformed into symbolic typology. Ancient Israel was surrounded by enemies—the Canaanite peoples with whom it fought for territory, marauders like the Midianites to the east and the Amalekites to the south, and the great empires of Mesopotamia and Egypt. Historical survival required nearly continued armed conflict. But distinctions are made among enemies, and Amalek here becomes the very type of ruthless foe that seeks to annihilate Israel." *The Five Books of Moses,* 415.

16. This contrast and its significance were pointed out to me by Nachum Danzig.

17. His campaign against Amalek persisted for many generations. Saul, Israel's first king, had a chance to fight, but he refused, sparing the Amalekite king, Agag. His disobedience cost him the kingdom (1 Sam. 15:1–35).

18. The puzzling invocation of the Lord's hand echoes the mysterious effect of Moses's raised hands during the battle.

19. See Chapter Eleven. We will be interested to see how Moses relates to his own flesh-and-blood descendants.

20. For evidence, we will examine carefully how they regard him in the next chapter, when his father-in-law Jethro comes and finds Moses sitting morning until night before the people, exactly as ruler and judge.

21. This may, in fact, have prepared Moses to accept Jethro's forthcoming advice about delegating responsibility for judging (see Chapter Eleven).

22. Although the content of what is said to them differs greatly, will not Moses's and the prophets' experience of the Voice that calls them be rather like Homer's recognition of divine power speaking through him: "Sing, muse"?

23. The formulation of this sentence I owe to Richie Lewis.

ELEVEN Jethro's Visit

1. Some readers get around the apparent inconsistency by arguing that Rephidim is, after all, close to Sinai: the rock from which Moses struck the water was at Horeb

(17:6), which is the location of the mountain in question. Mount Horeb is the same as Mount Sinai, is the same as the mountain of God. Others insist that the Jethro story is, in fact, temporally out of place and that it took place *after* the giving of the law at Sinai (reported in Chapters Nineteen and following), a view that they support by noting that Moses will tell Jethro (in this chapter) that he is making known to the people "the statutes of God (*chuqqe ha'elohim*) and His laws (*torothav*)" (18:16).

2. As Rashi puts it, "There is no early or late in the Torah."

3. As a result, it may occur to someone to suggest that Jethro, too, is a "godsend." We return to this idea later in this chapter.

4. My thanks to Judah Mandelbaum for this last observation.

5. Although I think that the people who worry about chronology are asking the wrong question, for what it is worth I incline to the view that the story is not out of chronological order. Had the Law already been given at Sinai, Jethro would not have advised Moses: "And you shall teach them the statutes and the laws, and shall make known to them the way wherein they must walk, and the work that they must do" (18:20).

6. The Hebrew word *kohen* can mean both priest and chief ruler. We do not know whether Jethro was just a priest or rather a priest-king like Melchizedek (Gen. 14:19–21).

7. The word father-in-law occurs thirteen times in this account of Jethro's visit. But see also Note 30 of this chapter.

8. This is the second Eliezer (*My-God-is-[my]-help*) in the Bible. The first one, Abraham's servant, successfully (with God's help, so he said) found a wife for Isaac—Rebekah—at a foreign well, securing God's Way for another generation. Moses's Eliezer—whose mother Moses met at a well—is named for God's political, rather than domestic, assistance. With his giant-of-a-father devoting himself to founding and politics, securing God's Way for a whole people, Eliezer himself will do nothing, never even gaining another mention in the text.

9. Very likely to set up the contrast, in Hebrew the verse begins with the verb, "And came Jethro" (*vayyavo' yithro*), a replica of "And came Amalek" (*vayyavo' 'amaleq*). Two different outside nations *came*, but their purposes and intentions could not have been more opposed.

10. Cassuto, *A Commentary on the Book of Exodus*, 215.

11. We can easily imagine why Moses is so delighted to see Jethro. Not since he left his father-in-law to go down to Egypt has Moses had a suitable companion. Not once has he been in the presence of a (friendly) person of comparable stature and intellect—Aaron is not such a one—with whom he could speak freely and hope to be understood. (I owe this suggestion to Jerome Marcus.)

12. It was Jethro who summoned Moses home and gave him a wife, without Moses's even asking for one: "And Moses was content to dwell with *the man;* and he gave Moses Zipporah his daughter" (2:21; emphasis added).

13. There is another reference in the Jethro story to this same Garden of Eden verse. Jethro will later say that it is "*not good*" (*lo' tov*) for Moses to be judging *alone*

(18:17–18). The *only* other appearance of "not good" in the Torah is in God's speech calling for the creation of woman. To man whose aloneness is not good, God gave woman; to Moses whose aloneness is not good, Jethro (in God's place) will give judges. We will later consider whether Jethro's "gift" is an adequate remedy for the problem of Moses's "aloneness."

14. Not, as Jethro had heard, for *Moses's* sake (see 18:1). Compare Moses's "delivered *them*" with his "delivered *me*," in etymologizing the name he gave his son Eliezer (18:4). We note that Moses does not say "delivered *us*." Moses still does not identify himself as belonging to the people.

15. The last clause is obscure, not least because it begs for a (missing) clause to compete the thought. Some traditional interpreters, suggesting that Jethro is pleased because of the Lord's *justice,* hold that the phrase points to God's measure-for-measure retribution against the Egyptians: as they schemed against Israel (for example, by drowning the firstborn sons), so the Lord retaliated (He drowned the Egyptian legions). Other interpreters, suggesting that Jethro is pleased because of the Lord's *power* and, translating the verb *zid* to mean "dealt proudly" (rather than "schemed"), suggest that the phrase points to the item-by-item defeat (through the plagues) of the things (for example, its "gods") of which Egypt boasted.

16. "Jethro, as a Midianite priest, appears to speak here as a henotheist rather than a monotheist, conceding the reality of other gods but affirming Y-H-V-H's unrivaled greatness." Alter, *The Five Books of Moses,* 417.

17. What I am calling "sacrifice" includes both the completely consumed burnt offering (*'olah;* from *'alah,* "to ascend") and the sacrifice proper (*zevach*), which is a meal shared with the divine and eaten before the altar.

18. If this is correct, Jethro would be following the respectful practices of those who offer a nondenominational grace at the start of a meal attended by people of multiple faiths.

19. Cassuto, *A Commentary on the Book of Exodus,* 217. Rashi deals with Moses's absence by citing a beautiful midrash from the Mechilta, showing Moses's great modesty and humility: Moses is not mentioned because Moses made himself invisible by playing waiter, serving his guests (a role that he learned from Abraham serving his guests in Genesis 18:8). My thanks to Nathan Laufer for bringing this passage to my attention.

20. It will be a long question whether—and, if so, when—Moses comes to see the *need* for the priestly activity and ritual observance. For now, that issue has been highlighted by the pregnant silence about him during the sacrifices, even if he is in fact present at the altar when Jethro initiates them.

21. The observation belongs to Hannah Mandelbaum. What makes the analogy finally inappropriate for the Israelite polity is that these different domains are not separated but integrated. See my discussion of the Ten Commandments in Chapter Thirteen.

22. Such a fate was precisely what Moses had been afraid of, for different reasons, in Chapter Nine: "lest they stone me" (17:4).

23. The phrase, "to inquire of God," will later be used to describe approaching an oracle for all sorts of revelations. In the only previous comparable usage, Rebekah "went to inquire of Y-H-V-H (*lidrosh 'eth-Y-H-V-H*)" because of her difficult pregnancy (Gen. 25:22). Here, in a judicial context, the people are seeking what only a "divine revelation" could provide in order to resolve a difficult interpersonal dispute.

24. Exodus 15:26. In the Lord's quoted remarks, He is clearly speaking about the future. At Marah, the text tells us that the Lord "made for them a statute and an ordinance (*hoq umishpat*)—[singular: only *one*]—and there He tested them." We doubt that Moses could be referring to that one statue and one ordinance. Also, he speaks here of *torathoth*, not of *mishpatim*.

25. Compare Joseph's statement to the butler and the baker, who each had troubling dreams that they could not interpret: "Do not interpretations belong to God (*'elohim*)? Pray tell it *me!*" (Gen. 40:8; emphasis added). Just as we had no independent confirmation that Joseph was indeed channeling divine dream interpretation, so we lack here any independent confirmation that Moses is speaking here for God.

26. The root means, "to gaze at." Jethro is suggesting that Moses should be able to *see* or to *visualize* the requisite virtues in the men he is looking to appoint. The verb will appear only one more time in Exodus, in Exodus 24 in a crucial place (see the discussion in Chapter Sixteen).

27. Jethro heard Moses's "three" formulations not in the way we heard them. By treating the first one, "The people come to me to inquire of God," as pointing to a distinct service the people want from Moses—petitioning the divine for favors—Jethro offers Moses a pagan priest's advice.

28. The verbal root is *zhr*, which can mean "to give light." Here, it is used in the causative form and means "to warn" or "to caution." Perhaps the two meanings are linked: "to enlighten by admonition."

29. That is, to holiness. My thanks to Judah Mandelbaum for this formulation.

30. Nathan Laufer (in a personal communication) has suggested an ingenious solution to the puzzle about Jethro's departure. It requires attending to a second discussion, in the book of Numbers, about Moses's father-in-law who appears there out of the blue. "And Moses said unto Hobab [presumably, another name for Jethro], the son of Reuel the Midianite, *Moses's father-in-law:* 'We are journeying unto the place of which the Lord said: "I will give it you." Come you with us, and we will do you *good;* for the Lord has spoken *good* concerning Israel.' And he [Moses's father-in-law] said unto him: 'I will not go; but *I will depart to mine own land, and to my kindred.*' And he [Moses] said: 'Leave us not, I pray you; forasmuch as you know how we are to encamp in the wilderness, you shall serve us for eyes. And it shall be, if you go with us, that with whatever *good* the Lord shall do *good* unto us, the same *good* will we do unto you'" (Num. 10:29–32; emphasis added). Here, Moses pleads with his father-in-law to stay, perhaps because he treasures his wisdom and company—explicitly because he wants to avail himself of Jethro's keen-sightedness, experience, and knowledge of the desert. Jethro, quite understandably, wants to return to his land and kin. Moses makes an-

other appeal, promising to share the Lord's blessings with Jethro. Jethro does not respond. We are not told the outcome: Did he stay or did he go? By contrast, in the account of Jethro's visit in Exodus, we are given only the outcome, but not any antecedent discussion that might shed light on its occurrence.

Citing abundant internal literary evidence, Laufer suggests that the verses in Numbers 10 were once part of the story of Jethro's visit in Exodus (at the end of his first day), from which they were excised and relocated. For example, he notes that the addition of this singular mention of "father-in-law (*hothen*)" would bring the total uses of the word (in this single split-story) to fourteen, in keeping with the fact that key words frequently appear in multiples of seven. According to Laufer, Moses, after failing to persuade Jethro to stay, sends him away freely but reluctantly, with a sigh. Laufer also makes several lovely suggestions why the story might have been rearranged. Nathan Laufer, "Moses' Misplaced Speech Inviting His Father-in-Law to Join the Israelites," *Jewish Bible Quarterly* 47, No. 4 (Oct.–Dec. 2019): 237–253.

If Laufer is correct about the rearrangement, it still invites the sorts of questions I have considered in the text. It also highlights the fact that Jethro must leave before the Law is given and that Moses may now be looking for another, more exalted, teacher.

TWELVE Covenant from the Mountain

1. This very compressed summary, as well as the ones that follow in the next two paragraphs, covers materials and arguments fully presented in my *The Beginning of Wisdom: Reading Genesis*. Especially relevant are the first two chapters: "Awesome Beginnings: Man, Heaven and the Created Order," and "The Follies of Freedom and Reason: The Story of the Garden of Eden (I)."

2. There is no agreement on the location of this Wilderness of Sinai or of Mount Sinai, and probably for good reason. "The text gives us no details that can help us to determine the site, and possibly this silence is not unintended. Just as the Torah did not desire to associate the theophany expressly with a specific time, even so it did not wish to link it with a definite place, so that a person should not be able to corporealize the memory of the event and declare: Here, upon this mountain, the Lord revealed Himself to the Children of Israel, and from here He uttered the Ten Commandments. It is fitting that the happening should remain shrouded in the mists of sanctity." Cassuto, *A Commentary on the Book of Exodus*, 225.

3. The entire experience with Jethro is saturated with references to *'elohim*. Despite (once) acknowledging the greatness of *Y-H-V-H*, Jethro offers sacrifices instead to *'elohim*. Aaron and the elders eat with Moses's father-in-law before *'elohim*. Jethro tells Moses, "May *'elohim* be with you," "Be you for the people before *'elohim*," and "Bring you the matters before *'elohim*." Jethro speaks about men who "fear *'elohim*." Finally, and most relevantly, Jethro puts before Moses the need to seek divine sanction for his legal and judicial reforms: "If you shall do this thing and [if] *'elohim commands you*. . . ."

4. We speak loosely and at risk of misleading. We do not mean to suggest that God lives on this mountain or, more generally, that He has a continuous "dwelling place" here or anywhere. Unlike for the Greeks, where Mount Olympus is literally the home of the Greek gods, God has no permanent "abode," and places in the Torah have no permanent sanctity. They are temporarily made holy by the Lord's Presence. Still, trying to think here like Moses, we are following Moses's own usage from the Song of the Sea: "You guided them to Your holy habitation" (15:13).

5. Comments Robert Alter, "The perfect poetic parallelism, both semantic and rhythmic, of this [first] sentence signals the lofty, strongly cadenced language, akin to epic in its grandeur, of the entire episode." *The Five Books of Moses*, 423. The phrase "house of Jacob" occurs here for the only time in the Torah.

6. Years ago, God had made such a covenant with Abraham and his descendants: a promise of offspring and land, on condition of circumcising male newborns. That covenant has, of course, not been abrogated. But we have no idea how well it had been remembered by the Israelites in Egypt. And it is not the basis of the new *national* covenant now being proposed.

7. Readers interested in thinking about the idea of covenant in the context of the United States should examine the "Mayflower Compact," sworn to before God by the Pilgrims arriving at Plymouth, Massachusetts, in 1620. It is the first American political document.

8. The word translated "treasure," *segullah,* comes from an unused root meaning "to shut up," as wealth is shut up for safekeeping. What the Israelites may have understood by the term, who can say? This is its first use in the Torah and its only use in Exodus.

9. Although the Lord mentions the "House of Jacob" *to Moses,* neither the patriarchs nor the previous covenant with Abraham are mentioned in the covenant with the people, neither here in the proposal nor later, in Exodus 20, when its principles are specified. The new covenant, for *peoplehood,* rests on a new and entirely different foundation.

10. If we try to get help from the text on this matter, we have to this point but few examples. The first priest mentioned in the Bible was Melchizedek, who was also (perhaps coincidentally) the king of Salem (Gen. 14:18). In Egypt, we heard of Potiphera, the priest of On (and the father-in-law of Joseph), and more generally of a whole class of priests whose land Joseph did not purchase when, during the famine, he bought all the land for Pharaoh (Gen. 41:45 and 50; 46:20; 47:22 and 26): in Egypt, the priests are clearly distinct from the ruler and his courtiers. In Exodus, we have recently spent time with Jethro, priest of Midian (and the father-in-law of Moses); we do not know whether he was also a ruler in Midian, but we saw that in dealing with Moses he offered practical advice about political matters.

11. I owe this insight and formulation to Eric Cohen.

12. "For all the community, they are all holy, and in their midst is the Lord: why should you [Moses and Aaron] raise yourselves up over the Lord's assembly?" (Num. 16:3)

13. The (future) hereditary priesthood in Israel will be a role one is born into and is not based on one's charisma or special talents at "divination" or prophecy. The priest is not a holy person, but a servant of God and the people, mediating between both.

14. The word *qadosh* does not occur at all in Genesis. The five previous uses in Exodus are found at 3:5 ("where you [Moses] stand is holy ground"); twice at 12:16 ("there shall be a holy convocation"—referring to future celebrations of Passover); at 15:13, in the Song of the Sea ("You guided them to Your holy habitation"); and at 16:23, referring to a seventh day free of manna gathering ("holy sabbath unto the Lord").

15. These two obligations gain special prominence in the so-called Holiness Code of Leviticus. "You shall be holy, for I *Y-H-V-H* your God am holy. You shall fear-revere every man his mother and his father, and you shall keep My sabbaths: I am *Y-H-V-H* your God" (Lev. 19:2–3).

16. We are struck by the use here of the word *goy*, "nation," instead of the expected word *'am*, "people." From the start, we have been tracking *people* formation, the more-than-merely-genealogical basis of communal identity. We have just learned that God intends to turn the house of Jacob into a people, as a result of the new covenant He will here propose. So why is the goal described as "holy *nation*," rather than "holy people"? One suggestion: Israel is meant to be more than a polity among the polities of the earth. In aspiration, it is called to be holy, as the Lord is holy. It is meant to transcend politics as usual, to live under the fatherhood of God, as His firstborn son. The more genealogical and familial term, *goy*, suitably elevated, may thus apply.

17. Dan Polisar comments, "It is indeed fascinating that, up until this point, the people have virtually no idea *why* God singled them out and took them out of Egypt. They know only that He had a covenant with their ancestors and that He wants them to serve Him. This also helps in part to explain their recent murmurings: they had no idea what their role or destiny was" (personal communication).

18. We should be clear. God's purpose is that human beings should live a righteous and holy life, comprising peaceful and just relations among themselves and enjoying appropriate relations with the divine. That purpose is for the first time being made explicit to the Israelites at Sinai. According to the text, hearkening to the Law given at Sinai—not following our unaided human reason—is the necessary *means* for achieving that goal.

19. The proposal hints at, but does not quite assert, the equal covenantal standing of all members of the community, say, on the principle that each human being is equally in God's image. So far the covenant is being offered to the collective. But, as we will see in the next chapter, God will speak the Ten Words to everyone directly, without intermediaries. And He will summon each individual to embrace the principles of the covenant: each of the "commandments" will be given in the second-person *singular*. The call to become a holy nation will come to each Israelite *equally*.

20. In explicating Israel's grand mission among the nations, we have not forgotten the question, raised earlier and not yet answered, regarding the bearing of such a mission on the practical demands of national self-preservation, involving economics

and national defense. These matters appear to be left for later: inspiring men to care for their souls is more necessary—and more difficult—than teaching them how to care for their comfort and safety.

21. While agreeing with my description, Amiad Cohen (personal communication) does not see it as a significant shortcoming. Seeing God's covenantal offer to Israel as akin to a proposal of marriage, he points out that human beings who plight their troth in marriage (also) do not really know what they are getting into or what precisely will be expected of them. Rather a marrying couple accepts their obligation to the *idea* of marriage, precisely because they cannot know in advance what it concretely means. The pledge of union is meant to sustain the relationship, come what may.

I accept the analogy and Cohen's deep insights. Nevertheless, I still find the people's response wanting. Unlike the marital vows, they do not promise "from this day forward, for better for worse, for richer for poorer, in sickness and in health, to love and to cherish, till death us do part." They say only that we will do what You *said*.

22. Before describing the spectacle, we should acknowledge a certain tension in the account. On the one hand, we are in the run-up to the momentous event, an as-it-were coronation of the Lord as the accepted sovereign of Israel, for which fireworks would be a most fitting display. On the other hand, the spectacle is explicitly said to serve the purpose of permanently attaching the people's trust (also) *to Moses*.

23. This position was articulated by Niv Liel, a student in my Exodus seminar at Shalem College, Jerusalem, 2016–2017. We will revisit these two alternatives at the end of the next chapter, after we see the people's reaction to what actually transpires at the mountain three days later.

24. There is another reading of this verse. Cassuto, assuming that, off camera, Moses had gone down with the message about the Lord's descending in a cloud, suggests that Moses, again back up on the mountain, is here reporting the people's willingness and readiness to hear the word of the Lord. *A Commentary on the Book of Exodus*, 228. Perhaps so. But Cassuto, like Moses, does not see any difficulty in the people's earlier response. Nor does he say why the people would have had to approve the manner of the Lord's approach.

25. See Genesis 35:2, where Jacob, having just been invited by God to return to Beth-El and make Him an altar, instructs his household to prepare for the encounter: "Put away the strange gods that are among you, and cleanse yourselves, and change your garments; and let us arise, and go up to Beth-el."

26. Moses's injunction against carnal desire fits with the divine injunction against merging with the mountain. The target is certain pagan ideas about sexuality and about relations between gods and humans, including the notion that sexual union is itself a way of engaging with the divine. (The biblical Hebrew word for "temple prostitute" is *qedeshah,* a perversion of everything *qadosh,* a woman who may see sexual activity as a way of worshipping the earthy gods or, alternatively, who may enjoy sexual activity *without* any higher dedication.)

27. Alter, *The Five Books of Moses,* 427.

THIRTEEN Principles for God's New Nation

1. I am not suggesting that accepting and obeying these injunctions depend on our ability to understand their rationale; as presented, they are to be followed solely because they were enjoined. But there is nothing impious in trying to understand them. They are, after all, presented in rational speech to a group of people who, presumably, must understand them well enough to agree to abide by them.

In explicating the text, we intend also to build a case for the enduring moral and political significance of the Decalogue—a universal significance that goes far beyond its opposition to murder, adultery, and theft and that does not depend on the pyrotechnics accompanying their first enunciation.

2. But see Deuteronomy 5:19, where Moses tells the people that God Himself wrote the ten words on the two tables of stone.

3. Recalling the puzzling end of Exodus 19, we remind ourselves that it is not clear who is speaking this brief introduction: Moses or (the nameless voice of) "the text."

4. This suggestion may surprise many readers, especially those who bring to the text the conviction that monotheism—the belief that there exists only one God—is the Bible's first and most significant teaching. But on careful reading of the text, one will look in vain for an explicit claim to that effect before Second Isaiah. Nonetheless, readers can with reason suspect that the Bible leans from the start to a teaching of monotheism: it begins by attributing the Creation of the heavens and the earth to but a singular Creator God. But at least for now, neither the text nor even Y-H-V-H will assert that there is no divinity other than He.

5. It is true that, by idealizing the human form in the ageless and immortal gods, the Greek poets tried to bridge the gap between humankind and the indifferent natural forces and eternal heavenly bodies. It is also true that, in Homer, the anthropomorphic gods had their favorites among the mortals. But these "relationships" were one-sided and based entirely on caprice and whim. By the very understanding of divinity, it was unthinkable that any eternal, beautiful, and self-sufficient god would care a fig for us "creatures-of-a-day"—the weak, perishable, ugly, and unlovable mortals whom they toyed with for sport.

6. Among readers who seek more theological explanations, the most likely reason, unstated, would be that God is incorporeal and transnatural. Yet relying only on the biblical text (and not on later theologizing), the claim that God is incorporeal is not, in fact, so easily settled. There are a number of passages, even in Exodus, in which God speaks of Himself in corporeal terms, most famously when He tells Moses that He will cover him with His hand and show him [only] His "back" (33:21–23). Such passages are usually treated as metaphorical, in line with the thought that only through such images can our limited human intelligence gain any inkling of the ineffable divine. And there are later passages, including some describing the present revelation, that seem to deny that God has any visible form (Deut. 4:12 and 4:15), and that connect that assertion to the proscription of making graven images. But the proper response to

this dilemma may be to remind ourselves that the Torah is not interested in such metaphysical and theological issues (see God's answer to Moses's question about His name in Chapter Three). The text should not be read as if it is obliged to answer latter-day questions, born of medieval theology or modern skepticism, about the "nature of God." (We will return to this matter in Chapter Eighteen, when considering the matter of God's Presence in the Tabernacle.)

7. We now collect these statues in secular museums and admire their makers without a whiff of reverence for the divinity they allegedly represent. One suspects that when the ancient Athenians came to the Parthenon, temple of Athena on the Acropolis, what they most esteemed there was not the golden goddess but the sculptural genius of Phidias who made her (and the political will of Pericles, who ordered the Parthenon built).

8. The classic example is Oedipus, who unwittingly killed his father and married his mother. His deeds, committed in ignorance and violating no explicit law, nonetheless constituted a pollution that affected not only his children (who were also his half-siblings) but also the entire land of Thebes, which suffered a plague on generation. We shall return to this primal iniquity and its effects on the next generations when we examine the injunction to honor one's father and mother.

9. My friend and former colleague Michael Fishbane, as part of an overall critique of my humanistic reading of the text, has rightly pointed out that my interpretation of these passages underemphasizes the stark and painful fact that innocent children and grandchildren will have visited upon them the iniquities of their fathers. His comments and my response can be found here: http://mosaicmagazine.com/response/2013/06/loyalty-service-and-the-god-of-israel-a-response-to-leon-r-kass/ and http://mosaicmagazine.com/response/2013/06/response-to-the-commentators/.

10. Lovers of justice, please note: what we children get in both cases is equally "unjust," in the sense of equally undeserved.

11. This interpretation makes sense of the fact that the injunction is put in terms not of "speaking" or "saying," but of "carrying" or "bearing" or "lifting up" the name of the Lord. This metaphor implies that the fault, deeper than the speech itself, lies in the attempted appropriation of God's power and authority. It also makes sense of the second part of the verse about the consequence of disobedience: "The Lord will not acquit [cleanse; *niqqah*] the one who takes up His name in vain." The Lord will not claim you or serve you just because you claim the Lord or His assistance. And you will not be cleansed—not now, not ever—from the stain of having done so. We note, in passing, that this injunction applies not only to someone vainly swearing an oath but also to anyone who may undertake to speak in the name of God, not excluding prophets and priests who frequently take up the name of the Lord and who are susceptible to the occupational hazard of thinking that they thereby speak for, or even in the place of, the divine. A community whose members obey this injunction will be less likely to suffer the despotism of god-pretending pharaohs or the oppression of god-trafficking priests.

12. We have already had a lengthy discussion of the meaning of manna and the seventh day of cease-time. See Chapter Nine, especially the sections "A Day of Ceas-

ing" and "The Torah of Manna." The reader may wish to review that material as part of the present discussion of the Sabbath.

13. In an earlier draft of this paragraph, I wrote about "a complete world of changeable beings" and "a mysterious aspect of Being that is beyond change." Richie Lewis correctly called me out on this dubious importation of the (Greek) metaphysical emphasis on motion and rest, change and changelessness and reminded me of my own earlier interpretation of God's anti-metaphysical answer to Moses's request for the divine name. On its face, 'ehyeh 'asher 'ehyeh bespeaks anything but changelessness (see Chapter Three). Here is a good example of the danger of approaching the text with alien questions and categories. "Is God beyond change?" may well be a "wrong question," a question one asks only because one is committed to a certain (in this case, positive) answer.

14. My thanks to Nathan Laufer for this suggestion.

15. To be sure, the politics of ancient Israel did not altogether embody this ideal (for example, non-Hebrew slaves did not enjoy the humane and mandatory manumission after seven years prescribed for Hebrew slaves)—although, I hasten to add, it is only on the basis of the Sabbath teaching's ideal that such practice could be found wanting. It is also true that regimes fully embracing this ideal are largely the creation of the Enlightenment, beginning in the eighteenth century. But the idea of equal human dignity and radical human equality is planted here. Like an unpopped kernel of popcorn, the whole result is present in embryo.

16. It is true that the Law given at Sinai does not forbid polygamy, despite the evident tensions in bigamous households—between wives and between their offspring—that cry out from the stories in Genesis (for example, Sarah and Hagar [and Isaac and Ishmael] and Rachel and Leah [and Joseph and his brothers]). The kings of Israel will later practice polygamy, Solomon on a massive scale. And the principle of honoring father and mother is, technically, compatible with polygamy: Jacob had four wives, but each son had only one mother and father. But I stand by my suggestion. The elevation of woman *as mother* to a position of respect equal to that of her husband as father is already a critique of regarding women merely as sexual objects. Also, a careful analysis of Leviticus 18, which forbids the many incestuous unions, shows that God's Way for Israel—devoted to transmission of a covenantal way of life—demands clarity of lineage and definite responsibility for children, desiderata best supplied by monogamous marriage.

17. In the famous "love test" in Act I, Scene I, of *King Lear*, Cordelia, Lear's youngest daughter, refuses to say how much she loves her father: "I love your majesty according to my bond, no more nor less." Prodded by her father to "mend your speech a little," she explains: "Good my lord,/ You have begot me, bred me, loved me. I/ return those duties as are right fit,/ Obey you, love you, and most honor you." According to Cordelia, duty requires her to obey her father for begetting her, love her father for "breeding" (that is, rearing) her, and honor her father for loving her. In speaking in terms of her filial duties, Cordelia sees herself under obligation to her father, as the Decalogue teaches. But she has a non-Israelite understanding of the *ground* of the honor

she owes—seeing it as mere payback in "exchange" for love received. Moreover, her speech to her father "no more nor less" seems (at least to this reader) to fall far short of what honoring him requires.

18. Dan Polisar suggests, in a private communication, that honoring parents is also the key to counteracting fratricidal hatred. As evidence, he points out that Joseph (eventually) treats his brothers well not out of brotherly love, but principally out of re- gard for his/their father. Likewise, Judah took responsibility for his brother Benjamin not because he liked him, but because of his concern for their father. We return to this point at the end of this chapter.

19. For a fuller analysis of these passages in the Garden of Eden story and of its complex account of human sexuality, see my *The Beginning of Wisdom*, Chapter Three, "The Vexed Question of Man and Woman: The Story of the Garden of Eden (II)."

20. See my *The Beginning of Wisdom*, Chapter Seven, "Paternity and Piety: Noah and His Sons."

21. Twisted parent–child relations are the theme of other Genesis stories: the incest practiced by Lot's (unnamed) daughters upon their father Lot, whom they made drunk for the purpose; Jacob's deception of his father Isaac in stealing the blessing intended for Esau; Reuben's supplanting his father in an incestuous liaison with Jacob's concubine, Bilhah; the brutal, mendacious, and near-patricidal dis- play of Joseph's bloodied coat to Jacob; and perhaps also Joseph's near-patricidal in- difference to his aged father's heartache, when he steals Benjamin away from Jacob for himself.

22. There is much more evidence to support this reading. Back in Genesis, dur- ing the covenant between the sacrificial pieces, God had told Abraham that it would be four hundred years before his people could inherit the Promised Land: "And in the fourth generation they shall come back hither; for the *iniquity ('avon) of the Amorite is not yet full*" (Gen. 15:16; emphasis added). The Amorites, Abraham is told, will be cast out of the land in the fourth generation because of their swelling iniquity—a perfect example of the Lord's promise (or threat) to "visit the iniquity ('avon) of the fathers onto the children unto the third and *fourth generation* of them that hate Me" (20:5; em- phasis added). Later, in Leviticus 18, right after issuing the commandments against incest and other abominable sexual practices, the Lord explicitly says that it is *these* practices that defiled the land: "And the land was defiled, therefore I did visit the iniq- uity thereof upon it, and the land vomited out her inhabitants" (Lev. 18:25). He goes on to say that if Israel defiles the land by the same practices, the land would vomit them out also "as it vomited out the nation that was before you" (Lev. 18:28). A mere five verses later, in the passage quoted in the text above, God reasserts the principle: "Fear/revere every man his mother and his father" (Lev. 19:3). (My thanks to Richie Lewis for point- ing the way to this interpretation.)

23. The triad of Life, Wife (or Marriage), and Property should be compared to the three foundational natural rights made famous by John Locke—Life, Liberty, and Property—that, suitably altered by Jefferson (Pursuit of Happiness instead of Property),

became the bedrock of American political thought. What might it mean, in the long run, for a society to treat liberty rather than marriage as one of its inviolables? We may soon find out.

24. The King James translation, "Thou shalt not kill," is thus misleading. The Hebrew word "to kill," *h-r-g*, differs from *r-ts-ch*, "to murder."

25. This injunction is a modification (by delimitation) of the Noahide law that addressed all homicide, without regard to questions of justice: "Whosoever sheds man's blood, by man shall his blood be shed; for in the image of God made He man" (Gen. 9:6). Marking an advance over the anarchic "state of nature" where might made right, the Noahide law taught that bloodshed must be avenged, a life for a life (but no more than a life for a life, and the life only that of the killer). The new principle at Sinai, though still esteeming human life most highly, by contrast countenances self-defense and capital punishment (see the ordinances, discussed in the next chapter): life is an enormous good, but justice may be higher.

26. In Deuteronomy, Moses's repetition of this injunction reads: "You shall not bear *vain* (*shav'*) witness against your neighbor" (Deut. 5:17; emphasis added). *Shav'* is the word God used to proscribe lifting up the Lord's name *in vain*.

27. Later in Exodus, when the Lord tells the Israelites that they must three times a year go up to the Lord (presumably at the Tabernacle) with their sacrifices, He reassures them that "no man shall covet (*yachmod*) your land when you go up to appear before the Lord your God three times a year" (34:24). "Coveting" in this context clearly means not just desiring but also *acting* to *seize* the land, and also likely the women and children, while the man is away sacrificing.

28. Offering additional evidence to support the crucial importance of the principle against coveting, Nathan Laufer calls attention to its "foundational" place on the engraved structure of the Decalogue: "The command [against coveting] appears at the bottom of the second table because it is its 'foundation stone': adherence to the four commands above it on that table rest on adherence to it. On the first table, the bottom command—honoring of one's father and mother—can also be seen as the foundation upon which the four commands above it rest: one's parents are the source of learning about the obligations owed to one's creators—both the Creator God and one's biological creators" (personal communication).

29. This is a classic case of synesthesia, a condition in which the object of one sense (say, sound, by hearing) is simultaneously perceived by one or more additional senses (say, by sight or smell). Translators and commentators notice this peculiarity, but try to make it go away by translating *ro'im* not as "saw," but as "perceived." They therefore miss the text's important clue to the people's state of soul.

30. Richie Lewis has perceptively suggested (personal communication) that these verses may be describing the people's reaction *during,* and not only *after,* the enunciation of the Decalogue. If true, it would make clear both that and why they heard nothing of the words.

31. In the episode of the golden calf (see Chapter Twenty).

32. The categories of "hierarchy" and "equity" are Aaron Wildavsky's; they complete the four "regimes"—after "slavery" and "anarchy"—that he follows through the biblical account of Israelite politics. See Wildavsky, *Moses as Political Leader*.

33. We will revisit the purpose of sacrifices when we come to the discussion of the Tabernacle, especially in Chapter Eighteen.

34. The prohibition against uncovering of nakedness uses the same language that will later be repeated at length in Leviticus 18 (the centerpiece of the Holiness Code), to describe all the many forbidden (incestuous) sexual unions: "You shall not uncover the nakedness of. . . ." The present final warning seeks to prevent the intrusion of immodesty and sexual activity—common among the Canaanites into whose land they are coming—into Israelite forms of worship. Later, in describing the clothing of the priests in the Tabernacle, the priests are told that they should wear drawers to cover their naked flesh that "shall reach from the loins to the thighs" (28:42).

FOURTEEN Ordinances for God's New Nation

1. The scholars derive this name from Exodus 24:7: "And he [Moses] took the book of the covenant (*sefer habberith*), and read it aloud to the people." I will have more to say soon about both groups of interpreters and about the adequacy of reading these materials purely or even mainly as "law" and of regarding them as intended primarily for judges deciding cases.

2. At the same time, we note that they appear to be part of a *larger* whole of divine instruction, comprising in addition the directives regarding the Tabernacle (given later in Exodus) and the so-called holiness code (presented in Leviticus). Traditional readers also add Moses's repetition of the law in Deuteronomy. One should consider why this portion (the ordinances or *mishpatim*), and this portion only, is presented at this juncture.

3. There are other less complete Mesopotamian legal collections, among them the laws of King Lipit-Ishtar of Isin and the laws of Eshnunna, an Amorite city-state, both from the nineteenth century BCE. There are also later tablets of Hittite law. Unfortunately, we have no available evidence of written Egyptian law, the law that would have been most familiar to the Israelites at Sinai, and against which they would likely have assessed the Lord's ordinances. For a succinct discussion of these ancient Near Eastern laws in relation to the ordinances of Exodus, see Nahum Sarna, *Exploring Exodus: The Origins of Biblical Israel* (New York: Schocken, 1996), Chapter 8, "The Laws: Exodus 21–24," and Moshe Greenberg, "Some Postulates of Biblical Criminal Law," in *Yehezkel Kaufmann Jubilee Volume* (Jerusalem: Magnes Press, Hebrew University, 1960). An English translation of the Code of Hammurabi is available online: http://oll .libertyfund.org/titles/hammurabi-the-code-of-hammurabi. Readers who wish to consult all the codes will find them translated in J. B. Pritchard, ed., *Ancient Near Eastern Texts Relating to the Old Testament*, 3rd ed. (Princeton University Press, 1969), and more recently in Martha T. Roth, *Law Collections from Mesopotamia and Asia Minor*, 2nd ed (Atlanta: Scholars Press, 1997).

4. The need for such governing law, we should also recall, was made plain by the events and discussions of Jethro's visit, discussed in Chapter Eleven.

5. I thank Richie Lewis for this insight.

6. These biblical scholars also believe that the core of the Book of the Covenant was already in existence before the Exodus and was inserted here in the narrative, perhaps to give it divine backing.

7. For example, the handful of verses about the goring ox get two and a half chapters in *Bava Kamma,* one of the talmudic tractates, in *Nezikin,* the order on "Damages."

8. In doing so, I more or less follow (albeit in a nonprofessional way) the practice of scholars interested in biblical law as law, considered apart from its role in Jewish (rabbinic) law and historical practice. See, for a classical treatment, David Daube, *Studies in Biblical Law* (Cambridge: Cambridge University Press, 1947). As already noted, I differ from most of these scholars in that I do not read the ordinances legalistically or only for their manifest content, but as part of the unfolding story of Israel's national formation in relation to the divine—and hence also for their political, educational, rhetorical, and spiritual significance.

9. Actually, He "continues," without break, from where we so rudely interrupted Him. In His previous sentence (reported at 20:23), the Lord completed His instructions about the altars with an injunction against building stairs in order to avoid the exposure of nakedness.

10. We will return to this question in the next chapter, when we consider Exodus 24:3, 4, and 7. The use of the verb "place," *sim,* for the presentation of any law occurs only one more time in the Torah, in the famous passage that precedes Moses's "Second Discourse," his repetition of the law: "And this is the Torah which Moses placed (*sam*) before the Children of Israel when they came forth out of Egypt" (Deut. 4:44).

11. Readers of these ordinances should be alert for other uses of the second-person singular, the standard form in the Decalogue but most uncommon in the ordinances. Why might a given law speak of "you," rather than of "one" or "a man" or "he"?

12. This general principle will soon be qualified by the addition, "unless chosen."

13. For a discussion of how and why the Torah embraces (only) a *gradual* evolution of the Law toward its primary intention, not demanding too much at first of human nature, see Maimonides, *Guide of the Perplexed,* III.32. Maimonides speaks there mainly about the laws concerning sacrifices and idolatry, but the principles are more widely applicable.

14. Cassuto, *A Commentary on the Book of Exodus,* 13 and 265–266. Another distinguished biblical scholar, Brevard S. Childs, elaborates the point in a more complicated and nuanced way, winding up with a somewhat ambiguous (though tentatively opposite) conclusion: "Recent study has made it clear that the term does not designate an ethnic group, but tended to be a pejorative designation of a legal or social status within the Ancient Near Eastern society of the second millennium. The Hebrews were the disadvantaged peoples, which were considered inferior and were employed in menial laboring jobs. In some thirty occurrences of the term in the Pentateuch the term

applies to the 'Hebrews' either in contrast to the Egyptians . . . or [later] in contrast to the Philistines. . . . This would imply that a term which once was used to designate the outsider had been accepted by the Israelites, at least for a time. In the later period the Hebrew slave became identified with the Jewish slave (Jer. 34:9). But already in Ex. 21:2 the term was losing its wider connotation and becoming identified with the Israelite. The contrast lies between being a Hebrew and a 'foreigner' (21:8)." Brevard S. Childs, *The Book of Exodus: A Critical, Theological Commentary* (Louisville: Westminster Press, 1974), 468.

Many (but not all) traditional Jewish interpreters hold that *'ivri*, "Hebrew," is an ethnic classification and always means "Israelite," one who descends from Ever, the descendant of Shem (Gen. 9:14–17). Its first usage in the Bible was in the account of the war of the kings (Gen. 14), where Abram is referred to as "Abram the Hebrew": Did this mean a "descendant of Ever" or "from across the river"?

15. The Lord will later make the point explicitly, at least regarding the Israelites: "For unto Me the Children of Israel are servants (*'avadim*); they are My servants (*'avadai*) whom I brought forth out of the land of Egypt: I am *Y-H-V-H* your God" (Lev. 25:55).

16. The traditional commentators are at pains to discover who such a woman might be. They conclude that she must be a non-Israelite slave, seeing that (as we will shortly learn) Israelite women ("daughters") enter into servitude (only?) as partners for the master or for his son—and should she displease the master, she is to be redeemed, rather than given to another. But from this conclusion, these same commentators are bothered by the fact that the ordinance endorses giving a non-Israelite wife to an Israelite indentured servant. I understand how they get to these questions, and I acknowledge their importance, but they do not arise from the plain sense of the text, which seems to be interested in the question of freedom versus family, not with the ethnicity of whom to marry. I might add that, to this point in the Torah, there has been no law or teaching about marriage (including issues of monogamy or polygamy or the permissibility of partners outside the covenantal community).

17. This case revisits the confrontation between Jacob and his father-in-law Laban, whom Jacob had served for twenty years, seven years for each of his two wives, Leah and Rachel (his "wages"), and six more for his flocks. When Jacob at last steals away with his burgeoning family to avoid a coming confrontation, Laban pursues him, and the two men argue out the justice of who belongs to whom. In a final failing effort, Laban asserts, "The daughters are my daughters and the children are my children and the flocks are my flocks, and all that you see is mine" (Gen. 31:43). Lest anyone conclude that the Lord now sides retroactively with Laban, we note, among other differences, that Jacob was Laban's nephew, not only his servant, and that Laban gave him his *daughters*, not his slave girls, and explicitly as his wages for service. Still, the case is close enough to shed light on the current ordinance, as we will see again soon.

18. Rashi (on 21:6) offers a couple of specific explanations along these lines: "What is the reason that the ear had to be pierced rather than any other limb of the *servant's* body? Rabban Jochanan ben Zaccai said: That ear which heard on Mount Sinai (20:13),

'Thou shalt not steal' and *yet its owner* went and *stole and was therefore sold as a slave—* let it be pierced! Or, in the case of him who sold himself *from destitution, having committed no theft, the reason is:* That ear which heard on Mount Sinai *when I said,* (Lev. 25:55) 'For unto Me the Children of Israel are servants' and *yet its owner* went and procured for himself *another* master—let it be pierced!" *Pentateuch: Exodus,* 108b (emphasis added).

19. Genesis has already presented two relevant cases. When Abraham's servant comes to Paddan-aram seeking a wife for Isaac, and finds the wonderful Rebekah at the well, her father and brother (Bethuel and Laban) decide to give her to him *without even consulting her.* After accepting the great bridal gifts from the servant, her brother and mother plead for delay in her departure, but Abraham's servant insists on leaving straightaway. Only then do they ask Rebekah whether she will go—meaning, "go *now.*" In one word, she answers, *'elekh,* "I will go" (Gen. 24:32–61). In the next generation, when Jacob appeals to his wives Rachel and Leah to leave with him before their father Laban makes trouble, they answer: "Is there yet any portion or inheritance for us in our father's house? Are we not accounted by him strangers? For *he has sold us,* and *has also quite devoured our price*" (Gen. 31:14–15; emphasis added).

20. No reason or motive is given for why she is sold. Plausible ones include payment of debts, personal gain, and a wish to improve his daughter's station in life. From the point of view of the text, however, the father's reasons and motives are irrelevant; what matters to the Lord and to the law is instead how she should be treated once in the master's house. The entire discussion also helps make clear why there is no separate ordinance about *sons* sold into service; they fall under the general case of the male servant who goes to labor and (therefore) goes out after six years.

21. The woman here is not given a writ of divorce, as will be a married woman who displeases her husband, owing to some indecency (infidelity or other) that she has committed. See Deuteronomy 24:1–4.

22. There is ambiguity about "these three things." Some commentators (including Abravanel and Cassuto) believe that they refer to the food, raiment, and conjugal rights mentioned in the previous verse—a verse, by the way, from which the Rabbis would later derive the primary duties of a husband to his wife. But most traditional exegetes and most modern scholars, emphasizing the verb *ya'aseh,* "do," think they refer to the deeds mentioned in the prior "if" clauses: if he does not keep her for himself, if he does not espouse her to his son, and if he does not allow her to be redeemed, should she displease him. If he fails to do all three, she goes out free, without ransom.

23. From learning what deeds deserve the ultimate punishment, we will discover something about what God and the Torah most esteem. Indeed, the entire order of the civil law—the sequence of topics considered—will illuminate the priorities the Torah assigns to the various human goods. We will return to this point later, after we have gone through the ordinances.

24. For an extensive discussion of the Noahide code, both in itself and in relation to the lawless antediluvian world, see my *The Beginning of Wisdom,* Chapter Six, "Elementary Justice: Man, Animals, and the Coming of Law and Covenant."

25. In the Code of Hammurabi, even unintentional homicide is punished by death. The need to take intention into account places great responsibility on judges, and the Rabbis develop extensive teachings on how they are to assess this matter.

26. Perhaps to overcome any resistance to invading holy places and to make sure that this unprecedented teaching impresses itself on the Israelites, the Lord puts this injunction in the second-person singular: you, yes *you*, should go into the sanctuary and bring this murderer to justice.

27. The stem *qll* is the antonym of the stem *kbd*. With respect to weight, the former means, "to be light"; the latter, "to be heavy." With respect to honor, the former means "to treat lightly"; the latter, "to treat as weighty or important." *Kabbed* was the word translated as "honor"—"treat weightily"—in the Decalogue's injunction to honor your father and your mother. Although the likely meaning here is "to curse" or "to call down evil upon" the parents, the range of meanings invites the suggestion that other forms of serious disrespect and contempt may also be capital offenses.

28. For example, the Code of Hammurabi prescribes cutting off the hand of anyone who strikes his father. It says nothing about striking one's mother.

29. Against the simple (or simplistic) and harsh reading, the rabbinic tradition wisely says that, for the offense to be capital, the blow must have been severe enough to bruise the parent (the Mechilta and Tractate Sanhedrin 85b). (My thanks to Nathan Laufer for pointing this out.) Readers interested in this general question should visit the case and trial of Dmitri Karamazov.

30. Recall that the first time Moses—and the reader—met any Hebrew slaves in Egypt they were either being beaten by an Egyptian taskmaster or fighting with each other (2:11–13). The verb used here for "strike," *nakkah*, was also used there in both cases.

31. We imagine, of course, that judges will hear and consider testimony about provocation, initiation, fault, premeditation, malice, and other aspects of the quarrel and that these matters may influence their judgment in the case. But it is striking that the ordinance, to teach the principle, focuses entirely on bodily harm and the need to compensate the one harmed.

32. My thanks to Bill Frucht for the central ideas of this paragraph.

33. It is from this passage, the first such formulation in Israelite (rather than Noahide) law, that Maimonides will later derive the principle of capital punishment for murder. *Mishneh Torah,* Book of Damages, Laws of Murder and Protecting Life, 1:1.

34. The analysis of these cases owes much to a commentary on the slavery ordinances written by a contemporary Israeli rabbi, Rav Elchanan Samet, available at http://etzion.org.il/en/slavery. He and most traditional rabbinic commentators also hold that these two ordinances apply to all bondmen and bondwomen, whether Israelite or foreign. Their identity is not specified, and the expression "he is his money" would seem to imply that the servant may not be covered by the law that requires manumission in the seventh year. The last ordinances in this section, treated shortly, will return to actions involving such slaves, where their unqualified humanity is even more strongly affirmed.

35. There is also an issue of responsibility, tied to a grammatical issue of many and one: *men* strive together and strike a pregnant woman (both verbs plural), but only "*he*"—who is that?—shall be fined. Taking off from this textual difficulty, and exploiting an unusual translation of *'ason,* Raymond Westbrook, a distinguished scholar of Jewish law, produced a remarkable and ingenious interpretation of this entire passage, emphasizing the question of whether one knows or does not know who caused the harm. Although I am finally not persuaded by his interpretation, I recommend it to the reader's attention. Raymond Westbrook, "Lex Talionis and Exodus 21:22–25," *Revue Biblique* 93, No. 1 (January 1986): 52–69. (I thank Richie Lewis for bringing it to my attention.)

36. Rashi, for example, interprets "no mischief" as "*no further mischief* with the woman," adding that the violator pays the husband for the lost child. *Pentateuch: Exodus,* 113. Cassuto, in contrast, interprets it as "the woman and the children do not die." *A Commentary on the Book of Exodus,* 275.

There is a further possible complication: the Septuagint (the Greek translation of the Hebrew Bible) starts from a Hebrew original that has *'ishon,* "little man," in place of *'ason,* "harm." As a result, the Septuagint reads the first part of this case as a miscarriage of an unformed fetus, and the second part (where there *is 'ishon*) as a premature delivery of a fetus bearing the human look—and its death becomes a murder. (I owe this last observation to Richie Lewis.)

37. Rabbinic commentators are divided on this point: one agrees with our reading, and another says that he pays only monetary damages, because even if he intended to kill the man who was fighting, *her* death was unintentional (Tractate Sanhedrin 79a). (I am grateful to Nathan Laufer for pointing this out to me.)

38. Readers may notice and object that several items in the list illustrating the *lex talionis* would hardly apply to the case under consideration. How would the woman be burned or suffer stripes (with a whip) from brawling men? The likely explanation is that the long list of identical paybacks was probably a stock formula used precisely to convey the idea of "measure for measure" and that one automatically gets the whole chorus whenever the principle needs to be invoked.

39. We notice that these ordinances thus tacitly criticize young Moses's first question to the brawling Israelites, "Why do you smite your neighbor?"—the question that drew down on him the harsh rejoinder, "Who made you a man ruler and judge over us?" (2:13–14).

40. I am indebted to Yuval Levin for some of the formulations in these last two paragraphs. There may also be a rhetorical reason for these concessions to human bloody-mindedness. We recall again that this entire legal package is part of the covenant on offer to the Children of Israel, for their approval. It must therefore speak in ways that they can understand and accept. They would hardly be willing to accept a law that, for example, meted out capital punishment merely for brawling or that insisted that one should turn the other cheek, rather than retaliate, against one who strikes you on the cheek (see Matt. 5:39).

41. See the footnote early in this chapter that gave examples of the horrendous bodily mutilations that masters in the Ancient Near East would perform on their slaves.

42. Recall the way that God informs Cain about how He learns of Abel's murder: "Thy brother's blood cries out to me from the ground" (Gen. 4:10). Blood, which is the life, belongs only in living bodies; the earth should be moistened only with water.

43. For example, in the Code of Hammurabi, the upper-class owner who, suitably warned, fails to tie up or cut off the horns of his goring ox, will pay monetary damages should his ox gore the *son* (nothing is said about a daughter) of another *upper-class* person. In the Code of Eshnunna, the owner of a known-to-gore ox must pay monetary compensation if he, having been warned, failed to cut off the ox's horns and the ox later kills a man.

44. The rabbinic tradition characteristically softens the punishment for the owner. It interprets "he shall be put to death" as referring (only) to a possible *heavenly* punishment. Because he was guilty (only) of negligent, not of intentional, homicide, they hold he cannot be executed (relying on Num. 35:31). Thus, according to the next verse, he *always* can redeem himself with money. Our interpretation, closer to the surface of the present text, holds that failure to take precautions with a habitual gorer is the equivalent of willful complicity in the death and hence is capitally liable. But it sees in the ordinances an opening to judicial *discretion:* yes, as a matter of principle, he deserves to die, but taking into account all the circumstances, you judges are *permitted* to soften the sentence and may even do so in most cases.

45. Two reasons support such a reading, one formal, one substantive. First, from the start of these ordinances, the general pattern in each series of cases is a primary case, introduced by the term *ki,* "when," followed by a series of modified cases, each one introduced by the term *'im,* "if," with each new case understood to be a variant on the *original.* In the present set of cases—oxen that gore and kill human beings—the primary "*ki*" case involves an ox not known to gore habitually, but that nevertheless fatally injures a man or woman. There, the ox is stoned, and the master pays no further fine or punishment (21:28). Our present case of the ox fatally injuring a *bond*man or *bond*woman is introduced by *'im;* compared with the primary case, the sole difference is that the owner must now also pay the slave's master for the loss of the slave's services (21:32). Second, I noted earlier the radical ordinance that demands the *life* of the master who beats to death *his own* slave. Why, then, is the willfully negligent owner of a known-to-gore ox capitally responsible for the death of adults and children, but not answerable with his life for the death of slaves? One way to avoid this inconsistency is to suggest that the ox in the last case is *not* one of the known-to-gore variety. (The more traditional way of avoiding this inconsistency is to hold that the death penalty was never—or almost never, save in the most egregious of cases—actually imposed and that judges would almost always allow ransom; in this case, the thirty shekels constitute such a fixed ransom.)

46. See, for example, Exodus 23:5 and 23:12, discussed in my next chapter.

47. For a rich discussion of these matters, see Greenberg, "Some Postulates of Biblical Criminal Law."

48. The transitional link, both substantive and linguistic, is provided by the recent mention of oxen and asses and by the harm that the animals suffer from the thief.

The Israelites, before their enslavement to Pharaoh, had been shepherds in a largely agricultural society; before Israel's descent into Egypt, the patriarchs had been nomadic shepherds. The future economy in the Promised Land has yet to be explicitly specified, but as several of the ordinances imply, it is likely to be agricultural.

49. We note that the homeowner is not enjoined or encouraged to kill the nocturnal thief; he is merely exempted from the customary capital punishment for homicide, owing to the danger to his life that he might reasonably believe he faced. The thief is not being punished; rather, the owner is protecting himself.

50. The highest standard of compensation ("the best") is also mandated by the fact that it is often impossible to assess how much lasting damage a field trampled by a beast has suffered, beyond what is visible at the time of the trampling. (I owe this suggestion to Nathan Laufer.)

51. The ordinance does not say that he must make restitution from "the best" of his field and vineyard. Two possibilities: either that stipulation is implied, carried over from the previous case of damage caused by an animal, or the kind of restitution demanded here may be from less than the best, owing to the lesser degree of responsibility for damage caused by the accidental character of the spread of wildfire.

52. Rashi, citing the Talmud, glosses this proviso with an example: "if the owner of the ox is not *employed* with the borrower in his work (*B. Mets.* 95b)." *Pentateuch: Exodus,* 119a.

53. Actually, there is one more ordinance, the last of the casuistic ones, that is usually included here with the civil law: the ordinance about the seduction of an unbetrothed virgin (22:15–16). For reasons that will become clear in the next chapter, I choose to take it up as a transitional introduction to what comes next.

FIFTEEN Beyond Civil Law, Beyond Justice

1. These matters will be taken up in Leviticus, in the so-called holiness code, and also in Deuteronomy.

2. Verse 15 begins with "And," implying that the Lord Himself thought this ordinance was in some way connected with the preceding one(s).

3. These matters are not specifically dealt with until Deuteronomy 22:23–29.

4. If unable to pay a monetary bride-price (*mohar*), the would-be husband must find some other way to pay for the privilege of marrying the woman. Such was the situation of the patriarch Jacob. Laban made him work seven years for Leah and seven more years for Rachel: if you want to marry my daughter, my impecunious nephew, you must pay the price in labor.

The only other use of the term *mohar* in the Torah occurs in the story of the rape of Dinah by Shechem, the prince of Shechem (Gen. 34), and there is little doubt that the present ordinance has that story in mind. After having humbled her, Shechem tries to make matters right with her family: "And Shechem said unto her father and unto her brothers: 'Let me find favor in your eyes, and what you shall say unto me I will give. Ask me never so much bride-price (*mohar*) and gift [to the family], and I will give according as you shall say unto me; but give me the damsel to wife'" (Gen. 34:11–12).

The offer was refused. Two of Dinah's brothers avenged the rape by slaughtering all the men of Shechem. (Later, the Deuteronomic law dealing with the rape of an un-betrothed virgin will speak not of a dowry but of a fine payable to the father; the man *must* marry the woman without possibility of divorce—to our ears, a terrible arrangement, although one that gives social and economic stability to an otherwise unmarriageable [because abased] woman.)

5. Nothing is said about the age of these virgins. But we should remember that they could be—and often likely were—very young girls. In the Ancient Near East girls were often betrothed by the age of eight or nine, and there are reports of marriages being consummated by intercourse at even younger ages. According to Rashi, the matriarch Rebekah was only three years old when she married Isaac, an idea that strikes us as most unlikely. For his calculation, see his commentary on Gen. 25:20. *Pentateuch with Targum Onkelos, Haphtaroth and Rashi's Commentary: Genesis,* tr. Rev. M. Rosenbaum and Dr. A. M. Silberman (New York: Hebrew Publishing Company).

6. The paradigmatic situation is the story of the rape of Dinah, the only story in Genesis about daughters. Readers of the present ordinance should keep all aspects of that story in mind.

7. The economic approach also provides a peaceful alternative to violence and revenge. Dinah's brothers refused to take a bride-price and instead slaughtered all the men of Shechem to avenge the violation of their sister.

8. This Jacob did not do with Dinah. On my reading of the Dinah story, he bears much responsibility for what happens to her. For a full discussion, see *The Beginning of Wisdom,* Chapter Sixteen, "Politics and Piety: Jacob Becomes Israel."

9. The apparent link is probably logical, but it is also linguistic: the antecedent ordinance (22:15–16) spoke of a seducer who lies (*shakhav*) with an unbetrothed virgin. Verse 17 deals with (among others) a woman (for example, like Jezebel) who will use her wiles to seduce a man to false gods; verse 18 speaks about men who lie (*shokhev*) with beasts.

10. My grouping of the three verses does not follow the Tradition. The Masoretic text gathered the first two ordinances together, but treated the last—about sacrifices—as the first of the following group. Instead I follow Cassuto, who groups the three ordinances together not only because they all impose the death penalty but especially because "they are all connected, directly or indirectly, with idolatry and its usages. All three ordinances are connected, therefore, with the hard struggle waged by the religion of Israel against the worship of idols." Cassuto, *A Commentary on the Book of Exodus,* 289. Going beyond Cassuto, I will try to show the logical interconnections *among* the three enjoined practices, as well as the link between the third one and the things that come next.

11. The famous witch of Endor, whom Saul prevails upon to summon the ghost of the dead prophet Samuel, is not called *mekhashefah*, but *'ov*, a necromancer or wizard, one who communicates with the dead.

12. Blood and frogs were the only two plagues that the Egyptian sorcerers and magicians could imitate. Turning life-sustaining water into blood is obviously deadly; less obviously, an infestation of *amphibians* is in fact the epitome of chaos. In the account of Creation (Genesis 1), order arose by the principle of distinction. Dry land was separated from the waters, and the living creatures were assigned their uniquely fitting habitat: fish in the sea, birds in the air, land animals (and man) on the earth. There were no boundary-crossing creatures. As we shall shortly see, the importance of observing the cosmic distinctions is crucial to the Israelite idea of holiness. See also in my *The Hungry Soul*, the chapter on the Jewish dietary laws, "Sanctified Eating: A Memorial of Creation."

13. A partial justification for this turn to Canaan, admittedly taken out of textual order, comes from the Torah's only other use of the term sorcerer, *mekhashef*: "When you come into the land which the Lord your God gives you, you shall not learn to do after the abominations of those nations. There *shall not be found among you* any one that makes his son or his daughter to pass through the fire, one that uses divination, a soothsayer, or an enchanter, or a *sorcerer* (*mekhashef*), or a charmer, or one that consults a ghost or a familiar spirit, or a necromancer. For whosoever does these things is an *abomination* (to'evah) *unto the Lord;* and *because* of these abominations the Lord your God is driving them out from before you. You shall be *whole-hearted with the Lord your God*" (Deut. 18:9–13; emphasis added).

The passage treats the sorcerer (male) in the context of (other) "abominations" unto the Lord, for which He will drive the Canaanites out of their land—abominations that Israel is told it must *permanently* keep out of the Promised Land. (We shall soon take up the subjects of "abominations" and their elimination from the land, and the related subject of idolatry.)

The next two apodictic statements here in Exodus also clearly point to the iniquities of Canaan.

14. According to the *Tseror Hamor*, a biblical commentary by the fifteenth-century Spanish rabbi Avraham Sabba, the sorceress is not herself a seducer, but a person with magical aphrodisiac potions that can assist a man in his (thus-far) failed attempts at seduction. (My thanks to Nathan Laufer for pointing this out to me.) But whether as seducer or as aide to seducers, the sorceress seems to be especially connected with matters sexual.

15. Knowledge of "nature"—this is the first known use of "nature" in all of Greek literature—is the remedy for willing dehumanization. It appears to function like the Bible's "awe-fear-reverence of/for the Lord."

16. The story of Jezebel is told in the books of Kings (beginning in 1 Kings 16). She comes to a gruesome end. Just before her death, Jehu, the man responsible for killing her, tells the king, Joram (Jezebel's son), why she must die: "And it came to pass,

when Joram saw Jehu, that he said: 'Is it peace, Jehu?' And he answered: 'What peace, so long as the *harlotries* (*zenune*) of your mother Jezebel and her *sorceries* (*ukheshafeha*) are so many?'" (2 Kings 9:22; emphasis added). It is important to note that the charge against Jezebel was made not in a legal court but only here, by her executioner.

This is therefore an appropriate place to add that there is no basis, either in Jewish texts or in later Jewish tradition, for using this ordinance in Exodus to persecute women as "witches" (or as possessed by devils), as was often done in Christendom during medieval times and even later (the Salem witch trials took place in Massachusetts at the end of the seventeenth century). Jewish sages early on denied the existence of demons and the efficacy of so-called witchcraft, and there are no known legal cases in Judaism where someone was judicially convicted of sorcery.

17. Additional support for the notion that women may seduce and "bewitch" men toward idolatry comes in a later passage in Exodus (34:11–17), after the episode with the golden calf. Repeating His warnings about the Canaanites, the Lord concludes, "Lest you make a covenant with the inhabitants of the land, and they go astray after their gods, and do sacrifice unto their gods, and they call you, and you eat of their sacrifice; and you take of their daughters unto your sons, and their daughters go astray after their gods, and *make your sons go astray after their gods*" (34:15–16; emphasis added).

18. In the Bible's first creation story (Gen. 1), man and the terrestrial animals are both created on the same day, but man is distinguished from them (only) by being "in the image of God"; that is, by being "god*like*." For an extensive discussion of the biblical account of the articulated order of the world and the special place of the human being within it, see my *The Beginning of Wisdom*, Chapter One, "Awesome Beginnings: Man, Heaven and the Created Order."

19. Renamed more neutrally in our day as "zoophilia," it is apparently practiced by significant numbers of people in modern Western societies, with multiple websites for enthusiasts. It even has attracted ethical defenders, among them Princeton's Peter Singer, who regards opposition to bestiality to be irrational, the product of a mistaken anthropocentrism. This denial of a uniquely human dignity is precisely the attitude that the Bible is opposing in these ordinances.

That most people today are still disgusted by even the idea of bestiality—and I apologize for dwelling on it so long—is the result of centuries lived under this biblical teaching. But this disgust had to be culturally taught: that bestiality has to be condemned in the strongest possible terms should be taken as evidence that human beings are not *naturally* repelled by the idea. Far from it.

20. Cassuto, *A Commentary on the Book of Exodus*, 290.

21. "*THIS, at last,* is bone of my bone and flesh of my flesh" (Gen. 2:23; emphasis added). For an extensive discussion of the biblical anthropology of human sexuality (uninstructed), see my *The Beginning of Wisdom*, Chapter Three, "The Vexed Question of Man and Woman: The Story of the Garden of Eden (II)."

I am not alone in attributing sexual significance to man's first encounter with the animals. A midrash has it that Adam had intercourse with each of the animals, one by one, but was unsatisfied (*Yebamoth 63a*). Rashi, putting it more delicately, says that the man complained that each of the animals already had a tender mate, but that he had none. It was this complaint, reflecting newly awakened desire, that led immediately to the creation of woman (*Pentateuch: Genesis,* commenting on Gen. 2:20).

22. It can be argued that such a charge—like the very name "bestiality"—is an insult to the animals and that the human proclivity toward sex with animals reflects the liberation of desire from the constraints of animal instinct that is one of the fruits of human reason. Just a few sentences after Aristotle, in the *Politics*, declares that man alone among the animals has *logos* (speech and reason), he adds that "separated from law and justice, he is the worst of all the animals" and that "without virtue he is the most unholy and most savage [of the animals], and the worst with regard to sex and eating" (Book I, Chapter ii, at 1153a 31–36)—by which I take it he means incest, bestiality, and cannibalism. It is only *human* sexuality that becomes what Freud called "polymorphously perverse."

23. Sorcery will be called "an abomination unto the Lord" in Deuteronomy 18:9–13, quoted in Note 13. Bestiality will be cited as an abomination in Leviticus 18, the chapter on forbidden unions, the avoidance of which is a central part of the so-called holiness code.

24. For an excellent discussion of the concept of abomination in relation to moral theory, see Jeffrey Stout, *Ethics After Babel* (Cambridge: James Clarke & Co., 1988), Chapter 7, "Moral Abominations." Stout's analysis suggests that an abomination is an object, event, or act that transgresses boundaries that define and protect a culture's view of cosmic and social order. Like the Torah, Stout understands that different cultures, drawing boundaries differently, abominate different things. Unlike the Torah, he does not undertake to judge among them.

25. In two places in Numbers (21:2 and 21:3) and in five places in Deuteronomy (2:34, 3:6, 7:2, 13:16, and 20:17), the verb is used to describe the complete and utter destruction of the Canaanite cities, leaving nothing for spoils or plunder. *Charam* is what Saul would later refuse to do to the Amalekites, for which disobedience he lost his kingship.

26. In our prosperous cosmopolitan age, enjoying easy and widespread international travel, we modern readers, especially in Western countries, have trouble even imagining the dangers foreigners face at the hands of the natives, should they take up residence in countries not their own. We are shocked when one of our nationals living abroad is harassed or imprisoned for no reason other than xenophobia. But the biblical view of the perils had plenty of company in the premodern world. The ancient Greeks made a big point about the importance of hospitality, precisely because they understood that it was not the uninstructed human way. They regarded Zeus (the ruler of the gods, in his capacity as Zeus Xenios) as the protector of strangers and beggars, who were absolutely in need of his protection. And the folk teaching that one should treat a stranger kindly because he just might be a god in disguise was in fact an acknowledgment of the precariousness of not being in your own home: it can only be by divine assistance that sojourning people are kept alive at all. (I owe this last suggestion to Amy Kass.)

27. See, for example, Exodus 23:9, Leviticus 19:34, and Deuteronomy 10:19.

28. We recall Mel Brooks's 2,000-year-old man, describing the first national anthem: "Let them all go to hell except for cave 76."

29. The connection is made explicit in Deuteronomy when Moses retells the story of the giving of the law and summarizes the divine teachings: "He [the Lord] does execute justice for the orphan and the widow, and loves the stranger, in giving him food and raiment. Love you [plural] therefore the stranger; for you were strangers in the land of Egypt" (Deut. 10:18–19).

30. The Torah does not talk at all about gifts of money to the poor, and in the society envisioned here there is not yet the giving of alms or charity. Instead, there are agricultural gifts of *food* (the leavings of the harvest) and there are *loans* of money. The latter one expects to be paid back.

31. See, for example, Isaiah 8:21–22: "and it shall happen that, when they shall be hungry, they will be enraged, and will curse by their king and by their God; and whether they turn their faces upward, or look unto the earth, they behold distress and darkness, the gloom of anguish, and outspread thick darkness." The precise formulation in this passage is not *exactly* on target, for it speaks of cursing *by* their king and *by* God, rather than of cursing *them*. But no direct object of the curse is mentioned, and it seems that the people are blaming the powers that be—in heaven and on earth—for their miserable condition.

32. Cassuto argues that the lapidary formulation of these injunctions suggests that they reflect a more ancient and known tradition, found elsewhere in the Ancient Near East, instructing both the priests of the local temples and the shepherds, herdsmen, and farmers who work on the temple estates about the proper order of the offerings to the gods. He cites Hittite law that gives such instructions in great detail and that prescribes the penalty of extinction for the entire household of anyone who transgresses this commandment. Cassuto, *A Commentary on the Book of Exodus*, 294.

Readers of Genesis may recall that in the story of Cain and Abel, containing the account of mankind's first offerings to the divine, God favors the offerings of Abel who offered the "*firstlings* of his flock." Cain is not said to offer the *first* fruit.

33. Partly from this injunction, the rabbinic tradition would later derive humane and respectful rules of slaughter. For an extended discussion of the meaning of the Noahide code and covenant, see my *The Beginning of Wisdom*, Chapter Six, "Elementary Justice: Man, Animals, and the Coming of Law and Covenant."

34. For an extended philosophical exploration of the meaning of eating, from nature to culture, see my *The Hungry Soul*, especially Chapter Six, "Sanctified Eating," which includes a discussion of the dietary laws of Leviticus in the context of the Bible's views of eating.

35. The Lord will later make the point most explicitly: "You [plural] shall do no unrighteousness in judgment; you [singular] shall not respect the person of the poor, nor favor ("defer to"; *tehdar*) the person of the mighty; but in righteousness shall you judge your neighbor" (Lev. 19:15).

36. The word for "false" in that formulation is *shaqer*, but when the Decalogue is repeated in Deuteronomy, *shav'* is used instead: "Neither shall you bear false witness (*'ed shav'*) against your neighbor" (Deut. 5:17).

37. The citations for *chamas* are Genesis 6:11, 13; for *rasha'*, Genesis 18:23, 25. In the remaining uses, *chamas* is used by Jacob to name the cruelty of his sons, Simeon and Levi (Gen. 49:5), who slaughtered all the men of Shechem to avenge the rape of their sister; and *rasha'* is used to describe one of the street-brawling Hebrews whom Moses addressed on his second day outside Pharaoh's palace (Ex. 2:13). The new echoes of the antediluvian violence and the Flood extend the allusions we noted at the end of the last section in discussing not eating like dogs; the echoes of Sodomite wickedness toward strangers extend the allusions we noted in the discussion of how to treat the stranger (*ger*); the echo of the story of the brawling Hebrews reminds us that fighting is universally the (uninstructed) proclivity of men. In addition, the word *riv*, here translated as "dispute," was used but once in Genesis: "And there was a strife (*riv*) between the herdsmen of Abram's cattle and the herdsmen of Lot's cattle" (Gen. 13:7), which strife was settled only because Abram decided to separate from Lot and offered Lot the first choice of land.

38. Bill Frucht asks, "Could these ordinances be about episodes of political hysteria? Are they warnings not to listen to demagogues, join violent mass political movements, or spread what we now call fake news?" (personal communication).

39. A profound discussion of this counterintuitive point appears in the *Nicomachean Ethics* during the discussion of beneficence (ix.7). In examining why the benefactor loves the recipient more than the recipient loves the benefactor, Aristotle argues that the benefactor's deed—and therefore also the benefactor—"lives" in the recipient. Since everyone loves (his own) "being," and since the doer *exists* in his deeds, which (in the case of generous deeds) now reside in the recipient, the recipient becomes, in a sense, the benefactor at work. The love one usually feels for oneself extends also to one's neighbor *as a result of* acts of beneficence.

40. Actually, Cassuto, using a very strange translation of the word *'evyon* in the next verse, claims that the Lord makes this point explicitly: "You shall not pervert the judgment (*mishpat*) due to *your adversary* (*'evyonekha*) [instead of "your poor"] in his dispute [at law]." As far as I can determine, *'evyon* is always translated as "poor," and the Brown-Driver-Briggs lexicon does not give a single entry where the word means "adversary." But the usually careful Cassuto suggests that we have here a noun (elsewhere unattested in Hebrew) derived from a different stem, *'b(h)*, meaning "to refuse, be unwilling" in other Semitic languages. Hence, he interprets the noun as "opponent" or "adversary," a synonym for the earlier "enemy" and "one who hates." Cassuto supports this reading with several arguments: we have just had an ordinance about not perverting judgment due to the poor; in addition, the second-person pronominal suffix, "your," makes little sense if applied to "poor." Finally, in a textual structure in which the ordinances arrive fairly cleanly divided into groups of three, an ordinance about "your adversary" would perfectly complete the triad—"your enemy," "one who hates you," and "your adversary." See Cassuto, *A Commentary on the Book of Exodus*, 298. I

find this alternative reading very attractive, but I cannot find the linguistic evidence to support the translation on which it rests.

41. This is, of course, not the Torah's last word on this matter. Later, in Leviticus, the Lord summons the Israelites to "Be ye holy, as I the Lord your God am holy" (Lev. 19:2), and details multiple facets of such holiness. In the context of injunctions that echo the ordinances we are discussing here (including exhortations against false swearing, corruption in judging, and rumor mongering), the Lord extends the points made here. He opposes smoldering resentments, taking revenge, and grudge bearing, and (famously) enjoins *love* of neighbor: "You shall not hate your brother in your heart; you shall surely rebuke your neighbor, and not bear sin because of him. You shall not take vengeance, nor bear any grudge against the children of your people, but you shall love your neighbor as yourself: I am *Y-H-V-H*" (Lev. 19:17–18).

42. The verb translated "release" is *shamat,* from which is derived the name for the sabbatical year for the fields, *shemittah.* It is still reckoned in the modern state of Israel and observed by not a few of its farmers.

43. This passage, which appears in the context of the injunction about the Jubilee year, continues: "You shall neither sow your field nor prune your vineyard. That which grows of itself of your harvest you shall not reap, and the grapes of your undressed vine you shall not gather; it shall be a year of solemn rest (*shenath shabbathon*) for the land. And the Sabbath produce of the land shall be for you [plural]: for you [singular] and for your manservant and for your maidservant, and for your hired servant and for the strangers (*gerim*) who dwell with you" (Lev. 25:4–7). We shall have occasion to point out other differences between this "repetition" and the original passage in Exodus with which we are here concerned.

44. In contrast, the comparable passage in Leviticus, quoted in Note 43, says that the Sabbath yield shall be food for *him*—and for his servants and his strangers, all those under his roof. The poor and the wild beasts are not mentioned.

45. The latent question about sustenance in the *shemittah* year is taken up explicitly in the expanded discussion in Leviticus. God speaks about saving for the future, but if asked, He will provide the needed extra produce: "And if you shall say: 'What shall we eat the seventh year? Behold, we may not sow, nor gather in our increase'; then I will command My blessing upon you in the sixth year, and *it shall bring forth produce for the three years.* And you shall sow the eighth year, and eat of the produce, the old store; until the ninth year, until her produce comes in, you shall eat the old store. And the land shall not be sold in perpetuity; *for the land is Mine;* for you are strangers and settlers with Me" (Lev. 25:20–23; emphasis added). Our passage in Exodus ignores the problem, because it must be interested in making a different point.

46. Cassuto, *A Commentary on the Book of Exodus,* 301.

47. Here is the full passage. The context is the comparable teaching about the manna, the first experience of sabbatical desisting: "And you shall remember all the ways which the Lord your God has led you forty years in the wilderness, that He might afflict you, to prove you, to know what was in your heart, whether you would keep His commandments, or not. And He afflicted you, and suffered you to hunger, and fed you

with manna, which you knew not, neither did your fathers know; that He might make you know that man does not live by bread alone, but by every thing that proceeds out of the mouth of the Lord does man live" (Deut. 8:3).

48. Such, for example, was the self-understanding of the Egyptians who, during the seven lean years, were compelled to sell themselves into bondage to Joseph and Pharaoh: "Why should we die before your eyes, both we and our lands. Buy us and our land for bread, and we and our land shall be bondmen ('avadim) to Pharaoh" (Gen. 47:19).

49. Robert Alter points out the connection between the verb *nafash,* meaning "to breathe" and translated here in the passive as "be refreshed," and *nefesh,* "soul," the breath of life in a living creature; he connects both of these with the idea of a laborer panting from his work and rest as providing a long-wished-for deep breath of relief (Alter, *The Five Books of Moses,* 450). Hebrew readers will also hear in this term an echo of the phrase "soul (*nefesh*) of the stranger," which appeared but a few verses earlier (23:9). As I will suggest shortly, in the present context, it is a pregnant term.

50. As we will see in Chapter Twenty, no sooner does He stop repeating it than the people fall into idolatry.

51. Some scholars believe that the Canaanites also had a spring festival of flatbread (unleavened cakes); they read verse 15 as meaning "*That* festival, you *also* shall keep it," but, in your case, for an entirely different reason. The early summer festival of first fruits will later be called the Festival of Weeks (34:22); much later, it will be associated with the giving of the law at Mount Sinai—the event now on stage. The autumn harvest festival will later be called the Festival of Booths (or "Tabernacles"; Sukkot), said to commemorate the transient dwellings that the Lord made the Israelites occupy during their years of wandering after exiting Egypt (Lev. 23:42–43). For a wonderful treatment of these holidays in the Jewish liturgical calendar, tying the holidays to Israel's explicit encounters with the Lord during the "honeymoon" first year of her existence, see Laufer, *Rendezvous with God.*

52. The two *different* Hebrew words appearing in these verses that are translated "times," *regel* and *pa'am,* in the first instance both mean "foot." The first is more restricted to the anatomical foot; the second refers also to the "tap" of the foot—hence, the relation to "time," as measured by marking time and tapping of feet. It is a lovely touch to begin the call for pilgrimages with the mention of "feet," *regalim.*

As for the festivals' social purpose, Maimonides comments, "They are also useful in the establishment of friendship, which must exist among people living in political societies." *Guide of the Perplexed,* III.43.

53. However, when this injunction is revisited, in the renewed covenant after the episode with the golden calf, the connection with Passover is made explicit: "You shall not offer the blood of My sacrifice with leaven; neither shall the sacrifice of *the Feast of Passover* remain all night until morning" (34:25; emphasis added).

54. "No meal-offering, which you shall bring unto the Lord, shall be made with leaven; for you shall make no leaven, nor any honey, smoke as an offering made by fire unto the Lord" (Lev. 2:11).

55. Readers of Genesis may wonder whether this may tacitly be a comment on the meal offered by Abraham to the three men (later revealed to be angels) when they came to his tent: "And Abraham ran unto the herd, and fetched a calf tender and good, and gave it unto the servant; and he hastened to dress it. And he took curd, and milk, and the calf that he had dressed, and set it before them" (Gen 18:7–8). But although he mixed milk and meat—the calf was served with cow's milk and curd—nothing was said about *boiling* the calf in its mother's milk. Abraham clearly offered his honored guests the best he had; but, in contrast to the putative Canaanite practice, there was no effort at culinary delicacy or luxury in his preparation.

56. Cassuto, *A Commentary on the Book of Exodus*, 305.

57. This reading, which I do not finally support, has the singular merit of making sense out of the people's later speech and deeds, when Moses does not come down from the mountain after forty days and forty nights. When they see that Moses has disappeared, they demand that Aaron make them gods *"who shall go before us"* (32:1), who would henceforth lead them in Moses's stead to the Promised Land.

58. We are reminded of the surprise that Abram felt when, promptly answering God's call and going to possess the land of Canaan to which the Lord had sent him, he discovered, as the text says wryly, "And the Canaanite was then in the land" (Gen. 12:6). Why, who else would you expect to be in the land of Canaan? It was precisely at this point that the Lord appeared to reassure Abram, promising him (for the first time) that *this* was indeed the land that He would give to Abram's seed—which is to say, not to Abram. That promise is here being renewed, but the Canaanites are still in the land, now ready to be removed.

59. My thanks to Richie Lewis for the main ideas of this paragraph. The Lord will make the point more explicitly, some forty years later, when Israel arrives at the Jordan River, ready at last to enter the land. Speaking to Moses, He says, "Speak unto the Children of Israel, and say unto them: 'When you pass over the Jordan into the land of Canaan, then you shall drive out all the inhabitants of the land from before you, and destroy all their figured stones, and destroy all their molten images, and demolish all their high places. And you shall drive out the inhabitants of the land, and dwell therein; for *unto you have I given* the land to possess it. . . . But if you will not drive out the inhabitants of the land from before you, then *those that you let remain shall be as thorns in your eyes, and as pricks in your sides, and they shall harass you in the land wherein you dwell*. And it shall come to pass, that as I thought to do unto them, *so will I do unto you*'" (Num. 33:51–56; emphasis added).

60. The only other use in Exodus of this verb, translated as "panic," occurred when God panicked the Egyptians, just before they drowned (14:24); the only other use in Exodus of the noun *'emah*, translated as "terror," occurred in the Song of the Sea, right after the boast that "all the inhabitants of Canaan are melted away": "Terror and dread fall upon them; By the greatness of Your arm they are still as a stone; Till Your people pass over, O Lord" (15:16).

61. Some scholars, especially those devoted to source criticism, suggest that the present verses were inserted later, to deal with the seemingly embarrassing fact that it

took more than two centuries for the Israelites to finally conquer the land and to realize the divine promise. This allegedly retroactive qualification allows God to remove the embarrassment. Perhaps. But in keeping with our way of reading, we accept the text as it exists, and we will look—successfully, as it happens—for reasons *within* the text to explain the announcement of delay.

62. This insight I owe to Cassuto, *A Commentary on the Book of Exodus,* 309.

SIXTEEN Strange Goings-On

1. I was further encouraged along these lines by Robert Sacks's remarkable essay, "The Life and Death of Aaron the Priest."

2. Not everybody reads this as an addendum to the ordinances. Partly because the verb "said," *'amar,* is in the perfect form, Rashi, for one, claims that this command to Moses was in fact given much earlier, before even the Decalogue was pronounced, and that it refers to Moses's original ascent on the mountain. But my own reading of this speech does not depend on *when* it was uttered: the important linkages to what came before, and to what comes after, are more *logical* than chronological. Thus, this opening charge to Moses and his associates may function even as a thematic chapter heading for the events next to be described.

3. Nadab and Abihu were mentioned only once before, in the genealogy of Moses and Aaron (6:23). We wonder why the Lord summons by name (only and both) *these* two sons of Aaron, for he has four sons. If the idea was to choose the eldest, then only Nadab should be summoned. We happen to know, from reading ahead (Lev. 10:1–2), that Nadab and Abihu, in a wild and zealous act, will offer strange fire before the Lord and will be destroyed for doing so. Thus, we cannot help thinking that their presence and conduct in the present episode may contribute to their future misconduct and fate. In addition, their presence may also shed light on two themes, considered much earlier, that hover over our present scene: brothers and the risk of fratricide, and the iniquities of fathers visited upon their children.

4. I owe this suggestion to Nathan Laufer. I will return to it later.

5. "All that Y-H-V-H has said, we will do" (19:8).

6. And only the second instance of writing in the Torah. The previous mention of writing occurred after the battle against Amalek, when God commanded Moses to "write (*kethov*) this down in the book (*bassefer*)" (17:14).

7. This is the first time the word "tribe," *shevet,* has been used in Exodus. Its only previous use was in Jacob's final blessings of his sons (Gen. 49).

8. See our earlier discussions of the problematic character of the human impulse to sacrifice, in Chapter Seven (the section, "Fundamental Regulations: Sacrificing, Eating, and Procreating") and in Chapter Thirteen (the section, "Reactions on the Ground and the Need for Sacrifice"). For a full analysis of the problematic sacrifices of Cain and Noah, see my *The Beginning of Wisdom,* Chapter Four (the section titled "Sacrifice: Pride or Submission?") and Chapter Six (the section titled "The Ambiguous Sacrifice: Man's Evil Inclination").

9. Trying to make sense of the choice of the young, several commentators suggest that they are in fact the firstborn of each household, who were (again, according to the commentators) ipso facto the priests of the people, household by household, before the sin of the golden calf, after which they were replaced by the Levites (see Num. 3:12–13). In addition, Nathan Laufer suggests (personal communication) that (following Nachmanides's view that sacrifices are meant to substitute for the people who offer them) the sacrifices brought here by the firstborn are meant symbolically to redeem *themselves* from the Lord, to Whom they have been said to belong. This is an interesting reading, but there is nothing in the plain text to support it. Nothing is said about the firstborn (of each household), and many a firstborn would no longer be a youth.

We also note, but know not what to make of them, certain echoes—but with pointed differences—of the story of the binding of Isaac. Abraham, *following the Lord's command,* arose early in the morning (same words) to offer a burnt offering (same word); he brought along youths—also *ne'arim*—but they were told to wait below the mountain while Abraham and Isaac went up to offer sacrifice, whereas here they perform the sacrifices; Abraham built the altar (same words) on top of the mountain, whereas Moses builds it below. Moses "knows" from the start to sacrifice animals; Abraham learns this only at the end—although he too offers the ram (in place of the spared Isaac) without being told to do so. In the sequel, we will hear that the Lord stretched not out His hand against the "nobles" on the mountain after they "saw God"; Abraham was told by the angel not to stretch out his hand against the lad (*na'ar*) in a place named "The Lord Sees." Could the text be hinting that Moses, acting on his own, is out of step with Abraham and with God? Finally, we file away for later the possibility that Aaron's sons, Nadab and Abihu, might have been among the youths whom Moses sent to offer sacrifices to the Lord.

10. To anticipate: when the Lord provides His plan for the Tabernacle and the sacrifices that are to take place within it, the divine words become the frame and wrapping, and the blood is shed and animals offered only under divine order and measure. We take up this matter more fully in the next chapter.

11. There are other views. For example, Rashi regarded it as those books of the Bible—Genesis and the first half of Exodus—that report events up until the giving of the Law at Sinai. Rashi, *Pentateuch: Exodus,* 24:7. Alternatively, Cassuto favors the option of it being just a short general document confirming only the original terms of the covenant: that the people undertake to listen to the voice of the Lord and to keep His covenant (19:5), and that, in return, the Lord will take them to Him as a treasure among the peoples of the earth, and they will be to Him a kingdom of priests and a holy nation (19:5–6). Cassuto, *A Commentary on the Book of Exodus,* 312–313.

12. Against this reading, it will be pointed out, correctly, when the Lord (in Leviticus) prescribes how the priests should place blood on the altar (and when the priests do as the Lord had prescribed), the *same* verb, *zaraq,* there always translated "*sprinkle,*" is used. But that usage cannot be taken as evidence for what *Moses* does *here, uninstructed.* One might even suggest that the later practice of "sprinkling," commanded by God, was meant as a refinement or correction of Moses's less decorous strewing.

According to the Brown-Driver-Briggs lexicon, the verb *zaraq*, when its object is blood-in-a-bowl, is translated as "throw"; the biblical verse cited to illustrate this usage is our present one: "threw against the altar."

13. Alter, *The Five Books of Moses*, 456–457.

14. The burning bush, certainly a wonder, drew Moses's attention, but he approached it to *seek its cause*. It was the Lord's *spoken words* from out of the bush, not the spectacle, that moved Moses's soul and changed his life. As we discussed extensively in Chapter Three, this was the episode that elevated *hearing* over *seeing* as the Torah's preferred way of knowing—a matter to which we will shortly return.

15. Our analysis of this situation parallels our analysis of Miriam's leading the women in dance at the Sea of Reeds. There too we wondered whether a perfectly reasonable effort to enlist kinesthetic forms in support of the people's relation to God may have unleashed passions that could later lead the people astray.

16. *Ibn Ezra's Commentary on the Pentateuch: Exodus (Shemot)*, trans. and annotated by H. Norman Strickman and Arthur M. Silver (New York: Menorah Publishing, 1996), 524.

17. Quoted in Alter, *The Five Books of Moses*, 457.

18. Alter, *The Five Books of Moses*, 457.

19. Childs, *The Book of Exodus*, 506–507.

20. Readers who assume perfect obedience and fidelity on the part of the biblical characters—especially such notables as Moses, Aaron, and the elders—will likely say that the text does not *have* to mention that they prostrated themselves, because, of course, they did just as they were told. Such readers might even argue that the vision they were privileged to receive was a reward for their piety. Maybe so. But perhaps not. If Moses can be "inspired" to do things he was not told to do, cannot also the elders? More to the point, there are other things in the account that weigh against such an edifying interpolation and interpretation.

21. When, ten years ago, I read these three verses to an adult seminar on Exodus and asked what was going on, the first respondent—my wife—said: "It is as if they are on drugs." Never having used them, how could she have "seen" this so clearly?

22. In *chazah's* only previous use in the Bible, in Jethro's speech to Moses about finding judges, I translated it as "search out": "Moreover you shall search out (literally, 'see'; *chazah*) out of all the people able men, such as fear God, men of truth, hating unjust gain; and place such over them, to be rulers of thousands, rulers of hundreds, rulers of fifties, and rulers of tens" (18:17). This kind of "seeing" would involve seeing things that are invisible. How easily and accurately do we "see" such things? Do we not sometimes "see" only that which we imagine? The same question can also be raised about the more ordinary acts of seeing, denoted by the other verb, *ra'ah*; for example, in the Garden of Eden: "And the woman *saw* that the tree was . . . to be desired to make one *wise*" (Gen. 3:6; emphasis added). Was this really "seeing" or, rather, "imagining"?

23. Rashi, *Pentateuch: Exodus*, 24:10 (emphasis in original).

24. Nathan Laufer (in a personal communication) has offered a powerful interpretation of this episode, arguing that the vision is indeed a godsend. The premise of

his reading (a possibility already mentioned) is that God is, in this episode, mainly intent on shoring up Moses's credibility and authority with the people. And he makes a compelling case for the need to do so by rehearsing the many prior episodes of popular resistance to and rebellion against Moses's leadership. The Lord therefore summons the elders up the mountain, Laufer suggests, "not because He needs them to show obeisance to God or to bow down to or worship Him (what is the point of that?); but rather because He wants them to have precisely the vision that they have of God, to soak it up (what is meant by 'they ate and drank'), and to report back to the people with awe the amazing sight that they envision: 'Moses really does have a divine interlocutor at the top of the mountain. Why, we have seen him with our own eyes!'"

God does not strike the nobles down, Laufer continues, not because He is exercising forbearance in the face of their unanticipated misconduct, but "because of His over-riding agenda here: to make clear and strengthen, yet again, Moses's credibility as God's authentic messenger to the Israelite people. God is using these select people for His own purposes; there are no accidents here. It unfolds precisely as God knew it would."

As a "political" reading of these episodes, Laufer's interpretation is very attractive. But it abstracts from the "religious" focus of the narratives that immediately precede and follow: the (prior) warnings against Canaanite religion and the (forthcoming) elaborate instructions for the Tabernacle, the Israelite alternative that embodies a more elevated way for human beings to relate to the divine and establishes the fitting balance between awe and intimacy, distance and nearness, submission and elevation. In addition, we never hear later about the nobles or the elders coming to Moses's aid or boosting his credibility when the people again become restive. Moreover, in the sequel, the role of mediator between the people and God is taken away from the statesman Moses and turned over to the priests, to Aaron and his sons. A *visible approach* to the Lord will be provided in the Tabernacle, but only under measure, order, and divine instruction.

25. The root of the word translated "minister," *sh-r-th*, denotes high service, in contrast with *'eved*, a menial servant. It and its derivatives will be used nine more times in Exodus, once to again describe Joshua in relation to Moses (33:11) and the other eight times to refer to Aaron's service in the holy place (Tabernacle). We should be alert to these two very different "ministries."

26. Were we to continue the comparison with the story of the binding of Isaac, Joshua (Moses's eventual heir) would be in Isaac's place on ascending the mountain. But whereas Abraham after the event returned to his men alone, when Moses returns to the camp Joshua will again be with him.

27. This phrase, *kevod-Y-H-V-H*, "glory of the Lord," is generally understood to mean "appearance" or "manifestation" of the Lord to a human being—in our text, most often to Moses. One should not assume that such a "definition" has rendered the notion any less mysterious. What is the difference between the Lord and His "glory"? What, exactly, of "I-Will-Be-What-I-Will-Be" is becoming manifest to human eyes or

hearts or minds or souls? God only knows. (We will meet this again in Chapter Twenty-One, when Moses asks to be shown the Lord's glory.)

28. Cassuto, *A Commentary on the Book of Exodus*, 316.

29. This is triple the two days of preparation for the giving of the Decalogue given to the people before they encountered the Lord at the start of the revelations at Sinai (19:10–11).

SEVENTEEN "Let Them Make Me a Sanctuary"

1. Biblical scholars devoted to source criticism and the "Documentary Hypothesis" attribute this unexpected change of subject and style to the insertion of so-called priestly documents (P), which, among other things, are said to provide the priests with a biblical basis for their preeminence and rule. We, reading the text as an integrated narrative and intellectual whole, seek rather to discover *internal* textual and substantive *reasons* why the Tabernacle is necessary, why it appears where it does, why it is presented at such great length and in such detail, and what it contributes to the formation of the people of Israel.

2. Readers interested in pursuing these details and in getting help on some of the larger questions should consult the line-by-line commentary by Cassuto, *A Commentary on the Book of Exodus*, 319–406. See also Berman, *The Temple*, 21–56; Laufer, *Rendezvous with God*, 203–223; and Nehama Leibowitz, *New Studies in Shemot* (*Exodus*), trans. Aryeh Newman (Jerusalem: Haomanim Press, 1995), 459–548.

3. Actually, this is not quite accurate. In the lead-up to the Decalogue (Ex. 19), the Lord twice warns Moses to make sure that the priests (*kohanim*) should not break through to approach the mountain. We have no clear idea about whom He is speaking, seeing as no priests have been formally appointed. Traditional interpretation, on nontextual grounds, suggests that the priests at that stage were the firstborn sons in every household. Were that correct, there would have been upward of 100,000 priests—which is most unlikely.

4. To be precise, the building of the calf is not *literally*—but only *literarily* and *logically*—contemporaneous with Moses's receiving of the building plans. It begins only after Moses has been forty days on the mountain. But it occurs while and *because* Moses is detained on the mountain with God, learning about how to make the Tabernacle. The making of the calf therefore represents the *dramatic,* as well as *the* substantive, alternative to building the Tabernacle. The point is made by sandwiching it between the plans for the building (Ex. 25–31) and erecting the building according to plan (Ex. 35–40); see my discussion in Chapter Twenty.

5. For later comparison with the Tabernacle, we recall elements of the Babel story. A project of human reason, not of human wildness, it was founded on acts of bold and artful speech. The men first make bricks, from which they undertake to make a city and a tower with its top in heaven. Although they never rest from their labor, their project is never completed. They earn a name for themselves that means "meaninglessness," and none of the builders is individually known. Seeking to rival or control the

divine, they encounter God only when He descends to thwart their plans by confounding their speech; they never know Him. By contrast, the Tabernacle is founded on (God's) speech, measured and numbered; the pattern for it is in heaven, but it is brought down to earth; it is formed not from fired bricks, but from skins and cloth; the human makers, divinely inspired, will win individual fame for their (obedient) work. The Lord will descend not to destroy, but to dwell in their midst. Sabbath rest will be observed.

6. Let us recall also the sequence of events surrounding Noah's ark: violence over all the earth; building the divinely designed ark; drowning of the wicked with watery deliverance of a saving remnant in the ark; Noah's sacrifice; and the institution of the Noahide law for all humankind (Gen. 6-9). Here, in Exodus, we have the following sequence: violence in Egypt; drowning of Pharaoh's army and a watery deliverance of the Israelites at the Sea of Reeds; the Giving of the Law to Israel at Sinai; Moses's sacrifice and the elders' vision; Law for the divinely designed Tabernacle; the golden calf; and the actual building of the Tabernacle. And again, in (partial) chiasmus: in the first case, God's building project, Noah's uninstructed sacrifice, Noahide law; in the second case, Mosaic law, Moses's uninstructed sacrifice, God's building project.

7. Nathan Laufer has suggested a third guiding idea: the Tabernacle as a Palace for the Divine King. "If the people of Israel are to be God's 'kingdom of priests,' then God must be their king. The Ten Commandments and the ordinances that followed are the King's *law* to govern his kingdom; and the instructions for the Tabernacle are the instructions for the royal Palace in which His Presence would reside. If the command of the Sabbath was to create a 'Palace in Time,' then the command of the Tabernacle is to create a 'Palace in Space'" (private communication). There is much merit in this suggestion; it would explain the lavish expenditure and the need for detailed design, and it would enable us to see the priests as the king's courtiers. Also, as a metaphor, a "King's Palace" may be more accessible for twenty-first-century readers, who are likely to have trouble thinking about "God" "manifesting His Presence" in a "Sanctuary," to be mystically encountered by ordinary people. But we are more impressed with the way the Tabernacle *differs* from a permanent palace for a merely human monarch, beginning with its portability and concluding with its explicit purposes. We return to this subject in the final section of our last chapter.

8. Iron is excluded. Some commentators attribute its exclusion to iron's relative novelty, others to its use in weapons. The latter suggestion would echo God's earlier exclusion of *hewn* stones—presumably cut by the sword—from the making of any altars (20:21).

9. As Nahum Sarna points out, the verb translated "to dwell"

is not the common Hebrew stem *y-sh-v* [LK: used by Moses in the Song of the Sea] but the rarer *sh-k-n,* which . . . conveys the idea of a temporary lodging in a tent and characterizes the nomadic style of life. That is why the structure is called a *mishkan* . . . and why the verbal form is frequently used together with *'ohel,* the common word for "a tent," and in connection with nomads. The noun *mishkan* is often employed in synonymous parallelism with *'ohel,* and the other designations of the wilderness Tabernacle are the "Tent of the Pact [Covenant]" and the "Tent of Meeting." . . .

It functions to make perceptible and tangible the conception of God's immanence, that is, of the indwelling of the Divine Presence in the camp of Israel, to which the people may orient their hearts and minds. A postbiblical extension of this usage of the verb *sh-k-n* is the Hebrew term *shekhinah* for the Divine Presence.

JPS Torah Commentary: Exodus, 158.

10. There is a further ambiguity about the "who" of the construction. Although the Lord here clearly says that "they"—the people—shall build the Tabernacle, almost all the subsequent specific orders are addressed to Moses in the second-person singular: "And *you* shall make . . ." and "And *you* shall set . . ." Whether this means that Moses himself must do these things or, more likely, direct others in doing them is never made clear. The ambiguity does, however, serve to link Moses intimately with the people, more than he has been to this point and more than he has been inclined to be until now.

11. There is ample precedent in other ancient (including Ancient Near Eastern) societies for conveying astronomical lore in the images and proportions of religious shrines, available for the elite to discover. Archaeo-astronomers—students of the anthropology of astronomy—have shown how ancient building sites, like Stonehenge or Avebury in Britain, or the Great Pyramid in Egypt or the Mayan Palace of the Governor in the Yucatan, are aligned and structured in relation to risings of the sun and moon and the motions of the heavenly bodies. The Great Pyramid also embodies numbers and ratios related to astronomical phenomena. See, for example, Tompkins, *Secrets of the Great Pyramid.* No less a genius than Isaac Newton spent years looking for the secret scientific teaching embodied in the structure of Solomon's Temple. See Rob Iliffe, *Priest of Nature: The Religious Worlds of Isaac Newton* (Oxford: Oxford University Press, 2017). Might the *mishkan* be a portable Stonehenge—or, rather, a portable *anti*-Stonehenge?

12. The Babylonian towers, the *ziggurats,* were likely the place of astronomical observation: astronomy for the sake of astrology. The Babylonians were the first to measure the motions of the heavenly bodies, and they used that knowledge to guide their agricultural practices.

13. For a fuller discussion, see my *The Beginning of Wisdom,* Chapter Eight, "Babel: The Failure of Civilization."

14. When, beginning in Exodus 35, the construction actually begins, the order of manufacture will be reversed: the protecting "shell" of the Tabernacle will be made before the holy objects that get deposited inside.

15. The Ark will be 2.5 × 1.5 × 1.5 cubits (roughly 45 × 27 × 27 inches) in length, width, and height. (A cubit is the length of a man's arm, from elbow to tip of middle finger, approximately 18 inches.) Gold, we notice at the beginning, is going to be very

much in evidence; the word is used 105 times in the book of Exodus, 97 of them in connection with the sanctuary. The other eight mentions of gold occur in two parallel groupings of four: the first three refer to the jewelry that the Israelites receive from the Egyptians as they depart Egypt (3:22, 11:2, 12:35), and one occurs in God's warning against making (along with Him) gods of silver and gods of gold (20:20). The other four occur in the story of the golden calf; of the latter, the first three refer to golden earrings (32:2, 3, 24) used to make the calf, and the last occurs in Moses's report to God that the people have made them "gods of gold" (32:31). The alternatives are sharp and clear: either a golden sanctuary for God or golden "gods."

16. The word *kapporeth* is said by some to be derived from a Semitic root meaning "to cover"; others connect it to *kippur,* meaning "atonement"—as in *Yom Kippur,* the Day of Atonement, itself a "covering over" of sin and iniquity.

17. Perhaps the form was assumed to be known but not to be dwelt on, given that attention is called to the Ark below and the holy space opened up above. In Ezekiel's account of the Divine chariot (Ezek. 10:1–20), the cherubim are described as four-faced creatures (man, lion, ox, and eagle) that carry the chariot upon which rests the throne of glory. For present purposes, what they look like is unimportant; what dwells *above and below them* is all that matters.

18. For example, Don Isaac Abravanel, a fifteenth-century Spanish commentator asks, "How could He command them to do that which they had been specifically warned against?"

19. As we later learn of the sacrifices on the Altar, the offerings to the Lord are thoroughly burned, so that only the smell ascends. Libations are also poured, but only on the meat that is then thoroughly burned, and the wine vaporized. There is but a symbolic, not an actual, "feeding" of the Lord, by which rituals He is kept alive *for them.* In the Tabernacle proper, where the Table resides, there is not even a symbolic meal offered. (More on this later.)

20. In ignoring these details, we eschew speculation on the possible significances of the numbers, proportions, shapes, and colors involved, an interpretive project for another day.

21. Says Cassuto, "The altar, on which the sacrifices were offered, occupied a central cultic position, *and no shrine could possibly be without an altar.* It was *obvious* that in the Israelite sanctuary, *too,* there would be an altar; hence, from the very beginning, the word is used with the definite article." *A Commentary on the Book of Exodus,* 362 (emphasis added). Cassuto treats the sacrificial cult in Israel as an "obvious" instance of "us too." We are rather more inclined to treat it in the context not of Near Eastern history and culture, but of the Bible's long-standing explorations of the vexed human impulse to sacrifice, especially to a God Who does not "need" sacrifices. More on this later.

22. The precession of the equinox (roughly speaking: the changing place in the zodiac through which the sun rises on the day of the spring equinox, on or about March 20) from Taurus to Aries transformed the stellar calendar, in place for 2,160 years, no doubt with very disturbing cultural consequences. The Age of Aries, the Ram, con-

taining the birth of monotheism, was also the time of the rise of Israelite culture and religion. The destruction of the First Temple (587 BCE) takes place roughly two-thirds of the way through the Age of Aries. And that first two-thirds is again divided into thirds, punctuated by the Exodus from Egypt (around 1446 BCE) and the building of the First Temple (around 1000 BCE). The Age of Aries gave way to the Age of Pisces, Fishes, around the time of Jesus. (My thanks to Harvey Flaumenhaft for this tutorial in the importance of the astronomical transformations.)

23. John Ruskin, although a great admirer of the Tabernacle, recognized danger in the Tabernacle: the ex-slaves could associate its artistic splendor with the pagan gods they had seen worshipped in similar ways in Egypt. He wondered why God, ever inveighing against idolatry, "demand[ed] for Himself such honors, and accept[ed] for Himself such local dwelling, as had been paid and dedicated to idol gods by heathen worshippers."

> Was the glory of the tabernacle necessary to set forth or image His divine glory to the minds of His people? What! purple or scarlet necessary to the people who had seen the great river of Egypt run scarlet to the sea, under His condemnation? What! golden lamp and cherub necessary for those who had seen the fires of heaven falling like a mantle on Mount Sinai, and its golden courts opened to receive their mortal lawgiver? What! silver clasp and fillet necessary when they had seen the silver waves of the Red Sea clasp in their arched hollows the corpses of the horse and his rider? Nay—not so.
>
> There was but one reason, and that an eternal one; that as the covenant that He made with men was accompanied with some external sign of its continuance, and of His remembrance of it, so the acceptance of that covenant might be marked and signified by use, in some external sign of their love and obedience, and surrender of themselves and theirs to His will; and that their gratitude to Him, and continual remembrance of Him, might have at once their expression and their enduring testimony in the presentation to Him, not only of the firstlings of the herd and fold, not only of the fruits of the earth and the tithe of time, but of all treasures of wisdom and beauty; of the thought that invents, and the hand that labors; of wealth of wood, and weight of stone; of the strength of iron, and of the light of gold.

John Ruskin, *Seven Lamps of Architecture* (London: Smith, Elder, and Co., 1849), Chapter I, "The Lamp of Sacrifice," section VI.

EIGHTEEN "That I May Dwell Among Them"

1. Robert Alter astutely translates *ve'attah* in all three cases as, "As for you . . ." *The Five Books of Moses*, 471–473.

2. There is disagreement about whether the *Menorah* is lit twenty-four hours a day or only at night, with learned traditional authorities, citing textual passages, on both sides of the question. For those who say that the *Menorah* stayed lit round the clock, there is disagreement whether all the lamps stayed lit all day or only the westernmost one. If the purpose of the kindled light is functional, it is worth noting that the enclosed Holy Place would be dark also in the daytime, absent the lamp.

3. Please note (in v. 28:1) the two-by-two pairings of the sons, which anticipate their separate fates. Nadab and Abihu, the eldest pair, were present on the mountain with Aaron and the elders during the previous vision of the divine; they will be killed for overzealous performance of their priestly duties, offering strange fire before the Lord (Lev. 10:1–2). Eleazar will become the High Priest after Aaron dies, and Ithamar, the youngest, will play various supporting roles in the maintenance of the Tabernacle.

4. The Tradition mainly holds that humble Moses was simply delighted to allow his brother the limelight; in support, people point out that this portion of the Torah (*Tetsavveh*: 27:20–30:10) is the only portion of its last four books in which the name of Moses does not appear, a fact that they attribute to Moses's self-effacement for the sake of Aaron. But the same fact lends itself to an opposite interpretation: a foreshadowing of Moses's being eclipsed. One famous sixteenth-century commentator, Moshe Alshikh, recognized the problem of Moses's disappointment, though he thought that the Lord addressed it easily enough: "To comfort him and redress the balance God said: *Ve'attah*, 'Thou-thyself' i.e., you in person. Listen you, Moses: don't worry. It's all really you. You have a greater share in it than anyone. All fulfill themselves through you. . . . Your jealousy of the priestly role of Aaron and his sons is similarly ill-founded. Their achievement of this status is all your doing: 'thou-thyself bring Aaron near to thee.' Through your bringing near they will become worthy. Even the garments have no power to consecrate them as priests except through you." Quoted in Leibowitz, *New Studies in Shemot (Exodus)*, 526.

5. See Chapter Three, section titled "Moses Balks, Aaron Talks: Brotherhood and Rule." The reader is encouraged to reread those pages.

6. However, the Levite genealogy in Exodus 6 did more than hint to the reader—but not to Moses, who did not hear it—that Moses's line will die out and have no role in the Israelite future, while Aaron's line would rise to prominence. The mention of Aaron's sons—again by name—in the present passage reminds us of that future genealogical fact.

7. Consider further. The word "brother," in the singular, occurs only nine times in Exodus (after more than 100 times in Genesis), and four of those times are in this speech to Moses about the priestly garments. Earlier, in addition to the quoted passage about God's anger, Moses is twice told (7:1–2) that Aaron his brother will be his prophet before Pharaoh and will speak for him. Shockingly, the last two appearances of the word occur in Moses's call for fratricide after the golden calf—"slay every man his brother" (32:27); "every man upon his son and his brother" (32:29)—an episode for which his own brother Aaron was responsible and occurring *at the very time that Mo-*

ses is hearing about brother Aaron on the mountaintop. We are not wrong to keep this matter in mind.

8. And, while we are asking questions, why six? There will be later a *seventh* addition, the golden plate inscribed "Holy to the Lord," completing the visible picture with a specific reference to holiness—exactly like the hallowed seventh day, also Holy to the Lord.

9. The suggestion and formulation are Hannah Mandelbaum's.

10. People interested in seeing pictorial representations of, and in learning more about, the several priestly garments should visit the website of the Temple Institute, https://www.templeinstitute.org/beged/priestly_garments.htm.

11. Cassuto, *A Commentary on the Book of Exodus,* 379–380. Cassuto adds that the Bible is generally opposed to divination and therefore downplays the significance of the Urim and Thummim by saying almost nothing about them. He regards their presence at this early stage of people formation as a concession to the need of superstitious people to seek answers from the powers-that-be regarding all momentous happenings in their lives. And he points out that, after the time of King David, all allusion to these "objects" ceases altogether in the text, implying that people no longer came seeking such knowledge from oracles.

In support of Cassuto's interpretation, we note that the word "Urim" occurs only three more times (Lev. 8:8, Num. 27:21, Deut. 33:8) and "Thummim" only two more times (Lev. 8:8 and Deut. 33:8) in the Torah. And no case is presented where they are in fact used to render a decision or decide a course of action. (The seeming exception, in Numbers 27:21, can be shown not to be one, when one compares closely what was prescribed [Num. 27:18-21] with what was actually done [Num. 27:22–23].) In keeping with the downplaying of this activity, the end of the verse promptly drops the Urim and Thummim and refers back to the names of the Children of Israel: it is *they* and their *judgment* that will be on Aaron's heart when he goes in unto the Lord. (We will return soon, in the main text, to this question of their *judgment.*)

12. Private communication.

13. Here is the first explicit acknowledgment that being a priest is a dangerous business. There will be more on this soon.

14. The word *tsits* may come from a root, *natsats,* "to shine" or "to sparkle." It is, in every sense, the gleaming glory of the priest's attire, tied across his forehead.

15. These activities are discussed later, for example, in Numbers 18.

16. Cassuto, *A Commentary on the Book of Exodus,* 385 (emphasis in original).

17. Actually, the list of "the names of the Children of Israel who came to Egypt with Jacob"—with which the Book of Exodus began, and which is here echoed—already contains the clue of the disjunction: "And Joseph was in Egypt already" (1:6).

18. For an extended discussion of these matters, see Sacks, "The Life and Death of Aaron the Priest." "For the Torah, man is responsible for the ill effects of the conditions of his own existence, even though he may have in no way participated in their coming to be" (p. 259).

19. This too will be seen in the episode of the golden calf, featuring brother Aaron, soon to begin down below, and in our imaginations visible now, as it were, on the split-screen.

20. Ex. 39:28; Lev. 6:3, 16:4; Ezek. 44:18.

21. For example, among the Canaanites, an agricultural celebration of Sky Father's "impregnation" of Earth Mother (rain) was ritually reenacted by a having a woman taken sexually by a bull.

22. Everyone regards "fill their hands" as a metaphor for "install" or "consecrate," though the origin and the idea behind this image are uncertain. Cassuto says that the same idiom is found in Akkadian in the sense of "install," adding that the original meaning is "to fill the hands of the appointed person with the material for the work entrusted to him and with the tools required for executing it." *A Commentary on the Book of Exodus*, 386. But in the local contexts, we wonder whether the term might also have a more literal meaning, inviting us to look at what their hands are actually filled with, as they undertake their appointed office: in this case, the activity of sacrifice (and, also, de facto, the displacement of brother Moses). The idiom will recur with a shudder in the story of the golden calf, when Moses orders the Levites to kill their sons and brothers and, when they appear to have done so, to "fill your hands today for the Lord" (32:29; see Chapter Twenty) It is worth noting that those Levite hands will already have been filled before the actual *installation* of the priests, following the (mere) instructions presented here (reported in Lev. 8–9).

23. According to the Tradition, the person laying his hands on the animal should lean forward to the extent that, if the animal were to be removed away, he would fall down. The animal whose sacrifice will restore his owner's moral standing begins by literally holding him up bodily. (My thanks to Richie Lewis for pointing this out.)

24. This is the only use of the verb, *hizzah*, in Exodus, and the only time it is used with an imperative meaning in the Torah. Moses needs to be told to sprinkle, not throw, blood on people.

25. As noted earlier, this suggestion departs from the traditional understanding, which tends not to regard animal sacrifice as intrinsically problematic, seeing how much of it God (eventually) has commanded.

26. There is a tiny but significant difference between the Hebrew for "holiest holiness," *qodesh qodashim*—translated by others as "most holy"—and the physical place, "*The* Holy of Holies," *qodesh haqqodashim*: the presence of the definite article, *ha*, which indicates a thing, not a quality. However, while only the latter refers to a specific space, the crucial characteristic of supreme holiness they have in common. It is not a physical trait but a spiritual status. Both can be approached only by the High Priest. (Ordinary priests may have contact with the Holy; only the High Priest may deal with the Holiest Holy.)

27. The daily sacrifices join the daily lamp lighting and the showbread, as well as the daily offerings of incense (see Chapter Nineteen), as the quotidian duties of the priests. Working out the symbolic significance of this combination of daily rituals—

for example, as possible representatives of bodily life, light, food, and breath or soul—seems a potentially fruitful project.

28. I owe the fundamental insight of this paragraph and some of its formulations to Richie Lewis.

29. Robert Alter comments astutely: "One detects a certain tension between a conception of the sacred inherited from pagan cult and a new, monotheistic conception. According to the former, there exists an intricate technology of the sacred that confers holiness on a place and on the human officiants—the elaborate regimen of construction and dress and sacrifice and sprinkling with blood that has just been detailed. But now God reminds Israel that it is only through His glory, His free decision as deity to make His presence 'abide'—a nomad's term of temporary residence—in this place, that the Altar becomes consecrated. Without this divine initiative, all the choreography of the cult is unavailing. The manifestation of the 'glory' of the deity has polytheistic antecedents, though the strong emphasis on God's choice to abide in the midst of Israel is new." Alter, *The Five Books of Moses*, 483–484. To which we would add: the ritual practices, familiar to human beings everywhere, are not being copied, but rather employed to gradually redirect the human understanding of the character of the divine.

30. The point was made beautifully by Nachmanides, taking issue with Rashi on the reading of *leshokhni bethokham*, "to dwell among them": "But Rabbi Abraham Ibn Ezra explained [the verse to mean that] the purpose of My bringing them forth from the land of Egypt was only that I might dwell in their midst, and that this was the fulfillment of [the promise to Moses], *You shall serve G-d upon this mountain* [3:12]. He explained it well, and if it is so, there is in this matter a great secret. For in the plain sense of things it would appear that [the dwelling of] the Divine Glory in Israel was to fulfill a want below. But it is not so. It fulfilled a want above, being rather similar in thought to that which Scripture states, *Israel, in whom I will be glorified* (Isaiah 49:3). And Joshua said, [*For when the Canaanites . . . hear of it . . . and cut off our name from the earth,*] *and what wilt Thou do for Thy Great Name?* (Joshua 7:9)." Nachmanides, *Commentary on the Torah: Exodus*, trans. Rabbi Charles B. Chavel (Brooklyn: Shilo Publishing House, 1973), 506–507. The Lord God of Israel needs the recognition of His children for His living Presence in the world.

31. The latter prospect is made even more explicit in the description that follows the final completion of the Tabernacle, in the (almost) closing words of Exodus: "Then the cloud covered the Tent of Meeting, and the glory of the Lord filled the Tabernacle. And Moses was not able to enter into the Tent of Meeting, because the cloud abode thereon, and the glory of the Lord filled the Tabernacle" (40:34–35).

NINETEEN Beyond Animal Sacrifice

1. Although this altar has not been previously mentioned, "spices for the sweet incense" were on the list of items, mentioned at the beginning of the Lord's instructions, that the Israelites were asked to contribute for the Tabernacle (25:6). In Exodus

31, when summarizing the list of items that the artisans will produce, the Lord will list the Altar of Incense right after the Table and the Lampstand (31:8); later, when the text recounts the *construction* of the Tabernacle, the Altar of Incense will be included *with* the other items of furniture (Ex. 37)—all reasons to believe that its separated placement in *these* instructions is deliberate and significant.

2. The precise formula for composition of the incense is given in Exodus 30:34–36.

3. Here is the text: "And he shall take a censer full of coals of fire from off the altar before the Lord, and his hands full of sweet incense beaten small, and bring it within the veil. And he shall put the incense upon the fire before the Lord, that the cloud of the incense may cover the ark-cover that is upon the testimony, that he die not" (Lev. 16:12–13).

4. Traditional and scholarly commentators offer other attractive accounts of the purpose of the Altar of Incense, as well as the reason why it is not treated with the rest of the Tabernacle furniture. For example, Nachmanides says that the incense is burned for the glory of God, who has just made known that He will dwell among the Children of Israel: also, because incense "is of the attribute of justice," the burning of it checks the plague that the people have otherwise deserved. Nachmanides, *Commentary on the Torah: Exodus*, 507. Cassuto suggests that the description of the Golden Altar was not included earlier with the other Tabernacle furniture because it does not belong to God's "home," but rather to His worship *by humankind*. And he sees this paragraph as a lead-in to an account of the Tabernacle *service*, most of it to be given in Leviticus. *A Commentary on the Book of Exodus*, 390.

5. It will be the first of four additions to the instructions, to be followed by directions for the Laver, for the oil of anointment, and the spices for the incense, none of which we will discuss. (Each of these additions are preceded by the separating and framing remark, "And the Lord spoke unto Moses, saying" or, in one case, "And the Lord said to Moses.") The connections among these appear to be (at least with the first pair) more linguistic and moral, less logical and structural. All four paragraphs deal with guilt and atonement or the risk of death (or being cut off from one's people) for misconduct or both.

6. Recall that the contributions of materials for *building* the Tabernacle were voluntary and variable: each person would give as much as they wished. But once built, the assessments for *maintenance* of the Tabernacle will be compulsory and identical: each person contributes the same. The explanation for the latter is, as we say here, communal-political: each member's equal relation to God. It is also, as we will say soon, personal-spiritual: each person's equal need for atonement.

7. My thanks to Dan Polisar for the main ideas of this paragraph.

8. The verb *kafar*, "to cover over" or "to make atonement," is cognate with the noun *kofer*, "ransom." The difference between the two is subtle. One atones for some transgression; one pays ransom for one's life that would otherwise be forfeit for a transgression.

9. The ambiguity of census taking is conveyed also by the literal meaning of the Hebrew expression we translated as "taking the sum": "lift the head." Its only previous use came in Genesis, in the story about how Joseph interpreted the dreams of the chief butler and the chief baker, his fellow prisoners in jail. To both he predicted that in three days Pharaoh would "lift your head": but for the butler this meant being restored to his office, while for the baker it meant that he would be hung (Gen. 40). Having your head lifted in a muster for war invites thoughts about both kinds of "elevation."

10. This nervousness about census taking, so strange to our ears, was not in fact a peculiarly Israelite worry. According to Cassuto, in Mesopotamia the taking of the census was also thought to be dangerous, apparently because it implied a lack of faith in the deity; it was therefore tied to a religious ritual of purification. In fact, the entire census was named *tēbibtu*, "purification." *A Commentary on the Book of Exodus*, 394. Alter suggests that "assigning individuals in a mass an exact number set them up as vulnerable targets for malefic forces," and he cites the story of David's ill-fated census that triggered a plague (2 Sam. 24) in textual support of this idea. Alter, *The Five Books of Moses*, 486. But the ideas of ransoming *one's own* soul for *allowing* oneself to be numbered and doing so by contributions that will be used to support the Lord's sanctuary appear to be Israelite innovations. So too the ideas in the next paragraph.

11. Alas, there is apparently no etymological connection between *tsel*, "shadow," and *tselem*, "image," despite the fact that shadows are, famously in Socrates's image of the cave in Plato's *Republic*, the paradigmatic instance of "image" or "likeness." Still, the recognized pun would lead one to ponder such questions.

12. The expression *ruach 'elohim*, "divine spirit," has been used twice before in the Torah: at the beginning of the Creation, when the "*ruach 'elohim* hovered over the face of the waters" (Gen. 1:2), and in Pharaoh's attempt to explain Joseph's prophetic powers of dream interpretation ("Can we find one such as this—a man in whom is *ruach 'elohim*?"; Gen. 41:38). It will recur several times later in the Bible (for example, with Balaam and with Saul) to refer to the power of prophecy. The prophet *is* a prophet because he speaks in the name of God, infused with His spirit. The Lord here seems to be suggesting that the artist's inspiration to creativity is parallel to prophecy. The artist is closer to the prophet than to the priest. (I owe these observations and suggestions to Richie Lewis.) We will have occasion to return to *ruach 'elohim* in Chapter Twenty-Two, where the first of the two prior uses of the expression will be of paramount importance.

13. Cassuto, *A Commentary on the Book of Exodus*, 401–402.

14. This is the same unusual expression that appeared three times at the start of God's instructions about the appointment of brother Aaron and his sons to the priesthood and about the making of their garments (27:20, 28:1, 28:3); I suggested earlier that God was there addressing Moses's unstated interest in the question of his role in the Tabernacle (see the discussion of these passages and this usage in Chapter Eighteen). Here, by analogy, God may be addressing Moses's unstated concern about his role after he heard that it is Bezalel and his fellow artists who will be creating the Tabernacle.

15. Or like serving other self-serving "gods." In the Babylonian creation myth, *Enuma Elish,* the human beings were created to do all the work so that the chief god Marduk and the others might have rest. Only with *Y-H-V-H* is human service to the divine in the mutual interest of both. Both work, both rest—"the image" and "the Original."

16. The use of the infinitive construction in purpose clauses, as here "[in order] to know," leaves ambiguity regarding the subject: *Who* is to know, through Sabbath observance, that it is the Lord that sanctifies Israel? Traditional commentators do not agree. Rashi and Saadya Gaon hold that it is the nations of the world; Ibn Ezra argues that it means the Israelites themselves. In the present context, we incline to the latter view.

17. It is, of course, not obvious that Sabbath breaking, a "victimless crime," should even be considered in relation to these other severe "interpersonal" offenses. (Question: does bestiality count as an interpersonal—that is, ethical—offense?). Later Tradition would distinguish between offenses subject to both human and divine punishment (like murder and adultery) and offenses subject only to divine punishment (various so-called "religious" failings). But among the "religious" offenses, only Sabbath desecration—along with sacrificing children to Molech (Lev. 18:21)—was regarded by the Tradition as subject to *both human* and divine retribution. We will therefore try to see why human punishment might be in order for violating the Sabbath.

18. The singularity of the "making" that is Sabbath observance is paralleled by this literary fact: this is the only use of the expression, "to *make* the Sabbath, *la'asoth 'eth-hashabbath*," in the entire Torah.

19. The point is nicely made by Nehama Leibowitz who adds a lovely midrash supporting the idea that the relation between Israel and *the Sabbath* is also regarded as the relation between groom and bride: "R. Shimon b. Yochai taught: Thus the Sabbath addressed the Holy One Blessed be He (at the end of Creation): Lord of the universe! Everyone has a mate except me. Said the Holy One Blessed be He: The Congregation of Israel shall be thy mate. As soon as Israel stood at the foot of Mount Sinai, the Holy One Blessed be He said to them: Remember what I promised the Sabbath—the Congregation of Israel shall be thy mate. This is the meaning of the text: 'Remember the Sabbath day to keep it holy'" (Gen. Rabbah 11, 9). Leibowitz, *New Studies in Shemot (Exodus),* 540–541. We see here further evidence for the view that the story of the Tabernacle and its relation to the Sabbath should be understood in relation to the story of Creation, a point to which we will return thematically at the end, in Chapter Twenty-Two.

20. The root, *nefesh,* we translate as "soul," "that which breathes," in contradistinction to *basar,* "flesh." When God breathed the breath of life into a formed-clay earthling, "*adam* became a *nefesh,* a living soul" (Gen. 2:7).

21. Moses will in fact speak very soon afterward (a mere seven verses later in 32:7). It will take the episode of the golden calf, and God's retaliatory threat to destroy the Children of Israel, to incite speech in Moses's soul.

22. It bears emphasis that we are not told what is written on the tables. Tradition holds that it is the Decalogue, and there is later textual evidence to this effect in

Moses's retelling of the story (Deut. 10:4). But Moses, in his retelling, changes quite a number of things when recapitulating what transpired in Exodus; in doing so, he begins the tradition of the Oral Law, which adapts the written law to the special needs and circumstances of the times. At the present time, we have absolutely no idea of what was written on the original tables. From the text and context, a case can be made that the tables contain the instructions for building the Tabernacle, either alone or also with the ordinances and the Decalogue.

TWENTY The Covenant on Trial

1. This is, of course, a debatable inference. Ancient wisdom in moral matters holds that learning comes from doing, not the other way around; practice is the condition for understanding. (See, for example, Aristotle's *Nicomachean Ethics,* which argues that moral virtue arises from habituation in right conduct, adding that for those who know "the that" [right conduct], there is no need to add "the why" [1095b5–7].) For this reason, Jewish Tradition has celebrated this formula and the primacy of deeds, not words. But it would be a great stretch to attribute such understanding to the Israelite masses at Sinai. We therefore prefer our interpretation.

2. The consequences of violating the law and covenant are not announced until Leviticus 26:14–46.

3. Recall the following: Moses only reluctantly accepted the mission and then only with Aaron's help. He has shown impatience with the people for their slavish ways and lack of self-command. He speaks of the people always as "them" (or "the people" or "Your people"), *never* as "we" or "us." Although dutifully following God's orders on the people's behalf, he has held himself aloof from them, preferring instead to commune with the Lord (or even to joust with Pharaoh). Indeed, the story of the golden calf begins when—and *because*—Moses has tarried on the mountain forty days and nights, talking with the Lord. Did it really take that long for God to pronounce the instructions for the Tabernacle?

4. Choosing for oneself is, by definition, not obeying. Only through an act of *dis*obedience can someone show clearly that one is *freely* choosing for *oneself.* By contrast, an act one does in *conformity* with a command could be done freely (by one's own choice) or under compulsion (by slavish and fearful obedience to authority); from the outside, it would be impossible to tell which it is. For a fuller discussion of this point, see my *The Beginning of Wisdom,* Chapter Two, "The Follies of Freedom and Reason: The Story of the Garden of Eden (I)," especially 61–68.

5. The text does not in fact tell us exactly when they pressed Aaron to make them "gods." It says only "when they saw that Moses delayed." It could have been before forty days.

6. The people are right in thinking that they cannot do without Moses. But they do not yet know that their real need is for him to take command of them. They also show that human beings cannot live by speech and reason alone. Pagan worship had to erupt before it could be redirected to the Tabernacle and the Lord.

7. We are puzzled to find the people referring to the calf in plural: "these" and "gods." Cassuto has a plausible explanation: "The meaning of this proclamation is that they regarded the calf as an emblem of the Lord, and they considered this emblem itself worthy of divine honour, thus making the calf a partner, as it were, of the Lord. Hence the plural [subject and verb]. . . . This, then, was their sin: they transgressed against the commandment, 'You shall have no other gods before Me'—in My presence, associated with Me." *A Commentary on the Book of Exodus*, 413.

8. The verb *tsachaq* has a wide range of meanings, from making merry to mocking laughter, from sporting play to sexual activity. It is the same verb used to describe what Abimelech caught Isaac doing with Rebekah, thus proving that she was his wife, and not, as Isaac has told him, his sister (Gen. 26:8).

9. This argument notwithstanding, it is worth stressing that Aaron's failure at this critical juncture does not disqualify him for future leadership responsibilities. On the contrary, his more representative and mediating role will remain essential, and for reasons that have emerged in this episode. Soon after the end of Exodus we will find Aaron established (as the Lord had previously wished) as the High Priest in the Tabernacle, in charge (again) of the sacrifices and mediating between the people and God. Among other things, as we have already discussed, he will be charged, strangely, to *bear the iniquity of the holy things* (28:38)—a sign that he will continue to traffic in dangerous practices. But there, unlike here with the golden calf, he will operate not on his own but under strict instructions from the Lord. At the same time, his presence before the people will always remind them of their guilt for the golden calf.

It is also worth considering, as Assaf Inbari has suggested (in a personal communication) that the people's pagan worship, though condemnable, is also not disqualifying. They demonstrate that human beings cannot live by speech and reason alone. Their Dionysian outbreak may have been necessary before its elements could be incorporated into Tabernacle worship, albeit, as with Aaron's conduct, under strict rule.

10. Someone may well ask why the Lord didn't deliver this news to Moses sooner, in time for him to prevent the people's transgression. Is it possible that their sin was not only anticipated but also even necessary, both for their development and for Moses's?

11. The term "stiff-necked" refers to an ox that will not take the yoke. Hannah Mandelbaum suggests that the never-yoked young ox is a perfect image for the unyoked idolatrous people.

12. Why he does so we will soon consider.

13. We have already noted how little interest Moses has shown in family life.

14. Indirectly, Moses may be making an even subtler and more dangerous point: If you are not going to keep your self-sworn promises to the patriarchs, what good is your promise to make of *me* a great nation? Needless to say, Moses could not say such a thing out loud, but he could be forgiven for wondering here about the worth of God's promises.

15. The other five occur in the conversation that we will review in the next chapter.

16. Moses understood from the singing that the people were making love, not war.

17. Readers may wish to revisit our discussion of the one previous instance of dancing, led by Miriam after the victory at the Sea of Reeds. See the section titled "Miriam and the Dancing Women: Apollo or Dionysus?" in Chapter Eight.

18. "And he built an altar at the foot of the mountain" (24:4).

19. Sacks makes a good argument to suggest that it is the instructions for building the Tabernacle that are inscribed on the stone tables Moses shattered. If he is right, angry destruction of the tables at the sight of the golden calf would make perfect logical sense:

> Moses had seen through God's trick. The tabernacle was nothing more than a glorified and placatory substitute for the golden calf—even the altar still had horns!—and Moses would have none of it. But Aaron was a different sort of a man. In his own way, he had seen that room had to be made for the irrational side of the human soul: "This is thy God, O Israel, that brought thee out of the Land of Egypt." What he did not see is that wildness could only be tamed by the precision of number and the intricacy of art and formality, as is seen in the construction of the tabernacle.
>
> Moses's irrational reaction to the irrational meant that while he was the best of lawgivers, only Aaron could take onto himself the more dangerous position of High Priest.

Robert Sacks, "The Life and Death of Aaron the Priest," 252. Please note that Sacks is explaining but not justifying Moses's anger. By calling his action "irrational," Sacks raises questions about both Moses's "temper" and his lack of sympathy for the people's needs. There will be later occasions to wonder about the rightness of Moses's anger.

20. My thanks to Dore Feith for this last insight.

21. I owe this formulation to Amir Blumenkrantze, a student at Shalem College. It is at this moment perhaps that Moses not only accepts responsibility but also feels guilty for his part in the people's turn to idolatry.

22. Dan Polisar comments, "Forcing the people to eat this god also brings them back to their more heroic act of eating lamb, one of the gods of Egypt, before their departure from Egypt. By eating the 'god,' they are reminded that it is not superior to them and that it lacks any real power—just as they learned in Egypt when eating the lamb-god" (personal communication).

23. The formulation is Hannah Mandelbaum's. As we shall learn from the remainder of this story, Israelite cultural memory will record not only their sin of idolatry but also their ability to repent, surmount it, and persevere.

24. See Numbers 5:11–31. Such a suggestion should not be taken as mere psychologizing. Guilt can reorganize one's entire being, altering behavior and body, as well as mind.

25. Aaron here repeats verbatim what the people had said to him. But, in the sequel, he is anything but truthful in reporting his own actions.

26. We notice Aaron's deferential form of address. The relation of Aaron to Moses is no longer simply "brotherly"—that is, one of equality—if it ever was. Whereas the text went out of its way to identify Jethro as Moses's father-in-law, it has not since the very beginning referred to Aaron as Moses's brother, except in the instructions received regarding the appointment of the priests, discussed in Chapter Eighteen. Readers will recall that we found that identification fraught with premonitions of fratricide, if not literal, then effectual. (Moses will soon call for literal fratricide.)

27. It is unclear how many of the Levites actually follow Moses's orders to kill. We are told first that *all* the Levites came to Moses's side (32:26). But in the account of their deed, in accord with his command, the word "all" is missing (32:28). Did some Levites back out once they heard what was required, or did all of them participate? Did Aaron?

28. Someone might wonder: Is Moses's lifting up the Lord's name in vain?

29. A significant number, to be sure, but "only" 0.5 percent of the male population, a small-scale "decimation" and purging of the ranks.

30. I owe the medical analogy to Hannah Mandelbaum. Perhaps stretching the point, we may also compare the 3,000 dead—as far as we know, a random selection of the population—to the later example of the scapegoat (here, the "scape-calf-niks") chosen by lot and driven over the cliff on the Day of Atonement, symbolically to carry away the iniquities of the people. Antón Barba-Kay suggested to me a different explanation of the seemingly random killing: the apparent arbitrariness of the act perfectly conveys Moses's willful assertion of leadership, a move of which Machiavelli apparently approved (see *The Prince,* Chapter VI).

31. For a helpful discussion of the problem of translating *mile'u yedekhem*—"they filled your hands" or "fill your hands"—see Cassuto, *A Commentary on the Book of Exodus,* 422. Cassuto makes the case for the former. On this translation, Moses seems to be regarding the killing of the three thousand as an act of priestly sacrifice to the Lord, which act constitutes the de facto consecration or installation of the Levites as priests.

32. We recall that the first instance in the Bible of the Lord's anger occurred as a result of Moses's unwillingness to accept his mission (4:14). We speculated then that the reason for that anger was the Lord's anticipation of the likely fratricidal implications of the solution that Moses compelled him to adopt: the appointment of brother Aaron as Moses's second in command. It is even possible that Moses's wrathful deeds here will be later avenged in the Lord's severe (not to say excessive) response to his next significant act done in anger: his angry smiting of the rock in the wilderness of Zin, in defiance of God's command, for which misdeed Moses will be denied entrance to the Promised Land (see Num. 20).

TWENTY-ONE The Forgiving God and the Glorious Moses

1. It is unclear what book Moses is referring to, as there has been no prior mention of such a book of divine authorship. Does it mean the Torah that we are reading? Or does it refer rather to a "book of life," in which God inscribes a record of who shall

live? Or might it refer to a postulated log of the Lord's "Chosen Ones," analogous to the records kept by kings to keep track of the deeds of their favorites (see, for example, the chronicle of King Ahasuerus in the Book of Esther)? However this may be, the important point is that Moses asks to share the fate of "this people."

2. We may take this as evidence that God did not disapprove of the killing Moses authorized in the camp. It was not punishment enough; He had to smite more.

3. Cassuto notes a meaningful allusion and a suggestive pun in this verse. First, the verb "stripped themselves," *vayyithnatselu*, echoes "thus they despoiled [*vayenatselu*] the Egyptians" (12:36), the act that produced the jewelry that went into making the calf. Second, "these ornaments [*'adi*], with which the Israelites adorned themselves when they stood before Mount Sinai, may have appeared to them as witnesses . . . a testimony and memorial, as it were, to that sublime event and to the establishment of the covenant between them and the Lord. But now that they had broken the covenant, they were no longer worthy of wearing the symbol of the voided compact. The removal of the ornaments corresponds to the breaking of the tablets by Moses." Cassuto is referring to the linguistic similarity between the word for ornaments (*'adi*) and the word for witness (*'ed*). *A Commentary on the Book of Exodus*, 428.

4. The rest of the verse also adds to the "humanity" of the scene. "And he [Moses] would return to the camp, but his attendant Joshua son of Nun, a lad, would not budge from within the Tent" (33:11). The lad Joshua was either in the Tent while God was speaking with Moses or just outside. As one who was privy to the conversation between Moses and God, Joshua (here identified for the first time as the son of Nun) has his stature increase, enabling him to be later seen by the people as the legitimate heir to Moses. My thanks to Nathan Laufer for these insights.

5. Not long before, in teaching Moses His ordinances, God issued a warning about His messengers: "Heed his [the messenger's] voice, do not defy him, for he will not pardon your trespass" (23:21). Moses is rightly worried that the unknown messenger God has offered him will be an agent of divine retribution.

6. Cassuto glosses *"your ways"* as follows: "the principles by which Thy Court of Justice is guided, what criteria Thou dost employ in the bestowal of reward and punishment to people, and in what way man can obtain forgiveness from Thee for his sins, that I may be privileged *to know Thee*; and when I know Thy ways I shall know how to act and on what basis I may prevail on Thee to forgive my people and allow Thy Presence to dwell in their midst." *A Commentary on the Book of Exodus*, 433.

7. "The merit of Moses's prayer and the Lord's compassion had already changed the outlook. At first God had said to Moses, *Let me alone* [*hannicha li*] (xxxii:10), whereas now He said to him, *and I will give you rest* [*vahanichothi lakh*]. The parallelism underlines the radical change in the situation." Cassuto, *A Commentary on the Book of Exodus*, 434.

8. Ruth Martin comments: "God's 'shielded' revelation to Moses anticipates and allows the building of the Tabernacle, where man has access to God through a negotiation of revelation and veiling, access and distance." This remark appeared in a spectacular term paper on Exodus 32–34 written by Ms. Martin (then a college senior at

the University of Chicago; today, Ruth Martin Curry, a newly minted PhD in comparative literature at Northwestern) for my class on Exodus at University of Chicago in the spring of 2005 (quoted with permission). Her profound insights have since informed my entire reading of these chapters.

Here, once again, we choose not to probe the corporeal language the Lord uses to speak of Himself ("hand"; "back"; "face"). Those who have a preconceived notion of God as incorporeal will of course insist that this language *must* be metaphorical, a concession to us poor mortals who can have no other way of conceiving the divine. The Tradition interprets "God's back" as meaning "after the fact": human beings may know of God only in retrospect and only from learning of His deeds in the world. Perhaps so. But the text does not itself point to such an interpretation or any other. We therefore prefer to allow God's corporeal self-description to remain a mystery.

9. In God's compelling Moses to craft the tables, to replace the ones he shattered, Antón Barba-Kay sees a subtle analogy to Moses's forcing the people to drink the Golden Calf: both were forced to own and undo their misdeeds (personal communication).

10. For example, they are repeated often throughout the day in the several services for the Yom Kippur, the Day of Atonement—and for obvious reasons, given their emphasis on God's forgiving, merciful, and gracious character.

11. The word for merciful, *rachum*, is cognate with *rechem*, "womb," from the root *r-ch-m*, whose Aramaic and Akkadian cognates mean "love." Mercy is emblematically feminine.

12. This self-proclaimed characteristic reiterates what the Lord said in the second statement of the Decalogue—the one proscribing making images and worshipping them.

13. For example, like Jonah. Called by God to rouse the wicked people of Nineveh to repent, Jonah runs away from his mission because he will not be a party to God's mercy where His punishment was fully deserved. Later, when he explains his grievance against the Lord, Jonah (son of *Amittai*, "truth") recites the Lord's attributes disclosed here as part of the indictment (Jonah 4:2). But significantly, he omits mention of "abundant in truth"—Jonah's way of complaining that God always sacrifices justice to mercy. Jonah prefers the retributive God of the Flood to the merciful God of Sinai.

14. Although the Lord does not exactly say, 'I forgive you,' He surely speaks as if the people have been readmitted into full relationship with Him.

15. "Cultic poles," translating the Hebrew *'asherim*, were wooden poles associated with the worship of Asherah, a Canaanite fertility goddess.

16. Years later, there will be a second episode of mass idolatry that follows almost exactly this scenario: shared meals, whoring with Moabite women, and bowing down to their gods. On that occasion, the Lord will send a plague on the Children of Israel; twenty-four thousand will die (see Num. 25:1–9).

17. To repeat, the number forty gains its symbolic significance from the forty weeks of human gestation. On the surface, in all these cases, nothing appears to be happening, yet the world is pregnant with something momentous. At the end of the pe-

riod of forty (days, weeks, years), what was incubating stands forth fully revealed. The world is forever utterly transformed.

18. Martin, term paper, Note 8 (quoted with permission).

19. Just as they did, terrified, after the Lord's pronouncement, amid the pyrotechnics, of the Ten Commandments (20:15).

20. Ruth Martin comments, in connection with these verses, on the *need* to veil the sacred: "Concealment isn't necessarily an evil—sometimes concealment protects truth, rather than censors or disfigures it. . . . There is a certain truth only lost when sought—inquiry can destroy what it inquires into, or the inquirer can be destroyed by his inquiry. The sacred . . . must remain veiled to protect it from the inquiry that destroys. . . . Just as wanting to name God stems from the desire to order and appropriate knowledge, so sight seeks to consume. Both activities seek to know God in a way that denies His unknowability, His inherent mysteriousness. God conceals Himself in cloud, demands distance and reverence, not only for utilitarian purposes—to 'protect His privacy,' shield mortals from His overwhelming glory, or shame them into humility—but because obscurity is essential to His nature. His revelation *must* also conceal and mystify because that *is* Who He is." Martin, term paper, Note 8 (quoted with permission).

TWENTY-TWO The Completion(s) of the Tabernacle

1. They were previously addressed as a congregation (*'edah*) in connection with killing the Paschal lamb, marking their doors on Exodus eve, and the appearance of the glory of the Lord with His gift of the manna and the quail.

2. The thought, though not the precise formulation, is from Abraham Joshua Heschel's *The Sabbath: Its Meaning for Modern Man* (New York: Farrar Straus Giroux, 1951), "Prologue."

3. This echoes, perhaps, the people's immoderate zeal for the golden calf. But this time we will have a model for how such unrestraint should be handled: freedom can lead to excess, especially in relation to the divine, but law and command can provide measure.

4. We are also reminded of the gifts of silver, gold, and clothing that the Egyptians gave on their request to the departing Israelites on the night of the Exodus: "And the Lord gave the people favor in the sight of the (contrite) Egyptians, so that they let them have what they asked" (12:36). Here, Moses has given the (invisible) Lord favor in the sight of the (contrite) Israelites, so they let him (Him) have *more* than what he asked.

5. Rashi (Ex. 38:8) offers a lovely gloss: "Now Moses was about to reject them [the mirrors] since they were made to pander to their vanity, but the Holy One, blessed be He, said to him, 'Accept *them*; these are dearer to Me than all *the other contributions*, because through them the women reared *those* huge hosts in Egypt!' For when their husbands were tired through their crushing labor they used to bring them food and drink and induced them to eat. Then they would take the mirrors, and each gazed at herself in the mirror together with her husband, saying endearingly to him, 'See I am

handsomer than you!' Thus they awakened their husbands' affection and subsequently became the mothers of many children, as it is said (Song of Songs VIII.5), 'I awakened thy love under the apple-tree.'" Rashi, *Pentateuch: Exodus*, 212 (emphasis in original). This gloss regarding the women and their mirrors, along with the recent mention of the contributions of materials made by women (both absent from the instructions given to Moses before the episode with the golden calf), reminds us of the vital role of heroic women in the beginning stories of Exodus: the midwives, Moses's mother and sister, and Pharaoh's daughter—all defenders of life. Here, at the end of Exodus, hordes of nameless women donate their attractive and life-promoting advantages to the service of the Lord.

But there is a darker meaning of the contributions of the women, who "stood in array at the door of the Tent of Meeting." Among neighboring peoples, temple prostitutes (in Hebrew, *qedeshah*, related to *qadosh*, "holy") gathered before the sanctuary for the sexual coupling that was part of the religious observance. Much later, the aged priest Eli will be disturbed by reports of the conduct of his sons and how "they lay with the women who stood in array at the door to the Tent of Meeting" (1 Sam. 2:22). With this prospect in mind, the gift of their mirrors for the Laver implies the surrender of the instruments of seduction *not only of husbands*. They are fittingly incorporated into the wash stand, whereby the priests purify themselves before entering the Holy Place.

6. My thanks to Nathan Laufer for this astute suggestion.

7. The change in that dynamic and in those relationships will become manifest when, in Leviticus and Numbers, we hear reports of what actually happens after Aaron is finally installed as High Priest (in Lev. 8). Two examples will suffice. In Leviticus 9, after Aaron makes the sin offerings and the burnt offerings for himself and for the people, Aaron (and then Aaron and Moses together) bless the people, after which the glory of the Lord appears to the people; when His flame consumes the burnt offerings on the altar, the people shout and fall on their faces (Lev. 9:22–24). In Numbers 6–7, we hear more about what happened beginning on the very day the Tabernacle was erected: first, Moses receives from God the exact wording of the famous priestly blessing with which the priests are to bless the people (Num. 6:22–27); then the nobles of each of the tribes, in the name of those "political" divisions of the people that they lead, spontaneously bring large offerings to the Lord, to be processed by the Levites (Num. 7:1–88); finally, Moses goes into the Tent of Meeting to receive further instructions from the Lord about the lamps and the Levites (Num. 7:89–8:1–22). New activities of and new relations among the priests, the people, and Moses are called for by the existence of the Tabernacle.

8. This installation does not take place until the eighth chapter of Leviticus.

9. Exodus 40:19, 21, 23, 25, 27, 29, 32.

10. "And Moses went up into the mountain, and the cloud covered the mountain. And dwelt the glory of the Lord upon Mount Sinai, and the cloud covered it six days; and the seventh day He called unto Moses out of the midst of the cloud. . . . And Moses entered into the midst of the cloud" (24:15–18). There are numerous linguistic parallels between the scene at the end of Exodus 24 and the scene at the end of Exodus 40.

11. "And the Lord called unto Moses, and spoke unto him *out of the tent of meeting*, saying . . ." (Lev. 1:1; emphasis added). There follows seven chapters of instructions regarding additional sacrifices to be offered in the Tabernacle, and then, in Leviticus 8, instructions for the installation of Aaron as High Priest.

12. And vice versa.

13. Among the latter, see, for example, Joshua Berman, *The Temple*, 13–19; Cassuto, *A Commentary on the Book of Exodus*, 476–477; Leibowitz, *New Studies in Shemot (Exodus)*, 471–486; and Jon D. Levenson, *Creation and the Persistence of Evil: The Jewish Drama of Divine Omnipotence* (Princeton: Princeton University Press, 1994), Chapter 7: "Cosmos and Microcosm," 78–99. Earlier thinkers, from Philo and Josephus to Newton and Rosenzweig, also looked to the Tabernacle (or the Temple) as a microcosm of the universe.

14. Levenson, *Creation and the Persistence of Evil*, 86.

15. Levenson, *Creation and the Persistence of Evil*, 98–99 (emphasis in original). Conflating the Tabernacle and Solomon's Jerusalem Temple in his argument, he speaks in this passage of the Temple, not the Tabernacle, but for the purposes of his argument the substitution is irrelevant.

16. In the next several paragraphs, I borrow liberally, often verbatim, from my interpretation of the Creation story in my *The Beginning of Wisdom*, 36–45.

17. We note that man, like God, is also someone "who will be what he will be."

18. These are not just primitive or foolish notions. Whether among the ancient Babylonians or Egyptians or Persians, or among native Americans or modern-day Buddhists or deep ecologists who worship Gaia, we find human beings looking up to nature as something divine. Because human life is precariously dependent on sun and rain, the effort to appease, propitiate, and control the cosmic forces through worship and sacrifice and the reading of signs is a nearly ubiquitous feature of early human life, and certainly in the Ancient Near East. In the ziggurats of Babylon, the place where human beings first began to count the celestial happenings (and hence the target of the Bible's story of the Tower of Babel), the priests, watchfully yet apprehensively, conducted measurements of the heavenly motions, on the basis of which they sought knowledge useful for the life of the city—forerunners of the astrological aspiration that persists to the present day.

If these examples do not persuade, the Bible makes the point explicitly. In Deuteronomy, Moses exhorts the Israelites to remember the divine voice they heard at Mount Horeb: "Take you therefore good heed unto yourselves—for you *saw* no manner of likeness [*temunah*] on the day that the Lord *spoke* unto you in Horeb out of the midst of the fire—lest you become corrupt, and make you a graven image, even the form of any figure, the likeness of male or female, the likeness of any beast that is on the earth, the likeness of any winged fowl that flies in the heavens, the likeness of any thing that creeps on the ground, the likeness of any fish that is in the water under the earth, *and lest you lift up your eyes unto the heavens, and when you see the sun and the moon and the stars, even all the host of the heavens, you be drawn aside and worship them, and serve them, which the Lord your God has allotted unto all the peoples under all the heavens*" (Deut. 4:15–19; emphasis added).

Absent the special revelation and the giving of the Law at Mount Sinai, human beings would naturally be led to the worship of heaven. Their natural and astronomical turn is further linked, according to this passage, to idolatry: the creation and worship of visible images and likenesses. Absent *hearing* God's word, human beings would follow their eyes upward. Human beings, free and indeterminate, would *on their own* try to find their way in the world, based on their ordinary experiences; they would ultimately be led to orient themselves by the cosmic "gods" (and their anthropomorphic and zoomorphic representations).

19. This is not merely an ancient (Egyptian) alternative. Readers, I hope, will recognize in the formulation modern man's turn for salvation to his mechanistic science of nature and to science's beloved offspring: technological wizardry and its amoral wizards.

Acknowledgments

Thanks are owed to many people who helped me produce this book, beginning with my students at the University of Chicago and Shalem College and my friends and colleagues in Washington, DC, and Jerusalem, with whom I have studied Exodus in seminar-style discussions since 1998. I have been encouraged by their enthusiasm for the text, and I have benefited often from their insights. Their specific contributions are quoted in the text (with their kind permission) and acknowledged in the Notes.

Several friends and family members read portions of the manuscript and offered critical comments and useful suggestions: Antón Barba-Kay, Peter Berkowitz, Dore Feith, Michael Fishbane, Harvey Flaumenhaft, Rob Hochman, Miriam Kass, Neal Kozodoy, Robyn Krauthammer, Hannah Mandelbaum, Gil Meilaender, Dan Polisar, and Rabbi Meir Soloveichik. Eric Cohen and Yuval Levin read the entire manuscript and tendered helpful advice and comment. The friendship of these two thoughtful men ranks high among the blessings of my life.

Shawn Z. Aster, professor of Hebrew Bible at Bar Ilan and Yeshiva Universities, reviewed the near-final manuscript, correcting errors of Hebrew translation and transliteration and identifying problems of interpretation, uses of secondary sources, and treatment of Ancient Near Eastern history and culture. I am deeply in his debt.

I am grateful to Christopher DeMuth, Arthur Brooks, and Roger and Susan Hertog for providing me a most congenial home at the American Enterprise Institute, where the early parts of this project were completed.

The Tikvah Foundation provided a generous grant to support the publication of this book. Once again, my profound thanks to Eric Cohen, Tikvah's executive director, and to Roger Hertog for their unfailing support.

It has been my great good fortune to have landed at the Yale University Press and in the hands of its executive editor William Frucht. A wordsmith of the old school,

Bill has been over the manuscript with meticulous care, sanding and polishing every sentence with precision and grace. It has been an enormous pleasure to work with someone who knows what I am trying to say and who loves helping me say it better. My thanks also to Karen Olson for ably shepherding the manuscript to production, to Gail Naron Chalew for her superb copy editing, and to Mary Pasti of the Yale University Press and Brian Ostrander of Westchester Publishing Services for skillfully supervising and managing all phases of production. It has been a pleasure working with such a competent and gracious group of colleagues.

The drawing of the ground plan of the Wilderness Tabernacle is reprinted from *The JPS Torah Commentary: Exodus* by Nahum Sarna, by kind permission of The University of Nebraska Press. (Copyright 1991 by the Jewish Publication Society.)

To Rabbi Shmuel Herzfeld of Congregation Ohev Sholom in Washington, DC, my synagogue for the past five years, I owe a different kind of debt. Comforted by his loving pastoral attentions and inspired by his unequivocal spirituality, enthusiasm for Torah, and moral passion, I have experienced in his congregational community—for the first time in my life—an inkling of what it means to commune with what is highest and best.

I dedicate this volume to my four Israeli study partners, whose singular contributions I have acknowledged in the preface: Richie Lewis, Nathan Laufer, Daniel Polisar, and my granddaughter Hannah Mandelbaum. This book would never have been written without their encouragement and their sympathetic yet critical engagement with my interpretations. To Hannah, I owe something even more precious. It was her offer to study Torah with me over FaceTime that restored me to life in the wake of my dear Amy's passing. Thanks to Hannah, Amy's spirit now accompanies me on every page.

Index

Raamses, building of, 29, 454; plague
of firstborn sons, 34, 141, 142, 147, 153,
154–155, 159, 174–175, 179–180, 611n19,
623n35, 632n34; priests, 652n10; return
to as curse, 639n15; slavery instituted
by Joseph, 138, 349, 492, 675n48; sorcery
in, 383–384, 669n12; spoils given to
Israelites, 76, 180–183, 532, 636n26.
See also Pharaoh
elders: absence of, 100, 624n1; meeting
with God on Mount Sinai, 431–432,
441–446, 453, 454, 677nn2–3, 679nn20–21,
679n24
Eleazar (Aaron's son), 121, 476, 686n3
Eli, 699n5
Eliezer (Abraham's servant), 648n8
Eliezer (Moses's son), 121, 265, 266, 267,
622n29, 648n8, 649n14
Elim, 224, 240, 642n9
Elisheva (Aaron's wife), 121, 627n8
Ellison, John, 620n21
enemies: Canaanites, expulsion of,
419–422, 423–425, 618n12, 671n25,
676n58–61; treatment of, 402–403,
673nn39–40, 674n41
Engels, Friedrich, 629n11
ephod, 483–484, 488–489
equity, 337, 457–458, 559–560, 641n4
eros, 267–268
Esau, 80, 88, 89, 91, 245, 267, 334, 617n9,
645n3, 645n5, 646n10
Eshnunna, Code of, 660n3, 666n43
Esther, Book of, 246, 260, 696n1
Eve, 22, 163, 386, 455, 482n, 533, 623n34,
670n21
Exodus, Book of, 1, 14–16; authorship,
18; Genesis context, 12–14; importance
of, 1–3; interpretive approach to,
7–12; name, 21; on people formation,
5–7; philosophical approach to,
3–4; universal applicability, 4–5,
604–605
Ezekiel, Book of, 628n3

false witness, 332, 400–401, 659n26,
672n35, 673n36
family: honoring father and mother,
322–328, 334–335, 397, 657n16, 658n18,
658n22; moral obligations within,
396–397; Passover and households,
170–171; servitude and, 351–354,
662nn16–18; striking and cursing
father and mother, 323, 357–358,
664nn27–29. *See also* fratricide;
marriage
fear of God, 32–33, 164, 256, 336, 337, 358,
610n15
Feith, Dore, 695n20
fertility and fruitfulness: Egyptian, 136;
God's promise of, 109; of Israelites,
24–25, 608nn4–6
festivals. *See* seasonal festivals
fighting: acceptance by ordinances,
363–364; bodily injury from, 358–359,
664nn30–31; near pregnant women,
361–363, 665nn35–38
fire: liability for property damage, 374–375;
perpetual flame in Tabernacle, 477,
686n2; Sabbath and, 576; significance
of, 62–63. *See also* burning bush; cloud
and fire
firstborn sons: God's vs. Pharaoh's, 85–86;
patricide and, 165; priesthood and, 303
firstborn sons, plague of: iniquity of,
632n34; male infanticide against
Israelites and, 34, 623n35; meaning
of, 142, 147, 159, 174–175, 611n19; overview of events, 141, 153, 154–155, 179–180
firstborn sons, redemption of: in
covenant renewal, 566, 567; institution
of, 160–161; ordinance on, 398–399;
purpose of, 161–162, 161n, 166–167, 186,
189–191, 492; symbolic substitution in
Passover, 172
Fishbane, Michael, 656n9
flatbread (*matsah*), 166, 176, 188, 494
Flatbread, Festival of, 413, 675n51